William Shakespeare

THE COMPLETE WORKS

William Shakespeare

THE COMPLETE WORKS

VOLUME 3

. . .

TRAGEDIES

The Complete Works of William Shakespeare, Volume 3

This edition published by Tess Press, an imprint of
Black Dog & Leventhal Publishers, Inc.
151 West 19th Street, New York, NY 10011

Design by Edstudio Design
Manufactured in China

ISBN-10: 1-57912-654-5
ISBN-13: 978-1-57912-654-4

h g f e d c b a

Table of Contents

CORIOLANUS

CORIOLANUS

DRAMATIS PERSONAE

CAIUS MARCIUS, afterwards CAIUS MARCIUS CORIOLANUS.
TITUS LARTIUS, general against the Volscians.
COMINIUS, general against the Volscians.
MENENIUS AGRIPPA, friend to Coriolanus.
SICINIUS VELUTUS, tribune of the people.
JUNIUS BRUTUS, tribune of the people.
Young MARCUS, son to Coriolanus.
A Roman Herald.
TULLUS AUFIDIUS, general of the Volscians.
Lieutenant to Aufidius.
Conspirators with Aufidius.
A Citizen of Antium.
Two Volscian Guards.
VOLUMNIA, mother to Coriolanus.
VIRGILIA, wife to Coriolanus.
VALERIA, friend to Virgilia.
Gentlewoman, attending on Virgilia.
Roman and Volscian Senators, Patricians, Aediles, Lictors, Soldiers, Citizens, Messengers, Servants to Aufidius, and other Attendants.

SCENE: *Rome and the neighbourhood; Corioli and the neighbourhood; Antium.*

ACT ONE SCENE ONE

Rome. A street.

Enter a company of mutinous Citizens, *with staves, clubs, and other weapons.*

FIRST CITIZEN
Before we proceed any further, hear me speak.

ALL
Speak, speak.

FIRST CITIZEN
You are all resolved rather to die than to famish?

ALL
Resolved, resolved.

FIRST CITIZEN
First, you know Caius Marcius is chief enemy to the people.

ALL
We know't, we know't.

FIRST CITIZEN
Let us kill him, and we'll have corn at our own price Is't a verdict?

ALL
No more talking on't; let it be done: away, away!

SECOND CITIZEN
One word, good citizens.

FIRST CITIZEN
We are accounted poor citizens, the patricians good. What authority surfeits on would relieve us: if they would yield us but the superfluity, while it were wholesome, we might guess they relieved us humanely; but they think we are too dear: the leanness that afflicts us, the object of our misery, is as an inventory to particularise their abundance; our sufferance is a gain to them. Let us revenge this with our pikes, ere we become rakes: for the gods know I speak this in hunger for bread, not in thirst for revenge.

SECOND CITIZEN

Would you proceed especially against Caius Marcius?

ALL

Against him first: he's a very dog to the commonalty.

SECOND CITIZEN

Consider you what services he has done for his country? 26

FIRST CITIZEN

Very well; and could be content to give him good report for't, but that he pays himself with being proud.

SECOND CITIZEN

Nay, but speak not maliciously.

FIRST CITIZEN

I say unto you, what he hath done famously, he did it to that end: though soft-conscienced men can be content to say it was for his country, he did it to please his mother, and to be partly proud; which he is, even till the altitude of his virtue. 34

SECOND CITIZEN

What he cannot help in his nature, you account a vice in him. You must in no way say he is covetous.

FIRST CITIZEN

If I must not, I need not be barren of accusations; he hath faults, with surplus, to tire in repetition. [*Shouts within.*] What shouts are these? The other side o' the city is risen: why stay we prating here? To the Capitol!

ALL

Come, come. 41

FIRST CITIZEN

Soft! who comes here?

Enter MENENIUS AGRIPPA.

SECOND CITIZEN

Worthy Menenius Agrippa; one that hath always loved the people.

FIRST CITIZEN

He's one honest enough: would all the rest were so!

MENENIUS

What work's, my countrymen, in hand? Where go you
With bats and clubs? The matter? speak, I pray you.

FIRST CITIZEN

Our business is not unknown to the senate; they have had inkling this fortnight what we intend to do, which now we'll show 'em in deeds. They say poor suitors have strong breaths: they shall know we have strong arms too.

MENENIUS

Why, masters, my good friends, mine honest neighbours,
Will you undo yourselves?

FIRST CITIZEN

We cannot, sir, we are undone already.

MENENIUS

I tell you, friends, most charitable care
Have the patricians of you. For your wants,
Your suffering in this dearth, you may as well
Strike at the heaven with your staves as lift them 61
Against the Roman state, whose course will on
The way it takes, crackling ten thousand curbs
Of more strong link asunder than can ever
Appear in your impediment. For the dearth,
The gods, not the patricians, make it, and
Your knees to them, not arms, must help. Alack,
You are transported by calamity
Thither where more attends you, and you slander
The helms o' the state, who care for you like fathers,
When you curse them as enemies. 71

FIRST CITIZEN

Care for us! True, indeed! They ne'er cared for us yet: suffer us to famish, and their store-houses crammed with grain; make edicts for usury, to support usurers; repeal daily any wholesome act established against the rich, and provide more piercing statutes daily, to chain up and restrain the poor. If the wars eat us not up, they will; and there's all the love they bear us.

MENENIUS

Either you must 79
Confess yourselves wondrous malicious,
Or be accused of folly. I shall tell you
A pretty tale: it may be you have heard it;
But, since it serves my purpose, I will venture
To stale't a little more.

FIRST CITIZEN

Well, I'll hear it, sir: yet you must not think to fob off our disgrace with a tale: but, an 't please you, deliver.

MENENIUS

There was a time when all the body's members
Rebell'd against the belly, thus accused it: 89
That only like a gulf it did remain
I' the midst o' the body, idle and unactive,
Still cupboarding the viand, never bearing
Like labour with the rest, where the other instruments
Did see and hear, devise, instruct, walk, feel,
And, mutually participate, did minister
Unto the appetite and affection common
Of the whole body. The belly answer'd—

FIRST CITIZEN

Well, sir, what answer made the belly? 99

MENENIUS

Sir, I shall tell you. With a kind of smile,
Which ne'er came from the lungs, but even thus—
For, look you, I may make the belly smile
As well as speak—it tauntingly replied
To the discontented members, the mutinous parts
That envied his receipt; even so most fitly

As you malign our senators for that
They are not such as you.

FIRST CITIZEN
Your belly's answer? What!
The kingly-crowned head, the vigilant eye,
The counsellor heart, the arm our soldier, 110
Our steed the leg, the tongue our trumpeter.
With other muniments and petty helps
In this our fabric, if that they—

MENENIUS
What then?
'Fore me, this fellow speaks! What then? what then?

FIRST CITIZEN
Should by the cormorant belly be restrain'd,
Who is the sink o' the body,—

MENENIUS
Well, what then?

FIRST CITIZEN
The former agents, if they did complain,
What could the belly answer?

MENENIUS
I will tell you;
If you'll bestow a small—of what you have
little— 123
Patience awhile, you'll hear the belly's answer.

FIRST CITIZEN
Ye're long about it.

MENENIUS
Note me this, good friend;
Your most grave belly was deliberate,
Not rash like his accusers, and thus answer'd:
'True is it, my incorporate friends,' quoth he,
'That I receive the general food at first,
Which you do live upon; and fit it is,
Because I am the store-house and the shop
Of the whole body: but, if you do remember,
I send it through the rivers of your blood,
Even to the court, the heart, to the seat o'
the brain; 136
And, through the cranks and offices of man,
The strongest nerves and small inferior veins
From me receive that natural competency
Whereby they live: and though that all at once,
You, my good friends,'—this says the belly, mark
me,—

FIRST CITIZEN
Ay, sir; well, well.

MENENIUS
'Though all at once cannot
See what I do deliver out to each,
Yet I can make my audit up, that all
From me do back receive the flour of all,
And leave me but the bran.' What say you
to't? 149

FIRST CITIZEN
It was an answer: how apply you this?

MENENIUS
The senators of Rome are this good belly,
And you the mutinous members; for examine
Their counsels and their cares, digest things rightly
Touching the weal o' the common, you shall find
No public benefit which you receive
But it proceeds or comes from them to you
And no way from yourselves. What do you think,
You, the great toe of this assembly?

FIRST CITIZEN
I the great toe! why the great toe? 159

MENENIUS
For that, being one o' the lowest, basest, poorest,
Of this most wise rebellion, thou go'st foremost:
Thou rascal, that art worst in blood to run,
Lead'st first to win some vantage.
But make you ready your stiff bats and clubs:
Rome and her rats are at the point of battle;
The one side must have bale.

Enter CAIUS MARCIUS.

Hail, noble Marcius.

MARCIUS
Thanks. What's the matter, you dissentious rogues,
That, rubbing the poor itch of your opinion,
Make yourselves scabs?

FIRST CITIZEN
We have ever your good word.

MARCIUS
He that will give good words to thee will
flatter 173
Beneath abhorring. What would you have, you curs,
That like nor peace nor war? the one affrights you,
The other makes you proud. He that trusts to you,
Where he should find you lions, finds you hares;
Where foxes, geese: you are no surer, no,
Than is the coal of fire upon the ice,
Or hailstone in the sun. Your virtue is [1]
To make him worthy whose offence subdues him
And curse that justice did it. Who deserves
greatness 183
Deserves your hate; and your affections are
A sick man's appetite, who desires most that
Which would increase his evil. He that depends
Upon your favours swims with fins of lead
And hews down oaks with rushes. Hang ye!
Trust Ye?
With every minute you do change a mind,
And call him noble that was now your hate,
Him vile that was your garland. What's the matter,
That in these several places of the city
You cry against the noble senate, who, 194

Under the gods, keep you in awe, which else
Would feed on one another? What's their seeking?

MENENIUS
For corn at their own rates; whereof, they say,
The city is well stored.

MARCIUS
Hang 'em! They say!
They'll sit by the fire, and presume to know
What's done i' the Capitol; who's like to rise,
Who thrives and who declines; side factions and give out
Conjectural marriages; making parties strong
And feebling such as stand not in their liking
Below their cobbled shoes. They say there's grain enough!
Would the nobility lay aside their ruth,
And let me use my sword, I'ld make a quarry
With thousands of these quarter'd slaves, as high
As I could pick my lance.

MENENIUS
Nay, these are almost thoroughly persuaded;
For though abundantly they lack discretion,
Yet are they passing cowardly. But, I beseech you,
What says the other troop?

MARCIUS
They are dissolved: hang 'em!
They said they were an-hungry; sigh'd forth proverbs,
That hunger broke stone walls, that dogs must eat,
That meat was made for mouths, that the gods sent not
Corn for the rich men only: with these shreds
They vented their complainings; which being answer'd,
And a petition granted them, a strange one—
To break the heart of generosity,
And make bold power look pale—they threw their caps
As they would hang them on the horns o' the moon,
Shouting their emulation.

MENENIUS
What is granted them?

MARCIUS
Five tribunes to defend their vulgar wisdoms,
Of their own choice: one's Junius Brutus,
Sicinius Velutus, and I know not— 'Sdeath!
The rabble should have first unroof'd the city,
Ere so prevail'd with me: it will in time
Win upon power and throw forth greater themes
For insurrection's arguing.

MENENIUS
This is strange.

MARCIUS
Go, get you home, you fragments!

Enter a Messenger, *hastily.*

MESSENGER
Where's Caius Marcius?

MARCIUS
Here: what's the matter?

MESSENGER
The news is, sir, the Volsces are in arms.

MARCIUS
I am glad on't: then we shall ha' means to vent
Our musty superfluity. See, our best elders.

Enter COMINIUS, TITUS LARTIUS, *and other* Senators; JUNIUS BRUTUS *and* SICINIUS VELUTUS.

FIRST SENATOR
Marcius, 'tis true that you have lately told us;
The Volsces are in arms.

MARCIUS
They have a leader,
Tullus Aufidius, that will put you to't.
I sin in envying his nobility,
And were I any thing but what I am,
I would wish me only he.

COMINIUS
You have fought together.

MARCIUS
Were half to half the world by the ears and he.
Upon my party, I'ld revolt, to make
Only my wars with him: he is a lion
That I am proud to hunt.

FIRST SENATOR
Then, worthy Marcius,
Attend upon Cominius to these wars.

COMINIUS
It is your former promise.

MARCIUS
Sir, it is;
And I am constant. Titus Lartius, thou
Shalt see me once more strike at Tullus' face.
What, art thou stiff? stand'st out?

TITUS
No, Caius Marcius;
I'll lean upon one crutch and fight with t'other,
Ere stay behind this business.

MENENIUS
O, true-bred!

FIRST SENATOR
Your company to the Capitol; where, I know,
Our greatest friends attend us.

TITUS
[*To Cominius*] Lead you on.
[*To Marcius*] Follow Cominius; we must follow you;
Right worthy you priority.

COMINIUS
Noble Marcius!
FIRST SENATOR
[*To the Citizens*] Hence to your homes; be gone!
MARCIUS
Nay, let them follow:
The Volsces have much corn; take these rats thither
To gnaw their garners. Worshipful mutiners,
Your valour puts well forth: pray, follow.
[*Citizens steal away. Exeunt all but Sicinius and Brutus.*
SICINIUS
Was ever man so proud as is this Marcius?
BRUTUS
He has no equal.
SICINIUS
When we were chosen tribunes for the people,—
BRUTUS
Mark'd you his lip and eyes?
SICINIUS
Nay, but his taunts.
BRUTUS
Being moved, he will not spare to gird
the gods. 289
SICINIUS
Be-mock the modest moon.
BRUTUS
The present wars devour him: he is grown
Too proud to be so valiant.
SICINIUS
Such a nature,
Tickled with good success, disdains the shadow
Which he treads on at noon: but I do wonder
His insolence can brook to be commanded
Under Cominius.
BRUTUS
Fame, at the which he aims,
In whom already he's well graced, can not
Better be held nor more attain'd than by 298
A place below the first: for what miscarries
Shall be the general's fault, though he perform
To the utmost of a man, and giddy censure
Will then cry out of Marcius 'O if he
Had borne the business!'
SICINIUS
Besides, if things go well,
Opinion that so sticks on Marcius shall
Of his demerits rob Cominius.
BRUTUS
Come:
Half all Cominius' honours are to Marcius.
Though Marcius earn'd them not, and all his faults
To Marcius shall be honours, though indeed
In aught he merit not.
SICINIUS
Let's hence, and hear
How the dispatch is made, and in what fashion,
More than his singularity, he goes
Upon this present action.
BRUTUS
Let's along. [*Exeunt.*

ACT ONE SCENE TWO

Corioli. The Senate-house.

Enter TULLUS AUFIDIUS *and certain* Senators.

FIRST SENATOR
So, your opinion is, Aufidius,
That they of Rome are enter'd in our counsels
And know how we proceed.
AUFIDIUS
Is it not yours?
What ever have been thought on in this state,
That could be brought to bodily act ere Rome
Had circumvention? 'Tis not four days gone
Since I heard thence; these are the words: I think
I have the letter here; yes, here it is.
[*Reads*] 'they have press'd a power, but it is not known
Whether for east or west: the dearth is great;
The people mutinous; and it is rumour'd,
Cominius, Marcius your old enemy,
Who is of Rome worse hated than of you,
And Titus Lartius, a most valiant Roman,
These three lead on this preparation
Whither 'tis bent: most likely 'tis for you:
Consider of it.'
FIRST SENATOR
Our army's in the field:
We never yet made doubt but Rome was ready
To answer us.
AUFIDIUS
Nor did you think it folly
To keep your great pretences veil'd till when
They needs must show themselves; which in the hatching,
It seem'd, appear'd to Rome. By the discovery.
We shall be shorten'd in our aim, which was
To take in many towns ere almost Rome
Should know we were afoot.
SECOND SENATOR
Noble Aufidius,
Take your commission; hie you to your bands:
Let us alone to guard Corioli:
If they set down before 's, for the remove
Bring your army; but, I think, you'll find
They've not prepared for us.

AUFIDIUS
O, doubt not that;
I speak from certainties. Nay, more,
Some parcels of their power are forth already,
And only hitherward. I leave your honours.
If we and Caius Marcius chance to meet,
'Tis sworn between us we shall ever strike
Till one can do no more.

ALL
The gods assist you!

AUFIDIUS
And keep your honours safe!

FIRST SENATOR
Farewell.

SECOND SENATOR
Farewell.

ALL
Farewell. [*Exeunt.*

ACT ONE SCENE THREE

Rome. A room in Marcius' house.

Enter VOLUMNIA *and* VIRGILIA: *they set them down on two low stools, and sew.*

VOLUMNIA
I pray you, daughter, sing; or express yourself in a more comfortable sort: if my son were my husband, I should freelier rejoice in that absence wherein he won honour than in the embracements of his bed where he would show most love. When yet he was but tender-bodied and the only son of my womb, when youth with comeliness plucked all gaze his way, when for a day of kings' entreaties a mother should not sell him an hour from her beholding, I, considering how honour would become such a person. that it was no better than picture-like to hang by the wall, if renown made it not stir, was pleased to let him seek danger where he was like to find fame. To a cruel war I sent him; from whence he returned, his brows bound with oak. I tell thee, daughter, I sprang not more in joy at first hearing he was a man-child than now in first seeing he had proved himself a man. [2]

VIRGILIA
But had he died in the business, madam; how then?

VOLUMNIA
Then his good report should have been my son; I therein would have found issue. Hear me profess sincerely: had I a dozen sons, each in my love alike and none less dear than thine and my good Marcius, I had rather had eleven die nobly for their country than one voluptuously surfeit out of action.

Enter a Gentlewoman.

GENTLEWOMAN
Madam, the Lady Valeria is come to visit you.

VIRGILIA
Beseech you, give me leave to retire myself.

VOLUMNIA
Indeed, you shall not.
Methinks I hear hither your husband's drum,
See him pluck Aufidius down by the hair,
As children from a bear, the Volsces shunning him:
Methinks I see him stamp thus, and call thus:
'Come on, you cowards! you were got in fear,
Though you were born in Rome:' his bloody brow
With his mail'd hand then wiping, forth he goes,
Like to a harvest-man that's task'd to mow
Or all or lose his hire.

VIRGILIA
His bloody brow! O Jupiter, no blood!

VOLUMNIA
Away, you fool! it more becomes a man
Than gilt his trophy: the breasts of Hecuba,
When she did suckle Hector, look'd not lovelier
Than Hector's forehead when it spit forth blood
At Grecian sword, contemning. Tell Valeria, [3]
We are fit to bid her welcome.
[*Exit Gentlewoman.*

VIRGILIA
Heavens bless my lord from fell Aufidius!

VOLUMNIA
He'll beat Aufidius 'head below his knee
And tread upon his neck.

Enter VALERIA, *with an* Usher *and* Gentlewoman.

VALERIA
My ladies both, good day to you.

VOLUMNIA
Sweet madam.

VIRGILIA
I am glad to see your ladyship.

VALERIA
How do you both? you are manifest house-keepers.What are you sewing here? A fine spot, in good faith. How does your little son?

VIRGILIA
I thank your ladyship; well, good madam.

VOLUMNIA
He had rather see the swords, and hear a drum, than look upon his school-master.

VALERIA
O' my word, the father's son: I'll swear, 'tis a very pretty boy. O' my troth, I looked upon him o' Wednesday half an hour together: has such a confirmed countenance. I saw him run after a gilded butterfly: and when he caught it, he let it go again; and after it again;

and over and over he comes, and again; catched it again; or whether his fall enraged him, or how 'twas, he did so set his teeth and tear it; O, I warrant it, how he mammocked it! 65

VOLUMNIA

One on 's father's moods.

VALERIA

Indeed, la, 'tis a noble child.

VIRGILIA

A crack, madam.

VALERIA

Come, lay aside your stitchery; I must have you play the idle husewife with me this afternoon.

VIRGILIA

No, good madam; I will not out of doors.

VALERIA

Not out of doors!

VOLUMNIA

She shall, she shall. 73

VIRGILIA

Indeed, no, by your patience; I'll not over the threshold till my lord return from the wars.

VALERIA

Fie, you confine yourself most unreasonably: come, you must go visit the good lady that lies in.

VIRGILIA

I will wish her speedy strength, and visit her with my prayers; but I cannot go thither.

VOLUMNIA

Why, I pray you?

VIRGILIA

'Tis not to save labour, nor that I want love. 81

VALERIA

You would be another Penelope: yet, they say, all the yarn she spun in Ulysses' absence did but fill Ithaca full of moths. Come; I would your cambric were sensible as your finger, that you might leave pricking it for pity. Come, you shall go with us.

VIRGILIA

No, good madam, pardon me; indeed, I will not forth.

VALERIA

In truth, la, go with me; and I'll tell you excellent news of your husband. 90

VIRGILIA

O, good madam, there can be none yet.

VALERIA

Verily, I do not jest with you; there came news from him last night.

VIRGILIA

Indeed, madam?

VALERIA

In earnest, it's true; I heard a senator speak it. Thus it is: the Volsces have an army forth; against whom Cominius the general is gone, with one part of our Roman power: your lord and Titus Lartius are set down before their city Corioli; they nothing doubt prevailing and to make it brief wars. This is true, on mine honour; and so, I pray, go with us.

VIRGILIA

Give me excuse, good madam; I will obey you in every thing hereafter.

VOLUMNIA

Let her alone, lady: as she is now, she will but disease our better mirth.

VALERIA

In troth, I think she would. Fare you well, then. Come, good sweet lady. Prithee, Virgilia, turn thy solemness out o' door. and go along with us. 108

VIRGILIA

No, at a word, madam; indeed, I must not. I wish you much mirth.

VALERIA

Well, then, farewell. [*Exeunt.*

ACT ONE SCENE FOUR

Before Corioli.

Enter, with drum and colours, MARCIUS, TITUS LARTIUS, Captains *and* Soldiers. *To them a* Messenger.

MARCIUS

Yonder comes news. A wager they have met.

LARTIUS

My horse to yours, no.

MARCIUS

'Tis done.

LARTIUS

Agreed.

MARCIUS

Say, has our general met the enemy?

MESSENGER

They lie in view; but have not spoke as yet.

LARTIUS

So, the good horse is mine.

MARCIUS

I'll buy him of you.

LARTIUS

No, I'll nor sell nor give him: lend you him I will
For half a hundred years. Summon the town.

MARCIUS

How far off lie these armies?

MESSENGER

Within this mile and half.

MARCIUS

Then shall we hear their 'larum, and they ours.

Now, Mars, I prithee, make us quick in work,
That we with smoking swords may march from hence, 16
To help our fielded friends! Come, blow thy blast.

They sound a parley. Enter two Senators *with others on the walls.*

Tullus Aufidius, is he within your walls?

FIRST SENATOR
No, nor a man that fears you less than he, [4]
That's lesser than a little. [*Drums afar off.*
Hark! our drums
Are bringing forth our youth. We'll break our walls,
Rather than they shall pound us up: our gates,
Which yet seem shut, we have but pinn'd with rushes;
They'll open of themselves. [*Alarum afar off.*
Hark you. far off!
There is Aufidius; list, what work he makes
Amongst your cloven army.

MARCIUS
O, they are at it!

LARTIUS
Their noise be our instruction. Ladders, ho!

Enter the army of the Volsces.

MARCIUS
They fear us not, but issue forth their city.
Now put your shields before your hearts, and fight
With hearts more proof than shields. Advance, brave Titus:
They do disdain us much beyond our thoughts,
Which makes me sweat with wrath. Come on, my fellows:
He that retires I'll take him for a Volsce,
And he shall feel mine edge.

Alarum. The Romans are beat back to their trenches. Re-enter MARCIUS, *cursing.*

MARCIUS
All the contagion of the south light on you, 41
You shames of Rome? you herd of—Boils and plagues [5]
Plaster you o'er, that you may be abhorr'd
Further than seen and one infect another
Against the wind a mile! You souls of geese,
That bear the shapes of men, how have you run
From slaves that apes would beat! Pluto and hell!
All hurt behind; backs red, and faces pale
With flight and agued fear! Mend and charge home,
Or, by the fires of heaven, I'll leave the foe
And make my wars on you: look to't: come on; 53
If you'll stand fast, we'll beat them to their wives,
As they us to our trenches followed. [6]

Another alarum. The Volsces *fly, and* MARCIUS *follows them to the gates.*

So, now the gates are ope: now prove good seconds:
'Tis for the followers fortune widens them,
Not for the fliers: mark me, and do the like.
[*Enters the gates.*

FIRST SOLDIER
Fool-hardiness; not I.

SECOND SOLDIER
Nor I. [MARCIUS *is shut in.*

FIRST SOLDIER
See, they have shut him in.

ALL
To the pot, I warrant him. [*Alarum continues.*

Re-enter TITUS LARTIUS.

LARTIUS
What is become of Marcius?

ALL
Slain, sir, doubtless.

FIRST SOLDIER
Following the fliers at the very heels,
With them he enters; who, upon the sudden,
Clapp'd to their gates: he is himself alone,
To answer all the city.

LARTIUS
O noble fellow!
Who sensibly outdares his senseless sword,
And, when it bows, stands up. Thou art left, Marcius:
A carbuncle entire, as big as thou art,
Were not so rich a jewel. Thou wast a soldier
Even to Cato's wish, not fierce and terrible [7]
Only in strokes; but, with thy grim looks and
The thunder-like percussion of thy sounds,
Thou madst thine enemies shake, as if the world 79
Were feverous and did tremble.

Re-enter MARCIUS, *bleeding, assaulted by the enemy.*

FIRST SOLDIER
Look, sir.

LARTIUS
O, 'tis Marcius!
Let's fetch him off, or make remain alike.
[*They fight, and all enter the city.*

ACT ONE SCENE FIVE

Corioli. A street.

Enter certain Romans, *with spoils.*

FIRST ROMAN
This will I carry to Rome.

SECOND ROMAN
And I this.
THIRD ROMAN
A murrain on't! I took this for silver.
[*Alarum continues still afar off.*

Enter MARCIUS *and* TITUS LARTIUS *with a trumpet.*

MARCIUS
See here these movers that do prize their hours
At a crack'd drachm! Cushions, leaden spoons,
Irons of a doit, doublets that hangmen would
Bury with those that wore them, these base slaves,
Ere yet the fight be done, pack up: down with them!
And hark, what noise the general makes!
To him!
There is the man of my soul's hate, Aufidius,
Piercing our Romans: then, valiant Titus, take
Convenient numbers to make good the city;
Whilst I, with those that have the spirit, will haste
To help Cominius.
LARTIUS
Worthy sir, thou bleed'st;
Thy exercise hath been too violent
For a second course of fight.
MARCIUS
Sir, praise me not;
My work hath yet not warm'd me: fare you well:
The blood I drop is rather physical
Than dangerous to me: to Aufidius thus
I will appear, and fight.
LARTIUS
Now the fair goddess, Fortune,
Fall deep in love with thee; and her great charms
Misguide thy opposers' swords! Bold gentleman,
Prosperity be thy page!
MARCIUS
Thy friend no less
Than those she placeth highest! So, farewell.
LARTIUS
Thou worthiest Marcius! [*Exit Marcius.*
Go, sound thy trumpet in the market-place;
Call thither all the officers o' the town,
Where they shall know our mind: away!
[*Exeunt.*

ACT ONE SCENE SIX

Near the camp of Cominius.

Enter COMINIUS, *as it were in retire, with soldiers.*

COMINIUS
Breathe you, my friends: well fought; we are come off
Like Romans, neither foolish in our stands,
Nor cowardly in retire: believe me, sirs,
We shall be charged again. Whiles we have struck,
By interims and conveying gusts we have heard
The charges of our friends. Ye Roman gods! [8]
Lead their successes as we wish our own,
That both our powers, with smiling fronts encountering,
May give you thankful sacrifice.

Enter a Messenger.

Thy news?
MESSENGER
The citizens of Corioli have issued,
And given to Lartius and to Marcius battle:
I saw our party to their trenches driven,
And then I came away.
COMINIUS
Though thou speak'st truth,
Methinks thou speak'st not well.
How long is't since?
MESSENGER
Above an hour, my lord.
COMINIUS
'Tis not a mile; briefly we heard their drums:
How couldst thou in a mile confound an hour,
And bring thy news so late?
MESSENGER
Spies of the Volsces
Held me in chase, that I was forced to wheel
Three or four miles about, else had I, sir,
Half an hour since brought my report.
COMINIUS
Who's yonder,
That does appear as he were flay'd? O gods
He has the stamp of Marcius; and I have
Before-time seen him thus.
MARCIUS
[*Within*] Come I too late?
COMINIUS
The shepherd knows not thunder from a tabor
More than I know the sound of Marcius' tongue
From every meaner man.

Enter MARCIUS.

MARCIUS
Come I too late?
COMINIUS
Ay, if you come not in the blood of others,
But mantled in your own.
MARCIUS
O, let me clip ye
In arms as sound as when I woo'd, in heart
As merry as when our nuptial day was done,
And tapers burn'd to bedward!

COMINIUS
Flower of warriors,
How is't with Titus Lartius?
MARCIUS
As with a man busied about decrees:
Condemning some to death, and some to exile;
Ransoming him, or pitying, threatening the other;
Holding Corioli in the name of Rome,
Even like a fawning greyhound in the leash,
To let him slip at will.
COMINIUS
Where is that slave
Which told me they had beat you to your trenches? 53
Where is he? call him hither.
MARCIUS
Let him alone;
He did inform the truth: but for our gentlemen,
The common file—a plague! Tribunes for them!—
The mouse ne'er shunn'd the cat as they did budge
From rascals worse than they.
COMINIUS
But how prevail'd you?
MARCIUS
Will the time serve to tell? I do not think.
Where is the enemy? are you lords o' the field?
If not, why cease you till you are so?
COMINIUS
Marcius,
We have at disadvantage fought and did
Retire to win our purpose. 67
MARCIUS
How lies their battle? know you on which side
They have placed their men of trust?
COMINIUS
As I guess, Marcius,
Their bands i' the vaward are the Antiates,
Of their best trust; o'er them Aufidius,
Their very heart of hope.
MARCIUS
I do beseech you,
By all the battles wherein we have fought,
By the blood we have shed together, by the vows
We have made to endure friends, that you directly
Set me against Aufidius and his Antiates;
And that you not delay the present, but, 80
Filling the air with swords advanced and darts,
We prove this very hour.
COMINIUS
Though I could wish
You were conducted to a gentle bath
And balms applied to you, yet dare I never
Deny your asking: take your choice of those
That best can aid your action.
MARCIUS
Those are they
That most are willing: If any such be here—
As it were sin to doubt—that love this painting
Wherein you see me smear'd; if any fear
Lesser his person than an ill report; 92
If any think brave death outweighs bad life
And that his country's dearer than himself;
Let him alone, or so many so minded,
Wave thus, to express his disposition,
And follow Marcius.
[*They all shout and wave their swords, take him up in their arms, and cast up their caps.*
O, me alone! make you a sword of me?
If these shows be not outward, which of you
But is four Volsces? none of you but is
Able to bear against the great Aufidius
A shield as hard as his. A certain number,
Though thanks to all, must I select from all: the rest
Shall bear the business in some other fight,
As cause will be obey'd. Please you to march;
And four shall quickly draw out my command,
Which men are best inclined.
COMINIUS
March on, my fellows:
Make good this ostentation, and you shall
Divide in all with us. [*Exeunt.*

ACT ONE SCENE SEVEN

The gates of Corioli.

TITUS LARTIUS, *having set a guard upon Corioli, going with drum and trumpet toward* COMINIUS *and* CAIUS MARCIUS, *enters with* Lieutenant, *other* Soldiers, *and a* Scout.

LARTIUS
So, let the ports be guarded: keep your duties,
As I have set them down. If I do send, dispatch
Those centuries to our aid; the rest will serve
For a short holding: if we lose the field,
We cannot keep the town.
LIEUTENANT
Fear not our care, sir.
LARTIUS
Hence, and shut your gates upon's.
Our guider, come; to the Roman camp conduct us.
[*Exeunt.*

ACT ONE SCENE EIGHT

A field of battle.

Alarum as in battle. Enter, from opposite sides, MARCIUS *and* AUFIDIUS.

MARCIUS
I'll fight with none but thee; for I do hate thee
Worse than a promise-breaker.

AUFIDIUS
We hate alike:
Not Afric owns a serpent I abhor
More than thy fame and envy. Fix thy foot.

MARCIUS
Let the first budger die the other's slave,
And the gods doom him after!

AUFIDIUS
If I fly, Marcius,
Holloa me like a hare.

MARCIUS
Within these three hours, Tullus,
Alone I fought in your Corioli walls,
And made what work I pleased: 'tis not my blood
Wherein thou seest me mask'd; for thy revenge
Wrench up thy power to the highest.

AUFIDIUS
Wert thou the Hector
That was the whip of your bragg'd progeny,
Thou shouldst not scape me here.

[*They fight, and certain* Volsces *come to the aid of Aufidius. Marcius fights till they be driven in breathless.*

Officious, and not valiant, you have shamed me
In your condemned seconds. [*Exeunt.*

ACT ONE SCENE NINE

The Roman camp.

Flourish. Alarum. A retreat is sounded. Flourish. Enter, from one side, COMINIUS *with the* Romans; *from the other side,* MARCIUS, *with his arm in a scarf.*

COMINIUS
If I should tell thee o'er this thy day's work,
Thou'ldst not believe thy deeds: but I'll report it
Where senators shall mingle tears with smiles,
Where great patricians shall attend and shrug,
I'd the end admire, where ladies shall be frighted,
And, gladly quaked, hear more; where the dull tribunes,
That, with the fusty plebeians, hate thine honours,
Shall say against their hearts 'We thank the gods
Our Rome hath such a soldier.'
Yet camest thou to a morsel of this feast,
Having fully dined before.

Enter TITUS LARTIUS, *with his power, from the pursuit.*

LARTIUS
O general,
Here is the steed, we the caparison:
Hadst thou beheld—

MARCIUS
Pray now, no more: my mother,
Who has a charter to extol her blood,
When she does praise me grieves me. I have done
As you have done; that's what I can; induced
As you have been; that's for my country:
He that has but effected his good will
Hath overta'en mine act.

COMINIUS
You shall not be
The grave of your deserving; Rome must know
The value of her own: 'twere a concealment
Worse than a theft, no less than a traducement,
To hide your doings; and to silence that,
Which, to the spire and top of praises vouch'd,
Would seem but modest: therefore, I beseech you—
In sign of what you are, not to reward
What you have done— before our army hear me.

MARCIUS
I have some wounds upon me, and they smart
To hear themselves remember'd.

COMINIUS
Should they not,
Well might they fester 'gainst ingratitude,
And tent themselves with death. Of all the horses,
Whereof we have ta'en good and good store, of all
The treasure in this field achieved and city,
We render you the tenth, to be ta'en forth,
Before the common distribution, at
Your only choice.

MARCIUS
I thank you, general;
But cannot make my heart consent to take
A bribe to pay my sword: I do refuse it;
And stand upon my common part with those
That have beheld the doing.

[*A long flourish. They all cry* 'Marcius! Marcius!' *cast up their caps and lances: Cominius and Lartius stand bare.* [10]

MARCIUS
May these same instruments, which you profane,
Ne'er sound more! when drums and trumpets shall
I' the field prove flatterers, let courts and cities be
Made all of false-faced soothing!
When steel grows soft as the parasite's silk,

Let him be made a coverture for the wars!
No more, I say! For that I have not wash'd
My nose that bled, or foil'd some debile wretch,—
Which, without note, here's many else have done,—
You shout me forth
In acclamations hyperbolical; 57
As if I loved my little should be dieted
In praises sauced with lies.

COMINIUS
Too modest are you;
More cruel to your good report than grateful
To us that give you truly: by your patience,
If 'gainst yourself you be incensed, we'll put you,
Like one that means his proper harm, in manacles,
Then reason safely with you. Therefore, be it known,
As to us, to all the world, that Caius Marcius
Wears this war's garland: in token of the
which, 68
My noble steed, known to the camp, I give him,
With all his trim belonging; and from this time,
For what he did before Corioli, call him,
With all the applause and clamour of the host,
CAIUS MARCIUS CORIOLANUS! Bear
The addition nobly ever!
[*Flourish. Trumpets sound, and drums.*

ALL
Caius Marcius Coriolanus!

CORIOLANUS
I will go wash;
And when my face is fair, you shall perceive
Whether I blush or no: howbeit, I thank you.
I mean to stride your steed, and at all times
To undercrest your good addition
To the fairness of my power.

COMINIUS
So, to our tent;
Where, ere we do repose, we will write
To Rome of our success. You, Titus Lartius,
Must to Corioli back: send us to Rome
The best, with whom we may articulate,
For their own good and ours.

LARTIUS
I shall, my lord.

CORIOLANUS
The gods begin to mock me. I, that now
Refused most princely gifts, am bound to beg
Of my lord general.

COMINIUS
Take't; 'tis yours. What is't? 92

CORIOLANUS
I sometime lay here in Corioli
At a poor man's house; he used me kindly:
He cried to me; I saw him prisoner;
But then Aufidius was within my view,
And wrath o'erwhelm'd my pity: I request you
To give my poor host freedom.

COMINIUS
O, well begg'd!
Were he the butcher of my son, he should
Be free as is the wind. Deliver him, Titus.

LARTIUS
Marcius, his name?

CORIOLANUS
By Jupiter! forgot.
I am weary; yea, my memory is tired. 104
Have we no wine here?

COMINIUS
Go we to our tent:
The blood upon your visage dries; 'tis time
It should be look'd to: come. [*Exeunt.*

ACT ONE SCENE TEN

The camp of the Volsces.

A flourish. Cornets. Enter TULLUS AUFIDIUS, *bloody, with two or three* Soldiers.

AUFIDIUS
The town is ta'en!

FIRST SOLDIER
'Twill be deliver'd back on good condition.

AUFIDIUS
Condition!
I would I were a Roman; for I cannot,
Being a Volsce, be that I am. Condition!
What good condition can a treaty find
I' the part that is at mercy? Five times, Marcius,
I have fought with thee; o often hast thou beat me,
And wouldst do so, I think, should we encounter
As often as we eat. By the elements, 10
If e'er again I meet him beard to beard,
He's mine, or I am his: mine emulation
Hath not that honour in't it had; for where
I thought to crush him in an equal force,
True sword to sword, I'll potch at him some way
Or wrath or craft may get him.

FIRST SOLDIER
He's the devil.

AUFIDIUS
Bolder, though not so subtle. My valour's poison'd
With only suffering stain by him; for him
Shall fly out of itself: nor sleep nor sanctuary,
Being naked, sick, nor fane nor Capitol, 21
The prayers of priests nor times of sacrifice,
Embarquements all of fury, shall lift up
Their rotten privilege and custom 'gainst
My hate to Marcius: where I find him, were it

At home, upon my brother's guard, even there,
Against the hospitable canon, would I
Wash my fierce hand in's heart. Go you to the city;
Learn how 'tis held; and what they are that must
Be hostages for Rome.

FIRST SOLDIER
Will not you go?

AUFIDIUS
I am attended at the cypress grove: I pray
you— 33
'Tis south the city mills—bring me word thither
How the world goes, that to the pace of it
I may spur on my journey.

FIRST SOLDIER
I shall, sir. [*Exeunt.*

ACT TWO SCENE ONE

Rome. A public place.

Enter MENENIUS *with the two Tribunes of the people,* SICINIUS *and* BRUTUS.

MENENIUS
The augurer tells me we shall have news
to-night.

BRUTUS
Good or bad?

MENENIUS
Not according to the prayer of the people, for they love not Marcius. 5

SICINIUS
Nature teaches beasts to know their friends.

MENENIUS
Pray you, who does the wolf love?

SICINIUS
The lamb.

MENENIUS
Ay, to devour him; as the hungry plebeians would the noble Marcius.

BRUTUS
He's a lamb indeed, that baes like a bear.

MENENIUS
He's a bear indeed, that lives like a lamb. You two are old men: tell me one thing that I shall ask you.

BOTH
Well, sir.

MENENIUS
In what enormity is Marcius poor in, that you two have not in abundance?

BRUTUS
He's poor in no one fault, but stored with all. 17

SICINIUS
Especially in pride.

BRUTUS
And topping all others in boasting.

MENENIUS
This is strange now: do you two know how you are censured here in the city, I mean of us o' the right-hand file? do you?

BOTH
Why, how are we censured?

MENENIUS
Because you talk of pride now,—will you not be angry?

BOTH
Well, well, sir, well. 25

MENENIUS
Why, 'tis no great matter; for a very little thief of occasion will rob you of a great deal of patience: give your dispositions the reins, and be angry at your pleasures; at the least if you take it as a pleasure to you in being so. You blame Marcius for being proud?

BRUTUS
We do it not alone, sir.

MENENIUS
I know you can do very little alone; for your helps are many, or else your actions would grow wondrous single: your abilities are too infant-like for doing much alone. You talk of pride: O that you could turn your eyes toward the napes of your necks, and make but an interior survey of your good selves! O that you could!

BRUTUS
What then, sir?

MENENIUS
Why, then you should discover a brace of unmeriting, proud, violent, testy magistrates, alias fools, as any in Rome.

SICINIUS
Menenius, you are known well enough too. 43

MENENIUS
I am known to be a humorous patrician, and one that loves a cup of hot wine with not a drop of allaying Tiber in't; said to be something imperfect in favouring the first complaint; hasty and tinder-like upon too trivial motion; one that converses more with the buttock of the night than with the forehead of the morning: what I think I utter, and spend my malice in my breath. Meeting two such wealsmen as you are—I cannot call you Lycurguses— if the drink you give me touch my palate adversely, I make a crooked face at it. I can't say your worships have delivered the matter well, when I find the ass in compound with the major part of your syllables: and though I must be content to bear with those that say you are reverend grave men, yet they lie deadly that tell you you have good faces. If you see this in the map of my microcosm, follows it that I am known well enough too? what barm can your bisson

conspectuities glean out of this character, if I be known well enough too?

BRUTUS

Come, sir, come, we know you well enough.

MENENIUS

You know neither me, yourselves, nor any thing. You are ambitious for poor knaves' caps and legs: you wear out a good wholesome forenoon in hearing a cause between an orange-wife and a fosset-seller; and then rejourn the controversy of three pence to a second day of audience. When you are hearing a matter between party and party, if you chance to be pinched with the colic, you make faces like mummers; set up the bloody flag against all patience; and, in roaring for a chamber-pot, dismiss the controversy bleeding the more entangled by your hearing: all the peace you make in their cause is, calling both the parties knaves. You are a pair of strange ones. 76

BRUTUS

Come, come, you are well understood to be a perfecter giber for the table than a necessary bencher in the Capitol.

MENENIUS

Our very priests must become mockers, if they shall encounter such ridiculous subjects as you are. When you speak best unto the purpose, it is not worth the wagging of your beards; and your beards deserve not so honourable a grave as to stuff a botcher's cushion, or to be entombed in an ass's pack-saddle. Yet you must be saying, Marcius is proud; who in a cheap estimation, is worth predecessors since Deucalion, though peradventure some of the best of 'em were hereditary hangmen. God-den to your worships: more of your conversation would infect my brain, being the herdsmen of the beastly plebeians: I will be bold to take my leave of you.

[BRUTUS *and* SICINIUS *go aside.*

Enter VOLUMNIA, VIRGILIA, *and* VALERIA.

How now, my as fair as noble ladies,—and the moon, were she earthly, no nobler,—whither do you follow your eyes so fast? 94

VOLUMNIA

Honourable Menenius, my boy Marcius approaches; for the love of Juno, let's go.

MENENIUS

Ha! Marcius coming home!

VOLUMNIA

Ay, worthy Menenius; and with most prosperous approbation.

MENENIUS

Take my cap, Jupiter, and I thank thee. Hoo! Marcius coming home!

VOLUMNIA, VIRGILIA

Nay, 'tis true.

VOLUMNIA

Look, here's a letter from him: the state hath another, his wife another; and, I think, there's one at home for you. 105

MENENIUS

I will make my very house reel tonight: a letter for me!

VIRGILIA

Yes, certain, there's a letter for you; I saw't.

MENENIUS

A letter for me! it gives me an estate of seven years' health; in which time I will make a lip at the physician: the most sovereign prescription in Galen is but empiricutic, and, to this preservative, of no better report than a horse-drench. Is he not wounded? he was wont to come home wounded. 114

VIRGILIA

O, no, no, no.

VOLUMNIA

O, he is wounded; I thank the gods for't.

MENENIUS

So do I too, if it be not too much: brings a' victory in his pocket? the wounds become him.

VOLUMNIA

On's brows: Menenius, he comes the third time home with the oaken garland.

MENENIUS

Has he disciplined Aufidius soundly?

VOLUMNIA

Titus Lartius writes, they fought together, but Aufidius got off. 123

MENENIUS

And 'twas time for him too, I'll warrant him that: and he had stayed by him, I would not have been so fidiused for all the chests in Corioli, and the gold that's in them. Is the senate possessed of this?

VOLUMNIA

Good ladies, let's go. Yes, yes, yes; the senate has letters from the general, wherein he gives my son the whole name of the war: he hath in this action outdone his former deeds doubly. 131

VALERIA

In troth, there's wondrous things spoke of him.

MENENIUS

Wondrous! Ay, I warrant you, and not without his true purchasing.

VIRGILIA

The gods grant them true!

VOLUMNIA

True! pow, wow.

MENENIUS

True! I'll be sworn they are true.

Where is he wounded? [*To the Tribunes*] God save your good worships! Marcius is coming home: he has more cause to be proud. Where is he wounded?

VOLUMNIA

I' the shoulder and i' the left arm there will be large cicatrices to show the people, when he shall stand for his place. He received in the repulse of Tarquin seven hurts i' the body.

MENENIUS

One i' the neck, and two i' the thigh—there's nine that I know.

VOLUMNIA

He had, before this last expedition, twenty-five wounds upon him. 149

MENENIUS

Now it's twenty-seven: every gash was an enemy's grave. [*A shout and flourish*] Hark! the trumpets.

VOLUMNIA

These are the ushers of Marcius: before him he
carries noise, and behind him he leaves tears:
Death, that dark spirit, in 's nervy arm doth lie:
Which, being advanced, declines, and then men die.

A sennet. Trumpets sound. Enter COMINIUS *the general, and* TITUS LARTIUS; *between them*, CORIOLANUS, *crowned with an oaken garland; with* Captains *and* Soldiers, *and a* Herald.

HERALD

Know, Rome, that all alone Marcius did fight
Within Corioli gates: where he hath won, 157
With fame, a name to Caius Marcius; these
In honour follows Coriolanus.
Welcome to Rome, renowned Coriolanus!
[*Flourish.*

ALL

Welcome to Rome, renowned Coriolanus!

CORIOLANUS

No more of this; it does offend my heart:
Pray now, no more.

COMINIUS

Look, sir, your mother!

CORIOLANUS

O,
You have, I know, petition'd all the gods
For my prosperity! [*Kneels.*

VOLUMNIA

Nay, my good soldier, up;
My gentle Marcius, worthy Caius, and
By deed-achieving honour newly named,—
What is it?—Coriolanus must I call thee?—
But O, thy wife!

CORIOLANUS

My gracious silence, hail!
Wouldst thou have laugh'd had I come coffin'd home,
That weep'st to see me triumph? Ay, my dear,
Such eyes the widows in Corioli wear,
And mothers that lack sons.

MENENIUS

Now, the gods crown thee!

CORIOLANUS

And live you yet? [*To Valeria*] O my sweet lady, pardon.

VOLUMNIA

I know not where to turn: O, welcome home:
And welcome, general: and ye're welcome all.

MENENIUS

A hundred thousand welcomes. I could weep 181
And I could laugh, I am light and heavy. Welcome.
A curse begin at very root on's heart,
That is not glad to see thee! You are three
That Rome should dote on: yet, by the faith of men,
We have some old crab-trees here at home that will not
Be grafted to your relish. Yet welcome, warriors:
We call a nettle but a nettle and
The faults of fools but folly.

COMINIUS

Ever right.

CORIOLANUS

Menenius ever, ever.

HERALD

Give way there, and go on!

CORIOLANUS

[*To Volumnia and Virgilia*] Your hand, and yours:
Ere in our own house I do shade my head,
The good patricians must be visited;
From whom I have received not only greetings,
But with them change of honours.

VOLUMNIA

I have lived
To see inherited my very wishes
And the buildings of my fancy: only
There's one thing wanting, which I doubt not but
Our Rome will cast upon thee.

CORIOLANUS

Know, good mother,
I had rather be their servant in my way
Than sway with them in theirs.

COMINIUS

On, to the Capitol!
[*Flourish. Cornets. Exeunt in state, as before. Brutus and Sicinius come forward.*

BRUTUS

All tongues speak of him, and the bleared sights 209

VOLUMNIA Nay, my good soldier, up.

Are spectacled to see him: your prattling nurse
Into a rapture lets her baby cry
While she chats him: the kitchen malkin pins
Her richest lockram 'bout her reechy neck,
Clambering the walls to eye him: stalls, bulks, windows,
Are smother'd up, leads fill'd, and ridges horsed
With variable complexions, all agreeing
In earnestness to see him: seld-shown flamens
Do press among the popular throngs and puff
To win a vulgar station: or veil'd dames
Commit the war of white and damask in
Their nicely-gawded cheeks to the wanton spoil
Of Phoebus' burning kisses: such a pother
As if that whatsoever god who leads him
Were slily crept into his human powers
And gave him graceful posture.

SICINIUS
On the sudden,
I warrant him consul.

BRUTUS
Then our office may,
During his power, go sleep.
SICINIUS
He cannot temperately transport his honours
From where he should begin and end, but will [11]
Lose those he hath won.
BRUTUS
In that there's comfort.
SICINIUS
Doubt not
The commoners, for whom we stand, but they
Upon their ancient malice will forget
With the least cause these his new honours, which
That he will give them make I as little question
As he is proud to do't.
BRUTUS
I heard him swear,
Were he to stand for consul, never would he
Appear i' the market-place nor on him put
The napless vesture of humility;
Nor, showing, as the manner is, his wounds
To the people, beg their stinking breaths.
SICINIUS
'Tis right.
BRUTUS
It was his word: O, he would miss it rather
Than carry it but by the suit of the gentry to him
And the desire of the nobles.
SICINIUS
I wish no better
Than have him hold that purpose and to put it
In execution.
BRUTUS
'Tis most like he will.
SICINIUS
It shall be to him then as our good wills,
A sure destruction.
BRUTUS
So it must fall out
To him or our authorities. For an end,
We must suggest the people in what hatred
He still hath held them; that to's power he would
Have made them mules, silenced their pleaders and
Dispropertied their freedoms, holding them,
In human action and capacity,
Of no more soul nor fitness for the world
Than camels in the war, who have their provand
Only for bearing burdens, and sore blows
For sinking under them.
SICINIUS
This, as you say, suggested
At some time when his soaring insolence
Shall touch the people—which time shall not want, [12]
If he be put upon 't; and that's as easy
As to set dogs on sheep—will be his fire
To kindle their dry stubble; and their blaze
Shall darken him for ever.

Enter a Messenger.

BRUTUS
What's the matter?
MESSENGER
You are sent for to the Capitol. 'Tis thought
That Marcius shall be consul:
I have seen the dumb men throng to see him and
The blind to bear him speak: matrons flung gloves,
Ladies and maids their scarfs and handkerchers,
Upon him as he pass'd: the nobles bended,
As to Jove's statue, and the commons made
A shower and thunder with their caps and shouts:
I never saw the like.
BRUTUS
Let's to the Capitol;
And carry with us ears and eyes for the time,
But hearts for the event.
SICINIUS
Have with you. [*Exeunt.*

ACT TWO SCENE TWO

The same. The Capitol.

Enter two Officers, *to lay cushions.*

FIRST OFFICER
Come, come, they are almost here. How many stand for consulships?
SECOND OFFICER
Three, they say: but 'tis thought of every one Coriolanus will carry it.
FIRST OFFICER
That's a brave fellow; but he's vengeance proud, and loves not the common people.
SECOND OFFICER
Faith, there had been many great men that have flattered the people, who ne'er loved them; and there be many that they have loved, they know not wherefore; so that, if they love they know not why, they hate upon no better a ground: therefore, for Coriolanus neither to care whether they love or hate him manifests the true knowledge he has in their disposition; and out of his noble carelessness lets them plainly see't.
FIRST OFFICER
If he did not care whether he had their love or no, he waved indifferently 'twixt doing them neither good

nor harm: but he seeks their hate with greater devotion than can render it him; and leaves nothing undone that may fully discover him their opposite. Now, to seem to affect the malice and displeasure of the people is as bad as that which he dislikes, to flatter them for their love.

SECOND OFFICER

He hath deserved worthily of his country: and his ascent is not by such easy degrees as those who, having been supple and courteous to the people, bonneted, without any further deed to have them at an into their estimation and report: but he hath so planted his honours in their eyes, and his actions in their hearts, that for their tongues to be silent, and not confess so much, were a kind of ingrateful injury; to report otherwise, were a malice, that, giving itself the lie, would pluck reproof and rebuke from every ear that heard it.

FIRST OFFICER

No more of him; he is a worthy man: make way, they are coming. 34

A sennet. Enter, with Lictors before them, COMINIUS *the consul,* MENENIUS, CORIOLANUS, Senators, SICINIUS *and* BRUTUS. *The* Senators *take their places; the* Tribunes *take their Places by themselves.* CORIOLANUS *stands.*

MENENIUS

Having determined of the Volsces and
To send for Titus Lartius, it remains,
As the main point of this our after-meeting,
To gratify his noble service that
Hath thus stood for his country: therefore, please you
Most reverend and grave elders, to desire
The present consul, and last general
In our well-found successes, to report
A little of that worthy work perform'd
By Caius Marcius Coriolanus, whom 44
We met here both to thank and to remember
With honours like himself.

FIRST SENATOR

Speak, good Cominius:
Leave nothing out for length, and make us think
Rather our state's defective for requital
Than we to stretch it out. [*To the Tribunes*]
Masters o' the people,
We do request your kindest ears, and after,
Your loving motion toward the common body,
To yield what passes here.

SICINIUS

We are convented
Upon a pleasing treaty, and have hearts
Inclinable to honour and advance 57
The theme of our assembly.

BRUTUS

Which the rather
We shall be blest to do, if he remember
A kinder value of the people than
He hath hereto prized them at.

MENENIUS

That's off, that's off;
I would you rather had been silent. Please you
To hear Cominius speak?

BRUTUS

Most willingly;
But yet my caution was more pertinent
Than the rebuke you give it.

MENENIUS

He loves your people
But tie him not to be their bedfellow.
Worthy Cominius, speak. [*Coriolanus offers to go away.*] Nay, keep your place. 72

FIRST SENATOR

Sit, Coriolanus; never shame to hear
What you have nobly done.

CORIOLANUS

Your horrors' pardon:
I had rather have my wounds to heal again
Than hear say how I got them.

BRUTUS

Sir, I hope
My words disbench'd you not.

CORIOLANUS

No, sir: yet oft,
When blows have made me stay, I fled from words.
You soothed not, therefore hurt not: but your people,
I love them as they weigh.

MENENIUS

Pray now, sit down.

CORIOLANUS

I had rather have one scratch my head i' the sun
When the alarum were struck than idly sit 86
To hear my nothings monster'd. [*Exit.*

MENENIUS

Masters of the people,
Your multiplying spawn how can he flatter—
That's thousand to one good one—when you now see
He had rather venture all his limbs for honour
Than one on's ears to hear it? Proceed, Cominius.

COMINIUS

I shall lack voice: the deeds of Coriolanus
Should not be utter'd feebly. It is held
That valour is the chiefest virtue, and
Most dignifies the haver: if it be,
The man I speak of cannot in the world 97
Be singly counterpoised. At sixteen years,
When Tarquin made a head for Rome, he fought

Beyond the mark of others: our then dictator,
Whom with all praise I point at, saw him fight,
When with his Amazonian chin he drove
The bristled lips before him: be bestrid
An o'er-press'd Roman and i' the consul's view
Slew three opposers: Tarquin's self he met,
And struck him on his knee: in that day's feats,
When he might act the woman in the scene,
He proved best man i' the field, and for his meed 109
Was brow-bound with the oak. His pupil age
Man-enter'd thus, he waxed like a sea,
And in the brunt of seventeen battles since
He lurch'd all swords of the garland. For this last,
Before and in Corioli, let me say,
I cannot speak him home: he stopp'd the fliers;
And by his rare example made the coward
Turn terror into sport: as weeds before
A vessel under sail, so men obey'd 118
And fell below his stem: his sword, death's stamp,
Where it did mark, it took; from face to foot
He was a thing of blood, whose every motion
Was timed with dying cries: alone he enter'd
The mortal gate of the city, which he painted
With shunless destiny; aidless came off,
And with a sudden reinforcement struck
Corioli like a planet: now all's his:
When, by and by, the din of war gan pierce
His ready sense; then straight his doubled spirit 129
Re-quicken'd what in flesh was fatigate,
And to the battle came he; where he did
Run reeking o'er the lives of men, as if
'Twere a perpetual spoil: and till we call'd
Both field and city ours, he never stood
To ease his breast with panting.

MENENIUS
Worthy man!

FIRST SENATOR
He cannot but with measure fit the honours
Which we devise him.

COMINIUS
Our spoils he kick'd at,
And look'd upon things precious as they were
The common muck of the world: he covets less 142
Than misery itself would give; rewards
His deeds with doing them, and is content
To spend the time to end it.

MENENIUS
He's right noble:
Let him be call'd for.

FIRST SENATOR
Call Coriolanus.

OFFICER
He doth appear.

Re-enter CORIOLANUS.

MENENIUS
The senate, Coriolanus, are well pleased
To make thee consul.

CORIOLANUS
I do owe them still
My life and services.

MENENIUS
It then remains
That you do speak to the people.

CORIOLANUS
I do beseech you,
Let me o'erleap that custom, for I cannot 157
Put on the gown, stand naked and entreat them,
For my wounds' sake, to give their suffrage: please you
That I may pass this doing.

SICINIUS
Sir, the people
Must have their voices; neither will they bate
One jot of ceremony.

MENENIUS
Put them not to't:
Pray you, go fit you to the custom and
Take to you, as your predecessors have,
Your honour with your form.

CORIOLANUS
It is apart
That I shall blush in acting, and might well
Be taken from the people.

BRUTUS
Mark you that? 171

CORIOLANUS
To brag unto them, thus I did, and thus;
Show them the unaching scars which I should hide,
As if I had received them for the hire
Of their breath only!

MENENIUS
Do not stand upon't.
We recommend to you, tribunes of the people,
Our purpose to them: and to our noble consul
Wish we all joy and honour.

SENATORS
To Coriolanus come all joy and honour!
[*Flourish of cornets. Exeunt all but Sicinius and Brutus.*

BRUTUS
You see how he intends to use the people.

SICINIUS
May they perceive's intent! He will require them, 184

As if he did contemn what he requested
Should be in them to give.

BRUTUS

Come, we'll inform them
Of our proceedings here: on the marketplace,
I know, they do attend us. [*Exeunt.*

ACT TWO SCENE THREE

The same. The Forum.

Enter seven or eight Citizens.

FIRST CITIZEN

Once, if he do require our voices, we ought not to deny him.

SECOND CITIZEN

We may, sir, if we will.

THIRD CITIZEN

We have power in ourselves to do it, but it is a power that we have no power to do; for if he show us his wounds and tell us his deeds, we are to put our tongues into those wounds and speak for them; so, if he tell us his noble deeds, we must also tell him our noble acceptance of them. Ingratitude is monstrous, and for the multitude to be ingrateful, were to make a monster of the multitude: of the which we being members, should bring ourselves to be monstrous members.

FIRST CITIZEN

And to make us no better thought of, a little help will serve; for once we stood up about the corn, he himself stuck not to call us the many-headed multitude.

THIRD CITIZEN

We have been called so of many; not that our heads are some brown, some black, some auburn, some bald, but that our wits are so diversely coloured: and truly I think if all our wits were to issue out of one skull, they would fly east, west, north, south, and their consent of one direct way should be at once to all the points o' the compass.

SECOND CITIZEN

Think you so? Which way do you judge my wit would fly?

THIRD CITIZEN

Nay, your wit will not so soon out as another man's will;'tis strongly wedged up in a block-head, but if it were at liberty, 'twould, sure, southward.

SECOND CITIZEN

Why that way?

THIRD CITIZEN

To lose itself in a fog, where being three parts melted away with rotten dews, the fourth would return for conscience sake, to help to get thee a wife.

SECOND CITIZEN

You are never without your tricks: you may, you
may. 34

THIRD CITIZEN

Are you all resolved to give your voices? But that's no matter, the greater part carries it. I say, if he would incline to the people, there was never a worthier man.

Enter CORIOLANUS *in a gown of humility, with* MENENIUS.

Here he comes, and in the gown of humility: mark his behavior. We are not to stay all together, but to come by him where he stands, by ones, by twos, and by threes. He's to make his requests by particulars; wherein every one of us has a single honour, in giving him our own voices with our own tongues: therefore follow me, and I'll direct you how you shall go by him.

ALL

Content, content. [*Exeunt Citizens.*

MENENIUS

O sir, you are not right: have you not known
The worthiest men have done't?

CORIOLANUS

What must I say?
'I Pray, sir'—Plague upon't! I cannot bring
My tongue to such a pace:—'Look, sir, my wounds!
I got them in my country's service, when
Some certain of your brethren roar'd and ran
From the noise of our own drums.'

MENENIUS

O me, the gods!
You must not speak of that: you must desire
them 56
To think upon you.

CORIOLANUS

Think upon me! hang 'em!
I would they would forget me, like the virtues [13]
Which our divines lose by 'em.

MENENIUS

You'll mar all:
I'll leave you: pray you, speak to 'em, I pray you,
In wholesome manner. [*Exit.*

CORIOLANUS

Bid them wash their faces
And keep their teeth clean. [*Re-enter two of the Citizens.*] So, here comes a brace. [*Re-enter a third Citizen.*]
You know the cause, air, of my standing here.

THIRD CITIZEN

We do, sir; tell us what hath brought you to't. 68

CORIOLANUS

Mine own desert.

SECOND CITIZEN

Your own desert!

CORIOLANUS
Ay, but not mine own desire.

THIRD CITIZEN
How not your own desire?

CORIOLANUS
No, sir, 'twas never my desire yet to trouble the poor with begging.

THIRD CITIZEN
You must think, if we give you any thing, we hope to gain by you.

CORIOLANUS
Well then, I pray, your price o' the consulship? 77

FIRST CITIZEN
The price is to ask it kindly.

CORIOLANUS
Kindly! Sir, I pray, let me ha't: I have wounds to show you, which shall be yours in private. Your good voice, sir; what say you?

SECOND CITIZEN
You shall ha't, worthy sir.

CORIOLANUS
A match, sir. There's in all two worthy voices begged. I have your alms: adieu.

THIRD CITIZEN
But this is something odd.

SECOND CITIZEN
And 'twere to give again,—but 'tis no matter. 86
[*Exeunt the three Citizens.*

Re-enter two other Citizens.

CORIOLANUS
Pray you now, if it may stand with the tune of your voices that I may be consul, I have here the customary gown.

FOURTH CITIZEN
You have deserved nobly of your country, and you have not deserved nobly.

CORIOLANUS
Your enigma?

FOURTH CITIZEN
You have been a scourge to her enemies, you have been a rod to her friends; you have not indeed loved the common people.

CORIOLANUS
You should account me the more virtuous that I have not been common in my love. I will, sir, flatter my sworn brother, the people, to earn a dearer estimation of them; 'tis a condition they account gentle: and since the wisdom of their choice is rather to have my hat than my heart, I will practice the insinuating nod and be off to them most counterfeitly; that is, sir, I will counterfeit the bewitchment of some popular man and give it bountiful to the desirers. Therefore, beseech you, I may be consul.

FIFTH CITIZEN
We hope to find you our friend; and therefore give you our voices heartily.

FOURTH CITIZEN
You have received many wounds for your ountry.

CORIOLANUS
I will not seal your knowledge with showing them. I will make much of your voices, and so trouble you no further.

BOTH CITIZENS
The gods give you joy, sir, heartily! [*Exeunt.*

CORIOLANUS
Most sweet voices!
Better it is to die, better to starve, 113
Than crave the hire which first we do deserve.
Why in this woolvish toge should I stand here, [14]
To beg of Hob and Dick, that do appear,
Their needless vouches? Custom calls me to't:
What custom wills, in all things should we do't,
The dust on antique time would lie unswept,
And mountainous error be too highly heapt
For truth to o'er-peer. Rather than fool it so,
Let the high office and the honour go
To one that would do this. I am half through;
The one part suffer'd, the other will I do. 124

Re-enter three Citizens *more.*

Here come more voices.
Your voices: for your voices I have fought;
Watch'd for your voices; for your voices bear
Of wounds two dozen odd; battles thrice six
I have seen and heard of; for your voices have
Done many things, some less, some more: your voices:
Indeed I would be consul.

SIXTH CITIZEN
He has done nobly, and cannot go without any honest man's voice. 133

SEVENTH CITIZEN
Therefore let him be consul: the gods give him joy, and make him good friend to the people!

ALL CITIZENS
Amen, amen. God save thee, noble consul! [*Exeunt.*

CORIOLANUS
Worthy voices!

Re-enter MENENIUS, *with* BRUTUS *and* SICINIUS.

MENENIUS
You have stood your limitation; and the tribunes
Endue you with the people's voice: remains
That, in the official marks invested, you
Anon do meet the senate.

CORIOLANUS
Is this done?

SICINIUS
The custom of request you have discharged: 143
The people do admit you, and are summon'd
To meet anon, upon your approbation.
CORIOLANUS
Where? at the senate-house?
SICINIUS
There, Coriolanus.
CORIOLANUS
May I change these garments?
SICINIUS
You may, sir.
CORIOLANUS
That I'll straight do; and, knowing myself again,
Repair to the senate-house.
MENENIUS
I'll keep you company. Will you along?
BRUTUS
We stay here for the people.
SICINIUS
Fare you well.
[*Exeunt Coriolanus and Menenius.*
He has it now, and by his looks methink
'Tis warm at 's heart. 156
BRUTUS
With a proud heart he wore his humble weeds.
Will you dismiss the people?

Re-enter Citizens.

SICINIUS
How now, my masters! Have you chose this man?
FIRST CITIZEN
He has our voices, sir.
BRUTUS
We pray the gods he may deserve your loves.
SECOND CITIZEN
Amen, sir: to my poor unworthy notice,
He mock'd us when he begg'd our voices.
THIRD CITIZEN
Certainly
He flouted us downright.
FIRST CITIZEN
No, 'tis his kind of speech: he did not mock us.
SECOND CITIZEN
Not one amongst us, save yourself, but says 167
He used us scornfully: he should have show'd us
His marks of merit, wounds received for's country.
SICINIUS
Why, so he did, I am sure.
CITIZENS
No, no; no man saw 'em.
THIRD CITIZEN
He said he had wounds, which he could show in private;
And with his hat, thus waving it in scorn,
'I would be consul,' says he: 'aged custom,
But by your voices, will not so permit me;
Your voices therefore.' When we granted that,
Here was 'I thank you for your voices: thank you:
Your most sweet voices: now you have left your voices, 180
I have no further with you.' Was not this mockery?
SICINIUS
Why either were you ignorant to see't,
Or, seeing it, of such childish friendliness
To yield your voices?
BRUTUS
Could you not have told him
As you were lesson'd, when he had no power,
But was a petty servant to the state,
He was your enemy, ever spake against
Your liberties and the charters that you bear
I' the body of the weal; and now, arriving
A place of potency and sway o' the state,
If he should still malignantly remain
Fast foe to the plebeii, your voices might
Be curses to yourselves? You should have said
That as his worthy deeds did claim no less
Than what he stood for, so his gracious nature
Would think upon you for your voices and
Translate his malice towards you into love,
Standing your friendly lord.
SICINIUS
Thus to have said,
As you were fore-advised, had touch'd his spirit 202
And tried his inclination; from him pluck'd
Either his gracious promise, which you might,
As cause had call'd you up, have held him to;
Or else it would have gall'd his surly nature,
Which easily endures not article
Tying him to aught; so putting him to rage,
You should have ta'en the advantage of his choler
And pass'd him unelected.
BRUTUS
Did you perceive
He did solicit you in free contempt
When he did need your loves, and do you think
That his contempt shall not be bruising to you,
When he hath power to crush? Why, had your bodies 216
No heart among you? or had you tongues to cry
Against the rectorship of judgment?
SICINIUS
Have you
Ere now denied the asker? and now again
Of him that did not ask, but mock, bestow
Your sued-for tongues?

THIRD CITIZEN
He's not confirm'd; we may deny him yet.
SECOND CITIZEN
And will deny him:
I'll have five hundred voices of that sound.
FIRST CITIZEN
I twice five hundred and their friends to piece 'em. 227
BRUTUS
Get you hence instantly, and tell those friends,
They have chose a consul that will from them take
Their liberties: make them of no more voice
Than dogs that are as often beat for barking
As therefore kept to do so.
SICINIUS
Let them assemble,
And on a safer judgment all revoke
Your ignorant election; enforce his pride,
And his old hate unto you; besides, forget not
With what contempt he wore the humble weed,
How in his suit he scorn'd you; but your loves,
Thinking upon his services, took from you 239
The apprehension of his present portance,
Which most gibingly, ungravely, he did fashion
After the inveterate hate he bears you.
BRUTUS
Lay
A fault on us, your tribunes; that we laboured,
No impediment between, but that you must
Cast your election on him.
SICINIUS
Say, you chose him
More after our commandment than as guided
By your own true affections, and that your minds,
Pre-occupied with what you rather must do
Than what you should, made you against the grain 252
To voice him consul: lay the fault on us.
BRUTUS
Ay, spare us not. Say we read lectures to you,
How youngly he began to serve his country,
How long continued, and what stock he springs of,
The noble house o' the Marcians, from whence came
That Ancus Marcius, Numa's daughter's son,
Who, after great Hostilius, here was king;
Of the same house Publius and Quintus were,
That our beat water brought by conduits hither; 261
And [Censorinus,] nobly named so, [15]
Twice being [by the people chosen] censor,
Was his great ancestor.
SICINIUS
One thus descended,
That hath beside well in his person wrought
To be set high in place, we did commend
To your remembrances: but you have found,
Scaling his present bearing with his past,
That he's your fixed enemy, and revoke
Your sudden approbation.
BRUTUS
Say, you ne'er had done't—
Harp on that still—but by our putting on:
And presently, when you have drawn your number,
Repair to the Capitol.
ALL
We will so: almost all
Repent in their election. [*Exeunt Citizens.*
BRUTUS
Let them go on;
This mutiny were better put in hazard,
Than stay, past doubt, for greater:
If, as his nature is, he fall in rage
With their refusal, both observe and answer
The vantage of his anger.
SICINIUS
To the Capitol, come:
We will be there before the stream o' the people;
And this shall seem, as partly 'tis, their own,
Which we have goaded onward. [*Exeunt.*

ACT THREE SCENE ONE

Rome. A street.

Cornets. Enter CORIOLANUS, MENENIUS, *all the Gentry*, COMINIUS, TITUS LARTIUS, *and other Senators.*

CORIOLANUS
Tullus Aufidius then had made new head?
LARTIUS
He had, my lord; and that it was which caused
Our swifter composition.
CORIOLANUS
So then the Volsces stand but as at first,
Ready, when time shall prompt them, to make road.
Upon's again.
COMINIUS
They are worn, lord consul, so,
That we shall hardly in our ages see
Their banners wave again.
CORIOLANUS
Saw you Aufidius?
LARTIUS
On safe-guard he came to me; and did curse
Against the Volsces, for they had so vilely 12
Yielded the town: he is retired to Antium.
CORIOLANUS
Spoke he of me?

LARTIUS
He did, my lord.
CORIOLANUS
How? what?
LARTIUS
How often he had met you, sword to sword;
That of all things upon the earth he hated
Your person most, that he would pawn his fortunes
To hopeless restitution, so he might
Be call'd your vanquisher.
CORIOLANUS
At Antium lives he?
LARTIUS
At Antium.
CORIOLANUS
I wish I had a cause to seek him there,
To oppose his hatred fully. Welcome home.

Enter SICINIUS *and* BRUTUS.

Behold, these are the tribunes of the people,
The tongues o' the common mouth: I do despise them;
For they do prank them in authority,
Against all noble sufferance.
SICINIUS
Pass no further.
CORIOLANUS
Ha! what is that?
BRUTUS
It will be dangerous to go on: no further.
CORIOLANUS
What makes this change?
MENENIUS
The matter?
COMINIUS
Hath he not pass'd the noble and the common?
BRUTUS
Cominius, no.
CORIOLANUS
Have I had children's voices? 38
FIRST SENATOR
Tribunes, give way; he shall to the market-place.
BRUTUS
The people are incensed against him.
SICINIUS
Stop,
Or all will fall in broil.
CORIOLANUS
Are these your herd?
Must these have voices, that can yield them now
And straight disclaim their tongues? What are your offices?
You being their mouths, why rule you not their teeth?
Have you not set them on?
MENENIUS
Be calm, be calm.
CORIOLANUS
It is a purposed thing, and grows by plot,
To curb the will of the nobility:
Suffer't, and live with such as cannot rule 52
Nor ever will be ruled.
BRUTUS
Call't not a plot:
The people cry you mock'd them, and of late,
When corn was given them gratis, you repined;
Scandal'd the suppliants for the people, call'd them
Time-pleasers, flatterers, foes to nobleness.
CORIOLANUS
Why, this was known before.
BRUTUS
Not to them all.
CORIOLANUS
Have you inform'd them sithence?
BRUTUS
How! I inform them!
CORIOLANUS
You are like to do such business.
BRUTUS
Not unlike,
Each way, to better yours.
CORIOLANUS
Why then should I be consul? By yond clouds, 66
Let me deserve so ill as you, and make me
Your fellow tribune.
SICINIUS
You show too much of that
For which the people stir: if you will pass
To where you are bound, you must inquire your way,
Which you are out of, with a gentler spirit,
Or never be so noble as a consul,
Nor yoke with him for tribune.
MENENIUS
Let's be calm.
COMINIUS
The people are abused; set on. This paltering
Becomes not Rome, nor has Coriolanus
Deserved this so dishonour'd rub, laid falsely
I' the plain way of his merit.
CORIOLANUS
Tell me of corn!
This was my speech, and I will speak't again—
MENENIUS
Not now, not now.
FIRST SENATOR
Not in this heat, sir, now.
CORIOLANUS
Now, as I live, I will. My nobler friends,
I crave their pardons:

For the mutable, rank-scented many, let them
Regard me as I do not flatter, and
Therein behold themselves: I say again,
In soothing them, we nourish 'gainst our senate
The cockle of rebellion, insolence, sedition,
Which we ourselves have plough'd for, sow'd, and scatter'd,
By mingling them with us, the honour'd number,
Who lack not virtue, no, nor power, but that
Which they have given to beggars.

MENENIUS
Well, no more.

FIRST SENATOR
No more words, we beseech you.

CORIOLANUS
How! no more!
As for my country I have shed my blood,
Not fearing outward force, so shall my lungs
Coin words till their decay against those measles,
Which we disdain should tatter us, yet sought
The very way to catch them.

BRUTUS
You speak o' the people,
As if you were a god to punish, not
A man of their infirmity.

SICINIUS
'Twere well
We let the people know't.

MENENIUS
What, what? his choler?

CORIOLANUS
Choler!
Were I as patient as the midnight sleep,
By Jove, 'twould be my mind!

SICINIUS
It is a mind
That shall remain a poison where it is,
Not poison any further.

CORIOLANUS
Shall remain!
Hear you this Triton of the minnows? mark you
His absolute 'shall'?

COMINIUS
'Twas from the canon.

CORIOLANUS
'Shall'!
O good but most unwise patricians! why,
You grave but reckless senators, have you thus
Given Hydra here to choose an officer, [16]
That with his peremptory 'shall,' being but
The horn and noise o' the monster's, wants not spirit
To say he'll turn your current in a ditch,
And make your channel his? If he have power
Then vail your ignorance; if none, awake [17]
Your dangerous lenity. If you are learn'd,
Be not as common fools; if you are not,
Let them have cushions by you. You are plebeians,
If they be senators: and they are no less,
When, both your voices blended, the great'st taste
Most palates theirs. They choose their magistrate,
And such a one as he, who puts his 'shall, '
His popular 'shall' against a graver bench
Than ever frown in Greece. By Jove himself!
It makes the consuls base: and my soul aches
To know, when two authorities are up,
Neither supreme, how soon confusion
May enter 'twixt the gap of both and take
The one by the other.

COMINIUS
Well, on to the market-place.

CORIOLANUS
Whoever gave that counsel, to give forth
The corn o' the storehouse gratis, as 'twas used
Sometime in Greece,—

MENENIUS
Well, well, no more of that.

CORIOLANUS
Though there the people had more absolute power,
I say, they nourish'd disobedience, fed
The ruin of the state.

BRUTUS
Why, shall the people give
One that speaks thus their voice?

CORIOLANUS
I'll give my reasons,
More worthier than their voices. They know the corn
Was not our recompense, resting well assured
They ne'er did service for't: being press'd to the war,
Even when the navel of the state was touch'd,
They would not thread the gates. This kind of service
Did not deserve corn gratis. Being i' the war.
Their mutinies and revolts, wherein they show'd
Most valour, spoke not for them: the accusation
Which they have often made against the senate,
All cause unborn, could never be the motive
Of our so frank donation. Well, what then?
How shall this bisson multitude digest
The senate's courtesy? Let deeds express
What's like to be their words: 'we did request it;
We are the greater poll, and in true fear
They gave us our demands.' Thus we debase
The nature of our seats and make the rabble
Call our cares fears; which will in time
Break ope the locks o' the senate and bring in
The crows to peck the eagles.

MENENIUS
Come, enough.
BRUTUS
Enough, with over-measure.
CORIOLANUS
No, take more: 179
What may be sworn by, both divine and human,
Seal what I end withal! This double worship,
Where one part does disdain with cause, the other
Insult without all reason, where gentry, title, wisdom,
Cannot conclude but by the yea and no
Of general ignorance,—it must omit
Real necessities, and give way the while
To unstable slightness: purpose so barr'd, it follows,
Nothing is done to purpose. Therefore, beseech you,—
You that will be less fearful than discreet, 189
That love the fundamental part of state
More than you doubt the change on't, that prefer
A noble life before a long, and wish
†To jump a body with a dangerous physic
That's sure of death without it, at once pluck out
The multitudinous tongue; let them not lick
The sweet which is their poison: your dishonour
Mangles true judgment and bereaves the state
Of that integrity which should become't,
Not having the power to do the good it would,
For the in which doth control't.
BRUTUS
Has said enough. 201
SICINIUS
Has spoken like a traitor, and shall answer
As traitors do.
CORIOLANUS
Thou wretch, despite o'erwhelm thee!
What should the people do with these bald tribunes?
On whom depending, their obedience fails
To the greater bench: in a rebellion,
When what's not meet, but what must be, was law,
Then were they chosen: in a better hour,
Let what is meet be said it must be meet, 210
And throw their power i' the dust.
BRUTUS
Manifest treason!
SICINIUS
This a consul? no.
BRUTUS
The aediles, ho!

Enter an Aedile.

Let him be apprehended.
SICINIUS
Go, call the people: [*Exit Aedile.*] in whose name myself
Attach thee as a traitorous innovator,
A foe to the public weal: obey, I charge thee,
And follow to thine answer.
CORIOLANUS
Hence, old goat!
SENATORS, &c
We'll surety him.
COMINIUS
Aged sir, hands off.
CORIOLANUS
Hence, rotten thing! or I shall shake thy bones
Out of thy garments.
SICINIUS
Help, ye citizens! 226

Enter a rabble of Citizens *(Plebeians), with the* Aediles.

MENENIUS
On both sides more respect.
SICINIUS
Here's he that would take from you all your power.
BRUTUS
Seize him, Aediles!
CITIZENS
Down with him! down with him!
SENATORS, &c
Weapons, weapons, weapons!
[*They all bustle about Coriolanus, crying*
'Tribunes!' 'Patricians!' 'Citizens!' 'What, ho!'
'Sicinius!' 'Brutus!' 'Coriolanus!' 'Citizens!'
'Peace, peace, peace!' 'Stay, hold, peace!'
MENENIUS
What is about to be? I am out of breath;
Confusion's near; I cannot speak. You, tribunes 237
To the people! Coriolanus, patience!
Speak, good Sicinius.
SICINIUS
Hear me, people; peace!
CITIZENS
Let's hear our tribune: peace Speak, speak, speak.
SICINIUS
You are at point to lose your liberties:
Marcius would have all from you; Marcius,
Whom late you have named for consul.
MENENIUS
Fie, fie, fie!
This is the way to kindle, not to quench.
FIRST SENATOR
To unbuild the city and to lay all flat.
SICINIUS
What is the city but the people?
CITIZENS
True,
The people are the city. 250

CORIOLANUS Hence, rotten thing! or I shall shake thy bones out of thy garments.

BRUTUS
By the consent of all, we were establish'd
The people's magistrates.
CITIZENS
You so remain.
MENENIUS
And so are like to do.
COMINIUS
That is the way to lay the city flat;
To bring the roof to the foundation,
And bury all, which yet distinctly ranges,
In heaps and piles of ruin.
SICINIUS
This deserves death.
BRUTUS
Or let us stand to our authority,
Or let us lose it. We do here pronounce,
Upon the part o' the people, in whose power
We were elected theirs, Marcius is worthy
Of present death.
SICINIUS
Therefore lay hold of him;
Bear him to the rock Tarpeian, and from thence
Into destruction cast him.
BRUTUS
Aediles, seize him!
CITIZENS
Yield, Marcius, yield!
MENENIUS
Hear me one word;
Beseech you, tribunes, hear me but a word.
AEDILE
Peace, peace!
MENENIUS
[*To Brutus*] Be that you seem, truly your country's friend,
And temperately proceed to what you would
Thus violently redress.
BRUTUS
Sir, those cold ways, 277
That seem like prudent helps, are very poisonous
Where the disease is violent. Lay hands upon him,
And bear him to the rock.
CORIOLANUS
No, I'll die here.
[*Drawing his sword.*
There's some among you have beheld me fighting:
Come, try upon yourselves what you have seen me.

MENENIUS
Down with that sword! Tribunes, withdraw awhile.
BRUTUS
Lay hands upon him.
COMINIUS
Help Marcius, help,
You that be noble; help him, young and old!
CITIZENS
Down with him, down with him!
[In this mutiny, the Tribunes, the Aediles, and the People, are beat in.
MENENIUS
Go, get you to your house; be gone, away! [18]
All will be naught else.
SECOND SENATOR
Get you gone.
COMINIUS
Stand fast;
We have as many friends as enemies.
MENENIUS
Shall it be put to that?
FIRST SENATOR
The gods forbid!
I prithee, noble friend, home to thy house;
Leave us to cure this cause.
MENENIUS
For 'tis a sore upon us,
You cannot tent yourself: be gone, beseech you.
COMINIUS
Come, sir, along with us.
CORIOLANUS
I would they were barbarians—as they are,
Though in Rome litter'd—not Romans—as they are not,
Though calved i' the porch o' the Capitol—
MENENIUS
Be gone;
Put not your worthy rage into your tongue;
One time will owe another.
CORIOLANUS
On fair ground
I could beat forty of them.
MENENIUS
I could myself
Take up a brace o' the best of them; yea, the two tribunes:
COMINIUS
But now 'tis odds beyond arithmetic;
And manhood is call'd foolery, when it stands
Against a falling fabric. Will you hence,
Before the tag return? whose rage doth rend
Like interrupted waters and o'erbear
What they are used to bear.
MENENIUS
Pray you, be gone:
I'll try whether my old wit be in request
With those that have but little: this must be patch'd
With cloth of any colour.
COMINIUS
Nay, come away. *[Exeunt Coriolanus, Cominius, and others.*
A PATRICIAN
This man has marr'd his fortune.
MENENIUS
His nature is too noble for the world:
He would not flatter Neptune for his trident,
Or Jove for's power to thunder. His heart's his mouth:
What his breast forges, that his tongue must vent;
And, being angry, does forget that ever
He heard the name of death. *[A noise within.*
Here's goodly work!
SECOND PATRICIAN
I would they were a-bed!
MENENIUS
I would they were in Tiber! What the vengeance!
Could he not speak 'em fair?

Re-enter BRUTUS *and* SICINIUS, *with the rabble.*

SICINIUS
Where is this viper
That would depopulate the city and
Be every man himself?
MENENIUS
You worthy tribunes,—
SICINIUS
He shall be thrown down the Tarpeian rock
With rigorous hands: he hath resisted law,
And therefore law shall scorn him further trial
Than the severity of the public power
Which he so sets at nought.
FIRST CITIZEN
He shall well know
The noble tribunes are the people's mouths,
And we their hands.
CITIZENS
He shall, sure on't.
MENENIUS
Sir, sir,—
SICINIUS
Peace!
MENENIUS
Do not cry havoc, where you should but hunt
With modest warrant.
SICINIUS
Sir, how comes't that you
Have holp to make this rescue?

MENENIUS
Hear me speak:
As I do know the consul's worthiness,
So can I name his faults,—
SICINIUS
Consul! what consul?
MENENIUS
The consul Coriolanus.
BRUTUS
He consul!
CITIZENS
No, no, no, no, no.
MENENIUS
If, by the tribunes' leave, and yours, good people,
I may be heard, I would crave a word or two;
The which shall turn you to no further harm
Than so much loss of time.
SICINIUS
Speak briefly then;
For we are peremptory to dispatch
This viperous traitor: to eject him hence
Were but one danger, and to keep him here
Our certain death: therefore it is decreed
He dies to-night.
MENENIUS
Now the good gods forbid
That our renowned Rome, whose gratitude
Towards her deserved children is enroll'd
In Jove's own book, like an unnatural dam
Should now eat up her own!
SICINIUS
He's a disease that must be cut away.
MENENIUS
O, he's a limb that has but a disease;
Mortal, to cut it off; to cure it, easy.
What has he done to Rome that's worthy death?
Killing our enemies, the blood he hath lost—
Which, I dare vouch, is more than that he hath,
By many an ounce—he dropp'd it for his country;
And what is left, to lose it by his country,
Were to us all, that do't and suffer it,
A brand to the end o' the world.
SICINIUS
This is clean kam.
BRUTUS
Merely awry: when he did love his country,
It honour'd him.
MENENIUS
The service of the foot
Being once gangrened, is not then respected
For what before it was.
BRUTUS
We'll hear no more.
Pursue him to his house, and pluck him thence:
Lest his infection, being of catching nature,
Spread further.
MENENIUS
One word more, one word.
This tiger-footed rage, when it shall find
The harm of unscann'd swiftness, will too late
Tie leaden pounds to's heels. Proceed by process;
Lest parties, as he is beloved, break out,
And sack great Rome with Romans.
BRUTUS
If it were so,—
SICINIUS
What do ye talk?
Have we not had a taste of his obedience?
Our aediles smote? ourselves resisted? Come.
MENENIUS
Consider this: he has been bred i' the wars
Since he could draw a sword, and is ill school'd
In bolted language; meal and bran together
He throws without distinction. Give me leave,
I'll go to him, and undertake to bring him
Where he shall answer, by a lawful form,
In peace, to his utmost peril.
FIRST SENATOR
Noble tribunes,
It is the humane way: the other course
Will prove too bloody, and the end of it
Unknown to the beginning.
SICINIUS
Noble Menenius,
Be you then as the people's officer.
Masters, lay down your weapons.
BRUTUS
Go not home.
SICINIUS
Meet on the market-place. We'll attend you there:
Where, if you bring not Marcius, we'll proceed
In our first way.
MENENIUS
I'll bring him to you.
[*To the Senators*] Let me desire your company: he must come,
Or what is worst will follow.
FIRST SENATOR
Pray you, let's to him. [*Exeunt.*

ACT THREE SCENE TWO

A room in CORIOLANUS'S *house.*

Enter CORIOLANUS *with Patricians.*

CORIOLANUS
Let them puff all about mine ears, present me

Death on the wheel or at wild horses' heels,
Or pile ten hills on the Tarpeian rock,
That the precipitation might down stretch
Below the beam of sight, yet will I still
Be thus to them.

A PATRICIAN
You do the nobler.

CORIOLANUS
I muse my mother
Does not approve me further, who was wont
To call them woollen vassals, things created
To buy and sell with groats, to show bare heads
In congregations, to yawn, be still and wonder,
When one but of my ordinance stood up
To speak of peace or war.

Enter VOLUMNIA.

I talk of you:
Why did you wish me milder? would you have me
False to my nature? Rather say I play
The man I am.

VOLUMNIA
O, sir, sir, sir,
I would have had you put your power well on,
Before you had worn it out.

CORIOLANUS
Let go.

VOLUMNIA
You might have been enough the man you are,
With striving less to be so; lesser had been
The thwartings of your dispositions, if [19]
You had not show'd them how ye were disposed
Ere they lack'd power to cross you.

CORIOLANUS
Let them hang.

A PATRICIAN
Ay, and burn too.

Enter MENENIUS *and* Senators.

MENENIUS
Come, come, you have been too rough, something too rough;
You must return and mend it.

FIRST SENATOR
There's no remedy;
Unless, by not so doing, our good city
Cleave in the midst, and perish.

VOLUMNIA
Pray, be counsell'd:
I have a heart as little apt as yours,
But yet a brain that leads my use of anger
To better vantage.

MENENIUS
Well said, noble woman?
Before he should thus stoop to the herd, but that [20]
The violent fit o' the time craves it as physic
For the whole state, I would put mine armour on,
Which I can scarcely bear.

CORIOLANUS
What must I do?

MENENIUS
Return to the tribunes.

CORIOLANUS
Well, what then? what then?

MENENIUS
Repent what you have spoke.

CORIOLANUS
For them! I cannot do it to the gods;
Must I then do't to them?

VOLUMNIA
You are too absolute;
Though therein you can never be too noble,
But when extremities speak. I have heard you say,
Honour and policy, like unsever'd friends,
I' the war do grow together: grant that, and tell me,
In peace what each of them by the other lose,
That they combine not there.

CORIOLANUS
Tush, tush!

MENENIUS
A good demand.

VOLUMNIA
If it be honour in your wars to seem
The same you are not, which, for your best ends,
You adopt your policy, how is it less or worse,
That it shall hold companionship in peace
With honour, as in war, since that to both
It stands in like request?

CORIOLANUS
Why force you this?

VOLUMNIA
Because that now it lies you on to speak
To the people; not by your own instruction,
Nor by the matter which your heart prompts you,
But with such words that are but roted in
Your tongue, though but bastards and syllables [21]
Of no allowance to your bosom's truth.
Now, this no more dishonours you at all
Than to take in a town with gentle words,
Which else would put you to your fortune and
The hazard of much blood.
I would dissemble with my nature where
My fortunes and my friends at stake required
I should do so in honour: I am in this, [22]
Your wife, your son, these senators, the nobles;
And you will rather show our general louts
How you can frown than spend a fawn upon 'em,

For the inheritance of their loves and safeguard
Of what that want might ruin. [23]

MENENIUS
Noble lady!
Come, go with us; speak fair: you may salve so,
Not what is dangerous present, but the loss 88
Of what is past.

VOLUMNIA
I prithee now, my son,
Go to them, with this bonnet in thy hand;
And thus far having stretch'd it—here be with them—
Thy knee bussing the stones—for in such business
Action is eloquence, and the eyes of the ignorant
More learned than the ears—waving thy head,
Which often, thus, correcting thy stout heart, [24]
Now humble as the ripest mulberry
That will not hold the handling: or say to them, 100
Thou art their soldier, and being bred in broils
Hast not the soft way which, thou dost confess,
Were fit for thee to use as they to claim,
In asking their good loves, but thou wilt frame
Thyself, forsooth, hereafter theirs, so far
As thou hast power and person.

MENENIUS
This but done,
Even as she speaks, why, their hearts were yours;
For they have pardons, being ask'd, as free
As words to little purpose.

VOLUMNIA
Prithee now,
Go, and be ruled: although I know thou hadst rather 113
Follow thine enemy in a fiery gulf
Than flatter him in a bower. Here is Cominius.

Enter COMINIUS.

COMINIUS
I have been i' the market-place; and, sir, 'tis fit
You make strong party, or defend yourself
By calmness or by absence: all's in anger.

MENENIUS
Only fair speech.

COMINIUS
I think 'twill serve, if he
Can thereto frame his spirit.

VOLUMNIA
He must, and will
Prithee now, say you will, and go about it.

CORIOLANUS
Must I go show them my unbarbed sconce?
Must I with base tongue give my noble heart
A lie that it must bear? Well, I will do't:
Yet, were there but this single plot to lose,
This mould of Marcius, they to dust should grind it
And throw't against the wind. To the market-place!
You have put me now to such a part which never
I shall discharge to the life.

COMINIUS
Come, come, we'll prompt you.

VOLUMNIA
I prithee now, sweet son, as thou hast said
My praises made thee first a soldier, so,
To have my praise for this, perform a part
Thou hast not done before.

CORIOLANUS
Well, I must do't:
Away, my disposition, and possess me 138
Some harlot's spirit! my throat of war be turn'd,
Which quired with my drum, into a pipe
Small as an eunuch, or the virgin voice
That babies lulls asleep! the smiles of knaves
Tent in my cheeks, and schoolboys' tears take up
The glasses of my sight! a beggar's tongue
Make motion through my lips, and my arm'd knees,
Who bow'd but in my stirrup, bend like his
That hath received an alms! I will not do't,
Lest I surcease to honour mine own truth
And by my body's action teach my mind
A most inherent baseness.

VOLUMNIA
At thy choice, then:
To beg of thee, it is my more dishonour
Than thou of them. Come all to ruin; let
Thy mother rather feel thy pride than fear
Thy dangerous stoutness, for I mock at death
With as big heart as thou. Do as thou list
Thy valiantness was mine, thou suck'dst it from me,
But owe thy pride thyself.

CORIOLANUS
Pray, be content: 160
Mother, I am going to the market-place;
Chide me no more. I'll mountebank their loves,
Cog their hearts from them, and come home beloved
Of all the trades in Rome. Look, I am going:
Commend me to my wife. I'll return consul;
Or never trust to what my tongue can do
I' the way of flattery further.

VOLUMNIA
Do your will. [*Exit.*

COMINIUS
Away! the tribunes do attend you: arm yourself
To answer mildly; for they are prepared
With accusations, as I hear, more strong 172
Than are upon you yet.

CORIOLANUS
The word is 'mildly.' Pray you, let us go:
Let them accuse me by invention, I
Will answer in mine honour.
MENENIUS
Ay, but mildly.
CORIOLANUS
Well, mildly be it then. Mildly! [*Exeunt.*

ACT THREE SCENE THREE

The same. The Forum.

Enter SICINIUS *and* BRUTUS.

BRUTUS
In this point charge him home, that he affects
Tyrannical power: if he evade us there,
Enforce him with his envy to the people,
And that the spoil got on the Antiates
Was ne'er distributed.

Enter an Aedile.

What, will he come?
AEDILE
He's coming.
BRUTUS
How accompanied?
AEDILE
With old Menenius, and those senators
That always favour'd him.
SICINIUS
Have you a catalogue
Of all the voices that we have procured
Set down by the poll?
AEDILE
I have; 'tis ready. 14
SICINIUS
Have you collected them by tribes?
AEDILE
I have.
SICINIUS
Assemble presently the people hither;
And when they bear me say 'It shall be so
I' the right and strength o' the commons, ' be it either
For death, for fine, or banishment, then let them,
If I say fine, cry 'Fine;' if death, cry 'Death.'
Insisting on the old prerogative
And power i' the truth o' the cause.
AEDILE
I shall inform them.
BRUTUS
And when such time they have begun to cry,
Let them not cease, but with a din confused
Enforce the present execution
Of what we chance to sentence.
AEDILE
Very well.
SICINIUS
Make them be strong and ready for this hint,
When we shall hap to give 't them.
BRUTUS
Go about it. [*Exit Aedile.*
Put him to choler straight: he hath been used
Ever to conquer, and to have his worth
Of contradiction: being once chafed, he cannot
Be rein'd again to temperance; then he speaks
What's in his heart; and that is there which looks
With us to break his neck.
SICINIUS
Well, here he comes. 40

Enter CORIOLANUS, MENENIUS, *and* COMINIUS, *with* Senators *and* Patricians.

MENENIUS
Calmly, I do beseech you.
CORIOLANUS
Ay, as an ostler, that for the poorest piece
Will bear the knave by the volume. The honour'd gods
Keep Rome in safety, and the chairs of justice
Supplied with worthy men! plant love among 's! [25]
Throng our large temples with the shows of peace, [26]
And not our streets with war!
FIRST SENATOR
Amen, amen.
MENENIUS
A noble wish.

Re-enter Aedile, *with* Citizens.

SICINIUS
Draw near, ye people.
AEDILE
List to your tribunes. Audience: peace, I say! 53
CORIOLANUS
First, hear me speak.
BOTH TRIBUNES
Well, say. Peace, ho!
CORIOLANUS
Shall I be charged no further than this present?
Must all determine here?
SICINIUS
I do demand,
If you submit you to the people's voices,
Allow their officers and are content
To suffer lawful censure for such faults
As shall be proved upon you?

CORIOLANUS
I am content.
MENENIUS
Lo, citizens, he says he is content:
The warlike service he has done, consider; think 66
Upon the wounds his body bears, which show
Like graves i' the holy churchyard.
CORIOLANUS
Scratches with briers,
Scars to move laughter only.
MENENIUS
Consider further,
That when he speaks not like a citizen,
You find him like a soldier: do not take
His rougher accents for malicious sounds, [27]
But, as I say, such as become a soldier,
Rather than envy you.
COMINIUS
Well, well, no more.
CORIOLANUS
What is the matter
That being pass'd for consul with full voice,
I am so dishonour'd that the very hour 80
You take it off again?
SICINIUS
Answer to us.
CORIOLANUS
Say, then: 'tis true, I ought so.
SICINIUS
We charge you, that you have contrived to take
From Rome all season'd office and to wind
Yourself into a power tyrannical;
For which you are a traitor to the people.
CORIOLANUS
How! traitor!
MENENIUS
Nay, temperately; your promise.
CORIOLANUS
The fires i' the lowest hell fold-in the people!
Call me their traitor! Thou injurious tribune!
Within thine eyes sat twenty thousand deaths,
In thy hand clutch'd as many millions, in 93
Thy lying tongue both numbers, I would say
'Thou liest' unto thee with a voice as free
As I do pray the gods.
SICINIUS
Mark you this, people?
CITIZENS
To the rock, to the rock with him!
SICINIUS
Peace!
We need not put new matter to his charge:
What you have seen him do and heard him speak,
Beating your officers, cursing yourselves,
Opposing laws with strokes and here defying
Those whose great power must try him; even this, 104
So criminal and in such capital kind,
Deserves the extremest death.
BRUTUS
But since he hath
Served well for Rome,—
CORIOLANUS
What do you prate of service?
BRUTUS
I talk of that, that know it.
CORIOLANUS
You?
MENENIUS
Is this the promise that you made your mother?
COMINIUS
Know, I pray you,—
CORIOLANUS
I' ll know no further:
Let them pronounce the steep Tarpeian death,
Vagabond exile, raying, pent to linger
But with a grain a day, I would not buy 117
Their mercy at the price of one fair word;
Nor check my courage for what they can give,
To have't with saying 'Good morrow.'
SICINIUS
For that he has,
As much as in him lies, from time to time
Envied against the people, seeking means
To pluck away their power, as now at last
Given hostile strokes, and that not in the presence
Of dreaded justice, but on the ministers
That do distribute it; in the name o' the people
And in the power of us the tribunes, we, 128
Even from this instant, banish him our city,
In peril of precipitation
From off the rock Tarpeian never more
To enter our Rome gates: i' the people's name,
I say it shall be so.
CITIZENS
It shall be so, it shall be so; let him away:
He's banish'd, and it shall be so.
COMINIUS
Hear me, my masters, and my common friends,—
SICINIUS
He's sentenced; no more hearing.
COMINIUS
Let me speak:
I have been consul, and can show for Rome
Her enemies' marks upon me. I do love
My country's good with a respect more tender,
More holy and profound, than mine own life,

My dear wife's estimate, her womb's increase,
And treasure of my loins; then if I would
Speak that,—

SICINIUS
We know your drift: speak what?

BRUTUS
There's no more to be said, but he is banish'd,
As enemy to the people and his country:
It shall be so.

CITIZENS
It shall be so, it shall be so.

CORIOLANUS
You common cry of curs! whose breath I hate 152
As reek o' the rotten fens, whose loves I prize
As the dead carcasses of unburied men
That do corrupt my air, I banish you;
And here remain with your uncertainty!
Let every feeble rumour shake your hearts!
Your enemies, with nodding of their plumes,
Fan you into despair! Have the power still
To banish your defenders; till at length
Your ignorance, which finds not till it feels, 161
Making not reservation of yourselves, [28]
Still your own foes, deliver you as most
Abated captives to some nation
That won you without blows! Despising,
For you, the city, thus I turn my back:
There is a world elsewhere.
[Exeunt Coriolanus, Cominius, Menenius, Senators, and Patricians.

AEDILE
The people's enemy is gone, is gone!

CITIZENS
Our enemy is banish'd! he is gone! Hoo! hoo!
[Shouting, and throwing up their caps.

SICINIUS
Go, see him out at gates, and follow him,
As he hath followed you, with all despite;
Give him deserved vexation. Let a guard 172
Attend us through the city.

CITIZENS
Come, come; let's see him out at gates; come.
The gods preserve our noble tribunes! Come.
[Exeunt.

ACT FOUR SCENE ONE

Rome. Before a gate of the city.
Enter CORIOLANUS, VOLUMNIA, VIRGILIA, MENENIUS, COMINIUS, *with the young Nobility of Rome.*

CORIOLANUS
Come, leave your tears: a brief farewell: the beast
With many heads butts me away. Nay, mother,
Where is your ancient courage? you were used
To say extremity was the trier of spirits;
That common chances common men could bear;
That when the sea was calm all boats alike
Show'd mastership in floating; fortune's blows, [29]
When most struck home, being gentle wounded, craves
A noble cunning: you were used to load me
With precepts that would make invincible 11
The heart that conn'd them.

VIRGILIA
O heavens! O heavens!

CORIOLANUS
Nay! prithee, woman,—

VOLUMNIA
Now the red pestilence strike all trades in Rome,
And occupations perish!

CORIOLANUS
What, what, what!
I shall be loved when I am lack'd. Nay, mother.
Resume that spirit, when you were wont to say,
If you had been the wife of Hercules,
Six of his labours you'ld have done, and saved
Your husband so much sweat. Cominius,
Droop not; adieu. Farewell, my wife, my mother: 24
I'll do well yet. Thou old and true Menenius,
Thy tears are salter than a younger man's,
And venomous to thine eyes. My sometime general,
I have seen thee stern, and thou hast oft beheld
Heart-hardening spectacles; tell these sad women
'Tis fond to wail inevitable strokes,
As 'tis to laugh at 'em. My mother, you wot well
My hazards still have been your solace: and
Believe't not lightly—though I go alone,
Like to a lonely dragon, that his fen 34
Makes fear'd and talk'd of more than seen—your son
Will or exceed the common or be caught
With cautelous baits and practice.

VOLUMNIA
My first son.
Whither wilt thou go? Take good Cominius
With thee awhile: determine on some course,
More than a wild exposture to each chance
That starts i' the way before thee.

CORIOLANUS
O the gods!

COMINIUS
I'll follow thee a month, devise with thee
Where thou shalt rest, that thou mayst hear of us
And we of thee: so if the time thrust forth 46

A cause for thy repeal, we shall not send
O'er the vast world to seek a single man,
And lose advantage, which doth ever cool
I' the absence of the needer.

CORIOLANUS
Fare ye well:
Thou hast years upon thee; and thou art too full
Of the wars' surfeits, to go rove with one
That's yet unbruised: bring me but out at gate.
Come, my sweet wife, my dearest mother, and
My friends of noble touch, when I am forth,
Bid me farewell, and smile. I pray you, come.
While I remain above the ground, you shall
Hear from me still, and never of me aught
But what is like me formerly.

MENENIUS
That's worthily
As any ear can hear. Come, let's not weep.
If I could shake off but one seven years
From these old arms and legs, by the good gods,
I'ld with thee every foot.

CORIOLANUS
Give me thy hand: Come. [*Exeunt.*

ACT FOUR SCENE TWO

The same. A street near the gate.

Enter SICINIUS, BRUTUS, *and an* Aedile.

SICINIUS
Bid them all home; he's gone, and we'll no further.
The nobility are vex'd, whom we see have sided
In his behalf.

BRUTUS
Now we have shown our power,
Let us seem humbler after it is done
Than when it was a-doing.

SICINIUS
Bid them home:
Say their great enemy is gone, and they
Stand in their ancient strength.

BRUTUS
Dismiss them home. [*Exit Aedile.*
Here comes his mother.

SICINIUS
Let's not meet her.

BRUTUS
Why?

SICINIUS
They say she's mad.

BRUTUS
They have ta'en note of us: keep on your way.

Enter VOLUMNIA, VIRGILIA, *and* MENENIUS.

VOLUMNIA
O, ye're well met: the hoarded plague o' the gods
Requite your love!

MENENIUS
Peace, peace; be not so loud.

VOLUMNIA
If that I could for weeping, you should hear,—
Nay, and you shall hear some.
[*To Brutus*] Will you be gone?

VIRGILIA
[*To Sicinius*] You shall stay too: I would I had the power
To say so to my husband.

SICINIUS
Are you mankind?

VOLUMNIA
Ay, fool; is that a shame? Note but this fool.
Was not a man my father? Hadst thou foxship
To banish him that struck more blows for Rome
Than thou hast spoken words?

SICINIUS
O blessed heavens!

VOLUMNIA
More noble blows than ever thou wise words;
And for Rome's good. I'll tell thee what; yet go:
Nay, but thou shalt stay too: I would my son
Were in Arabia, and thy tribe before him,
His good sword in his hand.

SICINIUS
What then?

VIRGILIA
What then!
He'ld make an end of thy posterity.

VOLUMNIA
Bastards and all.
Good man, the wounds that he does bear for Rome!

MENENIUS
Come, come, peace.

SICINIUS
I would he had continued to his country
As he began, and not unknit himself
The noble knot he made.

BRUTUS
I would he had.

VOLUMNIA
'I would he had'! 'Twas you incensed the rabble:
Cats, that can judge as fitly of his worth
As I can of those mysteries which heaven
Will not have earth to know.

BRUTUS
Pray, let us go.

VOLUMNIA
Now, pray, sir, get you gone:

You have done a brave deed. Ere you go, hear this:—
As far as doth the Capitol exceed
The meanest house in Rome, so far my son—
This lady's husband here, this, do you see—
Whom you have banish'd, does exceed you all.

BRUTUS
Well, well, we'll leave you.

SICINIUS
Why stay we to be baited
With one that wants her wits?

VOLUMNIA
Take my prayers with you. [*Exeunt Tribunes.*
I would the gods had nothing else to do
But to confirm my curses! Could I meet 'em
But once a-day, it would unclog my heart
Of what lies heavy to't.

MENENIUS
You have told them home;
And, by my troth, you have cause. You'll sup with me?

VOLUMNIA
Anger's my meat; I sup upon myself,
And so shall starve with feeding. Come, let's go:
Leave this faint puling and lament as I do,
In anger, Juno-like. Come, come, come.

MENENIUS
Fie, fie, fie! [*Exeunt.*

ACT FOUR SCENE THREE

A highway between Rome and Antium.

Enter a Roman *and a* Volsce, *meeting.*

ROMAN
I know you well, sir, and you know me: your name, I think, is Adrian.

VOLSCE
It is so, sir: truly, I have forgot you.

ROMAN
I am a Roman; and my services are, as you are, against 'em: know you me yet?

VOLSCE
Nicanor? no.

ROMAN
The same, sir.

VOLSCE
You had more beard when I last saw you; but your favour is well approved by your tongue. What's the news in Rome? I have a note from the Volscian state, to find you out there: you have well saved me a day's journey.

ROMAN
There hath been in Rome strange insurrections; the people against the senators, patricians, and nobles.

VOLSCE
Hath been! is it ended, then? Our state thinks not so: they are in a most warlike preparation, and hope to come upon them in the heat of their division.

ROMAN
The main blaze of it is past, but a small thing would make it flame again: for the nobles receive so to heart the banishment of that worthy Coriolanus, that they are in a ripe aptness to take all power from the people and to pluck from them their tribunes for ever. This lies glowing, I can tell you, and is almost mature for the violent breaking out.

VOLSCE
Coriolanus banished!

ROMAN
Banished, sir.

VOLSCE
You will be welcome with this intelligence, Nicanor.

ROMAN
The day serves well for them now. I have heard it said, the fittest time to corrupt a man's wife is when she's fallen out with her husband. Your noble Tullus Aufidius will appear well in these wars, his great opposer, Coriolanus, being now in no request of his country.

VOLSCE
He cannot choose. I am most fortunate, thus accidentally to encounter you: you have ended my business, and I will merrily accompany you home.

ROMAN
I shall, between this and supper, tell you most strange things from Rome; all tending to the good of their adversaries. Have you an army ready, say you?

VOLSCE
A most royal one; the centurions and their charges, distinctly billeted, already in the entertainment, and to be on foot at an hour's warning.

ROMAN
I am joyful to hear of their readiness, and am the man, I think, that shall set them in present action. So, sir, heartily well met, and most glad of your company.

VOLSCE
You take my part from me, sir; I have the most cause to be glad of yours.

ROMAN
Well, let us go together. [*Exeunt.*

ACT FOUR SCENE FOUR

Antium. Before AUFIDIUS'S house.

Enter CORIOLANUS *in mean apparel, disguised and muffled* .

CORIOLANUS
A goodly city is this Antium. City,
'Tis I that made thy widows: many an heir
Of these fair edifices 'fore my wars
Have I heard groan and drop: then know me not,
Lest that thy wives with spits and boys with stones
In puny battle slay me.

Enter a Citizen.

Save you, sir.

CITIZEN
And you.

CORIOLANUS
Direct me, if it be your will,
Where great Aufidius lies: is he in Antium?

CITIZEN
He is, and feasts the nobles of the state
At his house this night.

CORIOLANUS
Which is his house, beseech you?

CITIZEN
This, here before you.

CORIOLANUS
Thank you, sir: farewell. [*Exit Citizen.*
O world, thy slippery turns! Friends now fast sworn,
Whose double bosoms seem to wear one heart,
Whose house, whose bed, whose meal, and exercise,
Are still together, who twin, as 'twere, in love
Unseparable, shall within this hour,
On a dissension of a doit, break out
To bitterest enmity: so, fellest foes,
Whose passions and whose plots have broke their sleep,
To take the one the other, by some chance,
Some trick not worth an egg, shall grow dear friends
And interjoin their issues. So with me:
My birth-place hate I, and my love's upon
This enemy town. I'll enter: if he slay me,
He does fair justice; if he give me way,
I'll do his country service. [*Exit.*

ACT FOUR SCENE FIVE

The same. A hall in AUFIDIUS'S house.

Music within. Enter a Servingman.

FIRST SERVANT
Wine, wine, wine! What service is here! I think our fellows are asleep. [*Exit.*

Enter a second Servingman.

SECOND SERVANT
Where's Cotus? my master calls for him. Cotus! [*Exit.*

Enter CORIOLANUS.

CORIOLANUS
A goodly house: the feast smells well; but I
Appear not like a guest.

Re-enter the first Servingman.

FIRST SERVANT
What would you have, friend? whence are you? Here's no place for you: pray, go to the door. [*Exit.*

CORIOLANUS
I have deserved no better entertainment,
In being Coriolanus.

Re-enter second Servingman.

SECOND SERVANT
Whence are you, sir? Has the porter his eyes in his head, that he gives entrance to such companions? Pray, get you out.

CORIOLANUS
Away!

SECOND SERVANT
Away! get you away.

CORIOLANUS
Now thou'rt troublesome.

SECOND SERVANT
Are you so brave? I'll have you talked with anon.

Enter a third Servingman . *The first meets him.*

THIRD SERVANT
What fellow's this?

FIRST SERVANT
A strange one as ever I looked on: I cannot get him out of the house: prithee, call my master to him. [*Retires.*

THIRD SERVANT
What have you to do here, fellow? Pray you, avoid the house.

CORIOLANUS
Let me but stand; I will not hurt your hearth.

THIRD SERVANT
What are you?

CORIOLANUS
A gentleman.

THIRD SERVANT
A marvellous poor one.

CORIOLANUS
True, so I am.

THIRD SERVANT
Pray you, poor gentleman, take up some other station; here's no place for you; pray you, avoid: come.

CORIOLANUS
Follow your function, go, and batten on cold bits.
[*Pushes him away.*

THIRD SERVANT
What, you will not? Prithee, tell my master what a strange guest he has here.

SECOND SERVANT
And I shall. [*Exit.*

THIRD SERVANT
Where dwellest thou? 33

CORIOLANUS
Under the canopy.

THIRD SERVANT
Under the canopy?

CORIOLANUS
Ay.

THIRD SERVANT
Where's that?

CORIOLANUS
I' the city of kites and crows.

THIRD SERVANT
I' the city of kites and crows! What an ass it is!
Then thou dwellest with daws too?

CORIOLANUS
No, I serve not thy master.

THIRD SERVANT
How, sir! do you meddle with my master? 42

CORIOLANUS
Ay; 'tis an honester service than to meddle with thy mistress. Thou pratest, and pratest; serve with thy trencher, hence!
[*Beats him away. Exit third Servingman.*

Enter AUFIDIUS *with the second* Servingman.

AUFIDIUS
Where is this fellow?

SECOND SERVANT
Here, sir: I'ld have beaten him like a dog, but for disturbing the lords within. [*Retires.*

AUFIDIUS
Whence comest thou? what wouldst thou? thy name?

CORIOLANUS
If, Tullus, [*Unmuffling.* 50
Not yet thou knowest me, and, seeing me, dost not
Think me for the man I am, necessity
Commands me name myself.

AUFIDIUS
What is thy name? 54

CORIOLANUS
A name unmusical to the Volscians' ears,
And harsh in sound to thine.

AUFIDIUS
Say, what's thy name?
Thou hast a grim appearance, and thy face [31]
Bears a command in't; though thy tackle's torn.
Thou show'st a noble vessel: what's thy name?

CORIOLANUS
Prepare thy brow to frown: know'st thou me yet?

AUFIDIUS
I know thee not: thy name?

CORIOLANUS
My name is Caius Marcius, who hath done
To thee particularly and to all the Volsces
Great hurt and mischief; thereto witness may
My surname, Coriolanus: the painful service,
The extreme dangers and the drops of blood
Shed for my thankless country are requited
But with that surname; a good memory,
And witness of the malice and displeasure
Which thou shouldst bear me: only that name remains;
The cruelty and envy of the people, 72
Permitted by our dastard nobles, who
Have all forsook me, hath devour'd the rest;
And suffer'd me by the voice of slaves to be
Whoop'd out of Rome. Now this extremity
Hath brought me to thy hearth; not out of hope—
Mistake me not—to save my life, for if
I had fear'd death, of all the men i' the world
I would have 'voided thee, but in mere spite,
To be full quit of those my banishers,
Stand I before thee here. Then if thou hast
A heart of wreak in thee, that wilt revenge
Thine own particular wrongs and stop those maims
Of shame seen through thy country, speed thee straight,
And make my misery serve thy turn: so use it
That my revengeful services may prove
As benefits to thee, for I will fight
Against my canker'd country with the spleen
Of all the under fiends. But if so be
Thou darest not this and that to prove more fortunes
Thou'rt tired, then, in a word, I also am 94
Longer to live most weary, and present
My throat to thee and to thy ancient malice;
Which not to cut would show thee but a fool,
Since I have ever follow'd thee with hate,
Drawn tuns of blood out of thy country's breast,
And cannot live but to thy shame, unless
It be to do thee service.

AUFIDIUS
O Marcius, Marcius!
Each word thou hast spoke hath weeded from my heart
A root of ancient envy. If Jupiter 105
Should from yond cloud speak divine things,
And say 'tis true,' I'ld not believe them more
Than thee, all noble Marcius. Let me twine

Mine arms about that body, where against
My grained ash an hundred times hath broke
And scarr'd the moon with splinters: here I clip
The anvil of my sword, and do contest
As hotly and as nobly with thy love
As ever in ambitious strength I did
Contend against thy valour. Know thou first,
I loved the maid I married; never man
Sigh'd truer breath; but that I see thee here,
Thou noble thing! more dances my rapt heart
Than when I first my wedded mistress saw
Bestride my threshold. Why, thou Mars! I tell thee,
We have a power on foot; and I had purpose
Once more to hew thy target from thy brawn,
Or lose mine arm for't: thou hast beat me out
Twelve several times, and I have nightly since
Dreamt of encounters 'twixt thyself and me;
We have been down together in my sleep,
Unbuckling helms, fisting each other's throat,
And waked half dead with nothing. Worthy Marcius,
Had we no quarrel else to Rome, but that
Thou art thence banish'd, we would muster all
From twelve to seventy, and pouring war
Into the bowels of ungrateful Rome,
Like a bold flood o'er-bear. O, come, go in,
And take our friendly senators by the hands;
Who now are here, taking their leaves of me,
Who am prepared against your territories,
Though not for Rome itself.

CORIOLANUS
You bless me, gods!

AUFIDIUS
Therefore, most absolute sir, if thou wilt have
The leading of thine own revenges, take
The one half of my commission; and set down—
As best thou art experienced, since thou know'st
Thy country's strength and weakness,—thine own ways;
Whether to knock against the gates of Rome,
Or rudely visit them in parts remote,
To fright them, ere destroy. But come in:
Let me commend thee first to those that shall
Say yea to thy desires. A thousand welcomes!
And more a friend than e'er an enemy;
Yet, Marcius, that was much. Your hand: most welcome!

[Exeunt Coriolanus and Aufidius. The two Servingmen come forward.

FIRST SERVANT
Here's a strange alteration!

SECOND SERVANT
By my hand, I had thought to have strucken him with a cudgel: and yet my mind gave me his clothes made a false report of him.

FIRST SERVANT
What an arm he has! he turned me about with his finger and his thumb, as one would set up a top.

SECOND SERVANT
Nay, I knew by his face that there was something in him: he had, sir, a kind of face, methought,—I cannot tell how to term it.

FIRST SERVANT
He had so; looking as it were—would I were hanged, but I thought there was more in him than I could think.

SECOND SERVANT
So did I, I'll be sworn: he is simply the rarest man i' the world.

FIRST SERVANT
I think he is: but a greater soldier than he you wot on.

SECOND SERVANT
Who, my master?

FIRST SERVANT
Nay, it's no matter for that.

SECOND SERVANT
Worth six on him.

FIRST SERVANT
Nay, not so neither: but I take him to be the greater soldier.

SECOND SERVANT
Faith, look you, one cannot tell how to say that: for the defence of a town, our general is excellent.

FIRST SERVANT
Ay, and for an assault too.

Re-enter third Servingman.

THIRD SERVANT
O slaves, I can tell you news,—news, you rascals!

FIRST AND SECOND SERVANT
What, what, what? let's partake.

THIRD SERVANT
I would not be a Roman, of all nations; I had as lieve be a condemned man.

FIRSTAND SECOND SERVANT
Wherefore? wherefore?

THIRD SERVANT
Why, here's he that was wont to thwack our general, Caius Marcius.

FIRST SERVANT
Why do you say 'thwack our general '?

THIRD SERVANT
I do not say 'thwack our general;' but he was always good enough for him.

SECOND SERVANT
Come, we are fellows and friends: he was ever too hard for him; I have heard him say so himself.

FIRST SERVANT

He was too hard for him directly, to say the troth on't: before Corioli he scotched him and notched him like a carbon ado.

SECOND SERVANT

An he had been cannibally given, he might have broiled and eaten him too. 194

FIRST SERVANT

But, more of thy news?

THIRD SERVANT

Why, he is so made on here within, as if he were son and heir to Mars; set at upper end o' the table; no question asked him by any of the senators, but they stand bald before him: our general himself makes a mistress of him; sanctifies himself with's hand and turns up the white o' the eye to his discourse. But the bottom of the news is that our general is cut i' the middle and but one half of what he was yesterday; for the other has half, by the entreaty and grant of the whole table. He'll go, he says, and sowl the porter of Rome gates by the ears: he will mow all down before him, and leave his passage polled.

SECOND SERVANT

And he's as like to do't as any man I can imagine.

THIRD SERVANT

Do't! he will do't; for, look you, sir, he has as many friends as enemies; which friends, sir, as it were, durst not, look you, sir, show themselves, as we term it, his friends whilst he's in directitude.

FIRST SERVANT

Directitude! what's that?

THIRD SERVANT

But when they shall see, sir, his crest up again, and the man in blood, they will out of their burrows, like conies after rain, and revel all with him.

FIRST SERVANT

But when goes this forward?

THIRD SERVANT

To-morrow; to-day; presently; you shall have the drum struck up this afternoon: 'tis, as it were, a parcel of their feast, and to be executed ere they wipe their lips.

SECOND SERVANT

Why, then we shall have a stirring world again. This peace is nothing, but to rust iron, increase tailors, and breed ballad-makers.

FIRST SERVANT

Let me have war, say I; it exceeds peace as far as day does night; it's spritely, waking, audible, and full of vent. Peace is a very apoplexy, lethargy; mulled, deaf, sleepy, insensible; a getter of more bastard children than war's a destroyer of men. 227

SECOND SERVANT

'Tis so: and as war, in some sort, may be said to be a ravisher, so it cannot be denied but peace is a great maker of cuckolds.

FIRST SERVANT

Ay, and it makes men hate one another.

THIRD SERVANT

Reason; because they then less need one another. The wars for my money. I hope to see Romans as cheap as Volscians. They are rising, they are rising.

ALL

In, in, in, in! [*Exeunt.*

ACT FOUR SCENE SIX

Rome. A public place.

Enter SICINIUS *and* BRUTUS.

SICINIUS

We hear not of him, neither need we fear him;
His remedies are tame i' the present peace
And quietness of the people, which before
Were in wild hurry. Here do we make his friends
Blush that the world goes well, who rather had,
Though they themselves did suffer by't, behold
Dissentious numbers pestering streets than see
Our tradesmen with in their shops and going
About their functions friendly.

BRUTUS

We stood to't in good time. [*Enter Menenius.*] Is this Menenius? 11

SICINIUS

'Tis he, 'tis he: O, he is grown most kind of late.

BOTH TRIBUNES

Hail sir!

MENENIUS

Hail to you both!

SICINIUS

Your Coriolanus
Is not much miss'd, but with his friends:
The commonwealth doth stand, and so would do,
Were he more angry at it.

MENENIUS

All's well; and might have been much better, if
He could have temporized.

SICINIUS

Where is he, hear you?

MENENIUS

Nay, I hear nothing: his mother and his wife
Hear nothing from him.

Enter three or four Citizens.

CITIZENS

The gods preserve you both!

SICINIUS

God-den, our neighbours. 25

BRUTUS

God-den to you all, god-den to you all.

FIRST CITIZEN
Ourselves, our wives, and children, on our knees,
Are bound to pray for you both.
SICINIUS
Live, and thrive!
BRUTUS
Farewell, kind neighbours: we wish'd Coriolanus
Had loved you as we did.
CITIZENS
Now the gods keep you!
BOTH TRIBUNES
Farewell, farewell. [*Exeunt Citizens.*
SICINIUS
This is a happier and more comely time
Than when these fellows ran about the streets,
Crying confusion.
BRUTUS
Caius Marcius was
A worthy officer i' the war; but insolent,
O'ercome with pride, ambitious past all thinking,
Self-loving,—
SICINIUS
And affecting one sole throne,
Without assistance.
MENENIUS
I think not so.
SICINIUS
We should by this, to all our lamentation,
If he had gone forth consul, found it so.
BRUTUS
The gods have well prevented it, and Rome
Sits safe and still without him.

Enter an Aedile.

AEDILE
Worthy tribunes,
There is a slave, whom we have put in prison,
Reports, the Volsces with two several powers
Are enter'd in the Roman territories,
And with the deepest malice of the war
Destroy what lies before 'em.
MENENIUS
'Tis Aufidius,
Who, hearing of our Marcius' banishment,
Thrusts forth his horns again into the world;
Which were inshell'd when Marcius stood for Rome,
And durst not once peep out.
SICINIUS
Come, what talk you
Of Marcius?
BRUTUS
Go see this rumourer whipp'd. It cannot be
The Volsces dare break with us.
MENENIUS
Cannot be!
We have record that very well it can,
And three examples of the like have been
Within my age. But reason with the fellow,
Before you punish him, where he heard this,
Lest you shall chance to whip your information
And beat the messenger who bids beware
Of what is to be dreaded.
SICINIUS
Tell not me:
I know this cannot be.
BRUTUS
Not possible.

Enter a Messenger.

MESSENGER
The nobles in great earnestness are going
All to the senate-house: some news is come
That turns their countenances.
SICINIUS
'Tis this slave;—
Go whip him, 'fore the people's eyes:—his raising;
Nothing but his report.
MESSENGER
Yes, worthy sir,
The slave's report is seconded; and more,
More fearful, is deliver'd.
SICINIUS
What more fearful?
MESSENGER
It is spoke freely out of many mouths—
How probable I do not know—that Marcius,
Join'd with Aufidius, leads a power 'gainst Rome,
And vows revenge as spacious as between
The young'st and oldest thing.
SICINIUS
This is most likely!
BRUTUS
Raised only, that the weaker sort may wish
Good Marcius home again.
SICINIUS
The very trick on't.
MENENIUS
This is unlikely:
He and Aufidius can no more atone
Than violentest contrariety.

Enter a second Messenger.

SECOND MESSENGER
You are sent for to the senate:
A fearful army, led by Caius Marcius
Associated with Aufidius, rages

Upon our territories; and have already
O'erborne their way, consumed with fire, and took
What lay before them.

Enter COMINIUS.

COMINIUS
O, you have made good work!
MENENIUS
What news? what news? 105
COMINIUS
You have holp to ravish your own daughters and
To melt the city leads upon your pates,
To see your wives dishonour'd to your noses, —
MENENIUS
What's the news? what's the news?
COMINIUS
Your temples burned in their cement, and
Your franchises, whereon you stood, confined
Into an auger's bore.
MENENIUS
Pray now, your news?
You have made fair work, I fear me. —Pray, your news?—
If Marcius should be join'd with Volscians,—
COMINIUS
If!
He is their god: he leads them like a thing 117
Made by some other deity than nature,
That shapes man better; and they follow him,
Against us brats, with no less confidence
Than boys pursuing summer butterflies,
Or butchers killing flies.
MENENIUS
You have made good work,
You and your apron-men; you that stood so up much
Upon the voice of occupation and
The breath of garlic-eaters!
COMINIUS
He will shake
Your Rome about your ears.
MENENIUS
As Hercules
Did shake down mellow fruit. You have made fair work! 132
BRUTUS
But is this true, sir?
COMINIUS
Ay; and you'll look pale
Before you find it other. All the regions
Do smilingly revolt; and who resist
Are mock'd for valiant ignorance,
And perish constant fools. Who is't can blame him?
Your enemies and his find something in him.
MENENIUS
We are all undone, unless
The noble man have mercy.
COMINIUS
Who shall ask it?
The tribunes cannot do't for shame; the people
Deserve such pity of him as the wolf 144
Does of the shepherds: for his best friends, if they
Should say 'Be good to Rome,' they charged him even
As those should do that had deserved his hate,
And therein show'd like enemies.
MENENIUS
'Tis true:
If he were putting to my house the brand
That should consume it, I have not the face
To say 'Beseech you, cease.' You have made fair hands,
You and your crafts! you have crafted fair!
COMINIUS
You have brought
A trembling upon Rome, such as was never
So incapable of help.
BOTH TRIBUNES
Say not we brought it. 158
MENENIUS
How! Was it we? we loved him but, like beasts
And cowardly nobles, gave way unto your clusters,
Who did hoot him out o' the city.
COMINIUS
But I fear
They'll roar him in again. Tullus Aufidius,
The second name of men, obeys his points
As if he were his officer: desperation
Is all the policy, strength and defence,
That Rome can make against them.

Enter a troop of Citizens.

MENENIUS
Here come the clusters.
And is Aufidius with him? You are they
That made the air unwholesome, when you cast
Your stinking greasy caps in hooting at 171
Coriolanus' exile. Now he's coming;
And not a hair upon a soldier's head
Which will not prove a whip: as many coxcombs
As you threw caps up will he tumble down,
And pay you for your voices. 'Tis no matter;
If he could burn us all into one coal,
We have deserved it.
CITIZENS
Faith, we hear fearful news.
FIRST CITIZEN
For mine own part,
When I said, banish him, I said 'twas pity.

SECOND CITIZEN
And so did I.

THIRD CITIZEN
And so did I; and, to say the truth, so did very many of us: that we did, we did for the best; and though we willingly consented to his banishment, yet it was against our will.

COMINIUS
Ye're goodly things, you voices!

MENENIUS
You have made
Good work, you and your cry! Shall's to the Capitol?

COMINIUS
O, ay, what else? [*Exeunt Cominius and Menenius.*

SICINIUS
Go, masters, get you home; be not dismay'd:
These are a side that would be glad to have
This true which they so seem to fear. Go home,
And show no sign of fear.

FIRST CITIZEN
The gods be good to us! Come, masters, let's home. I ever said we were i' the wrong when we banished him.

SECOND CITIZEN
So did we all. But, come, let's home.
[*Exeunt Citizens.*

BRUTUS
I do not like this news.

SICINIUS
Nor I.

BRUTUS
Let's to the Capitol. Would half my wealth
Would buy this for a lie!

SICINIUS
Pray, let us go. [*Exeunt.*

ACT FOUR SCENE SEVEN

A camp, at a small distance from Rome.

Enter AUFIDIUS *and his* Lieutenant.

AUFIDIUS
Do they still fly to the Roman?

LIEUTENANT
I do not know what witchcraft's in him, but
Your soldiers use him as the grace 'fore meat,
Their talk at table, and their thanks at end;
And you are darken'd in this action, sir,
Even by your own.

AUFIDIUS
I cannot help it now,
Unless, by using means, I lame the foot
Of our design. He bears himself more proudlier,
Even to my person, than I thought he would
When first I did embrace him: yet his nature
In that's no changeling; and I must excuse
What cannot be amended.

LIEUTENANT
Yet I wish, sir,—
I mean for your particular,—you had not
Join'd in commission with him; but either
Had borne the action of yourself, or else
To him had left it solely.

AUFIDIUS
I understand thee well; and be thou sure,
When he shall come to his account, he knows not
What I can urge against him. Although it seems,
And so he thinks, and is no less apparent
To the vulgar eye, that he bears all things fairly.
And shows good husbandry for the Volscian state,
Fights dragon-like, and does achieve as soon
As draw his sword; yet he hath left undone
That which shall break his neck or hazard mine,
Whene'er we come to our account.

LIEUTENANT
Sir, I beseech you, think you he'll carry Rome?

AUFIDIUS
All places yield to him ere he sits down;
And the nobility of Rome are his:
The senators and patricians love him too:
The tribunes are no soldiers; and their people
Will be as rash in the repeal, as hasty
To expel him thence. I think he'll be to Rome
As is the osprey to the fish, who takes it
By sovereignty of nature. First he was
A noble servant to them; but he could not
Carry his honours even: whether 'twas pride,
Which out of daily fortune ever taints
The happy man; whether defect of judgment,
To fail in the disposing of those chances
Which he was lord of; or whether nature,
Not to be other than one thing, not moving
From the casque to the cushion, but commanding peace
Even with the same austerity and garb
As he controll'd the war; but one of these—
As he hath spices of them all, not all,
For I dare so far free him—made him fear'd,
So hated, and so banish'd: but he has a merit,
To choke it in the utterance. So our virtues
Lie in the interpretation of the time:
And power, unto itself most commendable, [32]
Hath not a tomb so evident as a chair
To extol what it hath done.
One fire drives out one fire; one nail, one nail;
Rights by rights falter, strengths by strengths do fail. [33]

Come, let's away. When, Caius, Rome is thine,
Thou art poor'st of all; then shortly art thou mine.
[*Exeunt.*

ACT FIVE SCENE ONE

Rome. A public place.
Enter MENENIUS, COMINIUS, SICINIUS, BRUTUS, *and others.*

MENENIUS
No, I'll not go: you hear what he hath said
Which was sometime his general; who loved him
In a most dear particular. He call'd me father:
But what o' that? Go, you that banish'd him;
A mile before his tent fall down, and knee
The way into his mercy: nay, if he coy'd
To hear Cominius speak, I'll keep at home.
COMINIUS
He would not seem to know me.
MENENIUS
Do you hear?
COMINIUS
Yet one time he did call me by my name:
I urged our old acquaintance, and the drops
That we have bled together. Coriolanus
He would not answer to; forbad all names;
He was a kind of nothing, titleless,
Till he had forged himself a name o' the fire
Of burning Rome.
MENENIUS
Why, so: you have made good work!
A pair of tribunes that have rack'd for Rome,
To make coals cheap,—a noble memory!
COMINIUS
I minded him how royal 'twas to pardon
When it was less expected: he replied,
It was a bare petition of a state 22
To one whom they had punish'd.
MENENIUS
Very well:
Could he say less?
COMINIUS
I offer'd to awaken his regard
For's private friends: his answer to me was,
He could not stay to pick them in a pile
Of noisome musty chaff: he said 'twas folly,
For one poor grain or two, to leave unburnt,
And still to nose the offence.
MENENIUS
For one poor grain or two!
I am one of those; his mother, wife, his child,
And this brave fellow too, we are the grains:
You are the musty chaff; and you are smelt
Above the moon: we must be burnt for you.
SICINIUS
Nay, pray, be patient: if you refuse your aid
In this so never-needed help, yet do not
Upbraid's with our distress. But, sure, if you
Would be your country's pleader, your good tongue,
More than the instant army we can make,
Might stop our countryman.
MENENIUS
No, I'll not meddle.
SICINIUS
Pray you, go to him.
MENENIUS
What should I do?
BRUTUS
Only make trial what your love can do 46
For Rome, towards Marcius.
MENENIUS
Well, and say that Marcius
Return me, as Cominius is return'd,
Unheard; what then?
But as a discontented friend, grief-shot
With his unkindness? say't be so?
SICINIUS
Yet your good will
Must have that thanks from Rome, after the measure
As you intended well.
MENENIUS
I'll undertake 't:
I think he'll hear me. Yet, to bite his lip
And hum at good Cominius, much unhearts me.
He was not taken well; he had not dined: 59
The veins unfill'd, our blood is cold, and then
We pout upon the morning, are unapt
To give or to forgive; but when we have stuff'd
These and these conveyances of our blood
With wine and feeding, we have suppler souls
Than in our priest-like fasts: therefore I'll watch him
Till he be dieted to my request,
And then I'll set upon him.
BRUTUS
You know the very road into his kindness,
And cannot lose your way.
MENENIUS
Good faith, I'll prove him, 70
Speed how it will. I shall ere long have knowledge
Of my success. [*Exit.*
COMINIUS
He'll never hear him.
SICINIUS
Not?
COMINIUS
I tell you, he does sit in gold, his eye

Red as 'twould burn Rome; and his injury
The gaoler to his pity. I kneel'd before him;
'Twas very faintly he said 'Rise;' dismiss'd me
Thus, with his speechless hand; what he would do,
He sent in writing after me; what he would not,
Bound with an oath to yield to his conditions: *34*
So that all hope is vain, 82
Unless his noble mother, and his wife;
Who, as I hear, mean to solicit him
For mercy to his country. Therefore, let's hence,
And with our fair entreaties haste them on.
[*Exeunt.*

ACT FIVE SCENE TWO

Entrance of the Volscian camp before Rome.
Two Sentinels on guard.

Enter to them, MENENIUS.

FIRST SENATOR
Stay: whence are you?

SECOND SENATOR
Stand, and go back.

MENENIUS
You guard like men; 'tis well: but, by your leave,
I am an officer of state, and come
To speak with Coriolanus.

FIRST SENATOR
From whence?

MENENIUS
From Rome.

FIRST SENATOR
You may not pass, you must return: our general
Will no more hear from thence.

SECOND SENATOR
You'll see your Rome embraced with fire before
To speak with Coriolanus.

MENENIUS
Good my friends,
If you have heard your general talk of Rome,
And of his friends there, it is lots to blanks,
My name hath touch'd your ears it is Menenius.

FIRST SENATOR
Be it so; go back: the virtue of your name
Is not here passable.

MENENIUS
I tell thee, fellow,
The general is my lover: I have been
The book of his good acts, whence men have read
His name unparallel'd, haply amplified;
For I have ever verified my friends,
Of whom he's chief, with all the size that verity
Would without lapsing suffer: nay, sometimes,
Like to a bowl upon a subtle ground, 25
I have tumbled past the throw; and in his praise
Have almost stamp'd the leasing: therefore, fellow,
I must have leave to pass.

FIRST SENATOR
Faith, sir, if you had told as many lies in his behalf as you have uttered words in your own, you should not pass here; no, though it were as virtuous to lie as to live chastely. Therefore, go back.

MENENIUS
Prithee, fellow, remember my name is Menenius, always factionary on the party of your general. 34

SECOND SENATOR
Howsoever you have been his liar, as you say you have, I am one that, telling true under him, must say, you cannot pass. Therefore, go back.

MENENIUS
Hath he dined, canst thou tell? for I would not speak with him till after dinner.

FIRST SENATOR
You are a Roman, are you?

MENENIUS
I am, as thy general is. 41

FIRST SENATOR
Then you should hate Rome, as he does. Can you, when you have pushed out your gates the very defender of them, and, in a violent popular ignorance, given your enemy your shield, think to front his revenges with the easy groans of old women, the virginal palms of your daughters, or withthe palsied intercession of such a decayed dotant asyou seem to be? Can you think to blow out the intended fire your city is ready to flame in, with such weak breath as this? No, you are deceived; therefore, back to Rome, and prepare for your execution: you are condemned, our general has sworn you out of reprieve and pardon.

MENENIUS
Sirrah, if thy captain knew I were here, he would use me with estimation.

SECOND SENATOR
Come, my captain knows you not.

MENENIUS
I mean, thy general.

FIRST SENATOR
My general cares not for you. Back, I say, go; lest I let forth your half-pint of blood; back,—that's the utmost of your having: back.

MENENIUS
Nay, but, fellow, fellow,—

Enter CORIOLANUS *and* AUFIDIUS.

CORIOLANUS
What's the matter?

MENENIUS

Now, you companion, I'll say an errand for you: You shall know now that I am in estimation; you shall perceive that a Jack guardant cannot office me from my son Coriolanus: guess, but by my entertainment with him, if thou standest not i' the state of hanging, or of some death more long in spectatorship, and crueller in suffering; behold now presently, and swoon for what's to come upon thee. [*To Coriolanus*] The glorious gods sit in hourly synod about thy particular prosperity, and love thee no worse than thy old father Menenius does! O my son, my son! thou art preparing fire for us; look thee, here's water to quench it. I was hardly moved to come to thee; but being assured none but myself could move thee, I have been blown out of your gates with sighs; and conjure thee to pardon Rome, and thy petitionary countrymen. The good gods assuage thy wrath, and turn the dregs of it upon this varlet here,—this, who, like a block, hath denied my access to thee. [35]

CORIOLANUS

Away!

MENENIUS

How! away!

CORIOLANUS

Wife, mother, child, I know not. My affairs
Are servanted to others: though I owe [36]
My revenge properly, my remission lies
In Volscian breasts. That we have been familiar,
Ingrate forgetfulness shall poison, rather
Than pity note how much. Therefore, be gone.
Mine ears against your suits are stronger than
Your gates against my force. Yet, for I loved thee,
Take this along; I writ it for thy sake
[*Gives a letter.*
And would have sent it. Another word, Menenius,
I will not hear thee speak. This man, Aufidius,
Was my beloved in Rome: yet thou behold'st!

AUFIDIUS

You keep a constant temper.

[*Exeunt Coriolanus and Aufidius.*

FIRST SENATOR

Now, sir, is your name Menenius?

SECOND SENATOR

'Tis a spell, you see, of much power: you know the way home again.

FIRST SENATOR

Do you hear how we are shent for keeping your greatness back?

SECOND SENATOR

What cause, do you think, I have to swoon?

MENENIUS

I neither care for the world nor your general: for such things as you, I can scarce think there's any, ye're so slight. He that hath a will to die by himself fears it not from another: let your general do his worst. For you, be that you are, long; and your misery increase with your age! I say to you, as I was said to, Away!
[*Exit.*

FIRST SENATOR

A noble fellow, I warrant him.

SECOND SENATOR

The worthy fellow is our general: he's the rock, the oak not to be wind-shaken. [*Exeunt.*

ACT FIVE SCENE THREE

The tent of Coriolanus.

Enter CORIOLANUS, AUFIDIUS, *and others.*

CORIOLANUS

We will before the walls of Rome to-morrow
Set down our host. My partner in this action,
You must report to the Volscian lords, how plainly
I have borne this business.

AUFIDIUS

Only their ends
You have respected; stopp'd your ears against
The general suit of Rome; never admitted
A private whisper, no, not with such friends
That thought them sure of you.

CORIOLANUS

This last old man,
Whom with a crack'd heart I have sent to Rome,
Loved me above the measure of a father;
Nay, godded me, indeed. Their latest refuge
Was to send him; for whose old love I have,
Though I show'd sourly to him, once more offer'd
The first conditions, which they did refuse
And cannot now accept; to grace him only
That thought he could do more, a very little
I have yielded to: fresh embassies and suits,
Nor from the state nor private friends, hereafter
Will I lend ear to. Ha! what shout is this?
[*Shout within.*
Shall I be tempted to infringe my vow
In the same time 'tis made? I will not.

Enter in mourning habits, VIRGILIA, VOLUMNIA, *leading young* MARCIUS, VALERIA, *and* Attendants.

My wife comes foremost; then the honour'd mould
Wherein this trunk was framed, and in her hand
The grandchild to her blood. But, out, affection!
All bond and privilege of nature, break!
Let it be virtuous to be obstinate.
What is that curt'sy worth? or those doves' eyes,

Which can make gods forsworn? I melt, and am not
Of stronger earth than others. My mother bows;
As if Olympus to a molehill should
In supplication nod: and my young boy
Hath an aspect of intercession, which
Great nature cries 'Deny not.' let the Volsces
Plough Rome and harrow Italy: I'll never
Be such a gosling to obey instinct, but stand,
As if a man were author of himself
And knew no other kin.

VIRGILIA
My lord and husband!

CORIOLANUS
These eyes are not the same I wore in Rome.

VIRGILIA
The sorrow that delivers us thus changed
Makes you think so.

CORIOLANUS
Like a dull actor now,
I have forgot my part, and I am out,
Even to a full disgrace. Best of my flesh,
Forgive my tyranny; but do not say
For that 'Forgive our Romans.' O, a kiss
Long as my exile, sweet as my revenge!
Now, by the jealous queen of heaven, that kiss
I carried from thee, dear; and my true lip
Hath virgin'd it e'er since. You gods! I prate,
And the most noble mother of the world
Leave unsaluted: sink, my knee, i' the earth; [*Kneels.*
Of thy deep duty more impression show
Than that of common sons.

VOLUMNIA
O, stand up blest!
Whilst, with no softer cushion than the flint,
I kneel before thee; and unproperly
Show duty, as mistaken all this while
Between the child and parent. [*Kneels.*

CORIOLANUS
What is this?
Your knees to me? to your corrected son?
Then let the pebbles on the hungry beach
Fillip the stars; then let the mutinous winds
Strike the proud cedars 'gainst the fiery sun;
Murdering impossibility, to make
What cannot be, slight work.

VOLUMNIA
Thou art my warrior;
I holp to frame thee. Do you know this lady?

CORIOLANUS
The noble sister of Publicola,
The moon of Rome, chaste as the icicle
That's curdied by the frost from purest snow
And hangs on Dian's temple: dear Valeria!

VOLUMNIA
This is a poor epitome of yours,
Which by the interpretation of full time
May show like all yourself.

CORIOLANUS
The god of soldiers,
With the consent of supreme Jove, inform
Thy thoughts with nobleness; that thou mayst prove
To shame unvulnerable, and stick i' the wars
Like a great sea-mark, standing every flaw,
And saving those that eye thee!

VOLUMNIA
Your knee, sirrah.

CORIOLANUS
That's my brave boy!

VOLUMNIA
Even he, your wife, this lady, and myself,
Are suitors to you.

CORIOLANUS
I beseech you, peace:
Or, if you'ld ask, remember this before:
The thing I have forsworn to grant may never
Be held by you denials. Do not bid me
Dismiss my soldiers, or capitulate
Again with Rome's mechanics: tell me not
Wherein I seem unnatural: desire not
To ally my rages and revenges with
Your colder reasons.

VOLUMNIA
O, no more, no more!
You have said you will not grant us any thing;
For we have nothing else to ask, but that
Which you deny already: yet we will ask;
That, if you fail in our request, the blame
May hang upon your hardness: therefore hear us.

CORIOLANUS
Aufidius, and you Volsces, mark; for we'll
Hear nought from Rome in private. Your request?

VOLUMNIA
Should we be silent and not speak, our raiment
And state of bodies would bewray what life
We have led since thy exile. Think with thyself
How more unfortunate than all living women
Are we come hither: since that thy sight, which should
Make our eyes flow with joy, hearts dance with comforts,
Constrains them weep and shake with fear and sorrow;
Making the mother, wife and child to see
The son, the husband and the father tearing
His country's bowels out. And to poor we
Thine enmity's most capital: thou barr'st us
Our prayers to the gods, which is a comfort

That all but we enjoy; for how can we,
Alas, how can we for our country pray.
Whereto we are bound, together with thy victory,
Whereto we are bound? alack, or we must lose
The country, our dear nurse, or else thy person,
Our comfort in the country. We must find
An evident calamity, though we had
Our wish, which side should win: for either thou
Must, as a foreign recreant, be led
With manacles thorough our streets, or else
Triumphantly tread on thy country's ruin,
And bear the palm for having bravely shed
Thy wife and children's blood. For myself, son,
I purpose not to wait on fortune till
These wars determine: if I cannot persuade
thee 134
Rather to show a noble grace to both parts
Than seek the end of one, thou shalt no sooner
March to assault thy country than to tread—
Trust to't, thou shalt not—on thy mother's womb,
That brought thee to this world.

VIRGILIA
Ay, and mine,
That brought you forth this boy, to keep your name
Living to time.

YOUNG MARCIUS
A' shall not tread on me;
I'll run away till I am bigger, but then I'll fight.

CORIOLANUS
Not of a woman's tenderness to be,
Requires nor child nor woman's face to see.
I have sat too long. [*Rising.*

VOLUMNIA
Nay, go not from us thus.
If it were so that our request did tend
To save the Romans, thereby to destroy
The Volsces whom you serve, you might condemn us,
As poisonous of your honour: no; our suit
Is, that you reconcile them: while the Volsces
May say 'this mercy we have show'd;' the Romans,
'This we received;' and each in either side
Give the all-hail to thee and cry 'Be blest
For making up this peace!' Thou know'st,
great son, 158
The end of war's uncertain, but this certain,
That, if thou conquer Rome, the benefit
Which thou shalt thereby reap is such a name,
Whose repetition will be dogg'd with curses;
Whose chronicle thus writ: 'the man was noble,
But with his last attempt he wiped it out;
Destroy'd his country, and his name remains
To the ensuing age abhorr'd.' Speak to me, son:
Thou hast affected the fine strains of honour,
To imitate the graces of the gods; 168
To tear with thunder the wide cheeks o' the air,
And yet to charge thy sulphur with a bolt
That should but rive an oak. Why dost not speak?
Think'st thou it honourable for a noble man
Still to remember wrongs? Daughter, speak you:
He cares not for your weeping. Speak thou, boy:
Perhaps thy childishness will move him more
Than can our reasons. There's no man in the world
More bound to 's mother; yet here he lets me prate
Like one i' the stocks. Thou hast never in
thy life 179
Show'd thy dear mother any courtesy,
When she, poor hen, fond of no second brood,
Has cluck'd thee to the wars and safely home,
Loaden with honour. Say my request's unjust,
And spurn me back: but if it be not so,
Thou art not honest; and the gods will plague thee,
That thou restrain'st from me the duty which
To a mother's part belongs. He turns away:
Down, ladies; let us shame him with our knees.
To his surname Coriolanus 'longs more pride
Than pity to our prayers. Down: an end;
This is the last: so we will home to Rome,
And die among our neighbours. Nay, behold 's:
This boy, that cannot tell what he would have,
But kneels and holds up bands for fellowship,
Does reason our petition with more strength
Than thou hast to deny 't. Come, let us go:
This fellow had a Volscian to his mother;
His wife is in Corioli and his child
Like him by chance. Yet give us our dispatch:
I am hush'd until our city be afire, 200
And then I'll speak a little.
[*He holds her by the hand, silent.*

CORIOLANUS
O mother, mother!
What have you done? Behold, the heavens do ope,
The gods look down, and this unnatural scene
They laugh at. O my mother, mother! O!
You have won a happy victory to Rome;
But, for your son,—believe it, O, believe it,
Most dangerously you have with him prevail'd,
If not most mortal to him. But, let come.
Aufidius, though I cannot make true wars,
I'll frame convenient peace. Now, good Aufidius,
Were you in my stead, would you have heard
A mother less? or granted less, Aufidius?

AUFIDIUS
I was moved withal.

CORIOLANUS
I dare be sworn you were:
And, sir, it is no little thing to make
Mine eyes to sweat compassion. But, good sir,
What peace you'll make, advise me: for my part,

I'll not to Rome, I'll back with you; and pray you,
Stand to me in this cause. O mother! wife!

AUFIDIUS

[*Aside*] I am glad thou hast set thy mercy and thy honour
At difference in thee: out of that I'll work
Myself a former fortune.

[*The Ladies make signs to Coriolanus.*

CORIOLANUS

Ay, by and by; [*To Volumnia, Virgilia, &c.*
But we will drink together; and you shall bear
A better witness back than words, which we,
On like conditions, will have counter-seal'd.
Come, enter with us. Ladies, you deserve
To have a temple built you: all the swords
In Italy, and her confederate arms,
Could not have made this peace.

[*Exeunt.*

ACT FIVE SCENE FOUR

Rome. A public place.

Enter MENENIUS *and* SICINIUS.

MENENIUS

See you yond coign o' the Capitol, yond corner-stone?

SICINIUS

Why, what of that?

MENENIUS

If it be possible for you to displace it with your little finger, there is some hope the ladies of Rome, especially his mother, may prevail with him. But I say there is no hope in't: our throats are sentenced and stay upon execution.

SICINIUS

Is't possible that so short a time can alter the condition of a man!

MENENIUS

There is differency between a grub and a butterfly; yet your butterfly was a grub. This Marcius is grown from man to dragon: he has wings; he is more than a creeping thing.

SICINIUS

He loved his mother dearly.

MENENIUS

So did he me: and he no more remembers his mother now than an eight-year-old horse. The tartness of his face sours ripe grapes: when he walks, he moves like an engine, and the ground shrinks before his treading: he is able to pierce a corslet with his eye; talks like a knell, and his hum is a battery. He sits in his state, as a thing made for Alexander. What he bids be done is finished with his bidding. He wants nothing of a god but eternity and a heaven to throne in.

SICINIUS

Yes, mercy, if you report him truly.

MENENIUS

I paint him in the character. Mark what mercy his mother shall bring from him: there is no more mercy in him than there is milk in a male tiger; that shall our poor city find: and all this is long of you.

SICINIUS

The gods be good unto us!

MENENIUS

No, in such a case the gods will not be good unto us. When we banished him, we respected not them; and, he returning to break our necks, they respect not us.

Enter a Messenger.

MESSENGER

Sir, if you'ld save your life, fly to your house:
The plebeians have got your fellow-tribune
And hale him up and down, all swearing, if
The Roman ladies bring not comfort home,
They'll give him death by inches.

Enter a second Messenger.

SICINIUS

What's the news?

SECOND MESSENGER

Good news, good news; the ladies have prevail'd,
The Volscians are dislodged, and Marcius gone:
A merrier day did never yet greet Rome,
No, not the expulsion of the Tarquins.

SICINIUS

Friend,
Art thou certain this is true? is it most certain?

SECOND MESSENGER

As certain as I know the sun is fire:
Where have you lurk'd, that you make doubt of it?
Ne'er through an arch so hurried the blown tide,
As the recomforted through the gates. Why, hark you! [*Trumpets; hautboys; drums beat; all together.*
The trumpets, sackbuts, psalteries and fifes,
Tabours and cymbals and the shouting Romans,
Make the sun dance. Hark you! [*A shout within.*

MENENIUS

This is good news:
I will go meet the ladies. This Volumnia
Is worth of consuls, senators, patricians,
A city full; of tribunes, such as you,
A sea and land full. You have pray'd well to-day:
This morning for ten thousand of your throats
I'ld not have given a doit. Hark, how they joy!,

[*Music still, with shouts.*

SICINIUS
First, the gods bless you for your tidings; next,
Accept my thankfulness.
SECOND MESSENGER
Sir, we have all
Great cause to give great thanks.
SICINIUS
They are near the city?
SECOND MESSENGER
Almost at point to enter.
SICINIUS
We will meet them,
And help the joy. [*Exeunt.*

ACT FIVE SCENE FIVE

The same. A street near the gate.

Enter two Senators *with* VOLUMNIA, VIRGILIA, VALERIA, *&c., passing over the stage, followed by Patricians, and others.*

FIRST SENATOR
Behold our patroness, the life of Rome!
Call all your tribes together, praise the gods,
And make triumphant fires; strew flowers before them:
Unshout the noise that banish'd Marcius,
Repeal him with the welcome of his mother;
Cry 'Welcome, ladies, welcome!'
ALL
Welcome, ladies, Welcome!
[*A flourish with drums and trumpets. Exeunt.*

ACT FIVE SCENE SIX

Antium. A public place.

Enter TULLUS AUFIDIUS, *with* Attendants.

AUFIDIUS
Go tell the lords o' the city I am here:
Deliver them this paper: having read it,
Bid them repair to the market-place; where I,
Even in theirs and in the commons' ears,
Will vouch the truth of it. Him I accuse
The city ports by this hath enter'd and
Intends to appear before the people, hoping
To purge herself with words: dispatch.
[*Exeunt Attendants.*

Enter three or four Conspirators of AUFIDIUS *faction.*

Most welcome!
FIRST CONSPIRATOR
How is it with our general?
AUFIDIUS
Even so
As with a man by his own alms empoison'd,
And with his charity slain.
SECOND CONSPIRATOR
Most noble sir,
If you do hold the same intent wherein
You wish'd us parties, we'll deliver you
Of your great danger.
AUFIDIUS
Sir, I cannot tell:
We must proceed as we do find the people.
THIRD CONSPIRATOR
The people will remain uncertain whilst
'Twixt you there's difference; but the fall of either
Makes the survivor heir of all.
AUFIDIUS
I know it;
And my pretext to strike at him admits
A good construction. I raised him, and I pawn'd
Mine honour for his truth: who being so heighten'd,
He water'd his new plants with dews of flattery,
Seducing so my friends; and, to this end,
He bow'd his nature, never known before
But to be rough, unswayable and free.
THIRD CONSPIRATOR
Sir, his stoutness
When he did stand for consul, which he lost
By lack of stooping,—
AUFIDIUS
That I would have spoke of:
Being banish'd for't, he came unto my hearth;
Presented to my knife his throat: I took him;
Made him joint-servant with me; gave him way
In all his own desires; nay, let him choose
Out of my files, his projects to accomplish,
My best and freshest men; served his designments
In mine own person; holp to reap the fame
Which he did end all his; and took some pride
To do myself this wrong: till, at the last,
I seem'd his follower, not partner, and
He waged me with his countenance, as if
I had been mercenary.
FIRST CONSPIRATOR
So he did, my lord:
The army marvell'd at it, and, in the last,
When he had carried Rome and that we look'd
For no less spoil than glory,—
AUFIDIUS
There was it:
For which my sinews shall be stretch'd upon him.
At a few drops of women's rheum, which are
As cheap as lies, he sold the blood and labour
Of our great action: therefore shall he die,

And I'll renew me in his fall. But, hark! [*Drums and trumpets sound, with great shouts of the People.*

FIRST CONSPIRATOR
Your native town you enter'd like a post,
And had no welcomes home; but he returns,
Splitting the air with noise.

SECOND CONSPIRATOR
And patient fools,
Whose children he hath slain, their base throats tear
With giving him glory.

THIRD CONSPIRATOR
Therefore, at your vantage,
Ere he express himself, or move the people
With what he would say, let him feel your sword,
Which we will second. When he lies along,
After your way his tale pronounced shall bury
His reasons with his body.

AUFIDIUS
Say no more:
Here come the lords.

Enter the Lords *of the city .*

ALL THE LORDS
You are most welcome home.

AUFIDIUS
I have not deserved it.
But, worthy lords, have you with heed perused
What I have written to you?

LORDS
We have.

FIRST LORD
And grieve to hear't.
What faults he made before the last, I think
Might have found easy fines: but there to end
Where he was to begin and give away
The benefit of our levies, answering us
With our own charge, making a treaty where
There was a yielding,—this admits no excuse.

AUFIDIUS
He approaches: you shall hear him.

Enter CORIOLANUS, *marching with drum and colours; commoners being with him.*

CORIOLANUS
Hail, lords! I am return'd your soldier,
No more infected with my country's love
Than when I parted hence, but still subsisting
Under your great command. You are to know
That prosperously I have attempted and
With bloody passage led your wars even to
The gates of Rome. Our spoils we have brought home
Do more than counterpoise a full third part
The charges of the action. We have made peace
With no less honour to the Antiates
Than shame to the Romans: and we here deliver,
Subscribed by the consuls and patricians,
Together with the seal o' the senate, what
We have compounded on.

AUFIDIUS
Read it not, noble lords;
But tell the traitor, in the high'st degree
He hath abused your powers.

CORIOLANUS
Traitor! how now!

AUFIDIUS
Ay, traitor, Marcius!

CORIOLANUS
Marcius!

AUFIDIUS
Ay, Marcius, Caius Marcius: dost thou think
I'll grace thee with that robbery, thy stol'n name
Coriolanus in Corioli?
You lords and heads o' the state, perfidiously
He has betray'd your business, and given up,
For certain drops of salt, your city Rome,
I say 'your city,' to his wife and mother;
Breaking his oath and resolution like
A twist of rotten silk, never admitting
Counsel o' the war, but at his nurse's tears
He whined and roar'd away your victory,
That pages blush'd at him and men of heart
Look'd wondering each at other.

CORIOLANUS
Hear'st thou, Mars?

AUFIDIUS
Name not the god, thou boy of tears!

CORIOLANUS
Ha!

AUFIDIUS
No more.

CORIOLANUS
Measureless liar, thou hast made my heart
Too great for what contains it. Boy! O slave!
Pardon me, lords, 'tis the first time that ever
I was forced to scold. Your judgments, my grave lords,
Must give this cur the lie: and his own notion—
Who wears my stripes impress'd upon him; that
Must bear my beating to his grave—shall join
To thrust the lie unto him.

FIRST LORD
Peace, both, and hear me speak.

CORIOLANUS
Cut me to pieces, Volsces; men and lads,
Stain all your edges on me. Boy! false hound!
If you have writ your annals true, 'tis there,
That, like an eagle in a dove-cote, I

Flutter'd your Volscians in Corioli:
Alone I did it. Boy!

AUFIDIUS
Why, noble lords,
Will you be put in mind of his blind fortune,
Which was your shame, by this unholy braggart,
'Fore your own eyes and ears?

ALL CONSPIRATOR
Let him die for't. 142

ALL THE PEOPLE
'Tear him to pieces.' 'Do it presently.' 'He killed my son.' 'My daughter.' 'He killed my cousin Marcus.'
'He killed my father.'

SECOND LORD
Peace, ho! no outrage: peace!
The man is noble and his fame folds-in
This orb o' the earth. His last offences to us
Shall have judicious hearing. Stand, Aufidius,
And trouble not the peace.

CORIOLANUS
O that I had him,
With six Aufidiuses, or more, his tribe, 153
To use my lawful sword!

AUFIDIUS
Insolent villain!

ALL CONSPIRATOR
Kill, kill, kill, kill, kill him!
[The Conspirators draw, and kill Coriolanus: Aufidius stands on his body.

LORDS
Hold, hold, hold, hold!

AUFIDIUS
My noble masters, hear me speak.

FIRST LORD
O Tullus,—

SECOND LORD
Thou hast done a deed whereat valour will weep.

THIRD LORD
Tread not upon him. Masters all, be quiet;
Put up your swords.

AUFIDIUS
My lords, when you shall know—as in this rage,
Provoked by him, you cannot—the great danger
Which this man's life did owe you, you'll rejoice
That he is thus cut off. Please it your honours
To call me to your senate, I'll deliver 167
Myself your loyal servant, or endure
Your heaviest censure.

FIRST LORD
Bear from hence his body;
And mourn you for him: let him be regarded
As the most noble corse that ever herald
Did follow to his urn.

SECOND LORD
His own impatience
Takes from Aufidius a great part of blame.
Let's make the best of it.

AUFIDIUS
My rage is gone;
And I am struck with sorrow. Take him up.
Help, three o' the chiefest soldiers; I'll be one.
Beat thou the drum, that it speak mournfully:
Trail your steel pikes. Though in this city he
Hath widow'd and unchilded many a one,
Which to this hour bewail the injury,
Yet he shall have a noble memory.
Assist. *[Exeunt, bearing the body of Coriolanus. A dead march sounded.*

Notes

1. Your virtue, – &c.; "your virtue is to speak well of him whom his own offences have subjected to justice; and to rail at those laws by which he whom you praise was punished" (Johnson).
2. Bound with oak, – as a mark of honour for saving the life of a citizen.
3. At Grecian sword, contemning, – &c.; Folio 1 reads 'At Grecian sword. *Contenning,* tell *Valeria,* ' &c.; the reading in the text is substantially Collier's; many emendations have been proposed; perhaps a slightly better version of the line would be gained by the omission of the comma.
4. That fears you less; – Johnson conjectured *'but fears you less';* Johnson and Capell conjectured *'that fears you more';* Schmidt, *'that fears you,—less.'* The meaning is obvious, though there is a confusion, due to the case of the double negative in *'nor'* and *'less.'*
5. You herd of—Boils, – Johnson's emendation. Folios 1, 2, *'you Heard of Byles';* Folios 3, 4, *'you Herd of Biles';* Rowe, *'you herds of biles';* Pope (ed. 1), *'you herds; of boils';* Pope (ed. 2), Theobald, *'you! herds of boils';* Collier MS., *'unheard of boils';* &c. &c.
6. Trenches followed; – so Folios 2, 3, 4; Folio 1, *'trenches followes';* Collier (ed. 1), *'trenches follow';* (ed. 2), *'trenches. Follow!';* Dyce, Lettsom conjectured *'trenches: follow me';* &c.
7. Cato's; – Theobald's emendation of Folios, *'Calues'* and *'Calves';* Rowe, *'Calvus.'*
8. Ye; – Folios, *'the.'*
9. Folios, *'O, me alone! make you a sword of me?';* the punctuation in the text is Capell's. Clarke's explanation, making the line imperative, seems the most plausible:—"O take me alone for weapon among you all! make yourselves a sword of me."
10. The chief departure from the folios in this doubtful passage is the substitution of *'coverture'* for *'overture,'* as conjectured by Tyrwhitt; *'him'* is seemingly used here instead of the neuter *'it.'*
11. End, i.e. – to where he should end.

12. Touch, – Hanmer's emendation; Folios, *'teach'*; Theobald, *'reach.'*
13. Virtues Which our divines lose by 'em, i.e. – 'which our divines preach to men in vain'; but the line is possibly corrupt.
14. Woolvish toge; – Steevens' conjecture, adopted by Malone; Folio 1 reads *'Wooluish tongue'*; Folios 2, 3, 4, *'Woolvish gowne'*; Capell, *'wolfish gown'*; Mason conjectured *'woolen gown, '* or *'foolish gown'*; Beckett conjectured *'woolish gown'*; Steevens conjectured *'woolvish tongue'*; Grant White conjectured *'foolish togue'*; Clarke, (?) *'wool'nish, ' i.e. 'woolenish.'*
15. Vide – Preface.
16. Hydra here; i.e. – 'the many-headed multitude'; so Folio 2.
17. i.e. – "let your admitted ignorance take a lower tone and defer to their admitted superiority" (Clarke).
18. Your; – Rowe's emendation of Folios, *'our.'*
19. Thwartings of; – Theobald's reading; Folios, *'things of'*; Rowe, *'things that thwart'*; Wright conjectured *'things that cross.'*
20. To the herd; – Warburton's suggestion, adopted by Theobald; Folios, *'to the heart'*; Collier MS., *'o' th' heart'*; &c.
21. Though but bastards and syllables; – Capell, *'but bastards'*; Seymour conjectured *'although but bastards, syllables'*; Badham conjectured *'thought's bastards, and but syllables.'*
22. I am in this; – Warburton, 'In this advice I speak as your wife, your son, ' &c.
23. That want, i.e. – the want of that inheritance.
24. Which often, thus, correcting thy stout heart; – Johnson, *'With often, '* &c.; Capell, *'And often'*; Staunton conjectured *'While often'*; Nicholson conjectured *'Whilesoften'*; Warburton, *'Which soften.'*
25. Among's, i.e. – among us; Folio 1, *'amongs'*; Folios 2, 3, 4, *'amongst you'*; Pope, *'amongst you'*; Capell, *'among us.'*
26. Throng, – Theobald's and Warburton's emendation of Folios, *'Through.'*
27. Accents, – Theobald's correction of Folios, *'actions.'*
28. Not; – Capell's correction of Folios, *'but.'*
29. Fortune's blows, When most struck home, being gentle wounded, craves A noble cunning; i.e. – "When Fortune's blows are most struck home, to be gentle, although wounded, demands a noble philosophy" (Clarke). Pope, *'gently warded'*; Hanmer, *'greatly warded'*; Collier MS., *'gentle-minded.'*
30. My birth-place hate I, and my love's upon'; – Capell's emendation. Folio 1 reads, *'My Birth-place have I, and my loues upon'*; Folios 2, 3, *'My Birth-lace I, and my lover upon'*; Folio 4, *'My Birth-place have I, and my Lover left; upon'*; Pope, *'My birth-place have I and my lovers left'*; Beckett conjectured *'My country have I and my lovers lost,'* &c.
31. Appearance; – Folio 1, *'appearance'* (probably the recognised form of the word, representing the pronunciation at the time).
32. The sense of the lines should be to this effect:—"Power is in itself most commendable, but the orator's chair, from which a man's past actions are extolled, is the inevitable tomb of his power." The passage is crude, and many suggestions have been advanced.
33. Fouler; – Dyce's ingenious reading, *'falter,'* is the best conjectural emendation of the line.
34. Many emendations have been proposed to clear up the obscurity of the line. It appears to mean either (i.) that Coriolanus bound Cominius by asn oath to yield to his conditions; or (ii.) that Coriolanus was bound by an oath as *to what he would not,* unless the Romans should yield to his conditions. Johnson proposed to read—

    "What he would not,
    Bound by an oath. To yield to his conditions,"—

    the rest being omitted. Many attempts have been made to improve the passage, but no proposal carries conviction with it.
35. Your; – so Folio 1, 2, 3; Folio 4, *'our.'*
36. Though I owe My revenge properly, i.e. – 'though revenge is my own, remission belongs to the Volscians.'

HAMLET-PRINCE OF DENMARK

HAMLET-PRINCE OF DENMARK

DRAMATIS PERSONAE

CLAUDIUS, king of Denmark.
HAMLET, son to the late, and nephew to the present king.
POLONIUS, lord chamberlain.
HORATIO, friend to Hamlet.
LAERTES, son to Polonius.
VOLTIMAND, courtier.
CORNELIUS, courtier.
ROSENCRANTZ, courtier.
GUILDENSTERN, courtier.
OSRIC, courtier.
A Gentleman.
A Priest.
MARCELLUS, officer.
BERNARDO, officer.
FRANCISCO, a soldier.
REYNALDO, servant to Polonius.
Players.
Two Clowns, grave-diggers.
FORTINBRAS prince of Norway.
A Captain.
English Ambassadors.
GERTRUDE, queen of Denmark, and mother to Hamlet.
OPHELIA, daughter to Polonius.
Lords, Ladies, Officers, Soldiers, Sailors, Messengers, and other Attendants.
Ghost of Hamlet's Father.

SCENE: *Denmark.*

ACT ONE SCENE ONE

Elsinore. A platform before the castle.
FRANCISCO *at his post. Enter to him* BERNARDO.

BERNARDO
Who's there?
FRANCISCO
Nay, answer me: stand, and unfold yourself.
BERNARDO
Long live the king!
FRANCISCO
Bernardo?
BERNARDO
He.
FRANCISCO
You come most carefully upon your hour.
BERNARDO
'Tis now struck twelve; get thee to bed, Francisco.
FRANCISCO
For this relief much thanks: 'tis bitter cold,
And I am sick at heart.
BERNARDO
Have you had quiet guard?
FRANCISCO
Not a mouse stirring.
BERNARDO
Well, good night.
If you do meet Horatio and Marcellus,
The rivals of my watch, bid them make haste.
FRANCISCO
I think I hear them. Stand, ho! Who's there?

Enter HORATIO *and* MARCELLUS.

HORATIO
Friends to this ground.

MARCELLUS
And liegemen to the Dane.

FRANCISCO
Give you good night.

MARCELLUS
O, farewell, honest soldier:
Who hath relieved you?

FRANCISCO
Bernardo has my place.
Give you good night. [*Exit.*

MARCELLUS
Holla! Bernardo!

BERNARDO
Say,
What, is Horatio there?

HORATIO
A piece of him.

BERNARDO
Welcome, Horatio: welcome, good Marcellus. 28

MARCELLUS
What, has this thing appear'd again to-night?

BERNARDO
I have seen nothing.

MARCELLUS
Horatio says 'tis but our fantasy,
And will not let belief take hold of him
Touching this dreaded sight, twice seen of us:
Therefore I have entreated him along
With us to watch the minutes of this night;
That if again this apparition come,
He may approve our eyes and speak to it.

HORATIO
Tush, tush, 'twill not appear.

BERNARDO
Sit down awhile; 39
And let us once again assail your ears,
That are so fortified against our story
What we have two nights seen.

HORATIO
Well, sit we down,
And let us hear Bernardo speak of this.

BERNARDO
Last night of all,
When yond same star that's westward from the pole
Had made his course to illume that part of heaven
Where now it burns, Marcellus and myself,
The bell then beating one,—

Enter Ghost.

MARCELLUS
Peace, break thee off; look, where it comes again! 50

BERNARDO
In the same figure, like the king that's dead.

MARCELLUS
Thou art a scholar; speak to it, Horatio.

BERNARDO
Looks it not like the king? mark it, Horatio.

HORATIO
Most like: it harrows me with fear and wonder.

BERNARDO
It would be spoke to.

MARCELLUS
Question it, Horatio.

HORATIO
What art thou that usurp'st this time of night,
Together with that fair and warlike form
In which the majesty of buried Denmark
Did sometimes march? by heaven I charge thee, speak!

MARCELLUS
It is offended.

BERNARDO
See, it stalks away! 63

HORATIO
Stay! speak, speak! I charge thee, speak!
[*Exit Ghost.*

MARCELLUS
'Tis gone, and will not answer.

BERNARDO
How now, Horatio! you tremble and look pale:
Is not this something more than fantasy?
What think you on't?

HORATIO
Before my God, I might not this believe
Without the sensible and true avouch
Of mine own eyes.

MARCELLUS
Is it not like the king?

HORATIO
As thou art to thyself:
Such was the very armour he had on 75
When he the ambitious Norway combated;
So frown'd he once, when, in an angry parle,
He smote the sledded Polacks on the ice. [1]
'Tis strange.

MARCELLUS
Thus twice before, and jump at this dead hour,
With martial stalk hath he gone by our watch.

HORATIO
In what particular thought to work I know not:
But in the gross and scope of my opinion,
This bodes some strange eruption to our state.

MARCELLUS
Good now, sit down, and tell me, he that knows, 85
Why this same strict and most observant watch

BERNARDO Looks it not like the king? Mark it, Horatio.

So nightly toils the subject of the land,
And why such daily cast of brazen cannon,
And foreign mart for implements of war;
Why such impress of shipwrights, whose sore task
Does not divide the Sunday from the week;
What might be toward, that this sweaty haste
Doth make the night joint-labourer with the day:
Who is't that can inform me?

HORATIO

That can I;
At least, the whisper goes so. Our last king,
Whose image even but now appear'd to us,
Was, as you know, by Fortinbras of Norway,
Thereto prick'd on by a most emulate pride,
Dared to the combat; in which our valiant Hamlet—
For so this side of our known world esteem'd him—
Did slay this Fortinbras; who, by a seal'd compact,
Well ratified by law and heraldry,
Did forfeit, with his life, all those his lands
Which he stood seized of, to the conqueror:
Against the which, a moiety competent
Was gaged by our king; which had return'd
To the inheritance of Fortinbras,
Had he been vanquisher; as, by the same covenant,
And carriage of the article design'd,
His fell to Hamlet. Now, sir, young Fortinbras,
Of unimproved mettle hot and full,
Hath in the skirts of Norway here and there
Shark'd up a list of lawless resolutes,
For food and diet, to some enterprise
That hath a stomach in't; which is no other—
As it doth well appear unto our state—
But to recover of us, by strong hand
And terms compulsatory, those foresaid lands
So by his father lost: and this, I take it,
Is the main motive of our preparations,
The source of this our watch and the chief head
Of this post-haste and romage in the land.

BERNARDO

I think it be no other but e'en so: [2]
Well may it sort that this portentous figure
Comes armed through our watch; so like the king
That was and is the question of these wars.

HORATIO
A mote it is to trouble the mind's eye.
In the most high and palmy state of Rome,
A little ere the mightiest Julius fell,
The graves stood tenantless and the sheeted dead
Did squeak and gibber in the Roman streets:
As stars with trains of fire and dews of blood,
Disasters in the sun; and the moist star
Upon whose influence Neptune's empire stands
Was sick almost to doomsday with eclipse:
And even the like precurse of fierce events,
As harbingers preceding still the fates
And prologue to the omen coming on.
Have heaven and earth together demonstrated
Unto our climatures and countrymen.—
But soft, behold! lo, where it comes again!

Re-enter Ghost.

I'll cross it, though it blast me. Stay, illusion!
If thou hast any sound, or use of voice,
Speak to me:
If there be any good thing to be done,
That may to thee do ease and grace to me,
Speak to me: [*Cock crows.*
If thou art privy to thy country's fate,
Which, happily, foreknowing may avoid,
O, speak!
Or if thou hast uphoarded in thy life
Extorted treasure in the womb of earth,
For which, they say, you spirits oft walk in death,
Speak of it: stay, and speak! Stop it, Marcellus.
MARCELLUS
Shall I strike at it with my partisan?
HORATIO
Do, if it will not stand.
BERNARDO
'Tis here!
HORATIO
'Tis here!
MARCELLUS
'Tis gone! [*Exit Ghost.*
We do it wrong, being so majestical,
To offer it the show of violence;
For it is, as the air, invulnerable,
And our vain blows malicious mockery.
BERNARDO
It was about to speak, when the cock crew.
HORATIO
And then it started like a guilty thing
Upon a fearful summons. I have heard,
The cock, that is the trumpet to the morn,
Doth with his lofty and shrill-sounding throat
Awake the god of day; and, at his warning,
Whether in sea or fire, in earth or air,
The extravagant and erring spirit hies
To his confine: and of the truth herein
This present object made probation.
MARCELLUS
It faded on the crowing of the cock.
Some say that ever 'gainst that season comes
Wherein our Saviour's birth is celebrated,
The bird of dawning singeth all night long:
And then, they say, no spirit dare stir abroad;
The nights are wholesome; then no planets strike,
No fairy takes, nor witch hath power to charm,
So hallow'd and so gracious is the time.
HORATIO
So have I heard and do in part believe it.
But, look, the morn, in russet mantle clad,
Walks o'er the dew of yon high eastward hill: [3]
Break we our watch up; and by my advice,
Let us impart what we have seen to-night
Unto young Hamlet; for, upon my life,
This spirit, dumb to us, will speak to him.
Do you consent we shall acquaint him with it,
As needful in our loves, fitting our duty?
MARCELLUS
Let's do't, I pray; and I this morning know
Where we shall find him most conveniently.
[*Exeunt.*

ACT ONE SCENE TWO

A room of state in the castle.

Enter the KING, QUEEN, HAMLET, POLONIUS, LAERTES, VOLTIMAND, CORNELIUS, Lords, *and* Attendants.

KING CLAUDIUS
Though yet of Hamlet our dear brother's death
The memory be green, and that it us befitted
To bear our hearts in grief and our whole kingdom
To be contracted in one brow of woe,
Yet so far hath discretion fought with nature
That we with wisest sorrow think on him,
Together with remembrance of ourselves.
Therefore our sometime sister, now our queen,
The imperial jointress to this warlike state, [4]
Have we, as 'twere with a defeated joy,—
With an auspicious and a dropping eye,
With mirth in funeral and with dirge in marriage,
In equal scale weighing delight and dole,—
Taken to wife: nor have we herein barr'd
Your better wisdoms, which have freely gone
With this affair along. For all, our thanks.
Now follows, that you know, young Fortinbras,
Holding a weak supposal of our worth,

Or thinking by our late dear brother's death
Our state to be disjoint and out of frame,
Colleagued with the dream of his advantage,
He hath not fail'd to pester us with message,
Importing the surrender of those lands
Lost by his father, with all bonds of law,
To our most valiant brother. So much for him.
Now for ourself and for this time of meeting:
Thus much the business is: we have here writ
To Norway, uncle of young Fortinbras,—
Who, impotent and bed-rid, scarcely hears
Of this his nephew's purpose,—to suppress
His further gait herein; in that the levies,
The lists and full proportions, are all made
Out of his subject: and we here dispatch
You, good Cornelius, and you, Voltimand,
For bearers of this greeting to old Norway;
Giving to you no further personal power
To business with the king, more than the scope
Of these delated articles allow.
Farewell, and let your haste commend your duty.

CORNELIUS, VOLTIMAND
In that and all things will we show our duty.

KING CLAUDIUS
We doubt it nothing: heartily farewell.
[*Exeunt Voltimand and Cornelius.*
And now, Laertes, what's the news with you?
You told us of some suit; what is't, Laertes?
You cannot speak of reason to the Dane,
And lose your voice: what wouldst thou beg, Laertes,
That shall not be my offer, not thy asking?
The head is not more native to the heart,
The hand more instrumental to the mouth,
Than is the throne of Denmark to thy father.
What wouldst thou have, Laertes?

LAERTES
My dread lord,
Your leave and favour to return to France;
From whence though willingly I came to Denmark,
To show my duty in your coronation,
Yet now, I must confess, that duty done,
My thoughts and wishes bend again toward France
And bow them to your gracious leave and pardon.

KING CLAUDIUS
Have you your father's leave? What says Polonius?

POLONIUS
He hath, my lord, wrung from me my slow leave [5]
By laboursome petition, and at last
Upon his will I seal'd my hard consent:
I do beseech you, give him leave to go.

KING CLAUDIUS
Take thy fair hour, Laertes; time be thine,
And thy best graces spend it at thy will!
But now, my cousin Hamlet, and my son,—

HAMLET
[*Aside*]
A little more than kin, and less than kind.

KING CLAUDIUS
How is it that the clouds still hang on you?

HAMLET
Not so, my lord; I am too much i' the sun.

QUEEN GERTRUDE
Good Hamlet, cast thy nighted colour off,
And let thine eye look like a friend on Denmark.
Do not for ever with thy vailed lids
Seek for thy noble father in the dust:
Thou know'st 'tis common; all that lives must die,
Passing through nature to eternity.

HAMLET
Ay, madam, it is common.

QUEEN GERTRUDE
If it be,
Why seems it so particular with thee?

HAMLET
Seems, madam! nay, it is; I know not 'seems.'
'Tis not alone my inky cloak, good mother,
Nor customary suits of solemn black,
Nor windy suspiration of forced breath,
No, nor the fruitful river in the eye,
Nor the dejected 'haviour of the visage,
Together with all forms, moods, shapes of grief,
That can denote me truly: these indeed seem,
For they are actions that a man might play:
But I have that within which passeth show;
These but the trappings and the suits of woe.

KING CLAUDIUS
'Tis sweet and commendable in your nature, Hamlet,
To give these mourning duties to your father:
But, you must know, your father lost a father;
That father lost, lost his, and the survivor bound
In filial obligation for some term
To do obsequious sorrow: but to persever
In obstinate condolement is a course
Of impious stubbornness; 'tis unmanly grief;
It shows a will most incorrect to heaven,
A heart unfortified, a mind impatient,
An understanding simple and unschool'd:
For what we know must be and is as common
As any the most vulgar thing to sense,
Why should we in our peevish opposition
Take it to heart? Fie! 'tis a fault to heaven,
A fault against the dead, a fault to nature,
To reason most absurd; whose common theme
Is death of fathers, and who still hath cried,
From the first corse till he that died to-day,
'This must be so.' We pray you, throw to earth
This unprevailing woe, and think of us

As of a father: for let the world take note,
You are the most immediate to our throne;
And with no less nobility of love
Than that which dearest father bears his son,
Do I impart toward you. For your intent
In going back to school in Wittenberg,
It is most retrograde to our desire:
And we beseech you, bend you to remain
Here, in the cheer and comfort of our eye,
Our chiefest courtier, cousin, and our son.

QUEEN GERTRUDE
Let not thy mother lose her prayers, Hamlet:
I pray thee, stay with us: go not to Wittenberg.

HAMLET
I shall in all my best obey you, madam.

KING CLAUDIUS
Why, 'tis a loving and a fair reply:
Be as ourself in Denmark. Madam, come;
This gentle and unforced accord of Hamlet
Sits smiling to my heart: in grace whereof,
No jocund health that Denmark drinks to-day,
But the great cannon to the clouds shall tell,
And the king's rouse the heavens all bruit again,
Re-speaking earthly thunder. Come away.
[*Exeunt all but Hamlet.*

HAMLET
O, that this too too solid flesh would melt,
Thaw and resolve itself into a dew!
Or that the Everlasting had not fix'd
His canon 'gainst self-slaughter! O God! God!
How weary, stale, flat and unprofitable,
Seem to me all the uses of this world!
Fie on't! ah fie! 'tis an unweeded garden,
That grows to seed; things rank and gross in nature
Possess it merely. That it should come to this!
But two months dead: nay, not so much, not two:
So excellent a king; that was, to this,
Hyperion to a satyr; so loving to my mother
That he might not beteem the winds of heaven
Visit her face too roughly. Heaven and earth!
Must I remember? why, she would hang on him,
As if increase of appetite had grown
By what it fed on: and yet, within a month—
Let me not think on't—Frailty, thy name is woman!—
A little month, or ere those shoes were old
With which she follow'd my poor father's body,
Like Niobe, all tears:—why she, even she—
O, God! a beast, that wants discourse of reason,
Would have mourn'd longer—married with my uncle,
My father's brother, but no more like my father
Than I to Hercules: within a month:
Ere yet the salt of most unrighteous tears
Had left the flushing in her galled eyes,
She married. O, most wicked speed, to post
With such dexterity to incestuous sheets!
It is not nor it cannot come to good:
But break, my heart; for I must hold my tongue.

Enter HORATIO, MARCELLUS, *and* BERNARDO.

HORATIO
Hail to your lordship!

HAMLET
I am glad to see you well:
Horatio,—or I do forget myself.

HORATIO
The same, my lord, and your poor servant ever.

HAMLET
Sir, my good friend; I'll change that name with you:
And what make you from Wittenberg, Horatio?
Marcellus?

MARCELLUS
My good lord—

HAMLET
I am very glad to see you. Good even, sir.
But what, in faith, make you from Wittenberg?

HORATIO
A truant disposition, good my lord.

HAMLET
I would not hear your enemy say so,
Nor shall you do mine ear that violence,
To make it truster of your own report
Against yourself: I know you are no truant.
But what is your affair in Elsinore?
We'll teach you to drink deep ere you depart.

HORATIO
My lord, I came to see your father's funeral.

HAMLET
I pray thee, do not mock me, fellow-student;
I think it was to see my mother's wedding.

HORATIO
Indeed, my lord, it follow'd hard upon.

HAMLET
Thrift, thrift, Horatio! the funeral baked meats
Did coldly furnish forth the marriage tables.
Would I had met my dearest foe in heaven
Or ever I had seen that day, Horatio!
My father!—methinks I see my father.

HORATIO
Where, my lord?

HAMLET
In my mind's eye, Horatio.

HORATIO
I saw him once; he was a goodly king.

HAMLET
He was a man, take him for all in all,
I shall not look upon his like again.

HORATIO
My lord, I think I saw him yesternight.
HAMLET
Saw? who? 197
HORATIO
My lord, the king your father.
HAMLET
The king my father!
HORATIO
Season your admiration for a while
With an attent ear, till I may deliver,
Upon the witness of these gentlemen,
This marvel to you.
HAMLET
For God's love, let me hear.
HORATIO
Two nights together had these gentlemen,
Marcellus and Bernardo, on their watch,
In the dead vast and middle of the night,
Been thus encounter'd. A figure like your father,
Armed at point exactly, cap-a-pe, 209
Appears before them, and with solemn march
Goes slow and stately by them: thrice he walk'd
By their oppress'd and fear surprised eyes,
Within his truncheon's length; whilst they, distill'd
Almost to jelly with the act of fear,
Stand dumb and speak not to him. This to me
In dreadful secrecy impart they did;
And I with them the third night kept the watch:
Where, as they had deliver'd, both in time,
Form of the thing, each word made true and good, 220
The apparition comes: I knew your father;
These hands are not more like.
HAMLET
But where was this?
MARCELLUS
My lord, upon the platform where we watch'd.
HAMLET
Did you not speak to it?
HORATIO
My lord, I did;
But answer made it none: yet once methought
It lifted up its head and did address
Itself to motion, like as it would speak;
But even then the morning cock crew loud,
And at the sound it shrunk in haste away,
And vanish'd from our sight.
HAMLET
'Tis very strange. 233
HORATIO
As I do live, my honour'd lord, 'tis true;
And we did think it writ down in our duty
To let you know of it.
HAMLET
Indeed, indeed, sirs, but this troubles me.
Hold you the watch to-night?
MARCELLUS, BERNARDO
We do, my lord.
HAMLET
Arm'd, say you?
MARCELLUS, BERNARDO
Arm'd, my lord.
HAMLET
From top to toe?
MARCELLUS, BERNARDO
My lord, from head to foot.
HAMLET
Then saw you not his face?
HORATIO
O, yes, my lord; he wore his beaver up.
HAMLET
What, look'd he frowningly? 246
HORATIO
A countenance more in sorrow than in anger.
HAMLET
Pale or red?
HORATIO
Nay, very pale.
HAMLET
And fix'd his eyes upon you?
HORATIO
Most constantly.
HAMLET
I would I had been there.
HORATIO
It would have much amazed you.
HAMLET
Very like, very like. Stay'd it long?
HORATIO
While one with moderate haste might tell a hundred.
MARCELLUS, BERNARDO
Longer, longer.
HORATIO
Not when I saw't.
HAMLET
His beard was grizzled,—no? 258
HORATIO
It was, as I have seen it in his life,
A sable silver'd.
HAMLET
I will watch to-night;
Perchance 'twill walk again.
HORATIO
I warrant it will.
HAMLET
If it assume my noble father's person,
I'll speak to it, though hell itself should gape

And bid me hold my peace. I pray you all,
If you have hitherto conceal'd this sight,
Let it be tenable in your silence still;
And whatsoever else shall hap to-night,
Give it an understanding, but no tongue: 270
I will requite your loves. So, fare you well:
Upon the platform, 'twixt eleven and twelve,
I'll visit you.

ALL
Our duty to your honour.

HAMLET
Your loves, as mine to you: farewell.
[*Exeunt all but Hamlet.*
My father's spirit in arms! all is not well;
I doubt some foul play: would the night were come!
Till then sit still, my soul: foul deeds will rise,
Though all the earth o'erwhelm them, to men's eyes. [*Exit.*

ACT ONE SCENE THREE

A room in Polonius' house.

Enter LAERTES *and* OPHELIA.

LAERTES
My necessaries are embark'd: farewell:
And, sister, as the winds give benefit
And convoy is assistant, do not sleep,
But let me hear from you.

OPHELIA
Do you doubt that?

LAERTES
For Hamlet and the trifling of his favour,
Hold it a fashion and a toy in blood,
A violet in the youth of primy nature,
Forward, not permanent, sweet, not lasting,
The perfume and suppliance of a minute;
No more.

OPHELIA
No more but so?

LAERTES
Think it no more: 13
For nature, crescent, does not grow alone
In thews and bulk, but, as this temple waxes, [6]
The inward service of the mind and soul
Grows wide withal. Perhaps he loves you now,
And now no soil nor cautel doth besmirch
The virtue of his will: but you must fear, [7]
His greatness weigh'd, his will is not his own;
For he himself is subject to his birth: [8]
He may not, as unvalued persons do,
Carve for himself; for on his choice depends
The safety and health of this whole state;
And therefore must his choice be circumscribed
Unto the voice and yielding of that body
Whereof he is the head. Then if he says he loves you,
It fits your wisdom so far to believe it
As he in his particular act and place [9]
May give his saying deed; which is no further
Than the main voice of Denmark goes withal.
Then weigh what loss your honour may sustain,
If with too credent ear you list his songs, 33
Or lose your heart, or your chaste treasure open
To his unmaster'd importunity.
Fear it, Ophelia, fear it, my dear sister,
And keep you in the rear of your affection,
Out of the shot and danger of desire.
The chariest maid is prodigal enough,
If she unmask her beauty to the moon:
Virtue itself 'scapes not calumnious strokes:
The canker galls the infants of the spring,
Too oft before their buttons be disclosed, 43
And in the morn and liquid dew of youth
Contagious blastments are most imminent.
Be wary then; best safety lies in fear:
Youth to itself rebels, though none else near.

OPHELIA
I shall the effect of this good lesson keep,
As watchman to my heart. But, good my brother,
Do not, as some ungracious pastors do,
Show me the steep and thorny way to heaven;
Whiles, like a puff'd and reckless libertine,
Himself the primrose path of dalliance treads,
And recks not his own rede.

LAERTES
O, fear me not. 55
I stay too long: but here my father comes.

Enter POLONIUS.

A double blessing is a double grace;
Occasion smiles upon a second leave.

POLONIUS
Yet here, Laertes! Aboard, aboard, for shame!
The wind sits in the shoulder of your sail,
And you are stay'd for. There; my blessing with thee!
And these few precepts in thy memory [10]
See thou character. Give thy thoughts no tongue,
Nor any unproportion'd thought his act. 64
Be thou familiar, but by no means vulgar.
Those friends thou hast, and their adoption tried,
Grapple them to thy soul with hoops of steel;
But do not dull thy palm with entertainment
Of each new-hatch'd, unfledged comrade.
Beware [11]
Of entrance to a quarrel, but being in,
Bear't that the opposed may beware of thee.
Give every man thy ear, but few thy voice;

Take each man's censure, but reserve thy judgement.
Costly thy habit as thy purse can buy,
But not express'd in fancy; rich, not gaudy;
For the apparel oft proclaims the man,
And they in France of the best rank and station
Are of a most select and generous chief in that. [12]
Neither a borrower nor a lender be;
For loan oft loses both itself and friend,
And borrowing dulls the edge of husbandry.
This above all: to thine own self be true,
And it must follow, as the night the day,
Thou canst not then be false to any man.
Farewell: my blessing season this in thee!

LAERTES
Most humbly do I take my leave, my lord.

POLONIUS
The time invites you; go; your servants tend.

LAERTES
Farewell, Ophelia; and remember well
What I have said to you.

OPHELIA
'Tis in my memory lock'd,
And you yourself shall keep the key of it.

LAERTES
Farewell. [*Exit.*

POLONIUS
What is't, Ophelia, be hath said to you?

OPHELIA
So please you, something touching the Lord Hamlet.

POLONIUS
Marry, well bethought:
'Tis told me, he hath very oft of late
Given private time to you; and you yourself
Have of your audience been most free and bounteous:
If it be so, as so 'tis put on me,
And that in way of caution, I must tell you,
You do not understand yourself so clearly
As it behoves my daughter and your honour.
What is between you? give me up the truth.

OPHELIA
He hath, my lord, of late made many tenders
Of his affection to me.

POLONIUS
Affection! pooh! you speak like a green girl,
Unsifted in such perilous circumstance.
Do you believe his tenders, as you call them?

OPHELIA
I do not know, my lord, what I should think.

POLONIUS
Marry, I'll teach you: think yourself a baby;
That you have ta'en these tenders for true pay,
Which are not sterling. Tender yourself more dearly;
Or—not to crack the wind of the poor phrase,
Running it thus—you'll tender me a fool. [13]

OPHELIA
My lord, he hath importuned me with love
In honourable fashion.

POLONIUS
Ay, fashion you may call it; go to, go to.

OPHELIA
And hath given countenance to his speech, my lord,
With almost all the holy vows of heaven.

POLONIUS
Ay, springes to catch woodcocks. I do know,
When the blood burns, how prodigal the soul
Lends the tongue vows: these blazes, daughter,
Giving more light than heat, extinct in both,
Even in their promise, as it is a-making,
You must not take for fire. From this time
Be somewhat scanter of your maiden presence;
Set your entreatments at a higher rate
Than a command to parley. For Lord Hamlet,
Believe so much in him, that he is young,
And with a larger tether may he walk
Than may be given you: in few, Ophelia,
Do not believe his vows; for they are brokers,
Not of that dye which their investments show,
But mere implorators of unholy suits,
Breathing like sanctified and pious bawds, [14]
The better to beguile. This is for all:
I would not, in plain terms, from this time forth,
Have you so slander any moment leisure,
As to give words or talk with the Lord Hamlet.
Look to't, I charge you: come your ways.

OPHELIA
I shall obey, my lord. [*Exeunt.*

ACT ONE SCENE FOUR

The platform.

Enter HAMLET, HORATIO, *and* MARCELLUS.

HAMLET
The air bites shrewdly; it is very cold.

HORATIO
It is a nipping and an eager air.

HAMLET
What hour now?

HORATIO
I think it lacks of twelve.

HAMLET
No, it is struck.

HORATIO
Indeed? I heard it not: then it draws near the season

Wherein the spirit held his wont to walk.
[A flourish of trumpets, and ordnance shot off, within.
What does this mean, my lord?

HAMLET
The king doth wake to-night and takes his rouse,
Keeps wassail, and the swaggering up-spring reels;
And, as he drains his draughts of Rhenish down,
The kettle-drum and trumpet thus bray out 13
The triumph of his pledge.

HORATIO
Is it a custom?

HAMLET
Ay, marry, is't:
But to my mind, though I am native here
And to the manner born, it is a custom
More honour'd in the breach than the observance. [15]
This heavy-headed revel east and west
Makes us traduced and tax'd of other nations:
They clepe us drunkards, and with swinish phrase
Soil our addition; and indeed it takes 24
From our achievements, though perform'd at height,
The pith and marrow of our attribute.
So, oft it chances in particular men,
That for some vicious mole of nature in them,
As, in their birth—wherein they are not guilty,
Since nature cannot choose his origin—
By the o'ergrowth of some complexion,
Oft breaking down the pales and forts of reason,
Or by some habit that too much o'er-leavens
The form of plausive manners, that these men,
Carrying, I say, the stamp of one defect, 35
Being nature's livery, or fortune's star,—
Their virtues else—be they as pure as grace,
As infinite as man may undergo—
Shall in the general censure take corruption
From that particular fault: the dram of eale [16]
Doth all the noble substance of a doubt
To his own scandal.

HORATIO
Look, my lord, it comes!

Enter Ghost.

HAMLET
Angels and ministers of grace defend us!
Be thou a spirit of health or goblin damn'd,
Bring with thee airs from heaven or blasts from hell,
Be thy intents wicked or charitable,
Thou comest in such a questionable shape
That I will speak to thee: I'll call thee Hamlet,
King, father, royal Dane: O, answer me!
Let me not burst in ignorance; but tell
Why thy canonized bones, hearsed in death,
Have burst their cerements; why the sepulchre,
Wherein we saw thee quietly inurn'd,
Hath oped his ponderous and marble jaws,
To cast thee up again. What may this mean,
That thou, dead corse, again in complete steel
Revisit'st thus the glimpses of the moon,
Making night hideous; and we fools of nature
So horridly to shake our disposition
With thoughts beyond the reaches of our souls?
Say, why is this? wherefore? what should we do?
[Ghost beckons Hamlet.

HORATIO
It beckons you to go away with it,
As if it some impartment did desire
To you alone.

MARCELLUS
Look, with what courteous action 66
It waves you to a more removed ground:
But do not go with it.

HORATIO
No, by no means.

HAMLET
It will not speak; then I will follow it.

HORATIO
Do not, my lord.

HAMLET
Why, what should be the fear?
I do not set my life in a pin's fee;
And for my soul, what can it do to that,
Being a thing immortal as itself?
It waves me forth again: I'll follow it.

HORATIO
What if it tempt you toward the flood, my lord,
Or to the dreadful summit of the cliff 73
That beetles o'er his base into the sea,
And there assume some other horrible form,
Which might deprive your sovereignty of reason
And draw you into madness? think of it: [17]
The very place puts toys of desperation,
Without more motive, into every brain
That looks so many fathoms to the sea
And hears it roar beneath.

HAMLET
It waves me still.
Go on; I'll follow thee.

MARCELLUS
You shall not go, my lord.

HAMLET
Hold off your hands. 90

HORATIO
Be ruled; you shall not go.

HAMLET
My fate cries out,
And makes each petty artery in this body

As hardy as the Nemean lion's nerve.
Still am I call'd. Unhand me, gentlemen.
By heaven, I'll make a ghost of him that lets me!
I say, away! Go on; I'll follow thee.
[Exeunt Ghost and Hamlet.

HORATIO
He waxes desperate with imagination.

MARCELLUS
Let's follow; 'tis not fit thus to obey him.

HORATIO
Have after. To what issue will this come?

MARCELLUS
Something is rotten in the state of Denmark.

HORATIO
Heaven will direct it.

MARCELLUS
Nay, let's follow him. *[Exeunt.*

ACT ONE SCENE FIVE

Another part of the platform.
Enter GHOST *and* HAMLET.

HAMLET
Where wilt thou lead me? speak;
I'll go no further.

GHOST
Mark me.

HAMLET
I will.

GHOST
My hour is almost come,
When I to sulphurous and tormenting flames
Must render up myself.

HAMLET
Alas, poor ghost!

GHOST
Pity me not, but lend thy serious hearing
To what I shall unfold.

HAMLET
Speak; I am bound to hear.

GHOST
So art thou to revenge, when thou shalt hear.

HAMLET
What?

GHOST
I am thy father's spirit,
Doom'd for a certain term to walk the night,
And for the day confined to fast in fires,
Till the foul crimes done in my days of nature
Are burnt and purged away. But that I am forbid
To tell the secrets of my prison-house,
I could a tale unfold whose lightest word
Would harrow up thy soul, freeze thy young blood,
Make thy two eyes, like stars, start from their spheres,
Thy knotted and combined locks to part
And each particular hair to stand on end,
Like quills upon the fretful porpentine:
But this eternal blazon must not be
To ears of flesh and blood. List, list, O, list! [18]
If thou didst ever thy dear father love—

HAMLET
O God!

GHOST
Revenge his foul and most unnatural murder.

HAMLET
Murder!

GHOST
Murder most foul, as in the best it is;
But this most foul, strange and unnatural.

HAMLET
Haste me to know't, that I, with wings as swift
As meditation or the thoughts of love,
May sweep to my revenge.

GHOST
I find thee apt;
And duller shouldst thou be than the fat weed
That roots itself in ease on Lethe wharf,
Wouldst thou not stir in this. Now, Hamlet, hear:
'Tis given out that, sleeping in my orchard,
A serpent stung me; so the whole ear of Denmark
Is by a forged process of my death
Rankly abused; but know, thou noble youth,
The serpent that did sting thy father's life
Now wears his crown.

HAMLET
O my prophetic soul!
My uncle!

GHOST
Ay, that incestuous, that adulterate beast,
With witchcraft of his wit, with traitorous gifts,—
O wicked wit and gifts, that have the power
So to seduce!—won to his shameful lust
The will of my most seeming-virtuous queen:
O Hamlet, what a falling-off was there!
From me, whose love was of that dignity
That it went hand in hand even with the vow
I made to her in marriage, and to decline
Upon a wretch whose natural gifts were poor
To those of mine!
But virtue, as it never will be moved,
Though lewdness court it in a shape of heaven,
So lust, though to a radiant angel link'd,
Will sate itself in a celestial bed,
And prey on garbage.
But, soft! methinks I scent the morning air;

Brief let me be. Sleeping within my orchard,
My custom always of the afternoon,
Upon my secure hour thy uncle stole,
With juice of cursed hebenon in a vial,
And in the porches of my ears did pour
The leperous distilment; whose effect
Holds such an enmity with blood of man
That swift as quicksilver it courses through
The natural gates and alleys of the body,
And with a sudden vigour it doth posset
And curd, like eager droppings into milk,
The thin and wholesome blood: so did it mine;
And a most instant tetter bark'd about,
Most lazar-like, with vile and loathsome crust,
All my smooth body.
Thus was I, sleeping, by a brother's hand
Of life, of crown, of queen, at once dispatch'd:
Cut off even in the blossoms of my sin,
Unhousel'd, disappointed, unaneled,
No reckoning made, but sent to my account
With all my imperfections on my head:
O, horrible! O, horrible! most horrible!
If thou hast nature in thee, bear it not;
Let not the royal bed of Denmark be
A couch for luxury and damned incest.
But, howsoever thou pursuest this act,
Taint not thy mind, nor let thy soul contrive
Against thy mother aught: leave her to heaven
And to those thorns that in her bosom lodge,
To prick and sting her. Fare thee well at once!
The glow-worm shows the matin to be near,
And 'gins to pale his uneffectual fire:
Adieu, adieu! Hamlet, remember me. [*Exit.*

HAMLET
O all you host of heaven! O earth! what else?
And shall I couple hell? O, fie! Hold, hold, my heart;
And you, my sinews, grow not instant old,
But bear me stiffly up. Remember thee!
Ay, thou poor ghost, while memory holds a seat
In this distracted globe. Remember thee!
Yea, from the table of my memory
I'll wipe away all trivial fond records,
All saws of books, all forms, all pressures past,
That youth and observation copied there;
And thy commandment all alone shall live
Within the book and volume of my brain,
Unmix'd with baser matter: yes, by heaven!
O most pernicious woman!
O villain, villain, smiling, damned villain!
My tables,—meet it is I set it down,
That one may smile, and smile, and be a villain;
At least I'm sure it may be so in Denmark:
[*Writing.*
So, uncle, there you are. Now to my word;
It is 'Adieu, adieu! remember me.'
I have sworn 't.

MARCELLUS, HORATIO
[*Within*] My lord, my lord,—

MARCELLUS
[*Within*] Lord Hamlet,—

HORATIO
[*Within*] Heaven secure him!

HAMLET
So be it!

HORATIO
[*Within*] Hillo, ho, ho, my lord!

HAMLET
Hillo, ho, ho, boy! come, bird, come.

Enter HORATIO *and* MARCELLUS.

MARCELLUS
How is't, my noble lord?

HORATIO
What news, my lord?

HAMLET
O, wonderful!

HORATIO
Good my lord, tell it.

HAMLET
No; you'll reveal it.

HORATIO
Not I, my lord, by heaven.

MARCELLUS
Nor I, my lord

HAMLET
How say you, then; would heart of man once think it?
But you'll be secret?

HORATIO, MARCELLUS
Ay, by heaven, my lord.

HAMLET
There's ne'er a villain dwelling in all Denmark
But he's an arrant knave.

HORATIO
There needs no ghost, my lord, come from the grave
To tell us this.

HAMLET
Why, right; you are i' the right;
And so, without more circumstance at all,
I hold it fit that we shake hands and part:
You, as your business and desire shall point you;
For every man has business and desire,
Such as it is; and for mine own poor part,
Look you, I'll go pray.

HORATIO
These are but wild and whirling words, my lord.

HAMLET
I'm sorry they offend you, heartily;
Yes, 'faith, heartily.

HORATIO
There's no offence, my lord.
HAMLET
Yes, by Saint Patrick, but there is, Horatio,
And much offence too. Touching this vision here,
It is an honest ghost, that let me tell you:
For your desire to know what is between us,
O'ermaster 't as you may. And now, good friends,
As you are friends, scholars and soldiers,
Give me one poor request.
HORATIO
What is't, my lord? we will.
HAMLET
Never make known what you have seen to-night.
HORATIO, MARCELLUS
My lord, we will not.
HAMLET
Nay, but swear't.
HORATIO
In faith,
My lord, not I.
MARCELLUS
Nor I, my lord, in faith.
HAMLET
Upon my sword.
MARCELLUS
We have sworn, my lord, already.
HAMLET
Indeed, upon my sword, indeed.
GHOST
[*Beneath*] Swear.
HAMLET
Ah, ha, boy! say'st thou so? art thou there, truepenny?
Come on—you hear this fellow in the cellarage—
Consent to swear.
HORATIO
Propose the oath, my lord.
HAMLET
Never to speak of this that you have seen,
Swear by my sword.
GHOST
[*Beneath*] Swear.
HAMLET
Hic et ubique? then we'll shift our ground.
Come hither, gentlemen,
And lay your hands again upon my sword:
Never to speak of this that you have heard,
Swear by my sword.
GHOST
[*Beneath*] Swear.
HAMLET
Well said, old mole! canst work i' the earth so fast?
A worthy pioner! Once more remove, good friends.
HORATIO
O day and night, but this is wondrous strange!
HAMLET
And therefore as a stranger give it welcome.
There are more things in heaven and earth, Horatio,
Than are dreamt of in your philosophy.
But come;
Here, as before, never, so help you mercy,
How strange or odd soe'er I bear myself,
As I perchance hereafter shall think meet
To put an antic disposition on,
That you, at such times seeing me, never shall,
With arms encumber'd thus, or this headshake,
Or by pronouncing of some doubtful phrase,
As 'Well, well, we know,' or 'We could, an if we would,'
Or 'If we list to speak,' or 'There be, an if they might,'
Or such ambiguous giving out, to note
That you know aught of me: this not to do,
So grace and mercy at your most need help you,
Swear.
GHOST
[*Beneath*] Swear.
HAMLET
Rest, rest, perturbed spirit! [*They swear.*] So, gentlemen,
With all my love I do commend me to you:
And what so poor a man as Hamlet is
May do, to express his love and friending to you,
God willing, shall not lack. Let us go in together;
And still your fingers on your lips, I pray.
The time is out of joint: O cursed spite,
That ever I was born to set it right!
Nay, come, let's go together. [*Exeunt.*

ACT TWO SCENE ONE

A room in Polonius' *house.*

Enter POLONIUS *and* REYNALDO. [19]

POLONIUS
Give him this money and these notes, Reynaldo.
REYNALDO
I will, my lord.
POLONIUS
You shall do marvellous wisely, good Reynaldo,
Before you visit him, to make inquire [20]
Of his behavior.
REYNALDO
My lord, I did intend it.
POLONIUS
Marry, well said; very well said.
Look you, sir,

Inquire me first what Danskers are in Paris;
And how, and who, what means, and where they keep,
What company, at what expense; and finding
By this encompassment and drift of question
That they do know my son, come you more nearer
Than your particular demands will touch it:
Take you, as 'twere, some distant knowledge of him;
As thus, 'I know his father and his friends,
And in part him: 'do you mark this, Reynaldo?

REYNALDO
Ay, very well, my lord.

POLONIUS
'And in part him; but' you may say 'not well:
But, if't be he I mean, he's very wild;
Addicted so and so:' and there put on him
What forgeries you please; marry, none so rank
As may dishonour him; take heed of that;
But, sir, such wanton, wild and usual slips
As are companions noted and most known
To youth and liberty.

REYNALDO
As gaming, my lord.

POLONIUS
Ay, or drinking, fencing, swearing, quarrelling,
Drabbing: you may go so far.

REYNALDO
My lord, that would dishonour him.

POLONIUS
'Faith, no; as you may season it in the charge.
You must not put another scandal on him,
That he is open to incontinency;
That's not my meaning; but breathe his faults so quaintly
That they may seem the taints of liberty,
The flash and outbreak of a fiery mind,
A savageness in unreclaimed blood,
Of general assault.

REYNALDO
But, my good lord,—

POLONIUS
Wherefore should you do this?

REYNALDO
Ay, my lord,
I would know that.

POLONIUS
Marry, sir, here's my drift;
And, I believe, it is a fetch of wit:
You laying these slight sullies on my son,
As 'twere a thing a little soil'd i' the working,
Mark you,
Your party in converse, him you would sound,
Having ever seen in the prenominate crimes
The youth you breathe of guilty, be assured
He closes with you in this consequence;
'Good sir,' or so, or 'friend,' or 'gentleman,'
According to the phrase or the addition
Of man and country.

REYNALDO
Very good, my lord.

POLONIUS
And then, sir, does he this—he does—what was I about to say? By the mass, I was about to say something: where did I leave?

REYNALDO
At 'closes in the consequence,' at 'friend or so,' and 'gentleman.'

POLONIUS
At 'closes in the consequence,' ay, marry;
He closes thus: 'I know the gentleman;
I saw him yesterday, or t' other day,
Or then, or then; with such, or such; and, as you say,
There was a' gaming; there o'ertook in's rouse;
There falling out at tennis:' or perchance,
'I saw him enter such a house of sale,'
Videlicet, a brothel, or so forth.
See you now;
Your bait of falsehood takes this carp of truth:
And thus do we of wisdom and of reach,
With windlasses and with assays of bias,
By indirections find directions out:
So by my former lecture and advice,
Shall you my son. You have me, have you not?

REYNALDO
My lord, I have.

POLONIUS
God be wi' you; fare you well.

REYNALDO
Good my lord!

POLONIUS
Observe his inclination in yourself.

REYNALDO
I shall, my lord.

POLONIUS
And let him ply his music.

REYNALDO
Well, my lord.

POLONIUS
Farewell! [*Exit Reynaldo.*

Enter OPHELIA.

How now, Ophelia! what's the matter?

OPHELIA
O, my lord, my lord, I have been so affrighted!

POLONIUS
With what, i' the name of God?

OPHELIA
My lord, as I was sewing in my closet,

Lord Hamlet, with his doublet all unbraced;
No hat upon his head; his stockings foul'd,
Ungarter'd, and down-gyved to his ancle;
Pale as his shirt; his knees knocking each other;
And with a look so piteous in purport
As if he had been loosed out of hell
To speak of horrors,—he comes before me.

POLONIUS
Mad for thy love?

OPHELIA
My lord, I do not know;
But truly, I do fear it.

POLONIUS
What said he?

OPHELIA
He took me by the wrist and held me hard;
Then goes he to the length of all his arm;
And, with his other hand thus o'er his brow,
He falls to such perusal of my face
As he would draw it. Long stay'd he so;
At last, a little shaking of mine arm
And thrice his head thus waving up and down,
He raised a sigh so piteous and profound
As it did seem to shatter all his bulk
And end his being: that done, he lets me go:
And, with his head over his shoulder turn'd,
He seem'd to find his way without his eyes;
For out o' doors he went without their helps,
And, to the last, bended their light on me.

POLONIUS
Come, go with me: I will go seek the king.
This is the very ecstasy of love,
Whose violent property fordoes itself
And leads the will to desperate undertakings
As oft as any passion under heaven
That does afflict our natures. I am sorry.
What, have you given him any hard words of late?

OPHELIA
No, my good lord, but, as you did command,
I did repel his letters and denied
His access to me.

POLONIUS
That hath made him mad.
I am sorry that with better heed and judgement
I had not quoted him: I fear'd he did but trifle,
And meant to wreck thee; but, beshrew my jealousy!
By heaven, it is as proper to our age
To cast beyond ourselves in our opinions
As it is common for the younger sort
To lack discretion. Come, go we to the king:
This must be known; which, being kept close, might move
More grief to hide than hate to utter love.

[*Exeunt.*

ACT TWO SCENE TWO

A room in the castle.

Enter KING, QUEEN, ROSENCRANTZ, GUILDENSTERN, *and* Attendants.

KING CLAUDIUS
Welcome, dear Rosencrantz and Guildenstern!
Moreover that we much did long to see you,
The need we have to use you did provoke
Our hasty sending. Something have you heard
Of Hamlet's transformation; so call it,
Sith nor the exterior nor the inward man
Resembles that it was. What it should be,
More than his father's death, that thus hath put him
So much from the understanding of himself,
I cannot dream of: I entreat you both,
That, being of so young days brought up with him,
And sith so neighbour'd to his youth and havior,
That you vouchsafe your rest here in our court
Some little time: so by your companies
To draw him on to pleasures, and to gather,
So much as from occasion you may glean,
Whether aught, to us unknown, afflicts him thus,
That, open'd, lies within our remedy.

QUEEN GERTRUDE
Good gentlemen, he hath much talk'd of you;
And sure I am two men there are not living
To whom he more adheres. If it will please you
To show us so much gentry and good will
As to expend your time with us awhile,
For the supply and profit of our hope,
Your visitation shall receive such thanks
As fits a king's remembrance.

ROSENCRANTZ
Both your majesties
Might, by the sovereign power you have of us,
Put your dread pleasures more into command
Than to entreatly.

GUILDENSTERN
But we both obey,
And here give up ourselves, in the full bent
To lay our service freely at your feet,
To be commanded.

KING CLAUDIUS
Thanks, Rosencrantz and gentle Guildenstern.

QUEEN GERTRUDE
Thanks, Guildenstern and gentle Rosencrantz:
And I beseech you instantly to visit
My too much changed son. Go, some of you,
And bring these gentlemen where Hamlet is.

GUILDENSTERN
Heavens make our presence and our practices
Pleasant and helpful to him!

QUEEN GERTRUDE
Ay, amen! [*Exeunt Rosencrantz, Guildenstern, and some Attendants.*

Enter POLONIUS.

POLONIUS
The ambassadors from Norway, my good lord,
Are joyfully return'd.

KING CLAUDIUS
Thou still hast been the father of good news.

POLONIUS
Have I, my lord? I assure my good liege,
I hold my duty, as I hold my soul,
Both to my God and to my gracious king:
And I do think, or else this brain of mine
Hunts not the trail of policy so sure
As it hath used to do, that I have found
The very cause of Hamlet's lunacy.

KING CLAUDIUS
O, speak of that; that do I long to hear.

POLONIUS
Give first admittance to the ambassadors;
My news shall be the fruit to that great feast.

KING CLAUDIUS
Thyself do grace to them, and bring them in.
[*Exit Polonius.*
He tells me, my dear Gertrude, he hath found
The head and source of all your son's distemper.

QUEEN GERTRUDE
I doubt it is no other but the main;
His father's death, and our o'erhasty marriage.

KING CLAUDIUS
Well, we shall sift him.

Re-enter POLONIUS, *with* VOLTIMAND *and* CORNELIUS.

Welcome, my good friends!
Say, Voltimand, what from our brother Norway?

VOLTIMAND
Most fair return of greetings and desires.
Upon our first, he sent out to suppress
His nephew's levies; which to him appear'd
To be a preparation 'gainst the Polack;
But, better look'd into, he truly found
It was against your highness: whereat grieved,
That so his sickness, age and impotence
Was falsely borne in hand, sends out arrests
On Fortinbras; which he, in brief, obeys;
Receives rebuke from Norway, and in fine
Makes vow before his uncle never more
To give the assay of arms against your majesty.
Whereon old Norway, overcome with joy,
Gives him three thousand crowns in annual fee, [22]
And his commission to employ those soldiers,
So levied as before, against the Polack:
With an entreaty, herein further shown,
[*Giving a paper.*
That it might please you to give quiet pass
Through your dominions for this enterprise,
On such regards of safety and allowance
As therein are set down.

KING CLAUDIUS
It likes us well;
And at our more consider'd time we'll read,
Answer, and think upon this business.
Meantime we thank you for your well-took labour:
Go to your rest; at night we'll feast together:
Most welcome home!
[*Exeunt Voltimand and Cornelius.*

POLONIUS
This business is well ended.
My liege, and madam, to expostulate
What majesty should be, what duty is,
Why day is day, night night, and time is time,
Were nothing but to waste night, day and time.
Therefore, since brevity is the soul of wit,
And tediousness the limbs and outward flourishes,
I will be brief: your noble son is mad:
Mad call I it; for, to define true madness,
What is't but to be nothing else but mad?
But let that go.

QUEEN GERTRUDE
More matter, with less art.

POLONIUS
Madam, I swear I use no art at all.
That he is mad, 'tis true: 'tis true 'tis pity;
And pity 'tis 'tis true: a foolish figure;
But farewell it, for I will use no art.
Mad let us grant him, then: and now remains
That we find out the cause of this effect,
Or rather say, the cause of this defect,
For this effect defective comes by cause:
Thus it remains, and the remainder thus.
Perpend.
I have a daughter—have while she is mine—
Who, in her duty and obedience, mark,
Hath given me this: now gather, and surmise.
[*Reads.*
'To the celestial and my soul's idol, the most beautified Ophelia,'—
That's an ill phrase, a vile phrase; 'beautified' is a vile phrase: but you shall hear.
Thus: [*Reads.*
'In her excellent white bosom, these, &c.'

QUEEN GERTRUDE
Came this from Hamlet to her?
POLONIUS
Good madam, stay awhile; I will be faithful. *[Reads.*
'Doubt thou the stars are fire;
Doubt that the sun doth move;
Doubt truth to be a liar;
But never doubt I love. 132
'O dear Ophelia, I am ill at these numbers;
I have not art to reckon my groans: but that
I love thee best, O most best, believe it.
Adieu.
'Thine evermore most dear lady, whilst this machine is to him, HAMLET.'
This, in obedience, hath my daughter shown me,
And more above, hath his solicitings,
As they fell out by time, by means and place,
All given to mine ear.
KING CLAUDIUS
But how hath she
Received his love?
POLONIUS
What do you think of me?
KING CLAUDIUS
As of a man faithful and honourable.
POLONIUS
I would fain prove so. But what might you think, 148
When I had seen this hot love on the wing—
As I perceived it, I must tell you that,
Before my daughter told me—what might you,
Or my dear majesty your queen here, think,
If I had play'd the desk or table-book,
Or given my heart a winking, mute and dumb,
Or look'd upon this love with idle sight;
What might you think? No, I went round to work,
And my young mistress thus I did bespeak:
'Lord Hamlet is a prince, out of thy star; 159
This must not be:' and then I prescripts gave her,
That she should lock herself from his resort,
Admit no messengers, receive no tokens.
Which done, she took the fruits of my advice;
And he, repulsed—a short tale to make—
Fell into a sadness, then into a fast,
Thence to a watch, thence into a weakness,
Thence to a lightness, and, by this declension,
Into the madness wherein now he raves, 168
And all we mourn for.
KING CLAUDIUS
Do you think 'tis this?
QUEEN GERTRUDE
It may be, very likely.
POLONIUS
Hath there been such a time—I'd fain know that—
That I have positive said ' 'Tis so,'
When it proved otherwise?
KING CLAUDIUS
Not that I know.
POLONIUS
[Pointing to his head and shoulders]
Take this from this, if this be otherwise:
If circumstances lead me, I will find
Where truth is hid, though it were hid indeed
Within the centre.
KING CLAUDIUS
How may we try it further?
POLONIUS
You know, sometimes he walks four hours together 182
Here in the lobby.
QUEEN GERTRUDE
So he does indeed.
POLONIUS
At such a time I'll loose my daughter to him:
Be you and I behind an arras then;
Mark the encounter: if he love her not
And be not from his reason fall'n thereon,
Let me be no assistant for a state,
But keep a farm and carters.
KING CLAUDIUS
We will try it.
QUEEN GERTRUDE
But, look, where sadly the poor wretch comes reading.
POLONIUS
Away, I do beseech you, both away:
I'll board him presently.
[Exeunt King, Queen, and Attendants.

Enter HAMLET, *reading.*

O, give me leave: 195
How does my good Lord Hamlet?
HAMLET
Well, God-a-mercy.
POLONIUS
Do you know me, my lord?
HAMLET
Excellent well; you are a fishmonger.
POLONIUS
Not I, my lord.
HAMLET
Then I would you were so honest a man.
POLONIUS
Honest, my lord!
HAMLET
Ay, sir; to be honest, as this world goes, is to be one man picked out of ten thousand.

POLONIUS
That's very true, my lord. 205

HAMLET
For if the sun breed maggots in a dead dog, being a god kissing carrion,—Have you a daughter?

POLONIUS
I have, my lord.

HAMLET
Let her not walk i' the sun: conception is a blessing: but not as your daughter may conceive. Friend, look to't.

POLONIUS
[*Aside*] How say you by that? Still harping on my daughter: yet he knew me not at first; he said I was a fishmonger: he is far gone, far gone: and truly in my youth I suffered much extremity for love; very near this. I'll speak to him again. What do you read, my lord?

HAMLET
Words, words, words.

POLONIUS
What is the matter, my lord?

HAMLET
Between who?

POLONIUS
I mean, the matter that you read, my lord.

HAMLET
Slanders, sir: for the satirical rogue says here that old men have grey beards, that their faces are wrinkled, their eyes purging thick amber and plum-tree gum and that they have a plentiful lack of wit, together with most weak hams: all which, sir, though I most powerfully and potently believe, yet I hold it not honesty to have it thus set down, for yourself, sir, should be old as I am, if like a crab you could go backward.

POLONIUS
[*Aside*] Though this be madness, yet there is method in 't. Will you walk out of the air, my lord?

HAMLET
Into my grave. 232

POLONIUS
Indeed, that is out o' the air. [*Aside*] How pregnant sometimes his replies are! a happiness that often madness hits on, which reason and sanity could not so prosperously be delivered of. I will leave him, and suddenly contrive the means of meeting between him and my daughter.—My honourable lord, I will most humbly take my leave of you.

HAMLET
You cannot, sir, take from me any thing that I will more willingly part withal: except my life, except my life, except my life.

POLONIUS
Fare you well, my lord.

HAMLET
These tedious old fools!

Enter ROSENCRANTZ *and* GUILDENSTERN.

POLONIUS
You go to seek the Lord Hamlet; there he is.

ROSENCRANTZ
[*To Polonius*] God save you, sir! [*Exit Polonius.*

GUILDENSTERN
My honoured lord!

ROSENCRANTZ
My most dear lord!

HAMLET
My excellent good friends! How dost thou, Guildenstern? Ah, Rosencrantz! Good lads, how do ye both? 251

ROSENCRANTZ
As the indifferent children of the earth.

GUILDENSTERN
Happy, in that we are not over-happy;
On fortune's cap we are not the very button.

HAMLET
Nor the soles of her shoe?

ROSENCRANTZ
Neither, my lord.

HAMLET
Then you live about her waist, or in the middle of her favours?

GUILDENSTERN
'Faith, her privates we.

HAMLET
In the secret parts of fortune? O, most true; she is a strumpet. What's the news?

ROSENCRANTZ
None, my lord, but that the world's grown honest.

HAMLET
Then is doomsday near: but your news is not true. Let me question more in particular: what have you, my good friends, deserved at the hands of fortune, that she sends you to prison thither?

GUILDENSTERN
Prison, my lord!

HAMLET
Denmark's a prison.

ROSENCRANTZ
Then is the world one. 269

HAMLET
A goodly one; in which there are many confines, wards and dungeons, Denmark being one o' the worst.

ROSENCRANTZ
We think not so, my lord.

HAMLET
Why, then, 'tis none to you; for there is nothing either good or bad, but thinking makes it so: to me it is a prison.

ROSENCRANTZ

Why then, your ambition makes it one; 'tis too narrow for your mind.

HAMLET

O God, I could be bounded in a nutshell and count myself a king of infinite space, were it not that I have bad dreams.

GUILDENSTERN

Which dreams indeed are ambition, for the very substance of the ambition is merely the shadow of a dream.

HAMLET

A dream itself is but a shadow.

ROSENCRANTZ

Truly, and I hold ambition of so airy and light a quality that it is but a shadow's shadow.

HAMLET

Then are our beggars bodies, and our monarchs and outstretched heroes the beggars' shadows. Shall we to the court? for, by my fay, I cannot reason.

ROSENCRANTZ, GUILDENSTERN

We'll wait upon you.

HAMLET

No such matter: I will not sort you with the rest of my servants, for, to speak to you like an honest man, I am most dreadfully attended. But, in the beaten way of friendship, what make you at Elsinore? [23]

ROSENCRANTZ

To visit you, my lord; no other occasion.

HAMLET

Beggar that I am, I am even poor in thanks; but I thank you: and sure, dear friends, my thanks are too dear a halfpenny. Were you not sent for? Is it your own inclining? Is it a free visitation? Come, deal justly with me: come, come; nay, speak.

GUILDENSTERN

What should we say, my lord?

HAMLET

Why, any thing, but to the purpose. You were sent for; and there is a kind of confession in your looks which your modesties have not craft enough to colour: I know the good king and queen have sent for you.

ROSENCRANTZ

To what end, my lord?

HAMLET

That you must teach me. But let me conjure you, by the rights of our fellowship, by the consonancy of our youth, by the obligation of our ever-preserved love, and by what more dear a better proposer could charge you withal, be even and direct with me, whether you were sent for, or no?

ROSENCRANTZ

[*Aside to Guildenstern*] What say you?

HAMLET

[*Aside*] Nay, then, I have an eye of you.—If you love me, hold not off.

GUILDENSTERN

My lord, we were sent for.

HAMLET

I will tell you why; so shall my anticipation prevent your discovery, and your secrecy to the king and queen moult no feather. I have of late—but wherefore I know not—lost all my mirth, forgone all custom of exercises; and indeed it goes so heavily with my disposition that this goodly frame, the earth, seems to me a sterile promontory, this most excellent canopy, the air, look you, this brave o'erhanging firmament, this majestical roof fretted with golden fire, why, it appears no other thing to me than a foul and pestilent congregation of vapours. What a piece of work is a man! how noble in reason! how infinite in faculty! in form and moving how express and admirable! in action how like an angel! in apprehension how like a god! the beauty of the world! the paragon of animals! And yet, to me, what is this quintessence of dust? man delights not me: no, nor woman neither, though by your smiling you seem to say so.

ROSENCRANTZ

My lord, there was no such stuff in my thoughts.

HAMLET

Why did you laugh then, when I said 'man delights not me'?

ROSENCRANTZ

To think, my lord, if you delight not in man, what lenten entertainment the players shall receive from you: we coted them on the way; and hither are they coming, to offer you service.

HAMLET

He that plays the king shall be welcome; his majesty shall have tribute of me; the adventurous knight shall use his foil and target; the lover shall not sigh gratis; the humorous man shall end his part in peace; the clown; shall make those laugh whose lungs are tick o' the sere; and the lady shall say her mind freely, or the blank verse shall halt for't. What players are they? [24]

ROSENCRANTZ

Even those you were wont to take delight in, the tragedians of the city.

HAMLET

How chances it they travel? their residence, both in reputation and profit, was better both ways.

ROSENCRANTZ

I think their inhibition comes by the means of the late innovation. [25]

HAMLET

Do they hold the same estimation they did when I was in the city? are they so followed?

ROSENCRANTZ
No, indeed, are they not.
HAMLET
How comes it? do they grow rusty?
ROSENCRANTZ
Nay, their endeavour keeps in the wonted pace: but there is, sir, an aery of children, little eyases, that cry out on the top of question, and are most tyrannically clapped for't: these are now the fashion, and so berattle the common stages—so they call them—that many wearing rapiers are afraid of goose-quills and dare scarce come thither. [26]
HAMLET
What, are they children? who maintains 'em? how are they escoted? Will they pursue the quality no longer than they can sing? will they not say afterwards, if they should grow themselves to common players—as it is most like, if their means are no better—their writers do them wrong, to make them exclaim against their own succession?
ROSENCRANTZ
'Faith, there has been much to do on both sides; and the nation holds it no sin to tarre them to controversy: there was, for a while, no money bid for argument, unless the poet and the player went to cuffs in the question.
HAMLET
Is't possible?
GUILDENSTERN
O, there has been much throwing about of brains.
HAMLET
Do the boys carry it away? 378
ROSENCRANTZ
Ay, that they do, my lord; Hercules and his load too. [27]
HAMLET
It is not very strange; for mine uncle is king of Denmark, and those that would make mows at him while my father lived, give twenty, forty, fifty, an hundred ducats a-piece for his picture in little. 'Sblood, there is something in this more than natural, if philosophy could find it out.

[*Flourish of trumpets within.*

GUILDENSTERN
There are the players.
HAMLET
Gentlemen, you are welcome to Elsinore. Your hands, come then: the appurtenance of welcome is fashion and ceremony: let me comply with you in this garb, lest my extent to the players, which, I tell you, must show fairly outward, should more appear like entertainment than yours. You are welcome: but my uncle-father and aunt-mother are deceived.
GUILDENSTERN
In what, my dear lord?
HAMLET
I am but mad north-north-west: when the wind is southerly I know a hawk from a handsaw.

Re-enter POLONIUS.

POLONIUS
Well be with you, gentlemen!
HAMLET
Hark you, Guildenstern; and you too: at each ear a hearer: that great baby you see there is not yet out of his swaddling-clouts.
ROSENCRANTZ
Happily he's the second time come to them; for they say an old man is twice a child.
HAMLET
I will prophesy he comes to tell me of the players; mark it. You say right, sir: o' Monday morning; 'twas so indeed.
POLONIUS
My lord, I have news to tell you.
HAMLET
My lord, I have news to tell you. When Roscius was an actor in Rome,— 410
POLONIUS
The actors are come hither, my lord.
HAMLET
Buz, buz!
POLONIUS
Upon mine honour,—
HAMLET
Then came each actor on his ass,—
POLONIUS
The best actors in the world, either for tragedy, comedy, history, pastoral, pastoral-comical, historical-pastoral, tragical-historical, tragical- comical-historical-pastoral, scene individable, or poem unlimited: Seneca cannot be too heavy, nor Plautus too light. For the law of writ and the liberty, these are the only men. 421
HAMLET
O Jephthah, judge of Israel, what a treasure hadst thou!
POLONIUS
What a treasure had he, my lord?
HAMLET
Why,
'One fair daughter, and no more, The which he loved passing well.'
POLONIUS
[*Aside*] Still on my daughter.
HAMLET
Am I not i' the right, old Jephthah?

POLONIUS
If you call me Jephthah, my lord, I have a daughter that I love passing well. 431
HAMLET
Nay, that follows not.
POLONIUS
What follows, then, my lord?
HAMLET
Why,
'As by lot, God wot,' and then, you know,
'It came to pass, as most like it was,'— the first row of the pious chanson will show you more; for look, where my abridgement comes. 438

Enter four or five Players.

You are welcome, masters; welcome all. I am glad to see thee well. Welcome, good friends. O, my old friend! thy face is valanced since I saw thee last: comest thou to beard me in Denmark? What, my young lady and mistress! By'r lady, your ladyship is nearer to heaven than when I saw you last, by the altitude of a chopine. Pray God, your voice, like a piece of uncurrent gold, be not cracked within the ring. Masters, you are all welcome. We'll e'en to't like French falconers, fly at any thing we see: we'll have a speech straight: come, give us a taste of your quality; come, a passionate speech.
FIRST PLAYER
What speech, my lord?
HAMLET
I heard thee speak me a speech once, but it was never acted; or, if it was, not above once; for the play, I remember, pleased not the million; 'twas caviare to the general: but it was—as I received it, and others, whose judgements in such matters cried in the top of mine—an excellent play, well digested in the scenes, set down with as much modesty as cunning. I remember, one said there were no sallets in the lines to make the matter savoury, nor no matter in the phrase that might indict the author of affectation; but called it an honest method, as wholesome as sweet, and by very much more handsome than fine. One speech in it I chiefly loved: 'twas Aeneas' tale to Dido; and thereabout of it especially, where he speaks of Priam's slaughter: if it live in your memory, begin at this line: let me see, let me see— [28]
'The rugged Pyrrhus, like the Hyrcanian beast,'— it is not so:—it begins with Pyrrhus:— 469
'The rugged Pyrrhus, he whose sable arms,
Black as his purpose, did the night resemble
When he lay couched in the ominous horse,
Hath now this dread and black complexion smear'd
With heraldry more dismal; head to foot
Now is he total gules; horridly trick'd
With blood of fathers, mothers, daughters, sons, 477
Baked and impasted with the parching streets,
That lend a tyrannous and damned light
To their lord's murder: roasted in wrath and fire,
And thus o'er-sized with coagulate gore,
With eyes like carbuncles, the hellish Pyrrhus
Old grandsire Priam seeks.'
So, proceed you. [29]
POLONIUS
'Fore God, my lord, well spoken, with good accent and good discretion.
FIRST PLAYER
'Anon he finds him
Striking too short at Greeks; his antique sword, 489
Rebellious to his arm, lies where it falls,
Repugnant to command: unequal match'd,
Pyrrhus at Priam drives; in rage strikes wide;
But with the whiff and wind of his fell sword
The unnerved father falls. Then senseless Ilium, [30]
Seeming to feel this blow, with flaming top
Stoops to his base, and with a hideous crash
Takes prisoner Pyrrhus' ear: for, lo! his sword,
Which was declining on the milky head 498
Of reverend Priam, seem'd i' the air to stick:
So, as a painted tyrant, Pyrrhus stood,
And like a neutral to his will and matter,
Did nothing.
But, as we often see, against some storm,
A silence in the heavens, the rack stand still,
The bold winds speechless and the orb below
As hush as death, anon the dreadful thunder
Doth rend the region, so, after Pyrrhus' pause,
Aroused vengeance sets him new a-work;
And never did the Cyclops' hammers fall
On Mars's armour forged for proof eterne
With less remorse than Pyrrhus' bleeding sword
Now falls on Priam.
Out, out, thou strumpet, Fortune! All you gods,
In general synod, 'take away her power;
Break all the spokes and fellies from her wheel,
And bowl the round nave down the hill of heaven,
As low as to the fiends!'
POLONIUS
This is too long. 518
HAMLET
It shall to the barber's, with your beard. Prithee, say on: he's for a jig or a tale of bawdry, or he sleeps: say on: come to Hecuba.
FIRST PLAYER
'But who, O, who had seen the mobled queen—'
HAMLET
'The mobled queen?'

POLONIUS

That's good; 'mobled queen' is good.

FIRST PLAYER

'Run barefoot up and down, threatening the flames
With bisson rheum; a clout upon that head
Where late the diadem stood, and for a robe,
About her lank and all o'er-teemed loins,
A blanket, in the alarm of fear caught up;
Who this had seen, with tongue in venom steep'd,
'Gainst Fortune's state would treason have pronounced:
But if the gods themselves did see her then
When she saw Pyrrhus make malicious sport
In mincing with his sword her husband's limbs,
The instant burst of clamour that she made,
Unless things mortal move them not at all,
Would have made milch the burning eyes of heaven, 539
And passion in the gods.'

POLONIUS

Look, whether he has not turned his colour and has tears in's eyes. Pray you, no more. [31]

HAMLET

'Tis well: I'll have thee speak out the rest soon. Good my lord, will you see the players well bestowed? Do you hear, let them be well used; for they are the abstract and brief chronicles of the time: after your death you were better have a bad epitaph than their ill report while you live.

POLONIUS

My lord, I will use them according to their desert.

HAMLET

God's bodykins, man, much better: use every man after his desert, and who should 'scape whipping? Use them after your own honour and dignity: the less they deserve, the more merit is in your bounty. Take them in.

POLONIUS

Come, sirs. 555

HAMLET

Follow him, friends: we'll hear a play to-morrow. [*Exit Polonius with all the Players but the First.*] Dost thou hear me, old friend; can you play the Murder of Gonzago?

FIRST PLAYER

Ay, my lord.

HAMLET

We'll ha't to-morrow night. You could, for a need, study a speech of some dozen or sixteen lines, which I would set down and insert in't, could you not? [32]

FIRST PLAYER

Ay, my lord. 565

HAMLET

Very well. Follow that lord; and look you mock him not. [*Exit First Player.*] My good friends, I'll leave you till night: you are welcome to Elsinore.

ROSENCRANTZ

Good my lord!

HAMLET

Ay, so, God be wi' ye; [*Exeunt Rosencrantz and Guildenstern.*] Now I am alone.

O, what a rogue and peasant slave am I!
Is it not monstrous that this player here,
But in a fiction, in a dream of passion,
Could force his soul so to his own conceit
That from her working all his visage wann'd,
Tears in his eyes, distraction in's aspect, 578
A broken voice, and his whole function suiting
With forms to his conceit? and all for nothing!
For Hecuba!
What's Hecuba to him, or he to Hecuba,
That he should weep for her? What would he do,
Had he the motive and the cue for passion
That I have? He would drown the stage with tears
And cleave the general ear with horrid speech,
Make mad the guilty and appal the free, 587
Confound the ignorant, and amaze indeed
The very faculties of eyes and ears.
Yet I,
A dull and muddy-mettled rascal, peak,
Like John-a-dreams, unpregnant of my cause,
And can say nothing; no, not for a king,
Upon whose property and most dear life
A damn'd defeat was made. Am I a coward?
Who calls me villain? breaks my pate across?
Plucks off my beard, and blows it in my face?
Tweaks me by the nose? gives me the lie i' the throat, 599
As deep as to the lungs? who does me this?
Ha!
'Swounds, I should take it: for it cannot be
But I am pigeon-liver'd and lack gall
To make oppression bitter. or ere this
I should have fatted all the region kites
With this slave's offal: bloody, bawdy villain!
Remorseless, treacherous, lecherous, kindless villain!
O, vengeance! 608
Why, what an ass am I! This is most brave,
That I, the son of a dear father murder'd,
Prompted to my revenge by heaven and hell,
Must, like a whore, unpack my heart with words,
And fall a-cursing, like a very drab,
A scullion!
Fie upon't! foh! About, my brain! I have heard [33]
That guilty creatures sitting at a play

Have by the very cunning of the scene
Been struck so to the soul that presently
They have proclaim'd their malefactions;
For murder, though it have no tongue, will speak
With most miraculous organ. I'll have these players
Play something like the murder of my father
Before mine uncle: I'll observe his looks;
I'll tent him to the quick: if he but blench,
I know my course. The spirit that I have seen
May be the devil: and the devil hath power
To assume a pleasing shape; yea, and perhaps
Out of my weakness and my melancholy,
As he is very potent with such spirits,
Abuses me to damn me: I'll have grounds
More relative than this: the play 's the thing
Wherein I'll catch the conscience of the
king. [*Exit.*

ACT THREE SCENE ONE

A room in the castle.

Enter KING, QUEEN, POLONIUS, OPHELIA, ROSENCRANTZ, *and* GUILDENSTERN.

KING CLAUDIUS
And can you, by no drift of circumstance,
Get from him why he puts on this confusion,
Grating so harshly all his days of quiet
With turbulent and dangerous lunacy?

ROSENCRANTZ
He does confess he feels himself distracted;
But from what cause he will by no means speak.

GUILDENSTERN
Nor do we find him forward to be sounded,
But, with a crafty madness, keeps aloof,
When we would bring him on to some confession
Of his true state.

QUEEN GERTRUDE
Did he receive you well?

ROSENCRANTZ
Most like a gentleman.

GUILDENSTERN
But with much forcing of his disposition.

ROSENCRANTZ
Niggard of question; but, of our demands,
Most free in his reply.

QUEEN GERTRUDE
Did you assay him?
To any pastime?

ROSENCRANTZ
Madam, it so fell out, that certain players
We o'er-raught on the way: of these we told him;
And there did seem in him a kind of joy
To hear of it: they are about the court,
And, as I think, they have already order
This night to play before him.

POLONIUS
'Tis most true:
And he beseech'd me to entreat your majesties
To hear and see the matter.

KING CLAUDIUS
With all my heart; and it doth much content me
To hear him so inclined.
Good gentlemen, give him a further edge,
And drive his purpose on to these delights.

ROSENCRANTZ
We shall, my lord.
[*Exeunt Rosencrantz and Guildenstern.*

KING CLAUDIUS
Sweet Gertrude, leave us too;
For we have closely sent for Hamlet hither,
That he, as 'twere by accident, may here
Affront Ophelia:
Her father and myself, lawful espials,
Will so bestow ourselves that, seeing, unseen,
We may of their encounter frankly judge,
And gather by him, as he is behaved,
If 't be the affliction of his love or no
That thus he suffers for.

QUEEN GERTRUDE
I shall obey you.
And for your part, Ophelia, I do wish
That your good beauties be the happy cause
Of Hamlet's wildness: so shall I hope your
virtues
Will bring him to his wonted way again,
To both your honours.

OPHELIA
Madam, I wish it may. [*Exit Queen.*

POLONIUS
Ophelia, walk you here. Gracious, so please you,
We will bestow ourselves. [*To Ophelia*] Read on this
book;
That show of such an exercise may colour
Your loneliness. We are oft to blame in this,—
'Tis too much proved—that with devotion's visage
And pious action we do sugar o'er
The devil himself.

KING CLAUDIUS
[*Aside*] O, 'tis too true!
How smart a lash that speech doth give my
conscience!
The harlot's cheek, beautied with plastering art,
Is not more ugly to the thing that helps it
Than is my deed to my most painted word:
O heavy burthen!

POLONIUS
I hear him coming: let's withdraw, my lord.
[*Exeunt King and Polonius.*

Enter HAMLET.

HAMLET
To be, or not to be: that is the question:
Whether 'tis nobler in the mind to suffer
The slings and arrows of outrageous fortune,
Or to take arms against a sea of troubles, [35]
And by opposing end them? To die: to sleep;
No more; and by a sleep to say we end
The heart-ache and the thousand natural shocks
That flesh is heir to, 'tis a consummation
Devoutly to be wish'd. To die, to sleep;
To sleep: perchance to dream: ay, there's the rub;
For in that sleep of death what dreams may come
When we have shuffled off this mortal coil,
Must give us pause: there's the respect
That makes calamity of so long life;
For who would bear the whips and scorns of time,
The oppressor's wrong, the proud man's contumely,
The pangs of despised love, the law's delay,
The insolence of office and the spurns
That patient merit of the unworthy takes,
When he himself might his quietus make
With a bare bodkin? who would fardels bear,
To grunt and sweat under a weary life,
But that the dread of something after death,
The undiscover'd country from whose bourn [36]
No traveller returns, puzzles the will
And makes us rather bear those ills we have
Than fly to others that we know not of?
Thus conscience does make cowards of us all;
And thus the native hue of resolution
Is sicklied o'er with the pale cast of thought,
And enterprises of great pith and moment
With this regard their currents turn awry,
And lose the name of action.—Soft you now!
The fair Ophelia! Nymph, in thy orisons
Be all my sins remember'd.

OPHELIA
Good my lord,
How does your honour for this many a day?

HAMLET
I humbly thank you; well, well, well.

OPHELIA
My lord, I have remembrances of yours,
That I have longed long to re-deliver;
I pray you, now receive them.

HAMLET
No, not I;
I never gave you aught.

OPHELIA
My honour'd lord, you know right well you did;
And, with them, words of so sweet breath composed
As made the things more rich: their perfume lost,
Take these again; for to the noble mind
Rich gifts wax poor when givers prove unkind.
There, my lord.

HAMLET
Ha, ha! are you honest?

OPHELIA
My lord?

HAMLET
Are you fair?

OPHELIA
What means your lordship?

HAMLET
That if you be honest and fair, your honesty should admit no discourse to your beauty.

OPHELIA
Could beauty, my lord, have better commerce than with honesty?

HAMLET
Ay, truly; for the power of beauty will sooner transform honesty from what it is to a bawd than the force of honesty can translate beauty into his likeness: this was sometime a paradox, but now the time gives it proof. I did love you once.

OPHELIA
Indeed, my lord, you made me believe so.

HAMLET
You should not have believed me; for virtue cannot so inoculate our old stock but we shall relish of it: I loved you not.

OPHELIA
I was the more deceived.

HAMLET
Get thee to a nunnery: why wouldst thou be a breeder of sinners? I am myself indifferent honest; but yet I could accuse me of such things that it were better my mother had not borne me: I am very proud, revengeful, ambitious, with more offences at my beck than I have thoughts to put them in, imagination to give them shape, or time to act them in. What should such fellows as I do crawling between earth and heaven? We are arrant knaves, all; believe none of us. Go thy ways to a nunnery. Where's your father?

OPHELIA
At home, my lord.

HAMLET
Let the doors be shut upon him, that he may play the fool no where but in's own house. Farewell.

OPHELIA
O, help him, you sweet heavens!

HAMLET

If thou dost marry, I'll give thee this plague for thy dowry: be thou as chaste as ice, as pure as snow, thou shalt not escape calumny. Get thee to a nunnery, go: farewell. Or, if thou wilt needs marry, marry a fool; for wise men know well enough what monsters you make of them. To a nunnery, go, and quickly too. Farewell.

OPHELIA

O heavenly powers, restore him!

HAMLET

I have heard of your paintings too, well enough; God has given you one face, and you make yourselves another: you jig, you amble, and you lisp, and nick-name God's creatures, and make your wantonness your ignorance. Go to, I'll no more on't; it hath made me mad. I say, we will have no more marriages: those that are married already, all but one, shall live; the rest shall keep as they are. To a nunnery, go. [37] [*Exit.*

OPHELIA

O, what a noble mind is here o'erthrown!
The courtier's, soldier's, scholar's, eye, tongue, sword;
The expectancy and rose of the fair state,
The glass of fashion and the mould of form,
The observed of all observers, quite, quite down!
And I, of ladies most deject and wretched,
That suck'd the honey of his music vows,
Now see that noble and most sovereign reason,
Like sweet bells jangled, out of tune and harsh;
That unmatch'd form and feature of blown youth
Blasted with ecstasy: O, woe is me,
To have seen what I have seen, see what I see!

Re-enter KING *and* POLONIUS.

KING CLAUDIUS

Love! his affections do not that way tend;
Nor what he spake, though it lack'd form a little,
Was not like madness. There's something in his soul,
O'er which his melancholy sits on brood;
And I do doubt the hatch and the disclose
Will be some danger: which for to prevent,
I have in quick determination
Thus set it down: he shall with speed to England,
For the demand of our neglected tribute:
Haply the seas and country different
With variable objects shall expel
This something-settled matter in his heart,
Whereon his brains still beating puts him thus
From fashion of himself. What think you on't?

POLONIUS

It shall do well: but yet do I believe
The origin and commencement of his grief
Sprung from neglected love. How now, Ophelia!
You need not tell us what Lord Hamlet said;
We heard it all. My lord, do as you please;
But, if you hold it fit, after the play
Let his queen mother all alone entreat him
To show his grief: let her be round with him;
And I'll be placed, so please you, in the ear
Of all their conference. If she find him not,
To England send him, or confine him where
Your wisdom best shall think.

KING CLAUDIUS

It shall be so:
Madness in great ones must not unwatch'd go.
[*Exeunt.*

ACT THREE SCENE TWO

A hall in the castle.

Enter HAMLET *and* Players.

HAMLET

Speak the speech, I pray you, as I pronounced it to you, trippingly on the tongue: but if you mouth it, as many of your players do, I had as lief the town-crier spoke my lines. Nor do not saw the air too much with your hand, thus, but use all gently; for in the very torrent, tempest, and, as I may say, the whirlwind of passion, you must acquire and beget a temperance that may give it smoothness. O, it offends me to the soul to hear a robustious periwig-pated fellow tear a passion to tatters, to very rags, to split the ears of the groundlings, who for the most part are capable of nothing but inexplicable dumb-shows and noise: I would have such a fellow whipped for o'erdoing Termagant; it out-herods Herod: pray you, avoid it.

FIRST PLAYER

I warrant your honour.

HAMLET

Be not too tame neither, but let your own discretion be your tutor: suit the action to the word, the word to the action; with this special observance, that you o'erstep not the modesty of nature: for any thing so overdone is from the purpose of playing, whose end, both at the first and now, was and is, to hold as 'twere, the mirror up to nature; to show virtue her own feature, scorn her own image, and the very age and body of the time his form and pressure. Now this overdone, or come tardy off, though it make the unskilful laugh, cannot but make the judicious grieve; the censure of the which one must in your allowance o'erweigh a whole theatre of others. O, there be players that I have seen play, and heard others praise, and that highly, not to speak it profanely, that, neither having the accent of Christians nor the gait of Christian. pagan, nor man, have so strutted and bellowed that I have thought some of nature's journeymen had made men and made them well, they imitated humanity so abominably. [38]

FIRST PLAYER

I hope we have reformed that indifferently with us, sir. 36

HAMLET

O, reform it altogether. And let those that play your clowns speak no more than is set down for them; for there be of them that will themselves laugh, to set on some quantity of barren spectators to laugh too; though, in the mean time, some necessary question of the play be then to be considered: that's villanous, and shows a most pitiful ambition in the fool that uses it. Go, make you ready. [39] [*Exeunt Players.*

Enter POLONIUS, ROSENCRANTZ, *and* GUILDENSTERN.

How now, my lord! I will the king hear this piece of work?

POLONIUS

And the queen too, and that presently.

HAMLET

Bid the players make haste. [*Exit Polonius.*] Will you two help to hasten them?

ROSENCRANTZ, GUILDENSTERN

We will, my lord.

[*Exeunt Rosencrantz and Guildenstern.*

HAMLET

What ho! Horatio!

Enter HORATIO.

HORATIO

Here, sweet lord, at your service.

HAMLET

Horatio, thou art e'en as just a man
As e'er my conversation coped withal. 54

HORATIO

O, my dear lord,—

HAMLET

Nay, do not think I flatter;
For what advancement may I hope from thee
That no revenue hast but thy good spirits,
To feed and clothe thee? Why should the poor be flatter'd?
No, let the candied tongue lick absurd pomp,
And crook the pregnant hinges of the knee
Where thrift may follow fawning. Dost thou hear?
Since my dear soul was mistress of her choice
And could of men distinguish, her election
Hath seal'd thee for herself; for thou hast been
As one, in suffering all, that suffers nothing, 68
A man that fortune's buffets and rewards
Hast ta'en with equal thanks: and blest are those
Whose blood and judgement are so well commingled,
That they are not a pipe for fortune's finger
To sound what stop she please. Give me that man
That is not passion's slave, and I will wear him
In my heart's core, ay, in my heart of heart,
As I do thee.—Something too much of this.—
There is a play to-night before the king; 77
One scene of it comes near the circumstance
Which I have told thee of my father's death:
I prithee, when thou seest that act afoot,
Even with the very comment of thy soul
Observe mine uncle: if his occulted guilt
Do not itself unkennel in one speech,
It is a damned ghost that we have seen,
And my imaginations are as foul
As Vulcan's stithy. Give him heedful note;
For I mine eyes will rivet to his face, 87
And after we will both our judgements join
In censure of his seeming.

HORATIO

Well, my lord:
If he steal aught the whilst this play is playing,
And 'scape detecting, I will pay the theft.

HAMLET

They are coming to the play; I must be idle:
Get you a place.

Danish march. A flourish. Enter KING, QUEEN, POLONIUS, OPHELIA, ROSENCRANTZ, GUILDENSTERN, *and others.*

KING CLAUDIUS

How fares our cousin Hamlet?

HAMLET

Excellent, i' faith; of the chameleon's dish: I eat the air, promise-crammed: you cannot feed capons so. 100

KING CLAUDIUS

I have nothing with this answer, Hamlet; these words are not mine.

HAMLET

No, nor mine now. [*To Polonius*] My lord, you played once i' the university, you say?

POLONIUS

That did I, my lord; and was accounted a good actor.

HAMLET

What did you enact?

POLONIUS

I did enact Julius Caesar: I was killed i' the
Capitol; Brutus killed me.

HAMLET

It was a brute part of him to kill so capital a calf there. Be the players ready?

ROSENCRANTZ

Ay, my lord; they stay upon your patience.

QUEEN GERTRUDE

Come hither, my dear Hamlet, sit by me.

HAMLET
No, good mother, here's metal more attractive.
POLONIUS
[*To the King*] O, ho! do you mark that?
HAMLET
Lady, shall I lie in your lap?
[*Lying down at Ophelia's feet.*
OPHELIA
No, my lord. 113
HAMLET
I mean, my head upon your lap?
OPHELIA
Ay, my lord.
HAMLET
Do you think I meant country matters?
OPHELIA
I think nothing, my lord.
HAMLET
That's a fair thought to lie between maids' legs.
OPHELIA
What is, my lord?
HAMLET
Nothing.
OPHELIA
You are merry, my lord.
HAMLET
Who, I? 122
OPHELIA
Ay, my lord.
HAMLET
O God, your only jig-maker. What should a man do but be merry? for, look you, how cheerfully my mother looks, and my father died within these two hours.
OPHELIA
Nay, 'tis twice two months, my lord.
HAMLET
So long? Nay then, let the devil wear black, for
I'll have a suit of sables. O heavens! die two months ago, and not forgotten yet? Then there's hope a great man's memory may outlive his life half a year: but, by'r lady, he must build churches, then; or else shall he suffer not thinking on, with the hobby-horse, whose epitaph is 'For, O, for, O, the hobby-horse is forgot.'

Hautboys play. The dumb-show enters. [40]

Enter a King *and a* Queen *very lovingly; the* Queen *embracing him, and he her. She kneels, and makes show of protestation unto him. He takes her up, and declines his head upon her neck: lays him down upon a bank of flowers: she, seeing him asleep, leaves him. Anon comes in a fellow, takes off his crown, kisses it, and pours poison in the* King's *ears, and exit. The* Queen *returns; finds the* King *dead, and makes passionate action. The* Poisoner, *with some two or three Mutes, comes in again, seeming to lament with her. The dead body is carried away. The* Poisoner *wooes the* Queen *with gifts: she seems loath and unwilling awhile, but in the end accepts his love.* [*Exeunt.*

OPHELIA
What means this, my lord?
HAMLET
Marry, this is miching mallecho; it means mischief.
OPHELIA
Belike this show imports the argument of the play. 150

Enter Prologue.

HAMLET
We shall know by this fellow: the players cannot keep counsel; they'll tell all.
OPHELIA
Will he tell us what this show meant?
HAMLET
Ay, or any show that you'll show him: be not you ashamed to show, he'll not shame to tell you what it means.
OPHELIA
You are naught, you are naught: I'll make the play.
PROLOGUE
For us, and for our tragedy,
Here stooping to your clemency, 159
We beg your hearing patiently. [*Exit.*
HAMLET
Is this a prologue, or the posy of a ring?
OPHELIA
'Tis brief, my lord.
HAMLET
As woman's love.

Enter two Players, King *and* Queen.

PLAYER KING
Full thirty times hath Phoebus' cart gone round
Neptune's salt wash and Tellus' orbed ground,
And thirty dozen moons with borrow'd sheen
About the world have times twelve thirties been,
Since love our hearts and Hymen did our hands
Unite commutual in most sacred bands. 169
PLAYER QUEEN
So many journeys may the sun and moon
Make again count o'er ere love be done!
But, woe is me, you are so sick of late,
So far from cheer and from your former state,
That I distrust you. Yet, though I distrust,
Discomfort you, my lord, it nothing must:
For women's fear and love holds quantity; [41]
In either aught, or in extremity. [42]
Now, what my love is, proof hath made you know;
And as my love is sized, my fear is so: 180

Where love is great, the littlest doubts are fear;
Where little fears grow great, great love grows there.

PLAYER KING
'Faith, I must leave thee, love, and shortly too;
My operant powers their functions leave to do:
And thou shalt live in this fair world behind,
Honour'd, beloved; and haply one as kind
For husband shalt thou—

PLAYER QUEEN
O, confound the rest!
Such love must needs be treason in my breast:
In second husband let me be accurst!
None wed the second but who kill'd the first.

HAMLET
[*Aside*] Wormwood, wormwood.

PLAYER QUEEN
The instances that second marriage move
Are base respects of thrift, but none of love:
A second time I kill my husband dead,
When second husband kisses me in bed.

PLAYER KING
I do believe you think what now you speak;
But what we do determine oft we break.
Purpose is but the slave to memory,
Of violent birth, but poor validity:
Which now, like fruit unripe, sticks on the tree;
But fall, unshaken, when they mellow be.
Most necessary 'tis that we forget
To pay ourselves what to ourselves is debt:
What to ourselves in passion we propose,
The passion ending, doth the purpose lose.
The violence of either grief or joy
Their own enactures with themselves destroy:
Where joy most revels, grief doth most lament;
Grief joys, joy grieves, on slender accident.
This world is not for aye, nor 'tis not strange
That even our loves should with our fortunes change;
For 'tis a question left us yet to prove,
Whether love lead fortune, or else fortune love.
The great man down, you mark his favourite flies; [43]
The poor advanced makes friends of enemies.
And hitherto doth love on fortune tend;
For who not needs shall never lack a friend,
And who in want a hollow friend doth try,
Directly seasons him his enemy.
But, orderly to end where I begun,
Our wills and fates do so contrary run
That our devices still are overthrown;
Our thoughts are ours, their ends none of our own:
So think thou wilt no second husband wed;
But die thy thoughts when thy first lord is dead.

PLAYER QUEEN
Nor earth to me give food, nor heaven light!
Sport and repose lock from me day and night!
To desperation turn my trust and hope!
An anchor's cheer in prison be my scope!
Each opposite that blanks the face of joy
Meet what I would have well and it destroy!
Both here and hence pursue me lasting strife,
If, once a widow, ever I be wife!

HAMLET
If she should break it now!

PLAYER KING
'Tis deeply sworn. Sweet, leave me here awhile;
My spirits grow dull, and fain I would beguile
The tedious day with sleep. [*Sleeps.*

PLAYER QUEEN
Sleep rock thy brain;
And never come mischance between us twain! [*Exit.*

HAMLET
Madam, how like you this play?

QUEEN GERTRUDE
The lady doth protests too much, methinks.

HAMLET
O, but she'll keep her word.

KING CLAUDIUS
Have you heard the argument? Is there no offence in 't?

HAMLET
No, no, they do but jest, poison in jest; no offence i' the world.

KING CLAUDIUS
What do you call the play?

HAMLET
The Mouse-trap. Marry, how? Tropically. This play is the image of a murder done in Vienna: Gonzago is the duke's name; his wife, Baptista; you shall see anon; 'tis a knavish piece of work: but what o' that? your majesty and we that have free souls, it touches us not: let the galled jade wince, our withers are unwrung. [44]

Enter LUCIANUS.

This is one Lucianus, nephew to the king.

OPHELIA
You are as good as a chorus, my lord.

HAMLET
I could interpret between you and your love, if I could see the puppets dallying.

OPHELIA
You are keen, my lord, you are keen.

HAMLET
It would cost you a groaning to take off my edge.

OPHELIA
Still better, and worse.

HAMLET

So you must take your husbands. Begin, murderer; pox, leave thy damnable faces, and begin. Come: 'the croaking raven doth bellow for revenge.' [45]

LUCIANUS

Thoughts black, hands apt, drugs fit, and time agreeing;
Confederate season, else no creature seeing;
Thou mixture rank, of midnight weeds collected,
With Hecate's ban thrice blasted, thrice infected,
Thy natural magic and dire property,
On wholesome life usurp immediately.

[*Pours the poison into the sleeper's ears.*

HAMLET

He poisons him i' the garden for's estate. His name's Gonzago: the story is extant, and writ in choice Italian: you shall see anon how the murderer gets the love of Gonzago's wife.

OPHELIA

The king rises.

HAMLET

What, frighted with false fire!

QUEEN GERTRUDE

How fares my lord?

POLONIUS

Give o'er the play.

KING CLAUDIUS

Give me some light: away!

ALL

Lights, lights, lights!

[*Exeunt all but Hamlet and Horatio.*

HAMLET

Why, let the stricken deer go weep,
The hart ungalled play;
For some must watch, while some must sleep:
So runs the world away.

Would not this, sir, and a forest of feathers—if the rest of my fortunes turn Turk with me—with two Provincial roses on my razed shoes, get me a fellowship in a cry of players, sir?

HORATIO

Half a share.

HAMLET

A whole one, I.
For thou dost know, O Damon dear,
This realm dismantled was
Of Jove himself; and now reigns here
A very, very—pajock.

HORATIO

You might have rhymed.

HAMLET

O good Horatio, I'll take the ghost's word for a thousand pound. Didst perceive?

HORATIO

Very well, my lord.

HAMLET

Upon the talk of the poisoning?

HORATIO

I did very well note him.

HAMLET

Ah, ha! Come, some music! come, the recorders!
For if the king like not the comedy,
Why then, belike, he likes it not, perdy.
Come, some music!

Re-enter ROSENCRANTZ *and* GUILDENSTERN.

GUILDENSTERN

Good my lord, vouchsafe me a word with you.

HAMLET

Sir, a whole history.

GUILDENSTERN

The king, sir,—

HAMLET

Ay, sir, what of him?

GUILDENSTERN

Is in his retirement marvellous distempered.

HAMLET

With drink, sir?

GUILDENSTERN

No, my lord, rather with choler.

HAMLET

Your wisdom should show itself more richer to signify this to his doctor; for, for me to put him to his purgation would perhaps plunge him into far more choler.

GUILDENSTERN

Good my lord, put your discourse into some frame and start not so wildly from my affair.

HAMLET

I am tame, sir: pronounce.

GUILDENSTERN

The queen, your mother, in most great affliction of spirit, hath sent me to you.

HAMLET

You are welcome.

GUILDENSTERN

Nay, good my lord, this courtesy is not of the right breed. If it shall please you to make me a wholesome answer, I will do your mother's commandment: if not, your pardon and my return shall be the end of my business.

HAMLET

Sir, I cannot.

GUILDENSTERN

What, my lord?

HAMLET

Make you a wholesome answer; my wit's diseased; but, sir, such answer as I can make, you shall command; or, rather, as you say, my mother: therefore no more, but to the matter: my mother, you say,—

ROSENCRANTZ

Then thus she says; your behaviour hath struck her into amazement and admiration. 339

HAMLET

O wonderful son, that can so astonish a mother! But is there no sequel at the heels of this mother's admiration? Impart.

ROSENCRANTZ

She desires to speak with you in her closet, ere you go to bed.

HAMLET

We shall obey, were she ten times our mother. Have you any further trade with us?

ROSENCRANTZ

My lord, you once did love me.

HAMLET

So I do still, by these pickers and stealers. 348

ROSENCRANTZ

Good my lord, what is your cause of distemper? you do, surely, bar the door upon your own liberty, if you deny your griefs to your friend.

HAMLET

Sir, I lack advancement.

ROSENCRANTZ

How can that be, when you have the voice of the king himself for your succession in Denmark?

HAMLET

Ay, sir, but 'While the grass grows,'—the proverb is something musty. 356

Re-enter Players *with recorders.*

O, the recorders! let me see one. To withdraw with you:—why do you go about to recover the wind of me, as if you would drive me into a toil?

GUILDENSTERN

O, my lord, if my duty be too bold, my love is too unmannerly.

HAMLET

I do not well understand that. Will you play upon this pipe?

GUILDENSTERN

My lord, I cannot.

HAMLET

I pray you.

GUILDENSTERN

Believe me, I cannot.

HAMLET

I do beseech you. 369

GUILDENSTERN

I know no touch of it, my lord.

HAMLET

'Tis as easy as lying: govern these ventages with your lingers and thumb, give it breath with your mouth, and it will discourse most eloquent music.

Look you, these are the stops.

GUILDENSTERN

But these cannot I command to any utterance of harmony; I have not the skill.

HAMLET

Why, look you now, how unworthy a thing you make of me! You would play upon me; you would seem to know my stops; you would pluck out the heart of my mystery; you would sound me from my lowest note to the top of my compass: and there is much music, excellent voice, in this little organ; yet cannot you make it speak. 'Sblood, do you think I am easier to be played on than a pipe? Call me what instrument you will, though you can fret me, yet you cannot play upon me.

Enter POLONIUS.

God bless you, sir! 384

POLONIUS

My lord, the queen would speak with you, and presently.

HAMLET

Do you see yonder cloud that's almost in shape of a camel?

POLONIUS

By the mass, and 'tis like a camel, indeed.

HAMLET

Methinks it is like a weasel.

POLONIUS

It is backed like a weasel.

HAMLET

Or like a whale? 392

POLONIUS

Very like a whale.

HAMLET

Then I will come to my mother by and by. They fool me to the top of my bent. I will come by and by.

POLONIUS

I will say so.

HAMLET

By and by is easily said. [*Exit Polonius.*] Leave me, friends. [*Exeunt all but Hamlet.*

'Tis now the very witching time of night,
When churchyards yawn and hell itself breathes out
Contagion to this world: now could I drink hot blood,
And do such bitter business as the day [46]
Would quake to look on. Soft! now to my mother. 405

O heart, lose not thy nature; let not ever
The soul of Nero enter this firm bosom:
Let me be cruel, not unnatural:
I will speak daggers to her, but use none;
My tongue and soul in this be hypocrites;
How in my words soever she be shent,
To give them seals never, my soul, consent! [*Exit.*

ACT THREE SCENE THREE

A room in the castle.

Enter KING, ROSENCRANTZ,
and GUILDENSTERN.

KING CLAUDIUS
I like him not, nor stands it safe with us
To let his madness range. Therefore prepare you;
I your commission will forthwith dispatch,
And he to England shall along with you:
The terms of our estate may not endure
Hazard so near as doth hourly grow
Out of his lunacies. [47]

GUILDENSTERN
We will ourselves provide:
Most holy and religious fear it is
To keep those many many bodies safe
That live and feed upon your majesty.

ROSENCRANTZ
The single and peculiar life is bound,
With all the strength and armour of the mind,
To keep itself from noyance; but much more
That spirit upon whose weal depend and rest
The lives of many. The cease of majesty
Dies not alone; but, like a gulf, doth draw
What's near it with it: it is a massy wheel,
Fix'd on the summit of the highest mount,
To whose huge spokes ten thousand lesser things
Are mortised and adjoin'd; which, when it falls,
Each small annexment, petty consequence,
Attends the boisterous ruin. Never alone
Did the king sigh, but with a general groan.

KING CLAUDIUS
Arm you, I pray you, to this speedy voyage;
For we will fetters put upon this fear,
Which now goes too free-footed.

ROSENCRANTZ, GUILDENSTERN
We will haste us.
[*Exeunt Rosencrantz and Guildenstern.*

Enter POLONIUS.

POLONIUS
My lord, he's going to his mother's closet:
Behind the arras I'll convey myself,
To hear the process; I'll warrant she'll tax him home:
And, as you said, and wisely was it said,
'Tis meet that some more audience than a mother,
Since nature makes them partial, should o'erhear
The speech, of vantage. Fare you well, my liege:
I'll call upon you ere you go to bed,
And tell you what I know.

KING CLAUDIUS
Thanks, dear my lord. [*Exit Polonius.*
O, my offence is rank, it smells to heaven;
It hath the primal eldest curse upon't,
A brother's murder. Pray can I not,
Though inclination be as sharp as will:
My stronger guilt defeats my strong intent;
And, like a man to double business bound,
I stand in pause where I shall first begin,
And both neglect. What if this cursed hand
Were thicker than itself with brother's blood,
Is there not rain enough in the sweet heavens
To wash it white as snow? Whereto serves mercy
But to confront the visage of offence?
And what's in prayer but this two-fold force,
To be forestalled ere we come to fall,
Or pardon'd being down? Then I'll look up;
My fault is past. But, O, what form of prayer
Can serve my turn? 'Forgive me my foul murder'?
That cannot be; since I am still possess'd
Of those effects for which I did the murder,
My crown, mine own ambition and my queen.
May one be pardon'd and retain the offence?
In the corrupted currents of this world
Offence's gilded hand may shove by justice,
And oft 'tis seen the wicked prize itself
Buys out the law: but 'tis not so above;
There is no shuffling, there the action lies
In his true nature; and we ourselves compell'd,
Even to the teeth and forehead of our faults,
To give in evidence. What then? what rests?
Try what repentance can: what can it not?
Yet what can it when one can not repent?
O wretched state! O bosom black as death!
O limed soul, that, struggling to be free,
Art more engaged! Help, angels! Make assay!
Bow, stubborn knees; and, heart with strings of
steel,
Be soft as sinews of the new-born babe!
All may be well. [*Retires and kneels.*

Enter HAMLET.

HAMLET
Now might I do it pat, now he is praying;
And now I'll do't. And so he goes to heaven;
And so am I revenged. That would be scann'd:
A villain kills my father; and for that,

I, his sole son, do this same villain send
To heaven.
O, this is hire and salary, not revenge. [48]
He took my father grossly, full of bread;
With all his crimes broad blown, as flush as May;
And how his audit stands who knows save heaven?
But in our circumstance and course of thought,
'Tis heavy with him: and am I then revenged,
To take him in the purging of his soul,
When he is fit and season'd for his passage?
No!
Up, sword; and know thou a more horrid hent:
When he is drunk asleep, or in his rage,
Or in the incestuous pleasure of his bed;
At gaming, swearing, or about some act
That has no relish of salvation in't;
Then trip him, that his heels may kick at heaven,
And that his soul may be as damn'd and black
As hell, whereto it goes. My mother stays:
This physic but prolongs thy sickly days. [*Exit.*

KING CLAUDIUS
[*Rising*] My words fly up, my thoughts remain below:
Words without thoughts never to heaven go.
[*Exit.*

ACT THREE SCENE FOUR

The Queen's closet.

Enter QUEEN *and* POLONIUS.

POLONIUS
He will come straight. Look you lay home to him:
Tell him his pranks have been too broad to bear with,
And that your grace hath screen'd and stood between
Much heat and him. I'll sconce me even here.
Pray you, be round with him.

HAMLET
[*Within*] Mother, mother, mother!

QUEEN GERTRUDE
I'll warrant you,
Fear me not: withdraw, I hear him coming.
[*Polonius hides behind the arras.*

Enter HAMLET.

HAMLET
Now, mother, what's the matter?

QUEEN GERTRUDE
Hamlet, thou hast thy father much offended.

HAMLET
Mother, you have my father much offended.

QUEEN GERTRUDE
Come, come, you answer with an idle tongue.

HAMLET
Go, go, you question with a wicked tongue.

QUEEN GERTRUDE
Why, how now, Hamlet!

HAMLET
What's the matter now?

QUEEN GERTRUDE
Have you forgot me?

HAMLET
No, by the rood, not so:
You are the queen, your husband's brother's wife;
And—would it were not so!—you are my mother.

QUEEN GERTRUDE
Nay, then, I'll set those to you that can speak.

HAMLET
Come, come, and sit you down; you shall not budge;
You go not till I set you up a glass
Where you may see the inmost part of you.

QUEEN GERTRUDE
What wilt thou do? thou wilt not murder me?
Help, help, ho!

POLONIUS
[*Behind*] What, ho! help, help, help!

HAMLET
[*Drawing*] How now! a rat? Dead, for a ducat, dead! [*Makes a pass through the arras.*

POLONIUS
[*Behind*] O, I am slain! [*Falls and dies.*

QUEEN GERTRUDE
O me, what hast thou done?

HAMLET
Nay, I know not:
Is it the king?

QUEEN GERTRUDE
O, what a rash and bloody deed is this!

HAMLET
A bloody deed! almost as bad, good mother,
As kill a king, and marry with his brother.

QUEEN GERTRUDE
As kill a king!

HAMLET
Ay, lady, 'twas my word.
[*Lifts up the array and discovers Polonius.*
Thou wretched, rash, intruding fool, farewell!
I took thee for thy better: take thy fortune;
Thou find'st to be too busy is some danger.
Leave wringing of your hands: peace! sit you down,
And let me wring your heart; for so I shall,
If it be made of penetrable stuff,
If damned custom have not brass'd it so
That it be proof and bulwark against sense.

QUEEN GERTRUDE
What have I done, that thou darest wag thy tongue
In noise so rude against me?
HAMLET
Such an act
That blurs the grace and blush of modesty,
Calls virtue hypocrite, takes off the rose
From the fair forehead of an innocent love
And sets a blister there, makes marriage-vows
As false as dicers' oaths: O, such a deed
As from the body of contraction plucks
The very soul, and sweet religion makes
A rhapsody of words: heaven's face doth glow;
Yea, this solidity and compound mass,
With tristful visage, as against the doom,
Is thought-sick at the act.
QUEEN GERTRUDE
Ay me, what act,
That roars so loud, and thunders in the index?
HAMLET
Look here, upon this picture, and on this,
The counterfeit presentment of two brothers.
See, what a grace was seated on this brow;
Hyperion's curls; the front of Jove himself;
An eye like Mars, to threaten and command;
A station like the herald Mercury
New-lighted on a heaven-kissing hill;
A combination and a form indeed,
Where every god did seem to set his seal,
To give the world assurance of a man:
This was your husband. Look you now, what follows:
Here is your husband; like a mildew'd ear,
Blasting his wholesome brother. Have you eyes?
Could you on this fair mountain leave to feed,
And batten on this moor? Ha! have you eyes?
You cannot call it love; for at your age
The hey-day in the blood is tame, it's humble,
And waits upon the judgement: and what judgement
Would step from this to this? Sense, sure, you have,[49]
Else could you not have motion; but sure, that sense
Is apoplex'd; for madness would not err,
Nor sense to ecstasy was ne'er so thrall'd
But it reserved some quantity of choice,
To serve in such a difference. What devil was't
That thus hath cozen'd you at hoodman-blind?
Eyes without feeling, feeling without sight,
Ears without hands or eyes, smelling sans all,
Or but a sickly part of one true sense
Could not so mope.
O shame! where is thy blush? Rebellious hell,
If thou canst mutine in a matron's bones,
To flaming youth let virtue be as wax,
And melt in her own fire: proclaim no shame
When the compulsive ardour gives the charge,
Since frost itself as actively doth burn
And reason panders will.
QUEEN GERTRUDE
O Hamlet, speak no more:
Thou turn'st mine eyes into my very soul;
And there I see such black and grained spots
As will not leave their tinct.
HAMLET
Nay, but to live
In the rank sweat of an enseamed bed,
Stew'd in corruption, honeying and making love
Over the nasty sty,—
QUEEN GERTRUDE
O, speak to me no more;
These words, like daggers, enter in mine ears;
No more, sweet Hamlet!
HAMLET
A murderer and a villain;
A slave that is not twentieth part the tithe
Of your precedent lord; a vice of kings;
A cutpurse of the empire and the rule,
That from a shelf the precious diadem stole,
And put it in his pocket!
QUEEN GERTRUDE
No more!
HAMLET
A king of shreds and patches,—

Enter Ghost.

Save me, and hover o'er me with your wings,
You heavenly guards! What would your gracious figure?
QUEEN GERTRUDE
Alas, he's mad!
HAMLET
Do you not come your tardy son to chide,
That, lapsed in time and passion, lets go by
The important acting of your dread command?
O, say!
GHOST
Do not forget: this visitation
Is but to whet thy almost blunted purpose.
But, look, amazement on thy mother sits:
O, step between her and her fighting soul:
Conceit in weakest bodies strongest works:
Speak to her, Hamlet.
HAMLET
How is it with you, lady?
QUEEN GERTRUDE
Alas, how is't with you,
That you do bend your eye on vacancy
And with the incorporal air do hold discourse?

Forth at your eyes your spirits wildly peep;
And, as the sleeping soldiers in the alarm, 141
Your bedded hair, like life in excrements,
Start up, and stands on end. O gentle son,
Upon the heat and flame of thy distemper
Sprinkle cool patience. Whereon do you look?

HAMLET
On him, on him! Look you, how pale he glares!
His form and cause conjoin'd, preaching to stones,
Would make them capable. Do not look upon me;
Lest with this piteous action you convert
My stern effects: then what I have to do
Will want true colour; tears perchance for blood. 152

QUEEN GERTRUDE
To whom do you speak this?

HAMLET
Do you see nothing there?

QUEEN GERTRUDE
Nothing at all; yet all that is I see.

HAMLET
Nor did you nothing hear?

QUEEN GERTRUDE
No, nothing but ourselves.

HAMLET
Why, look you there! look, how it steals away!
My father, in his habit as he lived!
Look, where he goes, even now, out at the portal! [*Exit Ghost.*

QUEEN GERTRUDE
This the very coinage of your brain:
This bodiless creation ecstasy
Is very cunning in.

HAMLET
Ecstasy!
My pulse, as yours, doth temperately keep time, 167
And makes as healthful music: it is not madness
That I have utter'd: bring me to the test,
And I the matter will re-word; which madness
Would gambol from. Mother, for love of grace,
Lay not that flattering unction to your soul,
That not your trespass, but my madness speaks:
It will but skin and film the ulcerous place,
Whiles rank corruption, mining all within,
Infects unseen. Confess yourself to heaven;
Repent what's past; avoid what is to come;
And do not spread the compost on the weeds,
To make them ranker. Forgive me this my virtue;
For in the fatness of these pursy times
Virtue itself of vice must pardon beg,
Yea, curb and woo for leave to do him good.

QUEEN GERTRUDE
O Hamlet, thou hast cleft my heart in twain.

HAMLET
O, throw away the worser part of it,
And live the purer with the other half.
Good night: but go not to mine uncle's bed;
Assume a virtue, if you have it not.
That monster, custom, who all sense doth eat, 189
Of habits devil, is angel yet in this,
That to the use of actions fair and good
He likewise gives a frock or livery,
That aptly is put on. Refrain to-night,
And that shall lend a kind of easiness
To the next abstinence: the next more easy;
For use almost can change the stamp of nature,
And either … . the devil, or throw him out [50]
With wondrous potency. Once more, good night: 199
And when you are desirous to be bless'd,
I'll blessing beg of you. For this same lord,
[*Pointing to Polonius.*
I do repent: but heaven hath pleased it so,
To punish me with this and this with me,
That I must be their scourge and minister.
I will bestow him, and will answer well
The death I gave him. So, again, good night.
I must be cruel, only to be kind:
Thus bad begins and worse remains behind.
One word more, good lady.

QUEEN GERTRUDE
What shall I do? 210

HAMLET
Not this, by no means, that I bid you do:
Let the bloat king tempt you again to bed;
Pinch wanton on your cheek; call you his mouse;
And let him, for a pair of reechy kisses,
Or paddling in your neck with his damn'd fingers,
Make you to ravel all this matter out,
That I essentially am not in madness,
But mad in craft. 'Twere good you let him know;
For who, that's but a queen, fair, sober, wise,
Would from a paddock, from a bat, a gib, 221
Such dear concernings hide? who would do so?
No, in despite of sense and secrecy,
Unpeg the basket on the house's top.
Let the birds fly, and, like the famous ape,
To try conclusions, in the basket creep,
And break your own neck down.

QUEEN GERTRUDE
Be thou assured, if words be made of breath,
And breath of life, I have no life to breathe
What thou hast said to me.

HAMLET
I must to England; you know that?

QUEEN GERTRUDE
Alack,
I had forgot: 'tis so concluded on.
HAMLET
There's letters seal'd: and my two schoolfellows,
Whom I will trust as I will adders fang'd,
They bear the mandate; they must sweep my way,
And marshal me to knavery. Let it work;
For 'tis the sport to have the enginer
Hoist with his own petar: and 't shall go hard
But I will delve one yard below their mines,
And blow them at the moon: O, 'tis most sweet,
When in one line two crafts directly meet.
This man shall set me packing:
I'll lug the guts into the neighbour room.
Mother, good night. Indeed this counsellor
Is now most still, most secret and most grave,
Who was in life a foolish prating knave.
Come, sir, to draw toward an end with you.
Good night, mother. [*Exeunt severally; Hamlet dragging in Polonius.*

ACT FOUR SCENE ONE

A room in the castle.

Enter KING, QUEEN, ROSENCRANTZ, *and* GUILDENSTERN.

KING CLAUDIUS
There's matter in these sighs, these profound heaves:
You must translate: 'tis fit we understand them.
Where is your son?
QUEEN GERTRUDE
Bestow this place on us a little while. [51] [*Exeunt Rosencrantz and Guildenstern.*
Ah, mine own lord, what have I seen to-night!
KING CLAUDIUS
What, Gertrude? How does Hamlet?
QUEEN GERTRUDE
Mad as the sea and wind, when both contend
Which is the mightier: in his lawless fit,
Behind the arras hearing something stir,
Whips out his rapier, cries, 'A rat, a rat!'
And, in this brainish apprehension, kills
The unseen good old man.
KING CLAUDIUS
O heavy deed!
It had been so with us, had we been there:
His liberty is full of threats to all;
To you yourself, to us, to every one.
Alas, how shall this bloody deed be answer'd?
It will be laid to us, whose providence
Should have kept short, restrain'd and out of haunt,
This mad young man: but so much was our love,
We would not understand what was most fit;
But, like the owner of a foul disease,
To keep it from divulging, let it feed
Even on the pith of Life. Where is he gone?
QUEEN GERTRUDE
To draw apart the body he hath kill'd:
O'er whom his very madness, like some ore
Among a mineral of metals base,
Shows itself pure; he weeps for what is done.
KING CLAUDIUS
O Gertrude, come away!
The sun no sooner shall the mountains touch,
But we will ship him hence: and this vile deed
We must, with all our majesty and skill,
Both countenance and excuse. Ho, Guildenstern!

Re-enter ROSENCRANTZ *and* GUILDENSTERN.

Friends both, go join you with some further aid:
Hamlet in madness hath Polonius slain,
And from his mother's closet hath he dragg'd him:
Go seek him out; speak fair, and bring the body
Into the chapel. I pray you, haste in this. [*Exeunt Rosencrantz and Guildenstern.*
Come, Gertrude, we'll call up our wisest friends;
And let them know, both what we mean to do,
And what's untimely done ... ...
Whose whisper o'er the world's diameter,
As level as the cannon to his blank,
Transports his poison'd shot, may miss our name,
And hit the woundless air. O, come away! [52]
My soul is full of discord and dismay. [*Exeunt.*

ACT FOUR SCENE TWO

Another room in the castle.

Enter HAMLET.

HAMLET
Safely stowed.
ROSENCRANTZ, GUILDENSTERN
[*Within*] Hamlet! Lord Hamlet!
HAMLET
But soft, What noise? who calls on Hamlet?
O, here they come.

Enter ROSENCRANTZ *and* GUILDENSTERN.

ROSENCRANTZ
What have you done, my lord, with the dead body?
HAMLET
Compounded it with dust, whereto 'tis kin.

ROSENCRANTZ
Tell us where 'tis, that we may take it thence
And bear it to the chapel.

HAMLET
Do not believe it.

ROSENCRANTZ
Believe what? 11

HAMLET
That I can keep your counsel and not mine own. Besides, to be demanded of a sponge! what replication should be made by the son of a king?

ROSENCRANTZ
Take you me for a sponge, my lord?

HAMLET
Ay, sir, that soaks up the king's countenance, his rewards, his authorities. But such officers do the king best service in the end: he keeps them, like an ape, in the corner of his jaw; first mouthed, to be last swallowed: when he needs what you have gleaned, it is but squeezing you, and, sponge, you shall be dry again. [53]

ROSENCRANTZ
I understand you not, my lord.

HAMLET
I am glad of it: a knavish speech sleeps in a foolish ear. [54]

ROSENCRANTZ
My lord, you must tell us where the body is, and go with us to the king.

HAMLET
The body is with the king, but the king is not with the body. The king is a thing—

GUILDENSTERN
A thing, my lord! 30

HAMLET
Of nothing: bring me to him. Hide fox, and all after. [55] [*Exeunt.*

ACT FOUR SCENE THREE

Another room in the castle.

Enter KING *attended.*

KING CLAUDIUS
I have sent to seek him, and to find the body.
How dangerous is it that this man goes loose!
Yet must not we put the strong law on him:
He's loved of the distracted multitude,
Who like not in their judgment, but their eyes;
And where 'tis so, the offender's scourge is weigh'd,
But never the offence. To bear all smooth and even,
This sudden sending him away must seem
Deliberate pause: diseases desperate grown
By desperate appliance are relieved, 11
Or not at all.

Enter ROSENCRANTZ.

How now! what hath befall'n?

ROSENCRANTZ
Where the dead body is bestow'd, my lord,
We cannot get from him.

KING CLAUDIUS
But where is he?

ROSENCRANTZ
Without, my lord; guarded, to know your pleasure.

KING CLAUDIUS
Bring him before us.

ROSENCRANTZ
Ho, Guildenstern! bring in my lord.

Enter HAMLET *and* GUILDENSTERN.

KING CLAUDIUS
Now, Hamlet, where's Polonius?

HAMLET
At supper.

KING CLAUDIUS
At supper! where? 22

HAMLET
Not where he eats, but where he is eaten: a certain convocation of politic worms are e'en at him. Your worm is your only emperor for diet: we fat all creatures else to fat us, and we fat ourselves for maggots: your fat king and your lean beggar is but variable service, two dishes, but to one table: that's the end.

KING CLAUDIUS
Alas, alas! [56]

HAMLET
A man may fish with the worm that hath eat of a king, and cat of the fish that hath fed of that worm. 32

KING CLAUDIUS
What dost you mean by this?

HAMLET
Nothing but to show you how a king may go a progress through the guts of a beggar.

KING CLAUDIUS
Where is Polonius?

HAMLET
In heaven; send hither to see: if your messenger find him not there, seek him i' the other place yourself. But indeed, if you find him not within this month, you shall nose him as you go up the stairs into the lobby.

KING CLAUDIUS
Go seek him there. 41
[*To some Attendants.*

HAMLET
He will stay till ye come. [*Exeunt Attendants.*

KING CLAUDIUS
Hamlet, this deed, for thine especial safety,—[57]
Which we do tender, as we dearly grieve
For that which thou hast done,—must send thee hence
With fiery quickness; therefore prepare thyself;[58]
The bark is ready, and the wind at help,
The associates tend, and every thing is bent
For England.
HAMLET
For England!
KING CLAUDIUS
Ay, Hamlet.
HAMLET
Good.
KING CLAUDIUS
So is it, if thou knew'st our purposes.
HAMLET
I see a cherub that sees them. But, come; for
England! Farewell, dear mother.
KING CLAUDIUS
Thy loving father, Hamlet.
HAMLET
My mother: father and mother is man and wife; man and wife is one flesh; and so, my mother. Come, for England! [*Exit.*
KING CLAUDIUS
Follow him at foot; tempt him with speed aboard;
Delay it not; I'll have him hence to-night:
Away! for every thing is seal'd and done
That else leans on the affair: pray you, make haste.
[*Exeunt Rosencrantz and Guildenstern.*
And, England, if my love thou hold'st at aught—
As my great power thereof may give thee sense,
Since yet thy cicatrice looks raw and red
After the Danish sword, and thy free awe
Pays homage to us—thou mayst not coldly set
Our sovereign process; which imports at full,
By letters congruing to that effect,
The present death of Hamlet. Do it, England;
For like the hectic in my blood he rages,
And thou must cure me: till I know 'tis done,
Howe'er my haps, my joys were ne'er begun.[59]
[*Exit.*

ACT FOUR SCENE FOUR

A plain in Denmark.

Enter FORTINBRAS, *a* Captain, *and* Soldiers, *marching.*

FORTINBRAS
Go, captain, from me greet the Danish king;
Tell him that, by his license, Fortinbras
Craves the conveyance of a promised march[60]
Over his kingdom. You know the rendezvous.
If that his majesty would aught with us,
We shall express our duty in his eye;
And let him know so.
CAPTAIN
I will do't, my lord.
FORTINBRAS
Go softly on. [*Exeunt Fortinbras and Soldiers.*

Enter HAMLET, ROSENCRANTZ, GUILDENSTERN, *and others.*

HAMLET
Good sir, whose powers are these?[61]
CAPTAIN
They are of Norway, sir.
HAMLET
How purposed, sir, I pray you?
CAPTAIN
Against some part of Poland.
HAMLET
Who commands them, sir?
CAPTAIN
The nephew to old Norway, Fortinbras.
HAMLET
Goes it against the main of Poland, sir,
Or some frontier?
CAPTAIN
Truly to speak, and with no addition,
We go to gain a little patch of ground
That hath in it no profit but the name.
To pay five ducats, five, I would not farm it;
Nor will it yield to Norway or the Pole
A ranker rate, should it be sold in fee.
HAMLET
Why, then the Polack never will defend it.
CAPTAIN
Yes, it is already garrison'd.
HAMLET
Two thousand souls and twenty thousand ducats
Will not debate the question of this straw:
This is the imposthume of much wealth and peace,
That inward breaks, and shows no cause without
Why the man dies. I humbly thank you, sir.
CAPTAIN
God be wi' you, sir. [*Exit.*
ROSENCRANTZ
Will't please you go, my lord?
HAMLET
I'll be with you straight. Go a little before.
[*Exeunt all except Hamlet.*
How all occasions do inform against me,
And spur my dull revenge! What is a man,

If his chief good and market of his time
Be but to sleep and feed? a beast, no more.
Sure, he that made us with such large discourse,
Looking before and after, gave us not
That capability and god-like reason
To fust in us unused. Now, whether it be
Bestial oblivion, or some craven scruple
Of thinking too precisely on the event,
A thought which, quarter'd, hath but one part wisdom
And ever three parts coward, I do not know
Why yet I live to say 'This thing's to do;'
Sith I have cause and will and strength and means
To do't. Examples gross as earth exhort me:
Witness this army of such mass and charge
Led by a delicate and tender prince,
Whose spirit with divine ambition puff'd
Makes mouths at the invisible event,
Exposing what is mortal and unsure
To all that fortune, death and danger dare,
Even for an egg-shell. Rightly to be great
Is not to stir without great argument,
But greatly to find quarrel in a straw
When honour's at the stake. How stand I then,
That have a father kill'd, a mother stain'd,
Excitements of my reason and my blood,
And let all sleep? while, to my shame, I see
The imminent death of twenty thousand men,
That, for a fantasy and trick of fame,
Go to their graves like beds, fight for a plot
Whereon the numbers cannot try the cause,
Which is not tomb enough and continent
To hide the slain? O, from this time forth,
My thoughts be bloody, or be nothing worth! [*Exit.*

ACT FOUR SCENE FIVE

Elsinore. A room in the castle.

Enter QUEEN, HORATIO, *and a* Gentleman.

QUEEN GERTRUDE
I will not speak with her.

GENTLEMAN
She is importunate, indeed distract:
Her mood will needs be pitied.

QUEEN GERTRUDE
What would she have?

GENTLEMAN
She speaks much of her father; says she hears
There's tricks i' the world; and hems, and beats her heart;
Spurns enviously at straws; speaks things in doubt,
That carry but half sense: her speech is nothing,
Yet the unshaped use of it doth move
The hearers to collection; they aim at it,
And botch the words up fit to their own thoughts;
Which, as her winks, and nods, and gestures yield them,
Indeed would make one think there might be thought,
Though nothing sure, yet much unhappily.

HORATIO
'Twere good she were spoken with: for she may strew [62]
Dangerous conjectures in ill-breeding minds.

QUEEN GERTRUDE
Let her come in. [*Exit Horatio.*
To my sick soul, as sin's true nature is,
Each toy seems prologue to some great amiss:
So full of artless jealousy is guilt,
It spills itself in fearing to be spilt.

Re-enter HORATIO, *with* OPHELIA.

OPHELIA
Where is the beauteous majesty of Denmark?

QUEEN GERTRUDE
How now, Ophelia!

OPHELIA
[*Sings*] How should I your true love know
From another one?
By his cockle hat and staff,
And his sandal shoon.

QUEEN GERTRUDE
Alas, sweet lady, what imports this song?

OPHELIA
Say you? nay, pray you, mark. [*Sings*] He is dead and gone, lady,
He is dead and gone;
At his head a grass-green turf,
At his heels a stone.

QUEEN GERTRUDE
Nay, but, Ophelia,—

OPHELIA
Pray you, mark. [*Sings*] White his shroud as the mountain snow,—

Enter KING.

QUEEN GERTRUDE
Alas, look here, my lord.

OPHELIA
[*Sings*] Larded with sweet flowers;
Which bewept to the grave did go [63]
With true-love showers.

KING CLAUDIUS
How do you, pretty lady?

OPHELIA
Well, God 'ild you! They say the owl was a baker's daughter. Lord, we know what we are, but know not what we may be.
God be at your table!
KING CLAUDIUS
Conceit upon her father.
OPHELIA
Pray you, let's have no words of this; but when they ask you what it means, say you this:
[*Sings*] To-morrow is Saint Valentine's day, [64]
All in the morning betime,
And I a maid at your window, 56
To be your Valentine.
Then up he rose, and donn'd his clothes,
And dupp'd the chamber-door;
Let in the maid, that out a maid
Never departed more.
KING CLAUDIUS
Pretty Ophelia!
OPHELIA
Indeed, la, without an oath, I'll make an end on't:
[*Sings*] By Gis and by Saint Charity,
Alack, and fie for shame! 65
Young men will do't, if they come to't;
By cock, they are to blame.
Quoth she, before you tumbled me,
You promised me to wed.
So would I ha' done, by yonder sun,
An thou hadst not come to my bed.
KING CLAUDIUS
How long hath she been thus?
OPHELIA
I hope all will be well. We must be patient: but I cannot choose but weep, to think they should lay him i' the cold ground. My brother shall know of it: and so I thank you for your good counsel. Come, my coach! Good night, ladies; good night, sweet ladies; good night, good night. [*Exit.*
KING CLAUDIUS
Follow her close; give her good watch,
I pray you. [*Exit Horatio.*
O, this is the poison of deep grief; it springs
All from her father's death. O Gertrude, Gertrude, [65]
When sorrows come, they come not single spies,
But in battalions. First, her father slain:
Next, your son gone; and he most violent author 86
Of his own just remove: the people muddied,
Thick and unwholesome in their thoughts and whispers,
For good Polonius' death; and we have done but greenly,
In hugger-mugger to inter him: poor Ophelia
Divided from herself and her fair judgement,
Without the which we are pictures, or mere beasts:
Last, and as much containing as all these,
Her brother is in secret come from France;
Feeds on his wonder, keeps himself in clouds, [66]
And wants not buzzers to infect his ear 98
With pestilent speeches of his father's death;
Wherein necessity, of matter beggar'd,
Will nothing stick our person to arraign
In ear and ear. O my dear Gertrude, this,
Like to a murdering-piece, in many places
Gives me superfluous death. [*A noise within.*
QUEEN GERTRUDE
Alack, what noise is this? [67]
KING CLAUDIUS
Where are my Switzers? Let them guard the door.

Enter another Gentleman.

What is the matter?
GENTLEMAN
Save yourself, my lord:
The ocean, overpeering of his list,
Eats not the flats with more impetuous haste
Than young Laertes, in a riotous head, 111
O'erbears your officers. The rabble call him lord;
And, as the world were now but to begin,
Antiquity forgot, custom not known,
The ratifiers and props of every word,
They cry 'Choose we: Laertes shall be king:'
Caps, hands, and tongues, applaud it to the clouds:
'Laertes shall be king, Laertes king!'
QUEEN GERTRUDE
How cheerfully on the false trail they cry!
O, this is counter, you false Danish dogs! 120
KING CLAUDIUS
The doors are broke. [*Noise within.*

Enter LAERTES, *armed*; Danes *following.*

LAERTES
Where is this king? Sirs, stand you all without.
DANES
No, let's come in.
LAERTES
I pray you, give me leave.
DANES
We will, we will. [*They retire without the door.*
LAERTES
I thank you; keep the door. O thou vile king,
Give me my father!
QUEEN GERTRUDE
Calmly, good Laertes.
LAERTES
That drop of blood that's calm proclaims me bastard,
Cries cuckold to my father, brands the harlot

Even here, between the chaste unsmirched brow [68]
Of my true mother.

KING CLAUDIUS
What is the cause, Laertes, 134
That thy rebellion looks so giant-like?
Let him go, Gertrude; do not fear our person:
There's such divinity doth hedge a king,
That treason can but peep to what it would,
Acts little of his will. Tell us, Laertes,
Why thou art thus incensed. Let him go, Gertrude.
Speak, man.

LAERTES
Where is my father?

KING CLAUDIUS
Dead.

QUEEN GERTRUDE
But not by him.

KING CLAUDIUS
Let him demand his fill.

LAERTES
How came he dead? I'll not be juggled with: 146
To hell, allegiance! vows, to the blackest devil!
Conscience and grace, to the profoundest pit!
I dare damnation. To this point I stand,
That both the worlds I give to negligence,
Let come what comes; only I'll be revenged
Most throoughly for my father.

KING CLAUDIUS
Who shall stay you?

LAERTES
My will, not all the world:
And for my means, I'll husband them so well,
They shall go far with little.

KING CLAUDIUS
Good Laertes,
If you desire to know the certainty 158
Of your dear father's death, is't writ in your revenge,
That, swoopstake, you will draw both friend and foe,
Winner and loser?

LAERTES
None but his enemies.

KING CLAUDIUS
Will you know them then?

LAERTES
To his good friends thus wide I'll ope my arms;
And like the kind life-rendering pelican,
Repast them with my blood.

KING CLAUDIUS
Why, now you speak
Like a good child and a true gentleman.
That I am guiltless of your father's death,
And am most sensibly in grief for it, 170
It shall as level to your judgement pierce
As day does to your eye.

DANES
[*Within*] Let her come in.

LAERTES
How now! what noise is that?

Re-enter OPHELIA.

O heat, dry up my brains! tears seven times salt,
Burn out the sense and virtue of mine eye!
By heaven, thy madness shall be paid by weight,
Till our scale turn the beam. O rose of May!
Dear maid, kind sister, sweet Ophelia!
O heavens! is't possible, a young maid's wits
Should be as mortal as an old man's life? [69]
Nature is fine in love, and where 'tis fine, 182
It sends some precious instance of itself
After the thing it loves.

OPHELIA
[*Sings*] They bore him barefaced on the bier
Hey non nonny, nonny, hey nonny;
And in his grave rain'd many a tear:— [70]
Fare you well, my dove!

LAERTES
Hadst thou thy wits, and didst persuade revenge,
It could not move thus.

OPHELIA
[*Sings*] You must sing a-down a-down,
An you call him a-down-a. 192
O, how the wheel becomes it! It is the false steward, that stole his master's daughter. [71]

LAERTES
This nothing's more than matter.

OPHELIA
There's rosemary, that's for remembrance; pray, love, remember: and there is pansies. that's for thoughts.

LAERTES
A document in madness, thoughts and remembrance fitted. 200

OPHELIA
There's fennel for you, and columbines: there's rue for you; and here's some for me: we may call it herb-grace o' Sundays: O, you must wear your rue with a difference. There's a daisy: I would give you some violets, but they withered all when my father died: they say he made a good end,—
[*Sings*] For bonny sweet Robin is all my joy.

LAERTES
Thought and affliction, passion, hell itself,
She turns to favour and to prettiness.

OPHELIA
[*Sings*] And will he not come again?
And will he not come again?

No, no, he is dead:
Go to thy death-bed:
He never will come again.
His beard was as white as snow,
All flaxen was his poll:
He is gone, he is gone, [72]
And we cast away moan:
God ha' mercy on his soul!
And of all Christian souls, I pray God. God be wi' ye. [*Exit.*

LAERTES
Do you see this, O God? 222

KING CLAUDIUS
Laertes, I must commune with your grief,
Or you deny me right. Go but apart,
Make choice of whom your wisest friends you will.
And they shall hear and judge 'twixt you and me:
If by direct or by collateral hand
They find us touch'd, we will our kingdom give,
Our crown, our life, and all that we can ours,
To you in satisfaction; but if not,
Be you content to lend your patience to us,
And we shall jointly labour with your soul
To give it due content.

LAERTES
Let this be so;
His means of death, his obscure funeral—
No trophy, sword, nor hatchment o'er his bones,
No noble rite nor formal ostentation—
Cry to be heard, as 'twere from heaven to earth,
That I must call't in question.

KING CLAUDIUS
So you shall;
And where the offence is let the great axe fall.
I pray you, go with me. [*Exeunt.*

ACT FOUR SCENE SIX

Another room in the castle.

Enter HORATIO *and a* Servant.

HORATIO
What are they that would speak with me?

SERVANT
Sailors, sir: they say they have letters for you. [73]

HORATIO
Let them come in. [*Exit Servant.*
I do not know from what part of the world
I should be greeted, if not from Lord Hamlet.

Enter Sailors.

FIRST SAILOR
God bless you, sir.

HORATIO
Let him bless thee too.

FIRST SAILOR
He shall, sir, an't please him. There's a letter for you, sir; it comes from the ambassador that was bound for England; if your name be Horatio, as I am let to know it is.

HORATIO
[*Reads*] 'Horatio, when thou shalt have overlooked this, give these fellows some means to the king: they have letters for him. Ere we were two days old at sea, a pirate of very warlike appointment gave us chase. Finding ourselves too slow of sail, we put on a compelled valour, and in the grapple I boarded them: on the instant they got clear of our ship; so I alone became their prisoner. They have dealt with me like thieves of mercy: but they knew what they did; I am to do a good turn for them. Let the king have the letters I have sent; and repair thou to me with as much speed as thou wouldst fly death. I have words to speak in thine ear will make thee dumb; yet are they much too light for the bore of the matter. These good fellows will bring thee where I am. Rosencrantz and Guildenstern hold their course for England: of them I have much to tell thee. Farewell.
'He that thou knowest thine, Hamlet.'
Come, I will make you way for these your letters;
And do't the speedier, that you may direct me
To him from whom you brought them. [*Exeunt.*

ACT FOUR SCENE SEVEN

Another room in the castle.

Enter KING *and* LAERTES.

KING CLAUDIUS
Now must your conscience my acquittance seal,
And you must put me in your heart for friend,
Sith you have heard, and with a knowing ear,
That he which hath your noble father slain
Pursued my life.

LAERTES
It well appears: but tell me
Why you proceeded not against these feats,
So crimeful and so capital in nature,
As by your safety, wisdom, all things else,
You mainly were stirr'd up.

KING CLAUDIUS
O, for two special reasons;
Which may to you, perhaps, seem much unsinew'd, 13
But yet to me they are strong. The queen his mother

Lives almost by his looks; and for myself—
My virtue or my plague, be it either which—
She's so conjunctive to my life and soul, [74]
That, as the star moves not but in his sphere,
I could not but by her. The other motive,
Why to a public count I might not go,
Is the great love the general gender bear him;
Who, dipping all his faults in their affection,
Would, like the spring that turneth wood to stone, 24
Convert his gyves to graces; so that my arrows,
Too slightly timber'd for so loud a wind, [75]
Would have reverted to my bow again,
And not where I had aimed them.

LAERTES
And so have I a noble father lost;
A sister driven into desperate terms,
Whose worth, if praises may go back again,
Stood challenger on mount of all the age
For her perfections: but my revenge will come.

KING CLAUDIUS
Break not your sleeps for that: you must not think 35
That we are made of stuff so flat and dull
That we can let our beard be shook with danger
And think it pastime. You shortly shall hear more:
I loved your father, and we love ourself;
And that, I hope, will teach you to imagine—

Enter a Messenger.

How now! what news?

MESSENGER
Letters, my lord, from Hamlet:
This to your majesty; this to the queen.

KING CLAUDIUS
From Hamlet! who brought them?

MESSENGER
Sailors, my lord, they say; I saw them not:
They were given me by Claudio; he received them 48
Of him that brought them.

KING CLAUDIUS
Laertes, you shall hear them. Leave us.
[*Exit Messenger.*

[*Reads*] 'High and mighty, You shall know I am set naked on your kingdom. To-morrow shall I beg leave to see your kingly eyes: when I shall, first asking your pardon thereunto, recount the occasion of my sudden and more strange return.

'HAMLET.'

What should this mean? Are all the rest come back? 57
Or is it some abuse and no such thing?

LAERTES
Know you the hand?

KING CLAUDIUS
'Tis Hamlet's character. 'Naked!'
And in a postscript here, he says 'alone.'
Can you advise me?

LAERTES
I'm lost in it, my lord. But let him come;
It warms the very sickness in my heart,
That I shall live and tell him to his teeth,
'Thus didest thou.'

KING CLAUDIUS
If it be so, Laertes—
As how should it be so? how otherwise?—
Will you be ruled by me?

LAERTES
Ay, my lord; 70
So you will not o'errule me to a peace.

KING CLAUDIUS
To thine own peace. If he be now return'd,
As checking at his voyage, and that he means
No more to undertake it, I will work him
To an exploit, now ripe in my device,
Under the which he shall not choose but fall:
And for his death no wind of blame shall breathe,
But even his mother shall uncharge the practice
And call it accident.

LAERTES
My lord, I will be ruled; [76]
The rather, if you could devise it so 81
That I might be the organ.

KING CLAUDIUS
It falls right.
You have been talk'd of since your travel much,
And that in Hamlet's hearing, for a quality
Wherein, they say, you shine: your sum of parts
Did not together pluck such envy from him
As did that one, and that, in my regard,
Of the unworthiest siege.

LAERTES
What part is that, my lord?

KING CLAUDIUS
A very riband in the cap of youth,
Yet needful too; for youth no less becomes
The light and careless livery that it wears 93
Than settled age his sables and his weeds,
Importing health and graveness. Two months since,
Here was a gentleman of Normandy:—
I've seen myself, and served against, the French,
And they can well on horseback: but this gallant
Had witchcraft in't; he grew unto his seat;
And to such wondrous doing brought his horse,
As he had been incorpsed and demi-natured

With the brave beast: so far he topp'd my thought,
That I, in forgery of shapes and tricks, 104
Come short of what he did.

LAERTES
A Norman was't?

KING CLAUDIUS
A Norman.

LAERTES
Upon my life, Lamond.

KING CLAUDIUS
The very same.

LAERTES
I know him well: he is the brooch indeed
And gem of all the nation.

KING CLAUDIUS
He made confession of you,
And gave you such a masterly report
For art and exercise in your defence
And for your rapier most especial,
That he cried out, 'twould be a sight indeed,
If one could match you: the scrimers of their nation, 119
He swore, had neither motion, guard, nor eye,
If you opposed them. Sir, this report of his
Did Hamlet so envenom with his envy
That he could nothing do but wish and beg
Your sudden coming o'er, to play with him.
Now, out of this,—

LAERTES
What out of this, my lord?

KING CLAUDIUS
Laertes, was your father dear to you?
Or are you like the painting of a sorrow,
A face without a heart?

LAERTES
Why ask you this? 130

KING CLAUDIUS
Not that I think you did not love your father;
But that I know love is begun by time;
And that I see, in passages of proof,
Time qualifies the spark and fire of it.
There lives within the very flame of love
A kind of wick or snuff that will abate it;
And nothing is at a like goodness still;
For goodness, growing to a plurisy,
Dies in his own too much: that we would do,
We should do when we would; for this 'would' changes 141
And hath abatements and delays as many
As there are tongues, are hands, are accidents;
And then this 'should' is like a spendthrift sigh,
That hurts by easing. But, to the quick o' the ulcer:—
Hamlet comes back: what would you undertake,
To show yourself your father's son in deed
More than in words?

LAERTES
To cut his throat i' the church.

KING CLAUDIUS
No place, indeed, should murder sanctuarize;
Revenge should have no bounds. But, good Laertes,
Will you do this, keep close within your chamber. 154
Hamlet return'd shall know you are come home:
We'll put on those shall praise your excellence
And set a double varnish on the fame
The Frenchman gave you, bring you in fine together
And wager on your heads: he, being remiss,
Most generous and free from all contriving,
Will not peruse the foils; so that, with ease,
Or with a little shuffling, you may choose
A sword unbated, and in a pass of practice
Requite him for your father.

LAERTES
I will do't: 165
And, for that purpose, I'll anoint my sword.
I bought an unction of a mountebank,
So mortal that, but dip a knife in it,
Where it draws blood no cataplasm so rare,
Collected from all simples that have virtue
Under the moon, can save the thing from death
That is but scratch'd withal: I'll touch my point
With this contagion, that, if I gall him slightly,
It may be death.

KING CLAUDIUS
Let's further think of this;
Weigh what convenience both of time and means 177
May fit us to our shape: if this should fail,
And that our drift look through our bad performance,
'Twere better not assay'd: therefore this project
Should have a back or second, that might hold,
If this should blast in proof. Soft! let me see:
We'll make a solemn wager on your cunnings:
I ha't:
When in your motion you are hot and dry—
And make your bouts more violent to that end—
And that he calls for drink, I'll have prepared him 188
A chalice for the nonce, whereon but sipping,
If he by chance escape your venom'd stuck,
Our purpose may hold there. [77]

Enter QUEEN.

How now, sweet queen!

QUEEN GERTRUDE
One woe doth tread upon another's heel,
So fast they follow: your sister's drown'd, Laertes.

LAERTES
Drown'd! O, where?

QUEEN GERTRUDE
There is a willow grows aslant a brook,
That shows his hoar leaves in the glassy stream;
There with fantastic garlands did she come
Of crow-flowers, nettles, daisies, and long purples
That liberal shepherds give a grosser name,
But our cold maids do dead men's fingers call them:
There, on the pendent boughs her coronet weeds
Clambering to hang, an envious sliver broke;
When down her weedy trophies and herself
Fell in the weeping brook. Her clothes spread wide;
And, mermaid-like, awhile they bore her up:
Which time she chanted snatches of old tunes; [79]
As one incapable of her own distress,
Or like a creature native and indued
Unto that element: but long it could not be
Till that her garments, heavy with their drink,
Pull'd the poor wretch from her melodious lay
To muddy death.

LAERTES
Alas, then, she is drown'd?

QUEEN GERTRUDE
Drown'd, drown'd.

LAERTES
Too much of water hast thou, poor Ophelia,
And therefore I forbid my tears: but yet
It is our trick; nature her custom holds,
Let shame say what it will: when these are gone,
The woman will be out. Adieu, my lord:
I have a speech of fire, that fain would blaze,
But that this folly douts it. [78] [*Exit.*

KING CLAUDIUS
Let's follow, Gertrude:
How much I had to do to calm his rage!
Now fear I this will give it start again;
Therefore let's follow. [*Exeunt.*

ACT FIVE SCENE ONE

A churchyard.

Enter two Clowns, *with spades, &c.*

FIRST CLOWN
Is she to be buried in Christian burial that wilfully seeks her own salvation?

SECOND CLOWN
I tell thee she is; and therefore make her grave straight: the crowner hath sat on her, and finds it Christian burial.

FIRST CLOWN
How can that be, unless she drowned herself in her own defence?

SECOND CLOWN
Why, 'tis found so.

FIRST CLOWN
It must be 'se offendendo;' it cannot be else. For here lies the point: if I drown myself wittingly, it argues an act: and an act hath three branches; it is, to act, to do, and to perform: argal, she drowned herself wittingly.

SECOND CLOWN
Nay, but hear you, goodman delver,—

FIRST CLOWN
Give me leave. Here lies the water; good: here stands the man; good: if the man go to this water, and drown himself, it is, will he, nill he, he goes,—mark you that; but if the water come to him and drown him, he drowns not himself: argal, he that is not guilty of his own death shortens not his own life.

SECOND CLOWN
But is this law?

FIRST CLOWN
Ay, marry, is't; crowner's quest law.

SECOND CLOWN
Will you ha' the truth on't? If this had not been a gentlewoman, she should have been buried out o' Christian burial.

FIRST CLOWN
Why, there thou say'st: and the more pity that great folk should have countenance in this world to drown or hang themselves, more than their even Christian. Come, my spade. There is no ancient gentleman but gardeners, ditchers, and grave-makers: they hold up Adam's profession.

SECOND CLOWN
Was he a gentleman?

FIRST CLOWN
He was the first that ever bore arms.

SECOND CLOWN
Why, he had none. [80]

FIRST CLOWN
What, art a heathen? How dost thou understand the Scripture? The Scripture says 'Adam digged:' could he dig without arms? I'll put another question to thee: if thou answerest me not to the purpose, confess thyself

SECOND CLOWN
Go to.

FIRST CLOWN
What is he that builds stronger than either the mason, the shipwright, or the carpenter?

SECOND CLOWN
The gallows-maker; for that frame outlives a thousand tenants.

FIRST CLOWN

I like thy wit well, in good faith: the gallows does well; but how does it well? it does well to those that do ill: now thou dost ill to say the gallows is built stronger than the church: argal, the gallows may do well to thee. To't again, come.

SECOND CLOWN

'Who builds stronger than a mason, a shipwright, or a carpenter?'

FIRST CLOWN

Ay, tell me that, and unyoke.

SECOND CLOWN

Marry, now I can tell.

FIRST CLOWN

To't.

SECOND CLOWN

Mass, I cannot tell.

Enter HAMLET *and* HORATIO, *at a distance.*

FIRST CLOWN

Cudgel thy brains no more about it, for your dull ass will not mend his pace with beating; and, when you are asked this question next, say 'a grave-maker:' the houses that he makes last till doomsday. Go, get thee to Yaughan: fetch me a stoup of liquor. [*Exit Second Clown.*

[*He digs and sings.*

In youth, when I did love, did love,
Methought it was very sweet,
To contract, O, the time, for, ah, my behove,
O, methought, there was nothing meet.

HAMLET

Has this fellow no feeling of his business, that he sings at grave-making?

HORATIO

Custom hath made it in him a property of easiness.

HAMLET

'Tis e'en so: the hand of little employment hath the daintier sense.

FIRST CLOWN

[*Sings*]
But age, with his stealing steps,
Hath claw'd me in his clutch,
And hath shipped me intil the land,
As if I had never been such.

[*Throws up a skull.*

HAMLET

That skull had a tongue in it, and could sing once: how the knave jowls it to the ground, as if it were Cain's jaw-bone, that did the first murder! It might be the pate of a politician, which this ass now o'er-reaches; one that would circumvent God, might it not?

HORATIO

It might, my lord.

HAMLET

Or of a courtier; which could say 'Good morrow, sweet lord! How dost thou, good lord?' This might be my lord such-a-one, that praised my lord such-a-one's horse, when he meant to beg it; might it not?

HORATIO

Ay, my lord.

HAMLET

Why, e'en so: and now my Lady Worm's; chapless, and knocked about the mazzard with a sexton's spade: here's fine revolution, an we had the trick to see't. Did these bones cost no more the breeding, but to play at loggats with 'em? mine ache to think on't.

FIRST CLOWN

[Sings]
A pick-axe, and a spade, a spade,
For and a shrouding sheet:
O, a pit of clay for to be made
For such a guest is meet.

[*Throws up another skull.*

HAMLET

There's another: why may not that be the skull of a lawyer? Where be his quiddities now, his quillets, his cases, his tenures, and his tricks? why does he suffer this rude knave now to knock him about the sconce with a dirty shovel, and will not tell him of his action of battery? Hum! This fellow might be in's time a great buyer of land, with his statutes, his recognizances, his fines, his double vouchers, his recoveries: is this the fine of his fines, and the recovery of his recoveries, to have his fine pate full of fine dirt? will his vouchers vouch him no more of his purchases, and double ones too, than the length and breadth of a pair of indentures? The very conveyances of his lands will hardly lie in this box; and must the inheritor himself have no more, ha?

HORATIO

Not a jot more, my lord.

HAMLET

Is not parchment made of sheep-skins?

HORATIO

Ay, my lord, and of calf-skins too.

HAMLET

They are sheep and calves which seek out assurance in that. I will speak to this fellow. Whose grave's this, sirrah?

FIRST CLOWN

Mine, sir.
[*Sings*] O, a pit of clay for to be made
For such a guest is meet.

HAMLET

I think it be thine, indeed; for thou liest in't.

FIRST CLOWN

You lie out on't, sir, and therefore it is not yours: for my part, I do not lie in't, and yet it is mine.

HAMLET

'Thou dost lie in't, to be in't and say it is thine: 'tis for the dead, not for the quick; therefore thou liest.

FIRST CLOWN

'Tis a quick lie, sir; 'twill away gain, from me to you. 123

HAMLET

What man dost thou dig it for?

FIRST CLOWN

For no man, sir.

HAMLET

What woman, then?

FIRST CLOWN

For none, neither.

HAMLET

Who is to be buried in't?

FIRST CLOWN

One that was a woman, sir; but, rest her soul, she's dead.

HAMLET

How absolute the knave is! we must speak by the card, or equivocation will undo us. By the Lord, Horatio, these three years I have taken note of it; the age is grown so picked that the toe of the peasant comes so near the heel of the courtier, he galls his kibe. How long hast thou been a grave-digger?

FIRST CLOWN

All the days i' the year, I came to't that day that our last king Hamlet overcame Fortinbras.

HAMLET

How long is that since?

FIRST CLOWN

Cannot you tell that? every fool can tell that: it was the very day that young Hamlet was born; he that is mad, and sent into England.

HAMLET

Ay, marry, why was he sent into England?

FIRST CLOWN

Why, because he was mad: he shall recover his wits there; or, if he do not, it's no great matter there.

HAMLET

Why?

FIRST CLOWN

'Twill, not be seen in him there; there the men are as mad as he. 148

HAMLET

How came he mad?

FIRST CLOWN

Very strangely, they say.

HAMLET

How strangely?

FIRST CLOWN

Faith, e'en with losing his wits.

HAMLET

Upon what ground?

FIRST CLOWN

Why, here in Denmark: I have been sexton here, man and boy, thirty years.

HAMLET

How long will a man lie i' the earth ere he rot! 156

FIRST CLOWN

I' faith, if he be not rotten before he die—as we have many pocky corses now-a-days, that will scarce hold the laying in—he will last you some eight year or nine year: a tanner will last you nine year.

HAMLET

Why he more than another?

FIRST CLOWN

Why, sir, his hide is so tanned with his trade, that he will keep out water a great while; and your water is a sore decayer of your whoreson dead body. Here's a skull now; this skull has lain in the earth three and twenty years. 166

HAMLET

Whose was it?

FIRST CLOWN

A whoreson mad fellow's it was: whose do you think it was?

HAMLET

Nay, I know not.

FIRST CLOWN

A pestilence on him for a mad rogue! a' poured a flagon of Rhenish on my head once. This same skull, sir, was Yorick's skull, the king's jester.

HAMLET

This? 174

FIRST CLOWN

E'en that.

HAMLET

Let me see. [*Takes the skull.*] Alas, poor Yorick! I knew him, Horatio: a fellow of infinite jest, of most excellent fancy: he bath borne me on his back a thousand times; and now, how abhorred in my imagination it is! my gorge rims at it. Here hung those lips that I have kissed I know not how oft. Where be your gibes now? your gambols? your songs? your flashes of merriment, that were wont to set the table on a roar? Not one now, to mock your own grinning? quite chap-fallen? Now get you to my lady's chamber, and tell her, let her paint an inch thick, to this favour she must come; make her laugh at that. Prithee, Horatio, tell me one thing.

HORATIO

What's that, my lord?

HAMLET

Dost thou think Alexander looked o' this fashion i' the earth?

HAMLET Alas, poor Yorick! I knew him, Horatio.

HORATIO
E'en so. 191

HAMLET
And smelt so? pah!

[*Puts down the skull.*

HORATIO
E'en so, my lord.

HAMLET
To what base uses we may return, Horatio! Why may not imagination trace the noble dust of Alexander, till he find it stopping a bung-hole?

HORATIO
'Twere to consider too curiously, to consider so.

HAMLET
No, faith, not a jot; but to follow him thither with modesty enough, and likelihood to lead it: as thus: Alexander died, Alexander was buried, Alexander returneth into dust; the dust is earth; of earth we make loam; and why of that loam, whereto he was converted, might they not stop a beer-barrel?

Imperious Caesar, dead and turn'd to clay,
Might stop a hole to keep the wind away:
O, that that earth, which kept the world in awe,
Should patch a wall to expel the winter's flaw!
But soft! but soft! aside: here comes the king,

Enter Priest, *&c. in procession; the Corpse of* OPHELIA, LAERTES *and* Mourners *following*; KING, QUEEN, *their trains, &c.*

The queen, the courtiers: who is this they follow? 210
And with such maimed rites? This doth betoken
The corse they follow did with desperate hand
Fordo its own life: 'twas of some estate.
A very noble youth: mark.

[*Retiring with Horatio.*

LAERTES
What ceremony else?

HAMLET
That is Laertes,
A noble youth, mark.

LAERTES
What ceremony else?

FIRST PRIEST
Her obsequies have been as far enlarged
As we have weuranty: her death was doubtful;
And, but that great command o'ersways the order,
She should in ground unsanctified have lodged
Till the last trumpet; for charitable prayers,
Shards, flints and pebbles should be thrown on her;
Yet here she is allow'd her virgin crants,
Her maiden strewments and the bringing home
Of bell and burial.

LAERTES
Must there no more be done?

FIRST PRIEST
No more be done:
We should profane the service of the dead
To sing a requiem and such rest to her
As to peace-parted souls.

LAERTES
Lay her i' the earth:
And from her fair and unpolluted flesh
May violets spring! I tell thee, churlish priest,
A ministering angel shall my sister be,
When thou liest howling.

HAMLET
What, the fair Ophelia!

QUEEN GERTRUDE
Sweets to the sweet: farewell!
[*Scattering flowers.*
I hoped thou shouldst have been my Hamlet's wife;
I thought thy bride-bed to have deck'd, sweet maid,
And not have strew'd thy grave.

LAERTES
O, treble woe [81]
Fall ten times treble on that cursed head,
Whose wicked deed thy most ingenious sense
Deprived thee of! Hold off the earth awhile,
Till I have caught her once more in mine arms:
[*Leaps into the grave.*
Now pile your dust upon the quick and dead,
Till of this flat a mountain you have made,
To o'ertop old Pelion, or the skyish head
Of blue Olympus.

HAMLET
[*Advancing*] What is he whose grief
Bears such an emphasis? whose phrase of sorrow
Conjures the wandering stars, and makes them stand
Like wonder-wounded hearers? This is I,
Hamlet the Dane. [*Leaps into the grave.*

LAERTES
The devil take thy soul!
[*Grappling with him.*

HAMLET
Thou pray'st not well.
I prithee, take thy fingers from my throat;
For, though I am not splenitive and rash,
Yet have I something in me dangerous,
Which let thy wiseness fear: hold off thy hand.

KING CLAUDIUS
Pluck them asunder.

QUEEN GERTRUDE
Hamlet, Hamlet!

ALL
Gentlemen,—

HORATIO
Good my lord, be quiet.
[*The Attendants part them, and they come out of the grave.*

HAMLET
Why I will fight with him upon this theme
Until my eyelids will no longer wag.

QUEEN GERTRUDE
O my son, what theme?

HAMLET
I loved Ophelia: forty thousand brothers
Could not, with all their quantity of love,
Make up my sum. What wilt thou do for her?

KING CLAUDIUS
O, he is mad, Laertes.

QUEEN GERTRUDE
For love of God, forbear him.

HAMLET
'Swounds, show me what thou'lt do:
Woo't weep? woo't fight? woo't fast? woo't tear thyself?
Woo't drink up eisel? eat a crocodile [82]
I'll do't. Dost thou come here to whine?
To outface me with leaping in her grave?
Be buried quick with her, and so will I:
And, if thou prate of mountains, let them throw
Millions of acres on us, till our ground,
Singeing his pate against the burning zone,
Make Ossa like a wart! Nay, an thou'lt mouth,
I'll rant as well as thou.

QUEEN GERTRUDE
This is mere madness:
And thus awhile the fit will work on him;
Anon, as patient as the female dove,
When that her golden couplets are disclosed,
His silence will sit drooping.

HAMLET
Hear you, sir;
What is the reason that you use me thus?
I loved you ever: but it is no matter;
Let Hercules himself do what he may,
The cat will mew and dog will have his day. [*Exit.*

KING CLAUDIUS
I pray you, good Horatio, wait upon him. [*Exit Horatio.*
[*To Laertes*] Strengthen your patience in our last night's speech;
We'll put the matter to the present push.
Good Gertrude, set some watch over your son.
This grave shall have a living monument: 306
An hour of quiet shortly shall we see;
Till then, in patience our proceeding be. [*Exeunt.*

ACT FIVE SCENE TWO

A hall in the castle.

Enter HAMLET *and* HORATIO.

HAMLET
So much for this, sir: now shall you see the other;
You do remember all the circumstance?
HORATIO
Remember it, my lord?
HAMLET
Sir, in my heart there was a kind of fighting,
That would not let me sleep: methought I lay
Worse than the mutines in the bilboes. Rashly,
And praised be rashness for it, let us know,
Our indiscretion sometimes serves us well,
When our deep plots do pall: and that should teach us [83]
There's a divinity that shapes our ends, 11
Rough-hew them how we will,—
HORATIO
That is most certain.
HAMLET
Up from my cabin,
My sea-gown scarf'd about me, in the dark
Groped I to find out them; had my desire,
Finger'd their packet, and in fine withdrew
To mine own room again; making so bold,
My fears forgetting manners, to unseal
Their grand commission; where I found, Horatio,—
O royal knavery!—an exact command,
Larded with many several sorts of reasons 22
Importing Denmark's health and England's too,
With, ho! such bugs and goblins in my life,
That, on the supervise, no leisure bated,
No, not to stay the grinding of the axe,
My head should be struck off.
HORATIO
Is't possible?
HAMLET
Here's the commission: read it at more leisure.
But wilt thou hear me how I did proceed?
HORATIO
I beseech you.
HAMLET
Being thus be-netted round with villanies,—
Ere I could make a prologue to my brains, 33
They had begun the play—I sat me down, [84]
Devised a new commission, wrote it fair:
I once did hold it, as our statists do,
A baseness to write fair and labour'd much
How to forget that learning, but. sir, now
It did me yeoman's service: wilt thou know
The effect of what I wrote?
HORATIO
Ay, good my lord.
HAMLET
An earnest conjuration from the king,
As England was his faithful tributary,
As love between them like the palm might flourish, 45
As peace should still her wheaten garland wear
And stand a comma 'tween their amities,
And many such-like 'As'es of great charge,
That, on the view and knowing of these contents
Without debatement further, more or less,
He should the bearers put to sudden death,
Not shriving-time allow'd.
HORATIO
How was this seal'd?
HAMLET
Why, even in that was heaven ordinant.
I had my father's signet in my purse,
Which was the model of that Danish seal; 56
Folded the writ up in form of the other,
Subscribed it, gave't the impression, placed it safely,
The changeling never known. Now, the next day
Was our sea-fight; and what to this was sequent
Thou know'st already.
HORATIO
So Guildenstern and Rosencrantz go to't.
HAMLET
Why, man, they did make love to this employment; [85]
They are not near my conscience; their defeat
Does by their own insinuation grow:
'Tis dangerous when the baser nature comes
Between the pass and fell incensed points
Of mighty opposites.
HORATIO
Why, what a king is this!
HAMLET
Does it not, think'st thee, stand me now upon—
He that hath kill'd my king and whored my mother,
Popp'd in between the election and my hopes,
Thrown out his angle for my proper life,

And with such cozenage—is't not perfect conscience,
To quit him with this arm? and is't not to be damn'd,
To let this canker of our nature come
In further evil? 79

HORATIO
It must be shortly known to him from England
What is the issue of the business there.

HAMLET
It will be short: the interim is mine;
And a man's life's no more than to say 'One.'
But I am very sorry, good Horatio,
That to Laertes I forgot myself;
For, by the image of my cause, I see
The portraiture of his: I'll court his favours. [86]
But, sure, the bravery of his grief did put me
Into a towering passion.

HORATIO
Peace! who comes here? 90

Enter OSRIC.

OSRIC
Your lordship is right welcome back to Denmark.

HAMLET
I humbly thank you, sir. Dost know this water-fly?

HORATIO
No, my good lord.

HAMLET
Thy state is the more gracious; for 'tis a vice to know him. He hath much land, and fertile: let a beast be lord of beasts, and his crib shall stand at the king's mess: 'tis a chough; but, as I say, spacious in the possession of dirt. 98

OSRIC
Sweet lord, if your lordship were at leisure, I should impart a thing to you from his majesty.

HAMLET
I will receive it, sir, with all diligence of spirit. Put your bonnet to his right use; 'tis for the head.

OSRIC
I thank your lordship, it is very hot.

HAMLET
No, believe me, 'tis very cold; the wind is northerly. 105

OSRIC
It is indifferent cold, my lord, indeed.

HAMLET
But yet methinks it is very sultry and hot for my complexion. [87]

OSRIC
Exceedingly, my lord; it is very sultry,—as 'twere,—I cannot tell how. But, my lord, his majesty bade me signify to you that he has laid a great wager on your head: sir, this is the matter,—

HAMLET
I beseech you, remember—

[*Hamlet moves him to put on his hat.*

OSRIC
Nay, good my lord; for mine ease, in good faith. Sir, here is newly come to court Laertes; believe me, an absolute gentleman, full of most excellent differences, of very soft society and great showing: indeed, to speak feelingly of him, he is the card or calendar of gentry, for you shall find in him the continent of what part a gentleman would see. [88]

HAMLET
Sir, his definement suffers no perdition in you; though, I know, to divide him inventorially would dizzy the arithmetic of memory, and yet but yaw neither, in respect of his quick sail. But, in the verity of extolment, I take him to be a soul of great article; and his infusion of such dearth and rareness, as, to make true direction of him, his semblable is his mirror; and who else would trace him, his umbrage, nothing more.

OSRIC
Your lordship speaks most infallibly of him.

HAMLET
The concernancy, sir? why do we wrap the gentleman in our more rawer breath?

OSRIC
Sir? 132

HORATIO
Is't not possible to understand in another tongue? You will do't, sir, really. [89]

HAMLET
What imports the nomination of this gentleman?

OSRIC
Of Laertes?

HORATIO
His purse is empty already; all's golden words are spent.

HAMLET
Of him, sir.

OSRIC
I know you are not ignorant— 140

HAMLET
I would you did, sir; yet, in faith, if you did, it would not much approve me. Well, sir?

OSRIC
You are not ignorant of what excellence Laertes is—

HAMLET
I dare not confess that, lest I should compare with him in excellence; but, to know a man well, were to know himself.

OSRIC
I mean, sir, for his weapon; but in the imputation laid on him by them, in his meed he's unfellowed. 148

HAMLET
What's his weapon?
OSRIC
Rapier and dagger.
HAMLET
That's two of his weapons: but, well.
OSRIC
The king, sir, hath wagered with him six Barbary horses: against the which he has imponed, as I take it, six French rapiers and poniards, with their assigns, as girdle, hangers, and so: three of the carriages, in faith, are very dear to fancy, very responsive to the hilts, most delicate carriages, and of very liberal conceit. [90]
HAMLET
What call you the carriages?
HORATIO
I knew you must be edified by the margent ere you had done.
OSRIC
The carriages, sir, are the hangers.
HAMLET
The phrase would be more german to the matter, if we could carry cannon by our sides: I would it might be hangers till then. But, on: six Barbary horses against six French swords, their assigns, and three liberal-conceited carriages; that's the French bet against the Danish. Why is this 'imponed,' as you call it?
OSRIC
The king, sir, hath laid, that in a dozen passes between yourself and him, he shall not exceed you three hits: he hath laid on twelve for nine; and it would come to immediate trial, if your lordship would vouchsafe the answer.
HAMLET
How if I answer 'no'?
OSRIC
I mean, my lord, the opposition of your person in
trial. 175
HAMLET
Sir, I will walk here in the hall: if it please his majesty, 'tis the breathing time of day with me; let the foils be brought, the gentleman willing, and the king hold his purpose, I will win for him an I can; if not, I will gain nothing but my shame and the odd hits.
OSRIC
Shall I re-deliver you e'en so?
HAMLET
To this effect, sir; after what flourish your nature will.
OSRIC
I commend my duty to your lordship.
HAMLET
Yours, yours. [*Exit Osric.*] He does well to commend it himself; there are no tongues else for's turn.
HORATIO
This lapwing runs away with the shell on his head.
HAMLET
He did comply with his dug, before he sucked it. Thus has he—and many more of the same breed that I know the drossy age dotes on—only got the tune of the time and outward habit of encounter; a kind of yesty collection, which carries them through and through the most fond and winnowed opinions; and do but blow them to their trial, the bubbles are out. [91]

Enter a Lord.

LORD
My lord, his majesty commended him to you by young Osric, who brings back to him, that you attend him in the hall: he sends to know if your pleasure hold to play with Laertes, or that you will take longer time. [92]
HAMLET
I am constant to my purpose; they follow the king's pleasure: if his fitness speaks, mine is ready; now or
whensoever, provided I be so able as now. 202
LORD
The king and queen and all are coming down.
HAMLET [91]
In happy time.
LORD
The queen desires you to use some gentle entertainment to Laertes before you fall to play.
HAMLET
She well instructs me. [*Exit Lord.*
HORATIO
You will lose this wager, my lord.
HAMLET
I do not think so; since he went into France, I have been in continual practice; I shall win at the odds. But thou wouldst not think how ill all's here about my heart: but it is no matter.
HORATIO
Nay, good my lord,—
HAMLET
It is but foolery; but it is such a kind of gain-giving, as would perhaps trouble a woman.
HORATIO
If your mind dislike any thing, obey it: I will fore-
stall their repair hither, and say you are not fit. 217
HAMLET
Not a whit, we defy augury: there's a special providence in the fall of a sparrow. If it be now, 'tis not to come; if it be not to come, it will be now; if it be not now, yet it will come: the readiness is all: since no man has aught of what he leaves, what is't to leave betimes? Let be [93]

Enter KING, QUEEN, LAERTES, Lords, OSRIC, *and* Attendants *with foils, &c.*

KING CLAUDIUS
Come, Hamlet, come, and take this hand from me.
[The *King puts Laertes' hand into Hamlet's.*

HAMLET
Give me your pardon, sir: I've done you wrong;
But pardon't, as you are a gentleman.
This presence knows,
And you must needs have heard, how I am punish'd 229
With sore distraction. What I have done,
That might your nature, honour and exception
Roughly awake, I here proclaim was madness.
Was't Hamlet wrong'd Laertes? Never Hamlet:
If Hamlet from himself be ta'en away,
And when he's not himself does wrong Laertes,
Then Hamlet does it not, Hamlet denies it.
Who does it, then? His madness: if't be so,
Hamlet is of the faction that is wrong'd;
His madness is poor Hamlet's enemy. 239
Sir, in this audience, [94]
Let my disclaiming from a purposed evil
Free me so far in your most generous thoughts,
That I have shot mine arrow o'er the house,
And hurt my brother. [95]

LAERTES
I am satisfied in nature,
Whose motive, in this case, should stir me most
To my revenge: but in my terms of honour
I stand aloof; and will no reconcilement,
Till by some elder masters, of known honour,
I have a voice and precedent of peace, 250
To keep my name ungored. But till that time,
I do receive your offer'd love like love,
And will not wrong it.

HAMLET
I embrace it freely;
And will this brother's wager frankly play.
Give us the foils. Come on.

LAERTES
Come, one for me.

HAMLET
I'll be your foil, Laertes: in mine ignorance
Your skill shall, like a star i' the darkest night,
Stick fiery off indeed.

LAERTES
You mock me, sir.

HAMLET
No, by this hand.

KING CLAUDIUS
Give them the foils, young Osric. Cousin Hamlet, 264
You know the wager?

HAMLET
Very well, my lord;
Your grace hath laid the odds o' the weaker side.

KING CLAUDIUS
I do not fear it; I have seen you both:
But since he is better'd, we have therefore odds.

LAERTES
This is too heavy, let me see another.

HAMLET
This likes me well. These foils have all a length?
[*They prepare to play.*

OSRIC
Ay, my good lord.

KING CLAUDIUS
Set me the stoops of wine upon that table.
If Hamlet give the first or second hit,
Or quit in answer of the third exchange, 275
Let all the battlements their ordnance fire;
The king shall drink to Hamlet's better breath;
And in the cup an union shall he throw,
Richer than that which four successive kings
In Denmark's crown have worn. Give me the cups;
And let the kettle to the trumpet speak,
The trumpet to the cannoneer without,
The cannons to the heavens, the heavens to earth,
'Now the king drinks to Hamlet.' Come, begin:
And you, the judges, bear a wary eye. 287

HAMLET
Come on, sir.

LAERTES
Come, my lord. [*They play.*

HAMLET
One.

LAERTES
No.

HAMLET
Judgement.

OSRIC
A hit, a very palpable hit.

LAERTES
Well; again.

KING CLAUDIUS
Stay; give me drink. Hamlet, this pearl is thine;
Here's to thy health.
[*Trumpets sound, and cannon shot off within.*
Give him the cup.

HAMLET
I'll play this bout first; set it by awhile.
Come, [*They play.*] Another hit; what say you?

LAERTES
A touch, a touch, I do confess.

KING CLAUDIUS
Our son shall win.
QUEEN GERTRUDE
He's fat, and scant of breath. [96]
Here, Hamlet, take my napkin, rub thy brows:
The queen carouses to thy fortune, Hamlet.
HAMLET
Good madam!
KING CLAUDIUS
Gertrude, do not drink.
QUEEN GERTRUDE
I will, my lord; I pray you, pardon me.
KING CLAUDIUS
[*Aside*] It is the poison'd cup: it is too late.
HAMLET
I dare not drink yet, madam; by and by.
QUEEN GERTRUDE
Come, let me wipe thy face.
LAERTES
My lord, I'll hit him now.
KING CLAUDIUS
I do not think't.
LAERTES
[*Aside*] And yet 'tis almost 'gainst my conscience.
HAMLET
Come, for the third, Laertes: you but dally;
I pray you, pass with your best violence;
I am afeard you make a wanton of me. 317
LAERTES
Say you so? come on. [*They play.*
OSRIC
Nothing, neither way.
LAERTES
Have at you now!
[*Laertes wounds Hamlet; then in scuffling, they change rapiers, and Hamlet wounds Laertes.*
KING CLAUDIUS
Part them: they are incensed.
HAMLET
Nay, come, again. [*The Queen falls.*
OSRIC
Look to the queen there, ho!
HORATIO
They bleed on both sides. How is it, my lord?
OSRIC
How is't, Laertes?
LAERTES
Why, as a woodcock to mine own springe, Osric;
I am justly kill'd with mine own treachery.
HAMLET
How does the queen?
KING CLAUDIUS
She swounds to see them bleed.
QUEEN GERTRUDE
No, no, the drink, the drink,—O my dear Hamlet,— 332
The drink, the drink! I am poison'd. [*Dies.*
HAMLET
O villany! Ho! let the door be lock'd:
Treachery! Seek it out.
LAERTES
It is here, Hamlet: Hamlet, thou art slain;
No medicine in the world can do thee good;
In thee there is not half an hour of life;
The treacherous instrument is in thy hand,
Unbated and envenom'd: the foul practice
Hath turn'd itself onß me; lo, here I lie, 341
Never to rise again: thy mother's poison'd:
I can no more: the king, the king's to blame.
HAMLET
The point! envenom'd too!
Then, venom, to thy work. [*Stabs the King.*
ALL
Treason! treason!
KING CLAUDIUS
O, yet defend me, friends; I am but hurt.
HAMLET
Here, thou incestuous, murderous, damned Dane,
Drink off this potion. Is thy union here?
Follow my mother. [*King dies.*
LAERTES
He is justly served;
It is a poison temper'd by himself.
Exchange forgiveness with me, noble Hamlet:
Mine and my father's death come not upon thee, 355
Nor thine on me. [*Dies.*
HAMLET
Heaven make thee free of it! I follow thee.
I am dead, Horatio. Wretched queen, adieu!
You that look pale and tremble at this chance,
That are but mutes or audience to this act,
Had I but time—as this fell sergeant, death,
Is strict in his arrest—O, I could tell you—
But let it be. Horatio, I am dead;
Thou livest; report me and my cause aright
To the unsatisfied.
HORATIO
Never believe it: 367
I am more an antique Roman than a Dane:
Here's yet some liquor left.
HAMLET
As thou'rt a man,
Give me the cup: let go; by heaven, I'll have't.
O good Horatio, what a wounded name,
Things standing thus unknown, shall live behind me! [97]

FORTINBRAS This quarry cries on havoc.

If thou didst ever hold me in thy heart,
Absent thee from felicity awhile,
And in this harsh world draw thy breath in pain,
To tell my story. [*March afar off, and shot within.*
What warlike noise is this?

OSRIC
Young Fortinbras, with conquest come from
Poland, 381
To the ambassadors of England gives
This warlike volley.

HAMLET
O, I die, Horatio;
The potent poison quite o'er-crows my spirit:
I cannot live to hear the news from England;
But I do prophesy the election lights
On Fortinbras: he has my dying voice;
So tell him, with the occurrents, more and less,
Which have solicited. The rest is silence. [*Dies.*

HORATIO
Now cracks a noble heart. Good night, sweet
prince; 392
And flights of angels sing thee to thy rest!
Why does the drum come hither? [*March within.*

Enter FORTINBRAS, *the* English Ambassadors, *and others.*

FORTINBRAS
Where is this sight?

HORATIO
What is it ye would see?
If aught of woe or wonder, cease your search.

FORTINBRAS
This quarry cries on havoc. O proud death,
What feast is toward in thine eternal cell,
That thou so many princes at a shot
So bloodily hast struck?

FIRST AMBASSADOR
The sight is dismal;
And our affairs from England come too late:
The ears are senseless that should give us
hearing, 405
To tell him his commandment is fulfill'd,
That Rosencrantz and Guildenstern are dead:
Where should we have our thanks?

HORATIO
Not from his mouth,
Had it the ability of life to thank you:

He never gave commandment for their death.
But since, so jump upon this bloody question,
You from the Polack wars, and you from England,
Are here arrived, give order that these bodies
High on a stage be placed to the view;
And let me speak to the yet unknowing world
How these things came about: so shall you hear
Of carnal, bloody, and unnatural acts,
Of accidental judgements, casual slaughters,
Of deaths put on by cunning and forced cause, [97]
And, in this upshot, purposes mistook
Fall'n on the inventors' reads: all this can I
Truly deliver.

FORTINBRAS

Let us haste to hear it,
And call the noblest to the audience.
For me, with sorrow I embrace my fortune:
I have some rights of memory in this kingdom,
Which now to claim my vantage doth invite me.

HORATIO

Of that I shall have also cause to speak,
And from his mouth whose voice will draw on more:
But let this same be presently perform'd,
Even while men's minds are wild; lest more mischance,
On plots and errors, happen.

FORTINBRAS

Let four captains
Bear Hamlet, like a soldier, to the stage;
For he was likely, had he been put on,
To have proved most royally: and, for his passage,
The soldiers' music and the rites of war
Speak loudly for him.
Take up the bodies: such a sight as this
Becomes the field, but here shows much amiss.
Go, bid the soldiers shoot. [*A dead march. Exeunt, bearing off the dead bodies; after which a peal of ordnance is shot off.*

Notes

1. He smote the sledded Polacks on the ice; – Quarto 1, Quarto 2, Folio 1, *'pollax,'* variously interpreted as *'Polaeks,' 'poleauxe,'* &c.; there is very little to be said against the former interpretation, unless it be that 'the ambitious Norway' in the previous sentence would lead one to expect 'the sledded Polack,' a commendable reading originally proposed by Pope.
2. These lines occur in the Quartos, but are omitted in Folios.
3. Eastward, – so Quartos; Folios, *'easterne';* the latter reading was perhaps in Milton's mind, when he wrote:—

   "Now morn her rosy steps in th' eastern clime
   Advancing, sowed the earth with orient pearls."

   Par. Lost, v. 1.
4. To; – the reading of Quartos; Folios, *'of.'*
5. Omitted in Folios.
6. This temple; – so Quartos; Folios, *'his temple.'*
7. Wili, – so Quartos; Folios, *'fear.'*
8. Omitted in Quartos.
9. Particular act and place, – so Quartos; Folios, *'peculiar sect and force.'*
10. Polonius' precepts have been traced back to Euphues' advice to Philautus; the similarity is certainly striking *(vide* Rushtons's *Shakespeare's Euphuism);* others see in the passage a reference to Lord Burleigh's 'ten precepts,' enjoined upon Robert Cecil when about to set out on his travels (French's *Shakespeareana Genealogica, v.* Furness, Vol. II., p. 239).
11. Comrade – (accented on the second syllable), so Folio 1; Quartos (also Quarto 1), *'cowrage.'*
12. Are of a most select and generous chief in that; – so Folio 1; Quarto 1, *'are of a most select and general chiefe in that';* Quarto 2, *'Or of a most select and generous chiefe in that';* the line is obviously incorrect; the simplest emendation of the many proposed is the omission of the words *'of a'* and *'chief,'* which were probably due to marginal corrections of *'in'* and *'best'* in the previous line:—

    "Are most select and generous in that."

    (Collier *'choice'* for *'chief';* Staunton *'sheaf,' i.e.* set, clique, suggested by the Euphuistic phrase "gentlemen of the best sheaf").
13. Running, – Collier's conjecture; Quartos, *'Wrong';* Folio 1, *'Roaming';* Pope, *'Wronging';* Warburton, *'Wronging';* Theobald, *'Ranging.'* &c.
14. Bawds; – Theobald's emendation of *'bonds,'* the reading of Quartos and Folio 1.
15. Omitted in Folio 1 (also Quarto 1).
16. T*he dram of eale*
    Doth all the noble substance of a doubt
    To his own scandal; –

    This famous crux has taxed the ingenuity of generations of scholars, and some fifty various readings and interpretations have been proposed. The general meaning of the words is clear, emphasizing as they do the previous statement that as a man's virtues, be they as pure as grace, shall in the general censure take corruption from one particular fault, even so 'the dram of eale' reduces all the noble substance to its own low level.
    The difficulty of the passage lies in (i.) *'eale'* and (ii.) *'doth … of a doubt';* a simple explanation of (1) is that *'eale'* = *'e'il,' i.e. 'evil'* (similarly in Quarto 2, II. ii. 627, *'deale'* = *'de'ile'* = *'devil').* The chief objection to this plausible conjecture is that one would expect something rather more definite than 'dram of evil'; it is said, however, that *'eale'* is still used in the sense of 'reproach' in the western counties. Theobald proposed 'base,' probably having in mind the lines in *Cymbeline* (III. v. 88):—

    "From whose so many weights of baseness cannot
    A dram of worth be drawn."

As regards (ii.), no very plausible emendation has been proposed; *'of a doubt'* has been taken to be a printer's error for *'often dout,' 'oft endoubt,' 'offer doubt,' 'oft work out,'* &c. To the many questions which these words have called forth, the present writer is rash enough to add one more:—Could, perhaps, 'doth of a doubt' = deprives of the benefit of a doubt? Is there any instance of 'do' in XVIth century English = 'deprive'; the usage is common in modern English slang.

17. Omitted in Folio 1.
18. List, list, O list! – so Quartos; Folio 1, *'list, Hamlet, oh list.'*
19. The stage direction in Quartos:—*Enter old Polonius, with his man or two;* Folios, *Polonius and Reynaldo;* in Quarto 1, *Reynaldo* is called *Montano,* hence perhaps the reading of the later Quarto.
20. To make inquire; – so Quartos; Folios read, *'you make inquiry.'*
21. Omitted in Folios.
22. Three; – so Quarto 1 and Folios; Quartos read *'threescore.'*
23. The reading of Folios; omitted in Quartos.
24. The clown … sere, – omitted in Quartos; *vide* Glossary, "TICKLE O' THE SERE."
25. I think their inhibition comes by the means of the late innovation; vide – PREFACE.
26. Omitted in Quartos.
27. *Cp.:*—

    "I saw the children of Powles last night:
    And troth they pleas'd me pretty, pretty well,
    The apes, in time, will do it handsomely.
    —I like the audience that frequenteth there
    With much applause."
    Jack Drum's Entertainment (1601).

28. Aeneas' tale of Dido; – one cannot but believe that Hamlet's criticism of the play is throughout ironical, and that the speeches quoted are burlesque. "The fancy that a burlesque was intended," wrote Coleridge, "sinks below criticism; the lines, as epic narrative, are superb"; perhaps he would have changed his mind, and would have recognised them as mere parody, if he had read *Dido, Queen of Carthage,* a play left incomplete by Marlowe and finished by Nash *(cp.* e.g. Act II, Sc. i, which seems to be the very passage Shakespeare had in view).
29. Omitted in Folios.
30. Then senseless Ilium; – 527, *'mobled … good';* omitted in Quartos.
31. Whether, – Malone emendation; Quartos, Folios, *'where'* (*i.e. 'wh'ere = whether'*).
32. A speech of some dozen or sixteen lines; – there was much throwing about of brains in the attempt to find these lines in the play-scene in Act III. Sc. ii. "The discussion," as Furness aptly puts it, "is a tribute to Shakespeare's consummate art," and the view of this scholar commends itself—viz., that "in order to give an air of probability to what everyone would feel [otherwise] highly improbable, Shakespeare represents Hamlet as adapting an old play to his present needs by inserting in it some pointed lines."
33. :—

    "Hum, I have heard
    That guilty creatures, sitting at a play," &c.,

    Vide Heywood's *Apology for Actors,* where a number of these stories are collected; perhaps, however, Shakespeare had in mind the plot of *A Warning for Faire Women,* a play on this theme published in 1599, referring to a *cause célèbre* which befell at Lynn in Norfolk.
34. Niggard of question, but of our own demands most free; – Hanmer, *'Most free of our question, but to our demands most niggard';* Warburton, *'Most free of question, but of our demands most niggard';* Collier MS., *'niggard of our question, but to our demands most free.'*
35. To take arms against a sea of troubles, – &c.; the alleged confusion of metaphors in this passage was due to the commentator's ignorance, not to Shakespeare's; *vide* Glossary, *'take arms.'*
36. :—

    "The undiscovered country from whose bourne
    No traveller returns."
    In Catullus' *Elegy on a Sparrow,* occur the words:—

    "Qui nunc it per iter tenebricosum
    Illuc unde negant redire quenquam."

37. Paintings; – so (Quarto 1) Quartos; Folio 1, *'pratlings';* Folios 2, 3, 4, *'pratling';* Pope, *'painting';* Macdonald conjectured *'prancings.'*
38. Nor man; – so Quartos; Folios, *'or Norman.'*
39. There is a striking passage in Quarto 1, omitted in Quarto 2 and Folio, concerning those 'that keep one suit of jests, as a man is known by one suit of apparell'; the lines have a Shakespearian note, and are probably of great interest.
40. Much has been said to explain the introduction of the dumb-show; from the historical point of view its place in a court-play is not surprising, *vide* Glossary, 'DUMB SHOW.'
41. The reading of the Folios; Quarto is:—

    "For women feare too much, even as they love,
    And women's fear and love holds quantity."

    Johnson believed that a line was lost rhyming with *'love.'*
42. In neither ought, or in extremity; – Malone's emendation; Folios, *'In neither ought,'* &c.; Quartos, *'Eyther none, in neither ought,'* &c.
43. Favorite; – Folio 1, *'favourites,'* a reading for which much is to be said.
44. Vienna; – Quarto 1, *'Guyana';* for *'Gonzago,'* Quarto 1 reads *Albertus,* who is throughout called Duke; in Quarto 2 it is always *King;* except here where Hamlet says *'Gonzago is the Duke's name.'*
45. The croaking raven doth bellow for revenge; –

    Cp. "The screeking raven sits croaking for revenge,
    Whole herds of beasts comes bellowing for revenge."
    The True Tragedie of Rich. III.

46. Bitter business as the day; – so Folios; Quartos read *'business as the bitter day.'*
47. Lunacies; – so Folios; Quartos—*'browes.'*

48. Hire and salary; – so Folios; Quartos misprint, *'base and silly.'*
49. Omitted in Folios.
50. And either … the devil; – some such word as *'master,' 'quell,' 'shame,'* has been omitted in Quartos, which read *'and either the devil.'*
51. Omitted in Folios.
52. Folio 1 omits these lines, and ends scene with the words:—

    "And what's untimely done. Oh, come away,
    My soul is full of discord and dismay."
    Theobald proposed to restore the line by adding *'for, haply, slander.'*

53. Like an ape; – so Folios; Quartos, *'like an apple';* Farmer conjectured *'like an ape, an apple';* Singer, from Quarto 1, *'like an ape doth nuts';* Hudson (1879), *'as an ape doth nuts.'*
54. A knavish speech sleeps in a foolish ear; – a sentence proverbial since Shakespeare's time, but not known earlier.
55. Cp. – Psalm cxliv., *'Man is like a thing of naught';* 32-33, *'Hide fox, and all after,'* the reading of Folios; omitted in Quarto.
56. Omitted in Folios.
57. This deed, for thine; – so Quartos; Folios, *'deed of thine, for thine.'*
58. With fiery quickness; – so Folios; omitted in Quartos.
59. My haps, my joys were ne'er begun; – so Folios; Quartos, *'my haps, my joyes will nere begin';* Johnson conjectured *'my hopes, my joys are not begun';* Heath conjectured *"t may hap, my joys will ne'er begin';* Collier MS., *'my hopes, my joyes were ne're begun';* Tschischwitz, *'my joys will ne'er begun.'*
60. Craves; – so Quartos; Folios 1, 2, *'Claimes.'*
61. The reading of the Quartos; omitted in Folios.
62. Quartos and Folios assign these lines to Horatio; Blackstone re-arranged the lines as in the text.
63. Grave; – so Quarto 1, Folios; Quartos, *'ground'; 'did go';* Pope's emendation of Quartos; Folios, *'did not go.'*
64. Song in Quartos; omitted in Folios.
65. Death, O; – Quartos, *'death, and now behold.'*
66. Feeds on his wonder; – Johnson's emendation; Quartos, *'Feeds on this wonder';* Folios, *'keepes on his wonder';* Hanmer, *'Feeds on his anger.'*
67. Alack, what noise is this; – omitted in Quartos.
68. Unsmirched brows; – Grant White's emendation; Folio 1, *'unsmirched brow.'*
69. Omitted in Quartos.
70. Rain'd; – so Quartos; Folios 1, 2, *'raines.'*
71. It is the false steward, – &c.; the story has not yet been identified.
72. Cp. Eastward Hoe – (1604), by Jonson, Marston, and Chapman, for a travesty of the scene and this song (Act III. Sc. i.).
73. Sea-faring men; – so Quartos; Folios read *'Sailors.'*
74. She's so conjunctive; – so Folios; Quartos read *'She is so concline';* Quarto, 1676, *'She is so precious.'*
75. Loud a wind, – so Folios; Quartos 2, 3, *'loued Arm'd';* Quartos 4, 5, *'loued armes.'*
76. My lord … graveness; – omitted in Folios; so, too, 11. 115-124.
77. But stay, what noise?; – the reading of Quartos; omitted in Folios.
78. Douts; – Knight's emendation; Folio 1, *'doubts';* Quartos, *'drownes.'*
78. *'Tunes';* so Folio 1 and Quarto 1; Quarto 2, *'lauds'* (*i.e.* chants).
79. Is this … recoveries; – 130, 202, omitted in Quartos.
80. Treble woe; – the reading of Quartos 2, 3, 6; Folio 1, *'terrible woer';* Folios 2, 3, 4, *'terrible wooer.'*
81. Woo't drink up eisel; vide – Glossary, *'eisel';* the various emendations *'Weissel,' 'Yssel'* (a northern branch of the Rhine), *'Nile,' 'Nilus,'* are all equally unnecessary.
82. Pall; – so Quarto 2; Folio 1, *'parle';* Pope, *'fall.'*
83. They, i.e. – my brains.
84. Omitted in Quartos.
85. Court; – Rowe's emendation of Folios, *'count.'*
86. Or; – Folios read *'for.'*
87. These lines are omitted in Folios, which read, *'Sir, you are not ignorant of what excellence Laertes is at his weapon.'*
88. Another tongue; – Johnson conjectured *'a mother tongue';* Heath conjectured *'a mother tongue?'* No change is necessary; it's a bit of sarcasm.
89. Omitted in Folios.
90. Many more of the same breed; – so Quartos; Folio 1 reads, *'mine more of the same Beauy';* Folios 2, 3, 4, *'nine more of the same Beavy.'*
91. Omitted in Folios.
92. Since no man has aught of what he leaves, what is't to leave betimes? Let be. – The reading is taken partly from the Folios and partly from the Quartos; a long list of proposed emendations is given by the Cambridge editors.
93. Omitted in Quartos.
94. Brother; – so Quartos; Folios read *'mother.'*
95. He's fat and scant of breath; vide – Glossary, 'FAT.'
96. Live; – so Folios; Quartos, *'I leave.'*
97. Forced cause; – so Folios; Quartos read *'for no cause.'*

JULIUS CAESAR

JULIUS CAESAR

DRAMATIS PERSONAE

JULIUS CAESAR, triumvirs after the death of Julius Caesar.
OCTAVIUS CAESAR, triumvirs after the death of Julius Caesar.
MARCUS ANTONIUS, triumvirs after the death of Julius Caesar.
M. AEMILUS LEPIDUS, triumvirs after the death of Julius Caesar.
CICERO, senator.
PUBLIUS, senator.
POPILIUS LENA, senator.
MARCUS BRUTUS, conspirator against Julius Caesar.
CASSIUS, conspirator against Julius Caesar.
CASCA, conspirator against Julius Caesar.
TREBONIUS, conspirator against Julius Caesar.
LIGARIUS, conspirator against Julius Caesar.
DECIUS BRUTUS, conspirator against Julius Caesar.
METELLUS CIMBER, conspirator against Julius Caesar.
CINNA, conspirator against Julius Caesar.
FLAVIUS and MARULLUS, tribunes.
ARTEMIDORUS of Cnidos, a teacher of Rhetoric.
A Soothsayer.
CINNA, a poet. Another Poet
LUCILIUS, friend to Brutus and Cassius.
TITINIUS, friend to Brutus and Cassius.
MESSALA, friend to Brutus and Cassius.
Young CATO, friend to Brutus and Cassius.
VOLUMNIUS, friend to Brutus and Cassius.
VARRO, servant to Brutus.
CLITUS, servant to Brutus.
CLAUDIUS, servant to Brutus.
STRATO, servant to Brutus.
LUCIUS, servant to Brutus.
DARDANIUS, servant to Brutus.
PINDARUS, servant to Cassius.
CALPURNIA, wife to Caesar.
PORTIA, wife to Brutus.
Senators, Citizens, Guards, Attendants, &c.

SCENE: *Rome: the neighbourhood of Sardis: the neighbourhood of Philippi.*

ACT ONE SCENE ONE

Rome. A street.

Enter FLAVIUS, MARULLUS, *and certain* Commoners.

FLAVIUS
Hence! home, you idle creatures, get you home:
Is this a holiday? what! know you not,
Being mechanical, you ought not walk
Upon a labouring day without the sign
Of your profession? Speak, what trade art thou?
FIRST COMMONER
Why, sir, a carpenter.
MARULLUS
Where is thy leather apron and thy rule?
What dost thou with thy best apparel on?
You, sir, what trade are you?

SECOND COMMONER
Truly, sir, in respect of a fine workman, I am but, as you would say, a cobbler.

MARULLUS
But what trade art thou? answer me directly.

SECOND COMMONER
A trade, sir, that, I hope, I may use with a safe conscience: which is, indeed, sir, a mender of bad soles.

MARULLUS
What trade, thou knave? thou naughty knave, what trade?

SECOND COMMONER
Nay, I beseech you, sir, be not out with me: yet, if you be out, sir, I can mend you.

MARULLUS
What meanest thou by that? mend me, thou saucy fellow!

SECOND COMMONER
Why, sir, cobble you.

FLAVIUS
Thou art a cobbler, art thou?

SECOND COMMONER
Truly, sir, all that I live by is with the awl: I meddle with no tradesman's matters, nor women's matters, but with awl. I am, indeed, sir, a surgeon to old shoes; when they are in great danger, I recover them. As proper men as ever trod upon neat's leather have gone upon my handiwork. [1]

FLAVIUS
But wherefore art not in thy shop to-day?
Why dost thou lead these men about the streets?

SECOND COMMONER
Truly, sir, to wear out their shoes, to get myself into more work. But, indeed, sir, we make holiday, to see Caesar and to rejoice in his triumph.

MARULLUS
Wherefore rejoice? What conquest brings he home?
What tributaries follow him to Rome,
To grace in captive bonds his chariot-wheels?
You blocks, you stones, you worse than senseless things!
O you hard hearts, you cruel men of Rome,
Knew you not Pompey? Many a time and oft
Have you climb'd up to walls and battlements,
To towers and windows, yea, to chimney-tops,
Your infants in your arms, and there have sat
The live-long day, with patient expectation,
To see great Pompey pass the streets of Rome:
And when you saw his chariot but appear,
Have you not made an universal shout,
That Tiber trembled underneath her banks,
To hear the replication of your sounds
Made in her concave shores?
And do you now put on your best attire?
And do you now cull out a holiday?
And do you now strew flowers in his way
That comes in triumph over Pompey's blood?
Be gone!
Run to your houses, fall upon your knees,
Pray to the gods to intermit the plague
That needs must light on this ingratitude.

FLAVIUS
Go, go, good countrymen, and, for this fault,
Assemble all the poor men of your sort;
Draw them to Tiber banks, and weep your tears
Into the channel, till the lowest stream
Do kiss the most exalted shores of all.
[*Exeunt all the Commoners.*
See, whether their basest metal be not moved;
They vanish tongue-tied in their guiltiness.
Go you down that way towards the Capitol;
This way will I disrobe the images,
If you do find them deck'd with ceremonies.

MARULLUS
May we do so?
You know it is the feast of Lupercal.

FLAVIUS
It is no matter; let no images
Be hung with Caesar's trophies. I'll about,
And drive away the vulgar from the streets:
So do you too, where you perceive them thick.
These growing feathers pluck'd from Caesar's wing
Will make him fly an ordinary pitch,
Who else would soar above the view of men
And keep us all in servile fearfulness. [*Exeunt.*

ACT ONE SCENE TWO

A public place.
Flourish. Enter CAESAR; ANTONY, *for the course*; CALPURNIA, PORTIA, DECIUS CICERO, BRUTUS, CASSIUS, *and* CASCA; *a great crowd following, among them a* Soothsayer.

CAESAR
Calpurnia!

CASCA
Peace, ho! Caesar speaks.

CAESAR
Calpurnia!

CALPURNIA
Here, my lord.

CAESAR
Stand you directly in Antonius' way,
When he doth run his course. Antonius!

ANTONY
Caesar, my lord?

CAESAR
Forget not, in your speed, Antonius,
To touch Calpurnia; for our elders say,
The barren, touched in this holy chase,
Shake off their sterile curse.

ANTONY
I shall remember:
When Caesar says 'do this,' it is perform'd.

CAESAR
Set on; and leave no ceremony out. [*Flourish.*

SOOTHSAYER
Caesar!

CAESAR
Ha! who calls?

CASCA
Bid every noise be still: peace yet again!

CAESAR
Who is it in the press that calls on me?
I hear a tongue, shriller than all the music,
Cry 'Caesar!' Speak; Caesar is turn'd to hear.

SOOTHSAYER
Beware the ides of March.

CAESAR
What man is that?

BRUTUS
A soothsayer bids you beware the ides of March. [2]

CAESAR
Set him before me; let me see his face.

CASSIUS
Fellow, come from the throng; look upon Caesar.

CAESAR
What say'st thou to me now? speak once again.

SOOTHSAYER
Beware the ides of March.

CAESAR
He is a dreamer; let us leave him: pass. [*Sennet.*
Exeunt all except Brutus and Cassius.

CASSIUS
Will you go see the order of the course?

BRUTUS
Not I.

CASSIUS
I pray you, do.

BRUTUS
I am not gamesome: I do lack some part
Of that quick spirit that is in Antony.
Let me not hinder, Cassius, your desires;
I'll leave you.

CASSIUS
Brutus, I do observe you now of late:
I have not from your eyes that gentleness
And show of love as I was wont to have:
You bear too stubborn and too strange a hand
Over your friend that loves you.

BRUTUS
Cassius,
Be not deceived: if I have veil'd my look,
I turn the trouble of my countenance
Merely upon myself. Vexed I am
Of late with passions of some difference,
Conceptions only proper to myself,
Which give some soil perhaps to my behaviors;
But let not therefore my good friends be grieved—
Among which number, Cassius, be you one—
Nor construe any further my neglect,
Than that poor Brutus, with himself at war,
Forgets the shows of love to other men.

CASSIUS
Then, Brutus, I have much mistook your passion;
By means whereof this breast of mine hath buried
Thoughts of great value, worthy cogitations.
Tell me, good Brutus, can you see your face?

BRUTUS
No, Cassius; for the eye sees not itself.
But by reflection, by some other things.

CASSIUS
'Tis just:
And it is very much lamented, Brutus,
That you have no such mirrors as will turn
Your hidden worthiness into your eye,
That you might see your shadow. I have heard,
Where many of the best respect in Rome,
Except immortal Caesar, speaking of Brutus
And groaning underneath this age's yoke,
Have wish'd that noble Brutus had his eyes.

BRUTUS
Into what dangers would you lead me, Cassius,
That you would have me seek into myself
For that which is not in me?

CASSIUS
Therefore, good Brutus, be prepared to hear:
And since you know you cannot see yourself
So well as by reflection, I, your glass,
Will modestly discover to yourself
That of yourself which you yet know not of.
And be not jealous on me, gentle Brutus;
Were I a common laugher, or did use
To stale with ordinary oaths my love
To every new protester; if you know
That I do fawn on men and hug them hard
And after scandal them, or if you know
That I profess myself in banqueting
To all the rout, then hold me dangerous.
[*Flourish, and shout.*

BRUTUS
What means this shouting? I do fear, the people
Choose Caesar for their king.

CASSIUS
Ay, do you fear it?
Then must I think you would not have it so.

BRUTUS
I would not, Cassius; yet I love him well.
But wherefore do you hold me here so long?
What is it that you would impart to me?
If it be aught toward the general good,
Set honour in one eye and death i' the other,
And I will look on both indifferently:
For let the gods so speed me as I love
The name of honour more than I fear death.

CASSIUS
I know that virtue to be in you, Brutus,
As well as I do know your outward favour.
Well, honour is the subject of my story.
I cannot tell what you and other men
Think of this life; but, for my single self,
I had as lief not be as live to be
In awe of such a thing as I myself.
I was born free as Caesar; so were you:
We both have fed as well, and we can both
Endure the winter's cold as well as he:
For once, upon a raw and gusty day,
The troubled Tiber chafing with her shores,
Caesar said to me 'Darest thou, Cassius, now
Leap in with me into this angry flood,
And swim to yonder point?' Upon the word,
Accoutred as I was, I plunged in
And bade him follow; so indeed he did.
The torrent roar'd, and we did buffet it
With lusty sinews, throwing it aside
And stemming it with hearts of controversy;
But ere we could arrive the point proposed,
Caesar cried 'Help me, Cassius, or I sink!'
I, as Aeneas, our great ancestor,
Did from the flames of Troy upon his shoulder
The old Anchises bear, so from the waves of Tiber
Did I the tired Caesar. And this man
Is now become a god, and Cassius is
A wretched creature and must bend his body,
If Caesar carelessly but nod on him.
He had a fever when he was in Spain,
And when the fit was on him, I did mark
How he did shake: 'tis true, this god did shake:
His coward lips did from their colour fly,
And that same eye whose bend doth awe the world
Did lose his lustre: I did hear him groan:
Ay, and that tongue of his that bade the Romans
Mark him and write his speeches in their books,
Alas, it cried 'Give me some drink, Titinius,'
As a sick girl. Ye gods, it doth amaze me
A man of such a feeble temper should
So get the start of the majestic world
And bear the palm alone. [*Shout. Flourish.*

BRUTUS
Another general shout!
I do believe that these applauses are
For some new honours that are heap'd on Caesar.

CASSIUS
Why, man, he doth bestride the narrow world
Like a Colossus, and we petty men
Walk under his huge legs and peep about
To find ourselves dishonourable graves.
Men at some time are masters of their fates:
The fault, dear Brutus, is not in our stars,
But in ourselves, that we are underlings.
Brutus and Caesar: what should be in that 'Caesar'?
Why should that name be sounded more than yours?
Write them together, yours is as fair a name;
Sound them, it doth become the mouth as well;
Weigh them, it is as heavy; conjure with 'em,
Brutus will start a spirit as soon as Caesar.
Now, in the names of all the gods at once,
Upon what meat doth this our Caesar feed,
That he is grown so great? Age, thou art shamed!
Rome, thou hast lost the breed of noble bloods!
When went there by an age, since the great flood,
But it was famed with more than with one man?
When could they say till now, that talk'd of Rome,
That her wide walls encompass'd but one man? [3]
Now is it Rome indeed and room enough,
When there is in it but one only man.
O, you and I have heard our fathers say,
There was a Brutus once that would have brook'd
The eternal devil to keep his state in Rome
As easily as a king.

BRUTUS
That you do love me, I am nothing jealous;
What you would work me to, I have some aim:
How I have thought of this and of these times,
I shall recount hereafter; for this present,
I would not, so with love I might entreat you,
Be any further moved. What you have said
I will consider; what you have to say
I will with patience hear, and find a time
Both meet to hear and answer such high things.
Till then, my noble friend, chew upon this:
Brutus had rather be a villager
Than to repute himself a son of Rome
Under these hard conditions as this time
Is like to lay upon us.

CASSIUS
I am glad that my weak words
Have struck but thus much show of fire from Brutus.
BRUTUS
The games are done and Caesar is returning.
CASSIUS
As they pass by, pluck Casca by the sleeve;
And he will, after his sour fashion, tell you
What hath proceeded worthy note to-day.

Re-enter CAESAR *and his Train.*

BRUTUS
I will do so. But, look you, Cassius,
The angry spot doth glow on Caesar's brow,
And all the rest look like a chidden train:
Calpurnia's cheek is pale; and Cicero
Looks with such ferret and such fiery eyes
As we have seen him in the Capitol,
Being cross'd in conference by some senators.
CASSIUS
Casca will tell us what the matter is.
CAESAR
Antonius!
ANTONY
Caesar?
CAESAR
Let me have men about me that are fat;
Sleek-headed men and such as sleep o' nights:
Yond Cassius has a lean and hungry look;
He thinks too much: such men are dangerous.
ANTONY
Fear him not, Caesar; he's not dangerous;
He is a noble Roman and well given.
CAESAR
Would he were fatter! But I fear him not:
Yet if my name were liable to fear,
I do not know the man I should avoid
So soon as that spare Cassius. He reads much;
He is a great observer and he looks
Quite through the deeds of men: he loves no plays,
As thou dost, Antony; he hears no music;
Seldom he smiles, and smiles in such a sort
As if he mock'd himself and scorn'd his spirit
That could be moved to smile at any thing.
Such men as he be never at heart's ease
Whiles they behold a greater than themselves,
And therefore are they very dangerous.
I rather tell thee what is to be fear'd
Than what I fear; for always I am Caesar.
Come on my right hand, for this ear is deaf,
And tell me truly what thou think'st of him.
[*Sennet. Exeunt Caesar and all his Train, but Casca.*

CASCA
You pull'd me by the cloak; would you speak with me?
BRUTUS
Ay, Casca; tell us what hath chanced to-day,
That Caesar looks so sad.
CASCA
Why, you were with him, were you not?
BRUTUS
I should not then ask Casca what had chanced.
CASCA
Why, there was a crown offered him: and being offered him, he put it by with the back of his hand, thus; and then the people fell a-shouting.
BRUTUS
What was the second noise for?
CASCA
Why, for that too.
CASSIUS
They shouted thrice: what was the last cry for?
CASCA
Why, for that too.
BRUTUS
Was the crown offered him thrice?
CASCA
Ay, marry, was't, and he put it by thrice every time gentler than other, and at every putting-by mine honest neighbours shouted.
CASSIUS
Who offered him the crown?
CASCA
Why, Antony.
BRUTUS
Tell us the manner of it, gentle Casca.
CASCA
I can as well be hanged as tell the manner of it: it was mere foolery; I did not mark it. I saw Mark Antony offer him a crown;—yet 'twas not a crown neither, 'twas one of these coronets;—and, as I told you, he put it by once: but, for all that, to my thinking, he would fain have had it. Then he offered it to him again; then he put it by again: but, to my thinking, he was very loath to lay his fingers off it. And then he offered it the third time; he put it the third time by: and still as he refused it, the rabblement hooted and clapped their chopped hands and threw up their sweaty night-caps and uttered such a deal of stinking breath because Caesar refused the crown that it had almost choked Caesar; for he swounded and fell down at it: and for mine own part, I durst not laugh, for fear of opening my lips and receiving the bad air.
CASSIUS
But, soft, I pray you: what, did Caesar swound?
CASCA
He fell down in the market-place, and foamed at mouth, and was speechless.

BRUTUS
'Tis very like: he hath the failing sickness. [4]
CASSIUS
No, Caesar hath it not; but you and I
And honest Casca, we have the falling sickness.
CASCA
I know not what you mean by that; but, I am sure, Caesar fell down. If the rag-tag people did not clap him and hiss him, according as he pleased and displeased them, as they use to do the players in the theatre, I am no true man.
BRUTUS
What said he when he came unto himself?
CASCA
Marry, before he fell down, when he perceived the common herd was glad he refused the crown, he plucked me ope his doublet and offered them his throat to cut. An I had been a man of any occupation, if I would not have taken him at a word, I would I might go to hell among the rogues. And so he fell. When he came to himself again, he said, If he had done or said any thing amiss, he desired their worships to think it was his infirmity. Three or four wenches, where I stood, cried 'Alas, good soul!' and forgave him with all their hearts: but there's no heed to be taken of them; if Caesar had stabbed their mothers, they would have done no less.
BRUTUS
And after that, he came, thus sad, away?
CASCA
Ay.
CASSIUS
Did Cicero say any thing?
CASCA
Ay, he spoke Greek.
CASSIUS
To what effect?
CASCA
Nay, an I tell you that, I'll ne'er look you i' the face again: but those that understood him smiled at one another and shook their heads; but, for mine own part, it was Greek to me. I could tell you more news too: Marullus and Flavius, for pulling scarfs off Caesar's images, are put to silence. Fare you well. There was more foolery yet, if I could remember it.
CASSIUS
Will you sup with me to-night, Casca?
CASCA
No, I am promised forth.
CASSIUS
Will you dine with me to-morrow?
CASCA
Ay, if I be alive and your mind hold and your dinner worth the eating.
CASSIUS
Good: I will expect you.
CASCA
Do so. Farewell, both. *[Exit.*
BRUTUS
What a blunt fellow is this grown to be!
He was quick mettle when he went to school.
CASSIUS
So is he now in execution
Of any bold or noble enterprise,
However he puts on this tardy form.
This rudeness is a sauce to his good wit,
Which gives men stomach to digest his words
With better appetite.
BRUTUS
And so it is. For this time I will leave you:
To-morrow, if you please to speak with me,
I will come home to you; or, if you will,
Come home to me, and I will wait for you.
CASSIUS
I will do so: till then, think of the world. *[Exit Brutus.*
Well, Brutus, thou art noble; yet, I see,
Thy honourable metal may be wrought
From that it is disposed: therefore it is meet
That noble minds keep ever with their likes;
For who so firm that cannot be seduced?
Caesar doth bear me hard; but he loves Brutus:
If I were Brutus now and he were Cassius,
He should not humour me. I will this night, [5]
In several hands, in at his windows throw,
As if they came from several citizens,
Writings all tending to the great opinion
That Rome holds of his name; wherein obscurely
Caesar's ambition shall be glanced at:
And after this let Caesar seat him sure;
For we will shake him, or worse days endure.
[Exit.

ACT ONE SCENE THREE

The same. A street.

Thunder and lightning. Enter, from opposite sides, CASCA, *with his sword drawn, and* CICERO.

CICERO
Good even, Casca: brought you Caesar home?
Why are you breathless? and why stare you so?
CASCA
Are you not moved, when all the sway of earth
Shakes like a thing unfirm? O Cicero,
I have seen tempests, when the scolding winds
Have rived the knotty oaks, and I have seen

The ambitious ocean swell and rage and foam,
To be exalted with the threatening clouds:
But never till to-night, never till now,
Did I go through a tempest dropping fire.
Either there is a civil strife in heaven,
Or else the world, too saucy with the gods,
Incenses them to send destruction.

CICERO
Why, saw you any thing more wonderful?

CASCA
A common slave—you know him well by sight—
Held up his left hand, which did flame and burn
Like twenty torches join'd, and yet his hand,
Not sensible of fire, remain'd unscorch'd.
Besides—I ha' not since put up my sword—
Against the Capitol I met a lion,
Who glared upon me, and went surly by,
Without annoying me: and there were drawn
Upon a heap a hundred ghastly women,
Transformed with their fear; who swore they saw
Men all in fire walk up and down the streets.
And yesterday the bird of night did sit
Even at noon-day upon the market-place,
Hooting and shrieking. When these prodigies
Do so conjointly meet, let not men say
'These are their reasons; they are natural;' [6]
For, I believe, they are portentous things
Unto the climate that they point upon.

CICERO
Indeed, it is a strange-disposed time:
But men may construe things after their fashion,
Clean from the purpose of the things themselves.
Come Caesar to the Capitol to-morrow?

CASCA
He doth; for he did bid Antonius
Send word to you he would be there to-morrow.

CICERO
Good night then, Casca: this disturbed sky
Is not to walk in.

CASCA
Farewell, Cicero. [*Exit Cicero.*

Enter CASSIUS.

CASSIUS
Who's there?

CASCA
A Roman.

CASSIUS
Casca, by your voice.

CASCA
Your ear is good. Cassius, what night is this!

CASSIUS
A very pleasing night to honest men.

CASCA
Who ever knew the heavens menace so?

CASSIUS
Those that have known the earth so full of faults.
For my part, I have walk'd about the streets,
Submitting me unto the perilous night,
And, thus unbraced, Casca, as you see,
Have bared my bosom to the thunder-stone;
And when the cross blue lightning seem'd to open
The breast of heaven, I did present myself
Even in the aim and very flash of it.

CASCA
But wherefore did you so much tempt the heavens?
It is the part of men to fear and tremble,
When the most mighty gods by tokens send
Such dreadful heralds to astonish us.

CASSIUS
You are dull, Casca, and those sparks of life
That should be in a Roman you do want,
Or else you use not. You look pale and gaze
And put on fear and cast yourself in wonder,
To see the strange impatience of the heavens:
But if you would consider the true cause
Why all these fires, why all these gliding ghosts,
Why birds and beasts from quality and kind,
Why old men fool and children calculate, [7]
Why all these things change from their ordinance
Their natures and preformed faculties
To monstrous quality,—why, you shall find
That heaven hath infused them with these spirits,
To make them instruments of fear and warning
Unto some monstrous state.
Now could I, Casca, name to thee a man
Most like this dreadful night,
That thunders, lightens, opens graves, and roars
As doth the lion in the Capitol,
A man no mightier than thyself or me
In personal action, yet prodigious grown
And fearful, as these strange eruptions are.

CASCA
'Tis Caesar that you mean; is it not, Cassius?

CASSIUS
Let it be who it is: for Romans now
Have thews and limbs like to their ancestors;
But, woe the while! our fathers' minds are dead,
And we are govern'd with our mothers' spirits;
Our yoke and sufferance show us womanish.

CASCA
Indeed, they say the senators tomorrow
Mean to establish Caesar as a king;
And he shall wear his crown by sea and land,
In every place, save here in Italy.

CASSIUS
I know where I will wear this dagger then;
Cassius from bondage will deliver Cassius:
Therein, ye gods, you make the weak most strong;
Therein, ye gods, you tyrants do defeat:
Nor stony tower, nor walls of beaten brass,
Nor airless dungeon, nor strong links of iron,
Can be retentive to the strength of spirit;
But life, being weary of these worldly bars,
Never lacks power to dismiss itself.
If I know this, know all the world besides,
That part of tyranny that I do bear
I can shake off at pleasure. [*Thunder still.*

CASCA
So can I:
So every bondman in his own hand bears
The power to cancel his captivity.

CASSIUS
And why should Caesar be a tyrant then?
Poor man! I know he would not be a wolf,
But that he sees the Romans are but sheep:
He were no lion, were not Romans hinds.
Those that with haste will make a mighty fire
Begin it with weak straws: what trash is Rome,
What rubbish and what offal, when it serves
For the base matter to illuminate
So vile a thing as Caesar! But, O grief,
Where hast thou led me? I perhaps speak this
Before a willing bondman; then I know
My answer must be made. But I am arm'd,
And dangers are to me indifferent.

CASCA
You speak to Casca, and to such a man
That is no fleering tell-tale. Hold, my hand:
Be factious for redress of all these griefs,
And I will set this foot of mine as far
As who goes farthest.

CASSIUS
There's a bargain made.
Now know you, Casca, I have moved already
Some certain of the noblest-minded Romans
To undergo with me an enterprise
Of honourable dangerous consequence;
And I do know, by this, they stay for me
In Pompey's porch: for now, this fearful night,
There is no stir or walking in the streets;
And the complexion of the element
In favour's like the work we have in hand, [8]
Most bloody, fiery, and most terrible.

CASCA
Stand close awhile, for here comes one in haste.

CASSIUS
'Tis Cinna; I do know him by his gait;
He is a friend.

Enter CINNA.

Cinna, where haste you so?

CINNA
To find out you. Who's that? Metellus Cimber?

CASSIUS
No, it is Casca; one incorporate
To our attempts. Am I not stay'd for, Cinna?

CINNA
I am glad on't. What a fearful night is this!
There's two or three of us have seen strange sights.

CASSIUS
Am I not stay'd for? tell me.

CINNA
Yes, you are.
O Cassius, if you could
But win the noble Brutus to our party—

CASSIUS
Be you content: good Cinna, take this paper,
And look you lay it in the praetor's chair,
Where Brutus may but find it; and throw this
In at his window; set this up with wax
Upon old Brutus' statue: all this done,
Repair to Pompey's porch, where you shall find us.
Is Decius Brutus and Trebonius there?

CINNA
All but Metellus Cimber; and he's gone
To seek you at your house. Well, I will hie,
And so bestow these papers as you bade me.

CASSIUS
That done, repair to Pompey's theatre.
[*Exit Cinna.*
Come, Casca, you and I will yet ere day
See Brutus at his house: three parts of him
Is ours already, and the man entire
Upon the next encounter yields him ours.

CASCA
O, he sits high in all the people's hearts:
And that which would appear offence in us,
His countenance, like richest alchemy,
Will change to virtue and to worthiness.

CASSIUS
Him and his worth and our great need of him
You have right well conceited. Let us go,
For it is after midnight; and ere day
We will awake him and be sure of him. [*Exeunt.*

ACT TWO SCENE ONE

Rome. Brutus's orchard.

Enter BRUTUS.

BRUTUS
What, Lucius, ho!

I cannot, by the progress of the stars,
Give guess how near to day. Lucius, I say!
I would it were my fault to sleep so soundly.
When, Lucius, when? awake, I say! what, Lucius!

Enter LUCIUS.

LUCILIUS
Call'd you, my lord?
BRUTUS
Get me a taper in my study, Lucius:
When it is lighted, come and call me here.
LUCILIUS
I will, my lord. [*Exit.*
BRUTUS
It must be by his death: and for my part, 10
I know no personal cause to spurn at him,
But for the general. He would be crown'd:
How that might change his nature, there's the question.
It is the bright day that brings forth the adder;
And that craves wary walking. Crown him?—that;—
And then, I grant, we put a sting in him,
That at his will he may do danger with.
The abuse of greatness is, when it disjoins
Remorse from power: and, to speak truth of Caesar,
I have not known when his affections sway'd
More than his reason. But 'tis a common proof,
That lowliness is young ambition's ladder,
Whereto the climber-upward turns his face;
But when he once attains the upmost round.
He then unto the ladder turns his back,
Looks in the clouds, scorning the base degrees
By which he did ascend. So Caesar may.
Then, lest he may, prevent. And, since the quarrel
Will bear no colour for the thing he is,
Fashion it thus; that what he is, augmented,
Would run to these and these extremities:
And therefore think him as a serpent's egg
Which, hatch'd, would, as his kind, grow mischievous,
And kill him in the shell.

Re-enter LUCIUS.

LUCILIUS
The taper burneth in your closet, sir.
Searching the window for a flint, I found
This paper, thus seal'd up; and, I am sure,
It did not lie there when I went to bed.
[*Gives him the letter.*
BRUTUS
Get you to bed again; it is not day.
Is not to-morrow, boy, the ides of March? [9]
LUCILIUS
I know not, sir. 43
BRUTUS
Look in the calendar, and bring me word.
LUCILIUS
I will, sir. [*Exit.*
BRUTUS
The exhalations whizzing in the air
Give so much light that I may read by them.
[*Opens the letter and reads.*
'Brutus, thou sleep'st: awake, and see thyself.
Shall Rome, &c. Speak, strike, redress!
Brutus, thou sleep'st: awake!'
Such instigations have been often dropp'd
Where I have took them up. 52
'Shall Rome, &c.' Thus must I piece it out:
Shall Rome stand under one man's awe? What, Rome?
My ancestors did from the streets of Rome
The Tarquin drive, when he was call'd a king.
'Speak, strike, redress!' Am I entreated
To speak and strike? O Rome, I make thee promise;
If the redress will follow, thou receivest
Thy full petition at the hand of Brutus!

Re-enter LUCIUS.

LUCILIUS
Sir, March is wasted fourteen days.
[*Knocking within.*
BRUTUS
'Tis good. Go to the gate; somebody knocks.
[*Exit Lucius.* 63
Since Cassius first did whet me against Caesar,
I have not slept.
Between the acting of a dreadful thing
And the first motion, all the interim is
Like a phantasma, or a hideous dream:
The Genius and the mortal instruments
Are then in council; and the state of man,
Like to a little kingdom, suffers then
The nature of an insurrection.

Re-enter LUCIUS.

LUCILIUS
Sir, 'tis your brother Cassius at the door, 73
Who doth desire to see you.
BRUTUS
Is he alone?
LUCILIUS
No, sir, there are moe with him.
BRUTUS
Do you know them?
LUCILIUS
No, sir; their hats are pluck'd about their ears,
And half their faces buried in their cloaks,
That by no means I may discover them
By any mark of favour.

BRUTUS
Let 'em enter. [*Exit Lucius.*
They are the faction. O conspiracy,
Shamest thou to show thy dangerous brow by night,
When evils are most free? O, then by day
Where wilt thou find a cavern dark enough
To mask thy monstrous visage? Seek none, conspiracy;
Hide it in smiles and affability:
For if thou path, thy native semblance on, [10]
Not Erebus itself were dim enough
To hide thee from prevention.

Enter the conspirators, CASSIUS, CASCA, DECIUS, CINNA, METELLUS CIMBER, *and* TREBONIUS.

CASSIUS
I think we are too bold upon your rest:
Good morrow, Brutus; do we trouble you?
BRUTUS
I have been up this hour, awake all night.
Know I these men that come along with you?
CASSIUS
Yes, every man of them, and no man here
But honours you; and every one doth wish
You had but that opinion of yourself
Which every noble Roman bears of you.
This is Trebonius.
BRUTUS
He is welcome hither.
CASSIUS
This, Decius Brutus.
BRUTUS
He is welcome too.
CASSIUS
This, Casca; this, Cinna; and this, Metellus Cimber.
BRUTUS
They are all welcome.
What watchful cares do interpose themselves
Betwixt your eyes and night?
CASSIUS
Shall I entreat a word?
[*Brutus and Cassius whisper.*
DECIUS
Here lies the east: doth not the day break here?
CASCA
No.
CINNA
O, pardon, sir, it doth; and yon gray lines
That fret the clouds are messengers of day.
CASCA
You shall confess that you are both deceived.
Here, as I point my sword, the sun arises,
Which is a great way growing on the south,
Weighing the youthful season of the year.
Some two months hence up higher toward the north
He first presents his fire; and the high east
Stands, as the Capitol, directly here.
BRUTUS
Give me your hands all over, one by one.
CASSIUS
And let us swear our resolution.
BRUTUS
No, not an oath: if not the face of men,
The sufferance of our souls, the time's abuse,—
If these be motives weak, break off betimes,
And every man hence to his idle bed;
So let high-sighted tyranny range on,
Till each man drop by lottery. But if these,
As I am sure they do, bear fire enough
To kindle cowards and to steel with valour
The melting spirits of women, then, countrymen,
What need we any spur but our own cause,
To prick us to redress? what other bond
Than secret Romans, that have spoke the word,
And will not palter? and what other oath
Than honesty to honesty engaged,
That this shall be, or we will fall for it?
Swear priests and cowards and men cautelous,
Old feeble carrions and such suffering souls
That welcome wrongs; unto bad causes swear
Such creatures as men doubt; but do not stain
The even virtue of our enterprise,
Nor the insuppressive mettle of our spirits,
To think that or our cause or our performance
Did need an oath; when every drop of blood
That every Roman bears, and nobly bears,
Is guilty of a several bastardy,
If he do break the smallest particle
Of any promise that hath pass'd from him.
CASSIUS
But what of Cicero? shall we sound him?
I think he will stand very strong with us.
CASCA
Let us not leave him out.
CINNA
No, by no means.
METELLUS
O, let us have him, for his silver hairs
Will purchase us a good opinion
And buy men's voices to commend our deeds:
It shall be said, his judgement ruled our hands;
Our youths and wildness shall no whit appear,
But all be buried in his gravity.
BRUTUS
O, name him not: let us not break with him;
For he will never follow any thing
That other men begin.

CASSIUS
Then leave him out.
CASCA
Indeed he is not fit.
DECIUS
Shall no man else be touch'd but only Caesar?
CASSIUS
Decius, well urged: I think it is not meet,
Mark Antony, so well beloved of Caesar,
Should outlive Caesar: we shall find of him
A shrewd contriver; and, you know, his means,
If he improve them, may well stretch so far
As to annoy us all: which to prevent,
Let Antony and Caesar fall together.
BRUTUS
Our course will seem too bloody, Caius Cassius,
To cut the head off and then hack the limbs,
Like wrath in death and envy afterwards;
For Antony is but a limb of Caesar:
Let us be sacrificers, but not butchers, Caius.
We all stand up against the spirit of Caesar;
And in the spirit of men there is no blood:
O, that we then could come by Caesar's spirit,
And not dismember Caesar! But, alas,
Caesar must bleed for it! And, gentle friends,
Let's kill him boldly, but not wrathfully;
Let's carve him as a dish fit for the gods,
Not hew him as a carcass fit for hounds:
And let our hearts, as subtle masters do,
Stir up their servants to an act of rage,
And after seem to chide 'em. This shall make
Our purpose necessary and not envious:
Which so appearing to the common eyes,
We shall be call'd purgers, not murderers.
And for Mark Antony, think not of him;
For he can do no more than Caesar's arm
When Caesar's head is off.
CASSIUS
Yet I fear him;
For in the ingrafted love he bears to Caesar—
BRUTUS
Alas, good Cassius, do not think of him:
If he love Caesar, all that he can do
Is to himself, take thought and die for Caesar:
And that were much he should; for he is given
To sports, to wildness and much company.
TREBONIUS
There is no fear in him; let him not die;
For he will live, and laugh at this hereafter.
[*Clock strikes.*
BRUTUS
Peace! count the clock.
CASSIUS
The clock hath stricken three.
TREBONIUS
'Tis time to part.
CASSIUS
But it is doubtful yet,
Whether Caesar will come forth to-day, or no;
For he is superstitious grown of late,
Quite from the main opinion he held once
Of fantasy, of dreams and ceremonies:
It may be, these apparent prodigies,
The unaccustom'd terror of this night,
And the persuasion of his augurers,
May hold him from the Capitol to-day.
DECIUS
Never fear that: if he be so resolved,
I can o'ersway him; for he loves to hear
That unicorns may be betray'd with trees,
And bears with glasses, elephants with holes,
Lions with toils and men with flatterers;
But when I tell him he hates flatterers,
He says he does, being then most flattered.
Let me work;
For I can give his humour the true bent,
And I will bring him to the Capitol.
CASSIUS
Nay, we will all of us be there to fetch him.
BRUTUS
By the eighth hour: is that the uttermost?
CINNA
Be that the uttermost, and fail not then.
METELLUS
Caius Ligarius doth bear Caesar hard,
Who rated him for speaking well of Pompey:
I wonder none of you have thought of him.
BRUTUS
Now, good Metellus, go along by him:
He loves me well, and I have given him reasons;
Send him but hither, and I'll fashion him.
CASSIUS
The morning comes upon 's: we'll leave you, Brutus.
And, friends, disperse yourselves; but all remember
What you have said, and show yourselves true Romans.
BRUTUS
Good gentlemen, look fresh and merrily;
Let not our looks put on our purposes,
But bear it as our Roman actors do,
With untired spirits and formal constancy:
And so good morrow to you every one.
[*Exeunt all but Brutus.*
Boy! Lucius! Fast asleep? It is no matter;
Enjoy the honey-heavy dew of slumber:
Thou hast no figures nor no fantasies,
Which busy care draws in the brains of men;
Therefore thou sleep'st so sound.

Enter PORTIA.

PORTIA
Brutus, my lord!

BRUTUS
Portia, what mean you? wherefore rise you now?
It is not for your health thus to commit
Your weak condition to the raw cold morning.

PORTIA
Nor for yours neither. You've ungently, Brutus,
Stole from my bed: and yesternight, at supper,
You suddenly arose, and walk'd about,
Musing and sighing, with your arms across,
And when I ask'd you what the matter was,
You stared upon me with ungentle looks;
I urged you further; then you scratch'd your head,
And too impatiently stamp'd with your foot;
Yet I insisted, yet you answer'd not,
But, with an angry wafture of your hand,
Gave sign for me to leave you: so I did;
Fearing to strengthen that impatience
Which seem'd too much enkindled, and withal
Hoping it was but an effect of humour,
Which sometime hath his hour with every man.
It will not let you eat, nor talk, nor sleep,
And could it work so much upon your shape
As it hath much prevail'd on your condition,
I should not know you, Brutus. Dear my lord,
Make me acquainted with your cause of grief.

BRUTUS
I am not well in health, and that is all.

PORTIA
Brutus is wise, and, were he not in health,
He would embrace the means to come by it.

BRUTUS
Why, so I do. Good Portia, go to bed.

PORTIA
Is Brutus sick? and is it physical
To walk unbraced and suck up the humours
Of the dank morning? What, is Brutus sick,
And will he steal out of his wholesome bed,
To dare the vile contagion of the night
And tempt the rheumy and unpurged air
To add unto his sickness? No, my Brutus;
You have some sick offence within your mind,
Which, by the right and virtue of my place,
I ought to know of: and, upon my knees,
I charm you, by my once-commended beauty,
By all your vows of love and that great vow
Which did incorporate and make us one,
That you unfold to me, yourself, your half,
Why you are heavy, and what men to-night
Have had to resort to you: for here have been
Some six or seven, who did hide their faces
Even from darkness.

BRUTUS
Kneel not, gentle Portia.

PORTIA
I should not need, if you were gentle Brutus.
Within the bond of marriage, tell me, Brutus,
Is it excepted I should know no secrets
That appertain to you? Am I yourself
But, as it were, in sort or limitation,
To keep with you at meals, comfort your bed,
And talk to you sometimes? Dwell I but in the suburbs
Of your good pleasure? If it be no more,
Portia is Brutus' harlot, not his wife.

BRUTUS
You are my true and honourable wife,
As dear to me as are the ruddy drops
That visit my sad heart

PORTIA
If this were true, then should I know this secret.
I grant I am a woman; but withal
A woman that Lord Brutus took to wife:
I grant I am a woman; but withal
A woman well-reputed, Cato's daughter.
Think you I am no stronger than my sex,
Being so father'd and so husbanded?
Tell me your counsels, I will not disclose 'em:
I have made strong proof of my constancy,
Giving myself a voluntary wound
Here, in the thigh: can I bear that with patience.
And not my husband's secrets?

BRUTUS
O ye gods,
Render me worthy of this noble wife!
[*Knocking within.*
Hark, hark! one knocks: Portia, go in awhile;
And by and by thy bosom shall partake
The secrets of my heart.
All my engagements I will construe to thee,
All the charactery of my sad brows:
Leave me with haste. [*Exit Portia.*
Lucius, who's that knocks?

Re-enter LUCIUS *with* LIGARIUS.

LUCILIUS
Here is a sick man that would speak with you.

BRUTUS
Caius Ligarius, that Metellus spake of.
Boy, stand aside. Caius Ligarius! how?

LIGARIUS
Vouchsafe good morrow from a feeble tongue.

BRUTUS
O, what a time have you chose out, brave Caius,
To wear a kerchief! Would you were not sick!

PORTIA Tell me your counsels, I will not disclose 'em.

LIGARIUS
I am not sick, if Brutus have in hand
Any exploit worthy the name of honour.

BRUTUS
Such an exploit have I in hand, Ligarius,
Had you a healthful ear to hear of it.

LIGARIUS
By all the gods that Romans bow before,
I here discard my sickness! Soul of Rome!
Brave son, derived from honourable loins!
Thou, like an exorcist, hast conjured up
My mortified spirit. Now bid me run,
And I will strive with things impossible;
Yea, get the better of them. What's to do?

BRUTUS
A piece of work that will make sick men whole.

LIGARIUS
But are not some whole that we must make sick?

BRUTUS
That must we also. What it is, my Caius,
I shall unfold to thee, as we are going
To whom it must be done.

LIGARIUS
Set on your foot,
And with a heart new-fired I follow you,
To do I know not what: but it sufficeth
That Brutus leads me on.

BRUTUS
Follow me, then. [*Exeunt.*

ACT TWO SCENE TWO

Caesar's house.

Thunder and lightning. Enter CAESAR, *in his night-gown.*

CAESAR
Nor heaven nor earth have been at peace to-night:
Thrice hath Calpurnia in her sleep cried out,
'Help, ho! they murder Caesar!' Who's within?

Enter a Servant.

SERVANT
My lord?

CAESAR
Go bid the priests do present sacrifice
And bring me their opinions of success.
SERVANT
I will, my lord. [*Exit.*

Enter CALPURNIA.

CALPURNIA
What mean you, Caesar? think you to walk forth?
You shall not stir out of your house to-day.
CAESAR
Caesar shall forth: the things that threaten'd me
Ne'er look'd but on my back; when they shall see
The face of Caesar, they are vanished.
CALPURNIA
Caesar, I never stood on ceremonies,
Yet now they fright me. There is one within,
Besides the things that we have heard and seen,
Recounts most horrid sights seen by the watch.
A lioness hath whelped in the streets;
And graves have yawn'd, and yielded up their dead;
Fierce fiery warriors fought upon the clouds, [11]
In ranks and squadrons and right form of war,
Which drizzled blood upon the Capitol;
The noise of battle hurtled in the air,
Horses did neigh, and dying men did groan,
And ghosts did shriek and squeal about the streets.
O Caesar! these things are beyond all use,
And I do fear them.
CAESAR
What can be avoided
Whose end is purposed by the mighty gods?
Yet Caesar shall go forth; for these predictions
Are to the world in general as to Caesar.
CALPURNIA
When beggars die, there are no comets seen;
The heavens themselves blaze forth the death of princes.
CAESAR
Cowards die many times before their deaths;
The valiant never taste of death but once.
Of all the wonders that I yet have heard.
It seems to me most strange that men should fear;
Seeing that death, a necessary end,
Will come when it will come.

Re-enter Servant.

What say the augurers?
SERVANT
They would not have you to stir forth to-day.
Plucking the entrails of an offering forth,
They could not find a heart within the beast.
CAESAR
The gods do this in shame of cowardice:
Caesar should be a beast without a heart,
If he should stay at home to-day for fear.
No, Caesar shall not: danger knows full well
That Caesar is more dangerous than he:
We are two lions litter'd in one day, [12]
And I the elder and more terrible:
And Caesar shall go forth.
CALPURNIA
Alas, my lord,
Your wisdom is consumed in confidence.
Do not go forth to-day: call it my fear
That keeps you in the house, and not your own.
We'll send Mark Antony to the senate-house;
And he shall say you are not well to-day:
Let me, upon my knee, prevail in this.
CAESAR
Mark Antony shall say I am not well;
And, for thy humour, I will stay at home.

Enter DECIUS.

Here's Decius Brutus, he shall tell them so.
DECIUS
Caesar, all hail! good morrow, worthy Caesar:
I come to fetch you to the senate-house.
CAESAR
And you are come in very happy time,
To bear my greeting to the senators.
And tell them that I will not come to-day:
Cannot, is false, and that I dare not, falser:
I will not come to-day: tell them so, Decius.
CALPURNIA
Say he is sick.
CAESAR
Shall Caesar send a lie?
Have I in conquest stretch'd mine arm so far,
To be afraid to tell graybeards the truth?
Decius, go tell them Caesar will not come.
DECIUS
Most mighty Caesar, let me know some cause,
Lest I be laugh'd at when I tell them so.
CAESAR
The cause is in my will: I will not come;
That is enough to satisfy the senate.
But for your private satisfaction,
Because I love you, I will let you know:
Calpurnia here, my wife, stays me at home:
She dreamt to-night she saw my statua,
Which, like a fountain with an hundred spouts,
Did run pure blood: and many lusty Romans
Came smiling, and did bathe their hands in it:
And these does she apply for warnings, and portents,

And evils imminent; and on her knee
Hath begg'd that I will stay at home to-day.

DECIUS
This dream is all amiss interpreted;
It was a vision fair and fortunate:
Your statue spouting blood in many pipes,
In which so many smiling Romans bathed,
Signifies that from you great Rome shall suck
Reviving blood, and that great men shall press
For tinctures, stains, relics and cognizance.
This by Calpurnia's dream is signified.

CAESAR
And this way have you well expounded it.

DECIUS
I have, when you have heard what I can say:
And know it now: the senate have concluded
To give this day a crown to mighty Caesar.
If you shall send them word you will not come,
Their minds may change. Besides, it were a mock
Apt to be render'd, for some one to say
'Break up the senate till another time,
When Caesar's wife shall meet with better dreams.'
If Caesar hide himself, shall they' not whisper
'Lo, Caesar is afraid'?
Pardon me, Caesar; for my dear dear love
To your proceeding bids me tell you this;
And reason to my love is liable.

CAESAR
How foolish do your fears seem now, Calpurnia!
I am ashamed I did yield to them.
Give me my robe, for I will go.

Enter PUBLIUS, BRUTUS, LIGARIUS, METELLUS, CASCA, TREBONIUS, *and* CINNA.

And look where Publius is come to fetch me.

PUBLIUS
Good morrow, Caesar.

CAESAR
Welcome, Publius.
What, Brutus, are you stirr'd so early too?
Good morrow, Casca. Caius Ligarius,
Caesar was ne'er so much your enemy
As that same ague which has made you lean.
What is 't o'clock?

BRUTUS
Caesar, 'tis strucken eight.

CAESAR
I thank you for your pains and courtesy.

Enter ANTONY.

See! Antony, that revels long o' nights,
Is notwithstanding up. Good morrow, Antony.

ANTONY
So to most noble Caesar.

CAESAR
Bid them prepare within:
I am to blame to be thus waited for.
Now, Cinna: now, Metellus: what, Trebonius!
I have an hour's talk in store for you;
Remember that you call on me to-day:
Be near me, that I may remember you.

TREBONIUS
Caesar, I will: [*Aside*] and so near will I be,
That your best friends shall wish I had been further.

CAESAR
Good friends, go in, and taste some wine with me:
And we, like friends, will straightway go together.

BRUTUS
[*Aside*] That every like is not the same, O Caesar,
The heart of Brutus yearns to think upon!
[*Exeunt.*

ACT TWO SCENE THREE

A street near the Capitol.

Enter ARTEMIDORUS, *reading a paper.*

ARTEMIDORUS
'Caesar, beware of Brutus; take heed of Cassius; come not near Casca; have an eye to Cinna; trust not Trebonius; mark well Metellus Cimber: Decius Brutus loves thee not: thou hast wronged Caius Ligarius. There is but one mind in all these men, and it is bent against Caesar. If thou beest not immortal, look about you: security gives way to conspiracy. The mighty gods defend thee! Thy lover,
'ARTEMIDORUS'.
Here will I stand till Caesar pass along,
And as a suitor will I give him this.
My heart laments that virtue cannot live
Out of the teeth of emulation.
If thou read this, O Caesar, thou mayst live;
If not, the Fates with traitors do contrive. [*Exit.*

ACT TWO SCENE FOUR

Another part of the same street, before the house of Brutus.

Enter PORTIA *and* LUCIUS.

PORTIA
I prithee, boy, run to the senate-house;
Stay not to answer me, but get thee gone:
Why dost thou stay?

LUCILIUS
To know my errand, madam.

PORTIA
I would have had thee there, and here again,
Ere I can tell thee what thou shouldst do there.
O constancy, be strong upon my side,
Set a huge mountain 'tween my heart and tongue!
I have a man's mind, but a woman's might.
How hard it is for women to keep counsel!
Art thou here yet?

LUCILIUS
Madam, what should I do? 12
Run to the Capitol, and nothing else?
And so return to you, and nothing else?

PORTIA
Yes, bring me word, boy, if thy lord look well,
For he went sickly forth: and take good note
What Caesar doth, what suitors press to him.
Hark, boy! what noise is that?

LUCILIUS
I hear none, madam.

PORTIA
Prithee, listen well;
I heard a bustling rumour, like a fray,
And the wind brings it from the Capitol.

LUCILIUS
Sooth, madam, I hear nothing. 23

Enter the Soothsayer.

PORTIA
Come hither, fellow: which way hast thou been?

SOOTHSAYER
At mine own house, good lady.

PORTIA
What is 't clock?

SOOTHSAYER
About the ninth hour, lady.

PORTIA
Is Caesar yet gone to the Capitol?

SOOTHSAYER
Madam, not yet: I go to take my stand,
To see him pass on to the Capitol.

PORTIA
Thou hast some suit to Caesar, hast thou not?

SOOTHSAYER
That I have, lady: if it will please Caesar
To be so good to Caesar as to hear me,
I shall beseech him to befriend himself. 34

PORTIA
Why, know'st thou any harm's intended towards him?

SOOTHSAYER
None that I know will be, much that I fear may chance.
Good morrow to you. Here the street is narrow:
The throng that follows Caesar at the heels,
Of senators, of praetors, common suitors,
Will crowd a feeble man almost to death:
I'll get me to a place more void, and there
Speak to great Caesar as he comes along. [*Exit*.

PORTIA
I must go in. Ay, me, how weak a thing
The heart of woman is! O Brutus, 46
The heavens speed thee in thine enterprise!
Sure, the boy heard me: Brutus hath a suit
That Caesar will not grant. O, I grow faint.
Run, Lucius, and commend me to my lord;
Say I am merry: come to me again,
And bring me word what he doth say to thee.
[*Exeunt severally*.

ACT THREE SCENE ONE

Rome. Before the Capitol; the Senate sitting above.

A crowd of people; among them ARTEMIDORUS *and the* Soothsayer. *Flourish. Enter* CAESAR, BRUTUS, CASSIUS, CASCA, DECIUS, METELLUS, TREBONIUS, CINNA, ANTONY, LEPIDUS, POPILIUS, PUBLIUS, *and others*.

CAESAR
[*To the Soothsayer*] The ides of March are come.

SOOTHSAYER
Ay, Caesar; but not gone.

ARTEMIDORUS
Hail, Caesar! read this schedule.

DECIUS
Trebonius doth desire you to o'erread,
At your best leisure, this his humble suit.

ARTEMIDORUS
O Caesar, read mine first; for mine's a suit
That touches Caesar nearer: read it, great Caesar.

CAESAR
What touches us ourself shall be last served.

ARTEMIDORUS
Delay not, Caesar; read it instantly.

CAESAR
What, is the fellow mad?

PUBLIUS
Sirrah, give place. 11

CASSIUS
What, urge you your petitions in the street?
Come to the Capitol.
[*CAESAR goes up to the Senate-House, the rest following*.

POPILIUS
I wish your enterprise to-day may thrive.

CASSIUS
What enterprise, Popilius?

POPILIUS
Fare you well. [*Advances to Caesar.*
BRUTUS
What said Popilius Lena?
CASSIUS
He wish'd to-day our enterprise might thrive.
I fear our purpose is discovered.
BRUTUS
Look, how he makes to Caesar: mark him.
CASSIUS
Casca, be sudden, for we fear prevention.
Brutus, what shall be done? If this be known,
Cassius or Caesar never shall turn back,
For I will slay myself.
BRUTUS
Cassius, be constant:
Popilius Lena speaks not of our purposes;
For, look, he smiles, and Caesar doth not change.
CASSIUS
Trebonius knows his time; for, look you, Brutus.
He draws Mark Antony out of the way.
[*Exeunt Antony and Trebonius.*
DECIUS
Where is Metellus Cimber? Let him go,
And presently prefer his suit to Caesar.
BRUTUS
He is address'd: press near and second him.
CINNA
Casca, you are the first that rears your hand.
CAESAR
Are we all ready? What is now amiss
That Caesar and his senate must redress?
METELLUS
Most high, most mighty, and most puissant Caesar,
Metellus Cimber throws before thy seat
An humble heart,— [*Kneeling.*
CAESAR
I must prevent thee, Cimber.
These couchings and these lowly courtesies
Might fire the blood of ordinary men,
And turn pre-ordinance and first decree
Into the law of children. Be not fond, [13]
To think that Caesar bears such rebel blood
That will be thaw'd from the true quality
With that which melteth fools; I mean, sweet words,
Low-crooked court'sies and base spaniel-fawning.
Thy brother by decree is banished:
If thou dost bend and pray and fawn for him,
I spurn thee like a cur out of my way.
Know, Caesar doth not wrong, nor without cause [14]
Will he be satisfied.
METELLUS
Is there no voice more worthy than my own,
To sound more sweetly in great Caesar's ear
For the repealing of my banish'd brother?
BRUTUS
I kiss thy hand, but not in flattery, Caesar;
Desiring thee that Publius Cimber may
Have an immediate freedom of repeal.
CAESAR
What, Brutus!
CASSIUS
Pardon, Caesar; Caesar, pardon:
As low as to thy foot doth Cassius fall,
To beg enfranchisement for Publius Cimber.
CASSIUS
I could be well moved, if I were as you;
If I could pray to move, prayers would move me:
But I am constant as the northern star,
Of whose true-fix'd and resting quality
There is no fellow in the firmament.
The skies are painted with unnumber'd sparks,
They are all fire and every one doth shine,
But there's but one in all doth hold his place:
So in the world; 'tis furnish'd well with men,
And men are flesh and blood, and apprehensive;
Yet in the number I do know but one
That unassailable holds on his rank,
Unshaked of motion: and that I am he,
Let me a little show it, even in this;
That I was constant Cimber should be banish'd,
And constant do remain to keep him so.
CINNA
O Caesar,—
CAESAR
Hence! wilt thou lift up Olympus?
DECIUS
Great Caesar,—
CAESAR
Doth not Brutus bootless kneel?
CASCA
Speak, hands, for me!
[*Casca first, then the other Conspirators and Marcus Brutus stab Caesar.*
CAESAR
Et tu, Brute! Then fall, Caesar! [15] [*Dies.*
CINNA
Liberty! Freedom! Tyranny is dead!
Run hence, proclaim, cry it about the streets.
CASSIUS
Some to the common pulpits, and cry out
'Liberty, freedom, and enfranchisement!'
BRUTUS
People and senators, be not affrighted;
Fly not; stand stiff: ambition's debt is paid.

CASCA
Go to the pulpit, Brutus.
DECIUS
And Cassius too.
BRUTUS
Where's Publius?
CINNA
Here, quite confounded with this mutiny.
METELLUS
Stand fast together, lest some friend of Caesar's
Should chance—
BRUTUS
Talk not of standing. Publius, good cheer;
There is no harm intended to your person,
Nor to no Roman else: so tell them, Publius.
CASSIUS
And leave us, Publius; lest that the people,
Rushing on us, should do your age some mischief.
BRUTUS
Do so: and let no man abide this deed,
But we the doers.

Re-enter TREBONIUS.

CASSIUS
Where is Antony?
TREBONIUS
Fled to his house amazed:
Men, wives and children stare, cry out and run
As it were doomsday.
BRUTUS
Fates, we will know your pleasures:
That we shall die, we know; 'tis but the time
And drawing days out, that men stand upon.
CASSIUS
Why, he that cuts off twenty years of life
Cuts off so many years of fearing death.
BRUTUS
Grant that, and then is death a benefit:
So are we Caesar's friends, that have abridged
His time of fearing death. Stoop, Romans, stoop, [16]
And let us bathe our hands in Caesar's blood
Up to the elbows, and besmear our swords:
Then walk we forth, even to the market-place,
And, waving our red weapons o'er our heads,
Let's all cry 'Peace, freedom and liberty!'
CASSIUS
Stoop, then, and wash. How many ages hence
Shall this our lofty scene be acted over
In states unborn and accents yet unknown!
BRUTUS
How many times shall Caesar bleed in sport,
That now on Pompey's basis lies along
No worthier than the dust!
CASSIUS
So oft as that shall be,
So often shall the knot of us be call'd
The men that gave their country liberty.
DECIUS
What, shall we forth?
CASSIUS
Ay, every man away:
Brutus shall lead; and we will grace his heels
With the most boldest and best hearts of Rome.

Enter a Servant.

BRUTUS
Soft! who comes here? A friend of Antony's.
SERVANT
Thus, Brutus, did my master bid me kneel;
Thus did Mark Antony bid me fall down;
And being prostrate, thus he bade me say:
Brutus is noble, wise, valiant, and honest;
Caesar was mighty, bold, royal, and loving:
Say I love Brutus, and I honour him;
Say I fear'd Caesar, honour'd him and loved him.
If Brutus will vouchsafe that Antony
May safely come to him, and be resolved
How Caesar hath deserved to lie in death,
Mark Antony shall not love Caesar dead
So well as Brutus living; but will follow
The fortunes and affairs of noble Brutus
Thorough the hazards of this untrod state
With all true faith. So says my master Antony.
BRUTUS
Thy master is a wise and valiant Roman;
I never thought him worse.
Tell him, so please him come unto this place,
He shall be satisfied; and, by my honour,
Depart untouch'd.
SERVANT
I'll fetch him presently. [*Exit.*
BRUTUS
I know that we shall have him well to friend.
CASSIUS
I wish we may: but yet have I a mind
That fears him much; and my misgiving still
Falls shrewdly to the purpose.
BRUTUS
But here comes Antony.

Re-enter ANTONY.

Welcome, Mark Antony.
ANTONY
O mighty Caesar! dost thou lie so low?
Are all thy conquests, glories, triumphs, spoils,
Shrunk to this little measure? Fare thee well.
I know not, gentlemen, what you intend,

Who else must be let blood, who else is rank:
If I myself, there is no hour so fit
As Caesar's death hour, nor no instrument
Of half that worth as those your swords, made rich
With the most noble blood of all this world.
I do beseech ye, if you bear me hard,
Now, whilst your purpled hands do reek and smoke,
Fulfil your pleasure. Live a thousand years,
I shall not find myself so apt to die:
No place will please me so, no mean of death,
As here by Caesar, and by you cut off,
The choice and master spirits of this age.

BRUTUS
O Antony, beg not your death of us.
Though now we must appear bloody and cruel,
As, by our hands and this our present act,
You see we do, yet see you but our hands
And this the bleeding business they have done:
Our hearts you see not; they are pitiful;
And pity to the general wrong of Rome—
As fire drives out fire, so pity pity—
Hath done this deed on Caesar. For your part,
To you our swords have leaden points, Mark Antony:
Our arms, in strength of malice, and our hearts [17]
Of brothers' temper, do receive you in
With all kind love, good thoughts, and reverence.

CASSIUS
Your voice shall be as strong as any man's
In the disposing of new dignities.

BRUTUS
Only be patient till we have appeased
The multitude, beside themselves with fear,
And then we will deliver you the cause,
Why I, that did love Caesar when I struck him,
Have thus proceeded.

ANTONY
I doubt not of your wisdom.
Let each man render me his bloody hand:
First, Marcus Brutus, will I shake with you;
Next, Caius Cassius, do I take your hand;
Now, Decius Brutus, yours; now yours, Metellus;
Yours, Cinna; and, my valiant Casca, yours;
Though last, not last in love, yours, good Trebonius.
Gentlemen all,—alas, what shall I say?
My credit now stands on such slippery ground,
That one of two bad ways you must conceit me,
Either a coward or a flatterer.
That I did love thee, Caesar, O, 'tis true:
If then thy spirit look upon us now,
Shall it not grieve thee dearer than thy death,
To see thy Anthony making his peace,
Shaking the bloody fingers of thy foes,
Most noble! in the presence of thy corse?
Had I as many eyes as thou hast wounds,
Weeping as fast as they stream forth thy blood,
It would become me better than to close
In terms of friendship with thine enemies.
Pardon me, Julius! Here wast thou bay'd, brave hart;
Here didst thou fall; and here thy hunters stand,
Sign'd in thy spoil, and crimson'd in thy lethe.
O world, thou wast the forest to this hart;
And this, indeed, O world, the heart of thee.
How like a deer, strucken by many princes,
Dost thou here lie!

CASSIUS
Mark Antony,—

ANTONY
Pardon me, Caius Cassius:
The enemies of Caesar shall say this;
Then, in a friend, it is cold modesty.

CASSIUS
I blame you not for praising Caesar so;
But what compact mean you to have with us?
Will you be prick'd in number of our friends;
Or shall we on, and not depend on you?

ANTONY
Therefore I took your hands, but was, indeed,
Sway'd from the point, by looking down on Caesar.
Friends am I with you all and love you all,
Upon this hope, that you shall give me reasons
Why and wherein Caesar was dangerous.

BRUTUS
Or else were this a savage spectacle:
Our reasons are so full of good regard
That were you, Antony, the son of Caesar,
You should be satisfied.

ANTONY
That's all I seek:
And am moreover suitor that I may
Produce his body to the market-place;
And in the pulpit, as becomes a friend,
Speak in the order of his funeral.

BRUTUS
You shall, Mark Antony.

CASSIUS
Brutus, a word with you.
[*Aside to Brutus*] You know not what you do: do not consent
That Antony speak in his funeral:
Know you how much the people may be moved
By that which he will utter?

BRUTUS
By your pardon;
I will myself into the pulpit first,
And show the reason of our Caesar's death:
What Antony shall speak, I will protest
He speaks by leave and by permission,
And that we are contented Caesar shall

ANTONY How like a deer, strucken by many princes, dost thou here lie!

Have all true rites and lawful ceremonies.
It shall advantage more than do us wrong.

CASSIUS
I know not what may fall; I like it not.

BRUTUS
Mark Antony, here, take you Caesar's body.
You shall not in your funeral speech blame us,
But speak all good you can devise of Caesar,
And say you do't by our permission;
Else shall you not have any hand at all
About his funeral: and you shall speak
In the same pulpit whereto I am going,
After my speech is ended.

ANTONY
Be it so;
I do desire no more.

BRUTUS
Prepare the body then, and follow us.

[*Exeunt all but Antony.*

ANTONY
O, pardon me, thou bleeding piece of earth,
That I am meek and gentle with these butchers!
Thou art the ruins of the noblest man
That ever lived in the tide of times.
Woe to the hand that shed this costly blood!
Over thy wounds now do I prophesy,—
Which, like dumb mouths, do ope their ruby lips,
To beg the voice and utterance of my tongue—
A curse shall light upon the limbs of men; [18]
Domestic fury and fierce civil strife
Shall cumber all the parts of Italy;
Blood and destruction shall be so in use
And dreadful objects so familiar
That mothers shall but smile when they behold
Their infants quarter'd with the hands of war;
All pity choked with custom of fell deeds:
And Caesar's spirit, ranging for revenge,
With Ate by his side come hot from hell,
Shall in these confines with a monarch's voice
Cry 'Havoc,' and let slip the dogs of war;
That this foul deed shall smell above the earth
With carrion men, groaning for burial.

Enter a Servant.

You serve Octavius Caesar, do you not?

SERVANT
I do, Mark Antony.

ANTONY
Caesar did write for him to come to Rome.
SERVANT
He did receive his letters, and is coming;
And bid me say to you by word of mouth—
O Caesar!— [*Seeing the body.*
ANTONY
Thy heart is big, get thee apart and weep.
Passion, I see, is catching; for mine eyes,
Seeing those beads of sorrow stand in thine,
Began to water. Is thy master coming?
SERVANT
He lies to-night within seven leagues of Rome.
ANTONY
Post back with speed, and tell him what hath chanced:
Here is a mourning Rome, a dangerous Rome,
No Rome of safety for Octavius yet; 316
Hie hence, and tell him so. Yet, stay awhile;
Thou shalt not back till I have borne this corse
Into the market-place: there shall I try,
In my oration, how the people take
The cruel issue of these bloody men;
According to the which, thou shalt discourse
To young Octavius of the state of things.
Lend me your hand. [*Exeunt with Caesar's body.*

ACT THREE SCENE TWO

The Forum.

Enter BRUTUS *and* CASSIUS, *and a throng of Citizens.*

CITIZENS
We will be satisfied; let us be satisfied.
BRUTUS
Then follow me, and give me audience, friends.
Cassius, go you into the other street,
And part the numbers.
Those that will hear me speak, let 'em stay here;
Those that will follow Cassius, go with him;
And public reasons shall be rendered
Of Caesar's death.
FIRST CITIZEN
I will hear Brutus speak.
SECOND CITIZEN
I will hear Cassius; and compare their reasons,
When severally we hear them rendered. 11
[*Exit Cassius, with some of the Citizens. Brutus goes into the pulpit.*
THIRD CITIZEN
The noble Brutus is ascended: silence!
BRUTUS
Be patient till the last.

Romans, countrymen, and lovers! hear me for my cause, and be silent, that you may hear: believe me for mine honour, and have respect to mine honour, that you may believe: censure me in your wisdom, and awake your senses, that you may the better judge. If there be any in this assembly, any dear friend of Caesar's, to him I say, that Brutus' love to Caesar was no less than his. If then that friend demand why Brutus rose against Caesar, this is my answer:—Not that I loved Caesar less, but that I loved Rome more. Had you rather Caesar were living and die all slaves, than that Caesar were dead, to live all free men? As Caesar loved me, I weep for him; as he was fortunate, I rejoice at it; as he was valiant, I honour him: but, as he was ambitious, I slew him. There is tears for his love; joy for his fortune; honour for his valour; and death for his ambition. Who is here so base that would be a bondman? If any, speak; for him have I offended. Who is here so rude that would not be a Roman? If any, speak; for him have I offended. Who is here so vile that will not love his country? If any, speak; for him have I offended. I pause for a reply.
ALL
None, Brutus, none.
BRUTUS
Then none have I offended. I have done no more to Caesar than you shall do to Brutus. The question of his death is enrolled in the Capitol; his glory not extenuated, wherein he was worthy, nor his offences enforced, for which he suffered death.

Enter ANTONY *and others, with* CAESAR'S *body.*

Here comes his body, mourned by Mark Antony: who, though he had no hand in his death, shall receive the benefit of his dying, a place in the commonwealth; as which of you shall not? With this I depart—that, as I slew my best lover for the good of Rome, I have the same dagger for myself, when it shall please my country to need my death.
ALL
Live, Brutus! live, live!
FIRST CITIZEN
Bring him with triumph home unto his house.
SECOND CITIZEN
Give him a statue with his ancestors.
THIRD CITIZEN
Let him be Caesar.
FOURTH CITIZEN
Caesar's better parts
Shall be crown'd in Brutus.
FIRST CITIZEN
We'll bring him to his house
With shouts and clamours.
BRUTUS
My countrymen,—

SECOND CITIZEN
Peace, silence! Brutus speaks.
FIRST CITIZEN
Peace, ho!
BRUTUS
Good countrymen, let me depart alone,
And, for my sake, stay here with Antony:
Do grace to Caesar's corpse, and grace his speech
Tending to Caesar's glories; which Mark Antony,
By our permission, is allow'd to make.
I do entreat you, not a man depart,
Save I alone, till Antony have spoke. [*Exit.*
FIRST CITIZEN
Stay, ho! and let us hear Mark Antony.
THIRD CITIZEN
Let him go up into the public chair;
We'll hear him. Noble Antony, go up.
ANTONY
For Brutus' sake, I am beholding to you.
[*Goes into the pulpit.*
FOURTH CITIZEN
What does he say of Brutus?
THIRD CITIZEN
He says, for Brutus' sake,
He finds himself beholding to us all.
FOURTH CITIZEN
'Twere best he speak no harm of Brutus here.
FIRST CITIZEN
This Caesar was a tyrant.
THIRD CITIZEN
Nay, that's certain:
We are blest that Rome is rid of him.
SECOND CITIZEN
Peace! let us hear what Antony can say.
ANTONY
You gentle Romans,—
CITIZENS
Peace, ho! let us hear him.
ANTONY
Friends, Romans, countrymen, lend me your ears;
I come to bury Caesar, not to praise him.
The evil that men do lives after them;
The good is oft interred with their bones;
So let it be with Caesar. The noble Brutus
Hath told you Caesar was ambitious:
If it were so, it was a grievous fault,
And grievously hath Caesar answer'd it.
Here, under leave of Brutus and the rest—
For Brutus is an honourable man;
So are they all, all honourable men—
Come I to speak in Caesar's funeral.
He was my friend, faithful and just to me:
But Brutus says he was ambitious;
And Brutus is an honourable man.
He hath brought many captives home to Rome
Whose ransoms did the general coffers fill:
Did this in Caesar seem ambitious?
When that the poor have cried, Caesar hath wept:
Ambition should be made of sterner stuff:
Yet Brutus says he was ambitious;
And Brutus is an honourable man.
You all did see that on the Lupercal
I thrice presented him a kingly crown,
Which he did thrice refuse: was this ambition?
Yet Brutus says he was ambitious;
And, sure, he is an honourable man.
I speak not to disprove what Brutus spoke,
But here I am to speak what I do know.
You all did love him once, not without cause:
What cause withholds you then, to mourn for him?
O judgement! thou art fled to brutish beasts,
And men have lost their reason. Bear with me;
My heart is in the coffin there with Caesar,
And I must pause till it come back to me.
FIRST CITIZEN
Methinks there is much reason in his sayings.
SECOND CITIZEN
If thou consider rightly of the matter,
Caesar has had great wrong.
THIRD CITIZEN
Has he, masters?
I fear there will a worse come in his place.
FOURTH CITIZEN
Mark'd ye his words? He would not take the crown;
Therefore 'tis certain he was not ambitious.
FIRST CITIZEN
If it be found so, some will dear abide it.
SECOND CITIZEN
Poor soul! his eyes are red as fire with weeping.
THIRD CITIZEN
There's not a nobler man in Rome than Antony.
FOURTH CITIZEN
Now mark him, he begins again to speak.
ANTONY
But yesterday the word of Caesar might
Have stood against the world; now lies he there,
And none so poor to do him reverence.
O masters, if I were disposed to stir
Your hearts and minds to mutiny and rage,
I should do Brutus wrong, and Cassius wrong,
Who, you all know, are honourable men:
I will not do them wrong; I rather choose
To wrong the dead, to wrong myself and you,
Than I will wrong such honourable men.
But here's a parchment with the seal of Caesar;
I found it in his closet, 'tis his will:

Let but the commons hear this testament—
Which, pardon me, I do not mean to read—
And they would go and kiss dead Caesar's wounds
And dip their napkins in his sacred blood,
Yea, beg a hair of him for memory,
And, dying, mention it within their wills,
Bequeathing it as a rich legacy
Unto their issue.

FOURTH CITIZEN
We'll hear the will: read it, Mark Antony.

ALL
The will, the will! we will hear Caesar's will.

ANTONY
Have patience, gentle friends, I must not read it;
It is not meet you know how Caesar loved you.
You are not wood, you are not stones, but men;
And, being men, hearing the will of Caesar,
It will inflame you, it will make you mad:
'Tis good you know not that you are his heirs;
For, if you should, O, what would come of it!

FOURTH CITIZEN
Read the will; we'll hear it, Antony;
You shall read us the will, Caesar's will.

ANTONY
Will you be patient? will you stay awhile?
I have o'ershot myself to tell you of it:
I fear I wrong the honourable men
Whose daggers have stabb'd Caesar; I do fear it.

FOURTH CITIZEN
They were traitors: honourable men!

ALL
The will! the testament!

SECOND CITIZEN
They were villains, murderers: the will! read the will.

ANTONY
You will compel me, then, to read the will?
Then make a ring about the corpse of Caesar,
And let me show you him that made the will.
Shall I descend? and will you give me leave?

SEVERAL CITIZEN
Come down.

SECOND CITIZEN
Descend.

THIRD CITIZEN
You shall have leave. [*Antony comes down.*

FOURTH CITIZEN
A ring; stand round.

FIRST CITIZEN
Stand from the hearse, stand from the body.

SECOND CITIZEN
Room for Antony, most noble Antony.

ANTONY
Nay, press not so upon me; stand far off.

SEVERAL CITIZEN
Stand back; room; bear back.

ANTONY
If you have tears, prepare to shed them now.
You all do know this mantle: I remember
The first time ever Caesar put it on;
'Twas on a summer's evening, in his tent,
That day he overcame the Nervii:
Look, in this place ran Cassius' dagger through:
See what a rent the envious Casca made:
Through this the well-beloved Brutus stabb'd;
And as he pluck'd his cursed steel away,
Mark how the blood of Caesar follow'd it,
As rushing out of doors, to be resolved
If Brutus so unkindly knock'd, or no;
For Brutus, as you know, was Caesar's angel:
Judge, O you gods, how dearly Caesar loved him!
This was the most unkindest cut of all;
For when the noble Caesar saw him stab,
Ingratitude, more strong than traitors' arms,
Quite vanquish'd him: then burst his mighty heart;
And, in his mantle muffling up his face,
Even at the base of Pompey's statua,
Which all the while ran blood, great Caesar fell.
O, what a fall was there, my countrymen!
Then I, and you, and all of us fell down,
Whilst bloody treason flourish'd over us.
O, now you weep; and, I perceive, you feel
The dint of pity: these are gracious drops.
Kind souls, what, weep you when you but behold
Our Caesar's vesture wounded? Look you here,
Here is himself, marr'd, as you see, with traitors.

FIRST CITIZEN
O piteous spectacle!

SECOND CITIZEN
O noble Caesar!

THIRD CITIZEN
O woful day!

FOURTH CITIZEN
O traitors, villains!

FIRST CITIZEN
O most bloody sight!

SECOND CITIZEN
We will be revenged.

ALL
Revenge! About! Seek! Burn! Fire! Kill! Slay! Let not a traitor live!

ANTONY
Stay, countrymen.

FIRST CITIZEN
Peace there! hear the noble Antony.

SECOND CITIZEN
We'll hear him, we'll follow him, we'll die with him.
ANTONY
Good friends, sweet friends, let me not stir you up
To such a sudden flood of mutiny.
They that have done this deed are honourable:
What private griefs they have, alas, I know not,
That made them do it: they are wise and honourable,
And will, no doubt, with reasons answer you.
I come not, friends, to steal away your hearts:
I am no orator, as Brutus is;
But, as you know me all, a plain blunt man,
That love my friend; and that they know full well
That gave me public leave to speak of him:
For I have neither wit, nor words, nor worth,
Action, nor utterance, nor the power of speech,
To stir men's blood: I only speak right on;
I tell you that which you yourselves do know;
Show you sweet Caesar's wounds, poor poor dumb mouths,
And bid them speak for me: but were I Brutus,
And Brutus Antony, there were an Antony
Would ruffle up your spirits and put a tongue
In every wound of Caesar that should move
The stones of Rome to rise and mutiny.
ALL
We'll mutiny.
FIRST CITIZEN
We'll burn the house of Brutus.
THIRD CITIZEN
Away, then! come, seek the conspirators.
ANTONY
Yet hear me, countrymen; yet hear me speak.
ALL
Peace, ho! Hear Antony. Most noble Antony!
ANTONY
Why, friends, you go to do you know not what:
Wherein hath Caesar thus deserved your loves?
Alas, you know not: I must tell you then:
You have forgot the will I told you of.
ALL
Most true. The will! Let's stay and hear the will.
ANTONY
Here is the will and under Caesar's seal.
To every Roman citizen he gives,
To every several man, seventy five drachmas.
SECOND CITIZEN
Most noble Caesar! We'll revenge his death.
THIRD CITIZEN
O royal Caesar!
ANTONY
Hear me with patience.
ALL
Peace, ho!
ANTONY
Moreover, he hath left you all his walks,
His private arbours and new-planted orchards,
On this side Tiber; he hath left them you, [19]
And to your heirs for ever, common pleasures,
To walk abroad, and recreate yourselves.
Here was a Caesar! when comes such another?
FIRST CITIZEN
Never, never. Come, away, away!
We'll burn his body in the holy place,
And with the brands fire the traitors' houses.
Take up the body.
SECOND CITIZEN
Go fetch fire.
THIRD CITIZEN
Pluck down benches.
FOURTH CITIZEN
Pluck down forms, windows, any thing.
[*Exeunt Citizens with the body.*
ANTONY
Now let it work. Mischief, thou art afoot,
Take thou what course thou wilt!

Enter a Servant.

How now, fellow!
SERVANT
Sir, Octavius is already come to Rome.
ANTONY
Where is he?
SERVANT
He and Lepidus are at Caesar's house.
ANTONY
And thither will I straight to visit him:
He comes upon a wish. Fortune is merry,
And in this mood will give us any thing.
SERVANT
I heard him say, Brutus and Cassius
Are rid like madmen through the gates of Rome.
ANTONY
Belike they had some notice of the people,
How I had moved them. Bring me to Octavius.
[*Exeunt.*

ACT THREE SCENE THREE

A street.

Enter CINNA *the poet.*

CINNA
I dreamt to-night that I did feast with Caesar,
And things unluckily charge my fantasy:
I have no will to wander forth of doors,
Yet something leads me forth.

Enter Citizens.

FIRST CITIZEN
What is your name?

SECOND CITIZEN
Whither are you going?

THIRD CITIZEN
Where do you dwell?

FOURTH CITIZEN
Are you a married man or a bachelor?

SECOND CITIZEN
Answer every man directly. 9

FIRST CITIZEN
Ay, and briefly.

FOURTH CITIZEN
Ay, and wisely.

THIRD CITIZEN
Ay, and truly, you were best.

CINNA
What is my name? Whither am I going? Where do I dwell? Am I a married man or a bachelor? Then, to answer every man directly and briefly, wisely and truly: wisely I say, I am a bachelor.

SECOND CITIZEN
That's as much as to say, they are fools that marry: you'll bear me a bang for that, I fear. Proceed; directly. 19

CINNA
Directly, I am going to Caesar's funeral.

FIRST CITIZEN
As a friend or an enemy?

CINNA
As a friend.

SECOND CITIZEN
That matter is answered directly.

FOURTH CITIZEN
For your dwelling,—briefly.

CINNA
Briefly, I dwell by the Capitol.

THIRD CITIZEN
Your name, sir, truly.

CINNA
Truly, my name is Cinna.

FIRST CITIZEN
Tear him to pieces; he's a conspirator. 28

CINNA
I am Cinna the poet, I am Cinna the poet.

FOURTH CITIZEN
Tear him for his bad verses, tear him for his bad verses.

CINNA
I am not Cinna the conspirator.

FOURTH CITIZEN
It is no matter, his name's Cinna; pluck but his name out of his heart, and turn him going. 34

THIRD CITIZEN
Tear him, tear him! Come, brands ho! fire-brands: to Brutus', to Cassius'; burn all: some to Decius' house, and some to Casca's; some to Ligarius': away, go!
[*Exeunt.*

ACT FOUR SCENE ONE

A house in Rome.

ANTONY, OCTAVIUS, *and* LEPIDUS, *seated at a table.*

ANTONY
These many, then, shall die; their names are prick'd.

OCTAVIUS
Your brother too must die; consent you, Lepidus?

LEPIDUS
I do consent,—

OCTAVIUS
Prick him down, Antony.

LEPIDUS
Upon condition Publius shall not live,
Who is your sister's son, Mark Antony.

ANTONY
He shall not live; look, with a spot I damn him.
But, Lepidus, go you to Caesar's house;
Fetch the will hither, and we shall determine
How to cut off some charge in legacies.

LEPIDUS
What, shall I find you here? 12

OCTAVIUS
Or here, or at the Capitol. [*Exit Lepidus.*

ANTONY
This is a slight unmeritable man,
Meet to be sent on errands: is it fit,
The three-fold world divided, he should stand
One of the three to share it?

OCTAVIUS
So you thought him;
And took his voice who should be prick'd to die,
In our black sentence and proscription.

ANTONY
Octavius, I have seen more days than you:
And though we lay these honours on this man,
To ease ourselves of divers slanderous loads,
He shall but bear them as the ass bears gold,
To groan and sweat under the business,
Either led or driven, as we point the way;
And having brought our treasure where we will,
Then take we down his load, and turn him off,
Like to the empty ass, to shake his ears,
And graze in commons.

OCTAVIUS
You may do your will;
But he's a tried and valiant soldier.

ANTONY
So is my horse, Octavius; and for that
I do appoint him store of provender:
It is a creature that I teach to fight,
To wind, to stop, to run directly on,
His corporal motion govern'd by my spirit.
And, in some taste, is Lepidus but so;
He must be taught and train'd and bid go forth:
A barren-spirited fellow; one that feeds
On abjects, orts and imitations, [20]
Which, out of use and staled by other men,
Begin his fashion: do not talk of him,
But as a property. And now, Octavius,
Listen great things:—Brutus and Cassius
Are levying powers: we must straight make head:
Therefore let our alliance be combined,
Our best friends made, our means stretch'd; [21]
And let us presently go sit in council,
How covert matters may be best disclosed,
And open perils surest answered.

OCTAVIUS
Let us do so: for we are at the stake,
And bay'd about with many enemies;
And some that smile have in their hearts, I fear,
Millions of mischiefs. [*Exeunt.*

ACT FOUR SCENE TWO

Camp near Sardis. Before Brutus's tent.

Drum. Enter BRUTUS, LUCILIUS, LUCIUS, *and* Soldiers; TITINIUS *and* PINDARUS *meeting them.*

BRUTUS
Stand, ho!

LUCILIUS
Give the word, ho! and stand.

BRUTUS
What now, Lucilius! is Cassius near?

LUCILIUS
He is at hand; and Pindarus is come
To do you salutation from his master.

BRUTUS
He greets me well. Your master, Pindarus,
In his own change, or by ill officers,
Hath given me some worthy cause to wish
Things done, undone: but, if he be at hand,
I shall be satisfied.

PINDARUS
I do not doubt
But that my noble master will appear
Such as he is, full of regard and honour.

BRUTUS
He is not doubted. A word, Lucilius;
How he received you, let me be resolved.

LUCILIUS
With courtesy and with respect enough;
But not with such familiar instances,
Nor with such free and friendly conference,
As he hath used of old.

BRUTUS
Thou hast described
A hot friend cooling: ever note, Lucilius,
When love begins to sicken and decay,
It useth an enforced ceremony.
There are no tricks in plain and simple faith;
But hollow men, like horses hot at hand,
Make gallant show and promise of their mettle;
But when they should endure the bloody spur,
They fall their crests, and, like deceitful jades,
Sink in the trial. Comes his army on?

LUCILIUS
They mean this night in Sardis to be quarter'd;
The greater part, the horse in general,
Are come with Cassius.

BRUTUS
Hark! he is arrived.
[*Low march within.*
March gently on to meet him.

Enter CASSIUS *and his powers.*

CASSIUS
Stand, ho!

BRUTUS
Stand, ho! Speak the word along.

FIRST SOLDIER
Stand!

SECOND SOLDIER
Stand!

THIRD SOLDIER
Stand!

CASSIUS
Most noble brother, you have done me wrong.

BRUTUS
Judge me, you gods! wrong I mine enemies?
And, if not so, how should I wrong a brother?

CASSIUS
Brutus, this sober form of yours hides wrongs;
And when you do them—

BRUTUS
Cassius, be content;
Speak your griefs softly: I do know you well.

Before the eyes of both our armies here,
Which should perceive nothing but love from us,
Let us not wrangle: bid them move away;
Then in my tent, Cassius, enlarge your griefs,
And I will give you audience.

CASSIUS
Pindarus,
Bid our commanders lead their charges off
A little from this ground.

BRUTUS
Lucilius, do you the like; and let no man [22] 55
Come to our tent till we have done our conference.
Let Lucius and Titinius guard our door. [*Exeunt.*

ACT FOUR SCENE THREE

Brutus's tent.

Enter BRUTUS *and* CASSIUS.

CASSIUS
That you have wrong'd me doth appear in this:
You have condemn'd and noted Lucius Pella
For taking bribes here of the Sardians;
Wherein my letters, praying on his side,
Because I knew the man, were slighted off.

BRUTUS
You wrong'd yourself to write in such a case.

CASSIUS
In such a time as this it is not meet
That every nice offence should bear his comment.

BRUTUS
Let me tell you, Cassius, you yourself
Are much condemn'd to have an itching palm;
To sell and mart your offices for gold 11
To undeservers.

CASSIUS
I an itching palm!
You know that you are Brutus that speak this,
Or, by the gods, this speech were else your last.

BRUTUS
The name of Cassius honours this corruption,
And chastisement doth therefore hide his head.

CASSIUS
Chastisement!

BRUTUS
Remember March, the ides of March remember:
Did not great Julius bleed for justice' sake?
What villain touch'd his body, that did stab,
And not for justice? What, shall one of us,
That struck the foremost man of all this world
But for supporting robbers, shall we now
Contaminate our fingers with base bribes,
And sell the mighty space of our large honours
For so much trash as may be grasped thus?
I had rather be a dog, and bay the moon,
Than such a Roman.

CASSIUS
Brutus, bay not me;
I'll not endure it: you forget yourself,
To hedge me in; I am a soldier, I, 32
Older in practise, abler than yourself
To make conditions.

BRUTUS
Go to; you are not, Cassius.

CASSIUS
I am.

BRUTUS
I say you are not.

CASSIUS
Urge me no more, I shall forget myself;
Have mind upon your health, tempt me no
farther.

BRUTUS
Away, slight man!

CASSIUS
Is't possible?

BRUTUS
Hear me, for I will speak.
Must I give way and room to your rash choler?
Shall I be frighted when a madman stares? 45

CASSIUS
O ye gods, ye gods! must I endure all this?

BRUTUS
All this! ay, more: fret till your proud heart break;
Go show your slaves how choleric you are,
And make your bondmen tremble. Must I budge?
Must I observe you? must I stand and crouch
Under your testy humour? By the gods,
You shall digest the venom of your spleen,
Though it do split you; for, from this day forth,
I'll use you for my mirth, yea, for my laughter,
When you are waspish.

CASSIUS
Is it come to this? 56

BRUTUS
You say you are a better soldier:
Let it appear so; make your vaunting true,
And it shall please me well: for mine own part,
I shall be glad to learn of noble men.

CASSIUS
You wrong me every way; you wrong me, Brutus;
I said, an elder soldier, not a better:
Did I say 'better'?

BRUTUS
If you did, I care not.

CASSIUS
When Caesar lived, he durst not thus have moved me.

BRUTUS
Peace, peace! you durst not so have tempted him.

CASSIUS
I durst not! 67

BRUTUS
No.

CASSIUS
What, durst not tempt him!

BRUTUS
For your life you durst not.

CASSIUS
Do not presume too much upon my love;
I may do that I shall be sorry for.

BRUTUS
You have done that you should be sorry for.
There is no terror, Cassius, in your threats,
For I am arm'd so strong in honesty
That they pass by me as the idle wind,
Which I respect not. I did send to you
For certain sums of gold, which you denied me:
For I can raise no money by vile means: 79
By heaven, I had rather coin my heart,
And drop my blood for drachmas, than to wring
From the hard hands of peasants their vile trash
By any indirection: I did send
To you for gold to pay my legions,
Which you denied me: was that done like Cassius?
Should I have answer'd Caius Cassius so?
When Marcus Brutus grows so covetous,
To lock such rascal counters from his friends,
Be ready, gods, with all your thunderbolts;
Dash him to pieces!

CASSIUS
I denied you not.

BRUTUS
You did.

CASSIUS
I did not: he was but a fool that brought
My answer back. Brutus hath rived my heart:
A friend should bear his friend's infirmities,
But Brutus makes mine greater than they are.

BRUTUS
I do not, till you practise them on me.

CASSIUS
You love me not.

BRUTUS
I do not like your faults.

CASSIUS
A friendly eye could never see such faults. 100

BRUTUS
A flatterer's would not, though they do appear
As huge as high Olympus.

CASSIUS
Come, Antony, and young Octavius, come,
Revenge yourselves alone on Cassius,
For Cassius is aweary of the world;
Hated by one he loves; braved by his brother;
Check'd like a bondman; all his faults observed,
Set in a note-book, learn'd, and conn'd by rote,
To cast into my teeth. O, I could weep
My spirit from mine eyes! There is my dagger,
And here my naked breast; within, a heart
Dearer than Plutus' mine, richer than gold:
If that thou be'st a Roman, take it forth;
I, that denied thee gold, will give my heart:
Strike, as thou didst at Caesar; for, I know,
When thou didst hate him worst, thou lovedst him better
Than ever thou lovedst Cassius.

BRUTUS
Sheathe your dagger:
Be angry when you will, it shall have scope;
Do what you will, dishonour shall be humour.
O Cassius, you are yoked with a lamb 122
That carries anger as the flint bears fire;
Who, much enforced, shows a hasty spark,
And straight is cold again.

CASSIUS
Hath Cassius lived
To be but mirth and laughter to his Brutus,
When grief, and blood ill-temper'd, vexeth him?

BRUTUS
When I spoke that, I was ill-temper'd too.

CASSIUS
Do you confess so much? Give me your hand.

BRUTUS
And my heart too.

CASSIUS
O Brutus!

BRUTUS
What's the matter?

CASSIUS
Have not you love enough to bear with me,
When that rash humour which my mother gave me 136
Makes me forgetful?

BRUTUS
Yes, Cassius; and, from henceforth,
When you are over-earnest with your Brutus,
He'll think your mother chides, and leave you so.

POET
[*Within*] Let me go in to see the generals;
There is some grudge between 'em, 'tis not meet
They be alone.

LUCILIUS
[*Within*] You shall not come to them.

POET
[*Within*] Nothing but death shall stay me.

Enter Poet, *followed by* LUCILIUS, TITINIUS, *and* LUCIUS.

CASSIUS
How now! what's the matter? 146

POET
For shame, you generals! what do you mean? [23]
Love, and be friends, as two such men should be;
For I have seen more years, I'm sure, than ye.

CASSIUS
Ha, ha! how vilely doth this cynic rhyme! [24]

BRUTUS
Get you hence, sirrah; saucy fellow, hence!

CASSIUS
Bear with him, Brutus; 'tis his fashion.

BRUTUS
I'll know his humour, when he knows his time:
What should the wars do with these jigging fools?
Companion, hence!

CASSIUS
Away, away, be gone. [*Exit Poet.*

BRUTUS
Lucilius and Titinius, bid the commanders
Prepare to lodge their companies to-night. 158

CASSIUS
And come yourselves, and bring Messala with you
Immediately to us. [*Exeunt Lucilius and Titinius.*

BRUTUS
Lucius, a bowl of wine! [*Exit Lucius.*

CASSIUS
I did not think you could have been so angry.

BRUTUS
O Cassius, I am sick of many griefs.

CASSIUS
Of your philosophy you make no use,
If you give place to accidental evils.

BRUTUS
No man bears sorrow better. Portia is dead.

CASSIUS
Ha! Portia!

BRUTUS
She is dead.

CASSIUS
How 'scaped I killing when I cross'd you so? 169
O insupportable and touching loss!
Upon what sickness?

BRUTUS
Impatient of my absence,
And grief that young Octavius with Mark Antony
Have made themselves so strong:—for with her death
That tidings came;—with this she fell distract,
And, her attendants absent, swallow'd fire.

CASSIUS
And died so?

BRUTUS
Even so.

CASSIUS
O ye immortal gods!

Re-enter LUCIUS, *with wine and taper.*

BRUTUS
Speak no more of her. Give me a bowl of wine.
In this I bury all unkindness, Cassius.

CASSIUS
My heart is thirsty for that noble pledge. 182
Fill, Lucius, till the wine o'erswell the cup;
I cannot drink too much of Brutus' love.

BRUTUS
Come in, Titinius! [*Exit Lucius.*

Re-enter TITINIUS, *with* MESSALA.

Welcome, good Messala.
Now sit we close about this taper here,
And call in question our necessities.

CASSIUS
Portia, art thou gone?

BRUTUS
No more, I pray you.
Messala, I have here received letters,
That young Octavius and Mark Antony
Come down upon us with a mighty power,
Bending their expedition toward Philippi. 194

MESSALA
Myself have letters of the selfsame tenor.

BRUTUS
With what addition?

MESSALA
That by proscription and bills of outlawry,
Octavius, Antony, and Lepidus,
Have put to death an hundred senators.

BRUTUS
Therein our letters do not well agree;
Mine speak of seventy senators that died
By their proscriptions, Cicero being one.

CASSIUS
Cicero one!

MESSALA
Cicero is dead,
And by that order of proscription. 205
Had you your letters from your wife, my lord?

BRUTUS
No, Messala.

MESSALA
Nor nothing in your letters writ of her?

BRUTUS
Nothing, Messala.

MESSALA
That, methinks, is strange.

BRUTUS
Why ask you? hear you aught of her in yours?
MESSALA
No, my lord.
BRUTUS
Now, as you are a Roman, tell me true.
MESSALA
Then like a Roman bear the truth I tell:
For certain she is dead, and by strange manner.
BRUTUS
Why, farewell, Portia. We must die, Messala: 216
With meditating that she must die once,
I have the patience to endure it now.
MESSALA
Even so great men great losses should endure.
CASSIUS
I have as much of this in art as you,
But yet my nature could not bear it so.
BRUTUS
Well, to our work alive. What do you think
Of marching to Philippi presently?
CASSIUS
I do not think it good.
BRUTUS
Your reason?
CASSIUS
This it is:
'Tis better that the enemy seek us: 227
So shall he waste his means, weary his soldiers,
Doing himself offence; whilst we, lying still,
Are full of rest, defense, and nimbleness.
BRUTUS
Good reasons must, of force, give place to better.
The people 'twixt Philippi and this ground
Do stand but in a forced affection;
For they have grudged us contribution:
The enemy, marching along by them,
By them shall make a fuller number up,
Come on refresh'd, new-added, and encouraged;
From which advantage shall we cut him off,
If at Philippi we do face him there,
These people at our back.
CASSIUS
Hear me, good brother.
BRUTUS
Under your pardon. You must note beside,
That we have tried the utmost of our friends,
Our legions are brim-full, our cause is ripe:
The enemy increaseth every day;
We, at the height, are ready to decline.
There is a tide in the affairs of men,
Which, taken at the flood, leads on to fortune;
Omitted, all the voyage of their life 248
Is bound in shallows and in miseries.
On such a full sea are we now afloat;
And we must take the current when it serves,
Or lose our ventures.
CASSIUS
Then, with your will, go on;
We'll along ourselves, and meet them at Philippi.
BRUTUS
The deep of night is crept upon our talk,
And nature must obey necessity;
Which we will niggard with a little rest.
There is no more to say?
CASSIUS
No more. Good night:
Early to-morrow will we rise, and hence. 260
BRUTUS
Lucius! [*Enter Lucius.*] My gown. [*Exit Lucius.*] Farewell, good Messala:
Good night, Titinius. Noble, noble Cassius,
Good night, and good repose.
CASSIUS
O my dear brother!
This was an ill beginning of the night:
Never come such division 'tween our souls!
Let it not, Brutus.
BRUTUS
Every thing is well.
CASSIUS
Good night, my lord.
BRUTUS
Good night, good brother.
TITINIUS, MESSALA
Good night, Lord Brutus.
BRUTUS
Farewell, every one. [*Exeunt all but Brutus.*

Re-enter LUCIUS, *with the gown.*

Give me the gown. Where is thy instrument?
LUCILIUS
Here in the tent.
BRUTUS
What, thou speak'st drowsily? 276
Poor knave, I blame thee not; thou art o'er-watch'd.
Call Claudius and some other of my men;
I'll have them sleep on cushions in my tent.
LUCILIUS
Varro and Claudius!

Enter VARRO *and* CLAUDIUS.

VARRO
Calls my lord?
BRUTUS
I pray you, sirs, lie in my tent and sleep;
It may be I shall raise you by and by
On business to my brother Cassius.

VARPO
So please you, we will stand and watch your pleasure.
BRUTUS
I will not have it so: lie down, good sirs;
It may be I shall otherwise bethink me.
Look, Lucius, here's the book I sought for so;
I put it in the pocket of my gown.
[*Varro and Cladius lie down.*
LUCILIUS
I was sure your lordship did not give it me.
BRUTUS
Bear with me, good boy, I am much forgetful.
Canst thou hold up thy heavy eyes awhile,
And touch thy instrument a strain or two?
LUCILIUS
Ay, my lord, an't please you.
BRUTUS
It does, my boy:
I trouble thee too much, but thou art willing.
LUCILIUS
It is my duty, sir.
BRUTUS
I should not urge thy duty past thy might;
I know young bloods look for a time of rest.
LUCILIUS
I have slept, my lord, already.
BRUTUS
It was well done; and thou shalt sleep again;
I will not hold thee long: if I do live,
I will be good to thee. [*Music, and a song.*
This is a sleepy tune. O murderous slumber,
Lay'st thou thy leaden mace upon my boy,
That plays thee music? Gentle knave, good night;
I will not do thee so much wrong to wake thee:
If thou dost nod, thou break'st thy instrument;
I'll take it from thee; and, good boy, good night.
Let me see, let me see; is not the leaf turn'd down
Where I left reading? Here it is, I think.

Enter the Ghost of CAESAR.

How ill this taper burns! Ha! who comes here?
I think it is the weakness of mine eyes
That shapes this monstrous apparition.
It comes upon me. Art thou any thing?
Art thou some god, some angel, or some devil,
That makest my blood cold and my hair to stare?
Speak to me what thou art.
GHOST
Thy evil spirit, Brutus.
BRUTUS
Why comest thou?
GHOST
To tell thee thou shalt see me at Philippi.
BRUTUS
Well; then I shall see thee again?
GHOST
Ay, at Philippi.
BRUTUS
Why, I will see thee at Philippi, then.
[*Exit Ghost.*

Now I have taken heart thou vanishest:
Ill spirit, I would hold more talk with thee,
Boy, Lucius! Varro! Claudius! Sirs, awake!
Claudius!
LUCILIUS
The strings, my lord, are false.
BRUTUS
He thinks he still is at his instrument.
Lucius, awake!
LUCILIUS
My lord?
BRUTUS
Didst thou dream, Lucius, that thou so criedst out?
LUCILIUS
My lord, I do not know that I did cry.
BRUTUS
Yes, that thou didst: didst thou see any thing?
LUCILIUS
Nothing, my lord.
BRUTUS
Sleep again, Lucius. Sirrah Claudius! [*To Varro*] Fellow thou, awake!
VARPO
My lord?
CLAUDIUS
My lord?
BRUTUS
Why did you so cry out, sirs, in your sleep?
VARRO, CLAUDIUS
Did we, my lord?
BRUTUS
Ay: saw you any thing?
VARPO
No, my lord, I saw nothing.
CLAUDIUS
Nor I, my lord.
BRUTUS
Go and commend me to my brother Cassius;
Bid him set on his powers betimes before,
And we will follow.
VARRO, CLAUDIUS
It shall be done, my lord.
[*Exeunt.*

ACT FIVE SCENE ONE

The plains of Philippi.

Enter OCTAVIUS, ANTONY, *and their* army.

OCTAVIUS
Now, Antony, our hopes are answered:
You said the enemy would not come down,
But keep the hills and upper regions;
It proves not so: their battles are at hand;
They mean to warn us at Philippi here,
Answering before we do demand of them.

ANTONY
Tut, I am in their bosoms, and I know
Wherefore they do it: they could be content
To visit other places; and come down
With fearful bravery, thinking by this face
To fasten in our thoughts that they have courage;
But 'tis not so.

Enter a Messenger.

MESSENGER
Prepare you, generals:
The enemy comes on in gallant show;
Their bloody sign of battle is hung out,
And something to be done immediately.

ANTONY
Octavius, lead your battle softly on,
Upon the left hand of the even field.

OCTAVIUS
Upon the right hand I; keep thou the left.

ANTONY
Why do you cross me in this exigent?

OCTAVIUS
I do not cross you; but I will do so. [25] [*March.*

Drum. Enter BRUTUS , CASSIUS, *and their* Army; LUCILIUS , TITINIUS , MESSALA, *and others.*

BRUTUS
They stand, and would have parley.

CASSIUS
Stand fast, Titinius: we must out and talk.

OCTAVIUS
Mark Antony, shall we give sign of battle?

ANTONY
No, Caesar, we will answer on their charge.
Make forth; the generals would have some words.

OCTAVIUS
Stir not until the signal.

BRUTUS
Words before blows: is it so, countrymen?

OCTAVIUS
Not that we love words better, as you do.

BRUTUS
Good words are better than bad strokes, Octavius.

ANTONY
In your bad strokes, Brutus, you give good words: 32
Witness the hole you made in Caesar's heart,
Crying 'Long live! hail, Caesar!'

CASSIUS
Antony,
The posture of your blows are yet unknown;
But for your words, they rob the Hybla bees,
And leave them honeyless.

ANTONY
Not stingless too.

BRUTUS
O, yes, and soundless too;
For you have stol'n their buzzing, Antony,
And very wisely threat before you sting.

ANTONY
Villains, you did not so, when your vile daggers
Hack'd one another in the sides of Caesar: 44
You show'd your teeth like apes, and fawn'd like hounds,
And bow'd like bondmen, kissing Caesar's feet;
Whilst damned Casca, like a cur, behind
Struck Caesar on the neck. O you flatterers!

CASSIUS
Flatterers! Now, Brutus, thank yourself:
This tongue had not offended so to-day,
If Cassius might have ruled.

OCTAVIUS
Come, come, the cause: if arguing make us sweat,
The proof of it will turn to redder drops.
Look; 55
I draw a sword against conspirators;
When think you that the sword goes up again?
Never, till Caesar's three and thirty wounds [26]
Be well avenged; or till another Caesar
Have added slaughter to the sword of traitors.

BRUTUS
Caesar, thou canst not die by traitors' hands,
Unless thou bring'st them with thee.

OCTAVIUS
So I hope;
I was not born to die on Brutus' sword.

BRUTUS
O, if thou wert the noblest of thy strain,
Young man, thou couldst not die more honourable. 67

CASSIUS
A peevish schoolboy, worthless of such honour,
Join'd with a masker and a reveller!

ANTONY
Old Cassius still!

OCTAVIUS
Come, Antony, away!

Defiance, traitors, hurl we in your teeth:
If you dare fight to-day, come to the field;
If not, when you have stomachs.
[*Exeunt Octavius, Antony, and their army.*

CASSIUS
Why, now, blow wind, swell billow and swim bark!
The storm is up, and all is on the hazard.

BRUTUS
Ho, Lucilius! hark, a word with you.

LUCILIUS
[*Standing forth*] My lord?
[*Brutus and Lucilius converse apart.*

CASSIUS
Messala!

MESSALA
[*Standing forth*] What says my general?

CASSIUS
Messala, 82
This is my birth-day; as this very day
Was Cassius born. Give me thy hand, Messala:
Be thou my witness that against my will
As Pompey was, am I compell'd to set
Upon one battle all our liberties.
You know that I held Epicurus strong
And his opinion: now I change my mind,
And partly credit things that do presage.
Coming from Sardis, on our former ensign 91
Two mighty eagles fell, and there they perch'd,
Gorging and feeding from our soldiers' hands;
Who to Philippi here consorted us:
This morning are they fled away and gone;
And in their steads do ravens, crows and kites,
Fly o'er our heads and downward look on us,
As we were sickly prey: their shadows seem
A canopy most fatal, under which
Our army lies, ready to give up the ghost.

MESSALA
Believe not so.

CASSIUS
I but believe it partly; 102
For I am fresh of spirit and resolved
To meet all perils very constantly.

BRUTUS
Even so, Lucilius.

CASSIUS
Now, most noble Brutus,
The gods to-day stand friendly, that we may,
Lovers in peace, lead on our days to age!
But since the affairs of men rest still incertain,
Let's reason with the worst that may befall.
If we do lose this battle, then is this
The very last time we shall speak together: [27]
What are you then determined to do? 113

BRUTUS
Even by the rule of that philosophy
By which I did blame Cato for the death
Which he did give himself, I know not how,
But I do find it cowardly and vile,
For fear of what might fall, so to prevent
The time of life: arming myself with patience
To stay the providence of some high powers
That govern us below.

CASSIUS
Then, if we lose this battle,
You are contented to be led in triumph
Thorough the streets of Rome? 124

BRUTUS
No, Cassius, no: think not, thou noble Roman,
That ever Brutus will go bound to Rome;
He bears too great a mind. But this same day
Must end that work the ides of March begun;
And whether we shall meet again I know not.
Therefore our everlasting farewell take:
For ever, and for ever, farewell, Cassius!
If we do meet again, why, we shall smile;
If not, why then, this parting was well made.

CASSIUS
For ever, and for ever, farewell, Brutus!
If we do meet again, we'll smile indeed; 135
If not, 'tis true this parting was well made.

BRUTUS
Why, then, lead on. O, that a man might know
The end of this day's business ere it come!
But it sufficeth that the day will end,
And then the end is known. Come, ho! away!
[*Exeunt.*

ACT FIVE SCENE TWO

The same. The field of battle.
Alarum. Enter BRUTUS *and* MESSALA.

BRUTUS
Ride, ride, Messala, ride, and give these bills
Unto the legions on the other side. [*Loud alarum.*
Let them set on at once; for I perceive
But cold demeanor in Octavius' wing,
And sudden push gives them the overthrow.
Ride, ride, Messala: let them all come down. [*Exeunt.*

ACT FIVE SCENE THREE

Another part of the field.
Alarums. Enter CASSIUS *and* TITINIUS.

CASSIUS
O, look, Titinius, look, the villains fly!

Myself have to mine own turn'd enemy:
This ensign here of mine was turning back;
I slew the coward, and did take it from him.

TITINIUS
O Cassius, Brutus gave the word too early;
Who, having some advantage on Octavius,
Took it too eagerly: his soldiers fell to spoil,
Whilst we by Antony are all enclosed.

Enter PINDARUS.

PINDARUS
Fly further off, my lord, fly further off;
Mark Antony is in your tents, my lord:
Fly, therefore, noble Cassius, fly far off.

CASSIUS
This hill is far enough. Look, look, Titinius;
Are those my tents where I perceive the fire?

TITINIUS
They are, my lord.

CASSIUS
Titinius, if thou lovest me,
Mount thou my horse, and hide thy spurs in him,
Till he have brought thee up to yonder troops,
And here again; that I may rest assured
Whether yond troops are friend or enemy.

TITINIUS
I will be here again, even with a thought. [*Exit.*

CASSIUS
Go, Pindarus, get higher on that hill;
My sight was ever thick; regard Titinius,
And tell me what thou notest about the field.
[*Pindarus ascends the hill.*
This day I breathed first: time is come round,
And where I did begin, there shall I end;
My life is run his compass. Sirrah, what news?

PINDARUS
[*Above*] O my lord!

CASSIUS
What news?

PINDARUS
[*Above*] Titinius is enclosed round about
With horsemen, that make to him on the spur;
Yet he spurs on. Now they are almost on him.
Now, Titinius! Now some light. O, he lights too.
He's ta'en. [*Shout.*] And, hark! they shout for joy.

CASSIUS
Come down, behold no more.
O, coward that I am, to live so long,
To see my best friend ta'en before my face!
[*Pindarus descends.*
Come hither, sirrah:
In Parthia did I take thee prisoner;
And then I swore thee, saving of thy life,
That whatsoever I did bid thee do,
Thou shouldst attempt it. Come now, keep thine oath;
Now be a freeman: and with this good sword,
That ran through Caesar's bowels, search this bosom.
Stand not to answer: here, take thou the hilts;
And, when my face is cover'd, as 'tis now,
Guide thou the sword. [*Pindarus stabs him.*]
Caesar, thou art revenged,
Even with the sword that kill'd thee. [*Dies.*

PINDARUS
So, I am free; yet would not so have been,
Durst I have done my will. O Cassius,
Far from this country Pindarus shall run,
Where never Roman shall take note of him. [*Exit.*

Re-enter TITINIUS *with* MESSALA.

MESSALA
It is but change, Titinius; for Octavius
Is overthrown by noble Brutus' power,
As Cassius' legions are by Antony.

TITINIUS
These tidings will well comfort Cassius.

MESSALA
Where did you leave him?

TITINIUS
All disconsolate,
With Pindarus his bondman, on this hill.

MESSALA
Is not that he that lies upon the ground?

TITINIUS
He lies not like the living. O my heart!

MESSALA
Is not that he?

TITINIUS
No, this was he, Messala,
But Cassius is no more. O setting sun,
As in thy red rays thou dost sink to night,
So in his red blood Cassius' day is set;
The sun of Rome is set! Our day is gone;
Clouds, dews, and dangers come; our deeds are done!
Mistrust of my success hath done this deed.

MESSALA
Mistrust of good success hath done this deed.
O hateful error, melancholy's child,
Why dost thou show to the apt thoughts of men
The things that are not? O error, soon conceived,
Thou never comest unto a happy birth,
But kill'st the mother that engender'd thee!

TITINIUS
What, Pindarus! where art thou, Pindarus?

CASSIUS Come down, behold no more.

MESSALA
Seek him, Titinius, whilst I go to meet
The noble Brutus, thrusting this report
Into his ears; I may say, thrusting it;
For piercing steel and darts envenomed
Shall be as welcome to the ears of Brutus
As tidings of this sight.

TITINIUS
Hie you, Messala,
And I will seek for Pindarus the while. 89
[*Exit Messala.*
Why didst thou send me forth, brave Cassius?
Did I not meet thy friends? and did not they
Put on my brows this wreath of victory,
And bid me give it thee? Didst thou not hear their shouts?
Alas, thou hast misconstrued every thing!
But, hold thee, take this garland on thy brow;
Thy Brutus bid me give it thee, and I
Will do his bidding. Brutus, come apace,
And see how I regarded Caius Cassius.
By your leave, gods:—this is a Roman's part:
Come, Cassius' sword, and find Titinius' heart.
[*Kills himself.*

Alarum. Re-enter MESSALA, *with* BRUTUS, *young* CATO, STRATO, VOLUMNIUS, *and* LUCILIUS.

BRUTUS
Where, where, Messala, doth his body lie? 102

MESSALA
Lo, yonder, and Titinius mourning it.

BRUTUS
Titinius' face is upward.

CATO
He is slain.

BRUTUS
O Julius Caesar, thou art mighty yet!
Thy spirit walks abroad, and turns our swords
In our own proper entrails. [*Low alarums.*

CATO
Brave Titinius!
Look, whether he have not crown'd dead Cassius!

BRUTUS
Are yet two Romans living such as these?
The last of all the Romans, fare thee well!
It is impossible that ever Rome 113
Should breed thy fellow. Friends, I owe more tears
To this dead man than you shall see me pay.
I shall find time, Cassius, I shall find time.
Come, therefore, and to Thasos send his body:
His funerals shall not be in our camp,
Lest it discomfort us. Lucilius, come;
And come, young Cato; let us to the field.
Labeo and Flavius, set our battles on:
'Tis three o'clock; and, Romans, yet ere night
We shall try fortune in a second fight. [*Exeunt.*

ACT FIVE SCENE FOUR

Another part of the field.

Alarum. Enter fighting, Soldiers of both armies; then BRUTUS, *young* CATO, LUCILIUS, *and others.*

BRUTUS
Yet, countrymen, O, yet hold up your heads!
CATO
What bastard doth not? Who will go with me?
I will proclaim my name about the field:
I am the son of Marcus Cato, ho!
A foe to tyrants, and my country's friend;
I am the son of Marcus Cato, ho!
BRUTUS
And I am Brutus, Marcus Brutus, I;
Brutus, my country's friend; know me for Brutus!
[*Exit.*
LUCILIUS
O young and noble Cato, art thou down?
Why, now thou diest as bravely as Titinius;
And mayst be honour'd, being Cato's son.
FIRST SOLDIER
Yield, or thou diest.
LUCILIUS
Only I yield to die:
There is so much that thou wilt kill me straight;
[*Offering money.*
Kill Brutus, and be honour'd in his death.
FIRST SOLDIER
We must not. A noble prisoner!
SECOND SOLDIER
Room, ho! Tell Antony, Brutus is ta'en.
FIRST SOLDIER
I'll tell the news. Here comes the general.

Enter ANTONY.

Brutus is ta'en, Brutus is ta'en, my lord.
ANTONY
Where is he?
LUCILIUS
Safe, Antony; Brutus is safe enough:
I dare assure thee that no enemy 22
Shall ever take alive the noble Brutus:
The gods defend him from so great a shame!
When you do find him, or alive or dead,
He will be found like Brutus, like himself.
ANTONY
This is not Brutus, friend; but, I assure you,
A prize no less in worth: keep this man safe;
Give him all kindness: I had rather have
Such men my friends than enemies. Go on,
And see whether Brutus be alive or dead; 31
And bring us word unto Octavius' tent
How every thing is chanced. [*Exeunt.*

ACT FIVE SCENE FIVE

Another part of the field.

Enter BRUTUS, DARDANIUS, CLITUS , STRATO, *and* VOLUMNIUS.

BRUTUS
Come, poor remains of friends, rest on this rock.
CLITUS
Statilius show'd the torch-light, but, my lord,
He came not back: he is or ta'en or slain.
BRUTUS
Sit thee down, Clitus: slaying is the word;
It is a deed in fashion. Hark thee, Clitus.
[*Whispers.*
CLITUS
What, I, my lord? No, not for all the world.
BRUTUS
Peace then! no words.
CLITUS
I'll rather kill myself.
BRUTUS
Hark thee, Dardanius. [*Whispers.*
DARDANIUS
Shall I do such a deed?
CLITUS
O Dardanius!
DARDANIUS
O Clitus! 12
CLITUS
What ill request did Brutus make to thee?
DARDANIUS
To kill him, Clitus. Look, he meditates.

CLITUS
Now is that noble vessel full of grief,
That it runs over even at his eyes.
BRUTUS
Come hither, good Volumnius; list a word.
VOLUMNIUS
What says my lord?
BRUTUS
Why, this, Volumnius:
The ghost of Caesar hath appear'd to me
Two several times by night; at Sardis once,
And, this last night here in Philippi fields:
I know my hour is come.
VOLUMNIUS
Not so, my lord.
BRUTUS
Nay, I am sure it is, Volumnius.
Thou seest the world, Volumnius, how it goes;
Our enemies have beat us to the pit:
[Low alarums.
It is more worthy to leap in ourselves,
Than tarry till they push us. Good Volumnius,
Thou know'st that we two went to school together:
Even for that our love of old, I prithee,
Hold thou my sword-hilts, whilst I run on it.
VOLUMNIUS
That's not an office for a friend, my lord.
[Alarum still.
CLITUS
Fly, fly, my lord; there is no tarrying here.
BRUTUS
Farewell to you; and you; and you, Volumnius.
Strato, thou hast been all this while asleep;
Farewell to thee too, Strato. Countrymen, [28]
My heart doth joy that yet in all my life
I found no man but he was true to me.
I shall have glory by this losing day
More than Octavius and Mark Antony
By this vile conquest shall attain unto.
So fare you well at once; for Brutus' tongue
Hath almost ended his life's history:
Night hangs upon mine eyes; my bones would rest,
That have but labour'd to attain this hour.
[Alarum. Cry within, 'Fly, fly, fly!'
CLITUS
Fly, my lord, fly.
BRUTUS
Hence! I will follow.
[Exeunt Clitus, Dardanius, and Volumnius.
I prithee, Strato, stay thou by thy lord:
Thou art a fellow of a good respect;
Thy life hath had some smatch of honour in it:
Hold then my sword, and turn away thy face,
While I do run upon it. Wilt thou, Strato?
STRATO
Give me your hand first. Fare you well, my lord.
BRUTUS
Farewell, good Strato. [*Runs on his sword.*] Caesar, now be still:
I kill'd not thee with half so good a will. *[Dies.*

Alarum. Retreat. Enter OCTAVIUS, ANTONY, MESSALA, LUCILIUS, *and the army.*

OCTAVIUS
What man is that?
MESSALA
My master's man. Strato, where is thy master?
STRATO
Free from the bondage you are in, Messala:
The conquerors can but make a fire of him;
For Brutus only overcame himself,
And no man else hath honour by his death.
LUCILIUS
So Brutus should be found. I thank thee, Brutus,
That thou hast proved Lucilius' saying true.
OCTAVIUS
All that served Brutus, I will entertain them.
Fellow, wilt thou bestow thy time with me?
STRATO
Ay, if Messala will prefer me to you.
OCTAVIUS
Do so, good Messala.
MESSALA
How died my master, Strato?
STRATO
I held the sword, and he did run on it.
MESSALA
Octavius, then take him to follow thee,
That did the latest service to my master.
ANTONY
This was the noblest Roman of them all:
All the conspirators save only he
Did that they did in envy of great Caesar;
He only, in a general honest thought [29]
And common good to all, made one of them.
His life was gentle, and the elements
So mix'd in him that Nature might stand up
And say to all the world 'This was a man!'
OCTAVIUS
According to his virtue let us use him,
With all respect and rites of burial.
Within my tent his bones to-night shall lie,
Most like a soldier, order'd honourably.
So call the field to rest; and let's away,
To part the glories of this happy day. *[Exeunt.*

Notes

1. With awl. I; – Folios, *'withal I';* the correction was made by Farmer.
2. The line is evidently to be read thus:—

   "A soothsay'r bids you 'ware the ides of March."

3. Walls; – Rowe's emendation of Folios, *'walkes.'*
4. 'Tis very like: he hath; – Theobald's emendation; Folios, *"Tis very like he hath.'*
5. He should not humour me; i.e. – 'he (Brutus) should not influence me, as I have been influencing him'; others take 'he' to refer to Caesar, and Johnson explains the passage as follows:—"Caesar loves Brutus, but if Brutus and I were to change places, his (Caesar's love) should not humour me, so as to make me forget my principles."
6. These are their reasons; – Jervis conjectured *'These have their seasons';* Collier MS., *'These are the seasons.'*
7. Why old men fool and; – Mitford conjectured; Folios, *'Why old men. Fools, and';* Blackstone conjectured *'Why old men fools, and.'*
8. In favour's like; – Johnson reads *'In favour's, like';* Folios 1, 2, *'Is Fauors, like';* Folios 3, 4, *'Is Favours, like';* Rowe, *'Is feav'rous, like';* Capell, *'Is favour'd like';* &c. &c.
9. The ides of March; – Theobald's correction of Folios, *'the first of March.'*
10. For if thou path, thy native semblance on; – so Folio 2; Folios 1, 3, 4, *'For if thou path thy ...';* Pope, *'For if thou march, thy ...';* Singer conjectured *'For if thou put'st thy ...'* &c.; but there is no need to improve on the reading of Folio 2.
11. Fight; – so Folios; Dyce, *'fought';* Keightley, *'did fight.'*
12. Are; – Upton conjectured; Folios 1, 2, *'heare';* Folios 3, 4, *'hear';* Rowe, *'heard';* Theobald, *'were.'*
13. Law of children; – Johnson's emendation of Folios, *'lane of children';* Steevens conjectured *'line of c.';* Mason conjectured *'play of c.'* Mr. Fleay approves of the Folio reading, and explains *'lane'* in the sense of 'narrow conceits'; he compares the following lines from Jonson's *Staple of News:*—

    "A narrow-minded man! my thoughts do dwell
    All in a lane."

14. Know, Caesar, doth not wrong, nor without cause Will he be satisfied; – there is an interesting piece of literary history connected with these lines. In Ben Jonson's *Sylva* or *Discoveries* occurs the famous criticism on Shakespeare, where Jonson, after speaking of his love for Shakespeare, "on this side of idolatry, expresses a wish 'that he had blotted more.' " "His wit was in his own power; would the rule of it had been so too! Many times he fell into those things could not escape laughter: as when he said in the person of Caesar, one speaking to him, 'Caesar, thou dost me wrong,' he replied, *'Caesar did never wrong but with just cause,'* and such like; which were ridiculous. But he redeemed his vices with his virtues. There was ever more in him to be praised than to be pardoned." Again in his *Staple of News* (acted 1625), a character says, "Cry you mercy, *you never did wrong, but with just cause."* From these references it is inferred that in its original form the passage stood thus:—

    "METELLUS. *Caesar, thou dost me wrong.*
    CAESAR. *Know, Caesar doth not wrong, but with just cause,*
    Nor without cause will he be satisfied."

    It is impossible to determine whether Jonson misquoted, or whether (as seems more likely) his criticism effected its purpose, and the lines were changed by Shakespeare or by his editors.

15. Et tu, Brute; – according to Plutarch, Caesar called out in Latin to Casca, *'O vile traitor, Casca, what doest thou?'* Suetonius, however, states that Caesar addressed Brutus in Greek:—' "kal o', TEKVOV," *i.e. 'and thou, too, my son.'* The words *'Et tu, Brute,'* proverbial in Elizabethan times, must have been derived from the Greek; they are found in at least three works published earlier than *Julius Caesar:*—(i.) Eedes' Latin play, *Caesaris interfecti,* 1582; (ii.) *The True Tragedie of Richard, Duke of York,* 1595; (iii.) *Acolastus,* his *Afterwitte,* 1600. In Caesar's Legend, *Mirror for Magistrates,* 1587, these lines occur:—

    "O This, quoth I, is violence: then Cassius pierced my breast;
    And Brutus thou, my son, quoth I, whom erst I loved best."

16. These lines are given to Casca by Pope.
17. In strength of malice; – so Folios; Pope, *'exempt from malice';* Capell, *'no strength of malice';* Seymour, *'reproof of malice';* Collier MS., adopted by Craik, *'in strength of welcome';* Badham conjectured *'unstring their malice,'* &c. If any emendation is necessary, Capell's suggestion commends itself most; but *'in strength of malice'* may mean 'in the intensity of their hatred to Caesar's tyranny,' and this, as Grant White points out, suits the context.
18. Limbs of men; – so Folios; Hanmer, *'kind of men';* Johnson conjectured *'lives of'* or *'lymmes of men';* Jackson, *'imps of men';* Collier MS., adopted by Craik, *'loins of men';* Bulloch, *'limbs of Rome,'* &c.
19. On this side Tiber; – Theobald proposed *'that'* for *'this';* Caesar's gardens were on the left bank of the river. Shakespeare followed North's *Plutarch,* and North merely translated the words in Amyot.
20. Abjects, orts; – Staunton's reading; Theobald, *'abject orts';* Folios, *'Obiects, Arts';* Becket conjectured *'abject arts';* Gould conjectured *'objects, orts.'*
21. Our means stretch'd; – Folio 1, *'our meanes stretcht';* Folios 2, 3, 4, *'and our best meanes stretcht out';* Johnson, *'our best means stretcht';* Malone, *'our means stretch'd to the utmost.'*
22. Craik's suggestion that *'Lucilius'* and *'Lucius'* have been transposed in these lines has been accepted by many Editors. The Cambridge editors are of opinion that the error is due to the author and not to a transcriber, and have, therefore, not tampered with the text.
23. Cp. – "This Phaonius ... came into the chamber, and with a certain scoffing and mocking gesture, which he counterfeited of purpose, he rehearsed the verses which old Nestor said in Homer":—

    "My lords I pray you hearken both to me,
    For I have seen more years than suchie three."

    (North's *Plutarch*).

24. Vilely; – so Folio 4; Folios 1, 2, *'vildely';* Folio 3, *'vildly.'*
25. I will do so, i.e. – 'I will do as you wish, and keep on the left'; according to some Editors, the words may mean 'I will not wrangle, but will have my way.'

26. Three and thirty; – Theobald, *'three and twenty'* (the number given in *Plutarch*).
27. The last; – Rowe unnecessarily suggested, *'Thou last'*; but *cp.* North's *Plutarch,* "he (Brutus) lamented the death of Cassius, calling him *the last* of all the Romans."
28. Farewell to thee too, Strato: Countrymen; – Theobald's emendation of Folios, *'Farewell to thee, to Strato, Countrymen.'*
29. In a general honest thought And; – Collier MS., adopted by Craik, reads *'in a generous honest thought Of.'*

KING LEAR

KING LEAR

DRAMATIS PERSONAE

LEAR, king of Britain.
KING OF FRANCE.
DUKE OF BURGUNDY.
DUKE OF CORNWALL.
DUKE OF ALBANY.
EARL OF KENT.
EARL OF GLOUCESTER.
EDGAR, son to Gloucester.
EDMUND, bastard son to Gloucester.
CURAN, a courtier.
Old Man, tenant to Gloucester.
Doctor.
Fool.
OSWALD, steward to Goneril.
A Captain employed by Edmund.
Gentleman attendant on Cordelia.
A Herald.
Servants to Cornwall.
GONERIL, daughter to Lear.
REGAN, daughter to Lear.
CORDELIA, daughter to Lear.
Knights of Lear's train, Captains, Messengers, Soldiers, and Attendants.

SCENE: *Britain.*

ACT ONE SCENE ONE

King Lear's palace.

Enter KENT, GLOUCESTER, *and* EDMUND.

KENT
I thought the king had more affected the Duke of Albany than Cornwall.

GLOUCESTER
It did always seem so to us: but now, in the division of the kingdom, it appears not which of the dukes he values most; for equalities are so weighed, that curiosity in neither can make choice of either's moiety.

KENT
Is not this your son, my lord?

GLOUCESTER
His breeding, sir, hath been at my charge: I have so often blushed to acknowledge him, that now I am brazed to it.

KENT
I cannot conceive you.

GLOUCESTER
Sir, this young fellow's mother could: whereupon she grew round-wombed, and had, indeed, sir, a son for her cradle ere she had a husband for her bed. Do you smell a fault?

KENT
I cannot wish the fault undone, the issue of it being so proper.

GLOUCESTER
But I have, sir, a son by order of law, some year elder than this, who yet is no dearer in my account: though this knave came something saucily into the world before he was sent for, yet was his mother fair; there was good sport at his making, and the whoreson must be acknowledged. Do you know this noble gentleman, Edmund?

EDMUND
No, my lord.

GLOUCESTER
My lord of Kent: remember him hereafter as my honourable friend.
EDMUND
My services to your lordship.
KENT
I must love you, and sue to know you better.
EDMUND
Sir, I shall study deserving.
GLOUCESTER
He hath been out nine years, and away he shall again. The king is coming.

Sennet. Enter KING LEAR, CORNWALL, ALBANY, GONERIL, REGAN, CORDELIA, *and* Attendants.

KING LEAR
Attend the lords of France and Burgundy, Gloucester.
GLOUCESTER
I shall, my liege. [*Exeunt Gloucester and Edmund.*
KING LEAR
Meantime we shall express our darker purpose.
Give me the map there. Know that we have divided
In three our kingdom: and 'tis our fast intent
To shake all cares and business from our age; [1]
Conferring them on younger strengths,while we [2]
Unburthen'd crawl toward death. Our son of Cornwall,
And you, our no less loving son of Albany,
We have this hour a constant will to publish
Our daughters' several dowers, that future strife
May be prevented now. The princes, France and Burgundy,
Great rivals in our youngest daughter's love,
Long in our court have made their amorous sojourn,
And here are to be answer'd. Tell me, my daughters,—
Since now we will divest us, both of rule,
Interest of territory, cares of state,—
Which of you shall we say doth love us most?
That our largest bounty may extend
Where nature doth with merit challenge. Goneril, [3]
Our eldest-born, speak first.
GONERIL
Sir, I love you more than words can wield the matter;
Dearer than eye-sight, space, and liberty;
Beyond what can be valued, rich or rare;
No less than life, with grace, health, beauty, honour;
As much as child e'er loved, or father found;
A love that makes breath poor, and speech unable;
Beyond all manner of so much I love you.
CORDELIA
[*Aside*] What shall Cordelia do? [4]
Love, and be silent.
KING LEAR
Of all these bounds, even from this line to this,
With shadowy forests and with champains rich'd,
With plenteous rivers and wide-skirted meads,
We make thee lady: to thine and Albany's issue
Be this perpetual. What says our second daughter,
Our dearest Regan, wife to Cornwall? Speak.
REGAN
Sir, I am made
Of the self-same metal that my sister is,
And prize me at her worth. In my true heart
I find she names my very deed of love;
Only she comes too short: that I profess
Myself an enemy to all other joys,
Which the most precious square of sense possesses;
And find I am alone felicitate
In your dear highness' love.
CORDELIA
[*Aside*] Then poor Cordelia!
And yet not so; since, I am sure, my love's
More richer than my tongue. [5]
KING LEAR
To thee and thine hereditary ever
Remain this ample third of our fair kingdom;
No less in space, validity, and pleasure,
Than that conferr'd on Goneril. Now, our joy,
Although the last, not least; to whose young love [6]
The vines of France and milk of Burgundy
Strive to be interess'd; what can you say to draw
A third more opulent than your sisters? Speak.
CORDELIA
Nothing, my lord.
KING LEAR
Nothing!
CORDELIA
Nothing.
KING LEAR
Nothing will come of nothing: speak again.
CORDELIA
Unhappy that I am, I cannot heave
My heart into my mouth: I love your majesty
According to my bond; nor more nor less.
KING LEAR
How, how, Cordelia! mend your speech a little,
Lest it may mar your fortunes.
CORDELIA
Good my lord,
You have begot me, bred me, loved me: I
Return those duties back as are right fit,
Obey you, love you, and most honour you.
Why have my sisters husbands, if they say
They love you all? Haply, when I shall wed,
That lord whose hand must take my plight shall carry
Half my love with him, half my care and duty:
Sure, I shall never marry like my sisters, [7]

To love my father all.

KING LEAR
But goes thy heart with this?

CORDELIA
Ay, good my lord.

KING LEAR
So young, and so untender?

CORDELIA
So young, my lord, and true.

KING LEAR
Let it be so; thy truth, then, be thy dower:
For, by the sacred radiance of the sun,
The mysteries of Hecate, and the night; [8]
By all the operation of the orbs
From whom we do exist, and cease to be;
Here I disclaim all my paternal care,
Propinquity and property of blood,
And as a stranger to my heart and me
Hold thee, from this, for ever. The barbarous Scythian,
Or he that makes his generation messes
To gorge his appetite, shall to my bosom
Be as well neighbour'd, pitied, and relieved,
As thou my sometime daughter.

KENT
Good my liege,—

KING LEAR
Peace, Kent!
Come not between the dragon and his wrath.
I loved her most, and thought to set my rest
On her kind nursery. Hence, and avoid my sight!
So be my grave my peace, as here I give
Her father's heart from her! Call France; who stirs?
Call Burgundy. Cornwall and Albany,
With my two daughters' dowers digest this third:
Let pride, which she calls plainness, marry her.
I do invest you jointly with my power,
Pre-eminence, and all the large effects
That troop with majesty. Ourself, by monthly course,
With reservation of an hundred knights,
By you to be sustain'd, shall our abode
Make with you by due turns. Only we still retain
The name, and all the additions to a king;
The sway, revenue, execution of the rest,
Beloved sons, be yours: which to confirm,
This coronet part betwixt you. [*Giving the crown.*

KENT
Royal Lear,
Whom I have ever honour'd as my king,
Loved as my father, as my master follow'd,

KING LEAR Hence, and avoid my sight!

As my great patron thought on in my prayers,—
KING LEAR
The bow is bent and drawn, make from the shaft.
KENT
Let it fall rather, though the fork invade
The region of my heart: be Kent unmannerly,
When Lear is mad. What wilt thou do, old man? [9]
Think'st thou that duty shall have dread to speak,
When power to flattery bows? To plainness honour's bound,
When majesty stoops to folly. Reverse thy doom; [10]
And, in thy best consideration, check
This hideous rashness: answer my life my judgment,
Thy youngest daughter does not love thee least;
Nor are those empty-hearted whose low sound
Reverbs no hollowness.
KING LEAR
Kent, on thy life, no more.
KENT
My life I never held but as a pawn
To wage against thy enemies; nor fear to lose it,
Thy safety being the motive.
KING LEAR
Out of my sight!
KENT
See better, Lear; and let me still remain
The true blank of thine eye.
KING LEAR
Now, by Apollo,—
KENT
Now, by Apollo, king,
Thou swear'st thy gods in vain.
KING LEAR
O, vassal! miscreant! [*Laying his hand on his sword.*
ALBANY, CORNWALL
KENT
Dear sir, forbear.
Do;
Kill thy physician, and the fee bestow
Upon thy foul disease. Revoke thy doom;
Or, whilst I can vent clamour from my throat,
I'll tell thee thou dost evil.
KING LEAR
Hear me, recreant! [11]
On thine allegiance, hear me!
Since thou hast sought to make us break our vow,
Which we durst never yet, and with strain'd pride
To come between our sentence and our power,
Which nor our nature nor our place can bear,
Our potency made good, take thy reward.
Five days we do allot thee, for provision [12]
To shield thee from diseases of the world;
And on the sixth to turn thy hated back [13]
Upon our kingdom: if, on the tenth day following,
Thy banish'd trunk be found in our dominions,
The moment is thy death. Away! by Jupiter,
This shall not be revoked.
KENT
Fare thee well, king: sith thus thou wilt appear,
Freedom lives hence, and banishment is here.
[*To Cordelia*] The gods to their dear shelter take thee, maid,
That justly think'st, and hast most rightly said!
[*To Regan and Goneril*] And your large speeches may your deeds approve,
That good effects may spring from words of love.
Thus Kent, O princes, bids you all adieu;
He'll shape his old course in a country new. [*Exit.*

Flourish. Re-enter GLOUCESTER, *with* FRANCE, BURGUNDY, *and* Attendants.

GLOUCESTER
Here's France and Burgundy, my noble lord. [14]
KING LEAR
My lord of Burgundy.
We first address towards you, who with this king
Hath rivall'd for our daughter: what, in the least,
Will you require in present dower with her,
Or cease your quest of love?
BURGUNDY
Most royal majesty,
I crave no more than what your highness offer'd,
Nor will you tender less.
KING LEAR
Right noble Burgundy,
When she was dear to us, we did hold her so;
But now her price is fall'n. Sir, there she stands:
If aught within that little seeming substance,
Or all of it, with our displeasure pieced,
And nothing more, may fitly like your grace,
She's there, and she is yours.
BURGUNDY
I know no answer.
KING LEAR
Will you, with those infirmities she owes,
Unfriended, new-adopted to our hate,
Dower'd with our curse, and stranger'd with our oath,
Take her, or leave her?
BURGUNDY
Pardon me, royal sir;
Election makes not up on such conditions.
KING LEAR
Then leave her, sir; for, by the power that made me,

I tell you all her wealth. [*To France*] For you, great king,
I would not from your love make such a stray,
To match you where I hate! therefore beseech you
To avert your liking a more worthier way
Than on a wretch whom nature is ashamed
Almost to acknowledge hers.

KING OF FRANCE
This is most strange,
That she, that even but now was your best object,
The argument of your praise, balm of your age,
Most best, most dearest, should in this trice of time
Commit a thing so monstrous, to dismantle
So many folds of favour. Sure, her offence
Must be of such unnatural degree,
That monsters it, or your fore-vouch'd affection
Fall'n into taint: which to believe of her,
Must be a faith that reason without miracle
Could never plant in me.

CORDELIA
I yet beseech your majesty,—
If for I want that glib and oily art,
To speak and purpose not; since what I well intend,
I'll do't before I speak,—that you make known
It is no vicious blot, murder, or foulness,
No unchaste action, or dishonour'd step,
That hath deprived me of your grace and favour;
But even for want of that for which I am richer,
A still-soliciting eye, and such a tongue
As I am glad I have not, though not to have it
Hath lost me in your liking.

KING LEAR
Better thou [15]
Hadst not been born than not to have pleased me better.

KING OF FRANCE
Is it but this,—a tardiness in nature
Which often leaves the history unspoken
That it intends to do? My lord of Burgundy,
What say you to the lady? Love's not love
When it is mingled with regards that stand
Aloof from the entire point. Will you have her?
She is herself a dowry.

BURGUNDY
Royal Lear,
Give but that portion which yourself proposed,
And here I take Cordelia by the hand,
Duchess of Burgundy.

KING LEAR
Nothing: I have sworn; I am firm.

BURGUNDY
I am sorry, then, you have so lost a father
That you must lose a husband.

CORDELIA
Peace be with Burgundy!
Since that respects of fortune are his love, [16]
I shall not be his wife.

KING OF FRANCE
Fairest Cordelia, that art most rich, being poor;
Most choice, forsaken; and most loved, despised!
Thee and thy virtues here I seize upon:
Be it lawful I take up what's cast away.
Gods, gods! 'tis strange that from their cold'st neglect
My love should kindle to inflamed respect.
Thy dowerless daughter, king, thrown to my chance,
Is queen of us, of ours, and our fair France:
Not all the dukes of waterish Burgundy
Can buy this unprized precious maid of me.
Bid them farewell, Cordelia, though unkind:
Thou losest here, a better where to find.

KING LEAR
Thou hast her, France: let her be thine; for we
Have no such daughter, nor shall ever see
That face of hers again. Therefore be gone
Without our grace, our love, our benison.
Come, noble Burgundy. [*Flourish. Exeunt all but France, Goneril, Regan, and Cordelia.*

KING OF FRANCE
Bid farewell to your sisters.

CORDELIA
The jewels of our father, with wash'd eyes
Cordelia leaves you: I know you what you are;
And like a sister am most loath to call
Your faults as they are named. Use well our father:
To your professed bosoms I commit him:
But yet, alas, stood I within his grace,
I would prefer him to a better place.
So, farewell to you both.

REGAN
Prescribe not us our duties.

GONERIL
Let your study
Be to content your lord, who hath received you
At fortune's alms. You have obedience scanted,
And well are worth the want that you have wanted. [17]

CORDELIA
Time shall unfold what plaited cunning hides:
Who cover faults, at last shame them derides. [18]
Well may you prosper!

KING OF FRANCE
Come, my fair Cordelia. [*Exeunt France and Cordelia.*

GONERIL

Sister, it is not a little I have to say of what most nearly appertains to us both. I think our father will hence to-night.

REGAN

That's most certain, and with you; next month with us.

GONERIL

You see how full of changes his age is; the observation we have made of it hath not been little: he always loved our sister most; and with what poor judgment he hath now cast her off appears too grossly. [19]

REGAN

'Tis the infirmity of his age: yet he hath ever but slenderly known himself.

GONERIL

The best and soundest of his time hath been but rash; then must we look to receive from his age, not alone the imperfections of long-engraffed condition, but therewithal the unruly waywardness that infirm and choleric years bring with them.

REGAN

Such unconstant starts are we like to have from him as this of Kent's banishment.

GONERIL

There is further compliment of leavetaking between France and him. Pray you, let's hit together: if our father carry authority with such dispositions as he bears, this last surrender of his will but offend us.

REGAN

We shall further think on't.

GONERIL

We must do something, and i' the heat. [*Exeunt.*

ACT ONE SCENE TWO

The Earl of Gloucester's castle.

Enter EDMUND, *with a letter.*

EDMUND

Thou, nature, art my goddess; to thy law
My services are bound. Wherefore should I
Stand in the plague of custom, and permit
The curiosity of nations to deprive me,
For that I am some twelve or fourteen moon-shines
Lag of a brother? Why bastards? wherefore base?
When my dimensions are as well compact,
My mind as generous, and my shape as true,
As honest madam's issue? Why brand they us
With base? with baseness? bastardy? base, base? [20]
Who, in the lusty stealth of nature, take
More composition and fierce quality
Than doth, within a dull, stale, tired bed,
Go to the creating a whole tribe of fops,
Got 'tween asleep and wake? Well, then,
Legitimate Edgar, I must have your land:
Our father's love is to the bastard Edmund
As to the legitimate: fine word,—legitimate!
Well, my legitimate, if this letter speed,
And my invention thrive, Edmund the base
Shall top the legitimate. I grow; I prosper:
Now, gods, stand up for bastards!

Enter GLOUCESTER.

GLOUCESTER

Kent banish'd thus! and France in choler parted!
And the king gone to-night! subscribed his power!
Confined to exhibition! All this done
Upon the gad! Edmund, how now! what news?

EDMUND

So please your lordship, none.

[*Putting up the letter.*

GLOUCESTER

Why so earnestly seek you to put up that letter? [22]

EDMUND

I know no news, my lord.

GLOUCESTER

What paper were you reading?

EDMUND

Nothing, my lord.

GLOUCESTER

No? What needed, then, that terrible dispatch of it into your pocket? the quality of nothing hath not such need to hide itself. Let's see: come, if it be nothing, I shall not need spectacles.

EDMUND

I beseech you, sir, pardon me: it is a letter from my brother, that I have not all o'er-read; and for so much as I have perused, I find it not fit for your o'er-looking.

GLOUCESTER

Give me the letter, sir.

EDMUND

I shall offend, either to detain or give it. The contents, as in part I understand them, are to blame.

GLOUCESTER

Let's see, let's see.

EDMUND

I hope, for my brother's justification, he wrote this but as an essay or taste of my virtue.

GLOUCESTER

[*Reads*] 'This policy and reverence of age makes the world bitter to the best of our times; keeps our fortunes from us till our oldness cannot relish them. I begin to find an idle and fond bondage in the oppression of aged tyranny; who sways, not as it hath power, but as it is suffered. Come to me, that of this I may speak more.

If our father would sleep till I waked him, you should half his revenue for ever, and live the beloved of your brother,

EDGAR.'

Hum—conspiracy!—'Sleep till I waked him,—you should enjoy half his revenue,'—My son Edgar! Had he a hand to write this? a heart and brain to breed it in?—When came this to you? who brought it?

EDMUND

It was not brought me, my lord; there's the cunning of it; I found it thrown in at the casement of my closet.

GLOUCESTER

You know the character to be your brother's?

EDMUND

If the matter were good, my lord, I durst swear it were his; but, in respect of that, I would fain think it were not. 65

GLOUCESTER

It is his.

EDMUND

It is his hand, my lord; but I hope his heart is not in the contents.

GLOUCESTER

Hath he never heretofore sounded you in this business?

EDMUND

Never, my lord: but I have heard him oft maintain it to be fit, that, sons at perfect age, and fathers declining, the father should be as ward to the son, and the son manage his revenue.

GLOUCESTER

O villain, villain! His very opinion in the letter! Abhorred villain! Unnatural, detested, brutish villain! worse than brutish! Go, sirrah, seek him; I'll apprehend him: abominable villain! Where is he?

EDMUND

I do not well know, my lord. If it shall please you to suspend your indignation against my brother till you can derive from him better testimony of his intent, you shall run a certain course; where, if you violently proceed against him, mistaking his purpose, it would make a great gap in your own honour, and shake in pieces the heart of his obedience. I dare pawn down my life for him, that he hath wrote this to feel my affection to your honour, and to no further pretence of danger.

GLOUCESTER

Think you so?

EDMUND

If your honour judge it meet, I will place you where you shall hear us confer of this, and by an auricular assurance have your satisfaction; and that without any further delay than this very evening. 93

GLOUCESTER

He cannot be such a monster—

EDMUND

Nor is not, sure.

GLOUCESTER

To his father, that so tenderly and entirely loves him. Heaven and earth! Edmund, seek him out: wind me into him, I pray you: frame the business after your own wisdom. I would unstate myself, to be in a due resolution.

EDMUND

I will seek him, sir, presently: convey the business as I shall find means and acquaint you withal. 101

GLOUCESTER

These late eclipses in the sun and moon portend no good to us: though the wisdom of nature can reason it thus and thus, yet nature finds itself scourged by the sequent effects: love cools, friendship falls off, brothers divide: in cities, mutinies; in countries, discord; in palaces, treason; and the bond cracked 'twixt son and father. This villain of mine comes under the prediction; there's son against father: the king falls from bias of nature; there's father against child. We have seen the best of our time: machinations, hollowness, treachery, and all ruinous disorders, follow us disquietly to our graves. Find out this villain, Edmund; it shall lose thee nothing; do it carefully. And the noble and true-hearted Kent banished! his offence, honesty! 'Tis strange. [23] [*Exit.*

EDMUND

This is the excellent foppery of the world, that, when we are sick in fortune,—often the surfeit of our own behavior,—we make guilty of our disasters the sun, the moon, and the stars: as if we were villains by necessity; fools by heavenly compulsion; knaves, thieves, and treachers, by spherical predominance; drunkards, liars, and adulterers, by an enforced obedience of planetary influence; and all that we are evil in, by a divine thrusting on: an admirable evasion of whoremaster man, to lay his goatish disposition to the charge of a star! My father compounded with my mother under the dragon's tail; and my nativity was under Ursa major; so that it follows, I am rough and lecherous. Tut, I should have been that I am, had the maidenliest star in the firmament twinkled on my bastardizing. Edgar— [24]

Enter EDGAR.

and pat he comes like the catastrophe of the old comedy: my cue is villanous melancholy, with a sigh like Tom o' Bedlam. O, these eclipses do portend these divisions! fa, sol, la, mi.

EDGAR

How now, brother Edmund! what serious contemplation are you in? 138

EDMUND

I am thinking, brother, of a prediction I read this other day, what should follow these eclipses.

EDGAR

Do you busy yourself about that?

EDMUND

I promise you, the effects he writes of succeed unhappily; as of unnaturalness between the child and the parent; death, dearth, dissolutions of ancient amities; divisions in state, menaces and maledictions against king and nobles; needless diffidences, banishment of friends, dissipation of cohorts, nuptial breaches, and I know not what.

EDGAR

How long have you been a sectary astronomical?

EDMUND

Come, come; when saw you my father last?

EDGAR

Why, the night gone by.

EDMUND

Spake you with him?

EDGAR

Ay, two hours together. 152

EDMUND

Parted you in good terms? Found you no displeasure in him by word or countenance?

EDGAR

None at all.

EDMUND

Bethink yourself wherein you may have offended him: and at my entreaty forbear his presence till some little time hath qualified the heat of his displeasure; which at this instant so rageth in him, that with the mischief of your person it would scarcely allay. 160

EDGAR

Some villain hath done me wrong.

EDMUND

That's my fear. I pray you, have a continent forbearance till the spied of his rage goes slower; and, as I say, retire with me to my lodging, from whence I will fitly bring you to hear my lord speak: pray ye, go; there's my key: if you do stir abroad, go armed. [25]

EDGAR

Armed, brother!

EDMUND

Brother, I advise you to the best; go armed: I am no honest man if there be any good meaning towards you: I have told you what I have seen and heard; but faintly, nothing like the image and horror of it: pray you, away.

EDGAR

Shall I hear from you anon?

EDMUND

I do serve you in this business. [*Exit Edgar.*
A credulous father! and a brother noble,
Whose nature is so far from doing harms,
That he suspects none: on whose foolish honesty
My practises ride easy! I see the business.
Let me, if not by birth, have lands by wit: 178
All with me's meet that I can fashion fit. [*Exit.*

ACT ONE SCENE THREE

The Duke of Albany's palace.

Enter GONERIL, *and* OSWALD, *her steward.*

GONERIL

Did my father strike my gentleman for chiding of his fool?

OSWALD

Yes, madam.

GONERIL

By day and night he wrongs me; every hour
He flashes into one gross crime or other,
That sets us all at odds: I'll not endure it:
His knights grow riotous, and himself upbraids us
On every trifle. When he returns from hunting,
I will not speak with him; say I am sick:
If you come slack of former services,
You shall do well; the fault of it I'll answer.

OSWALD

He's coming, madam; I hear him. [*Horns within.*

GONERIL

Put on what weary negligence you please,
You and your fellows; I'ld have it come to question:
If he dislike it, let him to our sister,
Whose mind and mine, I know, in that are one,
Not to be over-ruled. Idle old man,
That still would manage those authorities
That he hath given away! Now, by my life,
Old fools are babes again; and must be used
With checks as flatteries,—when they are seen abused. [26]
Remember what I tell you. 23

OSWALD

Well, madam.

GONERIL

And let his knights have colder looks among you;
What grows of it, no matter; advise your fellows so:
I would breed from hence occasions, and I shall,
That I may speak: I'll write straight to my sister,
To hold my very course. Prepare for dinner. [*Exeunt.*

ACT ONE SCENE FOUR

A hall in the same.

Enter KENT, *disguised.*

KENT

If but as well I other accents borrow,

That can my speech defuse, my good intent
May carry through itself to that full issue
For which I razed my likeness. Now, banish'd Kent,
If thou canst serve where thou dost stand condemn'd,
So may it come, thy master, whom thou lovest,
Shall find thee full of labours.

Horns within. Enter LEAR, Knights, *and* Attendants.

KING LEAR
Let me not stay a jot for dinner; go get it ready. [*Exit an Attendant.*] How now! what art thou?

KENT
A man, sir.

KING LEAR
What dost thou profess? what wouldst thou with us?

KENT
I do profess to be no less than I seem; to serve him truly that will put me in trust: to love him that is honest; to converse with him that is wise, and says little; to fear judgment; to fight when I cannot choose; and to eat no fish.

KING LEAR
What art thou?

KENT
A very honest-hearted fellow, and as poor as the king.

KING LEAR
If thou be as poor for a subject as he is for a king, thou art poor enough. What wouldst thou?

KENT
Service.

KING LEAR
Who wouldst thou serve?

KENT
You.

KING LEAR
Dost thou know me, fellow?

KENT
No, sir; but you have that in your countenance which I would fain call master.

KING LEAR
What's that?

KENT
Authority.

KING LEAR
What services canst thou do?

KENT
I can keep honest counsel, ride, run, mar a curious tale in telling it, and deliver a plain message bluntly: that which ordinary men are fit for, I am qualified in; and the best of me is diligence.

KING LEAR
How old art thou?

KENT
Not so young, sir, to love a woman for singing, nor so old to dote on her for any thing: I have years on my back forty eight.

KING LEAR
Follow me; thou shalt serve me: if I like thee no worse after dinner, I will not part from thee yet. Dinner, ho, dinner! Where's my knave? my fool? Go you, and call my fool hither. [*Exit an Attendant.*

Enter OSWALD.

You, you, sirrah, where's my daughter?

OSWALD
So please you,— [*Exit.*

KING LEAR
What says the fellow there? Call the clotpoll back. [*Exit a Knight.*] Where's my fool, ho? I think the world's asleep.

Re-enter Knight.

How now! where's that mongrel?

KNIGHT
He says, my lord, your daughter is not well.

KING LEAR
Why came not the slave back to me when I called him.

KNIGHT
Sir, he answered me in the roundest manner, he would not.

KING LEAR
He would not!

KNIGHT
My lord, I know not what the matter is; but, to my judgment, your highness is not entertained with that ceremonious affection as you were wont; there's a great abatement of kindness appears as well in the general dependants as in the duke himself also and your daughter.

KING LEAR
Ha! sayest thou so?

KNIGHT
I beseech you, pardon me, my lord, if I be mistaken; for my duty cannot be silent when I think your highness wronged.

KING LEAR
Thou but rememberest me of mine own conception: I have perceived a most faint neglect of late; which I have rather blamed as mine own jealous curiosity than as a very pretence and purpose of unkindness: I will look further into't. But where's my fool? I have not seen him this two days.

KNIGHT

Since my young lady's going into France, sir, the fool hath much pined away.

KING LEAR

No more of that; I have noted it well. Go you, and tell my daughter I would speak with her. [*Exit an Attendant.*] Go you, call hither my fool.

[*Exit an Attendant.*

Re-enter OSWALD.

O, you sir, you, come you hither, sir: who am I, sir?

OSWALD

My lady's father.

KING LEAR

'My lady's father'! my lord's knave: your whoreson dog! you slave! you cur!

OSWALD

I am none of these, my lord; I beseech your pardon. 82

KING LEAR

Do you bandy looks with me, you rascal?

[*Striking him.*

OSWALD

I'll not be struck, my lord.

KENT

Nor tripped neither, you base football player.

[*Tripping up his heels.*

KING LEAR

I thank thee, fellow; thou servest me, and I'll love thee.

KENT

Come, sir, arise, away! I'll teach you differences: away, away! if you will measure your lubber's length again, tarry: but away! go to; have you wisdom? so.

[*Pushes Oswald out.*

KING LEAR

Now, my friendly knave, I thank thee: there's earnest of thy service. [*Giving Kent money.*

Enter Fool.

FOOL

Let me hire him too: here's my coxcomb.

[*Offering Kent his cap.*

KING LEAR

How now, my pretty knave! how dost thou?

FOOL

Sirrah, you were best take my coxcomb.

KENT

Why, fool? [27]

FOOL

Why, for taking one's part that's out of favour: nay, an thou canst not smile as the wind sits, thou'lt catch cold shortly: there, take my coxcomb: why, this fellow has banished two on's daughters, and did the third a blessing against his will; if thou follow him, thou must needs wear my coxcomb. How now, uncle! Would I had two coxcombs and two daughters!

KING LEAR

Why, my boy? 104

FOOL

If I gave them all my living, I'ld keep my coxcombs myself. There's mine; beg another of thy daughters.

KING LEAR

Take heed, sirrah; the whip.

FOOL

Truth's a dog must to kennel; he must be whipped out, when Lady the brach may stand by the fire and stink.

KING LEAR

A pestilent gall to me!

FOOL

Sirrah, I'll teach thee a speech.

KING LEAR

Do.

FOOL

Mark it, nuncle: 113
Have more than thou showest,
Speak less than thou knowest,
Lend less than thou owest,
Ride more than thou goest,
Learn more than thou trowest,
Set less than thou throwest;
Leave thy drink and thy whore,
And keep in-a-door,
And thou shalt have more
Than two tens to a score. 123

KENT

This is nothing, fool.

FOOL

Then 'tis like the breath of an unfee'd lawyer; you gave me nothing for't. Can you make no use of nothing, nuncle?

KING LEAR

Why, no, boy; nothing can be made out of nothing.

FOOL

[*To Kent*] Prithee, tell him, so much the rent of his land comes to: he will not believe a fool.

KING LEAR

A bitter fool! 131

FOOL

Dost thou know the difference, my boy, between a bitter fool and a sweet fool?

KING LEAR

No, lad; teach me.

FOOL

That lord that counsell'd thee
To give away thy land,
Come place him here by me,

Do thou for him stand:
The sweet and bitter fool
Will presently appear;
The one in motley here, 141
The other found out there.

KING LEAR
Dost thou call me fool, boy?

FOOL
All thy other titles thou hast given away; that thou wast born with.

KENT
This is not altogether fool, my lord.

FOOL
No, faith, lords and great men will not let me; if I had a monopoly out, they would have part on't: and ladies too, they will not let me have all fool to myself; they'll be snatching. Give me an egg, nuncle, and I'll give thee two crowns. [28]

KING LEAR
What two crowns shall they be? 152

FOOL
Why, after I have cut the egg i' the middle, and eat up the meat, the two crowns of the egg. When thou clovest thy crown i' the middle, and gavest away both parts, thou borest thy ass on thy back o'er the dirt: thou hadst little wit in thy bald crown, when thou gavest thy golden one away. If I speak like myself in this, let him be whipped that first finds it so. 159
[*Singing*] Fools had ne'er less wit in a year;
For wise men are grown foppish,
They know not how their wits to wear,
Their manners are so apish.

KING LEAR
When were you wont to be so full of songs, sirrah?

FOOL
I have used it, nuncle, ever since thou madest thy daughters thy mothers: for when thou gavest them the rod, and put'st down thine own breeches, 169
[*Singing*] Then they for sudden joy did weep,
And I for sorrow sung,
That such a king should play bo-peep,
And go the fools among.
Prithee, nuncle, keep a schoolmaster that can teach thy fool to lie: I would fain learn to lie.

KING LEAR
An you lie, sirrah, we'll have you whipped.

FOOL
I marvel what kin thou and thy daughters are: they'll have me whipped for speaking true, thou'lt have me whipped for lying; and sometimes I am whipped for holding my peace. I had rather be any kind o' thing than a fool: and yet I would not be thee, nuncle; thou hast pared thy wit o' both sides, and left nothing i' the middle: here comes one o' the parings.

Enter GONERIL.

KING LEAR
How now, daughter! what makes that frontlet on? Methinks you are too much of late i' the frown. 186

FOOL
Thou wast a pretty fellow when thou hadst no need to care for her frowning; now thou art an O without a figure: I am better than thou art now; I am a fool, thou art nothing. [*To Goneril*] Yes, forsooth, I will hold my tongue; so your face bids me, though you say nothing. Mum, mum,
He that keeps nor crust nor crum,
Weary of all, shall want some.
[*Pointing to Lear*] That's a shealed peascod.

GONERIL
Not only, sir, this your all-licensed fool,
But other of your insolent retinue 197
Do hourly carp and quarrel; breaking forth
In rank and not-to-be endured riots. Sir,
I had thought, by making this well known unto you,
To have found a safe redress; but now grow fearful,
By what yourself too late have spoke and done.
That you protect this course, and put it on
By your allowance; which if you should, the fault
Would not 'scape censure, nor the redresses sleep,
Which, in the tender of a wholesome weal,
Might in their working do you that offence,
Which else were shame, that then necessity
Will call discreet proceeding.

FOOL
For, you trow, nuncle,
The hedge-sparrow fed the cuckoo so long,
That it's had it head bit off by it young.
So, out went the candle, and we were left darkling.

KING LEAR
Are you our daughter?

GONERIL
Come, sir,
I would you would make use of that good wisdom, 218
Whereof I know you are fraught; and put away
These dispositions, that of late transform you
From what you rightly are.

FOOL
May not an ass know when the cart draws the horse? Whoop, Jug! I love thee.

KING LEAR
Doth any here know me? This is not Lear:
Doth Lear walk thus? speak thus? Where are his eyes?

Either his notion weakens, his discernings
Are lethargied—Ha! waking? 'tis not so. [29]
Who is it that can tell me who I am? 228

FOOL
Lear's shadow.

KING LEAR
I would learn that; for, by the marks of sovereignty, knowledge, and reason,
I should be false persuaded I had daughters.

FOOL
Which they will make an obedient father.

KING LEAR
Your name, fair gentlewoman?

GONERIL
This admiration, sir, is much o' the savour
Of other your new pranks. I do beseech you
To understand my purposes aright: 237
As you are old and reverend, you should be wise.
Here do you keep a hundred knights and squires;
Men so disorder'd, so debosh'd and bold,
That this our court, infected with their manners,
Shows like a riotous inn: epicurism and lust
Make it more like a tavern or a brothel
Than a graced palace. The shame itself doth speak
For instant remedy: be then desired
By her, that else will take the thing she begs,
A little to disquantity your train; 247
And the remainder, that shall still depend,
To be such men as may besort your age,
And know themselves and you.

KING LEAR
Darkness and devils!
Saddle my horses; call my train together:
Degenerate bastard! I'll not trouble thee.
Yet have I left a daughter.

GONERIL
You strike my people; and your disorder'd rabble
Make servants of their betters.

Enter ALBANY.

KING LEAR
Woe, that too late repents,— [*To Albany*] O, sir, are you come?
Is it your will? Speak, sir. Prepare my horses.
Ingratitude, thou marble-hearted fiend, 260
More hideous when thou show'st thee in a child
Than the sea-monster!

ALBANY
Pray, sir, be patient.

KING LEAR
[*To Goneril*] Detested kite! thou liest:
My train are men of choice and rarest parts,
That all particulars of duty know,
And in the most exact regard support
The worships of their name. O most small fault,
How ugly didst thou in Cordelia show!
That, like an engine, wrench'd my frame of nature 271
From the fix'd place; drew from heart all love,
And added to the gall. O Lear, Lear, Lear!
Beat at this gate, that let thy folly in, [*Striking his head.*
And thy dear judgment out! Go, go, my people.

ALBANY
My lord, I am guiltless, as I am ignorant
Of what hath moved you.

KING LEAR
It may be so, my lord.
Hear, nature, hear; dear goddess, hear!
Suspend thy purpose, if thou didst intend
To make this creature fruitful!
Into her womb convey sterility! 282
Dry up in her the organs of increase;
And from her derogate body never spring
A babe to honour her! If she must teem,
Create her child of spleen; that it may live,
And be a thwart disnatured torment to her!
Let it stamp wrinkles in her brow of youth;
With cadent tears fret channels in her cheeks;
Turn all her mother's pains and benefits
To laughter and contempt; that she may feel
How sharper than a serpent's tooth it is 292
To have a thankless child! Away, away! [*Exit.*

ALBANY
Now, gods that we adore, whereof comes this?

GONERIL
Never afflict yourself to know the cause;
But let his disposition have that scope
That dotage gives it.

Re-enter LEAR.

KING LEAR
What, fifty of my followers at a clap!
Within a fortnight!

ALBANY
What's the matter, sir?

KING LEAR
I'll tell thee: [*To Goneril*] Life and death! I am ashamed
That thou hast power to shake my manhood thus;
That these hot tears, which break from me perforce, 304
Should make thee worth them. Blasts and fogs upon thee!
The untented woundings of a father's curse
Pierce every sense about thee! Old fond eyes,
Beweep this cause again, I'll pluck ye out,
And cast you, with the waters that you lose,
To temper clay. Yea, it is come to this?

Let is be so: yet have I left a daughter,
Who, I am sure, is kind and comfortable:
When she shall hear this of thee, with her nails
She'll flay thy wolvish visage. Thou shalt find
That I'll resume the shape which thou dost think
I have cast off for ever: thou shalt, I warrant thee.
[*Exeunt Lear, Kent, and Attendants.*

GONERIL
Do you mark that, my lord?

ALBANY
I cannot be so partial, Goneril,
To the great love I bear you,—

GONERIL
Pray you, content. What, Oswald, ho!
[*To the Fool*] You, sir, more knave than fool, after your master.

FOOL
Nuncle Lear, nuncle Lear, tarry and take the fool with thee.
A fox, when one has caught her,
And such a daughter,
Should sure to the slaughter,
If my cap would buy a halter:
So the fool follows after. [*Exit.*

GONERIL
This man hath had good counsel:—a hundred knights!
'Tis politic and safe to let him keep
At point a hundred knights: yes, that, on every dream,
Each buzz, each fancy, each complaint, dislike,
He may enguard his dotage with their powers,
And hold our lives in mercy. Oswald, I say!

ALBANY
Well, you may fear too far.

GONERIL
Safer than trust too far:
Let me still take away the harms I fear,
Not fear still to be taken: I know his heart.
What he hath utter'd I have writ my sister:
If she sustain him and his hundred knights,
When I have show'd the unfitness,—

Re-enter OSWALD.

How now, Oswald!
What, have you writ that letter to my sister?

OSWALD
Yes, madam.

GONERIL
Take you some company, and away to horse:
Inform her full of my particular fear;
And thereto add such reasons of your own
As may compact it more. Get you gone;
And hasten your return. [*Exit Oswald.*] No, no, my lord,
This milky gentleness and course of yours
Though I condemn not, yet, under pardon,
You are much more attask'd for want of wisdom
Than praised for harmful mildness.

ALBANY
How far your eyes may pierce I can not tell:
Striving to better, oft we mar what's well.

GONERIL
Nay, then—

ALBANY
Well, well; the event. [*Exeunt.*

ACT ONE SCENE FIVE

Court before the same.

Enter LEAR, KENT, *and* Fool.

KING LEAR
Go you before to Gloucester with these letters. Acquaint my daughter no further with any thing you know than comes from her demand out of the letter. If your diligence be not speedy, I shall be there afore you.

KENT
I will not sleep, my lord, till I have delivered your letter. [*Exit.*

FOOL
If a man's brains were in's heels, were't not in danger of kibes?

KING LEAR
Ay, boy.

FOOL
Then, I prithee, be merry; thy wit shall ne'er go slip-shod.

KING LEAR
Ha, ha, ha!

FOOL
Shalt see thy other daughter will use thee kindly; for though she's as like this as a crab's like an apple, yet I can tell what I can tell.

KING LEAR
Why, what canst thou tell, my boy?

FOOL
She will taste as like this as a crab does to a crab. Thou canst tell why one's nose stands i' the middle on's face?

KING LEAR
No.

FOOL
Why, to keep one's eyes of either side's nose; that what a man cannot smell out, he may spy into.

KING LEAR
I did her wrong—

FOOL
Canst tell how an oyster makes his shell?
KING LEAR
No.
FOOL
Nor I neither; but I can tell why a snail has a house. 27
KING LEAR
Why?
FOOL
Why, to put his head in; not to give it away to his daughters, and leave his horns without a case.
KING LEAR
I will forget my nature. So kind a father! Be my horses ready?
FOOL
Thy asses are gone about 'em. The reason why the seven stars are no more than seven is a pretty reason.
KING LEAR
Because they are not eight? 35
FOOL
Yes, indeed: thou wouldst make a good fool.
KING LEAR
To take't again perforce! Monster ingratitude!
FOOL
If thou wert my fool, nuncle, I'ld have thee beaten for being old before thy time.
KING LEAR
How's that?
FOOL
Thou shouldst not have been old till thou hadst been wise.
KING LEAR
O, let me not be mad, not mad, sweet heaven! 43
Keep me in temper: I would not be mad!

Enter Gentleman.

How now! are the horses ready?
GENTLEMAN
Ready, my lord.
KING LEAR
Come, boy.
FOOL
She that's a maid now, and laughs at my departure,
Shall not be a maid long, unless things be cut shorter. [*Exeunt.*

ACT TWO SCENE ONE

The Earl of Gloucester's castle.

Enter EDMUND, *and* CURAN *meets him.*

EDMUND
Save thee, Curan.
CURAN
And you, sir. I have been with your father, and given him notice that the Duke of Cornwall and Regan his duchess will be here with him this night.
EDMUND
How comes that?
CURAN
Nay, I know not. You have heard of the news abroad; I mean the whispered ones, for they are yet but ear-kissing arguments?
EDMUND
Not I: pray you, what are they? 9
CURAN
Have you heard of no likely wars toward, 'twixt the Dukes of Cornwall and Albany? *30*
EDMUND
Not a word.
CURAN
You may do, then, in time. Fare you well, sir. [*Exit.*
EDMUND
The duke be here to-night? The better! best!
This weaves itself perforce into my business.
My father hath set guard to take my brother;
And I have one thing, of a queasy question,
Which I must act: briefness and fortune, work! 19
Brother, a word; descend: brother, I say!

Enter EDGAR.

My father watches: O sir, fly this place;
Intelligence is given where you are hid;
You have now the good advantage of the night:
Have you not spoken 'gainst the Duke of Cornwall?
He's coming hither: now, i' the night, i' the haste,
And Regan with him: have you nothing said
Upon his party 'gainst the Duke of Albany?
Advise yourself.
EDGAR
I am sure on't, not a word.
EDMUND
I hear my father coming: pardon me:
In cunning I must draw my sword upon you:
Draw; seem to defend yourself; now quit you well.
Yield: come before my father. Light, ho, here!
Fly, brother. Torches, torches! So, farewell. [*Exit Edgar.*
Some blood drawn on me would beget opinion. [*Wounds his arm.*
Of my more fierce endeavour: I have seen drunkards
Do more than this in sport. Father, father!
Stop, stop! No help?

Enter GLOUCESTER, *and* Servants *with torches.*

GLOUCESTER
Now, Edmund, where's the villain?

EDMUND
Here stood he in the dark, his sharp sword out, 40
Mumbling of wicked charms, conjuring the moon
To stand auspicious mistress,—

GLOUCESTER
But where is he?

EDMUND
Look, sir, I bleed.

GLOUCESTER
Where is the villain, Edmund?

EDMUND
Fled this way, sir. When by no means he could—

GLOUCESTER
Pursue him, ho! Go after. [*Exeunt some Servants.*
By no means what?

EDMUND
Persuade me to the murder of your lordship;
But that I told him, the revenging gods
'Gainst parricides did all their thunders bend; [31]
Spoke, with how manifold and strong a bond
The child was bound to the father; sir, in fine,
Seeing how loathly opposite I stood 54
To his unnatural purpose, in fell motion,
With his prepared sword, he charges home
My unprovided body, lanced mine arm:
But when he saw my best alarum'd spirits,
Bold in the quarrel's right, roused to the encounter,
Or whether gasted by the noise I made,
Full suddenly he fled.

GLOUCESTER
Let him fly far:
Not in this land shall he remain uncaught;
And found—dispatch. The noble duke my master, [32]
My worthy arch and patron, comes to-night: 66
By his authority I will proclaim it,
That he which finds him shall deserve our thanks,
Bringing the murderous coward to the stake;
He that conceals him, death.

EDMUND
When I dissuaded him from his intent,
And found him pight to do it, with curst speech
I threaten'd to discover him: he replied,
'Thou unpossessing bastard! dost thou think,
If I would stand against thee, would the reposal
Of any trust, virtue, or worth in thee 76
Make thy words faith'd? No: what I should deny,— [33]
As this I would: ay, though thou didst produce
My very character,—I'ld turn it all
To thy suggestion, plot, and damned practice:
And thou must make a dullard of the world,
If they not thought the profits of my death
Were very pregnant and potential spurs
To make thee seek it.'

GLOUCESTER
Strong and fasten'd villain!
Would he deny his letter? I never got him. [34]
[*Tucket within.*
Hark, the duke's trumpets! I know not why he comes.
All ports I'll bar; the villain shall not 'scape;
The duke must grant me that: besides, his picture
I will send far and near, that all the kingdom
May have the due note of him; and of my land,
Loyal and natural boy, I'll work the means
To make thee capable.

Enter CORNWALL, REGAN, *and* Attendants.

CORNWALL
How now, my noble friend! since I came hither,
Which I can call but now, I have heard strange news.

REGAN
If it be true, all vengeance comes too short 98
Which can pursue the offender. How dost, my lord?

GLOUCESTER
O, madam, my old heart is crack'd, it's crack'd!

REGAN
What, did my father's godson seek your life?
He whom my father named? your Edgar?

GLOUCESTER
O, lady, lady, shame would have it hid!

REGAN
Was he not companion with the riotous knights
That tend upon my father?

GLOUCESTER
I know not, madam: 'tis too bad, too bad.

EDMUND
Yes, madam, he was of that consort. [35]

REGAN
No marvel, then, though he were ill affected: 108
'Tis they have put him on the old man's death,
To have the expense and waste of his revenues. [36]
I have this present evening from my sister
Been well inform'd of them; and with such cautions,
That if they come to sojourn at my house,
I'll not be there.

CORNWALL
Nor I, assure thee, Regan.
Edmund, I hear that you have shown your father
A child-like office.

EDMUND
'Twas my duty, sir.

GLOUCESTER
He did bewray his practise; and received
This hurt you see, striving to apprehend him.
CORNWALL
Is he pursued?
GLOUCESTER
Ay, my good lord. 122
CORNWALL
If he be taken, he shall never more
Be fear'd of doing harm: make your own purpose,
How in my strength you please. For you, Edmund,
Whose virtue and obedience doth this instant
So much commend itself, you shall be ours:
Natures of such deep trust we shall much need;
You we first seize on.
EDMUND
I shall serve you, sir,
Truly, however else.
GLOUCESTER
For him I thank your grace.
CORNWALL
You know not why we came to visit you,— 133
REGAN
Thus out of season, threading dark-eyed night:
Occasions, noble Gloucester, of some poise,
Wherein we must have use of your advice:
Our father he hath writ, so hath our sister,
Of differences, which I least thought it fit
To answer from our home; the several messengers
From hence attend dispatch. Our good old friend,
Lay comforts to your bosom; and bestow
Your needful counsel to our business,
Which craves the instant use.
GLOUCESTER
I serve you, madam: 144
Your graces are right welcome. [*Exeunt.*

ACT TWO SCENE TWO

Before Gloucester's castle.

Enter KENT *and* OSWALD, *severally.*

OSWALD
Good dawning to thee, friend: art of this house?
KENT
Ay.
OSWALD
Where may we set our horses?
KENT
I' the mire.
OSWALD
Prithee, if thou lovest me, tell me.
KENT
I love thee not.
OSWALD
Why, then, I care not for thee.
KENT
If I had thee in Lipsbury pinfold, I would make thee care for me. 9
OSWALD
Why dost thou use me thus? I know thee not.
KENT
Fellow, I know thee.
OSWALD
What dost thou know me for?
KENT
A knave; a rascal; an eater of broken meats; a base, proud, shallow, beggarly, three-suited, hundred-pound, filthy, worsted-stocking knave; a lily-livered, action-taking knave, a whoreson, glass-gazing, super-serviceable finical rogue; one-trunk-inheriting slave; one that wouldst be a bawd, in way of good service, and art nothing but the composition of a knave, beggar, coward, pandar, and the son and heir of a mongrel bitch: one whom I will beat into clamorous whining, if thou deniest the least syllable of thy addition.
OSWALD
Why, what a monstrous fellow art thou, thus to rail on one that is neither known of thee nor knows thee! 25
KENT
What a brazen-faced varlet art thou, to deny thou knowest me! Is it two days ago since I tripped up thy heels, and beat thee before the king? Draw, you rogue: for, though it be night, yet the moon shines; I'll make a sop o' the moonshine of you: draw, you whoreson cullionly barber-monger, draw. [*Drawing his sword.*
OSWALD
Away! I have nothing to do with thee.
KENT
Draw, you rascal: you come with letters against the king; and take vanity the puppet's part against the royalty of her father: draw, you rogue, or I'll so carbonado your shanks: draw, you rascal; come your ways.
OSWALD
Help, ho! murder! help!
KENT
Strike, you slave; stand, rogue, stand; you neat slave, strike. [*Beating him.*
OSWALD
Help, ho! murder! murder!

Enter EDMUND, *with his rapier drawn,*
CORNWALL, REGAN, GLOUCESTER,
and Servants.

EDMUND
How now! What's the matter?

KENT
With you, goodman boy, an you please: come, I'll flesh ye; come on, young master.
GLOUCESTER
Weapons! arms! What's the matter here? 44
CORNWALL
Keep peace, upon your lives:
He dies that strikes again. What is the matter?
REGAN
The messengers from our sister and the king.
CORNWALL
What is your difference? speak.
OSWALD
I am scarce in breath, my lord.
KENT
No marvel, you have so bestirred your valour. You cowardly rascal, nature disclaims in thee: a tailor made thee. 52
CORNWALL
Thou art a strange fellow: a tailor make a man?
KENT
Ay, a tailor, sir: a stone-cutter or painter could not have made him so ill, though he had been but two hours at the trade. [37]
CORNWALL
Speak yet, how grew your quarrel?
OSWALD
This ancient ruffian, sir, whose life I have spared at suit of his gray beard,—
KENT
Thou whoreson zed! thou unnecessary letter! My lord, if you will give me leave, I will tread this unbolted villain into mortar, and daub the wall of a jakes with him. Spare my gray beard, you wagtail?
CORNWALL
Peace, sirrah!
You beastly knave, know you no reverence?
KENT
Yes, sir; but anger hath a privilege.
CORNWALL
Why art thou angry?
KENT
That such a slave as this should wear a sword,
Who wears no honesty. Such smiling rogues as these,
Like rats, oft bite the holy cords atwain 71
Which are too intrinse t' unloose; smooth every passion [38]
That in the natures of their lords rebel;
Bring oil to fire, snow to their colder moods;
Renege, affirm, and turn their halcyon beaks
With every gale and vary of their masters,
Knowing nought, like dogs, but following.
A plague upon your epileptic visage!
Smile you my speeches, as I were a fool?
Goose, if I had you upon Sarum plain,
I'ld drive ye cackling home to Camelot. 82
CORNWALL
What, art thou mad, old fellow?
GLOUCESTER
How fell you out? say that.
KENT
No contraries hold more antipathy
Than I and such a knave.
CORNWALL
Why dost thou call him a knave? What's his offence?
KENT
His countenance likes me not.
CORNWALL
No more, perchance, does mine, nor his, nor hers.
KENT
Sir, 'tis my occupation to be plain:
I have seen better faces in my time
Than stands on any shoulder that I see 92
Before me at this instant.
CORNWALL
This is some fellow,
Who, having been praised for bluntness, doth affect
A saucy roughness, and constrains the garb
Quite from his nature: he cannot flatter, he,
An honest mind and plain, he must speak truth!
An they will take it, so; if not, he's plain.
These kind of knaves I know, which in this plainness
Harbour more craft and more corrupter ends
Than twenty silly ducking observants
That stretch their duties nicely. 104
KENT
Sir, in good sooth, in sincere verity,
Under the allowance of your great aspect,
Whose influence, like the wreath of radiant fire
On flickering Phoebus' front,—
CORNWALL
What mean'st by this?
KENT
To go out of my dialect, which you discommend so much. I know, sir, I am no flatterer: he that beguiled you in a plain accent was a plain knave; which for my part I will not be, though I should win your displeasure to entreat me to 't. 114
CORNWALL
What was the offence you gave him?
OSWALD
I never gave him any:
It pleased the king his master very late
To strike at me, upon his misconstruction;
When he, conjunct and flattering his displeasure,
Tripp'd me behind; being down, insulted, rail'd,

And put upon him such a deal of man,
That worthied him, got praises of the king
For him attempting who was self-subdued;
And, in the fleshment of this dread exploit,
Drew on me here again.

KENT
None of these rogues and cowards
But Ajax is their fool.

CORNWALL
Fetch forth the stocks!
You stubborn ancient knave, you reverend braggart,
We'll teach you—

KENT
Sir, I am too old to learn:
Call not your stocks for me: I serve the king;
On whose employment I was sent to you:
You shall do small respect, show too bold malice
Against the grace and person of my master,
Stocking his messenger.

CORNWALL
Fetch forth the stocks! As I have life and honour,
There shall he sit till noon.

REGAN
Till noon! till night, my lord; and all night too.

KENT
Why, madam, if I were your father's dog,
You should not use me so.

REGAN
Sir, being his knave, I will.

CORNWALL
This is a fellow of the self-same colour
Our sister speaks of. Come, bring away the stocks!
[*Stocks brought out.*

GLOUCESTER
Let me beseech your grace not to do so:
His fault is much, and the good king his master [39]
Will check him for 't: your purposed low correction
Is such as basest and contemned'st wretches
For pilferings and most common trespasses
Are punish'd with: the king must take it ill, [40]
That he's so slightly valued in his messenger,
Should have him thus restrain'd.

CORNWALL
I'll answer that.

REGAN
My sister may receive it much more worse,
To have her gentleman abused, assaulted,
For following her affairs. Put in his legs. [41]
[*Kent is put in the stocks.*
Come, my good lord, away.
[*Exeunt all but Gloucester and Kent.*

GLOUCESTER
I am sorry for thee, friend; 'tis the duke's pleasure,
Whose disposition, all the world well knows,
Will not be rubb'd nor stopp'd: I'll entreat for thee.

KENT
Pray, do not, sir: I have watched and travell'd hard;
Some time I shall sleep out, the rest I'll whistle.
A good man's fortune may grow out at heels:
Give you good morrow!

GLOUCESTER
The duke's to blame in this; 'twill be ill taken.
[*Exit.*

KENT
Good king, that must approve the common saw,
That out of heaven's benediction comest [42]
To the warm sun!
Approach, thou beacon to this under globe,
That by thy comfortable beams I may
Peruse this letter! Nothing almost sees miracles [43]
But misery: I know 'tis from Cordelia,
Who hath most fortunately been inform'd
Of my obscured course; and shall find time [44]
From this enormous state, seeking to give
Losses their remedies. All weary and o'erwatch'd,
Take vantage, heavy eyes, not to behold
This shameful lodging.
Fortune, good night: smile once more: turn thy wheel!
[*Sleeps.*

ACT TWO SCENE THREE

A wood.

Enter EDGAR.

EDGAR
I heard myself proclaim'd;
And by the happy hollow of a tree
Escaped the hunt. No port is free; no place,
That guard, and most unusual vigilance,
Does not attend my taking. Whiles I may 'scape,
I will preserve myself: and am bethought
To take the basest and most poorest shape
That ever penury, in contempt of man,
Brought near to beast: my face I'll grime with filth;
Blanket my loins: elf all my hair in knots;
And with presented nakedness out-face
The winds and persecutions of the sky.
The country gives me proof and precedent
Of Bedlam beggars, who, with roaring voices,
Strike in their numb'd and mortified bare arms
Pins, wooden pricks, nails, sprigs of rosemary;
And with this horrible object, from low farms,

Poor pelting villages, sheep-cotes, and mills,
Sometime with lunatic bans, sometime with prayers,
Enforce their charity. Poor Turlygod! poor Tom!
That's something yet: Edgar I nothing am. [*Exit.*

ACT TWO SCENE FOUR

Before Gloucester's *castle. Kent in the stocks.*

Enter LEAR, Fool, *and* Gentleman.

KING LEAR
'Tis strange that they should so depart from home,
And not send back my messenger.

GENTLEMAN
As I learn'd,
The night before there was no purpose in them
Of this remove.

KENT
Hail to thee, noble master!

KING LEAR
Ha!
Makest thou this shame thy pastime?

KENT
No, my lord.

FOOL
Ha, ha! he wears cruel garters. Horses are tied by the heads, dogs and bears by the neck, monkeys by the loins, and men by the legs: when a man's over-lusty at legs, then he wears wooden nether-stocks.

KING LEAR
What's he that hath so much thy place mistook
To set thee here?

KENT
It is both he and she;
Your son and daughter.

KING LEAR
No.

KENT
Yes.

KING LEAR
No, I say.

KENT
I say, yea.

KING LEAR
No, no, they would not. [45]

KENT
Yes, they have.

KING LEAR
By Jupiter, I swear, no.

KENT
By Juno, I swear, ay.

KING LEAR
They durst not do't;
They could not, would not do't; 'tis worse than murder,
To do upon respect such violent outrage:
Resolve me, with all modest haste, which way
Thou mightst deserve, or they impose, this usage,
Coming from us.

KENT
My lord, when at their home
I did commend your highness' letters to them,
Ere I was risen from the place that show'd
My duty kneeling, came there a reeking post,
Stew'd in his haste, half breathless, panting forth
From Goneril his mistress salutations;
Deliver'd letters, spite of intermission,
Which presently they read: on whose contents,
They summon'd up their meiny, straight took horse;
Commanded me to follow, and attend
The leisure of their answer; gave me cold looks:
And meeting here the other messenger,
Whose welcome, I perceived, had poison'd mine,—
Being the very fellow that of late
Display'd so saucily against your highness,—
Having more man than wit about me, drew:
He raised the house with loud and coward cries.
Your son and daughter found this trespass worth
The shame which here it suffers.

FOOL
Winter's not gone yet, if the wild-geese fly that way.
Fathers that wear rags
Do make their children blind;
But fathers that bear bags
Shall see their children kind.
Fortune, that arrant whore,
Ne'er turns the key to the poor.
But, for all this, thou shalt have as many dolours for thy daughters as thou canst tell in a year.

KING LEAR
O, how this mother swells up toward my heart!
Hysterica passio, down, thou climbing sorrow,
Thy element's below! Where is this daughter?

KENT
With the earl, sir, here within.

KING LEAR
Follow me not;
Stay here. [*Exit.*

GENTLEMAN
Made you no more offence but what you speak of?

KENT
None.
How chance the king comes with so small a train?

FOOL
And thou hadst been set i' the stocks for that question, thou hadst well deserved it.

KENT
Why, fool?
FOOL
We'll set thee to school to an ant, to teach thee there's no labouring i' the winter. All that follow their noses are led by their eyes but blind men; and there's not a nose among twenty but can smell him that's stinking. Let go thy hold when a great wheel runs down a hill, lest it break thy neck with following it: but the great one that goes up the hill, let him draw thee after. When a wise man gives thee better counsel, give me mine again: I would have none but knaves follow it, since a fool gives it.

That sir which serves and seeks for gain,
And follows but for form,
Will pack when it begins to rain,
And leave thee in the storm,
But I will tarry; the fool will stay,
And let the wise man fly:
The knave turns fool that runs away;
The fool no knave, perdy.

KENT
Where learned you this, fool?
FOOL
Not i' the stocks, fool.

Re-enter LEAR, *with* GLOUCESTER.

KING LEAR
Deny to speak with me? They are sick? they are weary?
They have travell'd all the night? Mere fetches;
The images of revolt and flying off.
Fetch me a better answer.
GLOUCESTER
My dear lord,
You know the fiery quality of the duke;
How unremoveable and fix'd he is
In his own course.
KING LEAR
Vengeance! plague! death! confusion!
Fiery? what quality? Why, Gloucester, Gloucester,
I'ld speak with the Duke of Cornwall and his wife.
GLOUCESTER
Well, my good lord, I have inform'd them so. [46]
KING LEAR
Inform'd them! Dost thou understand me, man?
GLOUCESTER
Ay, my good lord.
KING LEAR
The king would speak with Cornwall; the dear father
Would with his daughter speak, commands her service: [47]
Are they inform'd of this? My breath and blood!
Fiery? the fiery duke? Tell the hot duke that—
No, but not yet: may be he is not well:
Infirmity doth still neglect all office
Whereto our health is bound; we are not ourselves
When nature, being oppress'd, commands the mind
To suffer with the body: I'll forbear;
And am fall'n out with my more headier will,
To take the indisposed and sickly fit
For the sound man. Death on my state! wherefore
[*Looking on Kent.*
Should he sit here? This act persuades me
That this remotion of the duke and her
Is practise only. Give me my servant forth.
Go tell the duke and 's wife I'ld speak with them,
Now, presently: bid them come forth and hear me,
Or at their chamber-door I'll beat the drum
Till it cry sleep to death.
GLOUCESTER
I would have all well betwixt you. [*Exit.*
KING LEAR
O me, my heart, my rising heart! but, down!
FOOL
Cry to it, nuncle, as the cockney did to the eels when she put 'em i' the paste alive; she knapped 'em o' the coxcombs with a stick, and cried 'Down, wantons, down!' 'Twas her brother that, in pure kindness to his horse, buttered his hay.

Enter CORNWALL, REGAN, GLOUCESTER, *and* Servants.

KING LEAR
Good morrow to you both.
CORNWALL
Hail to your grace!
[*Kent is set at liberty.*
REGAN
I am glad to see your highness.
KING LEAR
Regan, I think you are; I know what reason
I have to think so: if thou shouldst not be glad,
I would divorce me from thy mother's tomb,
Sepulchring an adultress. [*To Kent*] O, are you free?
Some other time for that. Beloved Regan,
Thy sister's naught: O Regan, she hath tied
Sharp-tooth'd unkindness, like a vulture, here:
[*Points to his heart.*
I can scarce speak to thee; thou'lt not believe
With how depraved a quality—O Regan!
REGAN
I pray you, sir, take patience: I have hope.
You less know how to value her desert
Than she to scant her duty.
KING LEAR
Say, how is that?

REGAN
I cannot think my sister in the least
Would fail her obligation: if, sir, perchance
She have restrain'd the riots of your followers,
'Tis on such ground, and to such wholesome end,
As clears her from all blame.

KING LEAR
My curses on her!

REGAN
O, sir, you are old.
Nature in you stands on the very verge 160
Of her confine: you should be ruled and led
By some discretion, that discerns your state
Better than you yourself. Therefore, I pray you,
That to our sister you do make return;
Say you have wrong'd her, sir.

KING LEAR
Ask her forgiveness?
Do you but mark how this becomes the house:
'Dear daughter, I confess that I am old;
[*Kneeling.*
Age is unnecessary: on my knees I beg
That you'll vouchsafe me raiment, bed, and food.'

REGAN
Good sir, no more; these are unsightly tricks:
Return you to my sister.

KING LEAR
[*Rising*] Never, Regan: 173
She hath abated me of half my train;
Look'd black upon me; struck me with her tongue,
Most serpent-like, upon the very heart:
All the stored vengeances of heaven fall
On her ingrateful top! Strike her young bones,
You taking airs, with lameness!

CORNWALL
Fie, sir, fie!

KING LEAR
You nimble lightnings, dart your blinding flames
Into her scornful eyes! Infect her beauty,
You fen-suck'd fogs, drawn by the powerful sun,
To fall and blast her pride! [48]

REGAN
O the blest gods! so will you wish on me, 186
When the rash mood is on.

KING LEAR
No, Regan, thou shalt never have my curse:
Thy tender-defted nature shall not give [49]
Thee o'er to harshness: her eyes are fierce; but thine
Do comfort and not burn. 'Tis not in thee
To grudge my pleasures, to cut off my train,
To bandy hasty words, to scant my sizes,
And in conclusion to oppose the bolt
Against my coming in: thou better know'st
The offices of nature, bond of childhood, 196
Effects of courtesy, dues of gratitude;
Thy half o' the kingdom hast thou not forgot,
Wherein I thee endow'd·

REGAN
Good sir, to the purpose.

KING LEAR
Who put my man i' the stocks? [*Tucket within.*

CORNWALL
What trumpet's that?

REGAN
I know't, my sister's: this approves her letter,
That she would soon be here.

Enter OSWALD.

Is your lady come?

KING LEAR
This is a slave, whose easy-borrow'd pride
Dwells in the fickle grace of her he follows.
Out, varlet, from my sight!

CORNWALL
What means your grace?

KING LEAR
Who stock'd my servant? Regan, I have good hope 211
Thou didst not know on't. Who comes here? O heavens,

Enter GONERIL.

If you do love old men, if your sweet sway
Allow obedience, if yourselves are old,
Make it your cause; send down, and take my part!
[*To Goneril*] Art not ashamed to look upon this beard?
O Regan, wilt thou take her by the hand?

GONERIL
Why not by the hand, sir? How have I offended?
All's not offence that indiscretion finds
And dotage terms so.

KING LEAR
O sides, you are too tough;
Will you yet hold? How came my man i' the stocks? 224

CORNWALL
I set him there, sir: but his own disorders
Deserved much less advancement.

KING LEAR
You! did you?

REGAN
I pray you, father, being weak, seem so.
If, till the expiration of your month,
You will return and sojourn with my sister,
Dismissing half your train, come then to me:
I am now from home, and out of that provision

Which shall be needful for your entertainment.

KING LEAR

Return to her, and fifty men dismiss'd?
No, rather I abjure all roofs, and choose
To wage against the enmity o' the air;
To be a comrade with the wolf and owl,—
Necessity's sharp pinch! Return with her?
Why, the hot-blooded France, that dowerless took
Our youngest born, I could as well be brought
To knee his throne, and, squire-like; pension beg
To keep base life afoot. Return with her?
Persuade me rather to be slave and sumpter
To this detested groom. [*Pointing at Oswald.*

GONERIL

At your choice, sir.

KING LEAR

I prithee, daughter, do not make me mad:
I will not trouble thee, my child; farewell:
We'll no more meet, no more see one another:
But yet thou art my flesh, my blood, my daughter;
Or rather a disease that's in my flesh,
Which I must needs call mine: thou art a boil,
A plague-sore, an embossed carbuncle,
In my corrupted blood. But I'll not chide thee;
Let shame come when it will, I do not call it:
I do not bid the thunder-bearer shoot,
Nor tell tales of thee to high-judging Jove:
Mend when thou canst; be better at thy leisure:
I can be patient; I can stay with Regan,
I and my hundred knights.

REGAN

Not altogether so:
I look'd not for you yet, nor am provided
For your fit welcome. Give ear, sir, to my sister;
For those that mingle reason with your passion
Must be content to think you old, and so—
But she knows what she does.

KING LEAR

Is this well spoken?

REGAN

I dare avouch it, sir: what, fifty followers?
Is it not well? What should you need of more?
Yea, or so many, sith that both charge and danger
Speak 'gainst so great a number? How, in one house,
Should many people, under two commands,
Hold amity? 'Tis hard; almost impossible.

GONERIL

Why might not you, my lord, receive attendance
From those that she calls servants or from mine?

REGAN

Why not, my lord? If then they chanced to slack you,
We could control them. If you will come to me,—
For now I spy a danger,—I entreat you
To bring but five and twenty: to no more
Will I give place or notice.

KING LEAR

I gave you all—

REGAN

And in good time you gave it.

KING LEAR

Made you my guardians, my depositaries;
But kept a reservation to be follow'd
With such a number. What, must I come to you
With five and twenty, Regan? said you so?

REGAN

And speak't again, my lord; no more with me.

KING LEAR

Those wicked creatures yet do look well-favour'd,
When others are more wicked: not being the worst
Stands in some rank of praise. [*To Goneril*] I'll go with thee:
Thy fifty yet doth double five-and-twenty,
And thou art twice her love.

GONERIL

Hear me, my lord;
What need you five and twenty, ten, or five,
To follow in a house where twice so many
Have a command to tend you?

REGAN

What need one?

KING LEAR

O, reason not the need: our basest beggars
Are in the poorest thing superfluous:
Allow not nature more than nature needs,
Man's life's as cheap as beast's: thou art a lady;
If only to go warm were gorgeous,
Why, nature needs not what thou gorgeous wear'st,
Which scarcely keeps thee warm. But, for true need,—
You heavens, give me that patience, patience I need!
You see me here, you gods, a poor old man,
As full of grief as age; wretched in both!
If it be you that stir these daughters' hearts
Against their father, fool me not so much
To bear it tamely; touch me with noble anger,
And let not women's weapons, water-drops,
Stain my man's cheeks! No, you unnatural hags,
I will have such revenges on you both,
That all the world shall—I will do such things,—
What they are, yet I know not: but they shall be
The terrors of the earth. You think I'll weep
No, I'll not weep:
I have full cause of weeping; but this heart
Shall break into a hundred thousand flaws,
Or ere I'll weep. O fool, I shall go mad!

[*Exeunt Lear, Gloucester, Kent, and Fool. Storm and tempest.*

CORNWALL
Let us withdraw; 'twill be a storm.
REGAN
This house is little: the old man and his people
Cannot be well bestow'd.
GONERIL
'Tis his own blame; hath put himself from rest,
And must needs taste his folly.
REGAN
For his particular, I'll receive him gladly,
But not one follower.
GONERIL
So am I purposed.
Where is my lord of Gloucester?
CORNWALL
Follow'd the old man forth: he is return'd.

Re-enter GLOUCESTER.

GLOUCESTER
The king is in high rage.
CORNWALL
Whither is he going?
GLOUCESTER
He calls to horse; but will I know not whither.
CORNWALL
'Tis best to give him way; he leads himself.
GONERIL
My lord, entreat him by no means to stay.
GLOUCESTER
Alack, the night comes on, and the bleak winds [50]
Do sorely ruffle; for many miles about
There's scarce a bush.
REGAN
O, sir, to wilful men,
The injuries that they themselves procure
Must be their schoolmasters. Shut up your doors:
He is attended with a desperate train;
And what they may incense him to, being apt
To have his ear abused, wisdom bids fear.
CORNWALL
Shut up your doors, my lord; 'tis a wild night:
My Regan counsels well; come out o' the storm.
[*Exeunt.*

ACT THREE SCENE ONE

A heath.

Storm still. Enter KENT *and a* Gentleman, *meeting.*

KENT
Who's there, besides foul weather?
GENTLEMAN
One minded like the weather, most unquietly.
KENT
I know you. Where's the king?
GENTLEMAN
Contending with the fretful element:
Bids the winds blow the earth into the sea,
Or swell the curled water 'bove the main,
That things might change or cease; tears his white hair, [51]
Which the impetuous blasts, with eyeless rage,
Catch in their fury, and make nothing of;
Strives in his little world of man to out-scorn
The to-and-fro-conflicting wind and rain.
This night, wherein the cub-drawn bear would couch,
The lion and the belly-pinched wolf
Keep their fur dry, unbonneted he runs,
And bids what will take all.
KENT
But who is with him?
GENTLEMAN
None but the fool; who labours to out-jest
His heart-struck injuries.
KENT
Sir, I do know you;
And dare, upon the warrant of my note,
Commend a dear thing to you. There is division,
Although as yet the face of it be cover'd
With mutual cunning, 'twixt Albany and Cornwall;
Who have—as who have not, that their great stars [52]
Throned and set high?— servants, who seem no less,
Which are to France the spies and speculations
Intelligent of our state; what hath been seen,
Either in snuffs and packings of the dukes,
Or the hard rein which both of them have borne
Against the old kind king; or something deeper,
Whereof perchance these are but furnishings;
But, true it is, from France there comes a power
Into this scatter'd kingdom; who already,
Wise in our negligence, have secret feet
In some of our best ports, and are at point
To show their open banner. Now to you:
If on my credit you dare build so far
To make your speed to Dover, you shall find
Some that will thank you, making just report
Of how unnatural and bemadding sorrow
The king hath cause to plain.
I am a gentleman of blood and breeding;
And, from some knowledge and assurance, offer
This office to you.
GENTLEMAN
I will talk further with you.

KENT
No, do not.
For confirmation that I am much more
Than my out-wall, open this purse, and take
What it contains. If you shall see Cordelia,—
As fear not but you shall,—show her this ring;
And she will tell you who your fellow is
That yet you do not know. Fie on this storm!
I will go seek the king. 57

GENTLEMAN
Give me your hand: have you no more to say?

KENT
Few words, but, to effect, more than all yet;
That, when we have found the king,—in which your pain
That way, I'll this,—he that first lights on him
Holla the other. [*Exeunt severally.*

ACT THREE SCENE TWO

Another part of the heath. Storm still.

Enter LEAR *and* Fool.

KING LEAR
Blow, winds, and crack your cheeks! rage! blow!
You cataracts and hurricanoes, spout
Till you have drench'd our steeples, drown'd the cocks!
You sulphurous and thought-executing fires,
Vaunt-couriers to oak-cleaving thunderbolts,
Singe my white head! And thou, all-shaking thunder,
Smite flat the thick rotundity o' the world! [53]
Crack nature's moulds, an germens spill at once, 9
That make ingrateful man! [54]

FOOL
O nuncle, court holy-water in a dry house is better than this rain-water out o' door. Good nuncle, in, and ask thy daughters' blessing: here's a night pities neither wise man nor fool.

KING LEAR
Rumble thy bellyful! Spit, fire! spout, rain!
Nor rain, wind, thunder, fire, are my daughters:
I tax not you, you elements, with unkindness;
I never gave you kingdom, call'd you children,
You owe me no subscription: then let fall
Your horrible pleasure: here I stand, your slave,
A poor, infirm, weak, and despised old man:
But yet I call you servile ministers, 22
That have with two pernicious daughters join'd [55]
Your high engender'd battles 'gainst a head
So old and white as this. O! O! 'tis foul!

FOOL
He that has a house to put's head in has a good head-piece.
The cod-piece that will house
Before the head has any,
The head and he shall louse;
So beggars marry many. 31
The man that makes his toe
What he his heart should make
Shall of a corn cry woe,
And turn his sleep to wake.
For there was never yet fair woman but she made mouths in a glass.

KING LEAR
No, I will be the pattern of all patience; [56]
I will say nothing.

Enter KENT.

KENT
Who's there?

FOOL
Marry, here's grace and a cod-piece; that's a wise man and a fool. 42

KENT
Alas, sir, are you here? things that love night
Love not such nights as these; the wrathful skies
Gallow the very wanderers of the dark,
And make them keep their caves: since I was man,
Such sheets of fire, such bursts of horrid thunder,
Such groans of roaring wind and rain, I never
Remember to have heard: man's nature cannot carry
The affliction nor the fear.

KING LEAR
Let the great gods,
That keep this dreadful pother o'er our heads,
Find out their enemies now. Tremble, thou wretch, 54
That hast within thee undivulged crimes,
Unwhipp'd of justice: hide thee, thou bloody hand;
Thou perjured, and thou simular man of virtue
That art incestuous: caitiff, to pieces shake,
That under covert and convenient seeming
Hast practised on man's life: close pent-up guilts,
Rive your concealing continents, and cry
These dreadful summoners grace. I am a man
More sinn'd against than sinning.

KENT
Alack, bare-headed! 64
Gracious my lord, hard by here is a hovel;
Some friendship will it lend you 'gainst the tempest:
Repose you there; while I to this hard house—
More harder than the stones whereof 'tis raised; [57]
Which even but now, demanding after you,
Denied me to come in—return, and force
Their scanted courtesy

KING LEAR

My wits begin to turn.
Come on, my boy: how dost, my boy? art cold?
I am cold myself. Where is this straw, my fellow?
The art of our necessities is strange, 77
That can make vile things precious. Come, your hovel.
Poor fool and knave, I have one part in my heart
That's sorry yet for thee. [58]

Fool. [*Singing*] He that has and a little tiny wit— [59]
With hey, ho, the wind and the rain,—
Must make content with his fortunes fit,
For the rain it raineth every day

KING LEAR

True, my good boy. Come, bring us to this hovel.
[*Exeunt King Lear and Kent.*

FOOL

This is a brave night to cool a courtezan.
I'll speak a prophecy ere I go: 98
When priests are more in word than matter;
When brewers mar their malt with water;
When nobles are their tailors' tutors;
No heretics burn'd, but wenches' suitors;
When every case in law is right;
No squire in debt, nor no poor knight;
When slanders do not live in tongues;
Nor cutpurses come not to throngs;
When usurers tell their gold i' the field;
And bawds and whores do churches build;
Then shall the realm of Albion 109
Come to great confusion:
Then comes the time, who lives to see 't,
That going shall be used with feet.
This prophecy Merlin shall make; for I live before his time. [60] [*Exit.*

ACT THREE SCENE THREE

Gloucester's castle.

Enter GLOUCESTER *and* EDMUND.

GLOUCESTER

Alack, alack, Edmund, I like not this unnatural dealing. When I desire their leave that I might pity him, they took from me the use of mine own house; charged me, on pain of their perpetual displeasure, neither to speak of him, entreat for him, nor any way sustain him.

EDMUND

Most savage and unnatural!

GLOUCESTER

Go to; say you nothing. There's a division betwixt the dukes; and a worse matter than that: I have received a letter this night; 'tis dangerous to be spoken; I have locked the letter in my closet: these injuries the king now bears will be revenged home; there's part of a power already footed: we must incline to the king. I will seek him, and privily relieve him: go you and maintain talk with the duke, that my charity be not of him perceived: if he ask for me. I am ill, and gone to bed. Though I die for it, as no less is threatened me, the king my old master must be relieved. There is some strange thing toward, Edmund; pray you, be careful. [*Exit.*

EDMUND

This courtesy, forbid thee, shall the duke
Instantly know; and of that letter too:
This seems a fair deserving, and must draw me
That which my father loses; no less than all:
The younger rises when the old doth fall. [*Exit.*

ACT THREE SCENE FOUR

The heath. Before a hovel.

Enter LEAR, KENT, *and* Fool.

KENT

Here is the place, my lord; good my lord, enter:
The tyranny of the open night's too rough
For nature to endure. [*Storm still.*

KING LEAR

Let me alone.

KENT

Good my lord, enter here.

KING LEAR

Wilt break my heart?

KENT

I had rather break mine own. Good my lord, enter.

KING LEAR

Thou think'st 'tis much that this contentious storm [61]
Invades us to the skin: so 'tis to thee;
But where the greater malady is fix'd,
The lesser is scarce felt. Thou'ldst shun a bear;
But if thy flight lay toward the raging sea, 14
Thou'ldst meet the bear i' the mouth. When the mind's free,
The body's delicate: the tempest in my mind
Doth from my senses take all feeling else
Save what beats there. Filial ingratitude!
Is it not as this mouth should tear this hand
For lifting food to't? But I will punish home:
No, I will weep no more. In such a night
To shut me out! Pour on; I will endure.
In such a night as this! O Regan, Goneril!

Your old kind father, whose frank heart gave all,—
O, that way madness lies; let me shun that;
No more of that.

KENT
Good my lord, enter here.

KING LEAR
Prithee, go in thyself: seek thine own ease:
This tempest will not give me leave to ponder
On things would hurt me more. But I'll go in.
[*To the Fool*] In, boy; go first. You houseless poverty,—
Nay, get thee in. I'll pray, and then I'll sleep.
[*Fool goes in.*
Poor naked wretches, whereso'er you are,
That bide the pelting of this pitiless storm, [62]
How shall your houseless heads and unfed sides,
Your loop'd and window'd raggedness, defend you
From seasons such as these? O, I have ta'en
Too little care of this! Take physic, pomp;
Expose thyself to feel what wretches feel,
That thou mayst shake the superflux to them,
And show the heavens more just.

EDGAR
[*Within*] Fathom and half, fathom and half! Poor Tom! [*The Fool runs out from the hovel.*

FOOL
Come not in here, nuncle, here's a spirit Help me, help me!

KENT
Give me thy hand. Who's there?

FOOL
A spirit, a spirit: he says his name's poor Tom.

KENT
What art thou that dost grumble there i' the straw? Come forth.

Enter EDGAR *disguised as a madman.*

EDGAR
Away! the foul fiend follows me!
Through the sharp hawthorn blows the cold wind. [63]
Hum! go to thy cold bed, and warm thee.

KING LEAR
Hast thou given all to thy two daughters?
And art thou come to this?

EDGAR
Who gives any thing to poor Tom? whom the foul fiend hath led through fire and through flame, and through ford and whirlipool e'er bog and quagmire; that hath laid knives under his pillow, and halters in his pew; set ratsbane by his porridge; made film proud of heart, to ride on a bay trotting-horse over four-inched bridges, to course his own shadow for a traitor. Bless thy five wits! Tom's a-cold,—O, do de, do de, do de. Bless thee from whirlwinds, star-blasting, and taking! Do poor Tom some charity, whom the foul fiend vexes: there could I have him now,—and there,—and there again, and there. [64] [*Storm still*

KING LEAR
What, have his daughters brought him to this pass?
Couldst thou save nothing? Didst thou give them all?

FOOL
Nay, he reserved a blanket, else we had been all shamed.

KING LEAR
Now, all the plagues that in the pendulous air
Hang fated o'er men's faults light on thy daughters!

KENT
He hath no daughters, sir.

KING LEAR
Death, traitor! nothing could have subdued nature
To such a lowness but his unkind daughters.
Is it the fashion, that discarded fathers
Should have thus little mercy on their flesh?
Judicious punishment! 'twas this flesh begot
Those pelican daughters.

EDGAR
Pillicock sat on Pillicock-hill:
Halloo, halloo, loo, loo!

FOOL
This cold night will turn us all to fools and madmen.

EDGAR
Take heed o' the foul fiend: obey thy parents; keep thy word justly; swear not; commit not with man's sworn spouse; set not thy sweet heart on proud array. Tom's a-cold. [65]

KING LEAR
What hast thou been?

EDGAR
A serving-man, proud in heart and mind; that curled my hair; wore gloves in my cap; served the lust of my mistress' heart, and did the act of darkness with her; swore as many oaths as I spake words, and broke them in the sweet face of heaven: one that slept in the contriving of lust, and waked to do it: wine loved I deeply, dice dearly: and in woman out-paramoured the Turk: false of heart, light of ear, bloody of hand; hog in sloth, fox in stealth, wolf in greediness, dog in madness, lion in prey. Let not the creaking of shoes nor the rustling of silks betray thy poor heart to woman: keep thy foot out of brothels, thy hand out of plackets, thy pen from lenders' books, and defy the foul fiend.
Still through the hawthorn blows the cold wind:
Says suum, mun, ha, no, nonny.
Dolphin my boy, my boy, sessa! let him trot by. [66]
[*Storm still.*

EDGAR There could I have him now,—and there,—and there again,—and there.

KING LEAR

Why, thou wert better in thy grave than to answer with thy uncovered body this extremity of the skies. Is man no more than this? Consider him well. Thou owest the worm no silk, the beast no hide, the sheep no wool, the cat no perfume. Ha! here's three on's are sophisticated! Thou art the thing itself: unaccommodated man is no more but such a poor bare, forked animal as thou art. Off, off, you lendings! come unbutton here. [*Tearing off his clothes.*

FOOL

Prithee, nuncle, be contented; 'tis a naughty night to swim in. Now a little fire in a wild field were like an old lecher's heart; a small spark, all the rest on's body cold. Look, here comes a walking fire.

Enter GLOUCESTER, *with a torch.*

EDGAR

This is the foul fiend Flibbertigibbet: he begins at curfew, and walks till the first cock; he gives the web and the pin, squints the eye, and makes the hare-lip; mildews the white wheat, and hurts the poor creature of earth.

S. Withold footed thrice the old;
He met the night-mare, and her nine-fold;
Bid her alight,
And her troth plight,
And, aroint thee, witch, aroint thee!

KENT

How fares your grace?

KING LEAR

What's he?

KENT

Who's there? What is't you seek?

GLOUCESTER

What are you there? Your names?

EDGAR

Poor Tom; that eats the swimming frog, the toad, the tadpole, the wall-newt and the water; that in the fury of his heart, when the foul fiend rages, eats cow-dung for sallets; swallows the old rat and the ditch-dog; drinks the green mantle of the standing pool; who is whipped from tithing to tithing, and stock-punished, and imprisoned; who hath had three suits to his back, six shirts to his body, horse to ride, and weapon to wear;

But mice and rats, and such small deer,
Have been Tom's food for seven long year. [67]

Beware my follower. Peace, Smulkin; peace, thou fiend!

GLOUCESTER
What, hath your grace no better company?
EDGAR
The prince of darkness is a gentleman:
Modo he's call'd, and Mahu.
GLOUCESTER
Our flesh and blood is grown so vile, my lord,
That it doth hate what gets it.
EDGAR
Poor Tom's a-cold.
GLOUCESTER
Go in with me: my duty cannot suffer
To obey in all your daughters' hard commands:
Though their injunction be to bar my doors,
And let this tyrannous night take hold upon you,
Yet have I ventured to come seek you out,
And bring you where both fire and food is ready.
KING LEAR
First let me talk with this philosopher.
What is the cause of thunder?
KENT
Good my lord, take his offer; go into the house.
KING LEAR
I'll talk a word with this same learned Theban.
What is your study?
EDGAR
How to prevent the fiend, and to kill vermin.
KING LEAR
Let me ask you one word in private.
KENT
Importune him once more to go, my lord;
His wits begin to unsettle.
GLOUCESTER
Canst thou blame him? [*Storm still.*
His daughters seek his death: ah, that good Kent!
He said it would be thus, poor banish'd man!
Thou say'st the king grows mad; I'll tell thee, friend,
I am almost mad myself: I had a son,
Now outlaw'd from my blood; he sought my life,
But lately, very late: I loved him, friend;
No father his son dearer: truth to tell thee,
The grief hath crazed my wits. What a night's this!
I do beseech your grace,—
KING LEAR
O, cry your mercy, sir.
Noble philosopher, your company.
EDGAR
Tom's a-cold.
GLOUCESTER
In, fellow, there, into the hovel: keep thee warm.
KING LEAR
Come, let's in all.
KENT
This way, my lord.
KING LEAR
With him;
I will keep still with my philosopher.
KENT
Good my lord, soothe him; let him take the fellow.
GLOUCESTER
Take him you on.
KENT
Sirrah, come on; go along with us.
KING LEAR
Come, good Athenian.
GLOUCESTER
No words, no words: hush.
EDGAR
Child Rowland to the dark tower came, [68]
His word was still,—Fie, foh, and fum, [69]
I smell the blood of a British man. [*Exeunt.*

ACT THREE SCENE FIVE

Gloucester's castle.

Enter CORNWALL *and* EDMUND.

CORNWALL
I will have my revenge ere I depart his house.
EDMUND
How, my lord, I may be censured, that nature thus gives way to loyalty, something fears me to think of.
CORNWALL
I now perceive, it was not altogether your brother's evil disposition made him seek his death; but a provoking merit, set a-work by a reprovable badness in himself.
EDMUND
How malicious is my fortune, that I must repent to be just! This is the letter he spoke of, which approves him an intelligent party to the advantages of France. O heavens! that this treason were not, or not I the detector!
CORNWALL
Go with me to the duchess.
EDMUND
If the matter of this paper be certain, you have mighty business in hand.
CORNWALL
True or false, it hath made thee earl of Gloucester. Seek out where thy father is, that he may be ready for our apprehension.
EDMUND
[*Aside*] If I find him comforting the king, it will stuff his suspicion more fully.—I will persevere in my

course of loyalty, though the conflict be sore between that and my blood.

CORNWALL

I will lay trust upon thee; and thou shalt find a dearer father in my love. [*Exeunt.*

ACT THREE SCENE SIX

A chamber in a farmhouse adjoining the castle.

Enter GLOUCESTER, LEAR, KENT, Fool, *and* EDGAR.

GLOUCESTER

Here is better than the open air; take it thankfully. I will piece out the comfort with what addition I can: I will not be long from you.

KENT

All the power of his wits have given way to his impatience: the gods reward your kindness! [*Exit Gloucester.*

EDGAR

Frateretto calls me; and tells me
Nero is an angler in the lake of darkness.
Pray, innocent, and beware the foul fiend.

FOOL

Prithee, nuncle, tell me whether a madman be a gentleman or a yeoman? 10

KING LEAR

A king, a king!

FOOL

No, he's a yeoman that has a gentleman to his son; for he's a mad yeoman that sees his son a gentleman before him.

KING LEAR

To have a thousand with red burning spits
Come hissing in upon 'em,—

EDGAR

The foul fiend bites my back.

FOOL

He's mad that trusts in the tameness of a wolf, a horse's health, a boy's love, or a whore's oath. 19

KING LEAR

It shall be done; I will arraign them straight.
[*To Edgar*] Come, sit thou here, most learned justicer;
[*To the Fool*] Thou, sapient sir, sit here. Now, you she foxes!

EDGAR

Look, where he stands and glares!
Wantest thou eyes at trial, madam?
Come o'er the bourn, Bessy, to me,— [70]

FOOL

Her boat hath a leak,
And she must not speak 29
Why she dares not come over to thee.

EDGAR

The foul fiend haunts poor Tom in the voice of a nightingale. Hopdance cries in Tom's belly for two white herring. Croak not, black angel; I have no food for thee.

KENT

How do you, sir? Stand you not so amazed:
Will you lie down and rest upon the cushions?

KING LEAR

I'll see their trial first. Bring in the evidence.
[*To Edgar*] Thou robed man of justice, take thy place;
[*To the Fool*] And thou, his yoke-fellow of equity,
Bench by his side: [*To Kent*] you are o' the commission, 41
Sit you too.

EDGAR

Let us deal justly. [71]
Sleepest or wakest thou, jolly shepherd?
Thy sheep be in the corn;
And for one blast of thy minikin mouth,
Thy sheep shall take no harm.
Pur! the cat is gray

KING LEAR

Arraign her first; 'tis Goneril. I here take my oath before this honourable assembly, she kicked the poor king her father. 51

FOOL

Come hither, mistress. Is your name Goneril?

KING LEAR

She cannot deny it.

FOOL

Cry you mercy, I took you for a joint-stool.

KING LEAR

And here's another, whose warp'd looks proclaim
What store her heart is made on. Stop her there!
Arms, arms, sword, fire! Corruption in the place!
False justicer, why hast thou let her 'scape?

EDGAR

Bless thy five wits! 59

KENT

O pity! Sir, where is the patience now,
That thou so oft have boasted to retain?

EDGAR

[*Aside*] My tears begin to take his part so much,
They'll mar my counterfeiting.

KING LEAR

The little dogs and all,
Tray, Blanch, and Sweet-heart, see, they bark at me.

EDGAR

Tom will throw his head at them. Avaunt, you curs!
Be thy mouth or black or white,
Tooth that poisons if it bite; 68

Mastiff, greyhound, mongrel grim,
Hound or spaniel, brach or lym,
Or bobtail tike or trundle-tail,
Tom will make them weep and wail:
For, with throwing thus my head,
Dogs leap the hatch, and all are fled.

Do de, de, de. Sessa! Come, march to wakes and fairs and market-towns. Poor Tom, thy horn is dry. [72]

KING LEAR

Then let them anatomize Regan; see what breeds about her heart. Is there any cause in nature that makes these hard hearts? [*To Edgar*] You, sir, I entertain for one of my hundred; only I do not like the fashion of your garments: you will say they are Persian attire: but let them be changed.

KENT

Now, good my lord, lie here and rest awhile.

KING LEAR

Make no noise, make no noise; draw the curtains: so, so, so. We'll go to supper i' he morning. So, so, so.

FOOL

And I'll go to bed at noon.

Re-enter GLOUCESTER.

GLOUCESTER

Come hither, friend: where is the king my master?

KENT

Here, sir; but trouble him not, his wits are gone.

GLOUCESTER

Good friend, I prithee, take him in thy arms;
I have o'erheard a plot of death upon him:
There is a litter ready; lay him in't,
And drive towards Dover, friend, where thou shalt meet [73]
Both welcome and protection. Take up thy master:
If thou shouldst dally half an hour, his life,
With thine, and all that offer to defend him,
Stand in assured loss: take up, take up;
And follow me, that will to some provision
Give thee quick conduct.

KENT

Oppressed nature sleeps:
This rest might yet have balm'd thy broken sinews,
Which, if convenience will not allow,
Stand in hard cure. [*To the Fool*] Come, help to bear thy master;
Thou must not stay behind.

GLOUCESTER

Come, come, away. [*Exeunt all but Edgar.*

EDGAR

When we our betters see bearing our woes,
We scarcely think our miseries our foes.
Who alone suffers suffers most i' the mind,
Leaving free things and happy shows behind:
But then the mind much sufferance doth o'er skip,
When grief hath mates, and bearing fellowship.
How light and portable my pain seems now,
When that which makes me bend makes the king bow,
He childed as I father'd! Tom, away!
Mark the high noises; and thyself bewray,
When false opinion, whose wrong thought defiles thee,
In thy just proof, repeals and reconciles thee.
What will hap more to-night, safe 'scape the king!
Lurk, lurk. [*Exit.*

ACT THREE SCENE SEVEN

Gloucester's castle.

Enter CORNWALL, REGAN, GONERIL, EDMUND, *and* Servants.

CORNWALL

Post speedily to my lord your husband; show him this letter: the army of France is landed. Seek out the villain Gloucester. [*Exeunt some of the Servants.*

REGAN

Hang him instantly.

GONERIL

Pluck out his eyes.

CORNWALL

Leave him to my displeasure. Edmund, keep you our sister company: the revenges we are bound to take upon your traitorous father are not fit for your beholding. Advise the duke, where you are going, to a most festinate preparation: we are bound to the like. Our posts shall be swift and intelligent betwixt us. Farewell, dear sister: farewell, my lord of Gloucester.

Enter OSWALD.

How now! where's the king?

OSWALD

My lord of Gloucester hath convey'd him hence:
Some five or six and thirty of his knights,
Hot questrists after him, met him at gate;
Who, with some other of the lords dependants,
Are gone with him towards Dover; where they boast
To have well-armed friends.

CORNWALL

Get horses for your mistress.

GONERIL

Farewell, sweet lord, and sister.

CORNWALL
Edmund, farewell.
[*Exeunt Goneril, Edmund, and Oswald.*
Go seek the traitor Gloucester,
Pinion him like a thief, bring him before us.
[*Exeunt other Servants.*
Though well we may not pass upon his life
Without the form of justice, yet our power
Shall do a courtesy to our wrath, which men
May blame, but not control. Who's there? the traitor?

Enter GLOUCESTER, *brought in by two or three.*

REGAN
Ingrateful fox! 'tis he.
CORNWALL
Bind fast his corky arms.
GLOUCESTER
What mean your graces? Good my friends, consider 33
You are my guests: do me no foul play, friends.
CORNWALL
Bind him, I say. [*Servants bind him.*
REGAN
Hard, hard. O filthy traitor!
GLOUCESTER
Unmerciful lady as you are, I'm none.
CORNWALL
To this chair bind him. Villain, thou shalt find—
[*Regan plucks his beard.*
GLOUCESTER
By the kind gods, 'tis most ignobly done
To pluck me by the beard.
REGAN
So white, and such a traitor!
GLOUCESTER
Naughty lady,
These hairs, which thou dost ravish from my chin,
Will quicken, and accuse thee: I am your host:
With robbers' hands my hospitable favours 45
You should not ruffle thus. What will you do?
CORNWALL
Come, sir, what letters had you late from France?
REGAN
Be simple answerer, for we know the truth.
CORNWALL
And what confederacy have you with the traitors
Late footed in the kingdom?
REGAN
To whose hands have you sent the lunatic king?
Speak.
GLOUCESTER
I have a letter guessingly set down,
Which came from one that's of a neutral heart,
And not from one opposed.
CORNWALL
Cunning.
REGAN
And false.
CORNWALL
Where hast thou sent the king? 58
GLOUCESTER
To Dover.
REGAN
Wherefore to Dover? Wast thou not charged at peril—
CORNWALL
Wherefore to Dover? Let him first answer that.
GLOUCESTER
I am tied to the stake, and I must stand the course.
REGAN
Wherefore to Dover, sir?
GLOUCESTER
Because I would not see thy cruel nails
Pluck out his poor old eyes; nor thy fierce sister
In his anointed flesh stick boarish fangs. [74]
The sea, with such a storm as his bare head
In hell-black night endured, would have buoy'd up, 69
And quench'd the stelled fires:
Yet, poor old heart, he holp the heavens to rain.
If wolves had at thy gate howl'd that stern time, [75]
Thou shouldst have said 'Good porter, turn the key,'
All cruels else subscribed: but I shall see [76]
The winged vengeance overtake such children.
CORNWALL
See't shalt thou never. Fellows, hold the chair.
Upon these eyes of thine I'll set my foot.
GLOUCESTER
He that will think to live till he be old,
Give me some help! O cruel! O you gods!
REGAN
One side will mock another; the other too.
CORNWALL
If you see vengeance,—
FIRST SERVANT
Hold your hand, my lord:
I have served you ever since I was a child;
But better service have I never done you
Than now to bid you hold.
REGAN
How now, you dog!
FIRST SERVANT
If you did wear a beard upon your chin,
I'd shake it on this quarrel. What do you mean?
CORNWALL
My villain! [*They draw and fight.*
FIRST SERVANT
Nay, then, come on, and take the chance of anger.

REGAN
Give me thy sword. A peasant stand up thus! 91
[*Takes a sword, and runs at him behind.*
FIRST SERVANT
O, I am slain! My lord, you have one eye left
To see some mischief on him. O! [*Dies.*
CORNWALL
Lest it see more, prevent it. Out, vile jelly!
Where is thy lustre now?
GLOUCESTER
All dark and comfortless. Where's my son Edmund?
Edmund, enkindle all the sparks of nature,
To quit this horrid act.
REGAN
Out, treacherous villain!
Thou call'st on him that hates thee: it was he
That made the overture of thy treasons to us;
Who is too good to pity thee. 103
GLOUCESTER
O my follies! then Edgar was abused.
Kind gods, forgive me that, and prosper him!
REGAN
Go thrust him out at gates, and let him smell
His way to Dover. [*Exit one with Gloucester.*
How is't, my lord? how look you?
CORNWALL
I have received a hurt: follow me, lady.
Turn out that eyeless villain; throw this slave
Upon the dunghill. Regan, I bleed apace:
Untimely comes this hurt: give me your arm.
[*Exit Cornwall, led by Regan.*
SECOND SERVANT
I'll never care what wickedness I do,
If this man come to good.
THIRD SERVANT
If she live long, 115
And in the end meet the old course of death,
Women will all turn monsters.
SECOND SERVANT
Let's follow the old earl, and get the Bedlam
To lead him where he would: his roguish madness
Allows itself to any thing.
THIRD SERVANT
Go thou: I'll fetch some flax and whites of eggs
To apply to his bleeding face. Now, heaven help him! [*Exeunt severally.*

ACT FOUR SCENE ONE

The heath.

Enter EDGAR.

EDGAR
Yet better thus, and known to be contemn'd,
Than still contemn'd and flatter'd. To be worst,
The lowest and most dejected thing of fortune,
Stands still in esperance, lives not in fear:
The lamentable change is from the best;
The worst returns to laughter. Welcome,then, [77]
Thou unsubstantial air that I embrace!
The wretch that thou hast blown unto the worst
Owes nothing to thy blasts. But who comes here?

Enter GLOUCESTER, *led by an* Old Man.

My father, poorly led? World, world, O world!
But that thy strange mutations make us hate thee, 12
Lie would not yield to age. [78]
OLD MAN
O, my good lord, I have been your tenant, and your father's tenant, these fourscore years.
GLOUCESTER
Away, get thee away; good friend, be gone:
Thy comforts can do me no good at all;
Thee they may hurt.
OLD MAN
Alack, sir, you cannot see your way.
GLOUCESTER
I have no way, and therefore want no eyes; 20
I stumbled when I saw: full oft 'tis seen,
Our means secure us, and our mere defects
Prove our commodities. O dear son Edgar,
The food of thy abused father's wrath!
Might I but live to see thee in my touch,
I'ld say I had eyes again!
OLD MAN
How now! Who's there?
EDGAR
[*Aside*] O gods! Who is't can say 'I am at the worst'?
I am worse than e'er I was.
OLD MAN
'Tis poor mad Tom.
EDGAR
[*Aside*] And worse I may be yet: the worst is not
So long as we can say 'This is the worst.' 32
OLD MAN
Fellow, where goest?
GLOUCESTER
Is it a beggar-man?
OLD MAN
Madman and beggar too.
GLOUCESTER
He has some reason, else he could not beg.
I' the last night's storm I such a fellow saw;
Which made me think a man a worm: my son
Came then into my mind; and yet my mind
Was then scarce friends with him: I have heard more since.
As flies to wanton boys, are we to the gods.

They kill us for their sport. [79]

EDGAR
[*Aside*] How should this be? 44
Bad is the trade that must play fool to sorrow,
Angering itself and others.—Bless thee, master!

GLOUCESTER
Is that the naked fellow?

OLD MAN
Ay, my lord.

GLOUCESTER
Then, prithee, get thee gone: if, for my sake,
Thou wilt o'ertake us, hence a mile or twain,
I' the way toward Dover, do it for ancient love;
And bring some covering for this naked soul,
Who I'll entreat to lead me.

OLD MAN
Alack, sir, he is mad.

GLOUCESTER
'Tis the times' plague, when madmen lead the blind.
Do as I bid thee, or rather do thy pleasure;
Above the rest, be gone. 57

OLD MAN
I'll bring him the best 'parel that I have,
Come on't what will. [*Exit.*

GLOUCESTER
Sirrah, naked fellow,—

EDGAR
Poor Tom's a-cold. [*Aside*] I cannot daub it further.

GLOUCESTER
Come hither, fellow.

EDGAR
[*Aside*] And yet I must.—Bless thy sweet eyes, they bleed.

GLOUCESTER
Know'st thou the way to Dover?

EDGAR
Both stile and gate, horse-way and foot-path. Poor Tom hath been scared out of his good wits: bless thee, good man's son, from the foul fiend! five fiends have been in poor Tom at once; of lust, as Obidicut; Hobbididence, prince of dumbness; Mahu, of stealing; Modo, of murder; Flibbertigibbet, of mopping and mowing, who since possesses chamber-maids and waiting-women. So, bless thee, master! [80]

GLOUCESTER
Here, take this purse, thou whom the heavens' plagues
Have humbled to all strokes: that I am wretched
Makes thee the happier: heavens, deal so still!
Let the superfluous and lust-dieted man, 78
That slaves your ordinance, that will not see
Because he doth not feel, feel your power quickly;
So distribution should undo excess,
And each man have enough. Dost thou know Dover?

EDGAR
Ay, master.

GLOUCESTER
There is a cliff, whose high and bending head
Looks fearfully in the confined deep:
Bring me but to the very brim of it,
And I'll repair the misery thou dost bear
With something rich about me: from that place
I shall no leading need.

EDGAR
Give me thy arm: 91
Poor Tom shall lead thee. [*Exeunt.*

ACT FOUR SCENE TWO

Before ALBANY'S *palace.*

Enter GONERIL *and* EDMUND.

GONERIL
Welcome, my lord: I marvel our mild husband
Not met us on the way.

Enter OSWALD.

Now, where's your master'?

OSWALD
Madam, within; but never man so changed.
I told him of the army that was landed;
He smiled at it: I told him you were coming:
His answer was 'The worse:' of Gloucester's treachery,
And of the loyal service of his son,
When I inform'd him, then he call'd me sot,
And told me I had turn'd the wrong side out:
What most he should dislike seems pleasant to him; 12
What like, offensive.

GONERIL
[*To Edmund*] Then shall you go no further.
It is the cowish terror of his spirit,
That dares not undertake: he'll not feel wrongs
Which tie him to an answer. Our wishes on the way
May prove effects. Back, Edmund, to my brother;
Hasten his musters and conduct his powers:
I must change arms at home, and give the distaff
Into my husband's hands. This trusty servant
Shall pass between us: ere long you are like to hear,
If you dare venture in your own behalf, 23
A mistress's command. Wear this; spare speech; [*Giving a favour.*
Decline your head: this kiss, if it durst speak,
Would stretch thy spirits up into the air:
Conceive, and fare thee well.

EDMUND
Yours in the ranks of death.

GONERIL
My most dear Gloucester! [*Exit Edmund.*

O, the difference of man and man!
To thee a woman's services are due:
My fool usurps my body. [81]

OSWALD
Madam, here comes my lord. [*Exit.*

Enter ALBANY.

GONERIL
I have been worth the whistle.

ALBANY
O Goneril!
You are not worth the dust which the rude wind
Blows in your face. I fear your disposition:
That nature, which contemns its origin,
Cannot be border'd certain in itself;
She that herself will sliver and disbranch
From her material sap, perforce must wither
And come to deadly use.

GONERIL
No more; the text is foolish.

ALBANY
Wisdom and goodness to the vile seem vile:
Filths savour but themselves. What have you done?
Tigers, not daughters, what have you perform'd?
A father, and a gracious aged man,
Whose reverence even the head-lugg'd bear would lick,
Most barbarous, most degenerate! have you madded.
Could my good brother suffer you to do it?
A man, a prince, by him so benefited!
If that the heavens do not their visible spirits
Send quickly down to tame these vile offences, [82]
It will come,
Humanity must perforce prey on itself,
Like monsters of the deep·

GONERIL
Milk-liver'd man!
That bear'st a cheek for blows, a head for wrongs;
Who hast not in thy brows an eye discerning
Thine honour from thy suffering; that not know'st
Fools do those villains pity who are punish'd
Ere they have done their mischief. Where's thy drum?
France spreads his banners in our noiseless land;
With plumed helm thy slayer begins threats; [83]
Whiles thou, a moral fool, sit'st still, and criest
'Alack, why does he so?'

ALBANY
See thyself, devil!
Proper deformity seems not in the fiend
So horrid as in woman.

GONERIL
O vain fool!

ALBANY
Thou changed and self-cover'd thing, for shame,
Be-monster not thy feature. Were't my fitness
To let these hands obey my blood,
They are apt enough to dislocate and tear
Thy flesh and bones: howe'er thou art a fiend,
A woman's shape doth shield thee.

GONERIL
Marry, your manhood now— [84]

Enter a Messenger.

ALBANY
What news?

MESSENGER
O, my good lord, the Duke of Cornwall's dead:
Slain by his servant, going to put out
The other eye of Gloucester.

ALBANY
Gloucester's eyes!

MESSENGER
A servant that he bred, thrill'd with remorse,
Opposed against the act, bending his sword
To his great master; who, thereat enraged,
Flew on him, and amongst them fell'd him dead;
But not without that harmful stroke, which since
Hath pluck'd him after.

ALBANY
This shows you are above,
You justicers, that these our nether crimes
So speedily can venge! But, O poor Gloucester!
Lost he his other eye?

MESSENGER
Both, both, my lord.
This letter, madam, craves a speedy answer;
'Tis from your sister.

GONERIL
[*Aside*] One way I like this well;
But being widow, and my Gloucester with her,
May all the building in my fancy pluck
Upon my hateful life: another way,
The news is not so tart.—I'll read, and answer.
[*Exit.*

ALBANY
Where was his son when they did take his eyes?

MESSENGER
Come with my lady hither.

ALBANY
He is not here.

MESSENGER
No, my good lord; I met him back again.

ALBANY
Knows he the wickedness?

MESSENGER
Ay, my good lord; 'twas he inform'd against him;

And quit the house on purpose, that their punishment
Might have the freer course.

ALBANY

Gloucester, I live
To thank thee for the love thou show'dst the king,
And to revenge thine eyes. Come hither, friend:
Tell me what more thou know'st. [*Exeunt.*

ACT FOUR SCENE THREE

The French camp near Dover.

Enter KENT *and a* Gentleman.

KENT

Why the King of France is so suddenly gone back know you the reason?

GENTLEMAN

Something he left imperfect in the state, which since his coming forth is thought of; which imports to the kingdom so much fear and danger, that his personal return was most required and necessary.

KENT

Who hath he left behind him general?

GENTLEMAN

The Marshal of France, Monsieur La Far. 8

KENT

Did your letters pierce the queen to any demonstration of grief?

GENTLEMAN

Ay, sir; she took them, read them in my presence;
And now and then an ample tear trill'd down
Her delicate cheek: it seem'd she was a queen
Over her passion; who, most rebel-like,
Sought to be king o'er her.

KENT

O, then it moved her.

GENTLEMAN

Not to a rage: patience and sorrow strove
Who should express her goodliest. You have seen
Sunshine and rain at once: her smiles and tears 19
Were like a better way: those happy smilets, [85]
That play'd on her ripe lip, seem'd not to know
What guests were in her eyes; which parted thence,
As pearls from diamonds dropp'd. In brief,
Sorrow would be a rarity most beloved,
If all could so become it.

KENT

Made she no verbal question?

GENTLEMAN

'Faith, once or twice she heaved the name of 'father'
Pantingly forth, as if it press'd her heart:
Cried 'Sisters! sisters! Shame of ladies! sisters!
Kent! father! sisters! What, i' the storm? i' the night? 31
Let pity not be believed!' There she shook [86]
The holy water from her heavenly eyes,
And clamour moisten'd: then away she started [87]
To deal with grief alone·

KENT

It is the stars,
The stars above us, govern our conditions;
Else one self mate and mate could not beget
Such different issues. You spoke not with her since?

GENTLEMAN

No.

KENT

Was this before the king return'd?

GENTLEMAN

No, since.

KENT

Well, sir, the poor distressed Lear's i' the town; 43
Who sometime, in his better tune, remembers
What we are come about, and by no means
Will yield to see his daughter.

GENTLEMAN

Why, good sir?

KENT

A sovereign shame so elbows him: his own unkindness,
That stripp'd her from his benediction, turn'd her
To foreign casualties, gave her dear rights
To his dog-hearted daughters, these things sting
His mind so venomously, that burning shame
Detains him from Cordelia.

GENTLEMAN

Alack, poor gentleman!

KENT

Of Albany's and Cornwall's powers you heard not?

GENTLEMAN

'Tis so, they are afoot.

KENT

Well, sir, I'll bring you to our master Lear,
And leave you to attend him: some dear cause
Will in concealment wrap me up awhile;
When I am known aright, you shall not grieve
Lending me this acquaintance. I pray you, go
Along with me. [*Exeunt.*

ACT FOUR SCENE FOUR

The same. A tent.

Enter, with drum and colours, CORDELIA, Doctor, *and* Soldiers.

CORDELIA

Alack, 'tis he: why, he was met even now

As mad as the vex'd sea; singing aloud;
Crown'd with rank fumiter and furrow-weeds,
With bur-docks, hemlock, nettles, cuckoo-flowers,
Darnel, and all the idle weeds that grow
In our sustaining corn. A century send forth;
Search every acre in the high-grown field,
And bring him to our eye. [*Exit an Officer.*
What can man's wisdom
In the restoring his bereaved sense?
He that helps him take all my outward worth.

DOCTOR
There is means, madam: 13
Our foster-nurse of nature is repose,
The which he lacks; that to provoke in him,
Are many simples operative, whose power
Will close the eye of anguish.

CORDELIA
All blest secrets,
All you unpublish'd virtues of the earth,
Spring with my tears! be aidant and remediate
In the good man's distress! Seek, seek for him;
Lest his ungovern'd rage dissolve the life
That wants the means to lead it.

Enter a Messenger.

MESSENGER
News, madam; 24
The British powers are marching hitherward.

CORDELIA
'Tis known before; our preparation stands
In expectation of them. O dear father,
It is thy business that I go about;
Therefore great France
My mourning and important tears hath pitied.
No blown ambition doth our arms incite,
But love, dear love, and our aged father's right:
Soon may I hear and see him! [*Exeunt.*

ACT FOUR SCENE FIVE

Gloucester's castle.

Enter REGAN *and* OSWALD.

REGAN
But are my brother's powers set forth?

OSWALD
Ay, madam.

REGAN
Himself in person there?

OSWALD
Madam, with much ado:
Your sister is the better soldier.

REGAN
Lord Edmund spake not with your lord at home? [88]

OSWALD
No, madam.

REGAN
What might import my sister's letter to him?

OSWALD
I know not, lady.

REGAN
'Faith, he is posted hence on serious matter.
It was great ignorance, Gloucester's eyes being out,
To let him live: where he arrives he moves 13
All hearts against us: Edmund, I think, is gone,
In pity of his misery, to dispatch
His nighted life: moreover, to descry
The strength o' the enemy.

OSWALD
I must needs after him, madam, with my letter.

REGAN
Our troops set forth to-morrow: stay with us;
The ways are dangerous.

OSWALD
I may not, madam:
My lady charged my duty in this business.

REGAN
Why should she write to Edmund? Might not you
Transport her purposes by word? Belike, 24
Something—I know not what: I'll love thee much,
Let me unseal the letter.

OSWALD
Madam, I had rather—

REGAN
I know your lady does not love her husband;
I am sure of that: and at her late being here
She gave strange oeillades and most speaking looks
To noble Edmund. I know you are of her bosom.

OSWALD
I, madam?

REGAN
I speak in understanding; you are; I know't:
Therefore I do advise you, take this note:
My lord is dead; Edmund and I have talk'd;
And more convenient is he for my hand 37
Than for your lady's: you may gather more.
If you do find him, pray you, give him this;
And when your mistress hears thus much from you,
I pray, desire her call her wisdom to her.
So, fare you well.
If you do chance to hear of that blind traitor,
Preferment falls on him that cuts him off.

OSWALD
Would I could meet him, madam! I should show

What party I do follow.
REGAN
Fare thee well. [*Exeunt.*

ACT FOUR SCENE SIX

Fields near Dover.
Enter GLOUCESTER, *and* EDGAR *dressed like a peasant.*

GLOUCESTER
When shall we come to the top of that same hill?
EDGAR
You do climb up it now: look, how we labour.
GLOUCESTER
Methinks the ground is even.
EDGAR
Horrible steep.
Hark, do you hear the sea?
GLOUCESTER
No, truly.
EDGAR
Why, then, your other senses grow imperfect
By your eyes' anguish.
GLOUCESTER
So may it be, indeed:
Methinks thy voice is alter'd; and thou speak'st
In better phrase and matter than thou didst.
EDGAR
You're much deceived: in nothing am I changed
But in my garments.
GLOUCESTER
Methinks you're better spoken. 14
EDGAR
Come on, sir; here's the place: stand still. How fearful
And dizzy 'tis, to cast one's eyes so low!
The crows and choughs that wing the midway air
Show scarce so gross as beetles: half way down
Hangs one that gathers samphire, dreadful trade!
Methinks he seems no bigger than his head:
The fishermen, that walk upon the beach,
Appear like mice; and yond tall anchoring bark,
Diminish'd to her cock; her cock, a buoy
Almost too small for sight: the murmuring surge, 26
That on the unnumber'd idle pebbles chafes,
Cannot be heard so high. I'll look no more;
Lest my brain turn, and the deficient sight
Topple down headlong.
GLOUCESTER
Set me where you stand.
EDGAR
Give me your hand: you are now within a foot
Of the extreme verge: for all beneath the moon
Would I not leap upright.
GLOUCESTER
Let go my hand.
Here, friend, 's another purse; in it a jewel
Well worth a poor man's taking: fairies and gods
Prosper it with thee! Go thou farther off; 38
Bid me farewell, and let me hear thee going.
EDGAR
Now fare you well, good sir.
GLOUCESTER
With all my heart.
EDGAR
Why I do trifle thus with his despair
Is done to cure it.
GLOUCESTER
[*Kneeling*] O you mighty gods!
This world I do renounce, and, in your sights,
Shake patiently my great affliction off:
If I could bear it longer, and not fall
To quarrel with your great opposeless wills,
My snuff and loathed part of nature should 49
Burn itself out. If Edgar live, O, bless him!
Now, fellow, fare thee well. [*He falls forward.*
EDGAR
Gone, sir: farewell.
And yet I know not how conceit may rob
The treasury of life, when life itself
Yields to the theft: had he been where he thought,
By this, had thought been past. Alive or dead?
Ho, you sir! friend! Hear you, sir! speak!
Thus might he pass indeed: yet he revives.
What are you, sir?
GLOUCESTER
Away, and let me die.
EDGAR
Hadst thou been aught but gossamer, feathers, air,
So many fathom down precipitating, 62
Thou'dst shiver'd like an egg: but thou dost breathe;
Hast heavy substance; bleed'st not; speak'st; art sound.
Ten masts at each make not the altitude
Which thou hast perpendicularly fell:
Thy life's a miracle. Speak yet again.
GLOUCESTER
But have I fall'n, or no?
EDGAR
From the dread summit of this chalky bourn.
Look up a-height; the shrill-gorged lark so far
Cannot be seen or heard: do but look up.
GLOUCESTER
Alack, I have no eyes. 73
Is wretchedness deprived that benefit,
To end itself by death? 'Twas yet some comfort,

When misery could beguile the tyrant's rage,
And frustrate his proud will.

EDGAR
Give me your arm:
Up: so. How is 't? Feel you your legs? You stand.

GLOUCESTER
Too well, too well.

EDGAR
This is above all strangeness.
Upon the crown o' the cliff, what thing was that
Which parted from you?

GLOUCESTER
A poor unfortunate beggar.

EDGAR
As I stood here below, methought his eyes
Were two full moons; he had a thousand noses, 86
Horns whelk'd and waved like the enridged sea:
It was some fiend; therefore, thou happy father,
Think that the clearest gods, who make them honours
Of men's impossibilities, have preserved thee.

GLOUCESTER
I do remember now: henceforth I'll bear
Affliction till it do cry out itself
'Enough, enough,' and die. That thing you speak of,
I took it for a man; often 'twould say
'The fiend, the fiend:' he led me to that place.

EDGAR
Bear free and patient thoughts. But who comes here? 97

Enter LEAR, *fantastically dressed with wild flowers.*

The safer sense will ne'er accommodate
His master thus.

KING LEAR
No, they cannot touch me for coining; I am the king himself.

EDGAR
O thou side-piercing sight!

KING LEAR
Nature's above art in that respect. There's your press-money. That fellow handles his bow like a crow-keeper: draw me a clothier's yard. Look, look, a mouse! Peace, peace; this piece of toasted cheese will do 't. There's my gauntlet; I'll prove it on a giant. Bring up the brown bills. O, well flown, bird! i' the clout, i' the clout: hewgh! Give the word.

EDGAR
Sweet marjoram.

KING LEAR
Pass.

GLOUCESTER
I know that voice.

KING LEAR
Ha! Goneril, with a white beard! They flattered me like a dog; and told me I had white hairs in my beard ere the black ones were there. To say 'ay' and 'no' to every thing that I said!—'Ay' and 'no' too was no good divinity. When the rain came to wet me once, and the wind to make me chatter; when the thunder would not peace at my bidding; there I found 'em, there I smelt 'em out. Go to, they are not men o' their words: they told me I was every thing; 'tis a lie, I am not ague-proof. *89*

GLOUCESTER
The trick of that voice I do well remember:
Is 't not the king?

KING LEAR
Ay, every inch a king: 124
When I do stare, see how the subject quakes.
I pardon that man's life. What was thy cause? Adultery?
Thou shalt not die: die for adultery! No:
The wren goes to 't, and the small gilded fly
Does lecher in my sight.
Let copulation thrive; for Gloucester's bastard son
Was kinder to his father than my daughters
Got 'tween the lawful sheets.
To 't, luxury, pell-mell! for I lack soldiers.
Behold yond simpering dame, 135
Whose face between her forks presages snow;
That minces virtue, and does shake the head
To hear of pleasure's name;
The fitchew, nor the soiled horse, goes to 't
With a more riotous appetite.
Down from the waist they are Centaurs,
Though women all above:
But to the girdle do the gods inherit,
Beneath is all the fiends';
There's hell, there's darkness, there's the sulphurous pit, 146
Burning, scalding, stench, consumption; fie, fie, fie! pah, pah! Give me an ounce of civet, good apothecary, to sweeten my imagination: there's money for thee.

GLOUCESTER
O, let me kiss that hand!

KING LEAR
Let me wipe it first; it smells of mortality.

GLOUCESTER
O ruin'd piece of nature! This great world
Shall so wear out to nought. Dost thou know me?

KING LEAR
I remember thine eyes well enough. Dost thou squiny at me? No, do thy worst, blind Cupid! I'll not love. Read thou this challenge; mark but the penning of it.

GLOUCESTER
Were all the letters suns, I could not see one.

EDGAR
I would not take this from report; it is,
And my heart breaks at it.

KING LEAR
Read.

GLOUCESTER
What, with the case of eyes?

KING LEAR
O, ho, are you there with me? No eyes in your head, nor no money in your purse? Your eyes are in a heavy case, your purse in a light; yet you see how this world goes.

GLOUCESTER
I see it feelingly.

KING LEAR
What, art mad? A man may see how this world goes with no eyes. Look with thine ears: see how yond justice rails upon yond simple thief. Hark, in thine ear: change places; and, handy-dandy, which is the justice, which is the thief? Thou hast seen a farmer's dog bark at a beggar?

GLOUCESTER
Ay, sir.

KING LEAR
And the creature run from the cur? There thou mightst behold the great image of authority: a dog's obeyed in office.
Thou rascal beadle, hold thy bloody hand!
Why dost thou lash that whore? Strip thine own back;
Thou hotly lust'st to use her in that kind
For which thou whipp'st her. The usurer hangs the cozener.
Through tatter'd clothes small vices do appear;
Robes and furr'd gowns hide all. Plate sin with gold,
And the strong lance of justice hurtless breaks:
Arm it in rags, a pigmy's straw does pierce it.
None does offend, none, I say, none; I'll able 'em:
Take that of me, my friend, who have the power
To seal the accuser's lips. Get thee glass eyes;
And like a scurvy politician, seem
To see the things thou dost not. Now, now, now, now:
Pull off my boots: harder, harder: so.

EDGAR
O, matter and impertinency mix'd! Reason in madness!

KING LEAR
If thou wilt weep my fortunes, take my eyes.
I know thee well enough; thy name is Gloucester:
Thou must be patient; we came crying hither:
Thou know'st, the first time that we smell the air,
We wawl and cry. I will preach to thee: mark.

GLOUCESTER
Alack, alack the day!

KING LEAR
When we are born, we cry that we are come
To this great stage of fools: this a good block;
It were a delicate stratagem, to shoe
A troop of horse with felt: I'll put 't in proof;
And when I have stol'n upon these sons-in-law,
Then, kill, kill, kill, kill, kill, kill!

Enter a Gentleman, *with* Attendants.

GENTLEMAN
O, here he is: lay hand upon him. Sir,
Your most dear daughter—

KING LEAR
No rescue? What, a prisoner? I am even
The natural fool of fortune. Use me well;
You shall have ransom. Let me have surgeons;
I am cut to the brains.

GENTLEMAN
You shall have any thing.

KING LEAR
No seconds? all myself?
Why, this would make a man a man of salt,
To use his eyes for garden water-pots,
Ay, and laying autumn's dust.

GENTLEMAN
Good sir,—

KING LEAR
I will die bravely, like a bridegroom. What!
I will be jovial: come, come; I am a king,
My masters, know you that.

GENTLEMAN
You are a royal one, and we obey you.

KING LEAR
Then there's life in't. Nay, if you get it, you shall get it with running. Sa, sa, sa, sa.

[*Exit running; Attendants follow.*

GENTLEMAN
A sight most pitiful in the meanest wretch,
Past speaking of in a king! Thou hast one daughter,
Who redeems nature from the general curse
Which twain have brought her to.

EDGAR
Hail, gentle sir.

GENTLEMAN
Sir, speed you: what's your will?

EDGAR
Do you hear aught, sir, of a battle toward?

GENTLEMAN
Most sure and vulgar: every one hears that,
Which can distinguish sound.

EDGAR
But, by your favour,
How near's the other army?

GENTLEMAN
Near and on speedy foot; the main descry
Stands on the hourly thought.

EDGAR
I thank you, sir: that's all.

GENTLEMAN
Though that the queen on special cause is here,
Her army is moved on.

EDGAR
I thank you, sir. [*Exit Gentleman.*

GLOUCESTER
You ever-gentle gods, take my breath from me:
Let not my worser spirit tempt me again
To die before you please!

EDGAR
Well pray you, father.

GLOUCESTER
Now, good sir, what are you?

EDGAR
A most poor man, made tame to fortune's blows;
Who, by the art of known and feeling sorrows,
Am pregnant to good pity. Give me your hand,
I'll lead you to some biding.

GLOUCESTER
Hearty thanks:
The bounty and the benison of heaven
To boot, and boot!

Enter OSWALD.

OSWALD
A proclaim'd prize! Most happy!
That eyeless head of thine was first framed flesh
To raise my fortunes. Thou old unhappy traitor,
Briefly thyself remember: the sword is out
That must destroy thee.

GLOUCESTER
Now let thy friendly hand
Put strength enough to't. [*Edgar interposes.*

OSWALD
Wherefore, bold peasant,
Darest thou support a publish'd traitor? Hence;
Lest that the infection of his fortune take
Like hold on thee. Let go his arm.

EDGAR
Chill not let go, zir, without vurther 'casion.

OSWALD
Let go, slave, or thou diest!

EDGAR
Good gentleman, go your gait, and let poor volk pass. An chud ha' bin zwaggered out of my life, 'twould not ha' bin zo long as 'tis by a vortnight. Nay, come not near th' old man; keep out, che vor ye, or ise try whether your costard or my ballow be the harder: ch'ill be plain with you.

OSWALD
Out, dunghill!

EDGAR
Chill pick your teeth, zir: come; no matter vor your foins.

[*They fight, and Edgar knocks him down.*

OSWALD
Slave, thou hast slain me: villain, take my purse:
If ever thou wilt thrive, bury my body;
And give the letters which thou find'st about me
To Edmund earl of Gloucester; seek him out
Upon the British party: O, untimely death! [*Dies.*

EDGAR
I know thee well: a serviceable villain;
As duteous to the vices of thy mistress
As badness would desire.

GLOUCESTER
What, is he dead?

EDGAR
Sit you down, father; rest you.
Let's see these pockets: the letters that he speaks of
May be my friends. He's dead; I am only sorry
He had no other death's-man. Let us see:
Leave, gentle wax; and, manners, blame us not:
To know our enemies' minds, we'ld rip their hearts;
Their papers, is more lawful.
[*Reads*] 'Let our reciprocal vows be remembered. You have many opportunities to cut him off: if your will want not, time and place will be fruitfully offered. There is nothing done, if he return the conqueror: then am I the prisoner, and his bed my goal; from the loathed warmth whereof deliver me, and supply the place for your labour.

'Your—wife, so I would say—
'Affectionate servant,
'GONERIL.'

O undistinguish'd space of woman's will!
A plot upon her virtuous husband's life;
And the exchange my brother! Here, in the sands,
Thee I'll rake up, the post unsanctified
Of murderous lechers: and in the mature time
With this ungracious paper strike the sight
Of the death-practised duke: for him 'tis well
That of thy death and business I can tell.

GLOUCESTER
The king is mad: how stiff is my vile sense,
That I stand up, and have ingenious feeling
Of my huge sorrows! Better I were distract:
So should my thoughts be sever'd from my griefs,
And woes by wrong imaginations lose
The knowledge of themselves.

EDGAR
Give me your hand: [*Drum afar off.*
Far off, methinks, I hear the beaten drum:
Come, father, I'll bestow you with a friend. [*Exeunt.*

ACT FOUR SCENE SEVEN

A tent in the French camp. LEAR *on a bed asleep, soft music playing*; Gentleman, *and others attending.*

Enter CORDELIA, KENT, *and* Doctor.

CORDELIA
O thou good Kent, how shall I live and work,
To match thy goodness? My life will be too short,
And every measure fail me.
KENT
To be acknowledged, madam, is o'erpaid.
All my reports go with the modest truth;
Nor more nor clipp'd, but so.
CORDELIA
Be better suited:
These weeds are memories of those worser hours:
I prithee, put them off.
KENT
Pardon me, dear madam;
Yet to be known shortens my made intent:
My boon I make it, that you know me not 13
Till time and I think meet.
CORDELIA
Then be't so, my good lord. [*To the Doctor*] How does the king?
DOCTOR
Madam, sleeps still.
CORDELIA
O you kind gods,
Cure this great breach in his abused nature!
The untuned and jarring senses, O, wind up
Of this child-changed father!
DOCTOR
So please your majesty
That we may wake the king: he hath slept long.
CORDELIA
Be govern'd by your knowledge, and proceed
I' the sway of your own will. Is he array'd?
GENTLEMAN
Ay, madam; in the heaviness of his sleep
We put fresh garments on him.
DOCTOR
Be by, good madam, when we do awake him;
I doubt not of his temperance.
CORDELIA
Very well.
DOCTOR
Please you, draw near. Louder the music there!
CORDELIA
O my dear father! Restoration hang
Thy medicine on my lips; and let this kiss
Repair those violent harms that my two sisters
Have in thy reverence made!
KENT
Kind and dear princess!
CORDELIA
Had you not been their father, these white flakes 38
Had challenged pity of them. Was this a face
To be opposed against the warring winds? [91]
To stand against the deep dread-bolted thunder?
In the most terrible and nimble stroke
Of quick, cross lightning? to watch—poor perdu!—
With this thin helm? Mine enemy's dog, [92]
Though he had bit me, should have stood that night
Against my fire; and wast thou fain, poor father,
To hovel thee with swine, and rogues forlorn,
In short and musty straw? Alack, alack! 49
'Tis wonder that thy life and wits at once
Had not concluded all. He wakes; speak to him.
DOCTOR
Madam, do you; 'tis fittest.
CORDELIA
How does my royal lord? How fares your majesty?
KING LEAR
You do me wrong to take me out o' the grave:
Thou art a soul in bliss; but I am bound
Upon a wheel of fire, that mine own tears
Do scald like moulten lead.
CORDELIA
Sir, do you know me?
KING LEAR
You are a spirit, I know: when did you die?
CORDELIA
Still, still, far wide! 61
DOCTOR
He's scarce awake: let him alone awhile.
KING LEAR
Where have I been? Where am I? Fair daylight?
I am mightily abused. I should e'en die with pity,
To see another thus. I know not what to say.
I will not swear these are my hands: let's see;
I feel this pin prick. Would I were assured
Of my condition!
CORDELIA
O, look upon me, sir,
And hold your hands in benediction o'er me:
No, sir, you must not kneel.
KING LEAR
Pray, do not mock me:
I am a very foolish fond old man, 73
Fourscore and upward, not an hour more nor less;
And, to deal plainly,
I fear I am not in my perfect mind.

Methinks I should know you, and know this man;
Yet I am doubtful for I am mainly ignorant
What place this is; and all the skill I have
Remembers not these garments; nor I know not
Where I did lodge last night. Do not laugh at me;
For, as I am a man, I think this lady
To be my child Cordelia.

CORDELIA
And so I am, I am.

KING LEAR
Be your tears wet? yes, 'faith. I pray, weep not:
If you have poison for me, I will drink it.
I know you, do not love me; for your sisters
Have, as I do remember, done me wrong:
You have some cause, they have not.

CORDELIA
No cause, no cause.

KING LEAR
Am I in France?

KENT
In your own kingdom, sir.

KING LEAR
Do not abuse me.

DOCTOR
Be comforted, good madam: the great rage,
You see, is kill'd in him: and yet it is danger [93]
To make him even o'er the time he has lost.
Desire him to go in; trouble him no more
Till further settling.

CORDELIA
Will't please your highness walk?

KING LEAR
You must bear with me:
Pray you now, forget and forgive: I am old and foolish. *[Exeunt all but Kent and Gentleman.*

GENTLEMAN
Holds it true, sir, that the Duke of Cornwall was so slain?

KENT
Most certain, sir.

GENTLEMAN
Who is conductor of his people?

KENT
As 'tis said, the bastard son of Gloucester.

GENTLEMAN
They say Edgar, his banished son, is with the Earl of Kent in Germany.

KENT
Report is changeable. 'Tis time to look about; the powers of the kingdom approach apace.

GENTLEMAN
The arbitrement is like to be bloody. Fare you well, sir. *[Exit.*

KENT
My point and period will be throughly wrought,
Or well or ill, as this day's battle's fought.
[Exit.

ACT FIVE SCENE ONE

The British camp, near Dover.

Enter, with drum and colours, EDMUND, REGAN, Gentlemen, *and* Soldiers .

EDMUND
Know of the duke if his last purpose hold,
Or whether since he is advised by aught
To change the course: he's full of alteration
And self-reproving: bring his constant pleasure.
[To a Gentleman, who goes out.

REGAN
Our sister's man is certainly miscarried.

EDMUND
'Tis to be doubted, madam.

REGAN
Now, sweet lord,
You know the goodness I intend upon you:
Tell me—but truly—but then speak the truth,
Do you not love my sister?

EDMUND
In honour'd love.

REGAN
But have you never found my brother's way
To the forfended place? [94]

EDMUND
That thought abuses you.

REGAN
I am doubtful that you have been conjunct
And bosom'd with her, as far as we call hers.

EDMUND
No, by mine honour, madam.

REGAN
I never shall endure her: dear my lord,
Be not familiar with her.

EDMUND
Fear me not:
She and the duke her husband!

Enter, with drum and colours, ALBANY, GONERIL, *and* Soldiers.

GONERIL
[Aside] I had rather lose the battle than that sister
Should loosen him and me.

ALBANY
Our very loving sister, well be-met.
Sir, this I hear; the king is come to his daughter,
With others whom the rigor of our state
Forced to cry out. Where I could not be honest,

I never yet was valiant: for this business,
It toucheth us, as France invades our land,
Not bolds the king, with others, whom, I fear, [95]
Most just and heavy causes make oppose.

EDMUND
Sir, you speak nobly.

REGAN
Why is this reason'd?

GONERIL
Combine together 'gainst the enemy;
For these domestic and particular broils 36
Are not the question here.

ALBANY
Let's then determine
With the ancient of war on our proceedings.

EDMUND
I shall attend you presently at your tent.

REGAN
Sister, you'll go with us?

GONERIL
No.

REGAN
'Tis most convenient; pray you, go with us.

GONERIL
[*Aside*] O, ho, I know the riddle.—I will go.

As they are going out, enter EDGAR *disguised.*

EDGAR
If e'er your grace had speech with man so poor,
Hear me one word.

ALBANY
I'll overtake you. Speak.
[*Exeunt all but Albany and Edgar.*

EDGAR
Before you fight the battle, ope this letter. 48
If you have victory, let the trumpet sound
For him that brought it: wretched though I seem,
I can produce a champion that will prove
What is vouched there. If you miscarry,
Your business of the world hath so an end,
And machination ceases. Fortune love you [96]

ALBANY
Stay till I have read the letter.

EDGAR
I was forbid it.
When time shall serve, let but the herald cry,
And I'll appear again.

ALBANY
Why, fare thee well: I will o'erlook thy paper. 59
[*Exit Edgar.*

Re-enter EDMUND.

EDMUND
The enemy's in view; draw up your powers.
Here is the guess of their true strength and forces
By diligent discovery; but your haste
Is now urged on you.

ALBANY
We will greet the time. [*Exit.*

EDMUND
To both these sisters have I sworn my love;
Each jealous of the other, as the stung
Are of the adder. Which of them shall I take?
Both? one? or neither? Neither can be enjoy'd,
If both remain alive: to take the widow
Exasperates, makes mad her sister Goneril; 70
And hardly shall I carry out my side,
Her husband being alive. Now then we'll use
His countenance for the battle; which being done,
Let her who would be rid of him devise
His speedy taking off. As for the mercy
Which he intends to Lear and to Cordelia,
The battle done, and they within our power,
Shall never see his pardon; for my state
Stands on me to defend, not to debate. 79
[*Exit.*

ACT FIVE SCENE TWO

A field between the two camps.

Alarum within. Enter, with drum and colours, LEAR, CORDELIA, *and* Soldiers, *over the stage; and exeunt*

Enter EDGAR *and* GLOUCESTER.

EDGAR
Here, father, take the shadow of this tree
For your good host; pray that the right may thrive:
If ever I return to you again,
I'll bring you comfort.

GLOUCESTER
Grace go with you, sir! [97] [*Exit Edgar.*

Alarum and retreat within. Re-enter EDGAR.

EDGAR
Away, old man; give me thy hand; away!
King Lear hath lost, he and his daughter ta'en:
Give me thy hand; come on.

GLOUCESTER
No farther, sir; a man may rot even here.

EDGAR
What, in ill thoughts again? Men must endure 9
Their going hence, even as their coming hither;
Ripeness is all: come on.

GLOUCESTER
And that's true too. [*Exeunt.*

ACT FIVE SCENE THREE

The British camp near Dover.

Enter, in conquest, with drum and colours, EDMUND, LEAR *and* CORDELIA, *prisoners;* Captain, Soldiers, *&c.*

EDMUND
Some officers take them away: good guard,
Until their greater pleasures first be known
That are to censure them.
CORDELIA
We are not the first
Who, with best meaning, have incurr'd the worst.
For thee, oppressed king, am I cast down;
Myself could else out-frown false fortune's frown.
Shall we not see these daughters and these sisters?
KING LEAR
No, no, no, no! Come, let's away to prison:
We two alone will sing like birds i' the cage:
When thou dost ask me blessing, I'll kneel down, 12
And ask of thee forgiveness: so we'll live,
And pray, and sing, and tell old tales, and laugh
At gilded butterflies, and hear poor rogues
Talk of court news; and we'll talk with them too,
Who loses and who wins; who's in, who's out;
And take upon's the mystery of things,
As if we were God's spies: and we'll wear out,
In a wall'd prison, packs and sects of great ones,
That ebb and flow by the moon.
EDMUND
Take them away.
KING LEAR
Upon such sacrifices, my Cordelia, 23
The gods themselves throw incense. Have I caught thee?
He that parts us shall bring a brand from heaven,
And fire us hence like foxes. Wipe thine eyes;
The good-years shall devour them, flesh and fell,
Ere they shall make us weep: we'll see 'em starve first.
Come. [*Exeunt King Lear and Cordelia, guarded.*
EDMUND
Come hither, captain; hark.
Take thou this note; [*Giving a paper*]; go follow them to prison:
One step I have advanced thee; if thou dost
As this instructs thee, thou dost make thy way
To noble fortunes: know thou this, that men
Are as the time is: to be tender-minded 38
Does not become a sword: thy great employment
Will not bear question; either say thou'lt do 't,
Or thrive by other means.
CAPTAIN
I'll do 't, my lord.
EDMUND
About it; and write happy when thou hast done.
Mark, I say, instantly; and carry it so
As I have set it down.
CAPTAIN
I cannot draw a cart, nor eat dried oats;
If it be man's work, I'll do 't. [*Exit.*

Flourish. Enter ALBANY, GONERIL, REGAN, *another* Captain, *and* Soldiers.

ALBANY
Sir, you have shown to-day your valiant strain, 48
And fortune led you well: you have the captives
That were the opposites of this day's strife:
We do require them of you, so to use them
As we shall find their merits and our safety
May equally determine.
EDMUND
Sir, I thought it fit
To send the old and miserable king
To some retention and appointed guard;
Whose age has charms in it, whose title more,
To pluck the common bosom on his side,
An turn our impress'd lances in our eyes 59
Which do command them. With him I sent the queen;
My reason all the same; and they are ready
To-morrow, or at further space, to appear
Where you shall hold your session. At this time
We sweat and bleed: the friend hath lost his friend;
And the best quarrels, in the heat, are cursed
By those that feel their sharpness:
The question of Cordelia and her father
Requires a fitter place.
ALBANY
Sir, by your patience,
I hold you but a subject of this war, 71
Not as a brother.
REGAN
That's as we list to grace him.
Methinks our pleasure might have been demanded,
Ere you had spoke so far. He led our powers;
Bore the commission of my place and person;
The which immediacy may well stand up,
And call itself your brother.
GONERIL
Not so hot:
In his own grace he doth exalt himself,
More than in your addition.
REGAN
In my rights,
By me invested, he compeers the best.

GONERIL
That were the most, if he should husband you. 85
REGAN
Jesters do oft prove prophets.
GONERIL
Holla, holla!
That eye that told you so look'd but a-squint.
REGAN
Lady, I am not well; else I should answer
From a full flowing stomach. General,
Take thou my soldiers, prisoners, patrimony;
Dispose of them, of me; the walls are thine: [98]
Witness the world, that I create thee here
My lord and master.
GONERIL
Mean you to enjoy him?
ALBANY
The let-alone lies not in your good will.
EDMUND
Nor in thine, lord.
ALBANY
Half-blooded fellow, yes. 98
REGAN
[*To Edmund*] Let the drum strike, and prove my title thine.
ALBANY
Stay yet; hear reason. Edmund, I arrest thee
On capital treason; and, in thine attaint,
This gilded serpent [*Pointing to Goneril*] For your claim, fair sister,
I bar it in the interest of my wife:
'Tis she is sub-contracted to this lord,
And I, her husband, contradict your bans.
If you will marry, make your loves to me,
My lady is bespoke.
GONERIL
An interlude!
ALBANY
Thou art arm'd, Gloucester: let the trumpet sound: 112
If none appear to prove upon thy head
Thy heinous, manifest, and many treasons,
There is my pledge [*throwing down a glove*]; I'll prove it on thy heart, [99]
Ere I taste bread, thou art in nothing less
Than I have here proclaim'd thee.
REGAN
Sick, O, sick!
GONERIL
[*Aside*] If not, I'll ne'er trust medicine. [100]
EDMUND
There's my exchange [*throwing down a glove*]: what in the world he is
That names me traitor, villain-like he lies:
Call by thy trumpet: he that dares approach,
On him, on you, who not? I will maintain 125
My truth and honour firmly.
ALBANY
A herald, ho!
EDMUND
A herald, ho, a herald!
ALBANY
Trust to thy single virtue; for thy soldiers,
All levied in my name, have in my name
Took their discharge.
REGAN
My sickness grows upon me.
ALBANY
She is not well; convey her to my tent.
[*Exit Regan, led.*

Enter a Herald.

Come hither, herald,—Let the trumpet sound,—
And read out this.
CAPTAIN
Sound, trumpet! [*A trumpet sounds.*
HERALD
[*Reads*] 'If any man of quality or degree within the lists of the army will maintain upon Edmund, supposed Earl of Gloucester, that he is a manifold traitor, let him appear by the third sound of the trumpet: he is bold in his defence.'
EDMUND
Sound! [*First trumpet.*
HERALD
Again! [*Second trumpet.*
HERALD
Again! [*Third trumpet.*
[*Trumpet answers within.*

Enter EDGAR, *at the third sound, armed, with a trumpet before him.*

ALBANY
Ask him his purposes, why he appears
Upon this call o' the trumpet.
HERALD
What are you? 147
Your name, your quality? and why you answer
This present summons?
EDGAR
Know, my name is lost;
By treason's tooth bare-gnawn and canker-bit:
Yet am I noble as the adversary
I come to cope.
ALBANY
Which is that adversary?

EDGAR
What's he that speaks for Edmund Earl of Gloucester?
EDMUND
Himself: what say'st thou to him?
EDGAR
Draw thy sword,
That, if my speech offend a noble heart,
Thy arm may do thee justice: here is mine.
Behold, it is the privilege of mine honours, [101]
My oath, and my profession: I protest,
Maugre thy strength, youth, place, and eminence,
Despite thy victor sword and fire-new fortune,
Thy valour and thy heart, thou art a traitor;
False to thy gods, thy brother, and thy father;
Conspirant 'gainst this high-illustrious prince;
And, from the extremest upward of thy head
To the descent and dust below thy foot,
A most toad-spotted traitor. Say thou 'No,'
This sword, this arm, and my best spirits, are bent
To prove upon thy heart, whereto I speak, thou liest.
EDMUND
In wisdom I should ask thy name;
But, since thy outside looks so fair and warlike,
And that thy tongue some say of breeding breathes,
What safe and nicely I might well delay
By rule of knighthood, I disdain and spurn:
Back do I toss these treasons to thy head; [102]
With the hell-hated lie o'erwhelm thy heart;
Which, for they yet glance by and scarcely bruise,
This sword of mine shall give them instant way,
Where they shall rest for ever. Trumpets, speak!
[*Alarums. They fight. Edmund falls.*
ALBANY
Save him, save him!
GONERIL
This is practise, Gloucester:
By the law of arms thou wast not bound to answer
An unknown opposite; thou art not vanquish'd,
But cozen'd and beguiled.
ALBANY
Shut your mouth, dame,
Or with this paper shall I stop it: Hold, sir:
Thou worse than any name, read thine own evil: [103]
No tearing, lady: I perceive you know it.
[*Gives the letter to Edmund.*
GONERIL
Say, if I do, the laws are mine, not thine:
Who can arraign me for't?
ALBANY
Most monstrous! oh! [104]
Know'st thou this paper?
GONERIL
Ask me not what I know. [105] [*Exit.*
ALBANY
Go after her: she's desperate; govern her.
EDMUND
What you have charged me with, that have I done;
And more, much more; the time will bring it out:
'Tis past, and so am I. But what art thou
That hast this fortune on me? If thou'rt noble,
I do forgive thee.
EDGAR
Let's exchange charity.
I am no less in blood than thou art, Edmund;
If more, the more thou hast wrong'd me.
My name is Edgar, and thy father's son.
The gods are just, and of our pleasant vices [106]
Make instruments to plague us:
The dark and vicious place where thee he got
Cost him his eyes.
EDMUND
Thou hast spoken right, 'tis true;
The wheel is come full circle: I am here.
ALBANY
Methought thy very gait did prophesy
A royal nobleness: I must embrace thee:
Let sorrow split my heart, if ever I
Did hate thee or thy father!
EDGAR
Worthy prince, I know't.
ALBANY
Where have you hid yourself?
How have you known the miseries of your father?
EDGAR
By nursing them, my lord. List a brief tale;
And when 'tis told, O, that my heart would burst!
The bloody proclamation to escape,
That follow'd me so near,—O, our lives' sweetness!
That we the pain of death would hourly die
Rather than die at once!—taught me to shift
Into a madman's rags; to assume a semblance
That very dogs disdain'd: and in this habit
Met I my father with his bleeding rings,
Their precious stones new lost: became his guide,
Led him, begg'd for him, saved him from despair;
Never,—O fault!—reveal'd myself unto him,
Until some half-hour past, when I was arm'd:
Not sure, though hoping, of this good success,
I ask'd his blessing, and from first to last
Told him my pilgrimage: but his flaw'd heart,

Alack, too weak the conflict to support!
'Twixt two extremes of passion, joy and grief,
Burst smilingly.

EDMUND
This speech of yours hath moved me,
And shall perchance do good: but speak you on; 248
You look as you had something more to say.

ALBANY
If there be more, more woeful, hold it in;
For I am almost ready to dissolve,
Hearing of this.

EDGAR
This would have seem'd a period
To such as love not sorrow; but another, [107]
To amplify too much, would make much more,
And top extremity.
Whilst I was big in clamour came there in a man,
Who, having seen me in my worst estate,
Shunn'd my abhorr'd society; but then, finding
Who 'twas that so endured, with his strong arms 261
He fasten'd on my neck, and bellow'd out
As he'ld burst heaven; threw him on my father;
Told the most piteous tale of Lear and him
That ever ear received: which in recounting
His grief grew puissant, and the strings of life
Began to crack: twice then the trumpets sounded,
And there I left him tranced.

ALBANY
But who was this?

EDGAR
Kent, sir, the banish'd Kent; who in disguise
Follow'd his enemy king, and did him service
Improper for a slave. 272

Enter a Gentleman, *with a bloody knife.*

GENTLEMAN
Help, help, O, help!

EDGAR
What kind of help?

ALBANY
Speak, man.

EDGAR
What means that bloody knife?

GENTLEMAN
'Tis hot, it smokes;
It came even from the heart of— O, she's dead!

ALBANY
Who dead? speak, man.

GENTLEMAN
Your lady, sir, your lady: and her sister
By her is poisoned; she hath confess'd it.

EDMUND
I was contracted to them both: all three
Now marry in an instant.

EDGAR
Here comes Kent.

ALBANY
Produce their bodies, be they alive or dead: 285
This judgment of the heavens, that makes us tremble,
Touches us not with pity. [*Exit Gentleman.*

Enter KENT.

O, is this he?
The time will not allow the compliment
Which very manners urges.

KENT
I am come
To bid my king and master aye good night:
Is he not here?

ALBANY
Great thing of us forgot!
Speak, Edmund, where's the king? and where's Cordelia?
See'st thou this object, Kent?
[*The bodies of Goneril and Regan are brought in.*

KENT
Alack, why thus?

EDMUND
Yet Edmund was beloved:
The one the other poison'd for my sake, 300
And after slew herself.

ALBANY
Even so. Cover their faces.

EDMUND
I pant for life: some good I mean to do,
Despite of mine own nature. Quickly send,
Be brief in it, to the castle; for my writ
Is on the life of Lear and on Cordelia:
Nay, send in time.

ALBANY
Run, run, O, run!

EDGAR
To who, my lord? Who hath the office? send
Thy token of reprieve.

EDMUND
Well thought on: take my sword, 311
Give it the captain.

ALBANY
Haste thee, for thy life. [*Exit Edgar.*

EDMUND
He hath commission from thy wife and me
To hang Cordelia in the prison, and
To lay the blame upon her own despair,
That she fordid herself.

ALBANY
The gods defend her! Bear him hence awhile.
[*Edmund is borne off.*

Re-enter LEAR, *with* CORDELIA *dead in his arms*; EDGAR, Captain, *and others following.*

KING LEAR
Howl, howl, howl, howl! O, you are men of stones:
Had I your tongues and eyes, I'ld use them so
That heaven's vault should crack. She's gone for ever! 322
I know when one is dead, and when one lives;
She's dead as earth. Lend me a looking-glass;
If that her breath will mist or stain the stone,
Why, then she lives.
KENT
Is this the promised end
EDGAR
Or image of that horror?
ALBANY
Fall, and cease!
KING LEAR
This feather stirs; she lives! if it be so,
It is a chance which does redeem all sorrows
That ever I have felt.
KENT
[*Kneeling*] O my good master!
KING LEAR
Prithee, away.
EDGAR
'Tis noble Kent, your friend.
KING LEAR
A plague upon you, murderers, traitors all!
I might have saved her; now she's gone for ever! 338
Cordelia, Cordelia! stay a little. Ha!
What is't thou say'st? Her voice was ever soft,
Gentle, and low, an excellent thing in woman.
I kill'd the slave that was a-hanging thee.
CAPTAIN
'Tis true, my lords, he did.
KING LEAR
Did I not, fellow?
I have seen the day, with my good biting falchion
I would have made them skip: I am old now,
And these same crosses spoil me. Who are you?
Mine eyes are not o' the best: I'll tell you straight.
KENT
If fortune brag of two she loved and hated, 349
One of them we behold. [108]
KING LEAR
This is a dull sight. Are you not Kent?
KENT
The same,
Your servant Kent: Where is your servant Caius?
KING LEAR
He's a good fellow, I can tell you that;
He'll strike, and quickly too: he's dead and rotten.
KENT
No, my good lord; I am the very man,—
KING LEAR
I'll see that straight.
KENT
That, from your first of difference and decay,
Have follow'd your sad steps.
KING LEAR
You are welcome hither.
KENT
Nor no man else: all's cheerless, dark, and deadly. 363
Your eldest daughters have fordone themselves,
And desperately are dead.
KING LEAR
Ay, so I think.
ALBANY
He knows not what he says: and vain it is
That we present us to him.
EDGAR
Very bootless.

Enter a Captain.

CAPTAIN
Edmund is dead, my lord.
ALBANY
That's but a trifle here.
You lords and noble friends, know our intent.
What comfort to this great decay may come
Shall be applied: for us we will resign,
During the life of this old majesty,
To him our absolute power: [*To Edgar and Kent*] you, to your rights: 377
With boot, and such addition as your honours
Have more than merited. All friends shall taste
The wages of their virtue, and all foes
The cup of their deservings. O, see, see!
KING LEAR
And my poor fool is hang'd! No, no, no life!
Why should a dog, a horse, a rat, have life,
And thou no breath at all? Thou'lt come no more,
Never, never, never, never, never!
Pray you, undo this button: thank you, sir.
Do you see this? Look on her, look, her lips, [109]
Look there, look there! [*Dies.*
EDGAR
He faints! My lord, my lord!
KENT
Break, heart; I prithee, break!

EDGAR
Look up, my lord.

KENT
Vex not his ghost: O, let him pass! he hates him much
That would upon the rack of this tough world
Stretch him out longer.

EDGAR
He is gone, indeed.

KENT
The wonder is, he hath endured so long:
He but usurp'd his life.

ALBANY
Bear them from hence. Our present business
Is general woe. [*To Kent and Edgar*] Friends of my soul, you twain
Rule in this realm, and the gored state sustain.

KENT
I have a journey, sir, shortly to go;
My master calls me, I must not say no.

ALBANY
The weight of this sad time we must obey;
Speak what we feel, not what we ought to say.
The oldest hath borne most: we that are young
Shall never see so much, nor live so long.

[*Exeunt, with a dead march*

Notes

1. From our age; – so Folios; Quartos *'of our state.'*
2. (While we … now); – 50–51, 164; I. ii. *('fine word, legitimate')*; 48 *('and reverence')*; I. iv. *('so may it come')*; 296; 345–356; omitted in Quartos.
3. "Where nature doth with merit challenge. Goneril"; – so Folios; Quartos read *'Where merit doth most challenge it.'*
4. Do; – so Quartos; Folios read *'speak.'*
5. Ponderous; – so Folios; Quartos, *'richer.'*
6. The last, not least; – so Quartos; Folios read *'our last and least.'*
7. (As of unnaturalness … come); – *('go armed')*; I. iii. I. iv. omitted in Folios.
8. Mysteries, – the reading of Folios 2, 3, 4; Quartos, *'mistresse'*; Folio 1, *'miseries.'*
9. What wouldst thou do, old man?; – "This is spoken on seeing his master put his hand to his sword" (Capell); Folios 1, 2, 3, *'wouldest'*; Quartos, *'wilt.'*
10. Stoops to folly; – so Quartos; Folios, *'falls to folly'* (Folio 3, *'fall to folly')*; *'Reverse thy doom'*; so Quarto; Folios read, *'reserue thy state.'*
11. Recreant; – omitted in Quartos.
12. Five; – so Folios; Quartos, *'Foure.'*
13. Sixth, – so Folios; Quartos, *'fift.'*
14. This line is given to Cordelia in Folios.
15. Better; – so Folios; Quartos, *'go to, go to, better.'*
16. Respects of fortune; – so Quartos; Folios, *'respect and fortunes.'*
17. Want; – Quartos, *'worth.'* Theobald explains the Folio reading. "You well deserve to meet with that *want* of love from your husband, which you have professed to want for our Father."
18. Shame them derides; – so Quartos; Folios, *'with shame derides'*; Warburton, *'with shame abides,'* &c.
19. Hath not been; – so Quartos; Folios, *'hath been.'*
20. So Folios; Quartos read, *'with base, base bastardie.'*
21. Top the; – Edward's conjecture of Quartos 1, 2, *'tooth'*; Quarto 3, *'too h'*; Folios 1, 2, *'to'th'*; Folios 3, 4, *'to th,'* &c.
22. That, i.e. – the matter, contents.
23. These late eclipses in the sun and moon portend no good; v. – Preface.
24. Surfeit; – so Quarto 1; Quartos 2, 3, *'surfet'*; Folios 1, 2, 3, *'surfets'*; Folio 4, *'surfeits'*; Collier conjectured *'forefit.'*
25. That's my fear … Brother, – so Folios; Quartos read *'That's my feare brother,'* omitting rest of speech.
26. With checks as flatteries, when they are seen abused; – Tyrwhitt's explanation seems the most plausible, "with checks, as well as flatterers, when they *(i.e.* flatterers) are seen to be abused." The emendators have been busy with the line without much success.
27. Kent. Why, fool?; – the reading of Quartos; Folios read *'Lear. Why my Boy?'*
28. Ladies; – Capell's emendation; Quartos, *'lodes'*; Collier, *'loads.'*
29. Ha! waking? – Quartos read *'sleeping or waking; ha! sure.'*
30. Omitted in Quartos 2, 3.
31. Their thunders; – so the Quartos; Folios, *'the thunder'*; Johnson, *'their thunder.'*
32. Dispatch; i.e. – 'dispatch him'; or perhaps, 'dispatch is the word.'
33. What I should deny; – so Quartos; Folios, *'What should I deny'*; Rowe, *'by what I should deny'*; Hanmer, *'what I'd deny'*; Warburton, 'when I should deny'; Schmidt, *'what, should I deny.'*
34. I never got him; – so Quartos; Folios, *'said he?'*
35. Of that consort; – so Folios; omitted in Quartos.
36. The waste and spoil of his; – Quarto 1, *'the wast and spoyle of his'*; Quartos 2, 3, *'these—and waste of this his'*; Quarto 1 (Dev. and Cap.) *'these—and waste of this his'*; Folio 1, *'th' expence and wast of his'*; Folios 2, 3, 4, *'th' expence and wast of.'*
37. Hours; – Folios, *'years.'*
38. Which are too intrinse to unloose; – Folio 1, *'are t' intrince'*; Folios 2, 3, 4, *'art t'intrince'*; Quartos, *'are to intrench'*; Pope, *'Too intricate'*; Theobald, *'Too 'intrinsecate'*; Hanmer, *'too intrinsick'*; *'to unloose'*; Folios, *'t'unloose'*; Quartos, *'toinloose'*; Seymour conjectured *'to enloose.'*
39. His fault … punish'd with; – omitted in Folios.
40. The king must take it ill; – Folios read *'the King his Master, needs must take it ill.'*
41. Omitted in Folios.
42. Out of heaven's benediction comest To the warm sun; cp. – Heywood's *'Dialogues on Proverbs'*; *'In your rennyng from hym to me, ye runne out of God's blessing into the warm sunne'*; *i.e.* from good to worse. Professor Skeat suggests to me that the proverb refers to the haste of the congregation to leave the shelter of the church, immediately after the priest's benediction, running from God's

blessing into the warm sun. This explanation seems by far the best that has been suggested.

43. Miracles; – so Folios; Quartos 1, 2, 3, *'my wracke'*; Quarto 1 (Bodl.), *'my rackles.'*
44. And shall … remedies; – many emendations have been proposed to remove the obscurity of the lines, but none can be considered satisfactory. Kent, it must be remembered, is 'all weary and o'er-watched.' Jennens suggested that Kent is reading disjointed fragments of Cordelia's letter. *'From this enormous state'* seems to mean 'in this abnormal state of affairs.'
45. Omitted in Folios.
46. Omitted in Quartos.
47. Commands her service; – so Quartos; Folios, *'commands, tends, service.'*
48. And blast her pride; – so Quartos; Folios, *'and blister'*; Collier MS. and S. Walker conjectured *'and blast her'*; Schmidt conjectured *'and blister pride.'*
49. Tender-hefted; – so Folios; Quarto 2, *'tender hested'*; Quarto 1, *'teder hested'*; Quarto 3, *'tender hasted'*; Rowe (Ed. 2) and Pope, *'tender hearted'*; &c.
50. Bleak; – so Quartos; Folios, *'high.'*
51. (Oppressed … behind); – vii. omitted in the Folios.
52. Omitted in the Quartos.
53. Smite; – so Quartos; Folios, *'strike.'*
54. Make; – Folios, *'makes.'*
55. Have … join'd; – the reading of Quartos; Folios read *'will … join.'*
56. No I will be the pattern of all patience; cp. – the description of Leir by Perillus in the old play:—*'But he, the myrrour of mild patience, Puts up all wrongs, and never gives reply.'*
57. More harder than the stones; – so Folios; Quartos *'More hard then is the stone.'*
58. That's sorry; – so Folios; Quartos, *'That sorrowes.'*
59. Cp. – I Clown's song in *Twelfth Night,* V. vi.
60. I live before his time; – according to the legend, Lear was contemporary with Joash, King of Judah. The whole prophecy, which does not occur in the Quartos, was probably an interpolation, tacked on by the actor who played the fool. The passage is an imitation of some lines formerly attributed to Chaucer, called *'Chaucer's Prophecy.'*
61. Contentious; – so Folios; Quarto 1 (some copies) *'tempestious'*; Quartos 2, 3, and Quarto 1 (some copies) *'crulentious.'*
62. Storm; – so Quartos; Folios, *'night.'*
63. Through the sharp hawthorn blows the cold wind; – probably the burden of an old song.
64. Knives under his pillow and halters in his pew – (to tempt him to suicide). Theobald pointed out that the allusion is to an incident mentioned in Harsnet's *Declaration.*
65. Thy word justly; – Pope's emendation; Quartos read, *'thy words justly'*; Folio 1, *'thy words Iustice.'*
66. Sessa; – Malone's emendation; Folio 1, *'Sesey,'* Quarto 1, *'caese'*; Quarto 2, *'cease'*; Capell, *'sesse'*; &c.
67. *Cp. 'The Romance of Sir Bevis of Hamptoun;—*

    "Rattes and myce and suche small dere,
    Was his meate that seuen yere."

68. Child Rowland to the dark tower came, – &c. Jamieson, in his *Illustrations of Northern Antiquities* (1814) has preserved the story as told him by a tailor in his youth; this Scottish Version has since been reprinted and studied (*Cp.* Childs' *English and Scottish Ballads,* and Jacob's *English Fairy Tales*).
69. His word was still – refers, of course, to the giant, and not to Childe Rowland. The same story (with the refrain *Fee fo fum, Here is the Englishman*) is alluded to in Peele's *Old Wives Tale,* and it is just possible that it may be the ultimate original of the plot of Milton's *Comus* (*v.* Preface, on *British* for *English*).
70. Come o'er the bourn, Bessy, to me. – Mr. Chappell (Popular Music of the Olden Time, p. 305, note) says, "The allusion is to an English ballad by William Birch, entitled, 'A Songe betwene the Quene's Majestie and England,' a copy of which is in the library of the Society of Antiquaries. England commences the dialogue, inviting Queen Elizabeth in the following words:—

    "Come over the born, Bessy, come over the born, Bessy,
    Swete Bessy, come over to me."

The date of Birch's song is 1558, and it is printed in full in the *Harleian Miscellany,* X. 260.

71. Put into verse by Theobald. Steevens quotes a line from an old song,

    "Sleepeyst thou, makyst thou, Jeffery Coke."

    found in *The Interlude of the Four Elements* (1519).
72. Thy horn is dry, – "A horn was usually carried about by every Tom of Bedlam, to receive such drink as the charitable might afford him, with whatever scraps of food they might give him" (Malone), &c.
73. "Every editor from Theobald downwards," as the Cambridge Editors observe, "except Hanmer, has reprinted this speech from the Quartos. In deference to this consensus of authority we have retained it, though, as it seems to us, internal evidence is conclusive against the supposition that the lines were written by Shakespeare."
74. Stick; – the reading of Folios; Quartos, *'rash.'*
75. Howl'd that stern; – Quartos, *'heard that dearne'*; Capell. *'howl'd that dearn'*; 'dearn' = obscure, dark, gloomy).
76. All cruels else subscribed; – so Quartos; Folios *'subscribe.'* The passage has been variously interpreted; the weight of authority favouring the Folio reading, Schmidt's explanation being perhaps the most plausible:— "Everything which is at other times cruel, shows feeling or regard; you alone have not done so." Furness makes the words part of the speech addressed to the porter, "acknowledge the claims of all creatures, however cruel they may be at other times," or "give up all cruel things else; *i.e.,* forget that they are cruel." This approximates to the interpretation given by Mr. Wright to the reading in the text, "all their other cruelties being yielded or forgiven."
77. Welcome … blasts; – vi. (*'Plate … lips'*); vii. omitted in the Quartos.
78. Life would not yield to age, i.e. – life would not gladly lapse into old age and death.

79. Kill; – Quarto 1, *'bitt'*; Quartos 2, 3, *'bit'*; (probably an error for *'hit'*).
80. (The whole scene); vii. omitted in the Folios.
81. My fool usurps my body; – so Folios; Quarto 1, *'A foole usurps my bed'*; Quarto 2, *'My foote usurps my head'*; Malone, *'My fool usurps my bed.'*
82. Tame these vile offences; – Schmidt conjectured *'take the vild offenders'*; Heath conjectured *'these vile'*; Quarto 1, *'this vild'*; Pope, *'the vile.'*
83. Thy state begins to threat; – Jennens conjectured; Quarto 1, *'thy state begins thereat'*; Quartos 2, 3, *'thy slaier begins threats'*; Theobald, *'thy slayer begins his threats,'* &c.
84. Your manhood! mew!; – some copies of Quarto 1 read *'manhood mew'*; others *'manhood now'*; so the later Quartos; according to the present reading *'mew'* is evidently a cat-like interjection of contempt.
85. Like a better way; – so Quartos; the passage seems to mean that her smiles and tears resembled sunshine and rain, but in a more beautiful manner; many emendations have been proposed—*'like a wetter May'* (Warburton); *'like a better May'* (Malone); *'like;—a better way'* (Boaden), &c.
86. Let pity not be believed; – Pope, *'Let pity ne'er believe it'*; Capell, *'Let it not be believed'* (but *'believed'* = 'believed to exist').
87. Clamour moisten'd; – I Capell's reading; Quartos *'And clamour moistened her'*; Theobald, *'And, clamour-motion'd'*; Grant White, *'And, clamour-moisten'd,'* &c.
88. Lord; – so Folios; Quartos read *'lady.'*
89. I had white hairs in my beard ere the black ones were there; i.e., – "I had the wisdom of age before I had attained to that of youth" (Capell).
90. Tame to; – so Folios; Quartos, *'lame by.'*
91. Opposed against the warring winds; – Quartos, *'Exposed'*; Folios, *'jarring.'*
92. Mine enemy's; – Folios *'Mine Enemies'*; Quartos 1, 2, *'Mine injurious'*; Quarto 2. *'Mine iniurious'*; Theobald, *'My very enemy's,'* &c.
93. Kill'd; – so Folios: Quartos *'cured'*; Collier conjectured *'quell'd.'*
94. Omitted in the Folios.
95. Mason's conjecture *'Not the old king'* for *'not bolds the king'* is worthy of mention. Albany's point is that the invading enemy is France and not the wronged king, together with others whom heavy causes compel to fight against them; otherwise *'not bolds the king'* = 'not as it emboldens the king'; an awkward and harsh construction.
96. And … ceases; – iii. omitted in the Quartos.
97. Mr. Spedding (*News Sh. Soc. Trans.,* Part I.) plausibly suggested that the Fifth Act really begins here, and that the battle takes place between Edgar's exit and reentrance, the imagination having leisure to fill with anxiety for the issue.
98. The walls are thine; – Theobald conjectured *'they all are thine'*; (but perhaps the castle-walls are referred to).
99. Prove it; – so Quartos; Folios, *'make it'*; Anon. conjecture *'mark it'*; Collier MS., *'make good.'*
100. Medicine, – Folios; Quartos, *'poyson.'*
101. The privilege of mine honours; – Pope's reading; Quartos read *'the priuiledge of my tongue'*; Folios, *'my priuiledge, The pruiledge of mine Honours.'* Edgar refers to *'the right of bringing the charge'* as the privilege of his profession as knight.
102. Omitted in Quarto 2; Quarto 1 reads *'Heere do I tosse those treasons to thy head.'*
103. Name; – Quartos read *'thing.'*
104. Most monstrous! know'st; – Steevens emendation; Quarto 1 reads *'Most monstrous knowst'*; Quartos 2, 3, *'Monster, knowst'*; Folios, *'Most monstrous! O know'st'*; Capell, *'Most monsterous! know'st'*; Edd. Globe Ed., *'Most monstrous! Oh! know'st.'*
105. Ask me not what I know; – the Folios give this line to Edmund; the Quartos to Goneril.
106. Vices … plague us; – so Folios; Quartos read *'vertues … scourge us'*; Hanmer, *'vices … plague and punish us'*; Keightley, *'vices … plague us in their time'*; Anon. conjecture *'vices … scourge us and to plague us'*; *cp.* 'Wherewith a man sinneth, by the same also shall he be punished,' *Wisdom* xi.
107. But another, – &c., *i.e.* "one more such circumstance only, by amplifying what is already too much, would add to it, and so exceed what seemed to be the limit of sorrow" (Wright).
108. One of them we behold, i.e. – each beholding the other sees one of fortune's two notable objects of love and hate; (? for *'we'* read *'ye,'* as has been suggested).
109. Look on her, look, her lips; – Johnson's emendation; Folio 1 reads *'Looke her lips'*; Folios, *'looke* (or *look) on her lips.'*
110. This speech is given in the Folios to Edgar, and probably it was so intended by the poet. It has been suggested that the first two lines should be given to Edgar, the last two to Albany.

MACBETH

MACBETH

DRAMATIS PERSONAE

DUNCAN, king of Scotland.
MALCOLM, his son.
DONALBAIN, his son.
MACBETH, general of the king's army.
BANQUO, general of the king's army.
MACDUFF, nobleman of Scotland.
LENNOX, nobleman of Scotland.
ROSS, nobleman of Scotland.
MENTEITH, nobleman of Scotland.
ANGUS, nobleman of Scotland.
CAITHNESS, nobleman of Scotland.
FLEANCE, son to Banquo.
SIWARD, Earl of Northumberland, general of the English forces.
Young SIWARD, his son.
SEYTON, an officer attending on Macbeth.
Boy, son to Macduff.
An English Doctor.
A Scotch Doctor.
A Soldier.
A Porter.
An Old Man
LADY MACBETH.
LADY MACDUFF.
Gentlewoman attending on Lady Macbeth.
HECATE.
Three Witches.
Apparitions.
Lords, Gentlemen, Officers, Soldiers, Murderers, Attendants, and Messengers.

SCENE: *Scotland: England.*

ACT ONE SCENE ONE

A desert place.

Thunder and lightning. Enter three Witches.

FIRST WITCH
When shall we three meet again [1]
In thunder, lightning, or in rain?
SECOND WITCH
When the hurlyburly's done,
When the battle's lost and won.
THIRD WITCH
That will be ere the set of sun.
FIRST WITCH
Where the place?
SECOND WITCH
Upon the heath.
THIRD WITCH
There to meet with Macbeth.
FIRST WITCH
I come, Graymalkin!
SECOND WITCH
Paddock calls.
THIRD WITCH
Anon.
ALL
Fair is foul, and foul is fair:
Hover through the fog and filthy air.

[*Exeunt.*

ACT ONE SCENE TWO

A camp near Forres.

Alarum within. Enter DUNCAN , MALCOLM , DONALBAIN , LENNOX, *with* Attendants, *meeting a bleeding* Sergeant.

DUNCAN
What bloody man is that? He can report,
As seemeth by his plight, of the revolt
The newest state.

MALCOLM
This is the sergeant
Who like a good and hardy soldier fought
'Gainst my captivity. Hail, brave friend!
Say to the king the knowledge of the broil
As thou didst leave it.

SERGEANT
Doubtful it stood;
As two spent swimmers, that do cling together
And choke their art. The merciless Macdonwald—
Worthy to be a rebel, for to that 12
The multiplying villanies of nature
Do swarm upon him—from the western isles
Of kerns and gallowglasses is supplied;
And fortune, on his damned quarrel smiling, [2]
Show'd like a rebel's whore: but all's too weak:
For brave Macbeth—well he deserves that name—
Disdaining fortune, with his brandish'd steel,
Which smoked with bloody execution,
Like valour's minion carved out his passage 21
Till he faced the slave; [3]
†Which ne'er shook hands, nor bade farewell to him,
Till he unseam'd him from the nave to the chaps,
And fix'd his head upon our battlements.

DUNCAN
O valiant cousin! worthy gentleman!

SERGEANT
As whence the sun 'gins his reflection
Shipwrecking storms and direful thunders break,
So from that spring whence comfort seem'd to come
Discomfort swells. Mark, king of Scotland, mark:
No sooner justice had with valour arm'd
Compell'd these skipping kerns to trust their heels, 33
But the Norweyan lord surveying vantage
With furbish'd arms and new supplies of men
Began a fresh assault.

DUNCAN
Dismay'd not this
Our captains, Macbeth and Banquo?

SERGEANT
Yes;
As sparrows eagles, or the hare the lion.
If I say sooth, I must report they were
As cannons overcharged with double cracks, so they
Doubly redoubled strokes upon the foe:
Except they meant to bathe in reeking wounds,
Or memorize another Golgotha, 45
I cannot tell.
But I am faint, my gashes cry for help.

DUNCAN
So well thy words become thee as thy wounds;
They smack of honour both. Go get him surgeons.
[*Exit Sergeant, attended.*
Who comes here?

Enter ROSS.

MALCOLM
The worthy thane of Ross.

LENNOX
What a haste looks through his eyes! So should he look
That seems to speak things strange.

ROSS
God save the king!

DUNCAN
Whence camest thou, worthy thane?

ROSS
From Fife, great king;
Where the Norweyan banners flout the sky
And fan our people cold. Norway himself,
With terrible numbers,
Assisted by that most disloyal traitor
The thane of Cawdor, began a dismal conflict;
Till that Bellona's bridegroom, lapp'd in proof,
Confronted him with self-comparisons,
Point against point rebellious, arm 'gainst arm,
Curbing his lavish spirit: and, to conclude,
The victory fell on us.

DUNCAN
Great happiness!

ROSS
That now
Sweno, the Norways' king, craves composition;
Nor would we deign him burial of his men 71
Till he disbursed at Saint Colme's inch
Ten thousand dollars to our general use.

DUNCAN
No more that thane of Cawdor shall deceive
Our bosom interest: go pronounce his present death,
And with his former title greet Macbeth.

ROSS
I'll see it done.

DUNCAN
What he hath lost noble Macbeth hath won.
[*Exeunt.*

ACT ONE SCENE THREE

A heath near Forres.

Thunder. Enter the three Witches.

FIRST WITCH
Where hath thou been, sister?
SECOND WITCH
Killing swine.
THIRD WITCH
Sister, where thou?
FIRST WITCH
A sailor's wife had chestnuts in her lap,
And munch'd, and munch'd, and munch'd:—
'Give me,' quoth I:
'Aroint thee, witch!' the rump-fed ronyon cries.
Her husband's to Aleppo gone, master o' the Tiger:
But in a sieve I'll thither sail,
And, like a rat without a tail,
I'll do, I'll do, and I'll do. 11
SECOND WITCH
I'll give thee a wind.
FIRST WITCH
Thou'rt kind.
THIRD WITCH
And I another.
FIRST WITCH
I myself have all the other,
And the very ports they blow, [4]
All the quarters that they know
I' the shipman's card.
I will drain him dry as hay:
Sleep shall neither night nor day 20
Hang upon his pent-house lid;
He shall live a man forbid:
Weary se'nnights nine times nine
Shall he dwindle, peak and pine:
Though his bark cannot be lost,
Yet it shall be tempest-tost.
Look what I have.
SECOND WITCH
Show me, show me.
FIRST WITCH
Here I have a pilot's thumb,
Wreck'd as homeward he did come.
[*Drum within.*
THIRD WITCH
A drum, a drum! 31
Macbeth doth come.
ALL
The weird sisters, hand in hand, [5]
Posters of the sea and land,
Thus do go about, about:
Thrice to thine and thrice to mine
And thrice again, to make up nine.
Peace! the charm's wound up.

Enter MACBETH *and* BANQUO.

MACBETH
So foul and fair a day I have not seen.
BANQUO
How far is't call'd to Forres? What are these
So wither'd and so wild in their attire, 41
That look not like the inhabitants o' the earth,
And yet are on't? Live you? or are you aught
That man may question? You seem to understand me,
By each at once her choppy finger laying
Upon her skinny lips: you should be women,
And yet your beards forbid me to interpret
That you are so.
MACBETH
Speak, if you can: what are you?
FIRST WITCH
All hail, Macbeth! hail to thee, thane of Glamis!
SECOND WITCH
All hail, Macbeth, hail to thee, thane of Cawdor!
THIRD WITCH
All hail, Macbeth, thau shalt be king hereafter! 52
BANQUO
Good sir, why do you start; and seem to fear
Things that do sound so fair? I' the name of truth,
Are ye fantastical, or that indeed
Which outwardly ye show? My noble partner
You greet with present grace and great prediction
Of noble having and of royal hope,
That he seems rapt withal: to me you speak not.
If you can look into the seeds of time,
And say which grain will grow and which will not,
Speak then to me, who neither beg nor fear
Your favours nor your hate.
FIRST WITCH
Hail!
SECOND WITCH
Hail!
THIRD WITCH
Hail!
FIRST WITCH
Lesser than Macbeth, and greater.
SECOND WITCH
Not so happy, yet much happier.
THIRD WITCH
Thou shalt get kings, though thou be none:
So all hail, Macbeth and Banquo!
FIRST WITCH
Banquo and Macbeth, all hail!
MACBETH
Stay, you imperfect speakers, tell me more: 72
By Sinel's death I know I am thane of Glamis;

MACBETH By Sinel's death I know I am thane of Glamis.

But how of Cawdor? the thane of Cawdor lives,
A prosperous gentleman; and to be king
Stands not within the prospect of belief,
No more than to be Cawdor. Say from whence
You owe this strange intelligence? or why
Upon this blasted heath you stop our way
With such prophetic greeting? Speak, I charge you.
[*Witches vanish.*

BANQUO
The earth hath bubbles, as the water has,
And these are of them. Whither are they vanish'd? 83

MACBETH
Into the air; and what seem'd corporal melted
As breath into the wind. Would they had stay'd!

BANQUO
Were such things here as we do speak about?
Or have we eaten on the insane root
That takes the reason prisoner?

MACBETH
Your children shall be kings.

BANQUO
You shall be king.

MACBETH
And thane of Cawdor too: went it not so?

BANQUO
To the selfsame tune and words. Who's here?

Enter ROSS *and* ANGUS.

ROSS
The king hath happily received, Macbeth,
The news of thy success; and when he reads
Thy personal venture in the rebels' fight,
His wonders and his praises do contend
Which should be thine or his: silenced with that,
In viewing o'er the rest o' the selfsame day,
He finds thee in the stout Norweyan ranks,
Nothing afeard of what thyself didst make,
Strange images of death. As thick as hail [6]
Came post with post; and every one did bear
Thy praises in his kingdom's great defence,
And pour'd them down before him.

ANGUS
We are sent 106
To give thee from our royal master thanks;

Only to herald thee into his sight,
Not pay thee.

ROSS
And, for an earnest of a greater honour,
He bade me, from him, call thee thane of Cawdor:
In which addition, hail, most worthy thane!
For it is thine.

BANQUO
What, can the devil speak true?

MACBETH
The thane of Cawdor lives: why do you dress me
In borrow'd robes?

ANGUS
Who was the thane lives yet;
But under heavy judgement bears that life 118
Which he deserves to lose. Whether he was combined
With those of Norway, or did line the rebel
With hidden help and vantage, or that with both
He labour'd in his country's wreck, I know not;
But treasons capital, confess'd and proved,
Have overthrown him.

MACBETH
[*Aside*] Glamis, and thane of Cawdor!
The greatest is behind.
[*To Ross and Angus*]
Thanks for your pains.
[*To Banquo*] Do you not hope your children shall be kings,
When those that gave the thane of Cawdor to me
Promised no less to them?

BANQUO
That trusted home 134
Might yet enkindle you unto the crown,
Besides the thane of Cawdor. But 'tis strange:
And oftentimes, to win us to our harm,
The instruments of darkness tell us truths,
Win us with honest trifles, to betray's
In deepest consequence.
Cousins, a word, I pray you.

MACBETH
[*Aside*] Two truths are told,
As happy prologues to the swelling act
Of the imperial theme.—I thank you, gentlemen.
[*Aside*] This supernatural soliciting 145
Cannot be ill, cannot be good: if ill,
Why hath it given me earnest of success,
Commencing in truth? I am thane of Cawdor:
If good, why do I yield to that suggestion
Whose horrid image doth unfix my hair
And make my seated heart knock at my ribs,
Against the use of nature? Present fears
Are less than horrible imaginings:
My thought, whose murder yet is but fantastical,
Shakes so my single state of man that function
Is smother'd in surmise, and nothing is 156
But what is not.

BANQUO
Look, how our partner's rapt.

MACBETH
[*Aside*] If chance will have me king, why, chance may crown me,
Without my stir.

BANQUO
New honours come upon him,
Like our strange garments, cleave not to their mould
But with the aid of use.

MACBETH
[*Aside*] Come what come may,
Time and the hour runs through the roughest day.

BANQUO
Worthy Macbeth, we stay upon your leisure.

MACBETH
Give me your favour: my dull brain was wrought
With things forgotten. Kind gentlemen, your pains 170
Are register'd where every day I turn
The leaf to read them. Let us toward the king.
Think upon what hath chanced, and, at more time,
The interim having weigh'd it, let us speak
Our free hearts each to other.

BANQUO
Very gladly.

MACBETH
Till then, enough. Come, friends. [*Exeunt.*

ACT ONE SCENE FOUR

Forres. The palace.

Flourish. Enter DUNCAN, MALCOLM, DONALBAIN , LENNOX, *and* Attendants.

DUNCAN
Is execution done on Cawdor? Are not
Those in commission yet return'd?

MALCOLM
My liege,
They are not yet come back. But I have spoke
With one that saw him die: who did report
That very frankly he confess'd his treasons,
Implor'd your highness' pardon and set forth
A deep repentance: nothing in his life
Became him like the leaving it; he died
As one that had been studied in his death
To throw away the dearest thing he owed, 11
As 'twere a careless trifle.

DUNCAN
There's no art
To find the mind's construction in the face:
He was a gentleman on whom I built
An absolute trust.

Enter MACBETH, BANQUO, ROSS, *and* ANGUS.

O worthiest cousin!
The sin of my ingratitude even now
Was heavy on me: thou art so far before
That swiftest wing of recompense is slow
To overtake thee. Would thou hadst less deserved,
That the proportion both of thanks and payment
Might have been mine! only I have left to say,
More is thy due than more than all can pay.

MACBETH
The service and the loyalty I owe,
In doing it, pays itself. Your highness' part
Is to receive our duties; and our duties
Are to your throne and state children and servants,
Which do but what they should, by doing every thing
Safe toward your love and honour.

DUNCAN
Welcome hither:
I have begun to plant thee, and will labour
To make thee full of growing. Noble Banquo,
That hast no less deserved, nor must be known
No less to have done so, let me infold thee 35
And hold thee to my heart.

BANQUO
There if I grow,
The harvest is your own.

DUNCAN
My plenteous joys,
Wanton in fulness, seek to hide themselves
In drops of sorrow. Sons, kinsmen, thanes,
And you whose places are the nearest, know
We will establish our estate upon
Our eldest, Malcolm, whom we name hereafter
The Prince of Cumberland; which honour must
Not unaccompanied invest him only, 46
But signs of nobleness, like stars, shall shine
On all deservers. From hence to Inverness,
And bind us further to you.

MACBETH
The rest is labour, which is not used for you:
I'll be myself the harbinger and make joyful
The hearing of my wife with your approach;
So humbly take my leave.

DUNCAN
My worthy Cawdor!

MACBETH
[*Aside*] The Prince of Cumberland! that is a step
On which I must fall down, or else o'erleap,
For in my way it lies. Stars, hide your fires;
Let not light see my black and deep desires:
The eye wink at the hand; yet let that be,
Which the eye fears, when it is done, to see. [*Exit.*

DUNCAN
True, worthy Banquo; he is full so valiant,
And in his commendations I am fed;
It is a banquet to me. Let's after him,
Whose care is gone before to bid us welcome:
It is a peerless kinsman. [*Flourish. Exeunt.*

ACT ONE SCENE FIVE

Inverness. Macbeth's castle.

Enter LADY MACBETH, *reading a letter.*

LADY MACBETH
'They met me in the day of success; and I have learned by the perfectest report, they have more in them than mortal knowledge. When I burned in desire to question them further, they made themselves air, into which they vanished. Whiles I stood rapt in the wonder of it, came missives from the king, who all-hailed me "Thane of Cawdor;" by which title, before, these weird sisters saluted me, and referred me to the coming on of time, with "Hail, king that shalt be!" This have I thought good to deliver thee, my dearest partner of greatness, that thou mightst not lose the dues of rejoicing, by being ignorant of what greatness is promised thee. Lay it to thy heart, and farewell.'
Glamis thou art, and Cawdor; and shalt be
What thou art promised: yet do I fear thy nature;
It is too full o' the milk of human kindness
To catch the nearest way: thou wouldst be great;
Art not without ambition, but without 18
The illness should attend it: what thou wouldst highly,
That wouldst thou holily; wouldst not play false,
And yet wouldst wrongly win: thou'ldst have, great Glamis,
That which cries 'Thus thou must do, if thou have it;
And that which rather thou dost fear to do 7
Than wishest should be undone.' Hie thee hither,
That I may pour my spirits in thine ear;
And chastise with the valour of my tongue
All that impedes thee from the golden round,
Which fate and metaphysical aid doth seem
To have thee crown'd withal.

Enter a Messenger.

What is your tidings?

MESSENGER
The king comes here to-night.

LADY MACBETH
Thou'rt mad to say it:
Is not thy master with him? who, were't so,
Would have inform'd for preparation.

MESSENGER
So please you, it is true: our thane is coming:
One of my fellows had the speed of him,
Who, almost dead for breath, had scarcely more
Than would make up his message.

LADY MACBETH
Give him tending;
He brings great news. [*Exit Messenger.*
The raven himself is hoarse
That croaks the fatal entrance of Duncan 43
Under my battlements. Come, you spirits
That tend on mortal thoughts, unsex me here,
And fill me from the crown to the toe top-full
Of direst cruelty! make thick my blood;
Stop up the access and passage to remorse,
That no compunctious visitings of nature
Shake my fell purpose, nor keep peace between
The effect and it! Come to my woman's breasts,
And take my milk for gall, you murdering ministers,
Wherever in your sightless substances
You wait on nature's mischief! Come, thick night,
And pall thee in the dunnest smoke of hell,
That my keen knife see not the wound it makes,
Nor heaven peep through the blanket of the dark,
To cry 'Hold, hold!'

Enter MACBETH.

Great Glamis! worthy Cawdor!
Greater than both, by the all-hail hereafter!
Thy letters have transported me beyond
This ignorant present, and I feel now
The future in the instant.

MACBETH
My dearest love, 54
Duncan comes here to-night.

LADY MACBETH
And when goes hence?

MACBETH
To-morrow, as he purposes.

LADY MACBETH
O, never
Shall sun that morrow see!
Your face, my thane, is as a book where men
May read strange matters. To beguile the time,
Look like the time; bear welcome in your eye,
Your hand, your tongue: look like the innocent flower,
But be the serpent under't. He that's coming
Must be provided for: and you shall put
This night's great business into my dispatch;
Which shall to all our nights and days to come
Give solely sovereign sway and masterdom. 69

MACBETH
We will speak further.

LADY MACBETH
Only look up clear;
To alter favour ever is to fear:
Leave all the rest to me. [*Exeunt.*

ACT ONE SCENE SIX

Before Macbeth's castle.

Hautboys and torches. Enter DUNCAN, MALCOLM, DONALBAIN, BANQUO, LENNOX, MACDUFF, ROSS, ANGUS, *and* Attendants.

DUNCAN
This castle hath a pleasant seat; the air
Nimbly and sweetly recommends itself
Unto our gentle senses.

BANQUO
This guest of summer,
The temple-haunting martlet, does approve, [8]
By his loved mansionry, that the heaven's breath [9]
Smells wooingly here: no jutty, frieze, [10]
Buttress, nor coign of vantage, but this bird
Hath made his pendent bed and procreant cradle:
Where they most breed and haunt I have observed, [11]
The air is delicate.

Enter LADY MACBETH.

DUNCAN
See, see, our honour'd hostess! 13
The love that follows us sometime is our trouble,
Which still we thank as love. Herein I teach you
How you shall bid God 'ild us for your pains,
And thank us for your trouble.

LADY MACBETH
All our service
In every point twice done and then done double
Were poor and single business to contend
Against those honours deep and broad wherewith
Your majesty loads our house: for those of old,
And the late dignities heap'd up to them,
We rest your hermits.

DUNCAN
Where's the thane of Cawdor? 25
We coursed him at the heels, and had a purpose
To be his purveyor: but he rides well;
And his great love, sharp as his spur, hath holp him
To his home before us. Fair and noble hostess,
We are your guest to-night.

LADY MACBETH
Your servants ever
Have theirs, themselves and what is theirs, in compt,
To make their audit at your highness' pleasure,
Still to return your own.

DUNCAN
Give me your hand;
Conduct me to mine host: we love him highly,
And shall continue our graces towards him.
By your leave, hostess. [*Exeunt.*

ACT ONE SCENE SEVEN

Macbeth's castle.

Hautboys and torches. Enter a Sewer, *and divers* Servants *with dishes and service, and pass over the stage. Then enter* MACBETH.

MACBETH
If it were done when 'tis done, then 'twere well
It were done quickly: if the assassination
Could trammel up the consequence, and catch
With his surcease success; that but this blow
Might be the be-all and the end-all here,
But here, upon this bank and shoal of time, [12]
We'ld jump the life to come. But in these cases
We still have judgement here; that we but teach
Bloody instructions, which, being taught, return
To plague the inventor: this even-handed justice
Commends the ingredients of our poison'd chalice
To our own lips. He's here in double trust;
First, as I am his kinsman and his subject,
Strong both against the deed; then, as his host,
Who should against his murderer shut the door,
Not bear the knife myself. Besides, this Duncan
Hath borne his faculties so meek, hath been
So clear in his great office, that his virtues
Will plead like angels, trumpet-tongued, against
The deep damnation of his taking-off;
And pity, like a naked new-born babe,
Striding the blast, or heaven's cherubim, horsed
Upon the sightless couriers of the air,
Shall blow the horrid deed in every eye,
That tears shall drown the wind. I have no spur
To prick the sides of my intent, but only
Vaulting ambition, which o'erleaps itself
And falls on the other.

Enter LADY MACBETH.

How now! what news?

LADY MACBETH
He has almost supp'd: why have you left the chamber?

MACBETH
Hath he ask'd for me?

LADY MACBETH
Know you not he has?

MACBETH
We will proceed no further in this business:
He hath honour'd me of late; and I have bought
Golden opinions from all sorts of people,
Which would be worn now in their newest gloss,
Not cast aside so soon.

LADY MACBETH
Was the hope drunk
Wherein you dress'd yourself? hath it slept since?
And wakes it now, to look so green and pale
At what it did so freely? From this time
Such I account thy love. Art thou afeard
To be the same in thine own act and valour
As thou art in desire? Wouldst thou have that
Which thou esteem'st the ornament of life,
And live a coward in thine own esteem,
Letting 'I dare not' wait upon 'I would,'
Like the poor cat i' the adage? [13]

MACBETH
Prithee, peace:
I dare do all that may become a man;
Who dares do more is none. [14]

LADY MACBETH
What beast was't, then,
That made you break this enterprise to me?
When you durst do it, then you were a man;
And, to be more than what you were, you would
Be so much more the man. Nor time nor place
Did then adhere, and yet you would make both:
They have made themselves, and that their fitness now
Does unmake you. I have given suck, and know
How tender 'tis to love the babe that milks me:
I would, while it was smiling in my face,
Have pluck'd my nipple from his boneless gums,
And dash'd the brains out, had I so sworn as you
Have done to this.

MACBETH
If we should fail?

LADY MACBETH
We fail!
But screw your courage to the sticking-place,
And we'll not fail. When Duncan is asleep—
Whereto the rather shall his day's hard journey
Soundly invite him—his two chamberlains
Will I with wine and wassail so convince
That memory, the warder of the brain,
Shall be a fume, and the receipt of reason
A limbeck only: when in swinish sleep

Their drenched natures lie as in a death,
What cannot you and I perform upon
The unguarded Duncan? what not put upon 76
His spongy officers, who shall bear the guilt
Of our great quell?

MACBETH
Bring forth men-children only;
For thy undaunted mettle should compose
Nothing but males. Will it not be received,
When we have mark'd with blood those sleepy two
Of his own chamber and used their very daggers,
That they have done't?

LADY MACBETH
Who dares receive it other,
As we shall make our griefs and clamour roar
Upon his death?

MACBETH
I am settled, and bend up
Each corporal agent to this terrible feat. 89
Away, and mock the time with fairest show:
False face must hide what the false heart doth know.
[*Exeunt.*

ACT TWO SCENE ONE

Court of Macbeth's castle.

Enter BANQUO, *and* FLEANCE *bearing a torch before him.*

BANQUO
How goes the night, boy?

FLEANCE
The moon is down; I have not heard the clock.

BANQUO
And she goes down at twelve.

FLEANCE
I take't, 'tis later, sir.

BANQUO
Hold, take my sword. There's husbandry in heaven;
Their candles are all out. Take thee that too.
A heavy summons lies like lead upon me,
And yet I would not sleep: merciful powers,
Restrain in me the cursed thoughts that nature
Gives way to in repose!

Enter MACBETH, *and a* Servant *with a torch.*

Give me my sword.
Who's there?

MACBETH
A friend.

BANQUO
What, sir, not yet at rest? The king's a-bed:
He hath been in unusual pleasure, and
Sent forth great largess to your offices.
This diamond he greets your wife withal,
By the name of most kind hostess; and shut up
In measureless content.

MACBETH
Being unprepared,
Our will became the servant to defect;
Which else should free have wrought.

BANQUO
All's well.
I dreamt last night of the three weird sisters:
To you they have show'd some truth.

MACBETH
I think not of them:
Yet, when we can entreat an hour to serve,
We would spend it in some words upon that business,
If you would grant the time.

BANQUO
At your kind'st leisure.

MACBETH
If you shall cleave to my consent, when 'tis,
It shall make honour for you.

BANQUO
So I lose none
In seeking to augment it, but still keep
My bosom franchised and allegiance clear,
I shall be counsell'd.

MACBETH
Good repose the while!

BANQUO
Thanks, sir: the like to you! 38
[*Exeunt Banquo and Fleance.*

MACBETH
Go bid thy mistress, when my drink is ready,
She strike upon the bell. Get thee to bed.
[*Exit Servant.*
Is this a dagger which I see before me,
The handle toward my hand? Come, let me clutch thee.
I have thee not, and yet I see thee still.
Art thou not, fatal vision, sensible
To feeling as to sight? or art thou but
A dagger of the mind, a false creation,
Proceeding from the heat-oppressed brain?
I see thee yet, in form as palpable 49
As this which now I draw.
Thou marshall'st me the way that I was going;
And such an instrument I was to use.
Mine eyes are made the fools o' the other senses,
Or else worth all the rest; I see thee still,
And on thy blade and dudgeon gouts of blood,
Which was not so before. There's no such thing:
It is the bloody business which informs
Thus to mine eyes. Now o'er the one halfworld

Nature seems dead, and wicked dreams abuse
The curtain'd sleep; witchcraft celebrates [15]
Pale Hecate's offerings, and wither'd murder,
Alarum'd by his sentinel, the wolf,
Whose howl's his watch, thus with his stealthy pace,
With Tarquin's ravishing strides, towards his design [16]
Moves like a ghost. Thou sure and firm-set earth, [17]
Hear not my steps, which way they walk, for fear [18]
Thy very stones prate of my whereabout,
And take the present horror from the time,
Which now suits with it. Whiles I threat, he lives:
Words to the heat of deeds too cold breath gives.
[*A bell rings.*
I go, and it is done; the bell invites me.
Hear it not, Duncan; for it is a knell
That summons thee to heaven or to hell [*Exit.*

ACT TWO SCENE TWO

The same.

Enter LADY MACBETH.

LADY MACBETH
That which hath made them drunk hath made me bold;
What hath quench'd them hath given me fire.
Hark! Peace!
It was the owl that shriek'd, the fatal bellman,
Which gives the stern'st good-night. He is about it:
The doors are open; and the surfeited grooms
Do mock their charge with snores: I have drugg'd their possets,
That death and nature do contend about them,
Whether they live or die.

MACBETH
[*Within*] Who's there? what, ho!

LADY MACBETH
Alack, I am afraid they have awaked,
And 'tis not done. The attempt and not the deed
Confounds us. Hark! I laid their daggers ready;
He could not miss 'em. Had he not resembled
My father as he slept, I had done't.

Enter MACBETH.

My husband!

MACBETH
I have done the deed. Didst thou not hear a noise?

LADY MACBETH
I heard the owl scream and the crickets cry.
Did not you speak?

MACBETH
When?

LADY MACBETH
Now.

MACBETH
As I descended?

LADY MACBETH
Ay.

MACBETH
Hark!
Who lies i' the second chamber?

LADY MACBETH
Donalbain.

MACBETH
This is a sorry sight.
[*Looking on his hands.*

LADY MACBETH
A foolish thought, to say a sorry sight.

MACBETH
There's one did laugh in's sleep, and one cried 'Murder!'
That they did wake each other: I stood and heard them:
But they did say their prayers, and address'd them
Again to sleep.

LADY MACBETH
There are two lodged together.

MACBETH
One cried 'God bless us!' and 'Amen' the other;
As they had seen me with these hangman's hands.
Listening their fear, I could not say 'Amen,'
When they did say 'God bless us!'

LADY MACBETH
Consider it not so deeply.

MACBETH
But wherefore could not I pronounce 'Amen'?
I had most need of blessing, and 'Amen'
Stuck in my throat.

LADY MACBETH
These deeds must not be thought
After these ways; so, it will make us mad.

MACBETH
Methought I heard a voice cry 'Sleep no more! [19]
Macbeth does murder sleep', the innocent sleep,
Sleep that knits up the ravell'd sleeve of care,
The death of each day's life, sore labour's bath,
Balm of hurt minds, great nature's second course,
Chief nourisher in life's feast—

LADY MACBETH
What do you mean?

MACBETH
Still it cried 'Sleep no more!' to all the house: 47
'Glamis hath murder'd sleep, and therefore Cawdor
Shall sleep no more; Macbeth shall sleep no more.'

LADY MACBETH
Who was it that thus cried? Why, worthy thane,
You do unbend your noble strength, to think
So brainsickly of things. Go get some water,
And wash this filthy witness from your hand.
Why did you bring these daggers from the place?
They must lie there: go carry them; and smear
The sleepy grooms with blood.

MACBETH
I'll go no more: 58
I am afraid to think what I have done;
Look on't again I dare not.

LADY MACBETH
Infirm of purpose!
Give me the daggers: the sleeping and the dead
Are but as pictures: 'tis the eye of childhood
That fears a painted devil. If he do bleed,
I'll gild the faces of the grooms withal;
For it must seem their guilt.
[*Exit. Knocking within.*

MACBETH
Whence is that knocking?
How is't with me, when every noise appals me?
What hands are here? ha! they pluck out mine eyes.
Will all great Neptune's ocean wash this blood
Clean from my hand? No, this my hand will rather 73
The multitudinous seas incarnadine,
Making the green one red.

Re-enter LADY MACBETH.

LADY MACBETH
My hands are of your colour; but I shame
To wear a heart so white. [*Knocking within.*
I hear a knocking
At the south entry: retire we to our chamber;
A little water clears us of this deed:
How easy is it, then! Your constancy
Hath left you unattended. [*Knocking within.*
Hark! more knocking.
Get on your nightgown, lest occasion call us,
And show us to be watchers. Be not lost
So poorly in your thoughts.

MACBETH
To know my deed, 'twere best not know myself.
[*Knocking within.*
Wake Duncan with thy knocking! I would thou couldst! [*Exeunt.*

ACT TWO SCENE THREE

The same.

Knocking within. Enter a Porter.

PORTER
Here's a knocking indeed! If a man were porter of hell-gate, he should have old turning the key. [*Knocking within.*] Knock, knock, knock! Who's there, i' the name of Beelzebub? Here's a farmer, that hanged himself on the expectation of plenty: come in time; have napkins enow about you; here you'll sweat for't. [*Knocking within.*] Knock, knock! Who's there, in the other devil's name? Faith, here's an equivocator, that could swear in both the scales against either scale; who committed treason enough for God's sake, yet could not equivocate to heaven: O, come in, equivocator. [*Knocking within.*] Knock, knock, knock! Who's there? Faith, here's an English tailor come hither, for stealing out of a French hose: come in, tailor; here you may roast your goose. [*Knocking within.*] Knock, knock; never at quiet! What are you? But this place is too cold for hell. I'll devil-porter it no further: I had thought to have let in some of all professions that go the primrose way to the everlasting bonfire. [*Knocking within.*] Anon, anon! I pray you, remember the porter.
[*Opens the gate.*

Enter MACDUFF *and* LENNOX.

MACDUFF
Was it so late, friend, ere you went to bed,
That you do lie so late?

PORTER
'Faith sir, we were carousing till the second cock: and drink, sir, is a great provoker of three things.

MACDUFF
What three things does drink especially provoke? 26

PORTER
Marry, sir, nose-painting, sleep, and urine. Lechery, sir, it provokes, and unprovokes; it provokes the desire, but it takes away the performance: therefore, much drink may be said to be an equivocator with lechery: it makes him, and it mars him; it sets him on, and it takes him off; it persuades him, and disheartens him; makes him stand to, and not stand to; in conclusion, equivocates him in a sleep, and, giving him the lie, leaves him. 35

MACDUFF
I believe drink gave thee the lie last night.

PORTER
That it did, sir, i' the very throat on me: but I requited him for his lie; and, I think, being too strong

for him, though he took up my legs sometime, yet I made a shift to cast him.

MACDUFF
Is thy master stirring?

Enter MACBETH.

Our knocking has awaked him; here he comes.

LENNOX
Good morrow, noble sir.

MACBETH
Good morrow, both.

MACDUFF
Is the king stirring, worthy thane?

MACBETH
Not yet.

MACDUFF
He did command me to call timely on him: 47
I have almost slipp'd the hour.

MACBETH
I'll bring you to him.

MACDUFF
I know this is a joyful trouble to you;
But yet 'tis one.

MACBETH
The labour we delight in physics pain.
This is the door.

MACDUFF
I'll make so bold to call,
For 'tis my limited service. [*Exit.*

LENNOX
Goes the king hence to-day?

MACBETH
He does: he did appoint so.

LENNOX
The night has been unruly: where we lay,
Our chimneys were blown down; and, as they say, 60
Lamentings heard i' the air; strange screams of death,
And prophesying with accents terrible
Of dire combustion and confused events
New hatch'd to the woeful time: the obscure bird
Clamour'd the livelong night: some say, the earth
Was feverous and did shake.

MACBETH
'Twas a rough night.

LENNOX
My young remembrance cannot parallel
A fellow to it.

Re-enter MACDUFF.

MACDUFF
O horror, horror, horror! Tongue nor heart
Cannot conceive nor name thee!

MACBETH, LENNOX
What's the matter.

MACDUFF
Confusion now hath made his masterpiece!
Most sacrilegious murder hath broke ope
The Lord's anointed temple, and stole thence
The life o' the building!

MACBETH
What is 't you say? the life?

LENNOX
Mean you his majesty?

MACDUFF
Approach the chamber, and destroy your sight
With a new Gorgon: do not bid me speak;
See, and then speak yourselves.
[*Exeunt Macbeth and Lennox.*
Awake, awake!
Ring the alarum-bell. Murder and treason!
Banquo and Donalbain! Malcolm! awake!
Shake off this downy sleep, death's counterfeit,
And look on death itself! up, up, and see
The great doom's image! Malcolm! Banquo!
As from your graves rise up, and walk like sprites,
To countenance this horror! Ring the bell.
[*Bell rings.*

Enter LADY MACBETH.

LADY MACBETH
What's the business,
That such a hideous trumpet calls to parley
The sleepers of the house? speak, speak!

MACDUFF
O gentle lady,
'Tis not for you to hear what I can speak:
The repetition, in a woman's ear, 96
Would murder as it fell.

Enter BANQUO.

O Banquo, Banquo,
Our royal master 's murder'd!

LADY MACBETH
Woe, alas!
What, in our house?

BANQUO
Too cruel any where.
Dear Duff, I prithee, contradict thyself,
And say it is not so.

Re-enter MACBETH *and* LENNOX, *with* ROSS.

MACBETH
Had I but died an hour before this chance,
I had lived a blessed time; for, from this instant,
There 's nothing serious in mortality:
All is but toys: renown and grace is dead;

The wine of life is drawn, and the mere lees
Is left this vault to brag of.

Enter MALCOLM *and* DONALBAIN.

DONALBAIN
What is amiss?
MACBETH
You are, and do not know't:
The spring, the head, the fountain of your blood
Is stopp'd; the very source of it is stopp'd.
MACDUFF
Your royal father 's murdered.
MALCOLM
O, by whom?
LENNOX
Those of his chamber, as it seem'd, had done 't:
Their hands and faces were all badged with blood;
So were their daggers, which unwiped we found
Upon their pillows:
They stared, and were distracted; no man's life
Was to be trusted with them.
MACBETH
O, yet I do repent me of my fury,
That I did kill them.
MACDUFF
Wherefore did you so?
MACBETH
Who can be wise, amazed, temperate and furious,
Loyal and neutral, in a moment? No man:
The expedition of my violent love
Outrun the pauser, reason. Here lay Duncan,
His silver skin laced with his golden blood;
And his gash'd stabs look'd like a breach in nature
For ruin's wasteful entrance: there, the murderers,
Steep'd in the colours of their trade, their daggers
Unmannerly breech'd with gore: who could refrain,
That had a heart to love, and in that heart
Courage to make 's love known?
LADY MACBETH
Help me hence, ho!
MACDUFF
Look to the lady.
MALCOLM
[*Aside to Donalbain*] Why do we hold our tongues,
That most may claim this argument for ours?
DONALBAIN
[*Aside to Malcolm*] What should be spoken here, where our fate,
Hid in an auger-hole, may rush, and seize us?
Let 's away;
Our tears are not yet brew'd.
MALCOLM
[*Aside to Donalbain*] Nor our strong sorrow
Upon the foot of motion.
BANQUO
Look to the lady:
[*Lady Macbeth is carried out.*
And when we have our naked frailties hid,
That suffer in exposure, let us meet,
And question this most bloody piece of work,
To know it further. Fears and scruples shake us:
In the great hand of God I stand; and thence
Against the undivulged pretence I fight
Of treasonous malice.
MACDUFF
And so do I.
ALL
So all.
MACBETH
Let's briefly put on manly readiness,
And meet i' the hall together.
ALL
Well contented.
[*Exeunt all but Malcolm and Donalbain.*
MALCOLM
What will you do? Let's not consort with them:
To show an unfelt sorrow is an office
Which the false man does easy. I'll to England.
DONALBAIN
To Ireland, I; our separated fortune
Shall keep us both the safer: where we are,
There's daggers in men's smiles: the near in blood,
The nearer bloody.
MALCOLM
This murderous shaft that's shot
Hath not yet lighted, and our safest way
Is to avoid the aim.
Therefore, to horse;
And let us not b e dainty of leave-taking,
But shift away: there's warrant in that theft
Which steals itself, when there's no mercy left.
[*Exeunt.*

ACT TWO SCENE FOUR

Outside Macbeth's castle.

Enter ROSS *and an* Old Man.

OLD MAN
Threescore and ten I can remember well:
Within the volume of which time I have seen
Hours dreadful and things strange; but this sore night
Hath trifled former knowings.
ROSS
Ah, good father,
Thou seest, the heavens, as troubled with man's act,

Threaten his bloody stage: by the clock, 'tis day,
And yet dark night strangles the travelling lamp:
Is't night's predominance, or the day's shame,
That darkness does the face of earth entomb,
When living light should kiss it?

OLD MAN
'Tis unnatural,
Even like the deed that's done. On Tuesday last,
A falcon, towering in her pride of place,
Was by a mousing owl hawk'd at and kill'd.

ROSS
And Duncan's horses—a thing most strange and certain—
Beauteous and swift, the minions of their race,
Turn'd wild in nature, broke their stalls, flung out,
Contending 'gainst obedience, as they would make
War with mankind.

OLD MAN
'Tis said they eat each other.

ROSS
They did so, to the amazement of mine eyes
That look'd upon't. Here comes the good
Macduff.

Enter MACDUFF.

How goes the world, sir, now?

MACDUFF
Why, see you not?

ROSS
Is't known who did this more than bloody deed?

MACDUFF
Those that Macbeth hath slain.

ROSS
Alas, the day!
What good could they pretend?

MACDUFF
They were suborn'd:
Malcolm and Donalbain, the king's two sons,
Are stol'n away and fled; which puts upon them
Suspicion of the deed.

ROSS
'Gainst nature still!
Thriftless ambition, that wilt ravin up
Thine own life's means! Then 'tis most like
The sovereignty will fall upon Macbeth.

MACDUFF
He is already named, and gone to Scone
To be invested.

ROSS
Where is Duncan's body?

MACDUFF
Carried to Colmekill,
The sacred storehouse of his predecessors,
And guardian of their bones.

ROSS
Will you to Scone?

MACDUFF
No, cousin, I'll to Fife.

ROSS
Well, I will thither.

MACDUFF
Well, may you see things well done there: adieu!
Lest our old robes sit easier than our new!

ROSS
Farewell, father.

OLD MAN
God's benison go with you; and with those
That would make good of bad, and friends of foes!
[*Exeunt.*

ACT THREE SCENE ONE

Forres. The palace.

Enter BANQUO.

BANQUO
Thou hast it now: king, Cawdor, Glamis, all,
As the weird women promised, and, I fear,
Thou play'dst most foully for't: yet it was said
It should not stand in thy posterity,
But that myself should be the root and father
Of many kings. If there come truth from them—
As upon thee, Macbeth, their speeches shine—
Why, by the verities on thee made good,
May they not be my oracles as well,
And set me up in hope? But hush! no more.

Sennet sounded. Enter MACBETH, *as king*, LADY MACBETH, *as queen*, LENNOX, ROSS, *Lords, Ladies, and* Attendants.

MACBETH
Here's our chief guest.

LADY MACBETH
If he had been forgotten,
It had been as a gap in our great feast,
And all-thing unbecoming.

MACBETH
To-night we hold a solemn supper sir,
And I'll request your presence.

BANQUO
Let your highness
Command upon me; to the which my duties
Are with a most indissoluble tie
For ever knit.

MACBETH
Ride you this afternoon?

BANQUO
Ay, my good lord.

MACBETH
We should have else desired your good advice,
Which still hath been both grave and prosperous,
In this day's council; but we'll take to-morrow.
Is't far you ride?
BANQUO
As far, my lord, as will fill up the time
'Twixt this and supper: go not my horse the better,
I must become a borrower of the night
For a dark hour or twain.
MACBETH
Fail not our feast.
BANQUO
My lord, I will not.
MACBETH
We hear, our bloody cousins are bestow'd 33
In England and in Ireland, not confessing
Their cruel parricide, filling their hearers
With strange invention: but of that to-morrow,
When therewithal we shall have cause of state
Craving us jointly. Hie you to horse: adieu,
Till your return at night. Goes Fleance with you?
BANQUO
Ay, my good lord: our time does call upon 's.
MACBETH
I wish your horses swift and sure of foot;
And so I do commend you to their backs.
Farewell. [*Exit Banquo.* 42
Let every man be master of his time
Till seven at night: to make society
The sweeter welcome, we will keep ourself
Till supper-time alone: while then, God be with you! [*Exeunt all but Macbeth, and an attendant.*
Sirrah, a word with you: attend those men
Our pleasure?
ATTENDANT
They are, my lord, without the palace gate.
MACBETH
Bring them before us. [*Exit Attendant.*
To be thus is nothing;
But to be safely thus.—Our fears in Banquo
Stick deep; and in his royalty of nature 54
Reigns that which would be fear'd: 'tis much he dares;
And, to that dauntless temper of his mind,
He hath a wisdom that doth guide his valour
To act in safety. There is none but he
Whose being I do fear: and, under him,
My Genius is rebuked; as, it is said,
Mark Antony's was by Caesar. He chid the sisters
When first they put the name of king upon me,
And bade them speak to him: then prophet-like
They hail'd him father to a line of kings: 65
Upon my head they placed a fruitless crown,
And put a barren sceptre in my gripe,
Thence to be wrench'd with an unlineal hand,
No son of mine succeeding. If 't be so,
For Banquo's issue have I filed my mind;
For them the gracious Duncan have I murder'd;
Put rancours in the vessel of my peace
Only for them; and mine eternal jewel
Given to the common enemy of man,
To make them kings, the seed of Banquo kings! 75
Rather than so, come fate into the list.
And champion me to the utterance! Who's there!

Re-enter Attendant, *with two* Murderers.

Now go to the door, and stay there till we call. [*Exit Attendant.*
Was it not yesterday we spoke together?
FIRST MURDERER
It was, so please your highness.
MACBETH
Well then, now
Have you consider'd of my speeches? Know
That it was he in the times past which held you
So under fortune, which you thought had been
Our innocent self: this I made good to you
In our last conference, pass'd in probation with you, 86
How you were borne in hand, how cross'd, the instruments,
Who wrought with them, and all things else that might
To half a soul and to a notion crazed
Say 'Thus did Banquo.'
FIRST MURDERER
You made it known to us.
MACBETH
I did so, and went further, which is now
Our point of second meeting. Do you find
Your patience so predominant in your nature
That you can let this go? Are you so gospell'd
To pray for this good man and for his issue,
Whose heavy hand hath bow'd you to the grave
And beggar'd yours for ever?
FIRST MURDERER
We are men, my liege. 101
MACBETH
Ay, in the catalogue ye go for men;
As hounds and greyhounds, mongrels, spaniels, curs,
Shoughs, water-rugs and demi-wolves, are clept
All by the name of dogs: the valued file
Distinguishes the swift, the slow, the subtle,
The housekeeper, the hunter, every one
According to the gift which bounteous nature
Hath in him closed, whereby he does receive
Particular addition, from the bill 110

That writes them all alike: and so of men.
Now, if you have a station in the file,
Not i' the worst rank of manhood, say 't;
And I will put that business in your bosoms,
Whose execution takes your enemy off,
Grapples you to the heart and love of us,
Who wear our health but sickly in his life,
Which in his death were perfect.

SECOND MURDERER
I am one, my liege,
Whom the vile blows and buffets of the world
Have so incensed that I am reckless what 121
I do to spite the world.

FIRST MURDERER
And I another
So weary with disasters, tugg'd with fortune,
That I would set my lie on any chance,
To mend it, or be rid on't.

MACBETH
Both of you
Know Banquo was your enemy.

BOTH MURDERERS
True, my lord.

MACBETH
So is he mine; and in such bloody distance,
That every minute of his being thrusts
Against my near'st of life: and though I could
With barefaced power sweep him from my sight
And bid my will avouch it, yet I must not, 134
For certain friends that are both his and mine,
Whose loves I may not drop, but wail his fall
Who I myself struck down; and thence it is,
That I to your assistance do make love,
Masking the business from the common eye
For sundry weighty reasons.

SECOND MURDERER
We shall, my lord,
Perform what you command us.

FIRST MURDERER
Though our lives—

MACBETH
Your spirits shine through you. Within this hour at most
I will advise you where to plant yourselves;
Acquaint you with the perfect spy o' the time, [20]
The moment on't; for't must be done to-night,
And something from the palace; always thought
That I require a clearness: and with him—
To leave no rubs nor botches in the work—
Fleance his son, that keeps him company,
Whose absence is no less material to me
Than is his father's, must embrace the fate
Of that dark hour. Resolve yourselves apart:
I'll come to you anon.

BOTH MURDERERS
We are resolved, my lord.

MACBETH
I'll call upon you straight: abide within. 158
[*Exeunt Murderers.*
It is concluded. Banquo, thy soul's flight,
If it find heaven, must find it out to-night. [*Exit.*

ACT THREE SCENE TWO

The palace.

Enter LADY MACBETH *and a* Servant.

LADY MACBETH
Is Banquo gone from court?

SERVANT
Ay, madam, but returns again to-night.

LADY MACBETH
Say to the king, I would attend his leisure
For a few words.

SERVANT
Madam, I will. [*Exit.*

LADY MACBETH
Nought's had, all's spent,
Where our desire is got without content:
'Tis safer to be that which we destroy
Than by destruction dwell in doubtful joy.

Enter MACBETH.

How now, my lord! why do you keep alone,
Of sorriest fancies your companions making,
Using those thoughts which should indeed have died 13
With them they think on? Things without all remedy
Should be without regard: what's done is done.

MACBETH
We have scotch'd the snake, not kill'd it:
She'll close and be herself, whilst our poor malice
Remains in danger of her former tooth.
But let the frame of things disjoint, both the worlds suffer,
Ere we will eat our meal in fear and sleep
In the affliction of these terrible dreams
That shake us nightly: better be with the dead,
Whom we, to gain our peace, have sent to peace, [21] 26
Than on the torture of the mind to lie
In restless ecstasy. Duncan is in his grave;
After life's fitful fever he sleeps well;
Treason has done his worst: nor steel, nor poison,
Malice domestic, foreign levy, nothing,
Can touch him further.

LADY MACBETH
Come on;
Gentle my lord, sleek o'er your rugged looks;
Be bright and jovial among your guests to-night.
MACBETH
So shall I, love; and so, I pray, be you:
Let your remembrance apply to Banquo;
Present him eminence, both with eye and tongue:
Unsafe the while, that we
Must lave our honours in these flattering streams,
And make our faces vizards to our hearts,
Disguising what they are.
LADY MACBETH
You must leave this.
MACBETH
O, full of scorpions is my mind, dear wife!
Thou know'st that Banquo, and his Fleance, lives.
LADY MACBETH
But in them nature's copy's not eterne.
MACBETH
There's comfort yet; they are assailable;
Then be thou jocund: ere the bat hath flown
His cloister'd flight, ere to black Hecate's summons
The shard-borne beetle with his drowsy hums
Hath rung night's yawning peal, there shall be done
A deed of dreadful note.
LADY MACBETH
What's to be done?
MACBETH
Be innocent of the knowledge, dearest chuck,
Till thou applaud the deed. Come, seeling night,
Scarf up the tender eye of pitiful day;
And with thy bloody and invisible hand
Cancel and tear to pieces that great bond
Which keeps me pale! Light thickens; and the crow
Makes wing to the rooky wood:
Good things of day begin to droop and drowse;
While night's black agents to their preys do rouse.
Thou marvell'st at my words: but hold thee still:
Things bad begun make strong themselves by ill.
So, prithee, go with me. [*Exeunt.*

ACT THREE SCENE THREE

A park near the palace.

Enter three Murderers.

FIRST MURDERER
But who did bid thee join with us?
THIRD MURDERER
Macbeth.
SECOND MURDERER
He needs not our mistrust, since he delivers
Our offices and what we have to do
To the direction just.
FIRST MURDERER
Then stand with us.
The west yet glimmers with some streaks of day:
Now spurs the lated traveller apace
To gain the timely inn; and near approaches
The subject of our watch.
THIRD MURDERER
Hark! I hear horses.
BANQUO
[*Within*] Give us a light there, ho!
SECOND MURDERER
Then 'tis he: the rest
That are within the note of expectation
Already are i' the court.
FIRST MURDERER
His horses go about.
THIRD MURDERER
Almost a mile: but he does usually,
So all men do, from hence to the palace gate
Make it their walk.
SECOND MURDERER
A light, a light!

Enter BANQUO, *and* FLEANCE *with a torch.*

THIRD MURDERER
'Tis he.
FIRST MURDERER
Stand to't.
BANQUO
It will be rain to-night.
FIRST MURDERER
Let it come down. [*They set upon Banquo.*
BANQUO
O, treachery! Fly, good Fleance, fly, fly, fly!
Thou mayst revenge. O slave!
[*Dies. Fleance escapes.*
THIRD MURDERER
Who did strike out the light?
FIRST MURDERER
Was't not the way?
THIRD MURDERER
There's but one down; the son is fled.
SECOND MURDERER
We have lost
Best half of our affair.
FIRST MURDERER
Well, let's away, and say how much is done.
[*Exeunt.*

ACT THREE SCENE FOUR

The same. Hall in the palace.

A banquet prepared. Enter MACBETH, LADY MACBETH, ROSS, LENNOX, Lords, *and* Attendants.

MACBETH
You know your own degrees; sit down: at first
And last the hearty welcome.
LORDS
Thanks to your majesty.
MACBETH
Ourself will mingle with society,
And play the humble host.
Our hostess keeps her state, but in best time
We will require her welcome.
LADY MACBETH
Pronounce it for me, sir, to all our friends;
For my heart speaks they are welcome.
[*First* Murderer *appears at the door.*
MACBETH
See, they encounter thee with their hearts' thanks. 10
Both sides are even: here I'll sit i' the midst:
Be large in mirth; anon we'll drink a measure
The table round. [*Approaching the door.*]
There's blood on thy face.
MURDERER
'Tis Banquo's then.
MACBETH
'Tis better thee without than he within. [22]
Is he dispatch'd?
MURDERER
My lord, his throat is cut; that I did for him.
MACBETH
Thou art the best o' the cut-throats: yet he's good
That did the like for Fleance: if thou didst it,
Thou art the nonpareil.
FIRST MURDERER
Most royal sir,
Fleance is 'scaped. 23
MACBETH
Then comes my fit again: I had else been perfect,
Whole as the marble, founded as the rock,
As broad and general as the casing air:
But now I am cabin'd, cribb'd, confined, bound in
To saucy doubts and fears. But Banquo's safe?
FIRST MURDERER
Ay, my good lord: safe in a ditch he bides,
With twenty trenched gashes on his head;
The least a death to nature.
MACBETH
Thanks for that
There the grown serpent lies; the worm that's fled
Hath nature that in time will venom breed, 34
No teeth for the present. Get thee gone: to-morrow
We'll hear, ourselves, again. [*Exit Murderer.*
LADY MACBETH
My royal lord,
You do not give the cheer: the feast is sold
That is not often vouch'd, while 'tis a-making,
'Tis given with welcome: to feed were best at home;
From thence the sauce to meat is ceremony;
Meeting were bare without it.
MACBETH
Sweet remembrancer!
Now, good digestion wait on appetite,
And health on both!
LENNOX
May't please your highness sit.
[*The Ghost of Banquo enters, and sits in Macbeth's place.*
MACBETH
Here had we now our country's honour roof'd, 48
Were the graced person of our Banquo present;
Who may I rather challenge for unkindness
Than pity for mischance!
ROSS
His absence, sir,
Lays blame upon his promise. Please't your highness
To grace us with your royal company.
MACBETH
The table's full.
LENNOX
Here is a place reserved, sir.
MACBETH
Where?
LENNOX
Here, my good lord. What is't that moves your highness?
MACBETH
Which of you have done this?
LORDS
What, my good lord?
MACBETH
Thou canst not say I did it: never shake 62
Thy gory locks at me.
ROSS
Gentlemen, rise; his highness is not well.
LADY MACBETH
Sit, worthy friends: my lord is often thus,
And hath been from his youth: pray you, keep seat;
The fit is momentary; upon a thought
He will again be well: if much you note him,
You shall offend him and extend his passion:
Feed, and regard him not. Are you a man?

MACBETH
Ay, and a bold one, that dare look on that
Which might appal the devil.
LADY MACBETH
O proper stuff! 74
This is the very painting of your fear:
This is the air-drawn dagger which, you said,
Led you to Duncan. O, these flaws and starts,
Impostors to true fear, would well become
A woman's story at a winter's fire,
Authorized by her grandam. Shame itself!
Why do you make such faces? When all's done,
You look but on a stool.
MACBETH
Prithee, see there! behold! look! lo! how say you?
Why, what care I? If thou canst nod, speak too. 84
If charnel-houses and our graves must send
Those that we bury back, our monuments
Shall be the maws of kites.
[*Ghost vanishes.*
LADY MACBETH
What, quite unmann'd in folly?
MACBETH
If I stand here, I saw him.
LADY MACBETH
Fie, for shame!
MACBETH
Blood hath been shed ere now, i' the olden time,
Ere human statute purged the gentle weal;
Ay, and since too, murders have been perform'd
Too terrible for the ear: the time has been, [23]
That, when the brains were out, the man would die,
And there an end; but now they rise again,
With twenty mortal murders on their crowns,
And push us from our stools: this is more strange
Than such a murder is.
LADY MACBETH
My worthy lord,
Your noble friends do lack you.
MACBETH
I do forget.
Do not muse at me, my most worthy friends;
I have a strange infirmity, which is nothing
To those that know me. Come, love and health to all;
Then I'll sit down. Give me some wine; fill full.
I drink to the general joy o' the whole table,
And to our dear friend Banquo, whom we miss; 99
Would he were here! to all, and him, we thirst,
And all to all.
LORDS
Our duties, and the pledge.

Re-enter Ghost.

MACBETH
Avaunt! and quit my sight! let the earth hide thee!
Thy bones are marrowless, thy blood is cold;
Thou hast no speculation in those eyes
Which thou dost glare with!
LADY MACBETH
Think of this, good peers,
But as a thing of custom: 'tis no other;
Only it spoils the pleasure of the time.
MACBETH
What man dare, I dare: 110
Approach thou like the rugged Russian bear,
The arm'd rhinoceros, or the Hyrcan tiger;
Take any shape but that, and my firm nerves
Shall never tremble: or be alive again,
And dare me to the desert with thy sword;
†If trembling I inhabit then, protest me [24]
The baby of a girl. Hence, horrible shadow!
Unreal mockery, hence! [*Ghost vanishes.*
Why, so: being gone,
I am a man again. Pray you, sit still.
LADY MACBETH
You have displaced the mirth, broke the good meeting,
With most admired disorder.
MACBETH
Can such things be, 123
And overcome us like a summer's cloud,
Without our special wonder? You make me strange
Even to the disposition that I owe,
When now I think you can behold such sights,
And keep the natural ruby of your cheeks,
When mine is blanch'd with fear.
ROSS
What sights, my lord?
LADY MACBETH
I pray you, speak not; he grows worse and worse;
Question enrages him. At once, good night:
Stand not upon the order of your going,
But go at once.
LENNOX
Good night; and better health 135
Attend his majesty!
LADY MACBETH
A kind good night to all!
[*Exeunt all but Macbeth and Lady M.*
MACBETH
It will have blood; they say, blood will have blood: [25]
Stones have been known to move and trees to speak;
Augurs and understood relations have
By magot pies and choughs and rooks brought forth
The secret'st man of blood. What is the night?

LADY MACBETH
Almost at odds with morning, which is which.
MACBETH
How say'st thou, that Macduff denies his person
At our great bidding?
LADY MACBETH
Did you send to him, sir?
MACBETH
I hear it by the way; but I will send:
There's not a one of them but in his house
I keep a servant fee'd. I will to-morrow,
And betimes I will, to the weird sisters:
More shall they speak; for now I am bent to know,
By the worst means, the worst. For mine own good,
All causes shall give way: I am in blood
Stepp'd in so far that, should I wade no more,
Returning were as tedious as go o'er:
Strange things I have in head, that will to hand;
Which must be acted ere they may be scann'd.
LADY MACBETH
You lack the season of all natures, sleep. 159
MACBETH
Come, we'll to sleep. My strange and self-abuse
Is the initiate fear that wants hard use:
We are yet but young in deed. [26] [*Exeunt.*

ACT THREE SCENE FIVE

A Heath.

Thunder. Enter the three Witches *meeting* HECATE.

FIRST WITCH
Why, how now, Hecate! you look angerly.
HECATE
Have I not reason, beldams as you are,
Saucy and overbold? How did you dare
To trade and traffic with Macbeth
In riddles and affairs of death;
And I, the mistress of your charms,
The close contriver of all harms,
Was never call'd to bear my part,
Or show the glory of our art?
And, which is worse, all you have done
Hath been but for a wayward son,
Spiteful and wrathful, who, as others do,
Loves for his own ends, not for you. [27]
But make amends now: get you gone,
And at the pit of Acheron
Meet me i' the morning: thither he
Will come to know his destiny:
Your vessels and your spells provide,
Your charms and every thing beside.
I am for the air; this night I'll spend
Unto a dismal and a fatal end:
Great business must be wrought ere noon:
Upon the corner of the moon
There hangs a vaporous drop profound;
I'll catch it ere it come to ground:
And that distill'd by magic sleights
Shall raise such artificial sprites
As by the strength of their illusion
Shall draw him on to his confusion:
He shall spurn fate, scorn death, and bear
He hopes 'bove wisdom, grace and fear:
And you all know, security
Is mortals' chiefest enemy.
[*Music and a song within:* 'Come away, come away,' &c.
Hark! I am call'd; my little spirit, see,
Sits in a foggy cloud, and stays for me. [*Exit.*
FIRST WITCH
Come, let's make haste; she'll soon be back again.
[*Exeunt.*

ACT THREE SCENE SIX

Forres. The palace.

Enter LENNOX *and another* Lord.

LENNOX
My former speeches have but hit your thoughts,
Which can interpret further: only, I say,
Things have been strangely borne. The gracious Duncan
Was pitied of Macbeth: marry, he was dead:
And the right-valiant Banquo walk'd too late;
Whom, you may say, if't please you, Fleance kill'd,
For Fleance fled: men must not walk too late.
Who cannot want the thought how monstrous
It was for Malcolm and for Donalbain
To kill their gracious father? damned fact! 11
How it did grieve Macbeth! did he not straight
In pious rage the two delinquents tear,
That were the slaves of drink and thralls of sleep?
Was not that nobly done? Ay, and wisely too;
For 'twould have anger'd any heart alive
To hear the men deny't. So that, I say,
He has borne all things well: and I do think
That had he Duncan's sons under his key—
As, an't please heaven, he shall not—they should find
What 'twere to kill a father; so should Fleance.
But, peace! for from broad words and 'cause he fail'd 23
His presence at the tyrant's feast, I hear
Macduff lives in disgrace: sir, can you tell
Where he bestows himself?

LORD
The son of Duncan,
From whom this tyrant holds the due of birth
Lives in the English court, and is received
Of the most pious Edward with such grace
That the malevolence of fortune nothing
Takes from his high respect: thither Macduff
Is gone to pray the holy king, upon his aid
To wake Northumberland and warlike Siward:
That by the help of these—with Him above
To ratify the work—we may again
Give to our tables meat, sleep to our nights,
Free from our feasts and banquets bloody knives,
Do faithful homage and receive free honours:
All which we pine for now: and this report
Hath so exasperated the king that he
Prepares for some attempt of war.

LENNOX
Sent he to Macduff?

LORD
He did: and with an absolute 'Sir, not I,'
The cloudy messenger turns me his back,
And hums, as who should say 'You'll rue the time
That clogs me with this answer.'

LENNOX
And that well might
Advise him to a caution, to hold what distance
His wisdom can provide. Some holy angel
Fly to the court of England and unfold
His message ere he come, that a swift blessing
May soon return to this our suffering country
Under a hand accursed!

LORD
I'll send my prayers with him. [*Exeunt.*

ACT FOUR SCENE ONE

A cavern. In the middle, a boiling cauldron.

Thunder. Enter the three Witches.

FIRST WITCH
Thrice the brinded cat hath mew'd.

SECOND WITCH
Thrice and once the hedge-pig whined.

THIRD WITCH
Harpier cries 'Tis time, 'tis time.

FIRST WITCH
Round about the cauldron go;
In the poison'd entrails throw.
Toad, that under cold stone
Days and nights has thirtyone
Swelter'd venom sleeping got,
Boil thou first i' the charmed pot.

ALL
Double, double toil and trouble;
Fire burn, and cauldron bubble.

SECOND WITCH
Fillet of a fenny snake,
In the cauldron boil and bake;
Eye of newt and toe of frog,
Wool of bat and tongue of dog,
Adder's fork and blind-worm's sting,
Lizard's leg and howlet's wing,
For a charm of powerful trouble,
Like a hell-broth boil and bubble.

ALL
Double, double toil and trouble;
Fire burn, and cauldron bubble.

THIRD WITCH
Scale of dragon, tooth of wolf,
Witches' mummy, maw and gulf
Of the ravin'd salt-sea shark,
Root of hemlock digg'd i' the dark,
Liver of blaspheming Jew,
Gall of goat, and slips of yew
Silver'd in the moon's eclipse,
Nose of Turk and Tartar's lips,
Finger of birth-strangled babe
Ditch-deliver'd by a drab,
Make the gruel thick and slab:
Add thereto a tiger's chaudron,
For the ingredients of our cauldron.

ALL
Double, double toil and trouble;
Fire burn and cauldron bubble.

SECOND WITCH
Cool it with a baboon's blood,
Then the charm is firm and good.

Enter HECATE *to the other three Witches.*

HECATE
O, well done! I commend your pains;
And every one shall share i' the gains:
And now about the cauldron sing,
Live elves and fairies in a ring,
Enchanting all that you put in.
[*Music and a song:* 'Black spirits,' &c.
[*Hecate retires.*

SECOND WITCH
By the pricking of my thumbs,
Something wicked this way comes.
Open, locks,
Whoever knocks!

Enter MACBETH.

MACBETH
How now, you secret, black, and midnight hags!
What is't you do?

ALL
A deed without a name.

MACBETH
I conjure you, by that which you profess, 51
Howe'er you come to know it, answer me:
Though you untie the winds and let them fight
Against the churches; though the yesty waves
Confound and swallow navigation up;
Though bladed corn be lodged and trees blown down;
Though castles topple on their warders' heads;
Though palaces and pyramids do slope
Their heads to their foundations; though the treasure
Of nature's germens tumble all together,
Even till destruction sicken; answer me 63
To what I ask you.

FIRST WITCH
Speak.

SECOND WITCH
Demand.

THIRD WITCH
We'll answer.

FIRST WITCH
Say, if thou'dst rather hear it from our mouths,
Or from our masters?

MACBETH
Call 'em; let me see 'em.

FIRST WITCH
Pour in sow's blood, that hath eaten
Her nine farrow; grease that's sweaten
From the murderer's gibbet throw
Into the flame.

ALL
Come, high or low;
Thyself and office deftly show!

Thunder. First Apparition: *an armed Head.*

MACBETH
Tell me, thou unknown power,—

FIRST WITCH
He knows thy thought:
Hear his speech, but say thou nought. 79

FIRST APPARITION
Macbeth! Macbeth! Macbeth! beware Macduff;
Beware the thane of Fife. Dismiss me. Enough.
[*Descends.*

MACBETH
Whate'er thou art, for thy good caution, thanks;
Thou hast harp'd my fear aright: but one word more,—

FIRST WITCH
He will not be commanded: here's another,
More potent than the first.

Thunder. Second Apparition: *a bloody Child.*

SECOND APPARITION
Macbeth! Macbeth! Macbeth!

MACBETH
Had I three ears, I'ld hear thee.

SECOND APPARITION
Be bloody, bold, and resolute; laugh to scorn
The power of man, for none of woman born
Shall harm Macbeth. [*Descends.*

MACBETH
Then live, Macduff: what need I fear of thee?
But yet I'll make assurance double sure,
And take a bond of fate: thou shalt not live;
That I may tell pale-hearted fear it lies,
And sleep in spite of thunder.

Thunder. Third Apparition: *a Child crowned, with a tree in his hand.*

What is this
That rises like the issue of a king,
And wears upon his baby-brow the round
And top of sovereignty?

ALL
Listen, but speak not to't.

THIRD APPARITION
Be lion-mettled, proud; and take no care 101
Who chafes, who frets, or where conspirers are:
Macbeth shall never vanquish'd be until
Great Birnam wood to high Dunsinane hill
Shall come against him. [*Descends.*

MACBETH
That will never be:
Who can impress the forest, bid the tree
Unfix his earth-bound root? Sweet bodements! good!
Rebellion's head, rise never till the wood [29]
Of Birnam rise, and our high-placed Macbeth
Shall live the lease of nature, pay his breath
To time and mortal custom. Yet my heart
Throbs to know one thing: tell me, if your art
Can tell so much: shall Banquo's issue ever
Reign in this kingdom?

ALL
Seek to know no more.

MACBETH
I will be satisfied: deny me this,
And an eternal curse fall on you! Let me know.
Why sinks that cauldron? and what noise is this?
[*Hautboys.*

FIRST WITCH
Show!

SECOND WITCH
Show!

THIRD WITCH
Show!

ALL
Show his eyes, and grieve his heart;
Come like shadows, so depart! 132

A show of Eight Kings, *the last with a glass in his hand; Banquo's Ghost following.*

MACBETH
Thou art too like the spirit of Banquo; down!
Thy crown does sear mine eye-balls. And thy hair,
Thou other gold-bound brow, is like the first.
A third is like the former. Filthy hags!
Why do you show me this? A fourth! Start, eyes!
What, will the line stretch out to the crack of doom?
Another yet! A seventh! I'll see no more:
And yet the eighth appears, who bears a glass
Which shows me many more; and some I see
That two-fold balls and treble scepters carry:
Horrible sight! Now, I see, 'tis true;
For the blood-bolter'd Banquo smiles upon me,
And points at them for his. [*Apparitions vanish.*
What, is this so?

FIRST WITCH
Ay, sir, all this is so: but why
Stands Macbeth thus amazedly?
Come, sisters, cheer we up his sprites,
And show the best of our delights:
I'll charm the air to give a sound,
While you perform your antic round;
That this great king may kindly say,
Our duties did his welcome pay.

[*Music. The Witches dance, and then vanish, with Hecate.*

MACBETH
Where are they? Gone! Let this pernicious hour
Stand aye accursed in the calendar!
Come in, without there!

Enter LENNOX.

LENNOX
What's your grace's will?
MACBETH
Saw you the weird sisters?
LENNOX
No, my lord.
MACBETH
Came they not by you?
LENNOX
No, indeed, my lord.
MACBETH
Infected be the air whereon they ride;
And damn'd all those that trust them! I did hear
The galloping of horse: who was't came by?
LENNOX
'Tis two or three, my lord, that bring you word 166
Macduff is fled to England.
MACBETH
Fled to England!
LENNOX
Ay, my good lord.
MACBETH
Time, thou anticipatest my dread exploits:
The flighty purpose never is o'ertook
Unless the deed go with it: from this moment
The very firstlings of my heart shall be
The firstlings of my hand. And even now,
To crown my thoughts with acts, be it thought and done:
The castle of Macduff I will surprise; 177
Seize upon Fife; give to the edge o' the sword
His wife, his babes, and all unfortunate souls
That trace him in his line. No boasting like a fool:
This deed I'll do before this purpose cool.
But no more sights!—Where are these gentlemen?
Come, bring me where they are. [*Exeunt.*

ACT FOUR SCENE TWO

Fife. Macduff's castle.

Enter LADY MACDUFF, *her* Son, *and* ROSS.

LADY MACDUFF
What had he done, to make him fly the land?
ROSS
You must have patience, madam.
LADY MACDUFF
He had none:
His flight was madness: when our actions do not,
Our fears do make us traitors.
ROSS
You know not
Whether it was his wisdom or his fear.
LADY MACDUFF
Wisdom! to leave his wife, to leave his babes,
His mansion and his titles in a place
From whence himself does fly? He loves us not;
He wants the natural touch: for the poor wren,
The most diminutive of birds, will fight, 12
Her young ones in her nest, against the owl.
All is the fear and nothing is the love;
As little is the wisdom, where the flight
So runs against all reason.
ROSS
My dearest coz,
I pray you, school yourself: but for your husband,
He is noble, wise, judicious, and best knows
The fits o' the season. I dare not speak much further;
But cruel are the times, when we are traitors 30

And do not know ourselves, when we hold rumour [31]
From what we fear, yet know not what we fear,
But float upon a wild and violent sea
Each way and move. I take my leave of you: [32]
Shall not be long but I'll be here again:
Things at the worst will cease, or else climb upward
To what they were before. My pretty cousin,
Blessing upon you!

LADY MACDUFF
Father'd he is, and yet he's fatherless.

ROSS
I am so much a fool, should I stay longer,
It would be my disgrace and your discomfort:
I take my leave at once. [*Exit.*

LADY MACDUFF
Sirrah, your father's dead:
And what will you do now? How will you live?

SON
As birds do, mother.

LADY MACDUFF
What, with worms and flies?

SON
With what I get, I mean; and so do they.

LADY MACDUFF
Poor bird! thou'ldst never fear the net nor lime,
The pitfall nor the gin.

SON
Why should I, mother? Poor birds they are not set for.
My father is not dead, for all your saying.

LADY MACDUFF
Yes, he is dead: how wilt thou do for a father?

SON
Nay, how will you do for a husband?

LADY MACDUFF
Why, I can buy me twenty at any market.

SON
Then you'll buy 'em to sell again.

LADY MACDUFF
Thou speak'st with all thy wit; and yet, i' faith,
With wit enough for thee.

SON
Was my father a traitor, mother?

LADY MACDUFF
Ay, that he was.

SON
What is a traitor?

LADY MACDUFF
Why, one that swears and lies.

SON
And be all traitors that do so?

LADY MACDUFF
Every one that does so is a traitor, and must be hanged.

SON
And must they all be hanged that swear and lie?

LADY MACDUFF
Every one.

SON
Who must hang them?

LADY MACDUFF
Why, the honest men.

SON
Then the liars and swearers are fools, for there are liars and swearers enow to beat the honest men and hang up them.

LADY MACDUFF
Now, God help thee, poor monkey!
But how wilt thou do for a father?

SON
If he were dead, you'ld weep for him: if you would not, it were a good sign that I should quickly have a new father.

LADY MACDUFF
Poor prattler, how thou talk'st!

Enter a Messenger.

MESSENGER
Bless you, fair dame! I am not to you known,
Though in your state of honour I am perfect.
I doubt some danger does approach you nearly:
If you will take a homely man's advice,
Be not found here; hence, with your little ones.
To fright you thus, methinks, I am too savage;
To do worse to you were fell cruelty, [33]
Which is too nigh your person. Heaven preserve you!
I dare abide no longer. [*Exit.*

LADY MACDUFF
Whither should I fly?
I have done no harm. But I remember now
I am in this earthly world; where to do harm
Is often laudable, to do good sometime
Accounted dangerous folly: why then, alas,
Do I put up that womanly defence,
To say I have done no harm?

Enter Murderers.

What are these faces?

FIRST MURDERER
Where is your husband?

LADY MACDUFF
I hope, in no place so unsanctified
Where such as thou mayst find him.

FIRST MURDERER
He's a traitor.

SON
Thou liest, thou shag-hair'd villain!

FIRST MURDERER

What, you egg! *[Stabbing him.*

Young fry of treachery!

SON

He has kill'd me, mother:

Run away, I pray you! *[Dies.*

[Exit Lady Macduff, crying 'Murder!'

Exeunt Murderers, following her.

ACT FOUR SCENE THREE

England. Before the King's palace.

Enter MALCOLM *and* MACDUFF.

MALCOLM

Let us seek out some desolate shade, and there
Weep our sad bosoms empty.

MACDUFF

Let us rather
Hold fast the mortal sword, and like good men
Bestride our down fall'n birthdom: each new morn
New widows howl, new orphans cry, new sorrows
Strike heaven on the face, that it resounds
As if it felt with Scotland and yell'd out
Like syllable of dolour.

MALCOLM

What I believe I'll wail,
What know believe, and what I can redress,
As I shall find the time to friend, I will. 12
What you have spoke, it may be so perchance.
This tyrant, whose sole name blisters our tongues,
Was once thought honest: you have loved him well;
He hath not touch'd you yet. I am young; but something
You may deserve of him through me, and wisdom 34
To offer up a weak poor innocent lamb
To appease an angry god.

MACDUFF

I am not treacherous.

MALCOLM

But Macbeth is.
A good and virtuous nature may recoil
In an imperial charge. But I shall crave your pardon; 26
That which you are my thoughts cannot transpose:
Angels are bright still, though the brightest fell:
Though all things foul would wear the brows of grace,
Yet grace must still look so.

MACDUFF

I have lost my hopes.

MALCOLM

Perchance even there where I did find my doubts.
Why in that rawness left you wife and child,
Those precious motives, those strong knots of love,
Without leave-taking? I pray you,
Let not my jealousies be your dishonours,
But mine own safeties. You may be rightly just, 38
Whatever I shall think.

MACDUFF

Bleed, bleed, poor country!
Great tyranny! lay thou thy basis sure,
For goodness dare not cheque thee: wear thou thy wrongs;
The title is affeer'd! Fare thee well, lord:
I would not be the villain that thou think'st
For the whole space that's in the tyrant's grasp,
And the rich East to boot.

MALCOLM

Be not offended:
I speak not as in absolute fear of you.
I think our country sinks beneath the yoke;
It weeps, it bleeds; and each new day a gash
Is added to her wounds: I think withal
There would be hands uplifted in my right;
And here from gracious England have I offer
Of goodly thousands: but, for all this,
When I shall tread upon the tyrant's head,
Or wear it on my sword, yet my poor country
Shall have more vices than it had before,
More suffer and more sundry ways than ever,
By him that shall succeed.

MACDUFF

What should he be?

MALCOLM

It is myself I mean: in whom I know
All the particulars of vice so grafted 53
That, when they shall be open'd, black Macbeth
Will seem as pure as snow, and the poor state
Esteem him as a lamb, being compared
With my confineless harms.

MACDUFF

Not in the legions
Of horrid hell can come a devil more damn'd
In evils to top Macbeth.

MALCOLM

I grant him bloody,
Luxurious, avaricious, false, deceitful,
Sudden, malicious, smacking of every sin
That has a name: but there's no bottom, none,
In my voluptuousness: your wives, your daughters, 66
Your matrons and your maids, could not fill up
The cistern of my lust, and my desire
All continent impediments would o'erbear

That did oppose my will: better Macbeth
Than such an one to reign.

MACDUFF
Boundless intemperance
In nature is a tyranny; it hath been
The untimely emptying of the happy throne
And fall of many kings. But fear not yet
To take upon you what is yours: you may
Convey your pleasures in a spacious plenty,
And yet seem cold, the time you may so hoodwink.
We have willing dames enough; there cannot be
That vulture in you, to devour so many
As will to greatness dedicate themselves,
Finding it so inclined.

MALCOLM
With this there grows
In my most ill-composed affection such
A stanchless avarice that, were I king,
I should cut off the nobles for their lands,
Desire his jewels and this other's house:
And my more-having would be as a sauce
To make me hunger more; that I should forge
Quarrels unjust against the good and loyal,
Destroying them for wealth.

MACDUFF
This avarice
Sticks deeper, grows with more pernicious root
Than summer-seeming lust, and it hath been
The sword of our slain kings: yet do not fear;
Scotland hath foisons to fill up your will.
Of your mere own: all these are portable,
With other graces weigh'd.

MALCOLM
But I have none: the king-becoming graces,
As justice, verity, temperance, stableness,
Bounty, perseverance, mercy, lowliness,
Devotion, patience, courage, fortitude,
I have no relish of them, but abound
In the division of each several crime,
Acting it many ways. Nay, had I power, I should
Pour the sweet milk of concord into hell,
Uproar the universal peace, confound
All unity on earth.

MACDUFF
O Scotland, Scotland!

MALCOLM
If such a one be fit to govern, speak:
I am as I have spoken.

MACDUFF
Fit to govern!
No, not to live. O nation miserable,
With an untitled tyrant bloody-scepter'd,
When shalt thou see thy wholesome days again,
Since that the truest issue of thy throne
By his own interdiction stands accursed,
And does blaspheme his breed? Thy royal father
Was a most sainted king: the queen that bore thee,
Oftener upon her knees than on her feet,
Died every day she lived. Fare thee well! [35]
These evils thou repeat'st upon thyself
Have banish'd me from Scotland. O my breast,
Thy hope ends here!

MALCOLM
Macduff, this noble passion,
Child of integrity, hath from my soul
Wiped the black scruples, reconciled my thoughts
To thy good truth and honour. Devilish Macbeth
By many of these trains hath sought to win me
Into his power, and modest wisdom plucks me
From over-credulous haste: but God above
Deal between thee and me! for even now
I put myself to thy direction, and
Unspeak mine own detraction, here abjure
The taints and blames I laid upon myself,
For strangers to my nature. I am yet
Unknown to woman, never was forsworn,
Scarcely have coveted what was mine own,
At no time broke my faith, would not betray
The devil to his fellow and delight
No less in truth than life: my first false speaking
Was this upon myself: what I am truly,
Is thine and my poor country's to command:
Whither indeed, before thy here-approach,
Old Siward, with ten thousand warlike men,
Already at a point, was setting forth.
Now we'll together; and the chance of goodness
Be like our warranted quarrel! Why are you silent?

MACDUFF
Such welcome and unwelcome things at once
'Tis hard to reconcile.

Enter a Doctor.

MALCOLM
Well; more anon.—Comes the king forth, I pray you?

DOCTOR
Ay, sir; there are a crew of wretched souls
That stay his cure: their malady convinces
The great assay of art; but at his touch—
Such sanctity hath heaven given his hand—
They presently amend.

MALCOLM
I thank you, doctor. [*Exit Doctor.*

MACDUFF
What's the disease he means?

MALCOLM
'Tis call'd the evil:
A most miraculous work in this good king;

Which often, since my here-remain in England,
I have seen him do. How he solicits heaven,
Himself best knows: but strangely-visited people, 165
All swoln and ulcerous, pitiful to the eye,
The mere despair of surgery, he cures,
Hanging a golden stamp about their necks,
Put on with holy prayers: and 'tis spoken,
To the succeeding royalty he leaves
The healing benediction. With this strange virtue,
He hath a heavenly gift of prophecy,
And sundry blessings hang about his throne,
That speak him full of grace.

Enter ROSS.

MACDUFF
See, who comes here?
MALCOLM
My countryman; but yet I know him not. 176
MACDUFF
My ever-gentle cousin, welcome hither.
MALCOLM
I know him now. Good God, be times remove
The means that makes us strangers!
ROSS
Sir, amen.
MACDUFF
Stands Scotland where it did?
ROSS
Alas, poor country!
Almost afraid to know itself. It cannot
Be call'd our mother, but our grave; where nothing,
But who knows nothing, is once seen to smile:
Where sighs and groans and shrieks that rend the air
Are made, not mark'd; where violent sorrow seems
A modern ecstasy: the dead man's knell 189
Is there scarce ask'd for who; and good men's lives
Expire before the flowers in their caps,
Dying or ere they sicken.
MACDUFF
O, relation
Too nice, and yet too true!
MALCOLM
What's the newest grief?
ROSS
That of an hour's age doth hiss the speaker:
Each minute teems a new one.
MACDUFF
How does my wife?
ROSS
Why, well.
MACDUFF
And all my children?
ROSS
Well too.
MACDUFF
The tyrant has not batter'd at their peace?
ROSS
No; they were well at peace when I did leave 'em.
MACDUFF
Bet not a niggard of your speech: how goes't? 203
ROSS
When I came hither to transport the tidings,
Which I have heavily borne, there ran a rumour
Of many worthy fellows that were out;
Which was to my belief witness'd the rather,
For that I saw the tyrant's power a-foot:
Now is the time of help; your eye in Scotland
Would create soldiers, make our women fight,
To doff their dire distresses.
MALCOLM
Be't their comfort
We are coming thither: gracious England hath
Lent us good Siward and ten thousand men;
An older and a better soldier none 215
That Christendom gives out.
ROSS
Would I could answer
This comfort with the like! But I have words
That would be howl'd out in the desert air,
Where hearing should not latch them.
MACDUFF
What concern they?
The general cause? or is it a fee-grief
Due to some single breast?
ROSS
No mind that's honest
But in it shares some woe; though the main part
Pertains to you alone.
MACDUFF
If it be mine,
Keep it not from me, quickly let me have it.
ROSS
Let not your ears despise my tongue for ever,
Which shall possess them with the heaviest sound
That ever yet they heard.
MACDUFF
Hum! I guess at it.
ROSS
Your castle is surprised; your wife and babes
Savagely slaughter'd: to relate the manner,
Were, on the quarry of these murder'd deer,
To add the death of you.
MALCOLM
Merciful heaven!
What, man! ne'er pull your hat upon your brows;

Give sorrow words: the grief that does not speak
Whispers the o'er-fraught heart and bids it break. 242

MACDUFF
My children too?

ROSS
Wife, children, servants, all
That could be found.

MACDUFF
And I must be from thence!
My wife kill'd too?

ROSS
I have said.

MALCOLM
Be comforted:
Let's make us medicines of our great revenge,
To cure this deadly grief.

MACDUFF
He has no children. All my pretty ones?
Did you say all? O hell-kite! All?
What, all my pretty chickens and their dam
At one fell swoop?

MALCOLM
Dispute it like a man.

MACDUFF
I shall do so; 257
But I must also feel it as a man:
I cannot but remember such things were,
That were most precious to me. Did heaven look on,
And would not take their part? Sinful Macduff,
They were all struck for thee! naught that I am,
Not for their own demerits, but for mine,
Fell slaughter on their souls. Heaven rest them now!

MALCOLM
Be this the whetstone of your sword: let grief
Convert to anger; blunt not the heart, enrage it.

MACDUFF
O, I could play the woman with mine eyes 269
And braggart with my tongue! But, gentle heavens,
Cut short all intermission; front to front
Bring thou this fiend of Scotland and myself;
Within my sword's length set him; if he 'scape,
Heaven forgive him too!

MALCOLM
This tune goes manly. [36]
Come, go we to the king; our power is ready;
Our lack is nothing but our leave: Macbeth
Is ripe for shaking, and the powers above
Put on their instruments. Receive what cheer you may:
The night is long that never finds the day. 281

[*Exeunt.*

ACT FIVE SCENE ONE

Dunsinane. Ante-room in the castle.

Enter a Doctor of Physic *and a* Waiting-Gentlewoman.

DOCTOR
I have two nights watched with you, but can perceive no truth in your report. When was it she last walked?

GENTLEWOMAN
Since his majesty went into the field, I have seen her rise from her bed, throw her nightgown upon her, unlock her closet, take forth paper, fold it, write upon't, read it, afterwards seal it, and again return to bed; yet all this while in a most fast sleep. 7

DOCTOR
A great perturbation in nature, to receive at once the benefit of sleep, and do the effects of watching! In this slumbery agitation, besides her walking and other actual performances, what, at any time, have you heard her say?

GENTLEWOMAN
That, sir, which I will not report after her.

DOCTOR
You may to me: and 'tis most meet you should.

GENTLEWOMAN
Neither to you nor any one; having no witness to confirm my speech. 15

Enter LADY MACBETH, *with a taper.*

Lo you, here she comes! This is her very guise; and, upon my life, fast asleep. Observe her; stand close.

DOCTOR
How came she by that light?

GENTLEWOMAN
Why, it stood by her: she has light by her continually; 'tis her command.

DOCTOR
You see, her eyes are open.

GENTLEWOMAN
Ay, but their sense is shut. [37]

DOCTOR
What is it she does now? Look, how she rubs her hands. 24

GENTLEWOMAN
It is an accustomed action with her, to seem thus washing her hands: I have known her continue in this a quarter of an hour.

LADY MACBETH
Yet here's a spot.

DOCTOR
Hark! she speaks: I will set down what comes from her, to satisfy my remembrance the more strongly.

LADY MACBETH
Out, damned spot! out, I say!—One: two: why, then, 'tis time to do't.—Hell is murky!—Fie, my lord, fie! a

LADY MACBETH Out, damned spot! out, I say.

soldier, and afeard? What need we fear who knows it, when none can call our power to account?—Yet who would have thought the old man to have had so much blood in him.

DOCTOR

Do you mark that?

LADY MACBETH

The thane of Fife had a wife: where is she now?—

What, will these hands ne'er be clean?—No more o' that, my lord, no more o' that: you mar all with this starting.

DOCTOR

Go to, go to; you have known what you should not.

GENTLEWOMAN

She has spoke what she should not, I am sure of that: heaven knows what she has known.

LADY MACBETH

Here's the smell of the blood still: all the perfumes of Arabia will not sweeten this little hand. Oh, oh, oh!

DOCTOR

What a sigh is there! The heart is sorely charged.

GENTLEWOMAN

I would not have such a heart in my bosom for the dignity of the whole body.

DOCTOR

Well, well, well,—

GENTLEWOMAN

Pray God it be, sir.

DOCTOR

This disease is beyond my practise: yet I have known those which have walked in their sleep who have died holily in their beds.

LADY MACBETH

Wash your hands, put on your nightgown; look not so pale.—I tell you yet again, Banquo's buried; he cannot come out on's grave.

DOCTOR

Even so?

LADY MACBETH

To bed, to bed! there's knocking at the gate: come, come, come, come, give me your hand. What's done cannot be undone.—To bed, to bed, to bed!

[*Exit.*

DOCTOR
Will she go now to bed?
GENTLEWOMAN
Directly.
DOCTOR
Foul whisperings are abroad: unnatural deeds
Do breed unnatural troubles: infected minds
To their deaf pillows will discharge their secrets:
More needs she the divine than the physician.
God, God forgive us all! Look after her;
Remove from her the means of all annoyance,
And still keep eyes upon her. So, good night:
My mind she has mated, and amazed my sight.
I think, but dare not speak.
GENTLEWOMAN
Good night, good doctor. [*Exeunt.*

ACT FIVE SCENE TWO

The country near Dunsinane.

Drum and colours. Enter MENTEITH, CAITHNESS, ANGUS, LENNOX, *and* Soldiers.

MENTEITH
The English power is near, led on by Malcolm,
His uncle Siward and the good Macduff:
Revenges burn in them; for their dear causes
Would to the bleeding and the grim alarm
Excite the mortified man.
ANGUS
Near Birnam wood
Shall we well meet them; that way are they coming.
CAITHNESS
Who knows if Donalbain be with his brother?
LENNOX
For certain, sir, he is not: I have a file
Of all the gentry: there is Siward's son,
And many unrough youths that even now 11
Protest their first of manhood.
MENTEITH
What does the tyrant?
CAITHNESS
Great Dunsinane he strongly fortifies:
Some say he's mad; others that lesser hate him
Do call it valiant fury: but, for certain,
He cannot buckle his distemper'd cause
Within the belt of rule.
ANGUS
Now does he feel
His secret murders sticking on his hands;
Now minutely revolts upbraid his faith-breach;
Those he commands move only in command,
Nothing in love: now does he feel his title 23
Hang loose about him, like a giant's robe
Upon a dwarfish thief.
MENTEITH
Who then shall blame
His pester'd senses to recoil and start,
When all that is within him does condemn
Itself for being there?
CAITHNESS
Well, march we on,
To give obedience where 'tis truly owed:
Meet we the medicine of the sickly weal,
And with him pour we in our country's purge
Each drop of us.
LENNOX
Or so much as it needs,
To dew the sovereign flower and drown the weeds. 37
Make we our march towards Birnam.
[*Exeunt, marching.*

ACT FIVE SCENE THREE

Dunsinane. A room in the castle.

Enter MACBETH, *Doctor, and* Attendants.

MACBETH
Bring me no more reports; let them fly all:
Till Birnam wood remove to Dunsinane,
I cannot taint with fear. What's the boy Malcolm?
Was he not born of woman? The spirits that know
All mortal consequences have pronounced me thus:
'Fear not, Macbeth; no man that's born of woman
Shall e'er have power upon thee.' Then fly, false thanes, [38]
And mingle with the English epicures:
The mind I sway by and the heart I bear
Shall never sag with doubt nor shake with fear.

Enter a Servant.

The devil damn thee black, thou cream-faced loon! 13
Where got'st thou that goose look?
SERVANT
There is ten thousand—
MACBETH
Geese, villain!
SERVANT
Soldiers, sir.
MACBETH
Go, prick thy face, and over-red thy fear,
Thou lily-liver'd boy. What soldiers, patch?
Death of thy soul! those linen cheeks of thine
Are counsellors to fear. What soldiers, whey-face?

SERVANT
The English force, so please you.
MACBETH
Take thy face hence. [*Exit Servant.*
Seyton!—I am sick at heart,
When I behold—Seyton, I say!—This push
Will cheer me ever, or disseat me now. [39]
I have lived long enough: my way of life [40]
Is fall'n into the sear, the yellow leaf;
And that which should accompany old age,
As honour, love, obedience, troops of friends,
I must not look to have; but, in their stead,
Curses, not loud but deep, mouth-honour, breath,
Which the poor heart would fain deny, and dare not.
Seyton!

Enter SEYTON.

SEYTON
What is your gracious pleasure?
MACBETH
What news more? 36
SEYTON
All is confirm'd, my lord, which was reported.
MACBETH
I'll fight till from my bones my flesh be hack'd.
Give me my armour.
SEYTON
'Tis not needed yet.
MACBETH
I'll put it on.
Send out moe horses; skirr the country round; 43
Hang those that talk of fear. Give me mine armour.
How does your patient, doctor?
DOCTOR
Not so sick, my lord,
As she is troubled with thick-coming fancies,
That keep her from her rest.
MACBETH
Cure her of that.
Canst thou not minister to a mind diseased, 50
Pluck from the memory a rooted sorrow,
Raze out the written troubles of the brain
And with some sweet oblivious antidote
Cleanse the stuff'd bosom of that perilous stuff [41]
Which weighs upon the heart?
DOCTOR
Therein the patient
Must minister to himself.
MACBETH
Throw physic to the dogs; I'll none of it.
Come, put mine armour on; give me my staff.
Seyton, send out. Doctor, the thanes fly from me.
Come, sir, dispatch. If thou couldst, doctor, cast 61
The water of my land, find her disease,
And purge it to a sound and pristine health,
I would applaud thee to the very echo,
That should applaud again.—Pull't off, I say.—
What rhubarb, senna, or what purgative drug, [42]
Would scour these English hence? Hear'st thou of them?
DOCTOR
Ay, my good lord; your royal preparation
Makes us hear something.
MACBETH
Bring it after me. [43]
I will not be afraid of death and bane,
Till Birnam forest come to Dunsinane. 73
DOCTOR
[*Aside*] Were I from Dunsinane away and clear,
Profit again should hardly draw me here.
[*Exeunt.*

ACT FIVE SCENE FOUR

Country near Birnam wood.

Drum and colours. Enter MALCOLM, *old* SIWARD *and his* Son, MACDUFF, MENTEITH, CAITHNESS, ANGUS, LENNOX, ROSS, *and* Soldiers, *marching.*

MALCOLM
Cousins, I hope the days are near at hand
That chambers will be safe.
MENTEITH
We doubt it nothing.
SIWARD
What wood is this before us?
MENTEITH
The wood of Birnam.
MALCOLM
Let every soldier hew him down a bough
And bear't before him: thereby shall we shadow
The numbers of our host and make discovery
Err in report of us.
SOLDIERS
It shall be done.
SIWARD
We learn no other but the confident tyrant
Keeps still in Dunsinane, and will endure
Our setting down before 't.
MALCOLM
'Tis his main hope: 14
For where there is advantage to be given,
Both more and less have given him the revolt,
And none serve with him but constrained things
Whose hearts are absent too.

MACDUFF
Let our just censures
Attend the true event, and put we on
Industrious soldiership.
SIWARD
The time approaches
That will with due decision make us know
What we shall say we have and what we owe.
Thoughts speculative their unsure hopes relate,
But certain issue strokes must arbitrate: 26
Towards which advance the war.
[*Exeunt, marching.*

ACT FIVE SCENE FIVE

Dunsinane. Within the castle.

Enter MACBETH , SEYTON, *and* Soldiers, *with drum and colours.*

MACBETH
Hang out our banners on the outward walls;
The cry is still 'They come:' our castle's strength
Will laugh a siege to scorn: here let them lie
Till famine and the ague eat them up:
Were they not forced with those that should be ours,
We might have met them dareful, beard to beard,
And beat them backward home.
[*A cry of women within.*
What is that noise?
SEYTON
It is the cry of women, my good lord. [*Exit.*
MACBETH
I have almost forgot the taste of fears:
The time has been, my senses would have cool'd 11
To hear a night-shriek; and my fell of hair
Would at a dismal treatise rouse and stir
As life were in't: I have supp'd full with horrors;
Direness, familiar to my slaughterous thoughts,
Cannot once start me.

Re-enter SEYTON.

Wherefore was that cry?
SEYTON
The queen, my lord, is dead.
MACBETH
She should have died hereafter;
There would have been a time for such a word.
To-morrow, and to-morrow, and to-morrow,
Creeps in this petty pace from day to day 22
To the last syllable of recorded time,
And all our yesterdays have lighted fools
The way to dusty death. Out, out, brief candle!
Life's but a walking shadow, a poor player
That struts and frets his hour upon the stage
And then is heard no more: it is a tale
Told by an idiot, full of sound and fury,
Signifying nothing.

Enter a Messenger.

Thou comest to use thy tongue; thy story quickly.
MESSENGER
Gracious my lord, 32
I should report that which I say I saw,
But know not how to do it.
MACBETH
Well, say, sir.
MESSENGER
As I did stand my watch upon the hill,
I look'd toward Birnam, and anon, methought,
The wood began to move.
MACBETH
Liar and slave!
MESSENGER
Let me endure your wrath, if't be not so:
Within this three mile may you see it coming;
I say, a moving grove.
MACBETH
If thou speak'st false,
Upon the next tree shalt thou hang alive,
Till famine cling thee: if thy speech be sooth,
I care not if thou dost for me as much. 46
I pull in resolution, and begin
To doubt the equivocation of the fiend
That lies like truth: 'Fear not, till Birnam wood
Do come to Dunsinane:' and now a wood
Comes toward Dunsinane. Arm, arm, and out!
If this which he avouches does appear,
There is nor flying hence nor tarrying here.
I 'gin to be aweary of the sun,
And wish the estate o' the world were now
undone. 56
Ring the alarum-bell! Blow, wind! come, wrack!
At least we'll die with harness on our back.
[*Exeunt.*

ACT FIVE SCENE SIX

Dunsinane. Before the castle.

Drum and colours. Enter MALCOLM, *old* SIWARD, MACDUFF, *and their* Army, *with boughs.*

MALCOLM
Now near enough: your leafy screens throw down,
And show like those you are. You, worthy uncle,
Shall, with my cousin, your right-noble son,

Lead our first battle: worthy Macduff and we
Shall take upon 's what else remains to do,
According to our order.

SIWARD

Fare you well.
Do we but find the tyrant's power to-night,
Let us be beaten, if we cannot fight.

MACDUFF

Make all our trumpets speak; give them all breath, 11
Those clamorous harbingers of blood and death.
[*Exeunt.*

ACT FIVE SCENE SEVEN

Another part of the field.

Alarums. Enter MACBETH.

MACBETH

They have tied me to a stake; I cannot fly,
But, bear-like, I must fight the course. What's he
That was not born of woman? Such a one
Am I to fear, or none.

Enter Young SIWARD.

YOUNG SIWARD

What is thy name?

MACBETH

Thou'lt be afraid to hear it.

YOUNG SIWARD

No; though thou call'st thyself a hotter name
Than any is in hell.

MACBETH

My name's Macbeth.

YOUNG SIWARD

The devil himself could not pronounce a title
More hateful to mine ear.

MACBETH

No, nor more fearful.

YOUNG SIWARD

Thou liest, abhorred tyrant; with my sword 13
I'll prove the lie thou speak'st.
[*They fight and young Siward is slain.*

MACBETH

Thou wast born of woman
But swords I smile at, weapons laugh to scorn,
Brandish'd by man that's of a woman born. [*Exit.*

Alarums. Enter MACDUFF.

MACDUFF

That way the noise is. Tyrant, show thy face!
If thou be'st slain and with no stroke of mine,
My wife and children's ghosts will haunt me still.
I cannot strike at wretched kerns, whose arms
Are hired to bear their staves: either thou, Macbeth,
Or else my sword with an unbatter'd edge
I sheathe again undeeded. There thou shouldst be; 25
By this great clatter, one of greatest note
Seems bruited. Let me find him, fortune!
And more I beg not. [*Exit. Alarums.*

Enter MALCOLM *and old* SIWARD.

SIWARD

This way, my lord; the castle's gently render'd:
The tyrant's people on both sides do fight;
The noble thanes do bravely in the war;
The day almost itself professes yours,
And little is to do.

MALCOLM

We have met with foes
That strike beside us.

SIWARD

Enter, sir, the castle. 36
[*Exeunt. Alarums.*

ACT FIVE SCENE EIGHT

Another part of the field.

Enter MACBETH.

MACBETH

Why should I play the Roman fool, and die
On mine own sword? whiles I see lives, the gashes
Do better upon them.

Enter MACDUFF.

MACDUFF

Turn, hell-hound, turn!

MACBETH

Of all men else I have avoided thee:
But get thee back; my soul is too much charged
With blood of thine already.

MACDUFF

I have no words:
My voice is in my sword: thou bloodier villain
Than terms can give thee out!
[*They fight.*

MACBETH

Thou losest labour:
As easy mayst thou the intrenchant air
With thy keen sword impress as make me bleed: 14
Let fall thy blade on vulnerable crests;
I bear a charmed life, which must not yield,
To one of woman born.

MACDUFF

Despair thy charm;
And let the angel whom thou still hast served

Tell thee, Macduff was from his mother's womb
Untimely ripp'd.

MACBETH

Accursed be that tongue that tells me so,
For it hath cow'd my better part of man!
And be these juggling fiends no more believed,
That palter with us in a double sense;
That keep the word of promise to our ear,
And break it to our hope. I'll not fight with thee.

MACDUFF

Then yield thee, coward,
And live to be the show and gaze o' the time:
We'll have thee, as our rarer monsters are,
Painted upon a pole, and underwrit,
'Here may you see the tyrant.'

MACBETH

I will not yield,
To kiss the ground before young Malcolm's feet,
And to be baited with the rabble's curse.
Though Birnam wood be come to Dunsinane,
And thou opposed, being of no woman born,
Yet I will try the last. Before my body
I throw my warlike shield. Lay on, Macduff,
And damn'd be him that first cries 'Hold, enough!'
[*Exeunt, fighting. Alarums.*

Retreat. Flourish. Enter, with drum and colours, MALCOLM, *old* SIWARD, ROSS, *the other* Thanes, *and* Soldiers.

MALCOLM

I would the friends we miss were safe arrived.

SIWARD

Some must go off: and yet, by these I see,
So great a day as this is cheaply bought.

MALCOLM

Macduff is missing, and your noble son.

ROSS

Your son, my lord, has paid a soldier's debt:
He only lived but till he was a man;
The which no sooner had his prowess confirm'd
In the unshrinking station where he fought,
But like a man he died.

SIWARD

Then he is dead?

ROSS

Ay, and brought off the field: your cause of sorrow
Must not be measured by his worth, for then
It hath no end.

SIWARD

Had he his hurts before?

ROSS

Ay, on the front.

SIWARD

Why then, God's soldier be he!
Had I as many sons as I have hairs,
I would not wish them to a fairer death:
And so, his knell is knoll'd.

MALCOLM

He's worth more sorrow,
And that I'll spend for him.

SIWARD

He's worth no more:
They say he parted well, and paid his score:
And so, God be with him! Here comes newer comfort.

Re-enter MACDUFF, *with* MACBETH'S *head.*

MACDUFF

Hail, king! for so thou art: behold, where stands
The usurper's cursed head: the time is free:
I see thee compass'd with thy kingdom's pearl,
That speak my salutation in their minds;
Whose voices I desire aloud with mine:
Hail, King of Scotland!

ALL

Hail, King of Scotland! [*Flourish.*

MALCOLM

We shall not spend a large expense of time
Before we reckon with your several loves,
And make us even with you. My thanes and kinsmen,
Henceforth be earls, the first that ever Scotland
In such an honour named. What's more to do,
Which would be planted newly with the time,
As calling home our exiled friends abroad
That fled the snares of watchful tyranny;
Producing forth the cruel ministers
Of this dead butcher and his fiend-like queen,
Who, as 'tis thought, by self and violent hands
Took off her life; this, and what needful else
That calls upon us, by the grace of Grace,
We will perform in measure, time and place:
So, thanks to all at once and to each one,
Whom we invite to see us crown'd at Scone.
[*Flourish. Exeunt.*

Notes

1. Perhaps we should follow the punctuation of the Folio, and place a note of interrogation after *'again.'*
2. Damned quarrel; – Johnson's, perhaps unnecessary, emendation of Folios, *'damned quarry'* (*cp.* IV. iii. 235); but Holinshed uses 'quarrel' in the corresponding passage.
3. Many emendations and interpretations have been advanced for this passage; Koppel's explanation (*Shakespeare Studien,* 1896) is as follows:—"he faced the slave, who never found time for the preliminary formalities of a duel, *i.e.* shaking hands with and

bidding farewell to the opponent"; seemingly, however, *'which'* should have *'he'* (*i.e.* Macbeth) and not *'slave'* as its antecedent.

4. And the very ports they blow; – Johnson conjectured *'various'* for *'very'*; Pope reads *'points'* for *'ports'*; Clar. Press edd. *'orts'*; *'blow* = 'blow upon.'
5. Weird; – Folios, *'weyward'* (prob. = *'weird'*); Keightley, *'weyard.'*
6. As thick as hail Came post; – Rowe's emendation; Folios read *'As thick as tale Can post.'*
7. The difficulty of these lines arises from the repeated words *'that which'* and some editors have consequently placed the inverted commas after *'undone'*; but *'that which'* is probably due to the same expression in the previous line, and we should perhaps read *'and that's which'* or *'and that's what.'*
8. Martlet; – Rowe's emendation of Folios, *'Barlet.'*
9. Loved mansionry; – Theobald's emendation of Folios, *'loved mansonry'*; Pope (ed. 2), *'loved masonry.'*
10. Jutty, frieze; – Pope, *'jutting frieze'*; Staunton conjectured *'jutty, nor frieze,'* &c.
11. Most; – Rowe's emendation of Folios, *'must'*; Collier MS. *'much.'*
12. Shoal; – Theobald's emendation of Folios 1, 2, *'schoole.'*
13. Like the poor cat i' the adage; – 'The cat would eat fyshe, and would not wet her feete,' Heywood's *Proverbs;* the low Latin form of the same proverb is:—

    "Catus amat pisces, sed non vult tingere plantas."

14. Do more; – Rowe's emendation of Folios, *'no more.'*
15. Sleep; – Steevens conjectured *'sleeper,'* but no emendation is necessary; the pause after *'sleep'* is evidently equivalent to a syllable.
16. Tarquin's ravishing strides; – Pope's emendation; Folios, *'Tarquins ravishing sides.'*
17. Sure; – Pope's conjecture, adopted by Capell; Folios 1, 2, *'sowre.'*
18. Which way they walk; – Rowe's emendation; Folios, *'which they may walk.'*
19. There are no inverted commas in the Folios. The arrangement in the text is generally followed.
20. You with the perfect spy o' the time; – Johnson conjectured *'you with a'*; Tyrwhitt conjectured *'you with the perfect spot, the time'*; Beckett conjectured *'you with the perfectry o' the time'*; Grant White, from Collier MS., *'you, with a perfect spy, o' the time'*; Schmidt interprets *'spy'* to mean "an advanced guard; that time which will precede the time of the deed, and indicate that it is at hand"; according to others 'spy' = the person who gives the information; the simplest explanation is, perhaps, 'the exact spying out of the time,' *i.e.* 'the moment on't,' which in the text follows in apposition.
21. Our peace; – so Folio 1; Folios 2, 3, 4, *'our place.'*
22. 'Tis better thee without than he within; – probably *'he'* instead of *'him'* for the sake of effective antithesis with *'thee'*; unless, as is possible, *'he within'* = 'he in this room.'
23. Time has; – Folio 1, *'times has'*; Folios 2, 3, 4, *'times have'*; the reading of the First Folio is probably what Shakespeare intended.
24. If trembling I inhabit then; – various emendations have been proposed, *e.g. 'I inhibit,'* = *'me inhibit,' 'I inhibit thee,' 'I inherit,'* &c.; probably the text is correct, and the words mean 'If I then put on the habit of trembling,' *i.e.* 'If I invest myself in trembling' *(cp.* Koppel, p. 76).
25. The Folios read:—

    "It will have blood they say;
    Blood will have blood."

26. In deed; – Theobald's emendation of Folios, *'indeed'*; Hanmer, *'in deeds.'*
27. Loves; – Halliwell conjectured *'Lives'*; Staunton conjectured *'Loves evil.'*
28. The most pious Edward, i.e. – Edward the Confessor.
29. Rebellion's head; – Theobald's conjecture, adopted by Hanmer; Folios read *'Rebellious dead'*; Warburton's conjecture, adopted by Theobald, *'Rebellious head.'*
30. When we are traitors And do not know ourselves, i.e. – 'when we are accounted traitors, and do not know that we are, having no consciousness of guilt. Hanmer, *'know't o.'*; Keightley, *'know it ourselves'*; but no change seems necessary.
31. When we hold rumour, – &c.; *i.e.* 'when we interpret rumour in accordance with our fear, yet know not exactly what it is we fear.'
32. Each way and move; – Theobald conjectured *'Each way and wave'*; Capell, *'And move each way'*; Steevens conjectured *'And each way move'*; Johnson conjectured *'Each way, and move —'*; Jackson conjectured *'Each wail and moan'*; Ingleby conjectured *'Which way we move'*; Anonymous conjecture, *'And move each wave'*; Staunton conjectured *'Each sway and move'*; Daniel conjectured *'Each way it moves'*; Camb. edd. conjectured *'Each way and none'*; perhaps *'Each way we move'* is the simplest reading of the words.
33. Do worse, i.e. – "let her and her children be destroyed without warning" (Johnson); (Hanmer, *'do less'*; Capell, *'do less'*).
34. Deserve; – Warburton's emendation, adopted by Theobald; Folios 1, 2, *'discerne'*; Folios 3, 4, *'discern'*; —, *'and wisdom'*; there is some corruption of text here, probably a line has dropped out. Hanmer reads *''tis wisdom'*; Steevens conjectured *'and wisdom is it'*; Collier conjectured *'and 'tis wisdom'*; Staunton conjectured *'and wisdom 'tis'* or *'and wisdom bids'*; Keightley, *'and wisdom 'twere.'*
35. Died every day she lived, – "lived a life of daily mortification" (Delius).
36. Tune; – Rowe's emendation of Folios, *'time.'*
37. Sense is shut; – Rowe's emendation of Folios, *'sense are shut'*; S. Walker's conjecture, adopted by Dyce, *'sense' are shut.* The reading of the Folio probably gives the right reading, 'sense' being taken as a plural.
38. Then, i.e. – the thanes.
39. Cheer; – Percy's conjecture, adopted by Dyce, *'chair'*; —; *'disseat,'* Jennens's and Capell's conjecture, adopted by Steevens; Folio 1, *'dis-eate'*; Folios 2, 3, 4, *'disease'*; Bailey conjectured *disseize'*; Daniel conjectured *'defeat'*; Furness, *'dis-ease'*; Perring conjectured *'disheart.'*

40. Way of life; – Johnson proposed the unnecessary emendation *'May of life,'* and several editors have accepted the conjecture.
41. Stuff'd; – Folios 2, 3, 4, *'stuft';* Pope, *'full';* Steeven's conjecture, adopted by Hunter, *'foul';* Anonymous conjecture, *'fraught,' 'press'd';* Bailey conjectured *'stain'd';* Mull conjectured *'steep'd':* —; *'stuff';* so Folios 3, 4; Jackson conjectured *'tuft';* Collier (ed. 2). from Collier MS., *'grief';* Keightley, *'matter';* Anonymous conjecture, *'slough,' 'freight';* Kinnear conjectured *'fraught.'*
42. Senna; – so Folio 4; Folio 1, *'Cyme';* Folios 2, 3, *'Caeny';* Bulloch conjectured *'sirrah.'*
43. It, – i.e. the armour.

OTHELLO
THE MOOR OF VENICE

OTHELLO
THE MOOR OF VENICE

DRAMATIS PERSONAE

DUKE OF VENICE.
BRABANTIO, a senator.
Other Senators.
GRATIANO, brother to Brabantio.
LODOVICO, kinsman to Brabantio.
OTHELLO, a noble Moor in the service of the Venetian state.
CASSIO, his lieutenant.
IAGO, his ancient.
RODERIGO, a Venetian gentleman.
MONTANO, Othello's predecessor in the government of Cyprus.
Clown, servant to Othello.
DESDEMONA, daughter to Brabantio and wife to Othello.
EMILIA, wife to Iago.
BIANCA, mistress to Cassio.
Sailor, Messenger, Herald, Officers, Gentlemen, Musicians, and Attendants.

SCENE : *Venice: a Sea-port in Cyprus.*

ACT ONE SCENE ONE

Venice. A street.

Enter RODERIGO *and* IAGO.

RODERIGO
Tush! never tell me; I take it much unkindly
That thou, Iago, who hast had my purse
As if the strings were thine, shouldst know of this.

IAGO
'Sblood, but you will not hear me:
If ever I did dream of such a matter,
Abhor me.

RODERIGO
Thou told'st me thou didst hold him in thy hate.

IAGO
Despise me, if I do not. Three great ones of the city,
In personal suit to make me his lieutenant,
Off-capp'd to him: and, by the faith of man,
I know my price, I am worth no worse a place:
But he, as loving his own pride and purposes,
Evades them, with a bombast circumstance
Horribly stuff'd with epithets of war;
And, in conclusion, [1]
Nonsuits my mediators; for, 'Certes,' says he,
'I have already chose my officer.'
And what was he?
Forsooth, a great arithmetician,
One Michael Cassio, a Florentine,
A fellow almost damn'd in a fair wife; [2]
That never set a squadron in the field,
Nor the division of a battle knows
More than a spinster; unless the bookish theoric,
Wherein the toged consuls can propose
As masterly as he: mere prattle, without practice,
Is all his soldiership. But he, sir, had the election:
And I, of whom his eyes had seen the proof

At Rhodes, at Cyprus and on other grounds
Christian and heathen, must be be-lee'd and calm'd 32
By debitor and creditor: this counter-caster,
He, in good time, must his lieutenant be,
And I—God bless the mark!—his Moorship's ancient.

RODERIGO
By heaven, I rather would have been his hangman.

IAGO
Why, there's no remedy; 'tis the curse of service,
Preferment goes by letter and affection,
And not by old gradation, where each second
Stood heir to the first. Now, sir, be judge yourself,
Whether I in any just term am affined
To love the Moor.

RODERIGO
I would not follow him then. 44

IAGO
O, sir, content you;
I follow him to serve my turn upon him:
We cannot all be masters, nor all masters
Cannot be truly follow'd. You shall mark
Many a duteous and knee-crooking knave,
That, doting on his own obsequious bondage,
Wears out his time, much like his master's ass,
For nought but provender, and when he's old, cashier'd:
Whip me such honest knaves. Others there are
Who, trimm'd in forms and visages of duty,
Keep yet their hearts attending on themselves,
And, throwing but shows of service on their lords,
Do well thrive by them and when they have lined their coats
Do themselves homage: these fellows have some soul;
And such a one do I profess myself. For, sir,
It is as sure as you are Roderigo,
Were I the Moor, I would not be Iago:
In following him, I follow but myself;
Heaven is my judge, not I for love and duty,
But seeming so, for my peculiar end: 67
For when my outward action doth demonstrate
The native act and figure of my heart
In compliment extern, 'tis not long after
But I will wear my heart upon my sleeve
For daws to peck at: I am not what I am.

RODERIGO
What a full fortune does the thicklips owe,
If he can carry't thus!

IAGO
Call up her father,
Rouse him: make after him, poison his delight,
Proclaim him in the streets; incense her kinsmen,
And, though he in a fertile climate dwell, 78
Plague him with flies: though that his joy be joy,
Yet throw such changes of vexation on't, [3]
As it may lose some colour.

RODERIGO
Here is her father's house; I'll call aloud.

IAGO
Do, with like timorous accent and dire yell
As when, by night and negligence, the fire
Is spied in populous cities.

RODERIGO
What, ho, Brabantio! Signior Brabantio, ho!

IAGO
Awake! what, ho, Brabantio! thieves! thieves! thieves!
Look to your house, your daughter and your bags! 90
Thieves! thieves!

BRABANTIO *appears above, at a window.*

BRABANTIO
What is the reason of this terrible summons?
What is the matter there?

RODERIGO
Signior, is all your family within?

IAGO
Are your doors lock'd?

BRABANTIO
Why, wherefore ask you this?

IAGO
'Zounds, sir, you're robb'd; for shame, put on your gown;
Your heart is burst, you have lost half your soul;
Even now, now, very now, an old black ram
Is tupping your white ewe. Arise, arise;
Awake the snorting citizens with the bell, 101
Or else the devil will make a grandsire of you:
Arise, I say.

BRABANTIO
What, have you lost your wits?

RODERIGO
Most reverend signior, do you know my voice?

BRABANTIO
Not I: what are you?

RODERIGO
My name is Roderigo.

BRABANTIO
The worser welcome:
I have charged thee not to haunt about my doors:
In honest plainness thou hast heard me say
My daughter is not for thee; and now, in madness,
Being full of supper and distempering draughts,
Upon malicious bravery, dost thou come 113
To start my quiet.

RODERIGO
Sir, sir, sir,—
BRABANTIO
But thou must needs be sure
My spirit and my place have in them power
To make this bitter to thee.
RODERIGO
Patience, good sir.
BRABANTIO
What tell'st thou me of robbing? this is Venice;
My house is not a grange.
RODERIGO
Most grave Brabantio,
In simple and pure soul I come to you.
IAGO
'Zounds, sir, you are one of those that will not serve God, if the devil bid you. Because we come to do you service and you think we are ruffians, you'll have your daughter covered with a Barbary horse; you'll have your nephews neigh to you; you'll have coursers for cousins and gennets for germans.
BRABANTIO
What profane wretch art thou?
IAGO
I am one, sir, that comes to tell you your daughter and the Moor are now making the beast with two backs.
BRABANTIO
Thou art a villain.
IAGO
You are—a senator.
BRABANTIO
This thou shalt answer; I know thee, Roderigo.
RODERIGO
Sir, I will answer any thing. But, I beseech you,
If't be your pleasure and most wise consent,
As partly I find it is, that your fair daughter,
At this odd-even and dull watch o' the night,
Transported, with no worse nor better guard
But with a knave of common hire, a gondolier,
To the gross clasps of a lascivious Moor,—
If this be known to you and your allowance,
We then have done you bold and saucy wrongs;
But if you know not this, my manners tell me
We have your wrong rebuke. Do not believe
That, from the sense of all civility,
I thus would play and trifle with your reverence:
Your daughter, if you have not given her leave,
I say again, hath made a gross revolt;
Tying her duty, beauty, wit and fortunes
In an extravagant and wheeling stranger
Of here and every where. Straight satisfy yourself:
If she be in her chamber or your house,
Let loose on me the justice of the state
For thus deluding you.
BRABANTIO
Strike on the tinder, ho!
Give me a taper! call up all my people!
This accident is not unlike my dream:
Belief of it oppresses me already.
Light, I say! light! [*Exit above.*
IAGO
Farewell; for I must leave you:
It seems not meet, nor wholesome to my place,
To be produced—as, if I stay, I shall—
Against the Moor: for, I do know, the state,
However this may gall him with some check,
Cannot with safety cast him, for he's embark'd
With such loud reason to the Cyprus wars,
Which even now stand in act, that, for their souls,
Another of his fathom they have none,
To lead their business: in which regard,
Though I do hate him as I do hell-pains.
Yet, for necessity of present life,
I must show out a flag and sign of love,
Which is indeed but sign. That you shall surely find him,
Lead to the Sagittary the raised search;
And there will I be with him. So, farewell. [*Exit.*

Enter, below, BRABANTIO, *and* Servants *with torches.*

BRABANTIO
It is too true an evil: gone she is;
And what's to come of my despised time
Is nought but bitterness. Now, Roderigo,
Where didst thou see her? O unhappy girl!
With the Moor, say'st thou? Who would be a father!
How didst thou know 'twas she? O, she deceives me
Past thought! What said she to you? Get more tapers:
Raise all my kindred. Are they married, think you?
RODERIGO
Truly, I think they are.
BRABANTIO
O heaven! How got she out? O treason of the blood!
Fathers, from hence trust not your daughters' minds
By what you see them act. Is there not charms
By which the property of youth and maidhood
May be abused? Have you not read, Roderigo,
Of some such thing?
RODERIGO
Yes, sir, I have indeed.
BRABANTIO
Call up my brother. O, would you had had her!
Some one way, some another. Do you know
Where we may apprehend her and the Moor?

RODERIGO
I think I can discover him, if you please,
To get good guard and go along with me.
BRABANTIO
Pray you, lead on. At every house I'll call;
I may command at most. Get weapons, ho!
And raise some special officers of night.
On, good Roderigo: I'll deserve your pains.
[*Exeunt.*

ACT ONE SCENE TWO

Another street.

Enter OTHELLO, IAGO, *and* Attendants *with torches.*

IAGO
Though in the trade of war I have slain men,
Yet do I hold it very stuff o' the conscience
To do no contrived murder: I lack iniquity
Sometimes to do me service: nine or ten times
I had thought to have yerk'd him here under the ribs.
OTHELLO
'Tis better as it is.
IAGO
Nay, but he prated,
And spoke such scurvy and provoking terms
Against your honour
That, with the little godliness I have,
I did full hard forbear him. But, I pray you, sir,
Are you fast married? Be assured of this,
That the magnifico is much beloved,
And hath in his effect a voice potential
As double as the duke's: he will divorce you;
Or put upon you what restraint and grievance
The law, with all his might to enforce it on,
Will give him cable.
OTHELLO
Let him do his spite;
My services which I have done the signiory
Shall out-tongue his complaints. 'Tis yet to know,—
Which, when I know that boasting is an honour,
I shall promulgate—I fetch my life and being
From men of royal siege, and my demerits
May speak unbonneted to as proud a fortune
As this that I have reach'd: for know, Iago,
But that I love the gentle Desdemona,
I would not my unhoused free condition
Put into circumscription and confine
For the sea's worth. But, look! what lights come yond?
IAGO
Those are the raised father and his friends:
You were best go in.
OTHELLO
Not I; I must be found:
My parts, my title and my perfect soul
Shall manifest me rightly. Is it they?
IAGO
By Janus, I think no.

Enter CASSIO, *and certain* Officers *with torches.*

OTHELLO
The servants of the duke, and my lieutenant.
The goodness of the night upon you, friends!
What is the news?
CASSIO
The duke does greet you, general,
And he requires your haste-post-haste appearance,
Even on the instant.
OTHELLO
What is the matter, think you?
CASSIO
Something from Cyprus as I may divine:
It is a business of some heat: the galleys
Have sent a dozen sequent messengers
This very night at one another's heels,
And many of the consuls raised and met,
Are at the duke's already: you have been hotly call'd for;
When, being not at your lodging to be found,
The senate hath sent about three several guests
To search you out.
OTHELLO
'Tis well I am found by you.
I will but spend a word here in the house,
And go with you. [*Exit.*
CASSIO
Ancient, what makes he here?
IAGO
'Faith, he to-night hath boarded a land carack:
If it prove lawful prize, he's made for ever.
CASSIO
I do not understand.
IAGO
He's married.
CASSIO
To who?

Re-enter OTHELLO.

IAGO
Marry, to—Come, captain, will you go?
OTHELLO
Have with you.
CASSIO
Here comes another troop to seek for you.

IAGO
It is Brabantio. General, be advised;
He comes to bad intent.

Enter BRABANTIO, RODERIGO, *and* Officers *with torches and weapons.*

OTHELLO
Holla! stand there!
RODERIGO
Signior, it is the Moor.
BRABANTIO
Down with him, thief! [*They draw on both sides.*
IAGO
You, Roderigo! come, sir, I am for you.
OTHELLO
Keep up your bright swords, for the dew will rust them.
Good signior, you shall more command with years
Than with your weapons.
BRABANTIO
O thou foul thief, where hast thou stow'd my daughter?
Damn'd as thou art, thou hast enchanted her;
For I'll refer me to all things of sense,
If she in chains of magic were not bound,
Whether a maid so tender, fair and happy,
So opposite to marriage that she shunn'd
The wealthy curled darlings of our nation,
Would ever have, to incur a general mock,
Run from her guardage to the sooty bosom
Of such a thing as thou, to fear, not to delight.
Judge me the world, if 'tis not gross in sense [4]
That thou hast practised on her with foul charms,
Abused her delicate youth with drugs or minerals
That weaken motion: I'll have't disputed on; [5]
'Tis probable and palpable to thinking.
I therefore apprehend and do attach thee
For an abuser of the world, a practiser
Of arts inhibited and out of warrant.
Lay hold upon him: if he do resist,
Subdue him at his peril.
OTHELLO
Hold your hands,
Both you of my inclining, and the rest:
Were it my cue to fight, I should have known it
Without a prompter. Where will you that I go
To answer this your charge?
BRABANTIO
To prison, till fit time
Of law and course of direct session
Call thee to answer.
OTHELLO
What if I do obey?
How may the duke be therewith satisfied,
Whose messengers are here about my side,
Upon some present business of the state
To bring me to him?
FIRST OFFICER
'Tis true, most worthy signior;
The duke's in council and your noble self,
I am sure, is sent for.
BRABANTIO
How! the duke in council!
In this time of the night! Bring him away:
Mine's not an idle cause: the duke himself,
Or any of my brothers of the state,
Cannot but feel this wrong as 'twere their own;
For if such actions may have passage free,
Bond-slaves and pagans shall our statesmen be.
[*Exeunt.*

ACT ONE SCENE THREE

A council-chamber.

The DUKE *and* Senators *sitting at a table*; Officers *attending*.

DUKE OF VENICE
There is no composition in these news
That gives them credit.
FIRST SENATOR
Indeed, they are disproportion'd;
My letters say a hundred and seven galleys.
DUKE OF VENICE
And mine, a hundred and forty.
SECOND SENATOR
And mine, two hundred:
But though they jump not on a just account,—
As in these cases, where the aim reports,
'Tis oft with difference—yet do they all confirm
A Turkish fleet, and bearing up to Cyprus.
DUKE OF VENICE
Nay, it is possible enough to judgment:
I do not so secure me in the error,
But the main article I do approve
In fearful sense.
SAILOR
[*Within*] What, ho! what, ho! what, ho!
FIRST OFFICER
A messenger from the galleys.

Enter a Sailor.

DUKE OF VENICE
Now, what's the business?
SAILOR
The Turkish preparation makes for Rhodes;
So was I bid report here to the state [4]
By Signior Angelo.

DUKE OF VENICE
How say you by this change?
FIRST SENATOR
This cannot be,
By no assay of reason: 'tis a pageant,
To keep us in false gaze. When we consider
The importancy of Cyprus to the Turk,
And let ourselves again but understand,
That as it more concerns the Turk than Rhodes,
So may he with more facile question bear it,
For that it stands not in such warlike brace,
But altogether lacks the abilities
That Rhodes is dress'd in: if we make thought of this,
We must not think the Turk is so unskilful
To leave that latest which concerns him first,
Neglecting an attempt of ease and gain,
To wake and wage a danger profitless.
DUKE OF VENICE
Nay, in all confidence, he's not for Rhodes.
FIRST OFFICER
Here is more news.

Enter a Messenger.

MESSENGER
The Ottomites, reverend and gracious,
Steering with due course towards the isle of Rhodes,
Have there injointed them with an after fleet.
FIRST SENATOR
Ay, so I thought. How many, as you guess? [4]
MESSENGER
Of thirty sail: and now they do re-stem
Their backward course, bearing with frank appearance
Their purposes toward Cyprus. Signior Montano,
Your trusty and most valiant servitor,
With his free duty recommends you thus,
And prays you to believe him.
DUKE OF VENICE
'Tis certain, then, for Cyprus.
Marcus Luccicos, is not he in town?
FIRST SENATOR
He's now in Florence.
DUKE OF VENICE
Write from us to him; post-post-haste dispatch.
FIRST SENATOR
Here comes Brabantio and the valiant Moor.

Enter BRABANTIO, OTHELLO, IAGO, RODERIGO, *and* Officers.

DUKE OF VENICE
Valiant Othello, we must straight employ you
Against the general enemy Ottoman.
[*To Brabantio*] I did not see you; welcome, gentle signior;
We lack'd your counsel and your help tonight.
BRABANTIO
So did I yours. Good your grace, pardon me;
Neither my place nor aught I heard of business
Hath raised me from my bed, nor doth the general care
Take hold on me, for my particular grief
Is of so flood-gate and o'erbearing nature
That it engluts and swallows other sorrows
And it is still itself.
DUKE OF VENICE
Why, what's the matter?
BRABANTIO
My daughter! O, my daughter!
DUKE OF VENICE, SENATOR
Dead?
BRABANTIO
Ay, to me;
She is abused, stol'n from me, and corrupted
By spells and medicines bought of mountebanks;
For nature so preposterously to err,
Being not deficient, blind, or lame of sense,
Sans witchcraft could not. [4]
DUKE OF VENICE
Whoe'er he be that in this foul proceeding
Hath thus beguiled your daughter of herself
And you of her, the bloody book of law [6]
You shall yourself read in the bitter letter
After your own sense, yea, though our proper son
Stood in your action.
BRABANTIO
Humbly I thank your grace.
Here is the man, this Moor, whom now, it seems,
Your special mandate for the state-affairs
Hath hither brought.
DUKE OF VENICE, SENATOR
We are very sorry for't.
DUKE OF VENICE
[*To Othello*] What, in your own part, can you say to this?
BRABANTIO
Nothing, but this is so.
OTHELLO
Most potent, grave, and reverend signiors,
My very noble and approved good masters,
That I have ta'en away this old man's daughter,
It is most true; true, I have married her:
The very head and front of my offending
Hath this extent, no more. Rude am I in my speech,
And little bless'd with the soft phrase of peace:
For since these arms of mine had seven years' pith,
Till now some nine moons wasted, they have used
Their dearest action in the tented field,
And little of this great world can I speak,
More than pertains to feats of broil and battle, [7]

And therefore little shall I grace my cause
In speaking for myself. Yet, by your gracious patience,
I will a round unvarnish'd tale deliver
Of my whole course of love; what drugs, what charms,
What conjuration and what mighty magic,
For such proceeding I am charged withal,
I won his daughter.

BRABANTIO
A maiden never bold;
Of spirit so still and quiet, that her motion
Blush'd at herself; and she, in spite of nature,
Of years, of country, credit, every thing,
To fall in love with what she fear'd to look on!
It is a judgment maim'd and most imperfect
That will confess perfection so could err
Against all rules of nature, and must be driven
To find out practises of cunning hell,
Why this should be. I therefore vouch again
That with some mixtures powerful o'er the blood,
Or with some dram conjured to this effect,
He wrought upon her.

DUKE OF VENICE
To vouch this, is no proof,
Without more wider and more overt test [8]
Than these thin habits and poor likelihoods
Of modern seeming do prefer against him.

FIRST SENATOR
But, Othello, speak:
Did you by indirect and forced courses
Subdue and poison this young maid's affections?
Or came it by request and such fair question
As soul to soul affordeth?

OTHELLO
I do beseech you,
Send for the lady to the Sagittary,
And let her speak of me before her father:
If you do find me foul in her report,
The trust, the office I do hold of you,
Not only take away, but let your sentence [4]
Even fall upon my life.

DUKE OF VENICE
Fetch Desdemona hither.

OTHELLO
Ancient, conduct them; you best know the place.
[Exeunt Iago and Attendants.
And, till she come, as truly as to heaven
I do confess the vices of my blood, [4]
So justly to your grave ears I'll present
How I did thrive in this fair lady's love,
And she in mine.

DUKE OF VENICE
Say it, Othello.

OTHELLO
Her father loved me; oft invited me;
Still question'd me the story of my life,
From year to year, the battles, sieges, fortunes,
That I have pass'd.
I ran it through, even from my boyish days,
To the very moment that he bade me tell it;
Wherein I spake of most disastrous chances,
Of moving accidents by flood and field
Of hair-breadth scapes i' the imminent deadly breach,
Of being taken by the insolent foe
And sold to slavery, of my redemption thence
And portance in my travels' history: [9]
Wherein of antres vast and deserts idle,
Rough quarries, rocks and hills whose heads touch heaven,
It was my hint to speak,—such was the process;
And of the Cannibals that each other eat,
The Anthropophagi and men whose heads
Do grow beneath their shoulders. This to hear
Would Desdemona seriously incline:
But still the house-affairs would draw her thence:
Which ever as she could with haste dispatch,
She'ld come again, and with a greedy ear
Devour up my discourse: which I observing,
Took once a pliant hour, and found good means
To draw from her a prayer of earnest heart
That I would all my pilgrimage dilate,
Whereof by parcels she had something heard,
But not intentively: I did consent,
And often did beguile her of her tears,
When I did speak of some distressful stroke
That my youth suffer'd. My story being done,
She gave me for my pains a world of sighs: [10]
She swore, in faith, 'twas strange, 'twas passing strange,
'Twas pitiful, 'twas wondrous pitiful:
She wish'd she had not heard it, yet she wish'd
That heaven had made her such a man: she thank'd me,
And bade me, if I had a friend that loved her,
I should but teach him how to tell my story,
And that would woo her. Upon this hint I spake:
She loved me for the dangers I had pass'd,
And I loved her that she did pity them.
This only is the witchcraft I have used:
Here comes the lady; let her witness it.

Enter DESDEMONA , IAGO, *and* Attendants.

DUKE OF VENICE
I think this tale would win my daughter too.
Good Brabantio,
Take up this mangled matter at the best:
Men do their broken weapons rather use
Than their bare hands.

BRABANTIO
I pray you, hear her speak:
If she confess that she was half the wooer,
Destruction on my head, if my bad blame
Light on the man! Come hither, gentle mistress:
Do you perceive in all this noble company
Where most you owe obedience?

DESDEMONA
My noble father,
I do perceive here a divided duty:
To you I am bound for life and education;
My life and education both do learn me
How to respect you; you are the lord of duty;
I am hitherto your daughter: but here's my husband,
And so much duty as my mother show'd
To you, preferring you before her father,
So much I challenge that I may profess
Due to the Moor my lord.

BRABANTIO
God be wi' you! I have done.
Please it your grace, on to the state-affairs:
I had rather to adopt a child than get it.
Come hither, Moor:
I here do give thee that with all my heart
Which, but thou hast already, with all my heart [4]
I would keep from thee. For your sake, jewel,
I am glad at soul I have no other child:
For thy escape would teach me tyranny,
To hang clogs on them. I have done, my lord.

DUKE OF VENICE
Let me speak like yourself, and lay a sentence,
Which, as a grise or step, may help these lovers
Into your favour.
When remedies are past, the griefs are ended
By seeing the worst, which late on hopes depended.
To mourn a mischief that is past and gone
Is the next way to draw new mischief on.
What cannot be preserved when fortune takes
Patience her injury a mockery makes.
The robb'd that smiles steals something from the thief;
He robs himself that spends a bootless grief.

BRABANTIO
So let the Turk of Cyprus us beguile;
We lose it not, so long as we can smile.
He bears the sentence well that nothing bears
But the free comfort which from thence he hears,
But he bears both the sentence and the sorrow
That, to pay grief, must of poor patience borrow.
These sentences, to sugar, or to gall,
Being strong on both sides, are equivocal:
But words are words; I never yet did hear
That the bruised heart was pierced through the ear.
I humbly beseech you, proceed to the affairs of state.

DUKE OF VENICE
The Turk with a most mighty preparation makes for Cyprus. Othello, the fortitude of the place is best known to you; and though we have there a substitute of most allowed sufficiency, yet opinion, a sovereign mistress of effects, throws a more safer voice on you: you must therefore be content to slubber the gloss of your new fortunes with this more stubborn and boisterous expedition.

OTHELLO
The tyrant custom, most grave senators,
Hath made the flinty and steel couch of war
My thrice-driven bed of down: I do agnize
A natural and prompt alacrity
I find in hardness, and do undertake
These present wars against the Ottomites.
Most humbly therefore bending to your state,
I crave fit disposition for my wife.
Due reference of place and exhibition,
With such accommodation and besort
As levels with her breeding.

DUKE OF VENICE
If you please,
Be't at her father's.

BRABANTIO
I'll not have it so.

OTHELLO
Nor I.

DESDEMONA
Nor I; I would not there reside,
To put my father in impatient thoughts
By being in his eye. Most gracious duke,
To my unfolding lend your prosperous ear;
And let me find a charter in your voice,
To assist my simpleness.

DUKE OF VENICE
What would You, Desdemona?

DESDEMONA
That I did love the Moor to live with him,
My downright violence and storm of fortunes [11]
May trumpet to the world: my heart's subdued
Even to the very quality of my lord:
I saw Othello's visage in his mind,
And to his honour and his valiant parts
Did I my soul and fortunes consecrate.
So that, dear lords, if I be left behind,
A moth of peace, and he go to the war,
The rites for which I love him are bereft me,
And I a heavy interim shall support
By his dear absence. Let me go with him.

OTHELLO
Let her have your voices. [12]
Vouch with me, heaven, I therefore beg it not,
To please the palate of my appetite,

Nor to comply with heat—the young affects [13]
In me defunct—and proper satisfaction,
But to be free and bounteous to her mind:
And heaven defend your good souls, that you think
I will your serious and great business scant
For she is with me: no, when light-wing'd toys
Of feather'd Cupid seal with wanton dullness
My speculative and officed instruments,
That my disports corrupt and taint my business,
Let housewives make a skillet of my helm,
And all indign and base adversities
Make head against my estimation!

DUKE OF VENICE
Be it as you shall privately determine,
Either for her stay or going: the affair cries haste,
And speed must answer it.

FIRST SENATOR
You must away to-night.

OTHELLO
With all my heart.

DUKE OF VENICE
At nine i' the morning here w'll meet again.
Othello, leave some officer behind,
And he shall our commission bring to you;
With such things else of quality and respect
As doth import you.

OTHELLO
So please your grace, my ancient;
A man he is of honest and trust:
To his conveyance I assign my wife,
With what else needful your good grace shall think
To be sent after me.

DUKE OF VENICE
Let it be so.
Good night to every one.
[*To Brabantio*] And, noble signior,
If virtue no delighted beauty lack,
Your son-in-law is far more fair than black.

FIRST SENATOR
Adieu, brave Moor, use Desdemona well.

BRABANTIO
Look to her, Moor, if thou hast eyes to see:
She has deceived her father, and may thee.
[*Exeunt Duke, Senators, Officers, &c.*

OTHELLO
My life upon her faith! Honest Iago,
My Desdemona must I leave to thee:
I prithee, let thy wife attend on her:
And bring them after in the best advantage.
Come Desdemona; I have but an hour
Of love, of worldly matters and direction,
To spend with thee: we must obey the time.
[*Exeunt Othello and Desdemona.*

RODERIGO
Iago,—

IAGO
What say'st thou, noble heart?

RODERIGO
What will I do, thinkest thou?

IAGO
Why, go to bed, and sleep.

RODERIGO
I will incontinently drown myself.

IAGO
If thou dost, I shall never love thee after. Why, thou silly gentleman!

RODERIGO
It is silliness to live when to live is torment; and then have we a prescription to die when death is our physician.

IAGO
O villainous! I have looked upon the world for four times seven years; and since I could distinguish betwixt a benefit and an injury, I never found man that knew how to love himself. Ere I would say, I would drown myself for the love of a guinea-hen, I would change my humanity with a baboon.

RODERIGO
What should I do? I confess it is my shame to be so fond; but it is not in my virtue to amend it.

IAGO
Virtue! a fig! 'tis in ourselves that we are thus or thus. Our bodies are our gardens, to the which our wills are gardeners; so that if we will plant nettles, or sow lettuce, set hyssop and weed up thyme, supply it with one gender of herbs, or distract it with many, either to have it sterile with idleness, or manured with industry, why, the power and corrigible authority of this lies in our wills. If the balance of our lives had not one scale of reason to poise another of sensuality, the blood and baseness of our natures would conduct us to most preposterous conclusions: but we have reason to cool our raging motions, our carnal stings, our unbitted lusts, whereof I take this that you call love to be a sect or scion. [14]

RODERIGO
It cannot be.

IAGO
It is merely a lust of the blood and a permission of the will. Come, be a man. Drown thyself! drown cats and blind puppies. I have professed me thy friend and I confess me knit to thy deserving with cables of perdurable toughness; I could never better stead thee than now. Put money in thy purse; follow thou the wars; defeat thy favour with an usurped beard; I say, put money in thy purse. It cannot be that Desdemona should long continue her love to the Moor,—put

money in thy purse,—nor he his to her: it was a violent commencement, and thou shalt see an answerable sequestration:—put but money in thy purse. These Moors are changeable in their wills: fill thy purse with money:—the food that to him now is as luscious as locusts, shall be to him shortly as bitter as coloquintida. She must change for youth: when she is sated with his body, she will find the error of her choice: she must have change, she must: therefore put money in thy purse. If thou wilt needs damn thyself, do it a more delicate way than drowning. Make all the money thou canst: if sanctimony and a frail vow betwixt an erring barbarian and a supersubtle Venetian not too hard for my wits and all the tribe of hell, thou shalt enjoy her; therefore make money. A pox of drowning thyself! it is clean out of the way: seek thou rather to be hanged in compassing thy joy than to be drowned and go without her. [15, 16]

RODERIGO

Wilt thou be fast to my hopes, if I depend on the issue?

IAGO

Thou art sure of me:—go, make money:—I have told thee often, and I re-tell thee again and again, I hate the Moor: my cause is hearted; thine hath no less reason. Let us be conjunctive in our revenge against him; if thou canst cuckold him, thou dost thyself a pleasure, me a sport. There are many events in the womb of time which will be delivered. Traverse! go, provide thy money. We will have more of this to-morrow. Adieu.

RODERIGO

Where shall we meet i' the morning?

IAGO

At my lodging.

RODERIGO

I'll be with thee betimes.

IAGO

Go to; farewell. Do you hear, Roderigo? [17]

RODERIGO

What say you?

IAGO

No more of drowning, do you hear?

RODERIGO

I am changed: I'll go sell all my land. [*Exit.*

IAGO

Thus do I ever make my fool my purse;
For I mine own gain'd knowledge should profane,
If I would time expend with such a snipe,
But for my sport and profit. I hate the Moor,
And it is thought abroad, that 'twixt my sheets
He hath done my office: I know not if't be true;
But I, for mere suspicion in that kind,
Will do as if for surety. He holds me well;
The better shall my purpose work on him.
Cassio's a proper man: let me see now:
To get his place and to plume up my will
In double knavery—How, how? Let's see:—
After some time, to abuse Othello's ear
That he is too familiar with his wife.
He hath a person and a smooth dispose
To be suspected, framed to make women false.
The Moor is of a free and open nature,
That thinks men honest that but seem to be so,
And will as tenderly be led by the nose
As asses are.
I have't. It is engender'd. Hell and night
Must bring this monstrous birth to the world's light.
[*Exit.*

ACT TWO SCENE ONE

A Sea-port in Cyprus. An open place near the quay.

Enter MONTANO *and two Gentlemen.*

MONTANO

What from the cape can you discern at sea?

FIRST GENTLEMAN

Nothing at all: it is a highwrought flood;
I cannot, 'twixt the heaven and the main,
Descry a sail.

MONTANO

Methinks the wind hath spoke aloud at land;
A fuller blast ne'er shook our battlements:
If it hath ruffian'd so upon the sea,
What ribs of oak, when mountains melt on them,
Can hold the mortise? What shall we hear of this?

SECOND GENTLEMAN

A segregation of the Turkish fleet:
For do but stand upon the foaming shore,
The chidden billow seems to pelt the clouds;
The wind-shaked surge, with high and monstrous mane,
Seems to cast water on the burning bear,
And quench the guards of the ever-fixed pole:
I never did like molestation view
On the enchafed flood.

MONTANO

If that the Turkish fleet
Be not enshelter'd and embay'd, they are drown'd:
It is impossible they bear it out.

Enter a third Gentleman.

THIRD GENTLEMAN

News, lads! our wars are done.
The desperate tempest hath so bang'd the Turks,
That their designment halts: a noble ship of Venice

Hath seen a grievous wreck and sufferance
On most part of their fleet.

MONTANO
How! is this true?

THIRD GENTLEMAN
The ship is here put in,
A Veronesa; Michael Cassio,
Lieutenant to the warlike Moor Othello,
Is come on shore: the Moor himself at sea,
And is in full commission here for Cyprus.

MONTANO
I am glad on't; 'tis a worthy governor.

THIRD GENTLEMAN
But this same Cassio, though he speak of comfort
Touching the Turkish loss, yet he looks sadly,
And prays the Moor be safe; for they were parted
With foul and violent tempest.

MONTANO
Pray heavens he be;
For I have served him, and the man commands
Like a full soldier. Let's to the seaside, ho!
As well to see the vessel that's come in
As to throw out our eyes for brave Othello,
Even till we make the main and the aerial blue
An indistinct regard. [18]

THIRD GENTLEMAN
Come, let's do so:
For every minute is expectancy
Of more arrivance.

Enter CASSIO.

CASSIO
Thanks, you the valiant of this warlike isle,
That so approve the Moor! O, let the heavens
Give him defence against the elements,
For I have lost us him on a dangerous sea.

MONTANO
Is he well shipp'd?

CASSIO
His bark is stoutly timber'd, his pilot
Of very expert and approved allowance;
Therefore my hopes, not surfeited to death,
Stand in bold cure.
[*A cry within 'A sail, a sail, a sail!'*

Enter a fourth Gentleman.

CASSIO
What noise?

FOURTH GENTLEMAN
The town is empty; on the brow o' the sea
Stand ranks of people, and they cry 'A sail!'

CASSIO
My hopes do shape him for the governor.
[*Guns heard.*

SECOND GENTLEMAN
They do discharge their shot of courtesy:
Our friends at least.

CASSIO
I pray you, sir, go forth,
And give us truth who 'tis that is arrived.

SECOND GENTLEMAN
I shall. [*Exit.*

MONTANO
But, good lieutenant, is your general wived?

CASSIO
Most fortunately: he hath achieved a maid
That paragons description and wild fame;
One that excels the quirks of blazoning pens,
And in the essential vesture of creation
Does tire the ingener. [19]

Re-enter second Gentleman.

How now! who has put in?

SECOND GENTLEMAN
'Tis one Iago, ancient to the general.

CASSIO
Has had most favourable and happy speed:
Tempests themselves, high seas, and howling winds,
The gutter'd rocks and congregated sands,—
Traitors ensteep'd to clog the guiltless keel,—
As having sense of beauty, do omit
Their mortal natures, letting go safely by
The divine Desdemona.

MONTANO
What is she?

CASSIO
She that I spake of, our great captain's captain,
Left in the conduct of the bold Iago,
Whose footing here anticipates our thoughts
A se'nnight's speed. Great Jove, Othello guard,
And swell his sail with thine own powerful breath,
That he may bless this bay with his tall ship,
Make love's quick pants in Desdemona's arms,
Give renew'd fire to our extincted spirits,
And bring all Cyprus comfort! [20]

Enter DESDEMONA, EMILIA, IAGO, RODERIGO, *and* Attendants.

O, behold,
The riches of the ship is come on shore!
Ye men of Cyprus, let her have your knees.
Hail to thee, lady! and the grace of heaven,
Before, behind thee, and on every hand,
Enwheel thee round!

DESDEMONA
I thank you, valiant Cassio.
What tidings can you tell me of my lord?

CASSIO
He is not yet arrived: nor know I aught
But that he's well and will be shortly here. 102

DESDEMONA
O, but I fear—How lost you company?

CASSIO
The great contention of the sea and skies
Parted our fellowship—But, hark! a sail.
[*Within 'A sail, a sail!' Guns heard.*

SECOND GENTLEMAN
They give their greeting to the citadel:
This likewise is a friend.

CASSIO
See for the news. [*Exit Gentleman.*
Good ancient, you are welcome.
[*To Emilia*]
Welcome, mistress.
Let it not gall your patience, good Iago,
That I extend my manners; 'tis my breeding
That gives me this bold show of courtesy. 113
[*Kissing her.*

IAGO
Sir, would she give you so much of her lips
As of her tongue she oft bestows on me,
You'ld have enough.

DESDEMONA
Alas, she has no speech.

IAGO
In faith, too much;
I find it still, when I have list to sleep:
Marry, before your ladyship, I grant,
She puts her tongue a little in her heart,
And chides with thinking.

EMILIA
You have little cause to say so.

IAGO
Come on, come on; you are pictures out of doors, 125
Bells in your parlors, wild-cats in your kitchens,
Saints in your injuries, devils being offended,
Players in your housewifery, and housewives in your beds.

DESDEMONA
O, fie upon thee, slanderer!

IAGO
Nay, it is true, or else I am a Turk:
You rise to play and go to bed to work.

EMILIA
You shall not write my praise.

IAGO
No, let me not.

DESDEMONA
What wouldst thou write of me, if thou shouldst praise me?

IAGO
O gentle lady, do not put me to't;
For I am nothing, if not critical. 138

DESDEMONA
Come on assay. There's one gone to the harbour?

IAGO
Ay, madam.

DESDEMONA
I am not merry; but I do beguile
The thing I am, by seeming otherwise.
Come, how wouldst thou praise me?

IAGO
I am about it; but indeed my invention
Comes from my pate as birdlime does from frize;
It plucks out brains and all: but my Muse labours,
And thus she is deliver'd.
If she be fair and wise, fairness and wit, 148
The one's for use, the other useth it.

DESDEMONA
Well praised! How if she be black and witty?

IAGO
If she be black, and thereto have a wit,
She'll find a white that shall her blackness fit.

DESDEMONA
Worse and worse.

EMILIA
How if fair and foolish?

IAGO
She never yet was foolish that was fair;
For even her folly help'd her to an heir.

DESDEMONA
These are old fond paradoxes to make fools laugh i' the alehouse. What miserable praise hast thou for her that's foul and foolish?

IAGO
There's none so foul and foolish thereunto,
But does foul pranks which fair and wise ones do.

DESDEMONA
O heavy ignorance! thou praisest the worst best.
But what praise couldst thou bestow on a deserving woman indeed, one that, in the authority of her merit, did justly put on the vouch of very malice itself?

IAGO
She that was ever fair and never proud,
Had tongue at will and yet was never loud,
Never lack'd gold and yet went never gay, 168
Fled from her wish and yet said 'Now I may,'
She that being anger'd, her revenge being nigh,
Bade her wrong stay and her displeasure fly,
She that in wisdom never was so frail
To change the cod's head for the salmon's tail;
She that could think and ne'er disclose her mind,
See suitors following and not look behind, [18]
She was a wight, if ever such wight were,—

DESDEMONA
To do what? 177

IAGO
To suckle fools and chronicle small beer.

DESDEMONA
O most lame and impotent conclusion! Do not learn of him, Emilia, though he be thy husband. How say you, Cassio? is he not a most profane and liberal counsellor?

CASSIO
He speaks home, madam: You may relish him more in the soldier than in the scholar.

IAGO
[*Aside*] He takes her by the palm: ay, well said, whisper: with as little a web as this will I ensnare as great a fly as Cassio. Ay, smile upon her, do; I will gyve thee in thine own courtship. You say true; 'tis so, indeed: if such tricks as these strip you out of your lieutenantry, it had been better you had not kissed your three fingers so oft, which now again you are most apt to play the sir in. Very good; well kissed! an excellent courtesy! 'tis so, indeed. Yet again your fingers to your lips? would they were clyster-pipes for your sake! [*Trumpet within.*] The Moor! I know his trumpet. 196

CASSIO
'Tis truly so.

DESDEMONA
Let's meet him and receive him.

CASSIO
Lo, where he comes!

Enter OTHELLO *and* Attendants.

OTHELLO
O my fair warrior!

DESDEMONA
My dear Othello!

OTHELLO
It gives me wonder great as my content
To see you here before me. O my soul's joy!
If after every tempest come such calms,
May the winds blow till they have waken'd death!
And let the labouring bark climb hills of seas
Olympus-high and duck again as low 207
As hell's from heaven! If it were now to die,
'Twere now to be most happy; for, I fear,
My soul hath her content so absolute
That not another comfort like to this
Succeeds in unknown fate.

DESDEMONA
The heavens forbid
But that our loves and comforts should increase,
Even as our days do grow!

OTHELLO
Amen to that, sweet powers!
I cannot speak enough of this content;
It stops me here; it is too much of joy: 218
And this, and this, the greatest discords be [*Kissing her.*
That e'er our hearts shall make!

IAGO
[*Aside*] O, you are well tuned now!
But I'll set down the pegs that make this music,
As honest as I am.

OTHELLO
Come, let us to the castle.
News, friends; our wars are done, the Turks are drown'd.
How does my old acquaintance of this isle?
Honey, you shall be well desired in Cyprus;
I have found great love amongst them. O my sweet,
I prattle out of fashion, and I dote
In mine own comforts. I prithee, good Iago,
Go to the bay and disembark my coffers: 233
Bring thou the master to the citadel;
He is a good one, and his worthiness
Does challenge much respect. Come, Desdemona,
Once more, well met at Cyprus.
[*Exeunt Othello, Desdemona, and Attendants.*

IAGO
Do thou meet me presently at the harbour. Come hither. If thou be'st valiant,—as, they say, base men being in love have then a nobility in their natures more than is native to them,—list me. The lieutenant tonight watches on the court of guard:—first, I must tell thee this—Desdemona is directly in love with him. 244

RODERIGO
With him! why, 'tis not possible.

IAGO
Lay thy finger thus, and let thy soul be instructed. Mark me with what violence she first loved the Moor, but for bragging and telling her fantastical lies: and will she love him still for prating? let not thy discreet heart think it. Her eye must be fed; and what delight shall she have to look on the devil? When the blood is made dull with the act of sport, there should be, again to inflame it and to give satiety a fresh appetite, loveliness in favour, sympathy in years, manners and beauties; all which the Moor is defective in: now, for want of these required conveniences, her delicate tenderness will find itself abused, begin to heave the gorge, disrelish and abhor the Moor; very nature will instruct her in it and compel her to some second choice. Now, sir, this granted,—as it is a most

pregnant and unforced position—who stands so eminent in the degree of this fortune as Cassio does? a knave very voluble; no further conscionable than in putting on the mere form of civil and humane seeming, for the better compassing of his salt and most hidden loose affection? why, none; why, none: a slipper and subtle knave, a finder of occasions, that has an eye can stamp and counterfeit advantages, though true advantage never present itself; a devilish knave. Besides, the knave is handsome, young, and hath all those requisites in him that folly and green minds look after: a pestilent complete knave; and the woman hath found him already. [21]

RODERIGO
I cannot believe that in her; she's full of most blessed condition.

IAGO
Blessed fig's-end! the wine she drinks is made of grapes: if she had been blessed, she would never have loved the Moor. Blessed pudding! Didst thou not see her paddle with the palm of his hand? didst not mark that? [22]

RODERIGO
Yes, that I did; but that was but courtesy.

IAGO
Lechery, by this hand; an index and obscure prologue to the history of lust and foul thoughts. They met so near with their lips that their breaths embraced together. Villanous thoughts, Roderigo! when these mutualities so marshal the way, hard at hand comes the master and main exercise, the incorporate conclusion, Pish! But, sir, be you ruled by me: I have brought you from Venice. Watch you to-night; for the command, I'll lay't upon you. Cassio knows you not. I'll not be far from you: do you find some occasion to anger Cassio, either by speaking too loud, or tainting his discipline; or from what other course you please, which the time shall more favourably minister. [23]

RODERIGO
Well.

IAGO
Sir, he is rash and very sudden in choler, and haply may strike at you: provoke him, that he may; for even out of that will I cause these of Cyprus to mutiny; whose qualification shall come into no true taste again but by the displanting of Cassio. So shall you have a shorter journey to your desires by the means I shall then have to prefer them; and the impediment most profitably removed, without the which there were no expectation of our prosperity. [24]

RODERIGO
I will do this, if I can bring it to any
opportunity.

IAGO
I warrant thee. Meet me by and by at the citadel:
I must fetch his necessaries ashore. Farewell.

RODERIGO
Adieu. [*Exit.*

IAGO
That Cassio loves her, I do well believe it;
That she loves him, 'tis apt and of great credit:
The Moor, howbeit that I endure him not,
Is of a constant, loving, noble nature,
And I dare think he'll prove to Desdemona
A most dear husband. Now, I do love her too;
Not out of absolute lust, though peradventure
I stand accountant for as great a sin,
But partly led to diet my revenge,
For that I do suspect the lusty Moor
Hath leap'd into my seat; the thought whereof
Doth, like a poisonous mineral, gnaw my inwards;
And nothing can or shall content my soul
Till I am even'd with him, wife for wife,
Or failing so, yet that I put the Moor
At least into a jealousy so strong
That judgment cannot cure. Which thing to do,
If this poor trash of Venice, whom I trash [25]
For his quick hunting, stand the putting on,
I'll have our Michael Cassio on the hip,
Abuse him to the Moor in the rank garb—
For I fear Cassio with my night-cap too—
Make the Moor thank me, love me and reward me.
For making him egregiously an ass
And practising upon his peace and quiet
Even to madness. 'Tis here, but yet confused:
Knavery's plain face is never seen till used. [*Exit.*

ACT TWO SCENE TWO

A street.

Enter a Herald *with a proclamation*;
People *following*.

HERALD
It is Othello's pleasure, our noble and valiant general, that, upon certain tidings now arrived, importing the mere perdition of the Turkish fleet, every man put himself into triumph; some to dance, some to make bonfires, each man to what sport and revels his addiction leads him: for, besides these beneficial news, it is the celebration of his nuptial. So much was his pleasure should be proclaimed. All offices are open, and there is full liberty of feasting from this present hour of five till the bell have told eleven. Heaven bless the isle of Cyprus and our noble general Othello!
[*Exeunt.*

ACT TWO SCENE THREE

A hall in the castle.

Enter OTHELLO, DESDEMONA, CASSIO, *and* Attendants.

OTHELLO
Good Michael, look you to the guard to-night:
Let's teach ourselves that honourable stop,
Not to outsport discretion.

CASSIO
Iago hath direction what to do;
But, notwithstanding, with my personal eye
Will I look to't.

OTHELLO
Iago is most honest.
Michael, good night: to-morrow with your earliest
Let me have speech with you.
[*To Desdemona*] Come, my dear love,
The purchase made, the fruits are to ensue;
That profit's yet to come 'tween me and you.
Good night.
[*Exeunt Othello, Desdemona, and Attendants.*

Enter IAGO.

CASSIO
Welcome, Iago; we must to the watch.

IAGO
Not this hour, lieutenant; 'tis not yet ten o' the clock. Our general cast us thus early for the love of his Desdemona; who let us not therefore blame: he hath not yet made wanton the night with her; and she is sport for Jove.

CASSIO
She's a most exquisite lady.

IAGO
And, I'll warrant her, fun of game.

CASSIO
Indeed, she's a most fresh and delicate creature.

IAGO
What an eye she has! methinks it sounds a parley of provocation.

CASSIO
An inviting eye; and yet methinks right modest.

IAGO
And when she speaks, is it not an alarum to love?

CASSIO
She is indeed perfection.

IAGO
Well, happiness to their sheets! Come, lieutenant, I have a stoup of wine; and here without are a brace of Cyprus gallants that would fain have a measure to the health of black Othello.

CASSIO
Not to-night, good Iago: I have very poor and unhappy brains for drinking: I could well wish courtesy would invent some other custom of entertainment.

IAGO
O, they are our friends; but one cup: I'll drink for you.

CASSIO
I have drunk but one cup to-night, and that was craftily qualified too, and, behold, what innovation it makes here: I am unfortunate in the infirmity, and dare not task my weakness with any more. [26]

IAGO
What, man! 'tis a night of revels; the gallants desire it.

CASSIO
Where are they?

IAGO
Here at the door; I pray you, call them in.

CASSIO
I'll do't; but it dislikes me. [*Exit.*

IAGO
If I can fasten but one cup upon him,
With that which he hath drunk to-night already,
He'll be as full of quarrel and offence
As my young mistress' dog. Now, my sick fool Roderigo,
Whom love hath turn'd almost the wrong side out,
To Desdemona hath to-night caroused
Potations pottle-deep; and he's to watch:
Three lads of Cyprus, noble swelling spirits,
That hold their honours in a wary distance,
The very elements of this warlike isle,
Have I to-night fluster'd with flowing cups,
And they watch too. Now, 'mongst this flock of drunkards,
Am I to put our Cassio in some action
That may offend the isle.—But here they come:
If consequence do but approve my dream,
My boat sails freely, both with wind and stream.

Re-enter CASSIO *; with him* MONTANO *and* Gentlemen *; servants following with wine.*

CASSIO
'Fore God, they have given me a rouse already.

MONTANO
Good faith, a little one; not past a pint, as I am a soldier.

IAGO
Some wine, ho!
[*Sings*] And let me the canakin clink, clink;
And let me the canakin clink:
A soldier's but a man;

A life's but a span;
Why, then, let a soldier drink.
Some wine, boys!

CASSIO
'Fore God, an excellent song.

IAGO
I learned it in England, where, indeed, they are most potent in potting: your Dane, your German, and your swag-bellied Hollander—Drink, ho!—are nothing to your English.

CASSIO
Is your Englishman so expert in his drinking?

IAGO
Why, he drinks you, with facility, your Dane dead drunk; he sweats not to overthrow your Almain; he gives your Hollander a vomit, ere the next pottle can be filled.

CASSIO
To the health of our general!

MONTANO
I am for it, lieutenant; and I'll do you justice.

IAGO
O sweet England!
King Stephen was a worthy peer, [27]
His breeches cost him but a crown;
He held them sixpence all too dear,
With that he call'd the tailor lown.
He was a wight of high renown,
And thou art but of low degree:
'Tis pride that pulls the country down;
Then take thine auld cloak about thee.
Some wine, ho!

CASSIO
Why, this is a more exquisite song than the other.

IAGO
Will you hear't again?

CASSIO
No; for I hold him to be unworthy of his place that does those things. Well, God's above all; and there be souls must be saved, and there be souls must not be saved.

IAGO
It's true, good lieutenant.

CASSIO
For mine own part,—no offence to the general, nor any man of quality,—I hope to be saved.

IAGO
And so do I too, lieutenant.

CASSIO
Ay, but, by your leave, not before me; the lieutenant is to be saved before the ancient. Let's have no more of this; let's to our affairs.—Forgive us our sins!—Gentlemen, let's look to our business. Do not think, gentlemen. I am drunk: this is my ancient; this is my right hand, and this is my left:
I am not drunk now; I can stand well enough, and speak well enough.

ALL
Excellent well.

CASSIO
Why, very well then; you must not think then that I am drunk. [*Exit.*

MONTANO
To the platform, masters; come, let's set the watch.

IAGO
You see this fellow that is gone before;
He is a soldier fit to stand by Caesar
And give direction: and do but see his vice;
'Tis to his virtue a just equinox,
The one as long as the other: 'tis pity of him.
I fear the trust Othello puts him in,
On some odd time of his infirmity,
Will shake this island.

MONTANO
But is he often thus?

IAGO
'Tis evermore the prologue to his sleep:
He'll watch the horologe a double set,
If drink rock not his cradle.

MONTANO
It were well
The general were put in mind of it.
Perhaps he sees it not; or his good nature
Prizes the virtue that appears in Cassio,
And looks not on his evils: is not this true?

Enter RODERIGO.

IAGO
[*Aside to him*] How now, Roderigo!
I pray you, after the lieutenant; go. [*Exit Roderigo.*

MONTANO
And 'tis great pity that the noble Moor
Should hazard such a place as his own second
With one of an ingraft infirmity:
It were an honest action to say
So to the Moor.

IAGO
Not I, for this fair island:
I do love Cassio well; and would do much
To cure him of this evil—But, hark! what noise?
[*Cry within: 'Help! help!'*

Re-enter CASSIO, *driving in* RODERIGO.

CASSIO
You rogue! you rascal!

MONTANO
What's the matter, lieutenant?

CASSIO
A knave teach me my duty! 147
I'll beat the knave into a twiggen bottle.
RODERIGO
Beat me!
CASSIO
Dost thou prate, rogue? [*Striking Roderigo.*
MONTANO
Nay, good lieutenant; [*Staying him.*
I pray you, sir, hold your hand.
CASSIO
Let me go, sir,
Or I'll knock you o'er the mazzard.
MONTANO
Come, come, you're drunk.
CASSIO
Drunk! [*They fight*
IAGO
[*Aside to Roderigo*] Away, I say; go out, and cry a mutiny. [*Exit Roderigo.*
Nay, good lieutenant,—alas, gentlemen;—
Help, ho! — Lieutenant,—sir,—Montano,—sir; 161
Help, masters!—Here's a goodly watch indeed! [*Bell rings.*
Who's that which rings the bell?—Diablo, ho!
The town will rise: God's will, lieutenant, hold!
You will be shamed for ever.

Re-enter OTHELLO *and* Attendants.

OTHELLO
What is the matter here?
MONTANO
'Zounds, I bleed still; I am hurt to the death. [*Faints.*
OTHELLO
Hold, for your lives!
IAGO
Hold, ho! Lieutenant,—sir—Montano,—gentlemen,—
Have you forgot all sense of place and duty? [28]
Hold! the general speaks to you; hold, hold, for shame!
OTHELLO
Why, how now, ho! from whence ariseth this?
Are we turn'd Turks, and to ourselves do that
Which heaven hath forbid the Ottomites? 175
For Christian shame, put by this barbarous brawl:
He that stirs next to carve for his own rage
Holds his soul light; he dies upon his motion.
Silence that dreadful bell: it frights the isle
From her propriety. What is the matter, masters?
Honest Iago, that look'st dead with grieving,
Speak, who began this? on thy love, I charge thee.
IAGO
I do not know: friends all but now, even now, 183
In quarter, and in terms like bride and groom
Devesting them for bed; and then, but now—
As if some planet had unwitted men—
Swords out, and tilting one at other's breast,
In opposition bloody. I cannot speak
Any beginning to this peevish odds;
And would in action glorious I had lost
Those legs that brought me to a part of it!
OTHELLO
How comes it, Michael, you are thus forgot?
CASSIO
I pray you, pardon me; I cannot speak.
OTHELLO
Worthy Montano, you were wont be civil; 194
The gravity and stillness of your youth
The world hath noted, and your name is great
In mouths of wisest censure: what's the matter,
That you unlace your reputation thus
And spend your rich opinion for the name
Of a night-brawler? give me answer to it.
MONTANO
Worthy Othello, I am hurt to danger:
Your officer, Iago, can inform you,—
While I spare speech, which something now offends me, —
Of all that I do know: nor know I aught 205
By me that's said or done amiss this night;
Unless self-charity be sometimes a vice,
And to defend ourselves it be a sin
When violence assails us.
OTHELLO
Now, by heaven,
My blood begins my safer guides to rule;
And passion, having my best judgment collied,
Assays to lead the way: if I once stir,
Or do but lift this arm, the best of you
Shall sink in my rebuke. Give me to know
How this foul raut began, who set it on; 216
And he that is approved in this offence,
Though he had twinn'd with me, both at a birth,
Shall lose me. What! in a town of war,
Yet wild, the people's hearts brimful of fear,
To manage private and domestic quarrel,
In night, and on the court and guard of safety!
'Tis monstrous. Iago, who began't?
MONTANO
If partially affined, or leagued in office,
Thou dost deliver more or less than truth,
Thou art no soldier.
IAGO
Touch me not so near: 227

I had rather have this tongue cut from my mouth
Than it should do offence to Michael Cassio;
Yet, I persuade myself, to speak the truth
Shall nothing wrong him. Thus it is, general.
Montano and myself being in speech,
There comes a fellow crying out for help:
And Cassio following him with determined sword,
To execute upon him. Sir, this gentleman
Steps in to Cassio, and entreats his pause:
Myself the crying fellow did pursue,
Lest by his clamour—as it so fell out—
The town might fall in fright: he, swift of foot,
Outran my purpose; and I return'd the rather
For that I heard the clink and fall of swords,
And Cassio high in oath; which till to-night
I ne'er might say before. When I came back—
For this was brief—I found them close together,
At blow and thrust; even as again they were
When you yourself did part them.
More of this matter cannot I report:
But men are men; the best sometimes forget:
Though Cassio did some little wrong to him,
As men in rage strike those that wish them best,
Yet surely Cassio, I believe, received
From him that fled some strange indignity,
Which patience, could not pass.

OTHELLO

I know, Iago,
Thy honesty and love doth mince this matter,
Making it light to Cassio. Cassio, I love thee;
But never more be officer of mine.

Re-enter DESDEMONA, *attended.*

Look, if my gentle love be not raised up!
I'll make thee an example.

DESDEMONA

What's the matter?

OTHELLO

All's well now, sweeting; come away to bed.
Sir, for your hurts, myself will be your surgeon:
Lead him off. [*To Montano, who is led off.*
Iago, look with care about the town,
And silence those whom this vile brawl distracted.
Come, Desdemona: 'tis the soldiers' life
To have their balmy slumbers waked with strife.
[*Exeunt all but Iago and Cassio.*

IAGO

What, are you hurt, lieutenant?

CASSIO

Ay, past all surgery.

IAGO

Marry, heaven forbid!

CASSIO

Reputation, reputation, reputation! O, I have lost my reputation! I have lost the immortal part of myself, and what remains is bestial. My reputation, Iago, my reputation!

IAGO

As I am an honest man, I thought you had received some bodily wound; there is more sense in that than in reputation. Reputation is an idle and most false imposition: oft got without merit, and lost without deserving: you have lost no reputation at all, unless you repute yourself such a loser. What, man! there are ways to recover the general again: you are but now cast in his mood, a punishment more in policy than in malice; even so as one would beat his offenceless dog to affright an imperious lion: sue to him again, and he's yours.

CASSIO

I will rather sue to be despised than to deceive so good a commander with so slight, so drunken, and so indiscreet an officer. Drunk? and speak parrot? and squabble? swagger? swear? and discourse fustian with one's own shadow? O thou invisible spirit of wine, if thou hast no name to be known by, let us call thee devil!

IAGO

What was he that you followed with your sword? What had he done to you?

CASSIO

I know not.

IAGO

Is't possible?

CASSIO

I remember a mass of things, but nothing distinctly; a quarrel, but nothing wherefore. O God, that men should put an enemy in their mouths to steal away their brains! that we should, with joy, pleasance revel and applause, transform ourselves into beasts!

IAGO

Why, but you are now well enough: how came you thus recovered?

CASSIO

It hath pleased the devil drunkenness to give place to the devil wrath; one unperfectness shows me another, to make me frankly despise myself.

IAGO

Come, you are too severe a moraler: as the time, the place, and the condition of this country stands, I could heartily wish this had not befallen; but, since it is as it is, mend it for your own good.

CASSIO

I will ask him for my place again; he shall tell me I am a drunkard! Had I as many mouths as Hydra, such an answer would stop them all. To be now a sensible man, by and by a fool, and presently a beast! O strange! Every inordinate cup is unblessed and the ingredient is a devil.

IAGO

Come, come, good wine is a good familiar creature, if it be well used: exclaim no more against it. And, good lieutenant, I think you think I love you.

CASSIO

I have well approved it, sir. I drunk!

IAGO

You or any man living may be drunk! at a time, man. I'll tell you what you shall do. Our general's wife is now the general: may say so in this respect, for that he hath devoted and given up himself to the contemplation, mark, and denotement of her parts and graces: confess yourself freely to her; importune her help to put you in your place again: she is of so free, so kind, so apt, so blessed a disposition, she holds it a vice in her goodness not to do more than she is requested: this broken joint between you and her husband entreat her to splinter; and, my fortunes against any lay worth naming, this crack of your love shall grow stronger than it was before.

CASSIO[29]

You advise me well.

IAGO

I protest, in the sincerity of love and honest kindness.

CASSIO

I think it freely; and betimes in the morning I will beseech the virtuous Desdemona to undertake for me:
I am desperate of my fortunes if they cheque me here.

IAGO

You are in the right. Good night, lieutenant; I must to the watch.

CASSIO

Good night, honest Iago. [*Exit.*

IAGO

And what's he then that says I play the villain?
When this advice is free I give and honest,
Probal to thinking and indeed the course
To win the Moor again? For 'tis most easy
The inclining Desdemona to subdue
In any honest suit: she's framed as fruitful
As the free elements. And then for her
To win the Moor—were't to renounce his baptism,
All seals and symbols of redeemed sin,
His soul is so enfetter'd to her love,
That she may make, unmake, do what she list,
Even as her appetite shall play the god
With his weak function. How am I then a villain
To counsel Cassio to this parallel course,
Directly to his good? Divinity of hell!
When devils will the blackest sins put on,
They do suggest at first with heavenly shows,
As I do now: for whiles this honest fool
Plies Desdemona to repair his fortunes
And she for him pleads strongly to the Moor,
I'll pour this pestilence into his ear,
That she repeals him for her body's lust;
And by how much she strives to do him good,
She shall undo her credit with the Moor.
So will I turn her virtue into pitch,
And out of her own goodness make the net
That shall enmesh them all.

Re-enter RODERIGO.

How now, Roderigo!

RODERIGO

I do follow here in the chase, not like a hound that hunts, but one that fills up the cry. My money is almost spent; I have been to-night exceedingly well cudgelled; and I think the issue will be, I shall have so much experience for my pains, and so, with no money at all and a little more wit, return again to Venice.

IAGO

How poor are they that have not patience!
What wound did ever heal but by degrees?
Thou know'st we work by wit, and not by witchcraft;
And wit depends on dilatory time.
Does't not go well? Cassio hath beaten thee.
And thou, by that small hurt, hast cashier'd
Cassio:
Though other things grow fair against the sun,
Yet fruits that blossom first will first be ripe:
Content thyself awhile. By the mass, 'tis morning;
Pleasure and action make the hours seem short.
Retire thee; go where thou art billeted:
Away, I say; thou shalt know more hereafter:
Nay, get thee gone. [*Exit Roderigo.*] Two things are
to be done:
My wife must move for Cassio to her mistress;
I'll set her on;
Myself the while to draw the Moor apart,
And bring him jump when he may Cassio find
Soliciting his wife: ay, that's the way
Dull not device by coldness and delay. [*Exit.*

ACT THREE SCENE ONE

Before the castle.

Enter CASSIO *and some Musicians.*

CASSIO

Masters, play here; I will content your pains;
Something that's brief; and bid 'Good morrow, general.' [*Music.*

Enter Clown.

CLOWN

Why, masters, have your instruments been in Naples, that they speak i' the nose thus?

FIRST MUSICIAN
How, sir, how!
CLOWN
Are these, I pray you, wind-instruments?
FIRST MUSICIAN
Ay, marry, are they, sir.
CLOWN
O, thereby hangs a tail.
FIRST MUSICIAN
Whereby hangs a tale, sir?
CLOWN
Marry. sir, by many a wind-instrument that I know. But, masters, here's money for you: and the general so likes your music, that he desires you, for love's sake, to make no more noise with it. [30]
FIRST MUSICIAN
Well, sir, we will not.
CLOWN
If you have any music that may not be heard, to't again: but, as they say to hear music the general does not greatly care.
FIRST MUSICIAN
We have none such, sir.
CLOWN
Then put up your pipes in your bag, for I'll away: go; vanish into air; away!
[*Exeunt Musicians.*
CASSIO
Dost thou hear, my honest friend?
CLOWN
No, I hear not your honest friend; I hear you.
CASSIO
Prithee, keep up thy quillets. There's a poor piece of gold for thee: if the gentlewoman that attends the general's wife be stirring, tell her there's one Cassio entreats her a little favour of speech: wilt thou do this?
CLOWN
She is stirring, sir: if she will stir hither, I shall seem to notify unto her.
CASSIO
Do, good my friend. [*Exit Clown.*

Enter IAGO.

In happy time, Iago.
IAGO
You have not been a-bed, then?
CASSIO
Why, no; the day had broke
Before we parted. I have made bold, Iago,
To send in to your wife: my suit to her
Is, that she will to virtuous Desdemona
Procure me some access.
IAGO
I'll send her to you presently;
And I'll devise a mean to draw the Moor
Out of the way, that your converse and business
May be more free.
CASSIO
I humbly thank you for't. [*Exit Iago.*
I never knew
A Florentine more kind and honest. [31]

Enter EMILIA.

EMILIA
Good morrow, good Lieutenant: I am sorry
For your displeasure; but all will sure be well.
The general and his wife are talking of it;
And she speaks for you stoutly: the Moor replies,
That he you hurt is of great fame in Cyprus,
And great affinity and that in wholesome wisdom
He might not but refuse you, but he protests he loves you
And needs no other suitor but his likings
To take the safest occasion by the front [32]
To bring you in again.
CASSIO
Yet, I beseech you,
If you think fit, or that it may be done,
Give me advantage of some brief discourse
With Desdemona alone.
EMILIA
Pray you, come in:
I will bestow you where you shall have time
To speak your bosom freely.
CASSIO
I am much bound to you. [*Exeunt.*

ACT THREE SCENE TWO

A room in the castle.

Enter OTHELLO , IAGO, *and Gentlemen.*

OTHELLO
These letters give, Iago, to the pilot;
And by him do my duties to the senate:
That done, I will be walking on the works;
Repair there to me.
IAGO
Well, my good lord, I'll do't.
OTHELLO
This fortification, gentlemen, shall we see't?
GENTLEMAN
We'll wait upon your lordship. [*Exeunt.*

ACT THREE SCENE THREE

The garden of the castle.

Enter DESDEMONA, CASSIO, *and* EMILIA.

DESDEMONA
Be thou assured, good Cassio, I will do
All my abilities in thy behalf.
EMILIA
Good madam, do: I warrant it grieves my husband,
As if the case were his.
DESDEMONA
O, that's an honest fellow. Do not doubt, Cassio,
But I will have my lord and you again
As friendly as you were.
CASSIO
Bounteous madam,
Whatever shall become of Michael Cassio,
He's never any thing but your true servant.
DESDEMONA
I know't; I thank you. You do love my lord: 11
You have known him long; and be you well assured
He shall in strangeness stand no further off
Than in a polite distance.
CASSIO
Ay, but, lady,
That policy may either last so long,
Or feed upon such nice and waterish diet,
Or breed itself so out of circumstance,
That, I being absent and my place supplied,
My general will forget my love and service.
DESDEMONA
Do not doubt that; before Emilia here
I give thee warrant of thy place: assure thee,
If I do vow a friendship, I'll perform it
To the last article: my lord shall never rest;
I'll watch him tame and talk him out of patience; 33
His bed shall seem a school, his board a shrift;
I'll intermingle every thing he does
With Cassio's suit: therefore be merry, Cassio;
For thy solicitor shall rather die
Than give thy cause away.
EMILIA
Madam, here comes my lord.
CASSIO
Madam, I'll take my leave. 32
DESDEMONA
Why, stay, and hear me speak.
CASSIO
Madam, not now: I am very ill at ease,
Unfit for mine own purposes.
DESDEMONA
Well, do your discretion. [*Exit Cassio.*

Enter OTHELLO *and* IAGO.

IAGO
Ha! I like not that.
OTHELLO
What dost thou say?
IAGO
Nothing, my lord: or if—I know not what.
OTHELLO
Was not that Cassio parted from my wife?
IAGO
Cassio, my lord! No, sure, I cannot think it,
That he would steal away so guilty-like,
Seeing you coming.
OTHELLO
I do believe 'twas he. 44
DESDEMONA
How now, my lord!
I have been talking with a suitor here,
A man that languishes in your displeasure.
OTHELLO
Who is't you mean?
DESDEMONA
Why, your lieutenant, Cassio. Good my lord,
If I have any grace or power to move you,
His present reconciliation take;
For if he be not one that truly loves you,
That errs in ignorance and not in cunning,
I have no judgment in an honest face: 54
I prithee, call him back.
OTHELLO
Went he hence now?
DESDEMONA
Ay, sooth; so humbled
That he hath left part of his grief with me,
To suffer with him. Good love, call him back.
OTHELLO
Not now, sweet Desdemona; some other time.
DESDEMONA
But shall't be shortly?
OTHELLO
The sooner, sweet, for you.
DESDEMONA
Shall't be to-night at supper?
OTHELLO
No, not to-night.
DESDEMONA
To-morrow dinner, then?
OTHELLO
I shall not dine at home;
I meet the captains at the citadel.
DESDEMONA
Why, then, to-morrow night; or Tuesday morn; 69

On Tuesday noon, or night; on Wednesday morn:
I prithee, name the time, but let it not
Exceed three days: in faith, he's penitent;
And yet his trespass, in our common reason—
Save that, they say, the wars must make examples
Out of their best—is not almost a fault
To incur a private check. When shall he come?
Tell me, Othello: I wonder in my soul,
What you would ask me, that I should deny,
Or stand so mammering on. What! Michael Cassio, 80
That came a-wooing with you, and so many a time,
When I have spoke of you dispraisingly,
Hath ta'en your part; to have so much to do
To bring him in! Trust me, I could do much,—

OTHELLO
Prithee, no more: let him come when he will;
I will deny thee nothing.

DESDEMONA
Why, this is not a boon;
'Tis as I should entreat you wear your gloves,
Or feed on nourishing dishes, or keep you warm,
Or sue to you to do a peculiar profit
To your own person: nay, when I have a suit
Wherein I mean to touch your love indeed, 93
It shall be full of poise and difficult weight
And fearful to be granted.

OTHELLO
I will deny thee nothing:
Whereon, I do beseech thee, grant me this,
To leave me but a little to myself.

DESDEMONA
Shall I deny you? no: farewell, my lord.

OTHELLO
Farewell, my Desdemona: I'll come to thee straight.

DESDEMONA
Emilia, come. Be as your fancies teach you;
Whate'er you be, I am obedient.
[*Exeunt Desdemona and Emilia.*

OTHELLO
Excellent wretch! Perdition catch my soul, 103
But I do love thee! and when I love thee not,
Chaos is come again.

IAGO
My noble lord,—

OTHELLO
What dost thou say, Iago?

IAGO
Did Michael Cassio, when you woo'd my lady,
Know of your love?

OTHELLO
He did, from first to last: why dost thou ask?

IAGO
But for a satisfaction of my thought;
No further harm.

OTHELLO
Why of thy thought, Iago?

IAGO
I did not think he had been acquainted with her.

OTHELLO
O, yes; and went between us very oft.

IAGO
Indeed! 116

OTHELLO
Indeed! ay, indeed: discern'st thou aught in that?
Is he not honest?

IAGO
Honest, my lord!

OTHELLO
Honest! ay, honest.

IAGO
My lord, for aught I know.

OTHELLO
What dost thou think?

IAGO
Think, my lord!

OTHELLO
Think, my lord!
By heaven, he echoes me, [34]
As if there were some monster in his thought
Too hideous to be shown. Thou dost mean something:
I heard thee say even now, thou likedst not that, 129
When Cassio left my wife: what didst not like?
And when I told thee he was of my counsel
In my whole course of wooing, thou criedst 'Indeed!'
And didst contract and purse thy brow together,
As if thou then hadst shut up in thy brain
Some horrible conceit: if thou dost love me,
Show me thy thought.

IAGO
My lord, you know I love you.

OTHELLO
I think thou dost;
And, for I know thou'rt full of love and honesty,
And weigh'st thy words before thou givest them breath,
Therefore these stops of thine fright me the more: 143
For such things in a false disloyal knave
Are tricks of custom, but in a man that's just
They are close delations, working from the heart
That passion cannot rule.

IAGO
For Michael Cassio
I dare be sworn I think that he is honest.

OTHELLO
I think so too.
IAGO
Men should be what they seem;
Or those that be not, would they might seem none!
OTHELLO
Certain, men should be what they seem.
IAGO
Why, then, I think Cassio's an honest man.
OTHELLO
Nay, yet there's more in this:
I prithee, speak to me as to thy thinkings,
As thou dost ruminate, and give thy worst of thoughts [35]
The worst of words.
IAGO
Good my lord, pardon me:
Though I am bound to every act of duty,
I am not bound to that all slaves are free to.
Utter my thoughts? Why, say they are vile and false;
As where's that palace whereinto foul things
Sometimes intrude not? who has a breast so pure,
But some uncleanly apprehensions
Keep leets and law-days and in session sit
With meditations lawful?
OTHELLO
Thou dost conspire against thy friend, Iago,
If thou but think'st him wrong'd and makest his ear
A stranger to thy thoughts.
IAGO
I do beseech you—
Though I perchance am vicious in my guess,
As, I confess, it is my nature's plague
To spy into abuses, and oft my jealousy
Shapes faults that are not—that your wisdom yet,
From one that so imperfectly conceits,
Would take no notice, nor build yourself a trouble
Out of his scattering and unsure observance.
It were not for your quiet nor your good,
Nor for my manhood, honesty, or wisdom,
To let you know my thoughts.
OTHELLO
What dost thou mean?
IAGO
Good name in man and woman, dear my lord,
Is the immediate jewel of their souls:
Who steals my purse steals trash; 'tis something, nothing;
'Twas mine, 'tis his, and has been slave to thousands:
But he that filches from me my good name
Robs me of that which not enriches him
And makes me poor indeed.
OTHELLO
By heaven, I'll know thy thoughts.
IAGO
You cannot, if my heart were in your hand;
Nor shall not, whilst 'tis in my custody.
OTHELLO
Ha!
IAGO
O, beware, my lord, of jealousy;
It is the green-eyed monster which doth mock
The meat it feeds on; that cuckold lives in bliss
Who, certain of his fate, loves not his wronger;
But, O, what damned minutes tells he o'er
Who dotes, yet doubts, suspects, yet strongly loves!
OTHELLO [36]
O misery!
IAGO
Poor and content is rich and rich enough,
But riches fineless is as poor as winter
To him that ever fears he shall be poor.
Good heaven, the souls of all my tribe defend
From jealousy!
OTHELLO
Why, why is this?
Think'st thou I'ld make a lie of jealousy,
To follow still the changes of the moon
With fresh suspicions? No; to be once in doubt
Is once to be resolved: exchange me for a goat,
When I shall turn the business of my soul
To such exsufflicate and blown surmises,
Matching thy inference. 'Tis not to make me jealous
To say my wife is fair, feeds well, loves company,
Is free of speech, sings, plays and dances well;
Where virtue is, these are more virtuous:
Nor from mine own weak merits will I draw
The smallest fear or doubt of her revolt;
For she had eyes, and chose me. No, Iago;
I'll see before I doubt; when I doubt, prove;
And on the proof, there is no more but this,—
Away at once with love or jealousy!
IAGO
I am glad of it; for now I shall have reason
To show the love and duty that I bear you
With franker spirit: therefore, as I am bound,
Receive it from me. I speak not yet of proof.
Look to your wife; observe her well with Cassio;
Wear your eye thus, not jealous nor secure:
I would not have your free and noble nature,
Out of self-bounty, be abused; look to't:
I know our country disposition well;
In Venice they do let heaven see the pranks

They dare not show their husbands; their best conscience
Is not to leave't undone, but keep't unknown.
OTHELLO
Dost thou say so?
IAGO
She did deceive her father, marrying you;
And when she seem'd to shake and fear your looks,
She loved them most.
OTHELLO
And so she did.
IAGO
Why, go to then;
She that, so young, could give out such a seeming,
To seal her father's eyes up close as oak—
He thought 'twas witchcraft—but I am much to blame;
I humbly do beseech you of your pardon
For too much loving you.
OTHELLO
I am bound to thee for ever.
IAGO
I see this hath a little dash'd your spirits.
OTHELLO
Not a jot, not a jot.
IAGO
I' faith, I fear it has.
I hope you will consider what is spoke
Comes from my love. But I do see you're moved:
I am to pray you not to strain my speech
To grosser issues nor to larger reach
Than to suspicion. 263
OTHELLO
I will not.
IAGO
Should you do so, my lord,
My speech should fall into such vile success
As my thoughts aim not at. Cassio's my worthy friend—
My lord, I see you're moved.
OTHELLO
No, not much moved:
I do not think but Desdemona's honest.
IAGO
Long live she so! and long live you to think so!
OTHELLO
And yet, how nature erring from itself,—
IAGO
Ay, there's the point: as—to be bold with you—
Not to affect many proposed matches
Of her own clime, complexion, and degree,
Whereto we see in all things nature tends—
Foh! one may smell in such a will most rank,
Foul disproportion thoughts unnatural.
But pardon me; I do not in position
Distinctly speak of her; though I may fear
Her will, recoiling to her better judgement,
May fall to match you with her country forms
And happily repent.
OTHELLO
Farewell, farewell:
If more thou dost perceive, let me know more;
Set on thy wife to observe: leave me, Iago:
IAGO
[*Going*] My lord, I take my leave.
OTHELLO
Why did I marry? This honest creature doubtless
Sees and knows more, much more, than he unfolds.
IAGO
[*Returning*] My lord, I would I might entreat your honour
To scan this thing no further; leave it to time:
Though it be fit that Cassio have his place,
For, sure, he fills it up with great ability,
Yet, if you please to hold him off awhile,
You shall by that perceive him and his means:
Note, if your lady strain his entertainment 298
With any strong or vehement importunity;
Much will be seen in that. In the mean time,
Let me be thought too busy in my fears—
As worthy cause I have to fear I am—
And hold her free, I do beseech your honour.
OTHELLO
Fear not my government.
IAGO
I once more take my leave. [*Exit.*
OTHELLO
This fellow's of exceeding honesty,
And knows all qualities, with a learned spirit,
Of human dealings. If I do prove her haggard,
Though that her jesses were my dear heartstrings, 310
I'ld whistle her off and let her down the wind,
To pray at fortune. Haply, for I am black
And have not those soft parts of conversation
That chamberers have, or for I am declined
Into the vale of years,—yet that's not much—
She's gone. I am abused; and my relief
Must be to loathe her. O curse of marriage,
That we can call these delicate creatures ours,
And not their appetites! I had rather be a toad, 319
And live upon the vapour of a dungeon,
Than keep a corner in the thing I love
For others' uses. Yet, 'tis the plague of great ones;
Prerogatived are they less than the base;
'Tis destiny unshunnable, like death:
Even then this forked plague is fated to us
When we do quicken. Desdemona comes: [37]

Re-enter DESDEMONA *and* EMILIA.

If she be false, O, then heaven mocks itself!
I'll not believe't.

DESDEMONA
How now, my dear Othello!
Your dinner, and the generous islanders
By you invited, do attend your presence.

OTHELLO
I am to blame.

DESDEMONA
Why do you speak so faintly?
Are you not well?

OTHELLO
I have a pain upon my forehead here.

DESDEMONA
'Faith, that's with watching; 'twill away again:
Let me but bind it hard, within this hour
It will be well.

OTHELLO
Your napkin is too little:
[*He puts the handkerchief from him; and it drops.*
Let it alone. Come, I'll go in with you.

DESDEMONA
I am very sorry that you are not well.
[*Exeunt Othello and Desdemona.*

EMILIA
I am glad I have found this napkin:
This was her first remembrance from the Moor:
My wayward husband hath a hundred times
Woo'd me to steal it; but she so loves the token,
For he conjured her she should ever keep it,
That she reserves it evermore about her
To kiss and talk to. I'll have the work ta'en out,
And give't Iago: what he will do with it
Heaven knows, not I;
I nothing but to please his fantasy.

Re-enter IAGO.

IAGO
How now! what do you here alone?

EMILIA
Do not you chide; I have a thing for you.

IAGO
A thing for me? it is a common thing—

EMILIA
Ha!

IAGO
To have a foolish wife.

EMILIA
O, is that all? What will you give me now
For the same handkerchief?

IAGO
What handkerchief?

EMILIA
What handkerchief?
Why, that the Moor first gave to Desdemona;
That which so often you did bid me steal.

IAGO
Hast stol'n it from her?

EMILIA
No, 'faith; she let it drop by negligence.
And, to the advantage, I, being here, took't up.
Look, here it is.

IAGO
A good wench; give it me.

EMILIA
What will you do with 't, that you have been so earnest
To have me filch it?

IAGO
[*Snatching it*] Why, what's that to you?

EMILIA
If it be not for some purpose of import,
Give't me again: poor lady, she'll run mad
When she shall lack it.

IAGO
Be not acknown on 't; I have use for it.
Go, leave me. [*Exit Emilia.*
I will in Cassio's lodging lose this napkin,
And let him find it. Trifles light as air
Are to the jealous confirmations strong
As proofs of holy writ: this may do something.
The Moor already changes with my poison: [38]
Dangerous conceits are, in their natures, poisons.
Which at the first are scarce found to distaste,
But with a little act upon the blood.
Burn like the mines of sulphur. I did say so:
Look, where he comes!

Re-enter OTHELLO.

Not poppy, nor mandragora,
Nor all the drowsy syrups of the world,
Shall ever medicine thee to that sweet sleep
Which thou owedst yesterday.

OTHELLO
Ha! ha! false to me?

IAGO
Why, how now, general! no more of that.

OTHELLO
Avaunt! be gone! thou hast set me on the rack:
I swear 'tis better to be much abused
Than but to know't a little.

IAGO
How now, my lord!

OTHELLO
What sense had I of her stol'n hours of lust?
I saw't not, thought it not, it harm'd not me:
I slept the next night well, was free and merry;

I found not Cassio's kisses on her lips: 399
He that is robb'd, not wanting what is stol'n,
Let him not know't, and he's not robb'd at all.

IAGO

I am sorry to hear this.

OTHELLO

I had been happy, if the general camp,
Pioners and all, had tasted her sweet body,
So I had nothing known. O, now, for ever
Farewell the tranquil mind! farewell content!
Farewell the plumed troop, and the big wars,
That make ambition virtue! O, farewell! 408
Farewell the neighing steed, and the shrill trump,
The spirit-stirring drum, the ear-piercing fife,
The royal banner, and all quality,
Pride, pomp and circumstance of glorious war!
And, O you mortal engines, whose rude throats
The immortal Jove's dead clamours counterfeit,
Farewell! Othello's occupation's gone!

IAGO

Is't possible, my lord?

OTHELLO

Villain, be sure thou prove my love a whore,
Be sure of it; give me the ocular proof; 418
Or, by the worth of man's eternal soul,
Thou hadst been better have been born a dog
Than answer my waked wrath!

IAGO

Is't come to this?

OTHELLO

Make me to see't; or, at the least, so prove it,
That the probation bear no hinge nor loop
To hang a doubt on; or woe upon thy life!

IAGO

My noble lord,—

OTHELLO

If thou dost slander her and torture me,
Never pray more; abandon all remorse;
On horror's head horrors accumulate; 429
Do deeds to make heaven weep, all earth amazed;
For nothing canst thou to damnation add
Greater than that.

IAGO

O grace! O heaven forgive me!
Are you a man? have you a soul or sense?
God be wi' you; take mine office. O wretched fool.
That livest to make thine honesty a vice!
O monstrous world! Take note, take note, O world,
To be direct and honest is not safe.
I thank you for this profit; and from hence
I'll love no friend, sith love breeds such offence.

OTHELLO

Nay, stay: thou shouldst be honest.

IAGO

I should be wise, for honesty's a fool[38]
And loses that it works for.

OTHELLO

By the world,
I think my wife be honest and think she is not;
I think that thou art just and think thou art not.
I'll have some proof. Her name, that was as fresh
As Dian's visage, is now begrimed and black
As mine own face. If there be cords, or knives,
Poison, or fire, or suffocating streams,
I'll not endure it. Would I were satisfied!

IAGO

I see, sir, you are eaten up with passion:
I do repent me that I put it to you.
You would be satisfied?

OTHELLO

Would! nay, I will.

IAGO

And may: but, how? how satisfied, my lord?
Would you, the supervisor, grossly gape on—
Behold her topp'd?

OTHELLO

Death and damnation! O!

IAGO

It were a tedious difficulty, I think,
To bring them to that prospect: damn them then,
If ever mortal eyes do see them bolster
More than their own! What then? how then?
What shall I say? Where's satisfaction? 465
It is impossible you should see this,
Were they as prime as goats, as hot as monkeys,
As salt as wolves in pride, and fools as gross
As ignorance made drunk. But yet, I say,
If imputation and strong circumstances,
Which lead directly to the door of truth,
Will give you satisfaction, you may have't.

OTHELLO

Give me a living reason she's disloyal.

IAGO

I do not like the office: 474
But, sith I am enter'd in this cause so far,
Prick'd to't by foolish honesty and love,
I will go on. I lay with Cassio lately;
And, being troubled with a raging tooth,
I could not sleep.
There are a kind of men so loose of soul,
That in their sleeps will mutter their affairs:
One of this kind is Cassio:
In sleep I heard him say 'Sweet Desdemona,
Let us be wary, let us hide our loves;' 484
And then, sir, would he gripe and wring my hand,
Cry 'O sweet creature!' and then kiss me hard,
As if he pluck'd up kisses by the roots

That grew upon my lips; then laid his leg
Over my thigh, and sigh'd, and kiss'd; and then
Cried 'Cursed fate that gave thee to the Moor!'

OTHELLO
O monstrous! monstrous!

IAGO
Nay, this was but his dream.

OTHELLO
But this denoted a foregone conclusion:
'Tis a shrewd doubt, though it be but a dream.

IAGO
And this may help to thicken other proofs
That do demonstrate thinly.

OTHELLO
I'll tear her all to pieces.

IAGO
Nay, but be wise: yet we see nothing done;
She may be honest yet. Tell me but this,
Have you not sometimes seen a handkerchief
Spotted with strawberries in your wife's hand?

OTHELLO
I gave her such a one; 'twas my first gift.

IAGO
I know not that: but such a handkerchief—
I am sure it was your wife's—did I to-day
See Cassio wipe his beard with.

OTHELLO
If it be that,—

IAGO
If it be that, or any that was hers, [39]
It speaks against her with the other proofs.

OTHELLO
O, that the slave had forty thousand lives!
One is too poor, too weak for my revenge.
Now do I see 'tis true. Look here, Iago;
All my fond love thus do I blow to heaven.
'Tis gone.
Arise, black vengeance, from thy hollow cell! [40]
Yield up, O love, thy crown and hearted throne
To tyrannous hate! Swell, bosom, with thy fraught,
For 'tis of aspics' tongues!

IAGO
Yet be content.

OTHELLO
O, blood, blood, blood!

IAGO
Patience, I say; your mind perhaps may change.

OTHELLO
Never, Iago. Like to the Pontic sea, [38]
Whose icy current and compulsive course
Ne'er feels retiring ebb, but keeps due on
To the Propontic and the Hellespont, [41]
Even so my bloody thoughts, with violent pace,
Shall ne'er look back, ne'er ebb to humble love,
Till that a capable and wide revenge
Swallow them up. Now, by yond marble heaven,
[*Kneels*] In the due reverence of a sacred vow
I here engage my words.

IAGO
Do not rise yet.
[*Kneels*] Witness, you ever-burning lights above,
You elements that clip us round about,
Witness that here Iago doth give up
The execution of his wit, hands, heart,
To wrong'd Othello's service! Let him command,
And to obey shall be in me remorse,
What bloody business ever. [42]

[*They rise.*

OTHELLO
I greet thy love,
Not with vain thanks, but with acceptance bounteous,
And will upon the instant put thee to't:
Within these three days let me hear thee say
That Cassio's not alive.

IAGO
My friend is dead; 'tis done at your request:
But let her live.

OTHELLO
Damn her, lewd minx! O, damn her!
Come, go with me apart; I will withdraw,
To furnish me with some swift means of death
For the fair devil. Now art thou my lieutenant.

IAGO
I am your own for ever. [*Exeunt.*

ACT THREE SCENE FOUR

Before the castle.

Enter DESDEMONA, EMILIA, *and* Clown.

DESDEMONA
Do you know, sirrah, where Lieutenant Cassio lies?

CLOWN
I dare not say he lies any where.

DESDEMONA
Why, man?

CLOWN
He's a soldier, and for one to say a soldier lies, is stabbing.

DESDEMONA
Go to: where lodges he? [38]

CLOWN
To tell you where he lodges, is to tell you where I lie.

DESDEMONA
Can any thing be made of this?

CLOWN
I know not where he lodges, and for me to devise a lodging and say he lies here or he lies there, were to lie in mine own throat.

DESDEMONA
Can you inquire him out, and be edified by report?

CLOWN
I will catechise the world for him; that is, make questions, and by them answer.

DESDEMONA
Seek him, bid him come hither: tell him I have moved my lord on his behalf, and hope all will be well. 17

CLOWN
To do this is within the compass of man's wit: and therefore I will attempt the doing it. [*Exit.*

DESDEMONA
Where should I lose that handkerchief, Emilia?

EMILIA
I know not, madam.

DESDEMONA
Believe me, I had rather have lost my purse
Full of crusadoes: and, but my noble Moor
Is true of mind and made of no such baseness
As jealous creatures are, it were enough
To put him to ill thinking.

EMILIA
Is he not jealous?

DESDEMONA
Who, he? I think the sun where he was born 28
Drew all such humours from him.

EMILIA
Look, where he comes.

DESDEMONA
I will not leave him now till Cassio
Be call'd to him.

Enter OTHELLO.

How is't with you, my lord?

OTHELLO
Well, my good lady. [*Aside*] O, hardness to dissemble!—
How do you, Desdemona?

DESDEMONA
Well, my good lord.

OTHELLO
Give me your hand: this hand is moist, my lady.

DESDEMONA
It yet hath felt no age nor known no sorrow.

OTHELLO
This argues fruitfulness and liberal heart:
Hot, hot, and moist: this hand of yours requires
A sequester from liberty, fasting and prayer,
Much castigation, exercise devout;
For here's a young and sweating devil here,
That commonly rebels. 'Tis a good hand,
A frank one.

DESDEMONA
You may, indeed, say so;
For 'twas that hand that gave away my heart.

OTHELLO
A liberal hand: the hearts of old gave hands;
But our new heraldry is hands, not hearts. [43]

DESDEMONA
I cannot speak of this. Come now, your promise.

OTHELLO
What promise, chuck?

DESDEMONA
I have sent to bid Cassio come speak with you. 54

OTHELLO
I have a salt and sorry rheum offends me;
Lend me thy handkerchief.

DESDEMONA
Here, my lord.

OTHELLO
That which I gave you.

DESDEMONA
I have it not about me.

OTHELLO
Not?

DESDEMONA
No, indeed, my lord.

OTHELLO
That is a fault.
That handkerchief
Did an Egyptian to my mother give;
She was a charmer, and could almost read
The thoughts of people: she told her, while she kept it,
'Twould make her amiable and subdue my father
Entirely to her love, but if she lost it 69
Or made gift of it, my father's eye
Should hold her loathed and his spirits should hunt
After new fancies: she, dying, gave it me;
And bid me, when my fate would have me wive,
To give it her. I did so: and take heed on't; [44]
Make it a darling like your precious eye;
To lose't or give't away were such perdition
As nothing else could match.

DESDEMONA
Is't possible?

OTHELLO
'Tis true: there's magic in the web of it:
A sibyl, that had number'd in the world 81
The sun to course two hundred compasses,
In her prophetic fury sew'd the work;

The worms were hallow'd that did breed the silk;
And it was dyed in mummy which the skilful
Conserved of maidens' hearts.

DESDEMONA
Indeed! is't true?

OTHELLO
Most veritable; therefore look to't well.

DESDEMONA
Then would to God that I had never seen't!

OTHELLO
Ha! wherefore?

DESDEMONA
Why do you speak so startingly and rash?

OTHELLO
Is't lost? is't gone? speak, is it out o' the way? 92

DESDEMONA
Heaven bless us!

OTHELLO
Say you?

DESDEMONA
It is not lost; but what an if it were?

OTHELLO
How!

DESDEMONA
I say, it is not lost.

OTHELLO
Fetch't, let me see't.

DESDEMONA
Why, so I can, sir, but I will not now.
This is a trick to put me from my suit:
Pray you, let Cassio be received again.

OTHELLO
Fetch me the handkerchief: my mind misgives.

DESDEMONA
Come, come; 103
You'll never meet a more sufficient man.

OTHELLO
The handkerchief!

DESDEMONA
I pray, talk me of Cassio.

OTHELLO
The handkerchief!

DESDEMONA
A man that all his time
Hath founded his good fortunes on your love,
Shared dangers with you,—

OTHELLO
The handkerchief!

DESDEMONA
In sooth, you are to blame.

OTHELLO
Away! [*Exit.*

EMILIA
Is not this man jealous?

DESDEMONA
I ne'er saw this before. 115
Sure, there's some wonder in this handkerchief:
I am most unhappy in the loss of it.

EMILIA
'Tis not a year or two shows us a man:
They are all but stomachs, and we all but food;
They eat us hungerly, and when they are full,
They belch us. Look you, Cassio and my husband!

Enter CASSIO *and* IAGO.

IAGO
There is no other way; 'tis she must do't:
And, lo, the happiness! go, and importune her.

DESDEMONA
How now, good Cassio! what's the news with you?

CASSIO
Madam, my former suit: I do beseech you 126
That by your virtuous means I may again
Exist, and be a member of his love
Whom I with all the office of my heart
Entirely honour: I would not be delay'd.
If my offence be of such mortal kind
That nor my service past, nor present sorrows,
Nor purposed merit in futurity,
Can ransom me into his love again,
But to know so must be my benefit;
So shall I clothe me in a forced content, 136
And shut myself up in some other course, [45]
To fortune's alms.

DESDEMONA
Alas, thrice-gentle Cassio!
My advocation is not now in tune;
My lord is not my lord; nor should I know him,
Were he in favour as in humour alter'd.
So help me every spirit sanctified,
As I have spoken for you all my best
And stood within the blank of his displeasure
For my free speech! you must awhile be patient:
What I can do I will; and more I will 147
Than for myself I dare: let that suffice you.

IAGO
Is my lord angry?

EMILIA
He went hence but now,
And certainly in strange unquietness.

IAGO
Can he be angry? I have seen the cannon,
When it hath blown his ranks into the air,
And, like the devil, from his very arm
Puff'd his own brother:—and can he be angry?
Something of moment then: I will go meet him:
There's matter in't indeed, if he be angry.

DESDEMONA
I prithee, do so. [*Exit Iago.*
Something, sure, of state,
Either from Venice, or some unhatch'd practice
Made demonstrable here in Cyprus to him,
Hath puddled his clear spirit: and in such cases
Men's natures wrangle with inferior things,
Though great ones are their object. 'Tis even so;
For let our finger ache, and it indues
Our other healthful members even to that sense
Of pain: nay, we must think men are not gods,
Nor of them look for such observances
As fit the bridal. Beshrew me much, Emilia,
I was, unhandsome warrior as I am, [46]
Arraigning his unkindness with my soul;
But now I find I had suborn'd the witness,
And he's indicted falsely.

EMILIA
Pray heaven it be state-matters, as you think,
And no conception nor no jealous toy
Concerning you.

DESDEMONA
Alas the day! I never gave him cause.

EMILIA
But jealous souls will not be answer'd so;
They are not ever jealous for the cause, 179
But jealous for they are jealous: 'tis a monster
Begot upon itself, born on itself.

DESDEMONA
Heaven keep that monster from Othello's mind!

EMILIA
Lady, amen.

DESDEMONA
I will go seek him. Cassio, walk hereabout:
If I do find him fit, I'll move your suit
And seek to effect it to my uttermost.

CASSIO
I humbly thank your ladyship.
[*Exeunt Desdemona and Emilia.*

Enter BIANCA.

BIANCA
Save you, friend Cassio!

CASSIO
What make you from home?
How is it with you, my most fair Bianca? 190
I' faith, sweet love, I was coming to your house.

BIANCA
And I was going to your lodging, Cassio.
What, keep a week away? seven days and nights?
Eight score eight hours? and lovers' absent hours,
More tedious than the dial eight score times?
O weary reckoning!

CASSIO
Pardon me, Bianca:
I have this while with leaden thoughts been press'd:
But I shall, in a more continuate time,
Strike off this score of absence. Sweet Bianca,
[*Giving her Desdemona's handkerchief.*
Take me this work out.

BIANCA
O Cassio, whence came this? 203
This is some token from a newer friend:
To the felt absence now I feel a cause:
Is't come to this? Well, well.

CASSIO
Go to, woman!
Throw your vile guesses in the devil's teeth,
From whence you have them. You are jealous now
That this is from some mistress, some remembrance:
No, in good troth, Bianca.

BIANCA
Why, whose is it?

CASSIO
I know not, sweet: I found it in my chamber.
I like the work well: ere it be demanded—
As like enough it will—I'ld have it copied:
Take it, and do't; and leave me for this time.

BIANCA
Leave you! wherefore?

CASSIO
I do attend here on the general;
And think it no addition, nor my wish,
To have him see me woman'd.

BIANCA
Why, I pray you?

CASSIO
Not that I love you not. [38]

BIANCA
But that you do not love me.
I pray you, bring me on the way a little,
And say if I shall see you soon at night.

CASSIO
'Tis but a little way that I can bring you;
For I attend here: but I'll see you soon. 227

BIANCA
'Tis very good; I must be circumstanced.
[*Exeunt.*

ACT FOUR SCENE ONE

Cyprus. Before the castle.
Enter OTHELLO *and* IAGO.

IAGO
Will you think so?

OTHELLO
Think so, Iago!
IAGO
What,
To kiss in private?
OTHELLO
An unauthorised kiss.
IAGO
Or to be naked with her friend in bed
An hour or more, not meaning any harm?
OTHELLO
Naked in bed, Iago, and not mean harm!
It is hypocrisy against the devil:
They that mean virtuously, and yet do so,
The devil their virtue tempts, and they tempt heaven.
IAGO
So they do nothing, 'tis a venial slip:
But if I give my wife a handkerchief,—
OTHELLO
What then?
IAGO
Why, then, 'tis hers, my lord; and, being hers,
She may, I think, bestow't on any man.
OTHELLO
She is protectress of her honour too:
May she give that?
IAGO
Her honour is an essence that's not seen;
They have it very oft that have it not:
But, for the handkerchief,—
OTHELLO
By heaven, I would most gladly have forgot it.
Thou said'st, it comes o'er my memory,
As doth the raven o'er the infected house,
Boding to all—he had my handkerchief.
IAGO
Ay, what of that?
OTHELLO
That's not so good now.
IAGO
What,
If I had said I had seen him do you wrong?
Or heard him say,—as knaves be such abroad,
Who having, by their own importunate suit,
Or voluntary dotage of some mistress,
Convinced or supplied them, cannot choose
But they must blab—
OTHELLO
Hath he said any thing?
IAGO
He hath, my lord; but be you well assured,
No more than he'll unswear.
OTHELLO
What hath he said?
IAGO
'Faith, that he did—I know not what he did.
OTHELLO
What? what?
IAGO
Lie—
OTHELLO
With her?
IAGO
With her, on her; what you will.
OTHELLO
Lie with her! lie on her! We say lie on her, when they belie her. Lie with her! that's fulsome.—Handkerchief—confessions— handkerchief!—To confess, and be hanged for his labour;—first, to be hanged, and then to confess.—I tremble at it. Nature would not invest herself in such shadowing passion without some instruction. It is not words that shake me thus. Pish! Noses, ears, and lips.—Is't possible?—Confess—handkerchief!—O devil!— [*Falls in a trance.*
IAGO
Work on,
My medicine, work! Thus credulous fools are caught;
And many worthy and chaste dames even thus,
All guiltless, meet reproach. What, ho! my lord!
My lord, I say! Othello!

Enter CASSIO.

How now, Cassio!
CASSIO
What's the matter?
IAGO
My lord is fall'n into an epilepsy:
This is his second fit; he had one yesterday.
CASSIO
Rub him about the temples.
IAGO
No, forbear;
The lethargy must have his quiet course:
If not, he foams at mouth and by and by
Breaks out to savage madness. Look, he stirs:
Do you withdraw yourself a little while,
He will recover straight: when he is gone,
I would on great occasion speak with you. [*Exit Cassio.*
How is it, general? have you not hurt your head?
OTHELLO
Dost thou mock me?
IAGO
I mock you! no, by heaven.
Would you would bear your fortune like a man!

IAGO Work on, my medicine, work!

OTHELLO
A horned man's a monster and a beast.
IAGO
There's many a beast then in a populous city,
And many a civil monster.
OTHELLO
Did he confess it?
IAGO
Good sir, be a man;
Think every bearded fellow that's but yoked
May draw with you: there's millions now alive
That nightly lie in those unproper beds
Which they dare swear peculiar: your case is better. 84
O, 'tis the spite of hell, the fiend's arch-mock,
To lip a wanton in a secure couch,
And to suppose her chaste! No, let me know;
And knowing what I am, I know what she shall be.
OTHELLO
O, thou art wise; 'tis certain.
IAGO
Stand you awhile apart;
Confine yourself but in a patient list.
Whilst you were here o'erwhelmed with your grief— [47]
A passion most unsuiting such a man—
Cassio came hither: I shifted him away,
And laid good 'scuse upon your ecstasy, 96
Bade him anon return and here speak with me;
The which he promised. Do but encave yourself,
And mark the fleers, the gibes, and notable scorns,
That dwell in every region of his face;
For I will make him tell the tale anew,
Where, how, how oft, how long ago, and when
He hath, and is again to cope your wife:
I say, but mark his gesture. Marry, patience;
Or I shall say you are all in all in spleen,
And nothing of a man.
OTHELLO
Dost thou hear, Iago? 107
I will be found most cunning in my patience;
But—dost thou hear?—most bloody.
IAGO
That's not amiss;
But yet keep time in all. Will you withdraw?
[*Othello retires.*

Now will I question Cassio of Bianca,
A housewife that by selling her desires
Buys herself bread and clothes: it is a creature
That dotes on Cassio; as 'tis the strumpet's plague
To beguile many and be beguiled by one:
He, when he hears of her, cannot refrain
From the excess of laughter. Here he comes:

Re-enter CASSIO.

As he shall smile, Othello shall go mad; 119
And his unbookish jealousy must construe
Poor Cassio's smiles, gestures and light behavior,
Quite in the wrong. How do you now, lieutenant?

CASSIO
The worser that you give me the addition
Whose want even kills me.

IAGO
Ply Desdemona well, and you are sure on't.
[*Speaking lower*] Now, if this suit lay in Bianca's power,
How quickly should you speed!

CASSIO
Alas, poor caitiff!

OTHELLO
Look, how he laughs already! 129

IAGO
I never knew woman love man so.

CASSIO
Alas, poor rogue! I think, i' faith, she loves me.

OTHELLO
Now he denies it faintly, and laughs it out.

IAGO
Do you hear, Cassio?

OTHELLO
Now he importunes him
To tell it o'er: go to; well said, well said.

IAGO
She gives it out that you shall marry her:
Do you intend it?

CASSIO
Ha, ha, ha! 138

OTHELLO
Do you triumph, Roman? do you triumph?

CASSIO
I marry her! what? a customer! Prithee, bear some charity to my wit; do not think it so unwholesome. [48]
Ha, ha, ha!

OTHELLO
So, so, so, so: they laugh that win.

IAGO
'Faith, the cry goes that you shall marry her.

CASSIO
Prithee, say true.

IAGO
I am a very villain else.

OTHELLO
Have you scored me? Well. 147

CASSIO
This is the monkey's own giving out: she is persuaded I will marry her, out of her own love and flattery, not out of my promise.

OTHELLO
Iago beckons me; now he begins the story.

CASSIO
She was here even now; she haunts me in every place. I was the other day talking on the sea-bank with certain Venetians; and thither comes the bauble, and, by
this hand, she falls me thus about my neck— 155

OTHELLO [49]
Crying 'O dear Cassio!' as it were: his gesture imports it.

CASSIO
So hangs, and lolls, and weeps upon me; so hales, and pulls me: ha, ha, ha!

OTHELLO
Now he tells how she plucked him to my chamber. O, I see that nose of yours, but not that dog I shall throw it to.

CASSIO
Well, I must leave her company.

IAGO
Before me! look, where she comes.

CASSIO
'Tis such another fitchew! marry a perfumed
one. 166

Enter BIANCA.

What do you mean by this haunting of me?

BIANCA
Let the devil and his dam haunt you! What did you mean by that same handkerchief you gave me even now? I was a fine fool to take it. I must take out the work?—A likely piece of work, that you should find it in your chamber, and not know who left it there! This is some minx's token, and I must take out the work? There; give it your hobby-horse: wheresoever you had
it, I'll take out no work on't. 175

CASSIO
How now, my sweet Bianca! how now! how now!

OTHELLO
By heaven, that should be my handkerchief!

BIANCA
An you'll come to supper to-night, you may; an you will not, come when you are next prepared for. [*Exit*.

IAGO
After her, after her.

CASSIO
'Faith, I must; she'll rail in the street else. 181

IAGO
Will you sup there?
CASSIO
'Faith, I intend so.
IAGO
Well, I may chance to see you; for I would very fain speak with you.
CASSIO
Prithee, come; will you?
IAGO
Go to; say no more. [*Exit Cassio.*
OTHELLO
[*Advancing*] How shall I murder him, Iago?
IAGO
Did you perceive how he laughed at his vice? 189
OTHELLO
O Iago!
IAGO
And did you see the handkerchief?
OTHELLO
Was that mine?
IAGO
Yours, by this hand: and to see how he prizes the foolish woman your wife! she gave it him, and he hath given it his whore.
OTHELLO
I would have him nine years a-killing. A fine woman! a fair woman! a sweet woman!
IAGO
Nay, you must forget that. 198
OTHELLO
Ay, let her rot, and perish, and be damned to-night; for she shall not live: no, my heart is turned to stone; I strike it, and it hurts my hand. O, the world hath not a sweeter creature: she might lie by an emperor's side and command him tasks.
IAGO
Nay, that's not your way.
OTHELLO
Hang her! I do but say what she is: so delicate with her needle: an admirable musician: O! she will sing the savageness out of a bear: of so high and plenteous wit and invention:— 208
IAGO
She's the worse for all this.
OTHELLO
O, a thousand thousand times: and then, of so gentle a condition!
IAGO
Ay, too gentle.
OTHELLO
Nay, that's certain: but yet the pity of it, Iago!
O Iago, the pity of it, Iago!
IAGO
If you are so fond over her iniquity, give her patent to offend; for, if it touch not you, it comes near nobody. 217
OTHELLO
I will chop her into messes: cuckold me!
IAGO
O, 'tis foul in her.
OTHELLO
With mine officer!
IAGO
That's fouler.
OTHELLO
Get me some poison, Iago; this night: I'll not expostulate with her, lest her body and beauty unprovide my mind again: this night, Iago. 224
IAGO
Do it not with poison, strangle her in her bed, even the bed she hath contaminated.
OTHELLO
Good, good: the justice of it pleases: very good.
IAGO
And for Cassio, let me be his undertaker: you shall hear more by midnight.
OTHELLO
Excellent good. [*A trumpet within.*]
What trumpet is that same?
IAGO
Something from Venice, sure. 'Tis Lodovico
Come from the duke: and, see, your wife is with him.

Enter LODOVICO, DESDEMONA, *and* Attendants.

LODOVICO
Save you, worthy general!
OTHELLO
With all my heart, sir.
LODOVICO
The duke and senators of Venice greet you.
[*Gives him a letter.*
OTHELLO
I kiss the instrument of their pleasures.
[*Opens the letter, and reads.*
DESDEMONA
And what's the news, good cousin Lodovico?
IAGO
I am very glad to see you, signior;
Welcome to Cyprus.
LODOVICO
I thank you. How does Lieutenant Cassio?
IAGO
Lives, sir.

DESDEMONA
Cousin, there's fall'n between him and my lord
An unkind breach: but you shall make all well.
OTHELLO
Are you sure of that?
DESDEMONA
My lord?
OTHELLO
[*Reads*] 'This fail you not to do, as you will—' 250
LODOVICO
He did not call; he's busy in the paper.
Is there division 'twixt my lord and Cassio?
DESDEMONA
A most unhappy one: I would do much
To atone them, for the love I bear to Cassio.
OTHELLO
Fire and brimstone!
DESDEMONA
My lord?
OTHELLO
Are you wise?
DESDEMONA
What, is he angry?
LODOVICO
May be the letter moved him;
For, as I think, they do command him home,
Deputing Cassio in his government.
DESDEMONA
Trust me, I am glad on't.
OTHELLO
Indeed!
DESDEMONA
My lord?
OTHELLO
I am glad to see you mad.
DESDEMONA
Why, sweet Othello,—
OTHELLO
[*Striking her*] Devil! 267
DESDEMONA
I have not deserved this.
LODOVICO
My lord, this would not be believed in Venice,
Though I should swear I saw't: 'tis very much:
Make her amends; she weeps.
OTHELLO
O devil, devil!
If that the earth could teem with woman's tears,
Each drop she falls would prove a crocodile.
Out of my sight!
DESDEMONA
I will not stay to offend you. [*Going.*

LODOVICO
Truly, an obedient lady:
I do beseech your lordship, call her back. 279
OTHELLO
Mistress!
DESDEMONA
My lord?
OTHELLO
What would you with her, sir?
LODOVICO
Who, I, my lord?
OTHELLO
Ay; you did wish that I would make her turn:
Sir, she can turn, and turn, and yet go on,
And turn again; and she can weep, sir, weep;
And she's obedient, as you say, obedient,
Very obedient. Proceed you in your tears.
Concerning this, sir,—O well-painted passion!—
I am commanded home. Get you away;
I'll send for you anon. Sir, I obey the mandate, 291
And will return to Venice. Hence, avaunt! [*Exit Desdemona.*
Cassio shall have my place. And, sir, tonight,
I do entreat that we may sup together:
You are welcome, sir, to Cyprus.—Goats and monkeys! [*Exit.*
LODOVICO
Is this the noble Moor whom our full senate
Call all in all sufficient? Is this the nature [50]
Whom passion could not shake? whose solid virtue
The shot of accident, nor dart of chance,
Could neither graze nor pierce?
IAGO
He is much changed.
LODOVICO
Are his wits safe? is he not light of brain? 303
IAGO
He's that he is: I may not breathe my censure
What he might be: if what he might he is not,
I would to heaven he were!
LODOVICO
What, strike his wife!
IAGO
'Faith, that was not so well; yet would I knew
That stroke would prove the worst!
LODOVICO
Is it his use?
Or did the letters work upon his blood,
And new-create this fault?
IAGO
Alas, alas!
It is not honesty in me to speak
What I have seen and known. You shall observe him,
And his own courses will denote him so 316

That I may save my speech: do but go after,
And mark how he continues.

LODOVICO
I am sorry that I am deceived in him. [*Exeunt.*

ACT FOUR SCENE TWO

A room in the castle.

Enter OTHELLO *and* EMILIA.

OTHELLO
You have seen nothing then?

EMILIA
Nor ever heard, nor ever did suspect.

OTHELLO
Yes, you have seen Cassio and she together.

EMILIA
But then I saw no harm, and then I heard
Each syllable that breath made up between them.

OTHELLO
What, did they never whisper?

EMILIA
Never, my lord. 7

OTHELLO
Nor send you out o' the way?

EMILIA
Never.

OTHELLO
To fetch her fan, her gloves, her mask, nor nothing?

EMILIA
Never, my lord.

OTHELLO
That's strange.

EMILIA
I durst, my lord, to wager she is honest,
Lay down my soul at stake: if you think other,
Remove your thought; it doth abuse your bosom.
If any wretch have put this in your head,
Let heaven requite it with the serpent's curse!
For, if she be not honest, chaste, and true,
There's no man happy; the purest of their wives
Is foul as slander.

OTHELLO
Bid her come hither: go. [*Exit Emilia.*
She says enough; yet she's a simple bawd 22
That cannot say as much. This is a subtle whore,
A closet lock and key of villanous secrets:
And yet she'll kneel and pray; I have seen her do't.

Enter DESDEMONA *with* EMILIA.

DESDEMONA
My lord, what is your will?

OTHELLO
Pray, chuck, come hither.

DESDEMONA
What is your pleasure?

OTHELLO
Let me see your eyes;
Look in my face.

DESDEMONA
What horrible fancy's this?

OTHELLO
[*To Emilia*] Some of your function, mistress;
Leave procreants alone and shut the door;
Cough, or cry 'hem,' if any body come:
Your mystery, your mystery: nay, dispatch.
[*Exit Emilia.*

DESDEMONA
Upon my knees, what doth your speech import?
I understand a fury in your words,
But not the words.

OTHELLO
Why, what art thou?

DESDEMONA
Your wife, my lord; your true
And loyal wife.

OTHELLO
Come, swear it, damn thyself
Lest, being like one of heaven, the devils themselves
Should fear to seize thee: therefore be double damn'd:
Swear thou art honest.

DESDEMONA
Heaven doth truly know it.

OTHELLO
Heaven truly knows that thou art false as hell.

DESDEMONA
To whom, my lord? with whom? how am I false? 50

OTHELLO
O Desdemona! away! away! away!

DESDEMONA
Alas the heavy day! Why do you weep?
Am I the motive of these tears, my lord?
If haply you my father do suspect
An instrument of this your calling back,
Lay not your blame on me: If you have lost him,
Why, I have lost him too.

OTHELLO
Had it pleased heaven
To try me with affliction; had they rain'd
All kinds of sores and shames on my bare head.
Steep'd me in poverty to the very lips, 61
Given to captivity me and my utmost hopes,
I should have found in some place of my soul
A drop of patience: but, alas, to make me
A fixed figure for the time of scorn

To point his slow unmoving finger at!
Yet could I bear that too; well, very well:
But there, where I have garner'd up my heart,
Where either I must live, or bear no life;
The fountain from the which my current runs,
Or else dries up; to be discarded thence! 71
Or keep it as a cistern for foul toads
To knot and gender in! Turn thy complexion there,
Patience, thou young and rose-lipp'd cherubin,—
Ay, there, look grim as hell!

DESDEMONA
I hope my noble lord esteems me honest.

OTHELLO
O, ay; as summer flies are in the shambles,
That quicken even with blowing. O thou weed,
Who art so lovely fair and smell'st so sweet
That the sense aches at thee, would thou hadst ne'er been born!

DESDEMONA
Alas, what ignorant sin have I committed? 82

OTHELLO
Was this fair paper, this most goodly book,
Made to write 'whore' upon? What committed!
Committed! O thou public commoner!
I should make very forges of my cheeks,
That would to cinders burn up modesty,
Did I but speak thy deeds. What committed!
Heaven stops the nose at it and the moon winks,
The bawdy wind that kisses all it meets
Is hush'd within the hollow mine of earth,
And will not hear it. What committed! 92
Impudent strumpet!

DESDEMONA
By heaven, you do me wrong.

OTHELLO
Are you not a strumpet?

DESDEMONA
No, as I am a Christian:
If to preserve this vessel for my lord
From any other foul unlawful touch
Be not to be a strumpet, I am none.

OTHELLO
What, not a whore?

DESDEMONA
No, as I shall be saved.

OTHELLO
Is't possible?

DESDEMONA
O, heaven forgive us!

OTHELLO
I cry you mercy, then:
I took you for that cunning whore of Venice
That married with Othello. [*Raising his voice.*
You, mistress, 107
That have the office opposite to Saint Peter,
And keep the gate of hell!

Re-enter EMILIA.

You, you, ay, you!
We have done our course; there's money for your pains:
I pray you, turn the key and keep our counsel.
[*Exit.*

EMILIA
Alas, what does this gentleman conceive?
How do you, madam? how do you, my good lady?

DESDEMONA
'Faith, half asleep.

EMILIA
Good madam, what's the matter with my lord?

DESDEMONA
With who?

EMILIA
Why, with my lord, madam. 118

DESDEMONA
Who is thy lord?

EMILIA
He that is yours, sweet lady.

DESDEMONA
I have none: do not talk to me, Emilia;
I cannot weep; nor answer have I none,
But what should go by water. Prithee, tonight
Lay on my bed my wedding sheets: remember;
And call thy husband hither.

EMILIA
Here's a change indeed! [*Exit.*

DESDEMONA
'Tis meet I should be used so, very meet.
How have I been behaved, that he might stick
The small'st opinion on my least misuse? [51]

Re-enter EMILIA *with* IAGO.

IAGO
What is your pleasure, madam?
How is't with you? 131

DESDEMONA
I cannot tell. Those that do teach young babes
Do it with gentle means and easy tasks:
He might have chid me so; for, in good faith,
I am a child to chiding.

IAGO
What's the matter, lady?

EMILIA
Alas, Iago, my lord hath so bewhored her.
Thrown such despite and heavy terms upon her,
As true hearts cannot bear.

DESDEMONA
Am I that name, Iago?

IAGO
What name, fair lady?

DESDEMONA
Such as she says my lord did say I was.
EMILIA
He call'd her whore: a beggar in his drink
Could not have laid such terms upon his callat.
IAGO
Why did he so?
DESDEMONA
I do not know; I am sure I am none such.
IAGO
Do not weep, do not weep. Alas the day!
EMILIA
Hath she forsook so many noble matches,
Her father and her country and her friends,
To be call'd whore? would it not make one weep?
DESDEMONA
It is my wretched fortune.
IAGO
Beshrew him for't!
How comes this trick upon him?
DESDEMONA
Nay, heaven doth know.
EMILIA
I will be hang'd, if some eternal villain,
Some busy and insinuating rogue,
Some cogging, cozening slave, to get some office,
Have not devised this slander; I'll be hang'd else.
IAGO
Fie, there is no such man; it is impossible.
DESDEMONA
If any such there be, heaven pardon him!
EMILIA
A halter pardon him! and hell gnaw his bones!
Why should he call her whore? who keeps her company?
What place? what time? what form? what likelihood?
The Moor's abused by some most villanous knave,
Some base notorious knave, some scurvy fellow.
O heaven, that such companions thou'ldst unfold,
And put in every honest hand a whip
To lash the rascals naked through the world
Even from the east to the west!
IAGO
Speak within door.
EMILIA
O, fie upon them! Some such squire he was
That turn'd your wit the seamy side without,
And made you to suspect me with the Moor.
IAGO
You are a fool; go to.
DESDEMONA
O good Iago,
What shall I do to win my lord again?
Good friend, go to him; for, by this light of heaven,
I know not how I lost him. Here I kneel:
If e'er my will did trespass 'gainst his love,
Either in discourse of thought or actual deed,
Or that mine eyes, mine ears, or any sense,
Delighted them in any other form;
Or that I do not yet, and ever did,
And ever will—though he do shake me off
To beggarly divorcement—love him dearly,
Comfort forswear me! Unkindness may do much;
And his unkindness may defeat my life,
But never taint my love. I cannot say 'whore:'
It does abhor me now I speak the word;
To do the act that might the addition earn
Not the world's mass of vanity could make me.
IAGO
I pray you, be content; 'tis but his humour:
The business of the state does him offence,
And he does chide with you.
DESDEMONA
If 'twere no other,—
IAGO
'Tis but so, I warrant. [*Trumpets within.*
Hark, how these instruments summon to supper!
The messengers of Venice stay the meat: [52]
Go in, and weep not; all things shall be well.
[*Exeunt Desdemona and Emilia.*

Enter RODERIGO.

How now, Roderigo!
RODERIGO
I do not find that thou dealest justly with me.
IAGO
What in the contrary?
RODERIGO
Every day thou daffest me with some device, Iago; and rather, as it seems to me now, keepest from me all conveniency than suppliest me with the least advantage of hope. I will indeed no longer endure it, nor am I yet persuaded to put up in peace what already I have foolishly suffered.
IAGO
Will you hear me, Roderigo?
RODERIGO
'Faith, I have heard too much, for your words and performances are no kin together.
IAGO
You charge me most unjustly.
RODERIGO
With nought but truth. I have wasted myself out of my means. The jewels you have had from me to deliver to Desdemona would half have corrupted a

votarist: you have told me she hath received them and returned me expectations and comforts of sudden respect and acquaintance, but I find none.

IAGO

Well; go to; very well.

RODERIGO

Very well! go to! I cannot go to, man; nor 'tis not very well: nay, I think it is scurvy, and begin to find myself fobbed in it.

IAGO

Very well.

RODERIGO

I tell you 'tis not very well. I will make myself known to Desdemona: if she will return me my jewels, I will give over my suit and repent my unlawful solicitation; if not, assure yourself I will seek satisfaction of you.

IAGO

You have said now.

RODERIGO

Ay, and said nothing but what I protest intendment of doing.

IAGO

Why, now I see there's mettle in thee, and even from this instant to build on thee a better opinion than ever before. Give me thy hand, Roderigo: thou hast taken against me a most just exception; but yet, I protest, I have dealt most directly in thy affair.

RODERIGO

It hath not appeared.

IAGO

I grant indeed it hath not appeared, and your suspicion is not without wit and judgment. But, Roderigo, if thou hast that in thee indeed, which I have greater reason to believe now than ever, I mean purpose, courage and valour, this night show it: if thou the next night following enjoy not Desdemona, take me from this world with treachery and devise engines for my life.

RODERIGO

Well, what is it? is it within reason and compass?

IAGO

Sir, there is especial commission come from Venice to depute Cassio in Othello's place.

RODERIGO

Is that true? why, then Othello and Desdemona return again to Venice.

IAGO

O, no; he goes into Mauritania and takes away with him the fair Desdemona, unless his abode be lingered here by some accident: wherein none can be so determinate as the removing of Cassio.

RODERIGO

How do you mean, removing of him?

IAGO

Why, by making him uncapable of Othello's place; knocking out his brains.

RODERIGO

And that you would have me to do?

IAGO

Ay, if you dare do yourself a profit and a right.

He sups to-night with a harlotry, and thither will I go to him: he knows not yet of his horrorable fortune. If you will watch his going thence, which I will fashion to fall out between twelve and one, you may take him at your pleasure: I will be near to second your attempt, and he shall fall between us. Come, stand not amazed at it, but go along with me; I will show you such a necessity in his death that you shall think yourself bound to put it on him. It is now high supper-time, and the night grows to waste: about it.

RODERIGO

I will hear further reason for this.

IAGO

And you shall be satisfied. [*Exeunt.*

ACT FOUR SCENE THREE

Another room In the castle.

Enter OTHELLO, LODOVICO, DESDEMONA, EMILIA *and* Attendants.

LODOVICO

I do beseech you, sir, trouble yourself no further.

OTHELLO

O, pardon me; 'twill do me good to walk.

LODOVICO

Madam, good night; I humbly thank your ladyship.

DESDEMONA

Your honour is most welcome.

OTHELLO

Will you walk, sir?

O,—Desdemona,—

DESDEMONA

My lord?

OTHELLO

Get you to bed on the instant; I will be returned forthwith: dismiss your attendant there: look it be done.

DESDEMONA

I will, my lord.

[*Exeunt Othello, Lodovico, and Attendants.*

EMILIA

How goes it now? he looks gentler than he did.

DESDEMONA

He says he will return incontinent:
He hath commanded me to go to bed,
And bade me to dismiss you.

EMILIA
Dismiss me!
DESDEMONA
It was his bidding; therefore, good Emilia,
Give me my nightly wearing, and adieu:
We must not now displease him.
EMILIA
I would you had never seen him!
DESDEMONA
So would not I my love doth so approve him,
That even his stubbornness, his check, his frowns,— 22
Prithee, unpin me,—have grace and favour in them.
EMILIA
I have laid those sheets you bade me on the bed.
DESDEMONA
All's one. Good faith, how foolish are our minds! [53]
If I do die before thee prithee, shroud me
In one of those same sheets.
EMILIA
Come, come you talk.
DESDEMONA
My mother had a maid call'd Barbara: [54]
She was in love, and he she loved proved mad
And did forsake her: she had a song of 'willow;'
An old thing 'twas, but it express'd her fortune,
And she died singing it: that song to-night 34
Will not go from my mind; I have much to do,
But to go hang my head all at one side,
And sing it like poor Barbara. Prithee, dispatch.
EMILIA
Shall I go fetch your night-gown?
DESDEMONA
No, unpin me here.
This Lodovico is a proper man.
EMILIA
A very handsome man.
DESDEMONA
He speaks well.
EMILIA
I know a lady in Venice would have walked barefoot to Palestine for a touch of his nether lip. 44
DESDEMONA
[*Singing*] The poor soul sat sighing by a sycamore tree, [55]
Sing all a green willow; [56]
Her hand on her bosom, her head on her knee,
Sing willow, willow, willow:
The fresh streams ran by her, and murmur'd her moans;
Sing willow, willow, willow;
Her salt tears fell from her, and soften'd the stones;—
Lay by these:—
[*Singing*] Sing willow, willow, willow;
Prithee, hie thee; he'll come anon:— 57
[*Singing*] Sing all a green willow must be my garland.
Let nobody blame him; his scorn I approve,—
Nay, that's not next.—Hark! who is't that knocks?
EMILIA
It's the wind.
DESDEMONA
[*Singing*] I call'd my love false love; but what said he then?
Sing willow, willow, willow:
If I court moe women, you'll couch with moe men.—
So, get thee gone; good night. Mine eyes do itch;
Doth that bode weeping?
EMILIA
'Tis neither here nor there.
DESDEMONA
I have heard it said so. O, these men, these men! 72
Dost thou in conscience think,—tell me, Emilia,—
That there be women do abuse their husbands
In such gross kind?
EMILIA
There be some such, no question.
DESDEMONA
Wouldst thou do such a deed for all the world?
EMILIA
Why, would not you?
DESDEMONA
No, by this heavenly light!
EMILIA
Nor I neither by this heavenly light;
I might do't as well i' the dark.
DESDEMONA
Wouldst thou do such a deed for all the world?
EMILIA
The world's a huge thing: it is a great price.
For a small vice.
DESDEMONA
In troth, I think thou wouldst not. 85
EMILIA
In troth, I think I should; and undo't when I had done. Marry, I would not do such a thing for a joint-ring, nor for measures of lawn, nor for gowns, petticoats, nor caps, nor any petty exhibition; but for the whole world,—why, who would not make her husband a cuckold to make him a monarch? I should venture purgatory for't.
DESDEMONA
Beshrew me, if I would do such a wrong
For the whole world. 94

EMILIA
Why the wrong is but a wrong i' the world; and having the world for your labour, 'tis a wrong in your own world, and you might quickly make it right.

DESDEMONA
I do not think there is any such woman.

EMILIA
Yes, a dozen; and as many to the vantage as would store the world they played for.
But I do think it is their husbands' faults
If wives do fall: say that they slack their duties,
And pour our treasures into foreign laps,
Or else break out in peevish jealousies,
Throwing restraint upon us; or say they strike us,
Or scant our former having in despite;
Why, we have galls, and though we have some grace,
Yet have we some revenge. Let husbands know
Their wives have sense like them: they see and smell
And have their palates both for sweet and sour,
As husbands have. What is it that they do
When they change us for others? Is it sport?
I think it is: and doth affection breed it?
I think it doth: is't frailty that thus errs?
It is so too: and have not we affections,
Desires for sport, and frailty, as men have?
Then let them use us well: else let them know,
The ills we do, their ills instruct us so.

DESDEMONA
Good night, good night: heaven me such uses send,
Not to pick bad from bad, but by bad mend!
[*Exeunt.*

ACT FIVE SCENE ONE

Cyprus. A street.

Enter IAGO *and* RODERIGO.

IAGO
Here, stand behind this bulk; straight will he come:
Wear thy good rapier bare, and put it home:
Quick, quick; fear nothing; I'll be at thy elbow:
It makes us, or it mars us; think on that,
And fix most firm thy resolution.

RODERIGO
Be near at hand; I may miscarry in't.

IAGO
Here, at thy hand: be bold, and take thy stand.
[*Retires.*

RODERIGO
I have no great devotion to the deed;
And yet he hath given me satisfying reasons:
'Tis but a man gone. Forth, my sword: he dies.

IAGO
I have rubb'd this young quat almost to the sense,
And he grows angry. Now, whether he kill Cassio,
Or Cassio him, or each do kill the other,
Every way makes my gain: live Roderigo,
He calls me to a restitution large
Of gold and jewels that I bobb'd from him,
As gifts to Desdemona;
It must not be: if Cassio do remain,
He hath a daily beauty in his life
That makes me ugly; and, besides, the Moor
May unfold me to him; there stand I in much peril:
No, he must die. But so: I hear him coming.

Enter CASSIO.

RODERIGO
I know his gait, 'tis he.—Villain, thou diest!
[*Makes a pass at Cassio.*

CASSIO
That thrust had been mine enemy indeed,
But that my coat is better than thou know'st
I will make proof of thine.
[*Draws, and wounds Roderigo.*

RODERIGO
O, I am slain!
[*Iago from behind wounds Cassio in the leg, and exit.*

CASSIO
I am maim'd for ever. Help, ho! murder! murder!
[*Falls.*

Enter OTHELLO.

OTHELLO
The voice of Cassio: Iago keeps his word.

RODERIGO
O, villain that I am!

OTHELLO
It is even so.

CASSIO
O, help, ho! light! a surgeon!

OTHELLO
'Tis he:—O brave Iago, honest and just,
That hast such noble sense of thy friend's wrong!
Thou teachest me. Minion, your dear lies dead,
And your unblest fate hies: strumpet, I come.
Forth of my heart those charms, thine eyes, are blotted;
Thy bed, lust-stain'd, shall with lust's blood be spotted.
[*Exit.*

Enter LODOVICO *and* GRATIANO.

CASSIO
What, ho! no watch? no passage? murder! murder!

GRATIANO
'Tis some mischance; the cry is very direful.

CASSIO
O, help!
LODOVICO
Hark! 44
RODERIGO
O wretched villain!
LODOVICO
Two or three groan: it is a heavy night:
These may be counterfeits: let's think't unsafe
To come in to the cry without more help.
RODERIGO
Nobody come? then shall I bleed to death.
LODOVICO
Hark!

Re-enter IAGO, *with a light.*

GRATIANO
Here's one comes in his shirt, with light and weapons.
IAGO
Who's there? whose noise is this that ones on murder?
LODOVICO
We do not know.
IAGO
Did not you hear a cry?
CASSIO
Here, here! for heaven's sake, help me!
IAGO
What's the matter? 58
GRATIANO
This is Othello's ancient, as I take it.
LODOVICO
The same indeed; a very valiant fellow.
IAGO
What are you here that cry so grievously?
CASSIO
Iago? O, I am spoil'd, undone by villains!
Give me some help.
IAGO
O me, lieutenant! what villains have done this?
CASSIO
I think that one of them is hereabout,
And cannot make away.
IAGO
O treacherous villains!
What are you there? come in, and give some help.
[*To Lodovico and Gratiano.*
RODERIGO
O, help me here! 69
CASSIO
That's one of them.
IAGO
O murderous slave! O villain! [*Stabs Roderigo.*
RODERIGO
O damn'd Iago! O inhuman dog!
IAGO
Kill men i' the dark!—Where be these bloody thieves?—
How silent is this town!—Ho! murder! murder!—
What may you be? are you of good or evil?
LODOVICO
As you shall prove us, praise us.
IAGO
Signior Lodovico?
LODOVICO
He, sir.
IAGO
I cry you mercy. Here's Cassio hurt by villains.
GRATIANO
Cassio!
IAGO
How is't, brother!
CASSIO
My leg is cut in two.
IAGO
Marry, heaven forbid!
Light, gentlemen; I'll bind it with my shirt.

Enter BIANCA.

BIANCA
What is the matter, ho? who is't that cried?
IAGO
Who is't that cried!
BIANCA
O my dear Cassio! my sweet Cassio! O Cassio,
Cassio, Cassio!
IAGO
O notable strumpet! Cassio, may you suspect
Who they should be that have thus mangled you? 93
CASSIO
No.
GRATIANO
I am to find you thus: I have been to seek you.
IAGO
Lend me a garter. So. O, for a chair, [57]
To bear him easily hence!
BIANCA
Alas, he faints! O Cassio, Cassio, Cassio!
IAGO
Gentlemen all, I do suspect this trash
To be a party in this injury.
Patience awhile, good Cassio. Come, come;
Lend me a light. Know we this face or no?
Alas, my friend and my dear countryman
Roderigo! no:—yes, sure: O heaven! Roderigo.

BIANCA O, my dear Cassio! my sweet Cassio!

GRATIANO
What, of Venice?
IAGO
Even he, sir: did you know him?
GRATIANO
Know him! ay.
IAGO
Signior Gratiano? I cry you gentle pardon;
These bloody accidents must excuse my manners,
That so neglected you.
GRATIANO
I am glad to see you.
IAGO
How do you, Cassio? O, a chair, a chair!
GRATIANO
Roderigo!
IAGO
He, he 'tis he. [*A chair brought in.*
O, that's well said; the chair.
Some good man bear him carefully from hence;
I'll fetch the general's surgeon. [*To Bianca*] For you, mistress,
Save you your labour. He that lies slain here, Cassio,
Was my dear friend: what malice was between you?
CASSIO
None in the world; nor do I know the man.
IAGO
[*To Bianca.*] What, look you pale? O, bear him out o' the air.
[*Cassio and Roderigo are borne off.*
Stay you, good gentlemen. Look you pale, mistress? [58]
Do you perceive the gastness of her eye?
Nay, if you stare, we shall hear more anon. [59]
Behold her well; I pray you, look upon her:
Do you see, gentlemen? nay, guiltiness will speak,
Though tongues were out of use.

Enter EMILIA.

EMILIA
'Las, what's the matter? what's the matter, husband?
IAGO
Cassio hath here been set on in the dark
By Roderigo and fellows that are scaped:
He's almost slain, and Roderigo dead.
EMILIA
Alas, good gentleman! alas, good Cassio!
IAGO
This is the fruit of whoring. Prithee, Emilia,

OTHELLO Put out the light, and then—put out the light!

Go know of Cassio where he supp'd to-night.
[*To Bianca*] What, do you shake at that?

BIANCA
He supp'd at my house; but I therefore shake not.

IAGO
O, did he so? I charge you, go with me. 141

EMILIA
Fie, fie upon thee, strumpet!

BIANCA
I am no strumpet; but of life as honest
As you that thus abuse me.

EMILIA
As I! foh! fie upon thee!

IAGO
Kind gentlemen, let's go see poor Cassio dress'd.
Come, mistress, you must tell's another tale.
Emilia, run you to the citadel,
And tell my lord and lady what hath happ'd.
Will you go on? I pray. [*Aside*] This is the night
That either makes me or fordoes me quite.
[*Exeunt.*

ACT FIVE SCENE TWO

A bedchamber in the castle: DESDEMONA *in bed asleep*; a light burning.
Enter OTHELLO.

OTHELLO
It is the cause, it is the cause, my soul,—
Let me not name it to you, you chaste stars!—
It is the cause. Yet I'll not shed her blood;
Nor scar that whiter skin of hers than snow,
And smooth as monumental alabaster.
Yet she must die, else she'll betray more men.
Put out the light, and then put out the light:
If I quench thee, thou flaming minister,
I can again thy former light restore,
Should I repent me: but once put out thy light,
Thou cunning'st pattern of excelling nature,
I know not where is that Promethean heat
That can thy light relume. When I have pluck'd the rose,
I cannot give it vital growth again.

It must needs wither: I'll smell it on the tree.
[*Kissing her.*
Ah, balmy breath, that dost almost persuade
Justice to break her sword! One more, one more.
Be thus when thou art dead, and I will kill thee,
And love thee after. One more, and this the last:
So sweet was ne'er so fatal. I must weep, 21
But they are cruel tears: this sorrow's heavenly;
It strikes where it doth love. She wakes.
DESDEMONA
Who's there? Othello?
OTHELLO
Ay, Desdemona.
DESDEMONA
Will you come to bed, my lord?
OTHELLO
Have you pray'd to-night, Desdemona?
DESDEMONA
Ay, my lord.
OTHELLO
If you bethink yourself of any crime
Unreconciled as yet to heaven and grace,
Solicit for it straight.
DESDEMONA
Alas, my lord, what do you mean by that?
OTHELLO
Well, do it, and be brief; I will walk by: 33
I would not kill thy unprepared spirit;
No; heaven forfend! I would not kill thy soul.
DESDEMONA
Talk you of killing?
OTHELLO
Ay, I do.
DESDEMONA
Then heaven
Have mercy on me!
OTHELLO
Amen, with all my heart!
DESDEMONA
If you say so, I hope you will not kill me.
OTHELLO
Hum!
DESDEMONA
And yet I fear you; for you are fatal then
When your eyes roll so: why I should fear I know not,
Since guiltiness I know not; but yet I feel I fear.
OTHELLO
Think on thy sins.
DESDEMONA
They are loves I bear to you. 47
OTHELLO
Ay, and for that thou diest.
DESDEMONA
That death's unnatural that kills for loving.
Alas, why gnaw you so your nether lip?
Some bloody passion shakes your very frame:
These are portents: but yet I hope, I hope,
They do not point on me.
OTHELLO
Peace, and be still!
DESDEMONA
I will so. What's the matter?
OTHELLO
That handkerchief which I so loved and gave thee
Thou gavest to Cassio.
DESDEMONA
No, by my life and soul!
Send for the man, and ask him.
OTHELLO
Sweet soul, take heed, 60
Take heed of perjury; thou art on thy deathbed.
DESDEMONA
Ay, but not yet to die.
OTHELLO
Yes, presently:
Therefore confess thee freely of thy sin;
For to deny each article with oath
Cannot remove nor choke the strong conception
That I do groan withal. Thou art to die.
DESDEMONA
Then Lord have mercy on me!
OTHELLO
I say, amen.
DESDEMONA
And have you mercy too! I never did
Offend you in my life; never loved Cassio
But with such general warranty of heaven 72
As I might love; I never gave him token.
OTHELLO
By heaven, I saw my handkerchief in's hand.
O perjured woman! thou dost stone my heart,
And makest me call what I intend to do
A murder, which I thought a sacrifice:
I saw the handkerchief.
DESDEMONA
He found it then;
I never gave it him: send for him hither;
Let him confess a truth.
OTHELLO
He hath confess'd.
DESDEMONA
What, my lord?
OTHELLO
That he hath used thee.
DESDEMONA
How? unlawfully?
OTHELLO
Ay. 86

DESDEMONA
He will not say so.

OTHELLO
No, his mouth is stopp'd;
Honest Iago hath ta'en order for't.

DESDEMONA
O! my fear interprets: what, is he dead?

OTHELLO
Had all his hairs been lives, my great revenge
Had stomach for them all.

DESDEMONA
Alas! he is betray'd and I undone.

OTHELLO
Out, strumpet! weep'st thou for him to my face?

DESDEMONA
O, banish me, my lord, but kill me not!

OTHELLO
Down, strumpet!

DESDEMONA
Kill me to-morrow: let me live to-night! 97

OTHELLO
Nay, if you strive,—

DESDEMONA
But half an hour! [57]

OTHELLO
Being done, there is no pause.

DESDEMONA
But while I say one prayer!

OTHELLO
It is too late.

[*He stifles her.*

EMILIA
[*Within*] My lord, my lord! what, ho! my lord, my lord!

OTHELLO
What noise is this? Not dead? not yet quite dead?
I that am cruel am yet merciful;
I would not have thee linger in thy pain: So, so.

EMILIA
[*Within*] What, ho! my lord, my lord!

OTHELLO
Who's there?

EMILIA
[*Within*] O, good my lord, I would speak a word with you! 111

OTHELLO
Yes: 'tis Emilia. By and by. She's dead.
'Tis like she comes to speak of Cassio's death.—
The noise was here. Ha! no more moving?
Still as the grave. Shall she come in? were't good?—
I think she stirs again:—no. What's best to do?
If she come in, she'll sure speak to my wife:
My wife! my wife! what wife? I have no wife.
O insupportable! O heavy hour!
Methinks it should be now a huge eclipse
Of sun and moon, and that the affrighted globe
Should yawn at alteration.

EMILIA
[*Within*] I do beseech you 124
That I may speak with you, O, good my lord!

OTHELLO
I had forgot thee: O, come in, Emilia:
Soft; by and by. Let me the curtains draw.
Where art thou? [*Unlocks the door.*

Enter EMILIA.

What's the matter with thee now?

EMILIA
O, my good lord, yonder's foul murders done!

OTHELLO
What, now?

EMILIA
But now, my lord.

OTHELLO
It is the very error of the moon;
She comes more nearer earth than she was wont,
And makes men mad. 135

EMILIA
Cassio, my lord, hath kill'd a young Venetian
Call'd Roderigo.

OTHELLO
Roderigo kill'd!
And Cassio kill'd!

EMILIA
No, Cassio is not kill'd.

OTHELLO
Not Cassio kill'd! then murder's out of tune,
And sweet revenge grows harsh.

DESDEMONA
O, falsely, falsely murder'd!

EMILIA
Alas, what cry is that?

OTHELLO
That! what?

EMILIA
Out, and alas! that was my lady's voice. 146
Help! help, ho! help! O lady, speak again!
Sweet Desdemona! O sweet mistress, speak!

DESDEMONA
A guiltless death I die.

EMILIA
O, who hath done this deed?

DESDEMONA
Nobody; I myself. Farewell
Commend me to my kind lord: O, farewell!

[*Dies.*

OTHELLO
Why, how should she be murder'd?
EMILIA
Alas, who knows?
OTHELLO
You heard her say herself, it was not I.
EMILIA
She said so: I must needs report the truth.
OTHELLO
She's, like a liar, gone to burning hell:
'Twas I that kill'd her.
EMILIA
O, the more angel she, 159
And you the blacker devil!
OTHELLO
She turn'd to folly, and she was a whore.
EMILIA
Thou dost belie her, and thou art a devil.
OTHELLO
She was false as water.
EMILIA
Thou art rash as fire, to say
That she was false: O, she was heavenly true!
OTHELLO
Cassio did top her; ask thy husband else.
O, I were damn'd beneath all depth in hell,
But that I did proceed upon just grounds
To this extremity. Thy husband knew it all.
EMILIA
My husband! 170
OTHELLO
Thy husband.
EMILIA
That she was false to wedlock?
OTHELLO
Ay, with Cassio. Nay, had she been true,
If heaven would make me such another world
Of one entire and Perfect chrysolite,
I'ld not have sold her for it.
EMILIA
My husband!
OTHELLO
Ay, 'twas he that told me first:
An honest man he is, and hates the slime
That sticks on filthy deeds.
EMILIA
My husband!
OTHELLO
What needs this iteration, woman? I say thy husband. 183
EMILIA
O mistress, villany hath made mocks with love, [61]
My husband say that she was false!
OTHELLO
He, woman;
I say thy husband: dost understand the word?
My friend, thy husband, honest, honest Iago.
EMILIA
If he say so, may his pernicious soul
Rot half a grain a day! he lies to the heart:
She was too fond of her most filthy bargain.
OTHELLO
Ha!
EMILIA
Do thy worst:
This deed of thine is no more worthy heaven.
Than thou wast worthy her.
OTHELLO
Peace, you were best.
EMILIA
Thou hast not half that power to do me harm
As I have to be hurt. O gull! O dolt!
As ignorant as dirt! thou hast done a deed—
I care not for thy sword; I'll make thee known,
Though I lost twenty lives.— Help! help, ho! help!
The Moor hath kill'd my mistress! Murder! murder!

Enter MONTANO, GRATIANO, IAGO,
and others.

MONTANO
What is the matter? How now, general!
EMILIA
O, are you come, Iago? you have done well,
That men must lay their murders on your neck.
GRATIANO
What is the matter? 207
EMILIA
Disprove this villain, if thou be'st a man: [62]
He says thou told'st him that his wife was false:
I know thou didst not, thou'rt not such a villain:
Speak, for my heart is full.
IAGO
I told him what I thought, and told no more
Than what he found himself was apt and true.
EMILIA
But did you ever tell him she was false?
IAGO
I did.
EMILIA
You told a lie; an odious, damned lie; 216
Upon my soul, a lie, a wicked lie.
She false with Cassio!—did you say with Cassio?
IAGO
With Cassio, mistress. Go to, charm your tongue.
EMILIA
I will not charm my tongue; I am bound to speak:
My mistress here lies murder'd in her bed,— [57]

ALL
O heavens forfend!
EMILIA
And your reports have set the murder on.
OTHELLO
Nay, stare not, masters: it is true, indeed.
GRATIANO
'Tis a strange truth.
MONTANO
O monstrous act!
EMILIA
Villany, villany, villany!
I think upon't, I think: I smell't: O villany!—
I thought so then:—I'll kill myself for grief:—
O villany, villany!
IAGO
What, are you mad? I charge you, get you home.
EMILIA
Good gentlemen, let me have leave to speak:
'Tis proper I obey him, but not now.
Perchance, Iago, I will ne'er go home.
OTHELLO
O! O! O! [*He falls on the bed.*
EMILIA
Nay, lay thee down and roar;
For thou hast kill'd the sweetest innocent
That e'er did lift up eye.
OTHELLO
[*Rising*] O, she was foul!
I scarce did know you, uncle: there lies your niece,
Whose breath, indeed, these hands have newly stopp'd:
I know this act shows horrible and grim.
GRATIANO
Poor Desdemona! I am glad thy father's dead:
Thy match was mortal to him, and pure grief
Shore his old thread in twain: did he live now,
This sight would make him do a desperate turn,
Yea, curse his better angel from his side,
And fall to reprobation.
OTHELLO
'Tis pitiful; but yet Iago knows
That she with Cassio hath the act of shame
A thousand times committed; Cassio confess'd it:
And she did gratify his amorous works
With that recognizance and pledge of love
Which I first gave her; I saw it in his hand:
It was a handkerchief, an antique token
My father gave my mother.
EMILIA
O heaven! O heavenly powers!
IAGO
Come, hold your peace.
EMILIA
'Twill out, 'twill out: I peace!
No, I will speak as liberal as the north:
Let heaven and men and devils, let them all,
All, all, cry shame against me, yet I'll speak.
IAGO
Be wise, and get you home.
EMILIA
I will not. [*Iago offers to stab Emilia.*
GRATIANO
Fie!
Your sword upon a woman?
EMILIA
O thou dull Moor! that handkerchief thou speak'st of
I found by fortune and did give my husband;
For often, with a solemn earnestness,
More than indeed belong'd to such a trifle,
He begg'd of me to steal it.
IAGO
Villanous whore!
EMILIA
She give it Cassio! no, alas! I found it,
And I did give't my husband.
IAGO
Filth, thou liest!
EMILIA
By heaven, I do not, I do not, gentlemen.
O murderous coxcomb! what should such a fool
Do with so good a woman?
OTHELLO
Are there no stones in heaven
But what serve for the thunder?—Precious villain!
[*He runs at Iago: Iago, from behind, stabs Emilia, and exit.*
GRATIANO
The woman falls; sure, he hath kill'd his wife.
EMILIA
Ay, ay: O, lay me by my mistress' side.
GRATIANO
He's gone, but his wife's kill'd.
MONTANO
'Tis a notorious villain. Take you this weapon,
Which I have here recover'd from the Moor:
Come, guard the door without; let him not pass,
But kill him rather. I'll after that same villain,
For 'tis a damned slave.
[*Exeunt Montano and Gratiano.*
OTHELLO
I am not valiant neither,
But ever puny whipster gets my sword:
But why should honour outlive honesty?
Let it go all.

EMILIA
What did thy song bode, lady?
Hark, canst thou hear me? I will play the swan.
And die in music. [*Singing*] Willow, willow, willow.—
Moor, she was chaste; she loved thee, cruel Moor;
So come my soul to bliss, as I speak true; 301
So speaking as I think, I die, I die. [*Dies.*

OTHELLO
I have another weapon in this chamber;
It is a sword of Spain, the ice-brook's temper:—
O, here it is. Uncle, I must come forth.

GRATIANO
[*Within*] If thou attempt it, it will cost thee dear:
Thou hast no weapon, and perforce must suffer.

OTHELLO
Look in upon me then and speak with me,
Or, naked as I am, I will assault thee.

Re-enter GRATIANO.

GRATIANO
What is the matter?

OTHELLO
Behold, I have a weapon;
A better never did itself sustain 312
Upon a soldier's thigh: I have seen the day,
That, with this little arm and this good sword,
I have made my way through more impediments
Than twenty times your stop: but, O vain boast!
Who can control his fate? 'tis not so now.
Be not afraid, though you do see me weapon'd; [57]
Here is my journey's end, here is my butt,
And very sea-mark of my utmost sail.
Do you go back dismay'd? 'tis a lost fear;
Man but a rush against Othello's breast, 322
And he retires. Where should Othello go?
Now, how dost thou look now? O ill-starr'd wench!
Pale as thy smock! when we shall meet at compt,
This look of thine will hurl my soul from heaven,
And fiends will snatch at it. Cold, cold, my girl!
Even like thy chastity. O cursed slave!
Whip me, ye devils,
From the possession of this heavenly sight!
Blow me about in winds! roast me in sulphur!
Wash me in steep-down gulfs of liquid fire!
O Desdemona! Desdemona! dead!
Oh! Oh! Oh!

Enter LODOVICO. MONTANO, CASSIO *carried in a chair, and* Officers *with* IAGO, *prisoner.*

LODOVICO
Where is this rash and most unfortunate man?

OTHELLO
That's he that was Othello: here I am.

LODOVICO
Where is that viper? bring the villain forth.

OTHELLO
I look down towards his feet; but that's a fable.
If that thou best a devil, I cannot kill thee.
[*Wounds Iago.*

LODOVICO
Wrench his sword from him.

IAGO
I bleed, sir; but not kill'd.

OTHELLO
I am not sorry neither: I'ld have thee live;
For, in my sense, 'tis happiness to die. 343

LODOVICO
O thou Othello, thou wert once so good,
Fall'n in the practise of a damned slave,
What shall be said to thee?

OTHELLO
Why, any thing:
An honourable murderer, if you will;
For nought I did in hate, but all in honour.

LODOVICO
This wretch hath part confess'd his villany:
Did you and he consent in Cassio's death?

OTHELLO
Ay.

CASSIO
Dear general, I never gave you cause.

OTHELLO
I do believe it, and I ask your pardon.
Will you, I pray, demand that demi-devil 355
Why he hath thus ensnared my soul and body?

IAGO
Demand me nothing: what you know, you know:
From this time forth I never will speak word.

LODOVICO
What, not to pray?

GRATIANO
Torments will ope your lips.

OTHELLO
Well, thou dost best.

LODOVICO
Sir, you shall understand what hath befall'n,
Which, as I think, you know not. Here is a letter
Found in the pocket of the slain Roderigo;
And here another: the one of them imports
The death of Cassio to be undertook
By Roderigo.

OTHELLO
O villain!

CASSIO
Most heathenish and most gross!

LODOVICO
Now here's another discontented paper,

Found in his pocket too; and this, it seems,
Roderigo meant to have sent this damned villain;
But that belike Iago in the interim
Came in and satisfied him.

OTHELLO

O the pernicious caitiff!
How came you, Cassio, by that handkerchief
That was my wife's?

CASSIO

I found it in my chamber:
And he himself confess'd but even now
That there he dropp'd it for a special purpose
Which wrought to his desire.

OTHELLO

O fool! fool! fool!

CASSIO

There is besides in Roderigo's letter,
How he upbraids Iago, that he made him
Brave me upon the watch; whereon it came
That I was cast: and even but now he spake,
After long seeming dead, Iago hurt him,
Iago set him on.

LODOVICO

You must forsake this room, and go with us:
Your power and your command is taken off,
And Cassio rules in Cyprus. For this slave,
If there be any cunning cruelty
That can torment him much and hold him long,
It shall be his. You shall close prisoner rest,
Till that the nature of your fault be known
To the Venetian state. Come, bring him away. [63]

OTHELLO

Soft you; a word or two before you go.
I have done the state some service, and they know't.
No more of that. I pray you, in your letters,
When you shall these unlucky deeds relate,
Speak of me as I am; nothing extenuate,
Nor set down aught in malice: then must you speak
Of one that loved not wisely but too well;
Of one not easily jealous, but being wrought
Perplex'd in the extreme; of one whose hand,
Like the base Indian, threw a pearl away [64]
Richer than all his tribe; of one whose subdued eyes,
Albeit unused to the melting mood,
Drop tears as fast as the Arabian trees
Their medicinal gum. Set you down this;
And say besides, that in Aleppo once,
Where a malignant and a turban'd Turk
Beat a Venetian and traduced the state,
I took by the throat the circumcised dog,
And smote him, thus. *[Stabs himself.*

LODOVICO

O bloody period!

GRATIANO

All that's spoke is marr'd.

OTHELLO

I kiss'd thee ere I kill'd thee: no way but this;
Killing myself, to die upon a kiss.
[Falls on the bed, and dies.

CASSIO

This did I fear, but thought he had no weapon;
For he was great of heart.

LODOVICO

[*To Iago*] O Spartan dog,
More fell than anguish, hunger, or the sea!
Look on the tragic loading of this bed;
This is thy work: the object poisons sight;
Let it be hid. Gratiano, keep the house,
And seize upon the fortunes of the Moor,
For they succeed on you. To you, lord governor,
Remains the censure of this hellish villain;
The time, the place, the torture: O, enforce it!
Myself will straight aboard; and to the state
This heavy act with heavy heart relate.
[Exeunt.

Notes

1. Omitted in Folios and Quartos 2, 3.
2. A fellow almost damn'd in a fair wife; – if this alludes to Bianca, the phrase may possibly mean 'very near being married to a most fair wife.' Some explain, "A fellow whose ignorance of war would be condemned in a fair woman." The emendations proposed are unsatisfactory, and probably unnecessary.
3. Changes; – Folios read *'chances.'*
4. Omitted Quarto 1.
5. Weaken motion; – Rowe's emendation; Folios and Quartos 2, 3, *'weakens motion';* Pope (Ed. 2, Theobald) *'weaken notion';* Hammer, *'waken motion';* Keightley, *'wakens motion';* Anon. conjecture in Furness *'wake emotion,'* &c.
6. Bloody book of law; – "By the Venetian law the giving of love-potions was highly criminal" (Clarke).
7. Feats of broil; – Capell's emendation; Quarto 1, *'feate of broile';* Folio 1, *'Feats of Broiles,'* &c.
8. Certain; – so Quartos; Folios *'wider.'*
9. Portance in my; – so Folios and Quarto 2; Quarto 3, *'portence in my';* Quarto 1, *'with it all my';* Johnson conjectured *'portance in't; my';* &c.; *'travels";* the reading of Modern Edd. (Globe Ed.); Quartos, *'trauells';* Pope, *'travel's';* Folio 1, *'Trauellours';* Folios 2, 3, *'Travellers';* Folio 4, *'Traveller's';* Richardson conjectured *'travellous'* or *'travailous.'*
10. Sighs; – Folios, *'kisses';* Southern MS., *'thanks.'*
11. And storm of fortunes; – Quarto 1, *'and scorne of Fortunes,'* &c.

12. Let her have your voices – Dyce's correction; Folios, *'Let her have your voice'*; Quartos read:—

"Your voyces Lords; beseech you let her will
Haue a free way."

13. The young affects in me defunct; – Quartos, *'the young affects In my defunct'*; so Folio 1; Folios 2, 3, 4 *('effects')*. The reading of the text is the simplest and most plausible emendation of the many proposed, the words meaning 'the passions of youth which I have now outlived': *'proper satisfaction'* = 'my own gratification.'
14. Balance; – Folios, *'brain'* and *'braine'*; Theobald, *'beam.'*
15. Luscious as locusts; – "perhaps so mentioned from being placed together with wild honey in St. Matthew iii. 4" (Schmidt).
16. Omitted in Folios.
17. The reading in the text is that of the second and third Quartos; Quarto 1, adds after the words *'I am chang'd'*:—

"Goe to, farewell, put money enough in your purse";
omitting *'I'll go sell all my land.'*

18. (Didst not mark that? –); omitted in Quarto 1.
19. Tire the ingener; – Knight, Steevens conjectured; Folio 1, *'tyre the Ingenirer'*; Folios 2, 3, 4, *'tire the Ingeniver'*; Quarto 1, *'beare all Excellency —;* Quartos 2, 3, *'beare an excelency'*:—Johnson conjectured *'tire the ingenious verse'*; Pope, *'beare all excellency—'*
20. And ... Cyprus; – omitted in Folios.
21. A devilish knave; – omitted in Quartos.
22. Blest pudding; – Folios, *'Bless'd pudding'*; omitted in Quartos.
23. Comes the master and main; – so Folios; Quarto 1 reads *'comes the maine'*; Quartos 2, 3, *'comes Roderigo, the master and the maine.'*
24. Haply may; – Quartos read *'haply with his Trunchen may.'*
25. Poor trash of Venice, whom I trash; – Steevens' emendation; Quarto 1, *'poor trash ... I crush'*; Folios, Quartos 2, 3, *'poor Trash ... I trace'*; Theobald, Warburton conjectured *'poor brach ... I trace'*; Warburton (later conjectured) *'poor brach ... I cherish.'*
26. Here, i.e. – in my head.
27. These lines are from an old song called *'Take thy old cloak about thee,'* to be found in Percy's *Reliques*.
28. Sense of place; – Hanmer's emendation of Quartos, Folios, *'place of sense.'*
29. Some time; – so Quartos; Folios, *'a time'*; Grant White, *'one time.'*
30. For love's sake; – Quarto 1, *'of all loues.'*
31. Florentine, i.e. – 'even a Florentine'; Iago was a Venetian.
32. Omitted in Folios.
33. Watch him tame, i.e. – tame him by keeping him from sleep (as was done with hawks).
34. By heaven, he echoes me; – Quarto 1, *'By heauen he ecchoes me'*; Folios, *'Alas, thou echos't me'*; Quartos 2, 3, *'why dost thou ecchoe me.'*
35. Thy worst of thoughts; – so Folios, Quarto 2; Quarto 1, reads *'the worst of thoughts'*; Quarto 3, *'thy thoughts'*; perhaps we should read:—

"As thou dost rum'nate, give thy worst of thoughts."

36. Strongly; – so Quartos; Folios, *'soundly'*; Knight, *'fondly.'*
37. Desdemona comes; – so Quartos; Folios read *'Looke where she comes.'*
38. Omitted in Quarto 1.
39. Any that was hers; – Malone's emendation; Quartos, *'any, it was hers'*; Folio 1, *'any, it was hers'*; Folios 2, 3, 4, *'any if't was hers'*; Anon. conjecture *'any 'it' was hers.'*
40. Thy hollow cell; – so Quartos; Folios read *'the hollow hell'*; Warburton, *'th' unhallow'd cell.'*
41. Steevens compares the following passage in Holland's *Pliny*:—"And the sea Pontus ever more floweth and runneth out from Propontes, but the sea never retireth back again within Pontus."
42. Business ever; – Quartos, *'worke so euer'*; Collier, *'work soe'er'*; &c.
43. Our new heraldry, – (*vide* Preface).
44. Her, i.e. – to my wife (implied in *'wive'*).
45. Shut myself up in, – &c., *i.e.* 'Confine myself to some other course of life, awaiting fortune's charity'; Quarto 1, *'shoote my selfe up in'*; Capell, *'shoot myself upon'*; Rann, *'shape myself upon'*; Collier MS., *'shift myself upon.'*
46. Warrior; – Hanmer *'wrangler'*; *cp.* *'O my fair warrior'*; (II. i. 184).
47. Here o'erwhelmed; – Quarto 1, *'here ere while, mad.'*
48. (What, a customer! –); ii. 73-76; iii. 60-63, 87-104; omitted in Quarto 1.
49. And, by this hand, she falls me; – so Collier; Quarto 1, reads *'by this hand she fals'*; Folios, *'and falls me'*; Quartos 2, 3, *'fals me.'*
50. This the nature; – Pope's reading; Quartos, *'This the noble nature'*; Folios, *'Is this the nature.'*
51. Least misuse; – Quarto 1, *'greatest abuse'*; Collier MS., *'least misdeede.'*
52. The messengers of Venice stay the meat; – Knight's reading; Folio 1, *'The Messengers of Venice staies the meate'*; Folios 2, 3, 4, *'The Messenger of Venice staies the meate'*; Quarto 1, *'And the great Messengers of Venice stay'*; Quartos 2, 3, *'The meate, great Messengers of Venice stay.'*
53. All's one. Good faith; – Quarto 1, *'All's one good faith'*; Quartos 2, 3, *'All's one; good father'*; Folios, *'All's one: good Father.'*
54. Barbara; – Quartos read, *'Barbary'*; Folio 1, *'Barbarie.'*
55. &c.; The original of Desdemona's song is to be found in Percy's *Reliques* under the title of *'A Lover's Complaint, being forsaken of his Love,'* where the plaintive lover is a man.
56. Sighing; – Folios, *'singing'*; Quarto 3, *'singhing'*; Folio 1 (Dev.) *'sining.'*
57. Omitted in Quarto 1.
58. Gentlemen; – the reading of Folios; Quartos, *'Gentlewoman.'*
59. If you stare; – so Folios; Quartos 1, 2, *'an you stirre'*; Quarto 3, *'an you stirr'*; Anon. conjecture *'if you stay.'*
60. Put out the light, and then put out the light; i.e. – 'put out the light, and then put out the light of life.' The Cambridge Editors give some dozen variant methods of punctuating and reading the line, but it is perfectly clear as it stands.
61. Made mocks with love; – "taken advantage to play upon the weakness of passion" (Johnson).

62. Disprove this villain; – Capell, *'Disprove it, villain.'*
63. Bring away; – Quartos, *'bring him away';* Collier MS., *'bring them away.'*
64. Indian; – Folio 1, *'Iudean';* Theobald proposed *'Judian,'* adding, "I am satisfied in his *Judian* he is alluding to Herod, who, in a fit of blind jealosie, threw away such a jewel of a wife as *Mariamne* was to him." This interpretation was Warburton's. "This it is," as Coleridge put it, "for no-poets to comment on the greatest of poets! To make Othello say that he, who had killed his wife, was like Herod who had killed Mariamne!" Boswell aptly quotes from Habington's *Castara*—

"So the unskilful Indian those bright gems
Which might add majesty to diadems,
'Mong the waves scatters."

ROMEO AND JULIET

ROMEO AND JULIET

DRAMATIS PERSONAE

ESCALUS, prince of Verona.
PARIS, a young nobleman, kinsman to the prince.
MONTAGUE, head of two houses at variance with each other.
CAPULET, head of two houses at variance with each other.
An old man, cousin to Capulet.
ROMEO, son to Montague.
MERCUTIO, kinsman to the prince, and friend to Romeo.
BENVOLIO, nephew to Montague, and friend to Romeo.
TYBALT, nephew to Lady Capulet.
FRIAR LAURENCE, Franciscan.
FRIAR JOHN, Franciscan.
BALTHASAR, servant to Romeo.
SAMPSON, servant to Capulet.
GREGORY, servant to Capulet.
PETER, servant to Juliet's nurse.
ABRAHAM, servant to Montague.
An Apothecary.
Three Musicians.
Page to Paris; another Page; an officer.
LADY MONTAGUE, wife to Montague.
LADY CAPULET, wife to Capulet.
JULIET, daughter to Capulet.
Nurse to Juliet.
Citizens of Verona; several Men and Women, relations to both houses; Maskers, Guards, Watchmen, and Attendants.
Chorus.

SCENE: *Verona: Mantua.*

PROLOGUE. [1]

Two households, both alike in dignity,
In fair Verona, where we lay our scene,
From ancient grudge break to new mutiny,
Where civil blood makes civil hands unclean.
From forth the fatal loins of these two foes
A pair of star-cross'd lovers take their life;
Whose misadventured piteous overthrows
Do with their death bury their parents' strife.
The fearful passage of their death-mark'd love,
And the continuance of their parents' rage,
Which, but their children's end, nought could remove, 12
Is now the two hours' traffic of our stage;
The which if you with patient ears attend,
What here shall miss, our toil shall strive to mend.

ACT ONE SCENE ONE

Verona. A public place.

Enter SAMPSON *and* GREGORY, *of the house of Capulet, armed with swords and bucklers.*

SAMPSON
Gregory, o' my word, we'll not carry coals.

GREGORY
No, for then we should be colliers.
SAMPSON
I mean, an we be in choler, we'll draw.
GREGORY
Ay, while you live, draw your neck out o' the collar.
SAMPSON
I strike quickly, being moved.
GREGORY
But thou art not quickly moved to strike.
SAMPSON
A dog of the house of Montague moves me. 8
GREGORY
To move is to stir; and to be valiant is to stand: therefore, if thou art moved, thou runn'st away.
SAMPSON
A dog of that house shall move me to stand: I will take the wall of any man or maid of Montague's.
GREGORY
That shows thee a weak slave; for the weakest goes to the wall.
SAMPSON
True; and therefore women, being the weaker vessels, are ever thrust to the wall: therefore I will push Montague's men from the wall, and thrust his maids to the wall.
GREGORY
The quarrel is between our masters and us their men.
SAMPSON
'Tis all one, I will show myself a tyrant: when I have fought with the men, I will be cruel with the maids, and cut off their heads. [2]
GREGORY
The heads of the maids? 23
SAMPSON
Ay, the heads of the maids, or their maidenheads: take it in what sense thou wilt.
GREGORY
They must take it in sense that feel it.
SAMPSON
Me they shall feel while I am able to stand: and 'tis known I am a pretty piece of flesh.
GREGORY
'Tis well thou art not fish; if thou hadst, thou hadst been poor John. Draw thy tool; here comes two of the house of the Montagues.
SAMPSON
My naked weapon is out: quarrel: I will back thee. 33
GREGORY
How! turn thy back and run?
SAMPSON
Fear me not.
GREGORY
No, marry; I fear thee!
SAMPSON
Let us take the law of our sides; let them begin.
GREGORY
I will frown as I pass by, and let them take it as they list.
SAMPSON
Nay, as they dare. I will bite my thumb at them; which is a disgrace to them, if they bear it. 40

Enter ABRAHAM *and* BALTHASAR.

ABRAHAM
Do you bite your thumb at us, sir?
SAMPSON
I do bite my thumb, sir.
ABRAHAM
Do you bite your thumb at us, sir?
SAMPSON
[*Aside to Gregory*] Is the law of our side, if I say ay?
GREGORY
No.
SAMPSON
No, sir, I do not bite my thumb at you, sir, but I bite my thumb, sir.
GREGORY
Do you quarrel, sir?
ABRAHAM
Quarrel, sir! no, sir. 49
SAMPSON
If you do, sir, I am for you: I serve as good a man as you.
ABRAHAM
No better.
SAMPSON
Well, sir.
GREGORY
Say 'better:' here comes one of my master's kinsmen.
SAMPSON
Yes, better, sir.
ABRAHAM
You lie.
SAMPSON
Draw, if you be men. Gregory, remember thy swashing blow. [*They fight.*

Enter BENVOLIO.

BENVOLIO
Part, fools!
Put up your swords; you know not what you do.
[*Beats down their swords.*

Enter TYBALT.

TYBALT
What, art thou drawn among these heartless hinds?
Turn thee, Benvolio, look upon thy death.

BENVOLIO
I do but keep the peace: put up thy sword,
Or manage it to part these men with me.

TYBALT
What, drawn, and talk of peace! I hate the word,
As I hate hell, all Montagues, and thee:
Have at thee, coward! [*They fight.*

Enter several of both houses, who join the fray; then enter Citizens, *with clubs.*

FIRST CITIZEN
Clubs, bills, and partisans! strike! beat them down!
Down with the Capulets! down with the Montagues!

Enter CAPULET *in his gown, and* LADY CAPULET.

CAPULET
What noise is this? Give me my long sword, ho!

LADY CAPULET
A crutch, a crutch! why call you for a sword?

CAPULET
My sword, I say! Old Montague is come,
And flourishes his blade in spite of me.

Enter MONTAGUE *and* LADY MONTAGUE.

MONTAGUE
Thou villain Capulet,—Hold me not, let me go.

LADY MONTAGUE
Thou shalt not stir a foot to seek a foe.

Enter PRINCE, *with* Attendants.

PRINCE
Rebellious subjects, enemies to peace,
Profaners of this neighbour-stained steel,
Will they not hear? What, ho! you men, you beasts,
That quench the fire of your pernicious rage
With purple fountains issuing from your veins,
On pain of torture, from those bloody hands
Throw your mistemper'd weapons to the ground,
And hear the sentence of your moved prince.
Three civil brawls, bred of an airy word,
By thee, old Capulet, and Montague,
Have thrice disturb'd the quiet of our streets,
And made Verona's ancient citizens
Cast by their grave beseeming ornaments,
To wield old partisans, in hands as old,
Canker'd with peace, to part your canker'd hate:
If ever you disturb our streets again,
Your lives shall pay the forfeit of the peace.
For this time, all the rest depart away:
You, Capulet, shall go along with me:
And, Montague, come you this afternoon,
To know our further pleasure in this case,[3]
To old Free-town, our common judgement-place.
Once more, on pain of death, all men depart.
[Exeunt all but Montague, Lady Montague, and Benvolio.

MONTAGUE
Who set this ancient quarrel new abroach?
Speak, nephew, were you by when it began?

BENVOLIO
Here were the servants of your adversary,
And yours, close fighting ere I did approach:
I drew to part them: in the instant came
The fiery Tybalt, with his sword prepared,
Which, as he breathed defiance to my ears,
He swung about his head and cut the winds,
Who nothing hurt withal hiss'd him in scorn:
While we were interchanging thrusts and blows,
Came more and more and fought on part and part,
Till the prince came, who parted either part.

LADY MONTAGUE
O, where is Romeo? saw you him to-day?
Right glad I am he was not at this fray.

BENVOLIO
Madam, an hour before the worshipp'd sun
Peer'd forth the golden window of the east,
A troubled mind drave me to walk abroad;[4]
Where, underneath the grove of sycamore
That westward rooteth from the city's side,
So early walking did I see your son:
Towards him I made, but he was ware of me
And stole into the covert of the wood:
I, measuring his affections by my own,
That most are busied when they're most alone,[5]
Pursued my humour not pursuing his,
And gladly shunn'd who gladly fled from me.

MONTAGUE
Many a morning hath he there been seen,
With tears augmenting the fresh morning's dew,
Adding to clouds more clouds with his deep sighs;
But all so soon as the all-cheering sun
Should in the furthest east begin to draw
The shady curtains from Aurora's bed,
Away from light steals home my heavy son,
And private in his chamber pens himself,
Shuts up his windows, locks far daylight out
And makes himself an artificial night:
Black and portentous must this humour prove,
Unless good counsel may the cause remove.

BENVOLIO
My noble uncle, do you know the cause?

MONTAGUE
I neither know it nor can learn of him.

BENVOLIO
Have you importuned him by any means?

MONTAGUE
Both by myself and many other friends:
But he, his own affections' counsellor,
Is to himself—I will not say how true—
But to himself so secret and so close,
So far from sounding and discovery,
As is the bud bit with an envious worm,
Ere he can spread his sweet leaves to the air,
Or dedicate his beauty to the sun.[6]
Could we but learn from whence his sorrows grow,
We would as willingly give cure as know.

Enter ROMEO.

BENVOLIO
See, where he comes: so please you, step aside;
I'll know his grievance, or be much denied.
MONTAGUE
I would thou wert so happy by thy stay,
To hear true shrift. Come, madam, let's away.
[*Exeunt Montague and Lady.*
BENVOLIO
Good morrow, cousin.
ROMEO
Is the day so young?
BENVOLIO
But new struck nine.
ROMEO
Ay me! sad hours seem long.
Was that my father that went hence so fast?
BENVOLIO
It was. What sadness lengthens Romeo's hours?
ROMEO
Not having that, which, having, makes them short.
BENVOLIO
In love?
ROMEO
Out—
BENVOLIO
Of love?
ROMEO
Out of her favour, where I am in love.
BENVOLIO
Alas, that love, so gentle in his view,
Should be so tyrannous and rough in proof!
ROMEO
Alas, that love, whose view is muffled still,
Should, without eyes, see pathways to his will![7]
Where shall we dine? O me! What fray was here?
Yet, tell me not, for I have heard it all.
Here's much to do with hate, but more with love.
Why, then, O brawling love! O loving hate!
O any thing, of nothing first create!
O heavy lightness! serious vanity!
Mis-shapen chaos of well-seeming forms!
Feather of lead, bright smoke, cold fire, sick health!
Still-waking sleep, that is not what it is!
This love feel I, that feel no love in this.
Dost thou not laugh?
BENVOLIO
No, coz, I rather weep.
ROMEO
Good heart, at what?
BENVOLIO
At thy good heart's oppression.
ROMEO
Why, such is love's transgression.[8]
Griefs of mine own lie heavy in my breast,
Which thou wilt propagate, to have it prest
With more of thine: this love that thou hast shown
Doth add more grief to too much of mine own.
Love is a smoke raised with the fume of sighs;[9]
Being purged, a fire sparkling in lovers' eyes;
Being vex'd, a sea nourish'd with lovers' tears:
What is it else? a madness most discreet,
A choking gall and a preserving sweet.
Farewell, my coz.
BENVOLIO
Soft! I will go along;
An if you leave me so, you do me wrong.
ROMEO
Tut, I have lost myself; I am not here;
This is not Romeo, he's some other where.
BENVOLIO
Tell me in sadness, who is that you love.
ROMEO
What, shall I groan and tell thee?
BENVOLIO
Groan! why, no:
But sadly tell me who.
ROMEO
Bid a sick man in sadness make his will:[10]
Ah, word ill urged to one that is so ill!
In sadness, cousin, I do love a woman.
BENVOLIO
I aim'd so near, when I supposed you loved.
ROMEO
A right good mark-man! And she's fair I love.
BENVOLIO
A right fair mark, fair coz, is soonest hit.
ROMEO
Well, in that hit you miss: she'll not be hit
With Cupid's arrow; she hath Dian's wit;
And, in strong proof of chastity well arm'd,
From love's weak childish bow she lives unharm'd.[11]
She will not stay the siege of loving terms,

Nor bide the encounter of assailing eyes,
Nor ope her lap to saint-seducing gold:
O, she is rich in beauty, only poor,
That when she dies with beauty dies her store.[12]

BENVOLIO
Then she hath sworn that she will still live chaste?

ROMEO
She hath, and in that sparing makes huge waste,
For beauty starved with her severity
Cuts beauty off from all posterity.
She is too fair, too wise, wisely too fair,
To merit bliss by making me despair:
She hath forsworn to love, and in that vow
Do I live dead that live to tell it now.

BENVOLIO
Be ruled by me, forget to think of her.

ROMEO
O, teach me how I should forget to think.

BENVOLIO
By giving liberty unto thine eyes;
Examine other beauties.

ROMEO
'Tis the way
To call hers exquisite, in question more:
These happy masks that kiss fair ladies' brows
Being black put us in mind they hide the fair;
He that is strucken blind cannot forget
The precious treasure of his eyesight lost:
Show me a mistress that is passing fair,
What doth her beauty serve, but as a note
Where I may read who pass'd that passing fair?
Farewell: thou canst not teach me to forget.

BENVOLIO
I'll pay that doctrine, or else die in debt. [*Exeunt.*

ACT ONE SCENE TWO

A street.

Enter CAPULET, PARIS, *and* Servant.

CAPULET
But Montague is bound as well as I,
In penalty alike; and 'tis not hard, I think,
For men so old as we to keep the peace.

PARIS
Of honourable reckoning are you both;
And pity 'tis you lived at odds so long.
But now, my lord, what say you to my suit?

CAPULET
But saying o'er what I have said before:
My child is yet a stranger in the world;
She hath not seen the change of fourteen years;
Let two more summers wither in their pride,
Ere we may think her ripe to be a bride.

PARIS
Younger than she are happy mothers made.

CAPULET
And too soon marr'd are those so early made.
The earth hath swallow'd all my hopes but she,
She is the hopeful lady of my earth:[13]
But woo her, gentle Paris, get her heart,
My will to her consent is but a part;
An she agree, within her scope of choice,
Lies my consent and fair according voice.
This night I hold an old accustom'd feast,
Whereto I have invited many a guest,
Such as I love; and you, among the store,
One more, most welcome, makes my number more.
At my poor house look to behold this night
Earth-treading stars that make dark heaven light:[14]
Such comfort as do lusty young men feel[15]
When well-apparell'd April on the heel
Of limping winter treads, even such delight
Among fresh female buds shall you this night
Inherit at my house; hear all, all see,
And like her most whose merit most shall be:
Which on more view, of many mine being one [16]
May stand in number, though in reckoning none.
Come, go with me. [*To Servant, giving a paper.*
Go, sirrah, trudge about
Through fair Verona; find those persons out
Whose names are written there, and to them say,
My house and welcome on their pleasure stay.
[*Exeunt Capulet and Paris.*

SERVANT
Find them out whose names are written here! It is written, that the shoemaker should meddle with his yard, and the tailor with his last, the fisher with his pencil, and the painter with his nets; but I am sent to find those persons whose names are here writ, and can never find what names the writing person hath here writ. I must to the learned.—In good time.

Enter BENVOLIO *and* ROMEO.

BENVOLIO
Tut, man, one fire burns out another's burning,
One pain is lessen'd by another's anguish;
Turn giddy, and be holp by backward turning;
One desperate grief cures with another's languish:
Take thou some new infection to thy eye,
And the rank poison of the old will die.

ROMEO
Your plaintain-leaf is excellent for that.

BENVOLIO
For what, I pray thee?

ROMEO
For your broken shin.

BENVOLIO
Why, Romeo, art thou mad?
ROMEO
Not mad, but bound more than a madman is;
Shut up in prison, kept without my food,
Whipp'd and tormented and—God-den, good fellow.
SERVANT
God gi' god-den. I pray, sir, can you read?
ROMEO
Ay, mine own fortune in my misery.
SERVANT
Perhaps you have learned it without book: but, I pray, can you read any thing you see?
ROMEO
Ay, if I know the letters and the language.
SERVANT
Ye say honestly: rest you merry!
ROMEO
Stay, fellow; I can read. [*Reads.*
'Signior Martino and his wife and daughters; County Anselme and his beauteous sisters; the lady widow of Vitruvio; Signior Placentio and his lovely nieces; Mercutio and his brother Valentine; mine uncle Capulet, his wife and daughters; my fair niece Rosaline; Livia; Signior Valentio and his cousin Tybalt; Lucio and the lively Helena.'
A fair assembly: whither should they come?
SERVANT
Up.
ROMEO
Whither?
SERVANT
To supper; to our house.
ROMEO
Whose house?
SERVANT
My master's.
ROMEO
Indeed, I should have asked you that before.
SERVANT
Now I'll tell you without asking: my master is the great rich Capulet; and if you be not of the house of Montagues, I pray, come and crush a cup of wine.
Rest you merry! [*Exit.*
BENVOLIO
At this same ancient feast of Capulet's
Sups the fair Rosaline whom thou so lovest,
With all the admired beauties of Verona:
Go thither; and, with unattainted eye,
Compare her face with some that I shall show,
And I will make thee think thy swan a crow.
ROMEO
When the devout religion of mine eye
Maintains such falsehood, then turn tears to fires;
And these, who often drown'd could never die,
Transparent heretics, be burnt for liars!
One fairer than my love! the all-seeing sun
Ne'er saw her match since first the world begun.
BENVOLIO
Tut, you saw her fair, none else being by,
Herself poised with herself in either eye:
But in that crystal scales let there be weigh'd
Your lady's love against some other maid
That I will show you shining at this feast,
And she shall scant show well that now shows best.
ROMEO
I'll go along, no such sight to be shown,
But to rejoice in splendour of mine own. [*Exeunt.*

ACT ONE SCENE THREE

A room in Capulet's house.

Enter LADY CAPULET *and* Nurse.

LADY CAPULET
Nurse, where's my daughter? call her forth to me.
NURSE
Now, by my maidenhead, at twelve year old.
I bade her come. What, lamb! what, ladybird!
God forbid! Where's this girl? What, Juliet!

Enter JULIET.

JULIET
How now! who calls?
NURSE
Your mother.
JULIET
Madam, I am here.
What is your will?
LADY CAPULET
This is the matter:—Nurse, give leave awhile,
We must talk in secret:—nurse, come back again;
I have remember'd me, thou's hear our counsel.
Thou know'st my daughter's of a pretty age.
NURSE
Faith, I can tell her age unto an hour.
LADY CAPULET
She's not fourteen.
NURSE
I'll lay fourteen of my teeth,—
And yet, to my teen be it spoken, I have but four,—
She is not fourteen. How long is it now
To Lammas-tide?
LADY CAPULET
A fortnight and odd days.
NURSE
Even or odd, of all days in the year,
Come Lammas-eve at night shall she be fourteen.

Susan and she—God rest all Christian souls!—
Were of an age: well, Susan is with God;
She was too good for me; but, as I said,
On Lammas-eve at night shall she be fourteen;
That shall she, marry; I remember it well.
'Tis since the earthquake now eleven years;
And she was wean'd,—I never shall forget it,—
Of all the days of the year, upon that day:
For I had then laid wormwood to my dug,
Sitting in the sun under the dove-house wall;
My lord and you were then at Mantua:—
Nay, I do bear a brain:—but, as I said,
When it did taste the wormwood on the nipple
Of my dug and felt it bitter, pretty fool,
To see it tetchy and fall out with the dug!
'Shake' quoth the dove-house: 'twas no need, I trow, [17]
To bid me trudge:
And since that time it is eleven years;
For then she could stand alone; nay, by the rood,
She could have run and waddled all about;
For even the day before, she broke her brow:
And then my husband—God be with his soul!
A' was a merry man—took up the child:
'Yea,' quoth he, 'dost thou fall upon thy face?
Thou wilt fall backward when thou hast more wit;
Wilt thou not, Jule?' and, by my holidame,
The pretty wretch left crying and said, 'Ay.'
To see, now, how a jest shall come about!
I warrant, an I should live a thousand years,
I never should forget it: 'Wilt thou not, Jule?' quoth he;
And, pretty fool, it stinted and said 'Ay.'

LADY CAPULET
Enough of this; I pray thee, hold thy peace.

NURSE
Yes, madam, yet I cannot choose but laugh,
To think it should leave crying and say 'Ay.'
And yet, I warrant, it had upon its brow
A bump as big as a young cockerel's stone;
A parlous knock; and it cried bitterly:
'Yea,' quoth my husband, 'fall'st upon thy face?
Thou wilt fall backward when thou comest to age;
Wilt thou not, Jule?' it stinted and said 'Ay.'

JULIET
And stint thou too, I pray thee, nurse, say I.

NURSE
Peace, I have done. God mark thee to his grace!
Thou wast the prettiest babe that e'er I nursed:
An I might live to see thee married once,
I have my wish.

LADY CAPULET
Marry, that 'marry' is the very theme
I came to talk of. Tell me, daughter Juliet,
How stands your disposition to be married?

JULIET
It is an honour that I dream not of. [18]

NURSE
An honour! were not I thine only nurse,
I would say thou hadst suck'd wisdom from thy teat.

LADY CAPULET
Well, think of marriage now; younger than you,
Here in Verona, ladies of esteem,
Are made already mothers: by my count,
I was your mother much upon these years
That you are now a maid. Thus then in brief:
The valiant Paris seeks you for his love.

NURSE
A man, young lady! lady, such a man
As all the world—why, he's a man of wax.

LADY CAPULET
Verona's summer hath not such a flower.

NURSE
Nay, he's a flower; in faith, a very flower.

LADY CAPULET
What say you? can you love the gentleman?
This night you shall behold him at our feast;
Read o'er the volume of young Paris' face
And find delight writ there with beauty's pen;
Examine every married lineament,
And see how one another lends content
And what obscured in this fair volume lies
Find written in the margent of his eyes.
This precious book of love, this unbound lover,
To beautify him, only lacks a cover:
The fish lives in the sea, and 'tis much pride
For fair without the fair within to hide:
That book in many's eyes doth share the glory,
That in gold clasps locks in the golden story;
So shall you share all that he doth possess,
By having him, making yourself no less.

NURSE
No less! nay, bigger; women grow by men.

LADY CAPULET
Speak briefly, can you like of Paris' love?

JULIET
I'll look to like, if looking liking move:
But no more deep will I endart mine eye
Than your consent gives strength to make it fly.

Enter a Servant.

SERVANT
Madam, the guests are come, supper served up, you called, my young lady asked for, the nurse cursed in the pantry, and every thing in extremity. I must hence to wait; I beseech you, follow straight.

LADY CAPULET
We follow thee. [*Exit Servant.*
Juliet, the county stays.

NURSE
Go, girl, seek happy nights to happy days. [*Exeunt.*

ACT ONE SCENE FOUR

A street.

Enter ROMEO, MERCUTIO, BENVOLIO, *with five or six* Maskers, Torch-bearers, *and others.*

ROMEO
What, shall this speech be spoke for our excuse?
Or shall we on without apology?
BENVOLIO
The date is out of such prolixity:
We'll have no Cupid hoodwink'd with a scarf,
Bearing a Tartar's painted bow of lath,
Scaring the ladies like a crow-keeper;
Nor no without-book prologue, faintly spoke
After the prompter, for our entrance:
But let them measure us by what they will;
We'll measure them a measure, and be gone.
ROMEO
Give me a torch: I am not for this ambling;
Being but heavy, I will bear the light.
MERCUTIO
Nay, gentle Romeo, we must have you dance.
ROMEO
Not I, believe me: you have dancing shoes
With nimble soles: I have a soul of lead
So stakes me to the ground I cannot move.
MERCUTIO
You are a lover; borrow Cupid's wings,
And soar with them above a common bound.
ROMEO
I am too sore enpierced with his shaft
To soar with his light feathers, and so bound,
I cannot bound a pitch above dull woe:
Under love's heavy burden do I sink.
MERCUTIO
And, to sink it in, should you burden love;
Too great oppression for a tender thing.
ROMEO
Is love a tender thing? it is too rough,
Too rude, too boisterous, and it pricks like thorn.
MERCUTIO
If love be rough with you, be rough with love;
Prick love for pricking, and you beat love down.
Give me a case to put my visage in:
A visor for a visor! what care I
What curious eye doth quote deformities?
Here are the beetle brows shall blush for me.
BENVOLIO
Come, knock and enter; and no sooner in,
But every man betake him to his legs.
ROMEO
A torch for me: let wantons light of heart
Tickle the senseless rushes with their heels,
For I am proverb'd with a grandsire phrase;
I'll be a candle-holder, and look on.
The game was ne'er so fair, and I am done. [19]
MERCUTIO
Tut, dun's the mouse, the constable's own word:
If thou art dun, we'll draw thee from the mire [20]
Of this sir-reverence love, wherein thou stick'st [21]
Up to the ears. Come, we burn daylight, ho!
ROMEO
Nay, that's not so.
MERCUTIO
I mean, sir, in delay
We waste our lights in vain, like lamps by day. [22]
Take our good meaning, for our judgement sits
Five times in that ere once in our five wits.
ROMEO
And we mean well in going to this mask;
But 'tis no wit to go.
MERCUTIO
Why, may one ask?
ROMEO
I dream'd a dream to-night.
MERCUTIO
And so did I.
ROMEO
Well, what was yours?
MERCUTIO
That dreamers often lie.
ROMEO
In bed asleep, while they do dream things true.
MERCUTIO
O, then, I see Queen Mab hath been with you.
She is the fairies' midwife, and she comes
In shape no bigger than an agate-stone
On the fore-finger of an alderman,
Drawn with a team of little atomies
Athwart men's noses as they lie asleep;
Her waggon-spokes made of long spinners' legs,
The cover of the wings of grasshoppers,
The traces of the smallest spider's web,
The collars of the moonshine's watery beams,
Her whip of cricket's bone, the lash of film,
Her waggoner a small grey-coated gnat,
Not half so big as a round little worm
Prick'd from the lazy finger of a maid; [23]
Her chariot is an empty hazel-nut
Made by the joiner squirrel or old grub,
Time out o' mind the fairies' coachmakers.
And in this state she gallops night by night
Through lovers' brains, and then they dream of love;

O'er courtiers' knees, that dream on court'sies straight,
O'er lawyers' fingers, who straight dream on fees,
O'er ladies ' lips, who straight on kisses dream,
Which oft the angry Mab with blisters plagues,
Because their breaths with sweetmeats tainted are:
Sometime she gallops o'er a courtier's nose, [24]
And then dreams he of smelling out a suit;
And sometime comes she with a tithe-pig's tail
Tickling a parson's nose as a' lies asleep, 87
Then dreams he of another benefice:
Sometime she driveth o'er a soldier's neck,
And then dreams he of cutting foreign throats,
Of breaches, ambuscadoes, Spanish blades,
Of healths five-fathom deep; and then anon [25]
Drums in his ear, at which he starts and wakes,
And being thus frighted, swears a prayer or two
And sleeps again. This is that very Mab
That plats the manes of horses in the night,
And bakes the elf-locks in foul sluttish hairs,
Which once untangled, much misfortune bodes: [26]
This is the hag, when maids lie on their backs,
That presses them and learns them first to bear,
Making them women of good carriage:
This is she—

ROMEO
Peace, peace, Mercutio, peace!
Thou talk'st of nothing.

MERCUTIO
True, I talk of dreams,
Which are the children of an idle brain,
Begot of nothing but vain fantasy,
Which is as thin of substance as the air
And more inconstant than the wind, who wooes 111
Even now the frozen bosom of the north,
And, being anger'd, puffs away from thence,
Turning his face to the dew-dropping south. [27]

BENVOLIO
This wind, you talk of, blows us from ourselves;
Supper is done, and we shall come too late.

ROMEO
I fear, too early: for my mind misgives
Some consequence yet hanging in the stars
Shall bitterly begin his fearful date
With this night's revels and expires the term
Of a despised life closed in my breast 121
By some vile forfeit of untimely death.
But He, that hath the steerage of my course,
Direct my sail! On, lusty gentlemen.

BENVOLIO
Strike, drum. [*Exeunt.*

ACT ONE SCENE FIVE

A hall in Capulet's house.

Musicians *waiting. Enter* Servingmen, *with napkins.*

FIRST SERVANT
Where's Potpan, that he helps not to take away? He shift a trencher? he scrape a trencher!

SECOND SERVANT
When good manners shall lie all in one or two men's hands and they unwashed too, 'tis a foul thing.

FIRST SERVANT
Away with the joint-stools, remove the court-cupboard, look to the plate. Good thou, save me a piece of marchpane; and, as thou lovest me, let the porter let in Susan Grindstone and Nell. Antony, and Potpan!

SECOND SERVANT
Ay, boy, ready.

FIRST SERVANT
You are looked for and called for, asked for and sought for, in the great chamber.

SECOND SERVANT
We cannot be here and there too. Cheerly, boys; be brisk awhile, and the longer liver take all.

Enter CAPULET, *with* JULIET *and others of his house, meeting the* Guests *and* Maskers.

CAPULET
Welcome, gentlemen! ladies that have their toes
Unplagued with corns will have a bout with you. [28]
Ah ha, my mistress! which of you all 17
Will now deny to dance? she that makes dainty,
She, I'll swear, hath corns; am I come near ye now?
Welcome, gentlemen! I have seen the day
That I have worn a visor and could tell
A whispering tale in a fair lady's ear,
Such as would please: 'tis gone, 'tis gone, 'tis gone:
You are welcome, gentlemen! Come, musicians, play.
A hall, a hall! give room! and foot it, girls.
[*Music plays, and they dance.*
More light, you knaves; and turn the tables up,
And quench the fire, the room is grown too hot.
Ah, sirrah, this unlook'd-for sport comes well.
Nay, sit, nay, sit, good cousin Capulet;
For you and I are past our dancing days:
How long is't now since last yourself and I
Were in a mask?

SECOND CAPULET
By'r lady, thirty years.

CAPULET
What, man! 'tis not so much, 'tis not so much:
'Tis since the nuptial of Lucentio,
Come pentecost as quickly as it will,
Some five and twenty years; and then we mask'd.

SECOND CAPULET
'Tis more, 'tis more: his son is elder, sir; 38
His son is thirty.
CAPULET
Will you tell me that?
His son was but a ward two years ago.
ROMEO
[*To a Servingman*] What lady is that, which doth enrich the hand
Of yonder knight?
SERVANT
I know not, sir.
ROMEO
O, she doth teach the torches to burn bright!
It seems she hangs upon the cheek of night [29]
Like a rich jewel in an Ethiope's ear;
Beauty too rich for use, for earth too dear!
So shows a snowy dove trooping with crows,
As yonder lady o'er her fellows shows. 51
The measure done I'll watch her place of stand,
And, touching hers, make blessed my rude hand.
Did my heart love till now? forswear it, sight!
For I ne'er saw true beauty till this night.
TYBALT
This, by his voice, should be a Montague.
Fetch me my rapier, boy. What dares the slave
Come hither, cover'd with an antic face,
To fleer and scorn at our solemnity?
Now, by the stock and honour of my kin, 60
To strike him dead I hold it not a sin.
CAPULET
Why, how now, kinsman! wherefore storm you so?
TYBALT
Uncle, this is a Montague, our foe,
A villain that is hither come in spite,
To scorn at our solemnity this night.
CAPULET
Young Romeo is it?
TYBALT
'Tis he, that villain Romeo.
CAPULET
Content thee, gentle coz, let him alone;
He bears him like a portly gentleman;
And, to say truth, Verona brags of him
To be a virtuous and well goven'd youth: 71
I would not for the wealth of all the town
Here in my house do him disparagement:
Therefore be patient, take no note of him:
It is my will, the which if thou respect,
Show a fair presence and put off these frowns,
And ill-beseeming semblance for a feast.
TYBALT
It fits, when such a villain is a guest:
I'll not endure him.
CAPULET
He shall be endured:
What, goodman boy! I say, he shall: go to;
Am I the master here, or you? go to. 82
You'll not endure him! God shall mend my soul!
You'll make a mutiny among my guests!
You will set cock-a-hoop! you'll be the man!
TYBALT
Why, uncle, 'tis a shame.
CAPULET
Go to, go to;
You are a saucy boy: is't so, indeed?
This trick may chance to scathe you, I know what:
You must contrary me! marry 'tis time.
Well said, my hearts! You are a princox; go:
Be quiet, or—More light, more light! For shame!
I'll make you quiet. What, cheerly, my hearts! 93
TYBALT
Patience perforce with wilful choler meeting
Makes my flesh tremble in their different greeting.
I will withdraw: but this intrusion shall
Now seeming sweet convert to bitter gall. [*Exit.*
ROMEO
[*To Juliet*] If I profane with my unworthiest hand
This holy shrine, the gentle fine is this:
My lips, two blushing pilgrims, ready stand
To smooth that rough touch with a tender kiss.
JULIET
Good pilgrim, you do wrong your hand too much,
Which mannerly devotion shows in this;
For saints have hands that pilgrims' hands do touch, 105
And palm to palm is holy palmers' kiss.
ROMEO
Have not saints lips, and holy palmers too?
JULIET
Ay, pilgrim, lips that they must use in prayer.
ROMEO
O, then, dear saint, let lips do what hands do;
They pray, grant thou, lest faith turn to despair.
JULIET
Saints do not move, though grant for prayers' sake.
ROMEO
Then move not while my prayer's effect I take.
Thus from my lips, by yours, my sin is purged.
JULIET
Then have my lips the sin that they have took. 114
ROMEO
Sin from my lips? O trespass sweetly urged!
Give me my sin again.
JULIET
You kiss by the book.
NURSE
Madam, your mother craves a word with you.

ROMEO
What is her mother?
NURSE
Marry, bachelor,
Her mother is the lady of the house,
And a good lady, and a wise and virtuous:
I nursed her daughter, that you talk'd withal;
I tell you, he that can lay hold of her
Shall have the chinks.
ROMEO
Is she a Capulet?
O dear account! my life is my foe's debt.
BENVOLIO
Away, be gone; the sport is at the best.
ROMEO
Ay, so I fear; the more is my unrest.
CAPULET
Nay, gentlemen, prepare not to be gone;
We have a trifling foolish banquet towards.
Is it e'en so? why, then, I thank you all;
I thank you, honest gentlemen; good night.
More torches here! Come on then, let's to bed.
Ah, sirrah, by my fay, it waxes late:
I'll to my rest. [*Exeunt all but Juliet and Nurse.*
JULIET
Come hither, nurse. What is yond gentleman?
NURSE
The son and heir of old Tiberio.
JULIET
What's he that now is going out of door?
NURSE
Marry, that, I think, be young Petrucio.
JULIET
What's he that follows there, that would not dance?
NURSE
I know not.
JULIET
Go, ask his name: if he be married,
My grave is like to be my wedding bed.
NURSE
His name is Romeo, and a Montague;
The only son of your great enemy.
JULIET
My only love sprung from my only hate!
Too early seen unknown, and known too late!
Prodigious birth of love it is to me,
That I must love a loathed enemy.
NURSE
What's this? what's this?
JULIET
A rhyme I learn'd even now
Of one I danced withal. [*One calls within* 'Juliet.'
NURSE
Anon, anon!
Come, let's away; the strangers all are gone.
[*Exeunt.*

ACT TWO PROLOGUE.

Enter Chorus.

CHORUS
Now old desire doth in his death-bed lie,
And young affection gapes to be his heir:
That fair for which love groan'd for and would die,
With tender Juliet match'd, is now not fair.
Now Romeo is beloved and loves again,
Alike bewitched by the charm of looks,
But to his foe supposed he must complain,
And she steal love's sweet bait from fearful hooks:
Being held a foe, he may not have access
To breathe such vows as lovers use to swear;
And she as much in love, her means much less
To meet her new-beloved any where:
But passion lends them power, time means, to meet
Tempering extremities with extreme sweet. [*Exit.*

ACT TWO SCENE ONE

A lane by the wall of Capulet's orchard.
Enter ROMEO.

ROMEO
Can I go forward when my heart is here?
Turn back, dull earth, and find thy centre out.
[*He climbs the wall, and leaps down within it.*
Enter BENVOLIO *and* MERCUTIO.
BENVOLIO
Romeo! my cousin Romeo!
MERCUTIO
He is wise;
And, on my life, hath stol'n him home to bed.
BENVOLIO
He ran this way, and leap'd this orchard wall:
Call, good Mercutio.
MERCUTIO
Nay, I'll conjure too.
Romeo! humours! madman! passion! lover!
Appear thou in the likeness of a sigh:
Speak but one rhyme, and I am satisfied;
Cry but 'Ay me!' pronounce but 'love' and
'dove;' [30]
Speak to my gossip Venus one fair word,
One nick-name for her purblind son and heir,
Young Adam Cupid, he that shot so trim, [31, 32]
When King Cophetua loved the beggar-maid!

He heareth not, he stirreth not, he moveth not;
The ape is dead, and I must conjure him.
I conjure thee by Rosaline's bright eyes,
By her high forehead and her scarlet lip,
By her fine foot, straight leg and quivering thigh
And the demesnes that there adjacent lie,
That in thy likeness thou appear to us!

BENVOLIO
And if he hear thee, thou wilt anger him.

MERCUTIO
This cannot anger him: 'twould anger him
To raise a spirit in his mistress' circle
Of some strange nature, letting it there stand
Till she had laid it and conjured it down;
That were some spite: my invocation
Is fair and honest, and in his mistress' name
I conjure only but to raise up him.

BENVOLIO
Come, he hath hid himself among these trees,
To be consorted with the humorous night:
Blind is his love and best befits the dark.

MERCUTIO
If love be blind, love cannot hit the mark.
Now will he sit under a medlar tree,
And wish his mistress were that kind of fruit
As maids call medlars, when they laugh alone.
O, Romeo, that she were, O, that she were
An open et caetera, thou a poperin pear!
Romeo, good night: I'll to my truckle-bed;
This field-bed is too cold for me to sleep:
Come, shall we go?

BENVOLIO
Go, then; for 'tis in vain
To seek him here that means not to be found.
[*Exeunt.*

ACT TWO SCENE TWO

Capulet's orchard.

Enter ROMEO.

ROMEO
He jests at scars that never felt a wound.
[*Juliet appears above at a window.*
But, soft! what light through yonder window breaks?
It is the east, and Juliet is the sun.
Arise, fair sun, and kill the envious moon,
Who is already sick and pale with grief,
That thou her maid art far more fair than she:
Be not her maid, since she is envious;
Her vestal livery is but sick and green
And none but fools do wear it; cast it off.
It is my lady, O, it is my love!
O, that she knew she were!
She speaks yet she says nothing: what of that?
Her eye discourses; I will answer it.
I am too bold, 'tis not to me she speaks:
Two of the fairest stars in all the heaven,
Having some business, do entreat her eyes
To twinkle in their spheres till they return.
What if her eyes were there, they in her head?
The brightness of her cheek would shame those stars,
As daylight doth a lamp; her eyes in heaven
Would through the airy region stream so bright
That birds would sing and think it were not night.
See, how she leans her cheek upon her hand!
O, that I were a glove upon that hand,
That I might touch that cheek!

JULIET
Ay me!

ROMEO
She speaks:
O, speak again, bright angel! for thou art
As glorious to this night, being o'er my head,
As is a winged messenger of heaven
Unto the white-upturned wondering eyes
Of mortals that fall back to gaze on him
When he bestrides the lazy-pacing clouds
And sails upon the bosom of the air.

JULIET
O Romeo, Romeo! wherefore art thou Romeo?
Deny thy father and refuse thy name;
Or, if thou wilt not, be but sworn my love,
And I'll no longer be a Capulet.

ROMEO
[*Aside*] Shall I hear more, or shall I speak at this?

JULIET
'Tis but thy name that is my enemy;
Thou art thyself, though not a Montague.
What's Montague? it is nor hand, nor foot,
Nor arm, nor face, nor any other part [33]
Belonging to a man. O, be some other name!
What's in a name? that which we call a rose [34]
By any other name would smell as sweet;
So Romeo would, were he not Romeo call'd,
Retain thy dear perfection which he owes
Without that title. Romeo, doff thy name,
And for that name which is no part of thee
Take all myself.

ROMEO
I take thee at thy word:
Call me but love, and I'll be new baptized;
Henceforth I never will be Romeo.

JULIET
What man art thou that thus bescreen'd in night
So stumblest on my counsel?

ROMEO
By a name
I know not how to tell thee who I am:
My name, dear saint, is hateful to myself,
Because it is an enemy to thee;
Had I it written, I would tear the word.
JULIET
My ears have not yet drunk a hundred words
Of that tongue's utterance, yet I know the sound:
Art thou not Romeo and a Montague?
ROMEO
Neither, fair saint, if either thee dislike. [35]
JULIET
How camest thou hither, tell me, and wherefore?
The orchard walls are high and hard to climb,
And the place death, considering who thou art,
If any of my kinsmen find thee here.
ROMEO
With love's light wings did I o'er-perch these walls;
For stony limits cannot hold love out,
And what love can do that dares love attempt;
Therefore thy kinsmen are no let to me.
JULIET
If they do see thee, they will murder thee.
ROMEO
Alack, there lies more peril in thine eye
Than twenty of their swords: look thou but sweet,
And I am proof against their enmity.
JULIET
I would not for the world they saw thee here.
ROMEO
I have night's cloak to hide me from their sight;
And thou but love me, let them find me here:
My life were better ended by their hate,
Than death prorogued, wanting of thy love.
JULIET
By whose direction found'st thou out this place?
ROMEO
By love, who first did prompt me to inquire;
He lent me counsel and I lent him eyes.
I am no pilot; yet, wert thou as far
As that vast shore wash'd with the farthest sea,
I would adventure for such merchandise.
JULIET
Thou know'st the mask of night is on my face,
Else would a maiden blush bepaint my cheek
For that which thou hast heard me speak to-night
Fain would I dwell on form, fain, fain deny
What I have spoke: but farewell compliment!
Dost thou love me? I know thou wilt say 'Ay,'
And I will take thy word: yet, if thou swear'st,
Thou mayst prove false; at lovers' perjuries,
They say, Jove laughs. O gentle Romeo,
If thou dost love, pronounce it faithfully:
Of if thou think'st I am too quickly won,
I'll frown and be perverse and say thee nay,
So thou wilt woo: but else, not for the world.
In truth fair Montague, I am too fond,
And therefore thou mayst think my 'haviour light:
But trust me, gentleman, I'll prove more true
Than those that have more cunning to be strange.
I should have been more strange, I must confess,
But that thou overheard'st, ere I was ware,
My true love's passion: therefore pardon me,
And not impute this yielding to light love,
Which the dark night hath so discovered.
ROMEO
Lady, by yonder blessed moon I swear [36]
That tips with silver all these fruit-tree tops—
JULIET
O, swear not by the moon, the inconstant moon,
That monthly changes in her circled orb,
Lest that thy love prove likewise variable.
ROMEO
What shall I swear by?
JULIET
Do not swear at all;
Or, if thou wilt, swear by thy gracious self,
Which is the god of my idolatry,
And I'll believe thee.
ROMEO
If my heart's dear love—
JULIET
Well, do not swear: although I joy in thee,
I have no joy of this contract to-night:
It is too rash, too unadvised, too sudden;
Too like the lightning, which doth cease to be
Ere one can say 'It lightens.' Sweet, good night!
This bud of love, by summer's ripening breath,
May prove a beauteous flower when next we meet.
Good night, good night! as sweet repose and rest
Come to thy heart as that within my breast!
ROMEO
O, wilt thou leave me so unsatisfied?
JULIET
What satisfaction canst thou have to-night?
ROMEO
The exchange of thy love's faithful vow for mine.
JULIET
I gave thee mine before thou didst request it:
And yet I would it were to give again.
ROMEO
Wouldst thou withdraw it? for what purpose, love?
JULIET
But to be frank, and give it thee again.

And yet I wish but for the thing I have:
My bounty is as boundless as the sea,
My love as deep; the more I give thee,
The more I have, for both are infinite.
[*Nurse calls within.*
I hear some noise within; dear love, adieu!
Anon, good nurse! Sweet Montague, be true.
Stay but a little, I will come again. [*Exit, above.*

ROMEO
O blessed, blessed night! I am afeard.
Being in night, all this is but a dream,
Too flattering-sweet to be substantial.

Re-enter JULIET, *above.*

JULIET
Three words, dear Romeo, and good night indeed.
If that thy bent of love be honourable,
Thy purpose marriage, send me word to-morrow,
By one that I'll procure to come to thee,
Where and what time thou wilt perform the rite;
And all my fortunes at thy foot I'll lay
And follow thee my lord throughout the world.

NURSE
[*Within*] Madam!

JULIET
I come, anon.—But if thou mean'st not well,
I do beseech thee—

NURSE
[*Within*] Madam!

JULIET
By and by, I come:—
To cease thy suit, and leave me to my grief: [37]
To-morrow will I send.

ROMEO
So thrive my soul—

JULIET
A thousand times good night! [*Exit, above.*

ROMEO
A thousand times the worse, to want thy light.
Love goes toward love, as schoolboys from their books,
But love from love, toward school with heavy looks.
[*Retiring.*

Re-enter JULIET, *above.*

JULIET
Hist! Romeo, hist! O, for a falconer's voice,
To lure this tassel-gentle back again!
Bondage is hoarse, and may not speak aloud;
Else would I tear the cave where Echo lies,
And make her airy tongue more hoarse than mine,
With repetition of my Romeo's name.

ROMEO
It is my soul that calls upon my name:
How silver-sweet sound lovers' tongues by night,
Like softest music to attending ears!

JULIET
Romeo!

ROMEO
My dear?

JULIET
At what o'clock to-morrow
Shall I send to thee?

ROMEO
At the hour of nine.

JULIET
I will not fail: 'tis twenty years till then.
I have forgot why I did call thee back.

ROMEO
Let me stand here till thou remember it.

JULIET
I shall forget, to have thee still stand there,
Remembering how I love thy company.

ROMEO
And I'll still stay, to have thee still forget,
Forgetting any other home but this.

JULIET
'Tis almost morning; I would have thee gone:
And yet no further than a wanton's bird;
Who lets it hop a little from her hand,
Like a poor prisoner in his twisted gyves,
And with a silk thread plucks it back again,
So loving-jealous of his liberty.

ROMEO
I would I were thy bird.

JULIET
Sweet, so would I:
Yet I should kill thee with much cherishing.
Good night, good night! parting is such sweet sorrow,
That I shall say good night till it be morrow.
[*Exit above.*

ROMEO
Sleep dwell upon thine eyes, peace in thy breast!
Would I were sleep and peace, so sweet to rest!
Hence will I to my ghostly father's cell. [38]
His help to crave, and my dear hap to tell.
[*Exit.*

ACT TWO SCENE THREE

Friar Laurence's cell.

Enter FRIAR LAURENCE, *with a basket.*

FRIAR LAURENCE
The grey-eyed morn smiles on the frowning night, [39]
Chequering the eastern clouds with streaks of light,

And flecked darkness like a drunkard reels
From forth day's path and Titan's fiery wheels: [40]
Now, ere the sun advance his burning eye,
The day to cheer and night's dank dew to dry,
I must up-fill this osier cage of ours
With baleful weeds and precious-juiced flowers.
The earth that's nature's mother is her tomb;
What is her burying grave that is her womb,
And from her womb children of divers kind
We sucking on her natural bosom find,
Many for many virtues excellent,
None but for some and yet all different.
O, mickle is the powerful grace that lies
In herbs, plants, stones, and their true qualities:
For nought so vile that on the earth doth live
But to the earth some special good doth give,
Nor aught so good but strain'd from that fair use
Revolts from true birth, stumbling on abuse:
Virtue itself turns vice, being misapplied; 22
And vice sometimes by action dignified.
Within the infant rind of this small flower [41]
Poison hath residence and medicine power:
For this, being smelt, with that part cheers each part;
Being tasted, slays all senses with the heart.
Two such opposed kings encamp them still
In man as well as herbs, grace and rude will;
And where the worser is predominant,
Full soon the canker death eats up that plant.

Enter ROMEO.

ROMEO
Good morrow, father.
FRIAR LAURENCE
Benedicite! 33
What early tongue so sweet saluteth me?
Young son, it argues a distemper'd head
So soon to bid good morrow to thy bed:
Care keeps his watch in every old man's eye,
And where care lodges, sleep will never lie;
But where unbruised youth with unstuff'd brain
Doth couch his limbs, there golden sleep doth reign:
Therefore thy earliness doth me assure
Thou art up-roused by some distemperature;
Or, if not so, then here I hit it right,
Our Romeo hath not been in bed to-night.
ROMEO
That last is true; the sweeter rest was mine.
FRIAR LAURENCE
God pardon sin! wast thou with Rosaline?
ROMEO
With Rosaline, my ghostly father? no;
I have forgot that name, and that name's woe.
FRIAR LAURENCE
That's my good son: but where hast thou been, then?
ROMEO
I'll tell thee, ere thou ask it me again.
I have been feasting with mine enemy,
Where on a sudden one hath wounded me, 52
That's by me wounded: both our remedies
Within thy help and holy physic lies:
I bear no hatred, blessed man, for, lo,
My intercession likewise steads my foe.
FRIAR LAURENCE
Be plain, good son, and homely in thy drift;
Riddling confession finds but riddling shrift.
ROMEO
Then plainly know my heart's dear love is set
On the fair daughter of rich Capulet:
As mine on hers, so hers is set on mine;
And all combined, save what thou must combine 63
By holy marriage: when and where and how
We met, we woo'd and made exchange of vow,
I'll tell thee as we pass; but this I pray,
That thou consent to marry us to-day.
FRIAR LAURENCE
Holy Saint Francis, what a change is here!
Is Rosaline, whom thou didst love so dear,
So soon forsaken? young men's love then lies
Not truly in their hearts, but in their eyes.
Jesu Maria, what a deal of brine
Hath wash'd thy sallow cheeks for Rosaline!
How much salt water thrown away in waste,
To season love, that of it doth not taste!
The sun not yet thy sighs from heaven clears,
Thy old groans ring yet in my ancient ears;
Lo, here upon thy cheek the stain doth sit
Of an old tear that is not wash'd off yet:
If e'er thou wast thyself and these woes thine,
Thou and these woes were all for Rosaline:
And thou art changed? pronounce this sentence then,
Women may fall, when there's no strength in men. 84
ROMEO
Thou chid'st me oft for loving Rosaline.
FRIAR LAURENCE
For doting, not for loving, pupil mine.
ROMEO
And bad'st me bury love.
FRIAR LAURENCE
Not in a grave,
To lay one in, another out to have.
ROMEO
I pray thee, chide not: she whom I love now
Doth grace for grace and love for love allow;
The other did not so.
FRIAR LAURENCE
O, she knew well

Thy love did not read by rote and could not spell.
But come, young waverer, come, go with me,
In one respect I'll thy assistant be;
For this alliance may so happy prove,
To turn your households' rancour to pure love.

ROMEO
O, let us hence; I stand on sudden haste.

FRIAR LAURENCE
Wisely and slow; they stumble that run fast.
[*Exeunt.*

ACT TWO SCENE FOUR

A street.

Enter BENVOLIO *and* MERCUTIO.

MERCUTIO
Where the devil should this Romeo be?
Came he not home to-night?

BENVOLIO
Not to his father's; I spoke with his man.

MERCUTIO
Ah, that same pale hard-hearted wench, that Rosaline,
Torments him so, that he will sure run mad.

BENVOLIO
Tybalt, the kinsman of old Capulet,
Hath sent a letter to his father's house.

MERCUTIO
A challenge, on my life.

BENVOLIO
Romeo will answer it.

MERCUTIO
Any man that can write may answer a letter.

BENVOLIO
Nay, he will answer the letter's master, how he dares, being dared.

MERCUTIO
Alas, poor Romeo! he is already dead; stabbed with a white wench's black eye; shot thorough the ear with a.love-song; the very pin of his heart cleft with the blind bow-boy's butt-shaft: and is he a man to encounter Tybalt?

BENVOLIO
Why, what is Tybalt?

MERCUTIO
More than prince of cats, I can tell you. O, he is the courageous captain of complements. He fights as you sing prick-song, keeps time, distance, and proportion; rests me his minim rest, one, two, and the third in your bosom: the very butcher of a silk button, a duellist, a duellist; a gentleman of the very first house, of the first and second cause: ah, the immortal passado! the punto reverso! The hai!

BENVOLIO
The what?

MERCUTIO
The pox of such antic, lisping, affecting fantasticoes; these new tuners of accents! 'By Jesu, a very good blade! a very tall man! a very good whore!' Why, is not this a lamentable thing, grandsire, that we should be thus afflicted with these strange flies, these fashion-mongers, these perdona-mi's, who stand so much on the new form, that they cannot sit at ease on the old bench? O, their bones, their bones!

Enter ROMEO.

BENVOLIO
Here comes Romeo, here comes Romeo.

MERCUTIO
Without his roe, like a dried herring: O flesh, flesh, how art thou fishified! Now is he for the numbers that Petrarch flowed in: Laura to his lady was but a kitchen-wench; marry, she had a better love to be-rhyme her; Dido a dowdy; Cleopatra a gipsy; Helen and Hero hildings and harlots; This be a grey eye or so, but not to the purpose. Signior Romeo, bon jour! there's a French salutation to your French slop. You gave us the counterfeit fairly last night.

ROMEO
Good morrow to you both. What counterfeit did I give you?

MERCUTIO
The slip, sir, the slip; can you not conceive?

ROMEO
Pardon, good Mercutio, my business was great; and in such a case as mine a man may strain courtesy.

MERCUTIO
That's as much as to say, such a case as yours constrains a man to bow in the hams.

ROMEO
Meaning, to court'sy.

MERCUTIO
Thou hast most kindly hit it.

ROMEO
A most courteous exposition.

MERCUTIO
Nay, I am the very pink of courtesy.

ROMEO
Pink for flower.

MERCUTIO
Right.

ROMEO
Why, then is my pump well flowered.

MERCUTIO
Well said: follow me this jest now till thou hast worn out thy pump, that when the single sole of it is worn, the jest may remain after the wearing sole singular.

ROMEO
O single-soled jest, solely singular for the singleness! 65

MERCUTIO
Come between us, good Benvolio; my wits faint.

ROMEO
Switch and spurs, switch and spurs; or I'll cry a match.

MERCUTIO
Nay, if thy wits run the wild-goose chase, I have done, for thou hast more of the wild-goose in one of thy wits than, I am sure, I have in my whole five: was I with you there for the goose?

ROMEO
Thou wast never with me for any thing when thou wast not there for the goose.

MERCUTIO
I will bite thee by the ear for that jest.

ROMEO
Nay, good goose, bite not.

MERCUTIO
Thy wit is a very bitter sweeting; it is a most sharp sauce.

ROMEO
And is it not well served in to a sweet goose?

MERCUTIO
O here's a wit of cheveril, that stretches from an inch narrow to an ell broad!

ROMEO
I stretch it out for that word 'broad;' which added to the goose, proves thee far and wide a broad goose. 83

MERCUTIO
Why, is not this better now than groaning for love? now art thou sociable, now art thou Romeo; now art thou what thou art, by art as well as by nature: for this drivelling love is like a great natural, that runs lolling up and down to hide his bauble in a hole.

BENVOLIO
Stop there, stop there.

MERCUTIO
Thou desirest me to stop in my tale against the hair. 91

BENVOLIO
Thou wouldst else have made thy tale large.

MERCUTIO
O, thou art deceived; I would have made it short: for I was come to the whole depth of my tale; and meant, indeed, to occupy the argument no longer.

ROMEO
Here's goodly gear!

Enter Nurse *and* PETER.

MERCUTIO
A sail, a sail!

BENVOLIO
Two, two; a shirt and a smock.

NURSE
Peter! 99

PETER
Anon!

NURSE
My fan, Peter.

MERCUTIO
Good Peter, to hide her face; for her fan's the fairer face.

NURSE
God ye good morrow, gentlemen.

MERCUTIO
God ye good den, fair gentlewoman.

NURSE
Is it good den?

MERCUTIO
'Tis no less, I'll tell you, for the bawdy hand of the dial is now upon the prick of noon.

NURSE
Out upon you! what a man are you!

ROMEO
One, gentlewoman, that God hath made for himself to mar.

NURSE
By my troth, it is well said; 'for himself to mar,' quoth a'? Gentlemen, can any of you tell me where I may find the young Romeo?

ROMEO
I can tell you; but young Romeo will be older when you have found him than he was when you sought him: I am the youngest of that name, for fault of a worse.

Nurse. You say well. 118

MERCUTIO
Yea, is the worst well? very well took, i' faith; wisely, wisely.

NURSE
If you be he, sir, I desire some confidence with you.

BENVOLIO
She will indite him to some supper.

MERCUTIO
A bawd, a bawd, a bawd! So ho!

ROMEO
What hast thou found?

MERCUTIO
No hare, sir; unless a hare, sir, in a lenten pie, that is something stale and hoar ere it be spent. [*Sings*.

An old hare hoar, 127
And an old hare hoar,
Is very good meat in lent:
But a hare that is hoar
Is too much for a score,
When it hoars ere it be spent.

Romeo, will you come to your father's? we'll to dinner, thither.

ROMEO

I will follow you.

MERCUTIO

Farewell, ancient lady; farewell, [*singing*] 'lady, lady, lady.' 137

[*Exeunt Mercutio and Benvolio.*

NURSE

Marry, farewell! I pray you, sir, what saucy merchant was this, that was so full of his ropery?

ROMEO

A gentleman, nurse, that loves to hear himself talk, and will speak more in a minute than he will stand to in a month.

NURSE

An a' speak any thing against me, I'll take him down, an a' were lustier than he is, and twenty such Jacks; and if I cannot, I'll find those that shall. Scurvy knave! I am none of his flirt-gills; I am none of his skains-mates. And thou must stand by too, and suffer every knave to use me at his pleasure? [42]

PETER

I saw no man use you at his pleasure; if I had, my weapon should quickly have been out, I warrant you: I dare draw as soon as another man, if I see ocasion in a good quarrel, and the law on my side. 152

NURSE

Now, afore God, I am so vexed, that every part about me quivers. Scurvy knave! Pray you, sir, a word: and as I told you, my young lady bade me inquire you out; what she bade me say, I will keep to myself: but first let me tell ye, if ye should lead her into a fool's paradise, as they say, it were a very gross kind of behaviour, as they say: for the gentlewoman is young; and, therefore, if you should deal double with her, truly it were an ill thing to be offered to any gentlewoman, and very weak dealing. 161

ROMEO

Nurse, commend me to thy lady and mistress. I protest unto thee—

NURSE

Good heart, and, i' faith, I will tell her as much: Lord, Lord, she will be a joyful woman.

ROMEO

What wilt thou tell her, nurse? thou dost not mark me.

NURSE

I will tell her, sir, that you do protest; which, as I take it, is a gentlemanlike offer.

ROMEO

Bid her devise 169
Some means to come to shrift this afternoon;
And there she shall at Friar Laurence' cell
Be shrived and married. Here is for thy pains.

NURSE

No, truly, sir; not a penny.

ROMEO

Go to; I say you shall.

NURSE

This afternoon, sir? well, she shall be there.

ROMEO

And stay, good nurse, behind the abbey wall: 176
Within this hour my man shall be with thee,
And bring thee cords made like a tackled stair;
Which to the high top-gallant of my joy
Must be my convoy in the secret night.
Farewell; be trusty, and I'll quit thy pains:
Farewell; commend me to thy mistress.

NURSE

Now God in heaven bless thee! Hark, you, sir.

ROMEO

What say'st thou, my dear nurse?

NURSE

Is your man secret? Did you ne'er hear say,
Two may keep counsel, putting one away?

ROMEO

I warrant thee, my man's as true as steel. 187

NURSE

Well, sir; my mistress is the sweetest lady—Lord, Lord! when 'twas a little prating thing:—O, there is a nobleman in town, one Paris, that would fain lay knife aboard; but she, good soul, had as lief see a toad, a very toad, as see him. I anger her sometimes and tell her that Paris is the properer man; but, I'll warrant you, when I say so, she looks as pale as any clout in the versal world. Doth not rosemary and Romeo begin both with a letter? 196

ROMEO

Ay, nurse! what of that? both with an R.

NURSE

Ah. Mocker? that's the dog's name; R is for the—No; I know it begins with some other letter:—and she hath the prettiest sententious of it, of you and rosemary, that it would do you good to hear it.

ROMEO

Commend me to thy lady.

NURSE

Ay, a thousand times. [*Exit Romeo.*] Peter! 203

PETER

Anon!

NURSE

Peter, take my fan, and go before, and apace.

[*Exeunt.*

ACT TWO SCENE FIVE

Capulet's orchard.

Enter JULIET.

JULIET

The clock struck nine when I did send the nurse;

In half an hour she promised to return.
Perchance she cannot meet him: that's not so.
O, she is lame! love's heralds should be thoughts,
Which ten times faster glide than the sun's beams,
Driving back shadows over louring hills:
Therefore do nimble-pinion'd doves draw love,
And therefore hath the wind-swift Cupid wings.
Now is the sun upon the highmost hill
Of this day's journey, and from nine till twelve
Is three long hours, yet she is not come.
Had she affections and warm youthful blood,
She would be as swift in motion as a ball;
My words would bandy her to my sweet love,
And his to me:
But old folks, many feign as they were dead;
Unwieldy, slow, heavy and pale as lead.
O God, she comes!

Enter Nurse *and* PETER.

O honey nurse, what news?
Hast thou met with him? Send thy man away.

NURSE
Peter, stay at the gate. [*Exit Peter.*

JULIET
Now, good sweet nurse,—O Lord, why look'st thou sad?
Though news be sad, yet tell them merrily;
If good, thou shamest the music of sweet news
By playing it to me with so sour a face.

NURSE
I am a-weary, give me leave awhile:
Fie, how my bones ache! what a jaunt have I had!

JULIET
I would thou hadst my bones, and I thy news:
Nay, come, I pray thee, speak; good, good nurse, speak.

NURSE
Jesu, what haste? can you not stay awhile?
Do you not see that I am out of breath?

JULIET
How art thou out of breath, when thou hast breath
To say to me that thou art out of breath?
The excuse that thou dost make in this delay
Is longer than the tale thou dost excuse.
Is thy news good, or bad? answer to that;
Say either, and I'll stay the circumstance:
Let me be satisfied, is't good or bad?

NURSE
Well, you have made a simple choice; you know not how to choose a man: Romeo! no, not he; though his face be better than any man's, yet his leg excels all men's; and for a hand, and a foot, and a body, though they be not to be talked on, yet they are past compare: he is not the flower of courtesy, but I'll warrant him, as gentle as a lamb. Go thy ways, wench; serve God. What, have you dined at home?

JULIET
No, no: but all this did I know before.
What says he of our marriage? what of that?

NURSE
Lord, how my head aches! what a head have I!
It beats as it would fall in twenty pieces.
My back o' t' other side,—O, my back, my back!
Beshrew your heart for sending me about,
To catch my death with jaunting up and down!

JULIET
I' faith, I am sorry that thou art not well.
Sweet, sweet, sweet nurse, tell me, what says my love?

NURSE
Your love says, like an honest gentleman, and a courteous, and a kind, and a handsome, and, I warrant, a virtuous,—Where is your mother?

JULIET
Where is my mother! why, she is within;
Where should she be? How oddly thou repliest!
'Your love says, like an honest gentleman,
Where is your mother?'

NURSE
O God's lady dear!
Are you so hot? marry, come up, I trow;
Is this the poultice for my aching bones?
Henceforward do your messages yourself.

JULIET
Here's such a coil! come, what says Romeo?

NURSE
Have you got leave to go to shrift to-day?

JULIET
I have.

NURSE
Then hie you hence to Friar Laurence' cell;
There stays a husband to make you a wife:
Now comes the wanton blood up in your cheeks,
They'll be in scarlet straight at any news.
Hie you to church; I must another way,
To fetch a ladder, by the which your love
Must climb a bird's nest soon when it is dark:
I am the drudge and toil in your delight,
But you shall bear the burden soon at night.
Go; I'll to dinner; hie you to the cell.

JULIET
Hie to high fortune! Honest nurse, farewell.
[*Exeunt.*

ACT TWO SCENE SIX

Friar Laurence's cell.

Enter FRIAR LAURENCE *and* ROMEO.

FRIAR LAURENCE
So smile the heavens upon, this holy act,
That after hours with sorrow chide us not!

ROMEO

Amen, amen! but come what sorrow can,
It cannot countervail the exchange of joy
That one short minute gives me in her sight:
Do thou but close our hands with holy words,
Then love-devouring death do what he dare;
It is enough I may but call her mine.

FRIAR LAURENCE

These violent delights have violent ends
And in their triumph die, like fire and powder,
Which as they kiss consume: the sweetest honey
Is loathsome in his own deliciousness
And in the taste confounds the appetite:
Therefore love moderately; long love doth so;
Too swift arrives as tardy as too slow.

Enter JULIET.

Here comes the lady: O, so light a foot
Will ne'er wear out the everlasting flint:
A lover may bestride the gossamer
That idles in the wanton summer air,
And yet not fall; so light is vanity.

JULIET

Good even to my ghostly confessor.

FRIAR LAURENCE

Romeo shall thank thee, daughter, for us both.

JULIET

As much to him, else is his thanks too much.

ROMEO

Ah, Juliet, if the measure of thy joy
Be heap'd like mine and that thy skill be more
To blazon it, then sweeten with thy breath
This neighbour air, and let rich music's tongue
Unfold the imagined happiness that both
Receive in either by this dear encounter.

JULIET

Conceit, more rich in matter than in words,
Brags of his substance, not of ornament:
They are but beggars that can count their worth;
But my true love is grown to such excess
I cannot sum up sum of half my wealth. [43]

FRIAR LAURENCE

Come, come with me, and we will make short work;
For, by your leaves, you shall not stay alone
Till holy church incorporate two in one. [*Exeunt.*

ACT THREE SCENE ONE

A public place.

Enter MERCUTIO, BENVOLIO, Page *and* Servants.

BENVOLIO

I pray thee, good Mercutio, let's retire:
The day is hot, the Capulets abroad,
And, if we meet, we shall not escape a brawl;
For now, these hot days, is the mad blood stirring.

MERCUTIO

Thou art like one of those fellows that when he enters the confines of a tavern claps me his sword upon the table and says 'God send me no need of thee!' and by the operation of the second cup draws it on the drawer, when indeed there is no need.

BENVOLIO

Am I like such a fellow?

MERCUTIO

Come, come, thou art as hot a Jack in thy mood as any in Italy, and as soon moved to be moody, and as soon moody to be moved.

BENVOLIO

And what to?

MERCUTIO

Nay, an there were two such, we should have none shortly, for one would kill the other. Thou! why, thou wilt quarrel with a man that hath a hair more, or a hair less, in his beard than thou hast: thou wilt quarrel with a man for cracking nuts, having no other reason but because thou hast hazel eyes: what eye but such an eye would spy out such a quarrel? Thy head is as full of quarrels as an egg is full of meat, and yet thy head hath been beaten as addle as an egg for quarrelling: thou hast quarrelled with a man for coughing in the street, because he hath wakened thy dog that hath lain asleep in the sun: didst thou not fall out with a tailor for wearing his new doublet before Easter? with another, for tying his new shoes with old riband? and yet thou wilt tutor me from quarrelling!

BENVOLIO

An I were so apt to quarrel as thou art, any man should buy the fee-simple of my life for an hour and a quarter.

MERCUTIO

The fee-simple! O simple!

BENVOLIO

By my head, here come the Capulets.

MERCUTIO

By my heel, I care not.

Enter TYBALT *and others.*

TYBALT

Follow me close, for I will speak to them.
Gentlemen, good den: a word with one of you.

MERCUTIO

And but one word with one of us? couple it with something; make it a word and a blow.

TYBALT

You shall find me apt enough to that, sir, an you will give me occasion.

MERCUTIO
Could you not take some occasion without giving?
TYBALT
Mercutio, thou consort'st with Romeo,—
MERCUTIO
Consort! what, dost thou make us minstrels? an thou make minstrels of us, look to hear nothing but discords: here's my fiddlestick; here's that shall make you dance. 'Zounds, consort!
BENVOLIO
We talk here in the public haunt of men:
Either withdraw unto some private place,
And reason coldly of your grievances,
Or else depart; here all eyes gaze on us.
MERCUTIO
Men's eyes were made to look, and let them gaze;
I will not budge for no man's pleasure, I.

Enter ROMEO.

TYBALT
Well, peace be with you, sir: here comes my man.
MERCUTIO
But I'll be hanged, sir, if he wear your
livery: 56
Marry, go before to field, he'll be your follower;
Your worship in that sense may call him 'man.'
TYBALT
Romeo, the hate I bear thee can afford
No better term than this,—thou art a villain.
ROMEO
Tybalt, the reason that I have to love thee
Doth much excuse the appertaining rage
To such a greeting: villain am I none;
Therefore farewell; I see thou know'st me not.
TYBALT
Boy, this shall not excuse the injuries
That thou hast done me; therefore turn and
draw. 67
ROMEO
I do protest, I never injured thee,
But love thee better than thou canst devise,
Till thou shalt know the reason of my love:
And so, good Capulet,—which name I tender
As dearly as my own,—be satisfied.
MERCUTIO
O calm, dishonourable, vile submission!
Alla stoccata carries it away. [*Draws.*
Tybalt, you rat-catcher, will you walk?
TYBALT
What wouldst thou have with me? 76
MERCUTIO
Good king of cats, nothing but one of your nine lives; that I mean to make bold withal, and, as you shall use me hereafter, dry-beat the rest of the eight. Will you pluck your sword out of his pilcher by the ears? make haste, lest mine be about your ears ere it be out.
TYBALT
I am for you. [*Drawing.*
ROMEO
Gentle Mercutio, put thy rapier up.
MERCUTIO
Come, sir, your passado. [*They fight.*
ROMEO
Draw, Benvolio; beat down their weapons.
Gentlemen, for shame, forbear this outrage!
Tybalt, Mercutio, the prince expressly hath 98
Forbidden bandying in Verona streets:
Hold, Tybalt! good Mercutio!
[*Tybalt under Romeo's arm stabs Mercutio, and flies with his followers.*
MERCUTIO
I am hurt.
A plague o' both your houses! I am sped.
Is he gone, and hath nothing?
BENVOLIO
What, art thou hurt?
MERCUTIO
Ay, ay, a scratch, a scratch; marry, 'tis enough.
Where is my page? Go, villain, fetch a surgeon.
[*Exit Page.*
ROMEO
Courage, man; the hurt cannot be much.
MERCUTIO
No, 'tis not so deep as a well, nor so wide as a church-door; but 'tis enough, 'twill serve: ask me for to-morrow, and you shall find me a grave man. I am peppered, I warrant, for this world. A plague o' both your houses! 'Zounds, a dog, a rat, a mouse, a cat, to scratch a man to death! a braggart, a rogue, a villain, that fights by the book of arithmetic! Why the devil came you between us? I was hurt under your arm.
ROMEO
I thought all for the best. 116
MERCUTIO
Help me into some house, Benvolio,
Or I shall faint. A plague o' both your houses!
They have made worms' meat of me: I have it,
And soundly too: your houses!
[*Exeunt Mercutio and Benvolio.*
ROMEO
This gentleman, the prince's near ally,
My very friend, hath got his mortal hurt
In my behalf; my reputation stain'd
With Tybalt's slander,—Tybalt, that an hour
Hath been my kinsman! O sweet Juliet, [44]
Thy beauty hath made me effeminate
And in my temper soften'd valour's steel! 127

Re-enter BENVOLIO.

BENVOLIO
O Romeo, Romeo, brave Mercutio's dead!
That gallant spirit hath aspired the clouds,
Which too untimely here did scorn the earth.

ROMEO
This day's black fate on more days doth depend;
This but begins the woe others must end.

BENVOLIO
Here comes the furious Tybalt back again.

ROMEO
Alive, in triumph! and Mercutio slain!
Away to heaven, respective lenity,
And fire-eyed fury be my conduct now!

Re-enter TYBALT.

Now, Tybalt, take the villain back again,
That late thou gavest me; for Mercutio's soul
Is but a little way above our heads,
Staying for thine to keep him company:
Either thou, or I, or both, must go with him.

TYBALT
Thou, wretched boy, that didst consort him here,
Shalt with him hence.

ROMEO
This shall determine that. [*They fight; Tybalt falls.*

BENVOLIO
Romeo, away, be gone!
The citizens are up, and Tybalt slain.
Stand not amazed: the prince will doom thee death,
If thou art taken: hence, be gone, away!

ROMEO
O, I am fortune's fool!

BENVOLIO
Why dost thou stay? [*Exit Romeo.*

Enter Citizens, &c.

FIRST CITIZEN
Which way ran he that kill'd Mercutio?
Tybalt, that murderer, which way ran he?

BENVOLIO
There lies that Tybalt.

FIRST CITIZEN
Up, sir, go with me;
I charge thee in the prince's name, obey.

Enter Prince, *attended*; MONTAGUE, CAPULET, *their* Wives, *and others.*

PRINCE
Where are the vile beginners of this fray?

BENVOLIO
O noble prince, I can discover all
The unlucky manage of this fatal brawl:
There lies the man, slain by young Romeo,
That slew thy kinsman, brave Mercutio.

LADY CAPULET
Tybalt, my cousin! O my brother's child!
O prince! O cousin! husband! O, the blood is spilt
Of my dear kinsman! Prince, as thou art true,
For blood of ours, shed blood of Montague.
O cousin, cousin!

PRINCE
Benvolio, who began this bloody fray?

BENVOLIO
Tybalt, here slain, whom Romeo's hand did slay;
Romeo that spoke him fair, bade him bethink
How nice the quarrel was, and urged withal
Your high displeasure: all this uttered
With gentle breath, calm look, knees humbly bow'd,
Could not truce with the unruly spleen
Of Tybalt deaf to peace, but that he tilts
With piercing steel at bold Mercutio's breast,
Who, all as hot, turns deadly point to point,
And, with a martial scorn, with one hand beats
Cold death aside, and with the other sends
It back to Tybalt, whose dexterity,
Retorts it: Romeo he cries aloud,
'Hold, friends! friends, part!' and, swifter than his tongue,
His agile arm beats down their fatal points, [45]
And 'twixt them rushes; underneath whose arm
An envious thrust from Tybalt hit the life
Of stout Mercutio, and then Tybalt fled;
But by and by comes back to Romeo,
Who had but newly entertain'd revenge,
And to 't they go like lightning, for, ere I
Could draw to part them, was stout Tybalt slain.
And, as he fell, did Romeo turn and fly.
This is the truth, or let Benvolio die.

LADY CAPULET
He is a kinsman to the Montague;
Affection makes him false; he speaks not true:
Some twenty of them fought in this black strife,
And all those twenty could but kill one life.
I beg for justice, which thou, prince, must give;
Romeo slew Tybalt, Romeo must not live.

PRINCE
Romeo slew him, he slew Mercutio;
Who now the price of his dear blood doth owe?

MONTAGUE
Not Romeo, prince, he was Mercutio's friend;
His fault concludes but what the law should end,
The life of Tybalt.

PRINCE
And for that offence
Immediately we do exile him hence:
I have an interest in your hate's proceeding, [46]
My blood for your rude brawls doth lie a-bleeding;

But I'll amerce you with so strong a fine
That you shall all repent the loss of mine:
I will be deaf to pleading and excuses;
Nor tears nor prayers shall purchase out abuses:
Therefore use none: let Romeo hence in haste,
Else, when he's found, that hour is his last.
Bear hence this body, and attend our will:
Mercy but murders, pardoning those that kill.
[*Exeunt.*

ACT THREE SCENE TWO

Capulet's orchard.
Enter JULIET.

JULIET
Gallop apace, you fiery-footed steeds,
Towards Phoebus' lodging: such a waggoner
As Phaethon would whip you to the west,
And bring in cloudy night immediately.
Spread thy close curtain, love-performing night,
That runaway's eyes may wink, and Romeo [47]
Leap to these arms, untalk'd of and unseen.
Lovers can see to do their amorous rites
By their own beauties; or, if love be blind,
It best agrees with night. Come, civil night,
Thou sober-suited matron, all in black,
And learn me how to lose a winning match,
Play'd for a pair of stainless maidenhoods:
Hood my unmann'd blood, bating in my cheeks,
With thy black mantle; till strange love, grown bold,
Think true love acted simple modesty.
Come, night; come, Romeo; come, thou day in night;
For thou wilt lie upon the wings of night
Whiter than new snow on a raven's back.
Come, gentle night, come, loving, black-brow'd night,
Give me my Romeo; and, when he shall die,
Take him and cut him out in little stars,
And he will make the face of heaven so fine
That all the world will be in love with night
And pay no worship to the garish sun.
O, I have bought the mansion of a love,
But not possess'd it, and, though I am sold,
Not yet enjoy'd: so tedious is this day
As is the night before some festival
To an impatient child that hath new robes
And may not wear them. O, here comes my nurse,
And she brings news; and every tongue that speaks
But Romeo's name speaks heavenly eloquence.

Enter Nurse, *with cords.*

Now, nurse, what news? What hast thou there? the cords
That Romeo did thee fetch?

NURSE
Ay, ay, the cords. [*Throws them down.*

JULIET
Ay me! what news? why dost thou wring thy hands?

NURSE
Ah, well-a-day! he's dead, he's dead, he's dead!
We are undone, lady, we are undone!
Alack the day! he's gone, he's kill'd, he's dead!

JULIET
Can heaven be so envious?

NURSE
Romeo can,
Though heaven cannot: O Romeo, Romeo!
Who ever would have thought it? Romeo!

JULIET
What devil art thou, that dost torment me thus?
This torture should be roar'd in dismal hell.
Hath Romeo slain himself? say thou but 'I,'
And that bare vowel 'I' shall poison more
Than the death-darting eye of cockatrice:
I am not I, if there be such an I;
Or those eyes shut, that make thee answer 'I.'
If he be slain, say 'I'; or if not, no:
Brief sounds determine of my weal or woe.

NURSE
I saw the wound, I saw it with mine eyes,—
God save the mark!—here on his manly breast:
A piteous corse, a bloody piteous corse;
Pale, pale as ashes, all bedaub'd in blood,
All in gore-blood; I swounded at the sight.

JULIET
O, break, my heart! poor bankrupt, break at once!
To prison, eyes, ne'er look on liberty!
Vile earth, to earth resign; end motion here;
And thou and Romeo press one heavy bier!

NURSE
O Tybalt, Tybalt, the best friend I had!
O courteous Tybalt! honest gentleman!
That ever I should live to see thee dead!

JULIET
What storm is this that blows so contrary?
Is Romeo slaughter'd, and is Tybalt dead?
My dear-loved cousin, and my dearer lord? [48]
Then, dreadful trumpet, sound the general doom!
For who is living if those two are gone?

NURSE
Tybalt is gone, and Romeo banished;
Romeo that kill'd him, he is banished.

JULIET
O God! did Romeo's hand shed Tybalt's blood?

NURSE
It did, it did; alas the day, it did!

JULIET
O serpent heart, hid with a flowering face!

Did ever dragon keep so fair a cave?
Beautiful tyrant! fiend angelical!
Dove-feather'd raven! wolvish-ravening lamb! [49]
Despised substance of divinest show!
Just opposite to what thou justly seem'st,
A damned saint, an honourable villain! [50]
O nature, what hadst thou to do in hell, 84
When thou didst bower the spirit of a fiend
In moral paradise of such sweet flesh?
Was ever book containing such vile matter
So fairly bound? O, that deceit should dwell
In such a gorgeous palace!

NURSE
There's no trust,
No faith, no honesty in men; all perjured,
All forsworn, all naught, all dissemblers.
Ah, where's my man? give me some aqua vitae:
These griefs, these woes, these sorrows make me old.
Shame come to Romeo!

JULIET
Blister'd be thy tongue 97
For such a wish! he was not born to shame:
Upon his brow shame is ashamed to sit;
For 'tis a throne where honour may be crown'd
Sole monarch of the universal earth.
O, what a beast was I to chide at him!

NURSE
Will you speak well of him that kill'd your cousin? 104

JULIET
Shall I speak ill of him that is my husband?
Ah, poor my lord, what tongue shall smooth thy name,
When I, thy three-hours wife, have mangled it?
But, wherefore, villain, didst thou kill my cousin?
That villain cousin would have kill'd my husband:
Back, foolish tears, back to your native spring;
Your tributary drops belong to woe,
Which you, mistaking, offer up to joy.
My husband lives, that Tybalt would have slain;
And Tybalt's dead, that would have slain my husband:
All this is comfort; wherefore weep I then?
Some word there was, worser than Tybalt's death,
That murder'd me: I would forget it fain;
But, O, it presses to my memory, 118
Like damned guilty deeds to sinners' minds:
'Tybalt is dead, and Romeo—banished;'
That 'banished,' that one word 'banished,'
Hath slain ten thousand Tybalts. Tybalt's death
Was woe enough, if it had ended there:
Or, if sour woe delights in fellowship
And needly will be rank'd with other griefs,
Why follow'd not, when she said 'Tybalt's dead,'
Thy father, or thy mother, nay, or both, 127
Which modern lamentation might have moved?
But with a rearward following Tybalt's death,
'Romeo is banished,' to speak that word,
Is father, mother, Tybalt, Romeo, Juliet,
All slain, all dead. 'Romeo is banished!'
There is no end, no limit, measure, bound,
In that word's death; no words can that woe sound.
Where is my father, and my mother, nurse?

NURSE
Weeping and wailing over Tybalt's corse:
Will you go to them? I will bring you thither.

JULIET
Wash they his wounds with tears: mine shall be spent, 139
When theirs are dry, for Romeo's banishment.
Take up those cords: poor ropes, you are be-guiled,
Both you and I; for Romeo is exiled:
He made you for a highway to my bed;
But I, a maid, die maiden-widowed.
Come, cords, come, nurse; I'll to my wedding-bed;
And death, not Romeo, take my maidenhead!

NURSE
Hie to your chamber: I'll find Romeo
To comfort you: I wot well where he is.
Hark ye, your Romeo will be here at night:
I'll to him; he is hid at Laurence' cell.

JULIET
O, find him! give this ring to my true knight,
And bid him come to take his last farewell.
[*Exeunt.*

ACT THREE SCENE THREE

Friar Laurence's cell.

Enter FRIAR LAURENCE.

FRIAR LAURENCE
Romeo, come forth; come forth, thou fearful man:
Affliction is enamour'd of thy parts,
And thou art wedded to calamity.

Enter ROMEO.

ROMEO
Father, what news? what is the prince's doom?
What sorrow craves acquaintance at my hand,
That I yet know not?

FRIAR LAURENCE
Too familiar
Is my dear son with such sour company:
I bring thee tidings of the prince's doom.

ROMEO
What less than dooms-day is the prince's doom?

FRIAR LAURENCE
A gentler judgement vanish'd from his lips, 11

Not body's death, but body's banishment.

ROMEO
Ha, banishment! be merciful, say 'death;'
For exile hath more terror in his look,
Much more than death: do not say 'banishment.'

FRIAR LAURENCE
Hence from Verona art thou banished:
Be patient, for the world is broad and wide.

ROMEO
There is no world without Verona walls,
But purgatory, torture, hell itself.
Hence-banished is banish'd from the world,
And world's exile is death: then banished,
Is death mis-term'd: calling death banishment,
Thou cutt'st my head off with a golden axe,
And smilest upon the stroke that murders me.

FRIAR LAURENCE
O deadly sin! O rude unthankfulness!
Thy fault our law calls death; but the kind prince,
Taking my part, hath rush'd aside the law,
And turn'd that black word death to banishment:
This is dear mercy, and thou seest it not.

ROMEO
'Tis torture, and not mercy: heaven is here,
Where Juliet lives; and every cat and dog
And little mouse, every unworthy thing,
Live here in heaven and may look on her;
But Romeo may not: more validity,
More honourable state, more courtship lives
In carrion-flies than Romeo: they my seize
On the white wonder of dear Juliet's hand
And steal immortal blessing from her lips,
Who, even in pure and vestal modesty,
Still blush, as thinking their own kisses sin;
But Romeo may not; he is banished:
Flies may do this, but I from this must fly:
They are free men, but I am banished.
And say'st thou yet that exile is not death?
Hadst thou no poison mix'd, no sharp-ground knife,
No sudden mean of death, though ne'er so mean,
But 'banished' to kill me?—'banished'?
O friar, the damned use that word in hell;
Howlings attend it: how hast thou the heart,
Being a divine, a ghostly confessor,
A sin-absolver, and my friend profess'd,
To mangle me with that word 'banished'?

FRIAR LAURENCE
Thou fond mad man, hear me but speak a word;

ROMEO
O, thou wilt speak again of banishment.

FRIAR LAURENCE
I'll give thee armour to keep off that word:
Adversity's sweet milk, philosophy,
To comfort thee, though thou art banished.

ROMEO
Yet 'banished'? Hang up philosophy!
Unless philosophy can make a Juliet,
Displant a town, reverse a prince's doom,
It helps not, it prevails not: talk no more.

FRIAR LAURENCE
O, then I see that mad men have no ears.

ROMEO
How should they, when that wise men have no eyes?

FRIAR LAURENCE
Let me dispute with thee of thy estate.

ROMEO
Thou canst not speak of that thou dost not feel:
Wert thou as young as I, Juliet thy love,
An hour but married, Tybalt murdered,
Doting like me and like me banished,
Then mightst thou speak, then mightst thou tear thy hair,
And fall upon the ground, as I do now,
Taking the measure of an unmade grave.
[*Knocking within.*

FRIAR LAURENCE
Arise; one knocks; good Romeo, hide thyself.

ROMEO
Not I; unless the breath of heart sick groans,
Mist-like, infold me from the search of eyes.
[*Knocking.*

FRIAR LAURENCE
Hark, how they knock! Who's there? Romeo, arise;
Thou wilt be taken. Stay awhile! Stand up;
[*Knocking.*
Run to my study. By and by! God's will,
What simpleness is this! I come, I come! [*Knocking.*
Who knocks so hard? whence come you? what's your will?

NURSE
[*Within*] Let me come in, and you shall know my errand;
I come from Lady Juliet.

FRIAR LAURENCE
Welcome, then.

Enter Nurse.

NURSE
O holy friar, O, tell me, holy friar,
Where is my lady's lord, where's Romeo?

FRIAR LAURENCE
There on the ground, with his own tears made drunk.

NURSE
O, he is even in my mistress's case,
Just in her case! O woful sympathy!
Piteous predicament! Even so lies she,
Blubbering and weeping, weeping and blubbering.
Stand up, stand up; stand, and you be a man:

For Juliet's sake, for her sake, rise and stand;
Why should you fall into so deep an O?

ROMEO
Nurse!

NURSE
Ah sir! ah sir! Well, death's the end of all.

ROMEO
Spakest thou of Juliet? how is it with her?
Doth she not think me an old murderer,
Now I have stain'd the childhood of our joy
With blood removed but little from her own?
Where is she? and how doth she? and what says
My conceal'd lady to our cancell'd love?

NURSE
O, she says nothing, sir, but weeps and weeps;
And now falls on her bed; and then starts up,
And Tybalt calls; and then on Romeo cries,
And then down falls again.

ROMEO
As if that name,
Shot from the deadly level of a gun,
Did murder her; as that name's cursed hand
Murder'd her kinsman. O, tell me, friar, tell me,
In what vile part of this anatomy
Doth my name lodge? tell me, that I may sack
The hateful mansion. [*Drawing his sword.*

FRIAR LAURENCE
Hold thy desperate hand:
Art thou a man? thy form cries out thou art:
Thy tears are womanish; thy wild acts denote
The unreasonable fury of a beast:
Unseemly woman in a seeming man!
Or ill-beseeming beast in seeming both!
Thou hast amazed me; by my holy order,
I thought thy disposition better temper'd.
Hast thou slain Tybalt? wilt thou slay thyself?
And slay thy lady too that lives in thee,
By doing damned hate upon thyself?
Why rail'st thou on thy birth, the heaven, and earth?
Since birth, and heaven, and earth, all three
do meet
In thee at once; which thou at once wouldst lose.
Fie, fie, thou shamest thy shape, thy love, thy wit;
Which like a usurer, abound'st in all,
And usest none in that true use indeed
Which should bedeck thy shape, thy love, thy wit:
Thy noble shape is but a form of wax,
Digressing from the valour of a man;
Thy dear love sworn but hollow perjury,
Killing that love which thou hast vow'd to cherish;
Thy wit, that ornament to shape and love,
Mis-shapen in the conduct of them both,
Like powder in a skilless soldier's flask,
Is set a fire by thine own ignorance,
And thou dismember'd with thine own defence.
What, rouse thee, man! thy Juliet is alive,
For whose dear sake thou wast but lately dead;
There art thou happy: Tybalt would kill thee,
But thou slew'st Tybalt; there art thou happy too;
The law that threaten'd death becomes thy friend
And turns it to exile; there art thou happy:
A pack of blessings lights upon thy back;
Happiness courts thee in her best array;
But, like a misbehaved and sullen wench,
Thou pout'st upon thy fortune and thy love:
Take heed, take heed, for such die miserable.
Go, get thee to thy love, as was decreed,
Ascend her chamber, hence and comfort her:
But look thou stay not the watch be set,
For then thou canst not pass to Mantua;
Where thou shalt live, till we can find a time
To blaze your marriage, reconcile your friends,
Beg pardon of the prince, and call thee back
With twenty hundred thousand times more joy
Than thou went'st forth in lamentation.
Go before, nurse: commend me to thy lady;
And bid her hasten all the house to bed,
Which heavy sorrow makes them apt unto:
Romeo is coming.

NURSE
O Lord, I could have stay'd here all the night
To hear good counsel: O, what learning is!
My lord, I'll tell my lady you will come.

ROMEO
Do so, and bid my sweet prepare to chide.

NURSE
Here, sir, a ring she bid me give you, sir:
Hie you, make haste, for it grows very late. [*Exit.*

ROMEO
How well my comfort is revived by this!

FRIAR LAURENCE
Go hence; good night; and here stands all your state:
Either be gone before the watch be set,
Or by the break of day disguised from hence:
Sojourn in Mantua; I'll find out your man,
And he shall signify from time to time
Every good hap to you that chances here:
Give me thy hand; 'tis late: farewell; good night.

ROMEO
But that a joy past joy calls out on me,
It were grief, so brief to part with thee: Farewell.
[*Exeunt.*

ACT THREE SCENE FOUR

A room in Capulet's house.

Enter CAPULET, LADY CAPULET, *and* PARIS.

CAPULET
Things have fall'n out, sir, so unluckily,

That we have had no time to move our daughter:
Look you, she loved her kinsman Tybalt dearly,
And so did I:—Well, we were born to die.
'Tis very late, she'll not come down to-night:
I promise you, but for your company,
I would have been a-bed an hour ago.

PARIS
These times of woe afford no time to woo.
Madam, good night: commend me to your daughter.

LADY CAPULET
I will, and know her mind early to-morrow;
To-night she is mew'd up to her heaviness.

CAPULET
Sir Paris, I will make a desperate tender
Of my child's love: I think she will be ruled
In all respects by me; nay, more, I doubt it not.
Wife, go you to her ere you go to bed;
Acquaint her here of my son Paris' love;
And bid her, mark you me, on Wednesday next—
But, soft! what day is this?

PARIS
Monday, my lord,

CAPULET
Monday! ha, ha! Well, Wednesday is too soon,
O' Thursday let it be: o' Thursday, tell her,
She shall be married to this noble earl.
Will you be ready? do you like this haste?
We'll keep no great ado,—a friend or two;
For, hark you, Tybalt being slain so late,
It may be thought we held him carelessly,
Being our kinsman, if we revel much:
Therefore we'll have some half a dozen friends,
And there an end. But what say you to Thursday?

PARIS
My lord, I would that Thursday were to-morrow.

CAPULET
Well, get you gone: o' Thursday be it, then.
Go you to Juliet ere you go to bed,
Prepare her, wife, against this wedding-day.
Farewell, my lord. Light to my chamber, ho!
Afore me! it is so very late,
That we may call it early by and by.
Good night. [*Exeunt.*

ACT THREE SCENE FIVE

Capulet's orchard.

Enter ROMEO *and* JULIET *above, at the window.*

JULIET
Wilt thou be gone? it is not yet near day:
It was the nightingale, and not the lark,
That pierced the fearful hollow of thine ear;
Nightly she sings on yond pomegranate-tree:
Believe me, love, it was the nightingale.

ROMEO
It was the lark, the herald of the morn,
No nightingale: look, love, what envious streaks
Do lace the severing clouds in yonder east:
Night's candles are burnt out, and jocund day
Stands tiptoe on the misty mountain tops.
I must be gone and live, or stay and die.

JULIET
Yond light is not day-light, I know it, I:
It is some meteor that the sun exhales,
To be to thee this night a torch-bearer,
And light thee on thy way to Mantua:
Therefore stay yet; thou need'st not to be gone.

ROMEO
Let me be ta'en, let me be put to death;
I am content, so thou wilt have it so.
I'll say yon grey is not the morning's eye,
'Tis but the pale reflex of Cynthia's brow;
Nor that is not the lark, whose notes do beat
The vaulty heaven so high above our heads:
I have more care to stay than will to go:
Come, death, and welcome! Juliet wills it so.
How is't, my soul? let's talk; it is not day.

JULIET
It is, it is: hie hence, be gone, away!
It is the lark that sings so out of tune,
Straining harsh discords and unpleasing sharps.
Some say the lark makes sweet division;
This doth not so, for she divideth us:
Some say the lark and loathed toad change eyes; [52]
O, now I would they had changed voices too!
Since arm from arm that voice doth us affray,
Hunting thee hence with hunt's-up to the day,
O, now be gone; more light and light it grows.

ROMEO
More light and light; more dark and dark our woes!

Enter Nurse, *to the chamber.*

NURSE
Madam!

JULIET
Nurse?

NURSE
Your lady mother is coming to your chamber:
The day is broke; be wary, look about. [*Exit.*

JULIET
Then, window, let day in, and let life out.

ROMEO
Farewell, farewell! one kiss, and I'll descend.
[*He goeth down.*

JULIET
Art thou gone so? love, lord, ay, husband, friend!
I must hear from thee every day in the hour,
For in a minute there are many days:
O, by this count I shall be much in years
Ere I again behold my Romeo!
ROMEO
Farewell!
I will omit no opportunity
That may convey my greetings, love, to thee.
JULIET
O think'st thou we shall ever meet again?
ROMEO
I doubt it not; and all these woes shall serve
For sweet discourses in our time to come.
JULIET
O God, I have an ill-divining soul!
Methinks I see thee, now thou art below, [53]
As one dead in the bottom of a tomb;
Either my eyesight fails, or thou look'st pale.
ROMEO
And trust me, love, in my eye so do you:
Dry sorrow drinks our blood. Adieu, adieu! [*Exit.*
JULIET
O fortune, fortune! all men call thee fickle: 61
If thou art fickle, what dost thou with him.
That is renown'd for faith? Be fickle, fortune;
For then, I hope, thou wilt not keep him long,
But send him back.
LADY CAPULET
[*Within*] Ho, daughter! are you up?
JULIET
Who is't that calls? is it my lady mother?
Is she not down so late, or up so early?
What unaccustom'd cause procures her hither?

Enter LADY CAPULET.

LADY CAPULET
Why, how now, Juliet!
JULIET
Madam, I am not well.
LADY CAPULET
Evermore weeping for your cousin's death? 72
What, wilt thou wash him from his grave with tears?
An if thou couldst, thou couldst not make him live;
Therefore, have done: some grief shows much of love;
But much of grief shows still some want of wit.
JULIET
Yet let me weep for such a feeling loss.
LADY CAPULET
So shall you feel the loss, but not the friend
Which you weep for.
JULIET
Feeling so the loss,
I cannot choose but ever weep the friend.
LADY CAPULET
Well, girl, thou weep'st not so much for his death,
As that the villain lives which slaughter'd him.
JULIET
What villain, madam?
LADY CAPULET
That same villain, Romeo. 87
JULIET
[*Aside*] Villain and he be many miles asunder.—
God Pardon him! I do, with all my heart;
And yet no man like he doth grieve my heart.
LADY CAPULET
That is, because the traitor murderer lives.
JULIET
Ay, madam, from the reach of these my hands:
Would none but I might venge my cousin's death!
LADY CAPULET
We will have vengeance for it, fear thou not:
Then weep no more. I'll send to one in Mantua,
Where that same banish'd runagate doth live,
Shall give him such an unaccustom'd dram, 97
That he shall soon keep Tybalt company:
And then, I hope, thou wilt be satisfied.
JULIET
Indeed, I never shall be satisfied
With Romeo, till I behold him—dead—
Is my poor heart so for a kinsman vex'd:
Madam, if you could find out but a man
To bear a poison, I would temper it;
That Romeo should, upon receipt thereof, 105
Soon sleep in quiet. O, how my heart abhors
To hear him named, and cannot come to him.
To wreak the love I bore my cousin
Upon his body that hath slaughter'd him!
LADY CAPULET
Find thou the means, and I'll find such a man.
But now I'll tell thee joyful tidings, girl.
JULIET
And joy comes well in such a needy time:
What are they, I beseech your ladyship?
LADY CAPULET
Well, well, thou hast a careful father, child;
One who, to put thee from thy heaviness,
Hath sorted out a sudden day of joy, 116
That thou expect'st not nor I look'd not for.
JULIET
Madam, in happy time, what day is that?
LADY CAPULET
Marry, my child, early next Thursday morn,
The gallant, young and noble gentleman,
The County Paris, at Saint Peter's Church,

Shall happily make thee there a joyful bride.
JULIET
Now, by Saint Peter's Church and Peter too,
He shall not make me there a joyful bride.
I wonder at this haste; that I must wed
Ere he, that should be husband, comes to woo.
I pray you, tell my lord and father, madam,
I will not marry yet; and, when I do, I swear,
It shall be Romeo, whom you know I hate,
Rather than Paris. These are news indeed!
LADY CAPULET
Here comes your father; tell him so yourself,
And see how he will take it at your hands.

Enter CAPULET *and* Nurse.

CAPULET
When the sun sets, the air doth drizzle dew;
But for the sunset of my brother's son
It rains downright.
How now! a conduit, girl? what, still in tears?
Evermore showering? In one little body
Thou counterfeit'st a bark, a sea, a wind;
For still thy eyes, which I may call the sea,
Do ebb and flow with tears; the bark thy body is,
Sailing in this salt flood; the winds, thy sighs;
Who, raging with thy tears, and they with them,
Without a sudden calm, will overset
Thy tempest-tossed body. How now, wife!
Have you deliver'd to her our decree?
LADY CAPULET
Ay, sir; but she will none, she gives you thanks.
I would the fool were married to her grave!
CAPULET
Soft! take me with you, take me with you, wife.
How! will she none? doth she not give us thanks?
Is she not proud? doth she not count her blest,
Unworthy as she is, that we have wrought
So worthy a gentleman to be her bridegroom?
JULIET
Not proud, you have; but thankful, that you have:
Proud can I never be of what I hate;
But thankful even for hate, that is meant love.
CAPULET
How now, how now, chop-logic! What is this?
'Proud,' and 'I thank you,' and 'I thank you not;'
And yet 'not proud,' mistress minion, you, [54]
Thank me no thankings, nor proud me no prouds,
But fettle your fine joints 'gainst Thursday next,
To go with Paris to Saint Peter's Church,
Or I will drag thee on a hurdle thither.
Out, you green-sickness carrion! out, you baggage!
You tallow-face!
LADY CAPULET
Fie, fie! what, are you mad?
JULIET
Good father, I beseech you on my knees,
Hear me with patience but to speak a word.
CAPULET
Hang thee, young baggage! disobedient wretch!
I tell thee what: get thee to church o' Thursday,
Or never after look me in the face:
Speak not, reply not, do not answer me;
My fingers itch. Wife, we scarce thought us blest
That God had lent us but this only child; [55]
But now I see this one is one too much,
And that we have a curse in having her:
Out on her, hilding!
NURSE
God in heaven bless her!
You are to blame, my lord, to rate her so.
CAPULET
And why, my lady wisdom? hold your tongue,
Good prudence; smatter with your gossips, go.
NURSE
I speak no treason.
CAPULET
O, God ye god-den.

JULIET Good father, I beseech you on my knees,
hear me with patience but to speak a word.

NURSE
May not one speak?
CAPULET
Peace, you mumbling fool!
Utter your gravity o'er a gossip's bowl;
For here we need it not.
LADY CAPULET
You are too hot.
CAPULET
God's bread! it makes me mad:
Day, night, hour, tide, time, work, play,
Alone, in company, still my care hath been [56]
To have her match'd: and having now provided
A gentleman of noble parentage,
Of fair demesnes, youthful, and nobly train'd, [57]
Stuff'd, as they say, with honourable parts,
Proportion'd as one's thought would wish a man;
And then to have a wretched puling fool,
A whining mammet, in her fortune's tender,
To answer 'I'll not wed; I cannot love,
I am too young! I pray you, pardon me.'
But, an you will not wed, I'll pardon you:
Graze where you will, you shall not house with me:
Look to't, think on't, I do not use to jest.
Thursday is near; lay hand on heart, advise:
An you be mine, I'll give you to my friend;
And you be not, hang, beg, starve, die in the streets,
For, by my soul, I'll ne'er acknowledge thee,
Nor what is mine shall never do thee good:
Trust to't, bethink you; I'll not be forsworn. [*Exit.*
JULIET
Is there no pity sitting in the clouds,
That sees into the bottom of my grief?
O, sweet my mother, cast me not away!
Delay this marriage for a month, a week;
Or, if you do not, make the bridal bed
In that dim monument where Tybalt lies.
LADY CAPULET
Talk not to me, for I'll not speak a word:
Do as thou wilt, for I have done with thee. [*Exit.*
JULIET
O God!—O nurse, how shall this be prevented?
My husband is on earth, my faith in heaven;
How shall that faith return again to earth,
Unless that husband send it me from heaven
By leaving earth? comfort me, counsel me.
Alack, alack, that heaven should practise stratagems
Upon so soft a subject as myself!
What say'st thou? hast thou not a word of joy?
Some comfort, nurse.
NURSE
Faith, here it is.
Romeo is banish'd; and all the world to nothing,
That he dares ne'er come back to challenge you;
Or, if he do, it needs must be by stealth.
Then, since the case so stands as now it doth,
I think it best you married with the county.
O, he's a lovely gentleman!
Romeo's a dishclout to him: an eagle, madam,
Hath not so green, so quick, so fair an eye
As Paris hath. Beshrew my very heart,
I think you are happy in this second match,
For it excels your first: or if it did not,
Your first is dead; or 'twere as good he were,
As living here and you no use of him.
JULIET
Speakest thou from thy heart?
NURSE
And from my soul too;
Or else beshrew them both.
JULIET
Amen!
NURSE
What?
JULIET
Well, thou hast comforted me marvellous much.
Go in; and tell my lady I am gone,
Having displeased my father, to Laurence' cell,
To make confession and to be absolved.
NURSE
Marry, I will; and this is wisely done. [*Exit.*
JULIET
Ancient damnation! O most wicked fiend!
Is it more sin to wish me thus forsworn,
Or to dispraise my lord with that same tongue
Which she hath praised him with above compare
So many thousand times? Go, counsellor;
Thou and my bosom henceforth shall be twain.
I'll to the friar, to know his remedy:
If all else fail, myself have power to die. [*Exit.*

ACT FOUR SCENE ONE

Friar Laurence's cell.

Enter FRIAR LAURENCE *and* PARIS.

FRIAR LAURENCE
On Thursday, sir? the time is very short.
PARIS
My father Capulet will have it so;
And I am nothing slow to slack his haste. [58]
FRIAR LAURENCE
You say you do not know the lady's mind:
Uneven is the course, I like it not.

PARIS
Immoderately she weeps for Tybalt's death,
And therefore have I little talk'd of love;
For Venus smiles not in a house of tears.
Now, sir, her father counts it dangerous
That she doth give her sorrow so much sway,
And in his wisdom hastes our marriage,
To stop the inundation of her tears;
Which, too much minded by herself alone,
May be put from her by society:
Now do you know the reason of this haste.

FRIAR LAURENCE
[*Aside*] I would I knew not why it should be slow'd. *59*
Look, sir, here comes the lady towards my cell.

Enter JULIET.

PARIS
Happily met, my lady and my wife!

JULIET
That may be, sir, when I may be a wife.

PARIS
That may be must be, love, on Thursday next. 21

JULIET
What must be shall be.

FRIAR LAURENCE
That's a certain text.

PARIS
Come you to make confession to this father?

JULIET
To answer that, I should confess to you.

PARIS
Do not deny to him that you love me.

JULIET
I will confess to you that I love him.

PARIS
So will ye, I am sure, that you love me.

JULIET
If I do so, it will be of more price,
Being spoke behind your back, than to your face.

PARIS
Poor soul, thy face is much abused with tears.

JULIET
The tears have got small victory by that; 32
For it was bad enough before their spite.

PARIS
Thou wrong'st it, more than tears, with that report.

JULIET
That is no slander, sir, which is a truth;
And what I spake, I spake it to my face.

PARIS
Thy face is mine, and thou hast slander'd it.

JULIET
It may be so, for it is not mine own.
Are you at leisure, holy father, now;
Or shall I come to you at evening mass?

FRIAR LAURENCE
My leisure serves me, pensive daughter, now.
My lord, we must entreat the time alone. 42

PARIS
God shield I should disturb devotion!
Juliet, on Thursday early will I rouse ye:
Till then, adieu; and keep this holy kiss. [*Exit.*

JULIET
O, shut the door! and when thou hast done so,
Come weep with me; past hope, past cure, past help! *60*

FRIAR LAURENCE
Ah, Juliet, I already know thy grief;
It strains me past the compass of my wits:
I hear thou must, and nothing may prorogue it,
On Thursday next be married to this county.

JULIET
Tell me not, friar, that thou hear'st of this, 53
Unless thou tell me how I may prevent it:
If, in thy wisdom, thou canst give no help,
Do thou but call my resolution wise,
And with this knife I'll help it presently.
God join'd my heart and Romeo's, thou our hands;
And ere this hand, by thee to Romeo seal'd,
Shall be the label to another deed,
Or my true heart with treacherous revolt
Turn to another, this shall slay them both:
Therefore, out of thy long-experienced time,
Give me some present counsel, or, behold,
'Twixt my extremes and me this bloody knife
Shall play the umpire, arbitrating that
Which the commission of thy years and art
Could to no issue of true honour bring.
Be not so long to speak; I long to die,
If what thou speak'st speak not of remedy.

FRIAR LAURENCE
Hold, daughter: I do spy a kind of hope,
Which craves as desperate an execution
As that is desperate which we would prevent.
If, rather than to marry County Paris, 75
Thou hast the strength of will to slay thyself,
Then is it likely thou wilt undertake
A thing like death to chide away this shame,
That copest with death himself to scape from it;
And, if thou darest, I'll give thee remedy.

JULIET
O, bid me leap, rather than marry Paris,
From off the battlements of yonder tower;
Or walk in thievish ways; or bid me lurk
Where serpents are; chain me with roaring bears; 85

Or shut me nightly in a charnel-house,
O'er-cover'd quite with dead men's rattling bones,
With reeky shanks and yellow chapless-skulls;
Or bid me go into a new-made grave
And hide me with a dead man in his shroud;
Things that, to hear them told, have made me tremble;
And I will do it without fear or doubt,
To live an unstain'd wife to my sweet love.

FRIAR LAURENCE
Hold, then; go home, be merry, give consent
To marry Paris: Wednesday is to-morrow:
To-morrow night look that thou lie alone;
Let not thy nurse lie with thee in thy chamber:
Take thou this vial, being then in bed,
And this distilled liquor drink thou off;
When presently through all thy veins shall run
A cold and drowsy humour, for no pulse
Shall keep his native progress, but surcease:
No warmth, no breath, shall testify thou livest;
The roses in thy lips and cheeks shall fade
To paly ashes, thy eyes' windows fall,
Like death, when he shuts up the day of life;
Each part, deprived of supple government,
Shall, stiff and stark and cold, appear like death:
And in this borrow'd likeness of shrunk death
Thou shalt continue two and forty hours,
And then awake as from a pleasant sleep.
Now, when the bridegroom in the morning comes
To rouse thee from thy bed, there art thou dead:
Then, as the manner of our country is,
In thy best robes uncover'd on the bier
Thou shalt be borne to that same ancient vault
Where all the kindred of the Capulets lie.
In the mean time, against thou shalt awake,
Shall Romeo by my letters know our drift,
And hither shall he come: and he and I [61]
Will watch thy waking, and that very night
Shall Romeo bear thee hence to Mantua.
And this shall free thee from this present shame;
If no inconstant toy, nor womanish fear,
Abate thy valour in the acting it.

JULIET
Give me, give me! O, tell not me of fear!

FRIAR LAURENCE
Hold; get you gone, be strong and prosperous
In this resolve: I'll send a friar with speed
To Mantua, with my letters to thy lord.

JULIET
Love give me strength! and strength shall help afford.
Farewell, dear father! *[Exeunt.*

ACT FOUR SCENE TWO

Hall in Capulet's house.
Enter CAPULET, LADY CAPULET, Nurse, *and two* Servingmen.

CAPULET
So many guests invite as here are writ. *[Exit First Servant.*
Sirrah, go hire me twenty cunning cooks.

SECOND SERVANT
You shall have none ill, sir; for
I'll try if they can lick their fingers.

CAPULET
How canst thou try them so?

SECOND SERVANT
Marry, sir, 'tis an ill cook that cannot lick his own fingers: therefore he that cannot lick his fingers goes not with me.

CAPULET
Go, be gone. *[Exit Second Servant.*
We shall be much unfurnish'd for this time.
What, is my daughter gone to Friar Laurence?

NURSE
Ay, forsooth.

CAPULET
Well, he may chance to do some good on her:
A peevish self-will'd harlotry it is.

NURSE
See where she comes from shrift with merry look.

Enter JULIET.

CAPULET
How now, my headstrong! where have you been gadding?

JULIET
Where I have learn'd me to repent the sin
Of disobedient opposition
To you and your behests, and am enjoin'd
By holy Laurence to fall prostrate here,
And beg your pardon: pardon, I beseech you!
Henceforward I am ever ruled by you.

CAPULET
Send for the county; go tell him of this:
I'll have this knot knit up to-morrow morning.

JULIET
I met the youthful lord at Laurence' cell;
And gave him what becomed love I might,
Not stepping o'er the bounds of modesty.

CAPULET
Why, I am glad on't; this is well: stand up:
This is as't should be. Let me see the county;
Ay, marry, go, I say, and fetch him hither.
Now, afore God! this reverend holy friar,
All Our whole city is much bound to him.

JULIET
Nurse, will you go with me into my closet,
To help me sort such needful ornaments
As you think fit to furnish me to-morrow?
LADY CAPULET
No, not till Thursday; there is time enough.
CAPULET
Good nurse, go with her: we'll to church
to-morrow. [*Exeunt Juliet and Nurse.*
LADY CAPULET
We shall be short in our provision:
'Tis now near night.
CAPULET
Tush, I will stir about,
And all things shall be well, I warrant thee, wife:
Go thou to Juliet, help to deck up her;
I'll not to bed to-night; let me alone;
I'll play the housewife for this once. What, ho!
They are all forth. Well, I will walk myself
To County Paris, to prepare him up
Against to-morrow: my heart is wondrous light,
Since this same wayward girl is so reclaim'd.

ACT FOUR SCENE THREE

Juliet's chamber.

Enter JULIET *and* Nurse.

JULIET
Ay, those attires are best; but, gentle nurse,
I pray thee, leave me to myself to-night;
For I have need of many orisons
To move the heavens to smile upon my state,
Which, well thou know'st, is cross and full of sin.

Enter LADY CAPULET.

LADY CAPULET
What, are you busy, ho? need you my help?
JULIET
No, madam; we have cull'd such necessaries
As are behoveful for our state to-morrow:
So please you, let me now be left alone,
And let the nurse this night sit up with you;
For, I am sure, you have your hands full all,
In this so sudden business.
LADY CAPULET
Good night:
Get thee to bed, and rest; for thou hast need.
[*Exeunt Lady Capulet and Nurse.*
JULIET
Farewell! God knows when we shall meet again.
I have a faint cold fear thrills through my veins,
That almost freezes up the heat of life:
I'll call them back again to comfort me:
Nurse! What should she do here?
My dismal scene I needs must act alone.
Come, vial.
What if this mixture do not work at all?
Shall I be married then to-morrow morning?
No, no: this shall forbid it: lie thou there.
[*Laying down her dagger.*
What if it be a poison, which the friar
Subtly hath minister'd to have me dead,
Lest in this marriage he should be dishonour'd,
Because he married me before to Romeo?
I fear it is: and yet, methinks, I should not,
For he hath still been tried a holy man.
How if, when I am laid into the tomb,
I wake before the time that Romeo
Come to redeem me? there's a fearful point!
Shall I not, then, be stifled in the vault,
To whose foul mouth no healthsome air breathes in,
And there die strangled ere my Romeo comes?
Or, if I live, is it not very like,
The horrible conceit of death and night,
Together with the terror of the place,—
As in a vault, an ancient receptacle,
Where, for these many hundred years, the bones
Of all my buried ancestors are pack'd:
Where bloody Tybalt, yet but green in earth,
Lies festering in his shroud; where, as they say,
At some hours in the night spirits resort;—
Alack, alack, is it not like that I,
So early waking, what with loathsome smells,
And shrieks like mandrakes' torn out of the earth,
That living mortals, hearing them, run mad:—
O, if I wake, shall I not be distraught,
Environed with all these hideous fears?
And madly play with my forefather's joints?
And pluck the mangled Tybalt from his shroud?
And, in this rage, with some great kinsman's bone,
As with a club, dash out my desperate brains?
O, look! methinks I see my cousin's ghost
Seeking out Romeo, that did spit his body
Upon a rapier's point: stay, Tybalt, stay!
Romeo, I come! this do I drink to thee.
[*She falls upon her bed, within the curtains.*

ACT FOUR SCENE FOUR

Hall in Capulet's house.

Enter LADY CAPULET *and* Nurse.

LADY CAPULET
Hold, take these keys, and fetch more spices, nurse.
NURSE
They call for dates and quinces in the pastry.

Enter CAPULET.

CAPULET
Come, stir, stir, stir! the second cock hath crow'd,
The curfew-bell hath rung, 'tis three o'clock:
Look to the baked meats, good Angelica:
Spare not for cost.

NURSE
Go, you cot-quean, go,
Get you to bed; faith, you'll be sick to-morrow
For this night's watching.

CAPULET
No, not a whit: what! I have watch'd ere now
All night for lesser cause, and ne'er been sick.

LADY CAPULET
Ay, you have been a mouse-hunt in your time;
But I will watch you from such watching now.
[*Exeunt Lady Capulet and Nurse.*

CAPULET
A jealous-hood, a jealous-hood!

Enter three or four Servingmen, *with spits, logs, and baskets.*

Now, fellow,
What's there?

FIRST SERVANT
Things for the cook, sir; but I know not what.

CAPULET
Make haste, make haste. [*Exit First Serv.*] Sirrah, fetch drier logs:
Call Peter, he will show thee where they are.

SECOND SERVANT
I have a head, sir, that will find out logs,
And never trouble Peter for the matter. [*Exit.*

CAPULET
Mass, and well said; a merry whoreson, ha!
Thou shalt be logger-head. Good faith, 'tis day:
The county will be here with music straight,
For so he said he would: I hear him near.
[*Music within.*
Nurse! Wife! What, ho! What, nurse, I say!

Re-enter Nurse.

Go waken Juliet, go and trim her up;
I'll go and chat with Paris: hie, make haste,
Make haste; the bridegroom he is come already:
Make haste, I say. [*Exeunt.*

ACT FOUR SCENE FIVE

Juliet's chamber..

Enter Nurse.

NURSE
Mistress! what, mistress! Juliet! fast, I warrant her, she:
Why, lamb! why, lady! fie, you slug-a-bed!
Why, love, I say! madam! sweet-heart! why, bride!
What, not a word? you take your penny-worths now;
Sleep for a week; for the next night, I warrant,
The County Paris hath set up his rest,
That you shall rest but little. God forgive me,
Marry, and amen, how sound is she asleep!
I must needs wake her. Madam, madam, madam!
Ay, let the county take you in your bed: 11
He'll fright you up, i' faith. Will it not be?
[*Undraws the curtains.*
What, dress'd! and in your clothes! and down again!
I must needs wake you; Lady! lady! lady!
Alas, alas! Help, help! my lady's dead!
O, well-a-day, that ever I was born!
Some aqua vitae, ho! My lord! my lady!

Enter LADY CAPULET.

LADY CAPULET
What noise is here?

NURSE
O lamentable day!

LADY CAPULET
What is the matter?

NURSE
Look, look! O heavy day!

LADY CAPULET
O me, O me! My child, my only life,
Revive, look up, or I will die with thee! 24
Help, help! Call help.

Enter CAPULET.

CAPULET
For shame, bring Juliet forth; her lord is come.

NURSE
She's dead, deceased, she's dead; alack the day!

LADY CAPULET
Alack the day, she's dead, she's dead, she's dead!

CAPULET
Ha! let me see her: out, alas! she's cold;
Her blood is settled, and her joints are stiff;
Life and these lips have long been separated:
Death lies on her like an untimely frost
Upon the sweetest flower of all the field.

NURSE
O lamentable day!

LADY CAPULET
O woeful time! 35

CAPULET
Death, that hath ta'en her hence to make me wail,
Ties up my tongue, and will not let me speak.

Enter FRIAR LAURENCE *and* PARIS, *with* Musicians.

FRIAR LAURENCE
Come, is the bride ready to go to church?

CAPULET
Ready to go, but never to return.
O son! the night before thy wedding-day
Hath Death lain with thy wife. There she lies,
Flower as she was, deflowered by him.
Death is my son-in-law, Death is my heir;
My daughter he hath wedded: I will die,
And leave him all; life, living, all is Death's.

PARIS
Have I thought long to see this morning's face,
And doth it give me such a sight as this?

LADY CAPULET
Accursed, unhappy, wretched, hateful day!
Most miserable hour that e'er time saw
In lasting labour of his pilgrimage!
But one, poor one, one poor and loving child,
But one thing to rejoice and solace in,
And cruel death hath catch'd it from my sight!

NURSE
O woe! O woful, woful, woful day!
Most lamentable day, most woful day,
That ever, ever, I did yet behold!
O day! O day! O day! O hateful day!
Never was seen so black a day as this:
O woful day, O woful day!

PARIS
Beguiled, divorced, wronged, spited, slain!
Most detestable death, by thee beguiled,
By cruel cruel thee quite overthrown!
O love! O life! not life, but love in death!

CAPULET
Despised, distressed, hated, martyr'd, kill'd!
Uncomfortable time, why camest thou now
To murder, murder our solemnity?
O child! O child! my soul, and not my child!
Dead art thou! Alack! my child is dead;
And with my child my joys are buried.

FRIAR LAURENCE
Peace, ho, for shame! confusion's cure lives not
In these confusions. Heaven and yourself
Had part in this fair maid; now heaven hath all,
And all the better is it for the maid:
Your part in her you could not keep from death,
But heaven keeps his part in eternal life.
The most you sought was her promotion;
For 'twas your heaven she should be advanced:
And weep ye now, seeing she is advanced
Above the clouds, as high as heaven itself?
O, in this love, you love your child so ill,
That you run mad, seeing that she is well:
She's not well married that lives married long;
But she's best married that dies married young.
Dry up your tears, and stick your rosemary
On this fair corse; and, as the custom is,
In all her best array bear her to church:
For though fond nature bids us all lament,
Yet nature's tears are reason's merriment.

CAPULET
All things that we ordained festival,
Turn from their office to black funeral;
Our instruments to melancholy bells,
Our wedding cheer to a sad burial feast,
Our solemn hymns to sullen dirges change,
Our bridal flowers serve for a buried corse,
And all things change them to the contrary.

FRIAR LAURENCE
Sir, go you in; and, madam, go with him;
And go, Sir Paris; every one prepare
To follow this fair corse unto her grave:
The heavens do lour upon you for some ill;
Move them no more by crossing their high will.
[*Exeunt Capulet, Lady Capulet, Paris, and Friar.*

FIRST MUSICIAN
Faith, we may put up our pipes, and be gone.

NURSE
Honest good fellows, ah, put up, put up;
For, well you know, this is a pitiful case. [*Exit.*

FIRST MUSICIAN
Ay, by my troth, the case may be amended.

Enter PETER.

PETER
Musicians, O, musicians, 'Heart's ease, Heart's ease:'
O, an you will have me live, play 'Heart's ease.'

FIRST MUSICIAN
Why 'Heart's ease?'

PETER
O, musicians, because my heart itself plays 'My heart is full of woe:' O, play me some merry dump, to comfort me. [62]

FIRST MUSICIAN
Not a dump we; 'tis no time to play now.

PETER
You will not, then?

FIRST MUSICIAN
No.

PETER
I will then give it you soundly.

FIRST MUSICIAN
What will you give us?

PETER
No money, on my faith, but the gleek;
I will give you the minstrel.

FIRST MUSICIAN
Then will I give you the serving-creature.

PETER

Then will I lay the serving-creature's dagger on your pate. I will carry no crotchets: I'll re you, I'll fa you; do you note me?

FIRST MUSICIAN

An you re us and fa us, you note us.

SECOND MUSICIAN

Pray you, put up your dagger, and put out your wit.

PETER

Then have at you with my wit! I will dry-beat you with an iron wit, and put up my iron dagger. Answer me like men:

'When griping grief the heart doth wound, [63]
And doleful dumps the mind oppress,
Then music with her silver sound'—

why 'silver sound'? why 'music with her silver sound'? What say you, Simon Catling?

FIRST MUSICIAN

Marry, sir, because silver hath a sweet sound.

PETER

Pretty! what say you, Hugh Rebeck?

SECOND MUSICIAN

I say 'silver sound,' because musicians sound for silver.

PETER

Pretty too! What say you, James Soundpost?

THIRD MUSICIAN

Faith, I know not what to say.

PETER

O, I cry you mercy; you are the singer: I will say for you. It is 'music with her silver sound,' because musicians have no gold for sounding:

'Then music with her silver sound
With speedy help doth lend redress.' [*Exit.*

FIRST MUSICIAN

What a pestilent knave is this same!

SECOND MUSICIAN

Hang him, Jack! Come, we'll in here; tarry for the mourners, and stay dinner. [*Exeunt.*

ACT FIVE SCENE ONE

Mantua. A street.

Enter ROMEO.

ROMEO

If I may trust the flattering truth of sleep, [64]
My dreams presage some joyful news at hand:
My bosom's lord sits lightly in his throne;
And all this day an unaccustom'd spirit
Lifts me above the ground with cheerful thoughts.
I dreamt my lady came and found me dead—
Strange dream, that gives a dead man leave to think!—
And breathed such life with kisses in my lips,
That I revived, and was an emperor.
Ah me! how sweet is love itself possess'd,
When but love's shadows are so rich in joy!

Enter BALTHASAR, *booted.*

News from Verona!—How now, Balthasar!
Dost thou not bring me letters from the friar?
How doth my lady? Is my father well?
How fares my Juliet? that I ask again;
For nothing can be ill, if she be well.

BALTHASAR

Then she is well, and nothing can be ill:
Her body sleeps in Capel's monument,
And her immortal part with angels lives.
I saw her laid low in her kindred's vault,
And presently took post to tell it you:
O, pardon me for bringing these ill news,
Since you did leave it for my office, sir.

ROMEO

Is it even so? then I defy you, stars! [65]
Thou know'st my lodging: get me ink and paper,
And hire post-horses; I will hence to-night.

BALTHASAR

I do beseech you, sir, have patience: [66]
Your looks are pale and wild, and do import
Some misadventure.

ROMEO

Tush, thou art deceived:
Leave me, and do the thing I bid thee do.
Hast thou no letters to me from the friar?

BALTHASAR

No, my good lord.

ROMEO

No matter: get thee gone,
And hire those horses; I'll be with thee straight.
[*Exit Balthasar.*
Well, Juliet, I will lie with thee to-night.
Let's see for means: O mischief, thou art swift
To enter in the thoughts of desperate men!
I do remember an apothecary,—
And hereabouts he dwells,—which late I noted
In tatter'd weeds, with overwhelming brows,
Culling of simples; meagre were his looks,
Sharp misery had worn him to the bones:
And in his needy shop a tortoise hung,
An alligator stuff'd, and other skins
Of ill-shaped fishes; and about his shelves
A beggarly account of empty boxes,
Green earthen pots, bladders and musty seeds,
Remnants of packthread and old cakes of roses,
Were thinly scatter'd, to make up a show.
Noting this penury, to myself I said
'An if a man did need a poison now,
Whose sale is present death in Mantua,
Here lives a caitiff wretch would sell it him.'

O, this same thought did but forerun my need;
And this same needy man must sell it me.
As I remember, this should be the house.
Being holiday, the beggar's shop is shut.
What, ho! apothecary!

Enter Apothecary.

APOTHECARY
Who calls so loud?

ROMEO
Come hither, man. I see that thou art poor:
Hold, there is forty ducats: let me have
A dram of poison, such soon-speeding gear
As will disperse itself through all the veins
That the life-weary taker may fall dead
And that the trunk may be discharged of breath
As violently as hasty powder fired
Doth hurry from the fatal cannon's womb.

APOTHECARY
Such mortal drugs I have; but Mantua's law
Is death to any he that utters them.

ROMEO
Art thou so bare and full of wretchedness,
And fear'st to die? famine is in thy cheeks,
Need and oppression starveth in thine eyes,
Contempt and beggary hangs upon thy back;
The world is not thy friend nor the world's law;
The world affords no law to make thee rich;
Then be not poor, but break it, and take this.

APOTHECARY
My poverty, but not my will, consents.

ROMEO
I pay thy poverty, and not thy will.

APOTHECARY
Put this in any liquid thing you will,
And drink it off; and, if you had the strength
Of twenty men, it would dispatch you straight.

ROMEO
There 's thy gold, worse poison to men's souls,
Doing more murders in this loathsome world,
Than these poor compounds that thou mayst not sell.
I sell thee poison; thou hast sold me none.
Farewell: buy food, and get thyself in flesh.
Come, cordial and not poison, go with me
To Juliet's grave; for there must I use thee. [*Exeunt.*

ACT FIVE SCENE TWO

Friar Laurence's cell.

Enter FRIAR JOHN.

FRIAR JOHN
Holy Franciscan friar! brother, ho!

Enter FRIAR LAURENCE.

FRIAR LAURENCE
This same should be the voice of Friar John.
Welcome from Mantua: what says Romeo?
Or, if his mind be writ, give me his letter.

FRIAR JOHN
Going to find a bare-foot brother out,
One of our order, to associate me,
Here in this city visiting the sick,
And finding him, the searchers of the town,
Suspecting that we both were in a house
Where the infectious pestilence did reign,
Seal'd up the doors, and would not let us forth;
So that my speed to Mantua there was stay'd.

FRIAR LAURENCE
Who bare my letter, then, to Romeo?

FRIAR JOHN
I could not send it,—here it is again,—
Nor get a messenger to bring it thee,
So fearful were they of infection.

FRIAR LAURENCE
Unhappy fortune! by my brother-hood,
The letter was not nice but full of charge
Of dear import, and the neglecting it
May do much danger. Friar John, go hence;
Get me an iron crow, and bring it straight
Unto my cell.

FRIAR JOHN
Brother, I'll go and bring it thee. [*Exit.*

FRIAR LAURENCE
Now must I to the monument alone;
Within this three hours will fair Juliet wake:
She will beshrew me much that Romeo
Hath had no notice of these accidents;
But I will write again to Mantua,
And keep her at my cell till Romeo come;
Poor living corse, closed in a dead man's tomb!
[*Exit.*

ACT FIVE SCENE THREE

A churchyard; in it a tomb belonging to the Capulets.

Enter PARIS, *and his* Page *bearing flowers and a torch.*

PARIS
Give me thy torch, boy: hence, and stand aloof:
Yet put it out, for I would not be seen.
Under yond yew-trees lay thee all along,
Holding thine ear close to the hollow ground;
So shall no foot upon the churchyard tread,
Being loose, unfirm, with digging up of graves,
But thou shalt hear it; whistle then to me,

As signal that thou hear'st something approach.
Give me those flowers. Do as I bid thee, go.

PAGE
[*Aside*] I am almost afraid to stand alone 10
Here in the churchyard; yet I will adventure.
[*Retires.*

PARIS
Sweet flower, with flowers thy bridal bed I strew,—
O woe! thy canopy is dust and stones;—
Which with sweet water nightly I will dew,
Or, wanting that, with tears distill'd by moans:
The obsequies that I for thee will keep
Nightly shall be to strew thy grave and weep.
[*The Page whistles.*
The boy gives warning something doth approach.
What cursed foot wanders this way to-night,
To cross my obsequies and true love's rite? 21
What, with a torch! muffle me, night, awhile.
[*Retires.*

Enter ROMEO *and* BALTHASAR, *with a torch, mattock, &c.*

ROMEO
Give me that mattock and the wrenching iron.
Hold, take this letter: early in the morning
See thou deliver it to my lord and father.
Give me the light: upon thy life, I charge thee,
Whate'er thou hear'st or seeest, stand all aloof,
And do not interrupt me in my course.
Why I descend into this bed of death,
Is partly to behold my lady's face;
But chiefly to take thence from her dead finger
A precious ring, a ring that I must use 32
In dear employment: therefore hence, be gone:
But if thou, jealous, dost return to pry
In what I further shall intend to do,
By heaven, I will tear thee joint by joint
And strew this hungry churchyard with thy limbs:
The time and my intents are savage-wild,
More fierce and more inexorable far
Than empty tigers or the roaring sea.

BALTHASAR
I will be gone, sir, and not trouble you.

ROMEO
So shalt thou show me friendship. Take thou that: 43
Live, and be prosperous: and farewell, good fellow.

BALTHASAR
[*Aside*] For all this same, I'll hide me hereabout:
His looks I fear, and his intents I doubt. [*Retires.*

ROMEO
Thou detestable maw, thou womb of death,
Gorged with the dearest morsel of the earth,
Thus I enforce thy rotten jaws to open,
And, in despite, I'll cram thee with more food!
[*Opens the tomb.*

PARIS
This is that banish'd haughty Montague,
That murder'd my love's cousin, with which grief, 54
It is supposed, the fair creature died;
And here is come to do some villanous shame
To the dead bodies: I will apprehend him.
[*Comes forward.*
Stop thy unhallow'd toil, vile Montague!
Can vengeance be pursued further than death?
Condemned villain, I do apprehend thee:
Obey, and go with me; for thou must die.

ROMEO
I must indeed; and therefore came I hither.
Good gentle youth, tempt not a desperate man;
Fly hence, and leave me: think upon these gone; 65
Let them affright thee. I beseech thee, youth,
Put not another sin upon my head,
By urging me to fury: O, be gone!
By heaven, I love thee better than myself;
For I come hither arm'd against myself:
Stay not, be gone; live, and hereafter say,
A madman's mercy bade thee run away.

PARIS
I do defy thy conjurations,
And apprehend thee for a felon here.

ROMEO
Wilt thou provoke me? then have at thee, boy!
[*They fight.* 75

PAGE
O Lord, they fight! I will go call the watch. [*Exit.*

PARIS
O, I am slain! [*Falls.*] If thou be merciful,
Open the tomb, lay me with Juliet. [*Dies.*

ROMEO
In faith, I will. Let me peruse this face.
Mercutio's kinsman, noble County Paris!
What said my man, when my betossed soul
Did not attend him as we rode? I think
He told me Paris should have married Juliet:
Said he not so? or did I dream it so?
Or am I mad, hearing him talk of Juliet, 86
To think it was so? O, give me thy hand,
One writ with me in sour misfortune's book!
I'll bury thee in a triumphant grave;
A grave? O, no! a lantern, slaughter'd youth,
For here lies Juliet, and her beauty makes
This vault a feasting presence full of light.

Death, lie thou there, by a dead man interr'd.
[*Laying Paris in the tomb.*
How oft when men are at the point of death
Have they been merry! which their keepers call
A lightning before death: O, how may I
Call this a lightning? O my love! my wife!
Death, that hath suck'd the honey of thy breath,
Hath had no power yet upon thy beauty:
Thou art not conquer'd; beauty's ensign yet
Is crimson in thy lips and in thy cheeks,
And death's pale flag is not advanced there.
Tybalt, liest thou there in thy bloody sheet?
O, what more favour can I do to thee,
Than with that hand that cut thy youth in twain
To sunder his that was thine enemy?
Forgive me, cousin! Ah, dear Juliet,
Why art thou yet so fair? shall I believe
That unsubstantial death is amorous,
And that the lean abhorred monster keeps
Thee here in dark to be his paramour?
For fear of that, I still will stay with thee;
And never from this palace of dim night
Depart again: here, here will I remain
With worms that are thy chamber-maids; O, here
Will I set up my everlasting rest,
And shake the yoke of inauspicious stars
From this world-wearied flesh. Eyes, look your last!
Arms, take your last embrace! and, lips, O you
The doors of breath, seal with a righteous kiss
A dateless bargain to engrossing death!
Come, bitter conduct, come, unsavoury guide!
Thou desperate pilot, now at once run on
The dashing rocks thy sea-sick weary bark!
Here's to my love! [*Drinks.*] O true apothecary!
Thy drugs are quick. Thus with a kiss I die. [*Dies.*

Enter, at the other end of the churchyard, FRIAR LAURENCE, *with a lantern, crow, and spade.*

FRIAR LAURENCE
Saint Francis be my speed! how oft to-night
Have my old feet stumbled at graves! Who's there? [67]
BALTHASAR
Here's one a friend, and one that knows you well.
FRIAR LAURENCE
Bliss be upon you! Tell me, good my friend,
What torch is yond, that vainly lends his light
To grubs and eyeless skulls? as I discern,
It burneth in the Capel's monument.
BALTHASAR
It doth so, holy sir; and there's my master,
One that you love.
FRIAR LAURENCE
Who is it?
BALTHASAR
Romeo.
FRIAR LAURENCE
How long hath he been there?
BALTHASAR
Full half an hour.
FRIAR LAURENCE
Go with me to the vault.
BALTHASAR
I dare not, sir:
My master knows not but I am gone hence;
And fearfully did menace me with death,
If I did stay to look on his intents.
FRIAR LAURENCE
Stay, then; I'll go alone. Fear comes upon me:
O, much I fear some ill unlucky thing.
BALTHASAR
As I did sleep under this yew-tree here,
I dreamt my master and another fought,
And that my master slew him.
FRIAR LAURENCE
Romeo! [*Advances.*
Alack, alack, what blood is this, which stains
The stony entrance of this sepulchre?
What mean these masterless and gory swords
To lie discolour'd by this place of peace?

Enters the tomb.

Romeo! O, pale! Who else? what, Paris too?
And steep'd in blood? Ah, what an unkind hour
Is guilty of this lamentable chance!
The lady stirs. [*Juliet wakes.*
JULIET
O comfortable friar! where is my lord?
I do remember well where I should be,
And there I am. Where is my Romeo?
[*Noise within.*
FRIAR LAURENCE
I hear some noise. Lady, come from that nest
Of death, contagion, and unnatural sleep:
A greater power than we can contradict
Hath thwarted our intents. Come, come away.
Thy husband in thy bosom there lies dead;
And Paris too. Come, I'll dispose of thee
Among a sisterhood of holy nuns:
Stay not to question, for the watch is coming;
Come, go, good Juliet [*Noise again*], I dare no longer stay.
JULIET
Go, get thee hence, for I will not away. [*Exit Friar Laurence.*
What's here? a cup, closed in my true love's hand?
Poison, I see, hath been his timeless end:

O churl! drunk all, and left no friendly drop
To help me after? I will kiss thy lips;
Haply some poison yet doth hang on them,
To make me die with a restorative. [*Kisses him.*
Thy lips are warm.

FIRST WATCH
[*Within*] Lead, boy: which way?

JULIET
Yea, noise? then I'll be brief. O happy dagger!
[*Snatching Romeo's dagger.*
This is thy sheath [*Stabs herself*]; there rust, and let me die. [68] [*Falls on Romeo's body, and dies.*

Enter Watch, *with the* Page *of* PARIS.

PAGE
This is the place; there, where the torch doth burn.

FIRST WATCH
The ground is bloody; search about the churchyard:
Go, some of you, whoe'er you find attach.
Pitiful sight! here lies the county slain;
And Juliet bleeding, warm, and newly dead,
Who here hath lain these two days buried.
Go, tell the prince: run to the Capulets:
Raise up the Montagues: some others search:
We see the ground whereon these woes do lie;
But the true ground of all these piteous woes
We cannot without circumstance descry.

Re-enter some of the Watch, *with* BALTHASAR.

SECOND WATCH
Here's Romeo's man; we found him in the churchyard.

FIRST WATCH
Hold him in safety, till the prince come hither.

Re-enter others of the Watch, *with* FRIAR LAURENCE.

THIRD WATCH
Here is a friar, that trembles, sighs and weeps:
We took this mattock and this spade from him,
As he was coming from this churchyard side.

FIRST WATCH
A great suspicion: stay the friar too.

Enter the PRINCE *and* Attendants.

PRINCE
What misadventure is so early up,
That calls our person from our morning's rest?

Enter CAPULET, LADY CAPULET, *and others.*

CAPULET
What should it be, that they so shriek abroad?

LADY CAPULET
The people in the street cry Romeo,
Some Juliet, and some Paris; and all run,
With open outcry, toward our monument.

PRINCE
What fear is this which startles in our ears?

FIRST WATCH
Sovereign, here lies the County Paris slain;
And Romeo dead; and Juliet, dead before,
Warm and new kill'd.

PRINCE
Search, seek, and know how this foul murder comes.

FIRST WATCH
Here is a friar, and slaughtered Romeo's man;
With instruments upon them, fit to open
These dead men's tombs.

CAPULET
O heavens! O wife, look how our daughter bleeds!
This dagger hath mista'en,—for, lo, his house
Is empty on the back of Montague,—
And it mis-sheathed in my daughter's bosom! [69]

LADY CAPULET
O me! this sight of death is as a bell,
That warns my old age to a sepulchre.

Enter MONTAGUE *and others.*

PRINCE
Come, Montague; for thou art early up,
To see thy son and heir more early down.

MONTAGUE
Alas, my liege, my wife is dead to-night;
Grief of my son's exile hath stopp'd her breath: [70]
What further woe conspires against mine age?

PRINCE
Look, and thou shalt see.

MONTAGUE
O thou untaught! what manners is in this,
To press before thy father to a grave?

PRINCE
Seal up the mouth of outrage for a while,
Till we can clear these ambiguities,
And know their spring, their head, their true descent;
And then will I be general of your woes,
And lead you even to death: meantime forbear,
And let mischance be slave to patience.
Bring forth the parties of suspicion.

FRIAR LAURENCE
I am the greatest, able to do least,
Yet most suspected, as the time and place
Doth make against me, of this direful murder:
And here I stand, both to impeach and purge
Myself condemned and myself excused.

PRINCE
Then say at once what thou dost know in this.

FRIAR LAURENCE
I will be brief, for my short date of breath

Is not so long as is a tedious tale.
Romeo, there dead, was husband to that Juliet;
And she, there dead, that Romeo's faithful wife:
I married them; and their stol'n marriage-day
Was Tybalt's dooms-day, whose untimely death
Banish'd the new-made bridegroom from this city,
For whom, and not for Tybalt, Juliet pined.
You, to remove that siege of grief from her,
Betroth'd and would have married her perforce
To County Paris: then comes she to me,
And, with wild looks, bid me devise some mean
To rid her from this second marriage,
Or in my cell there would she kill herself.
Then gave I her, so tutor'd by my art,
A sleeping potion; which so took effect
As I intended, for it wrought on her
The form of death: meantime I writ to Romeo,
That he should hither come as this dire night,
To help to take her from her borrow'd grave,
Being the time the potion's force should cease.
But he which bore my letter, Friar John,
Was stay'd by accident, and yesternight
Return'd my letter back. Then all alone
At the prefixed hour of her waking,
Came I to take her from her kindred's vault;
Meaning to keep her closely at my cell,
Till I conveniently could send to Romeo:
But when I came, some minute ere the time
Of her awaking, here untimely lay
The noble Paris and true Romeo dead.
She wakes; and I entreated her come forth,
And bear this work of heaven with patience;
But then a noise did scare me from the tomb;
And she, too desperate, would not go with me,
But, as it seems, did violence on herself.
All this I know; and to the marriage
Her nurse is privy: and, if aught in this
Miscarried by my fault, let my old life
Be sacrificed, some hour before his time,
Unto the rigour of severest law.

PRINCE
We still have known thee for a holy man.
Where's Romeo's man? what can he say in this?

BALTHASAR
I brought my master news of Juliet's death;
And then in post he came from Mantua
To this same place, to this same monument.
This letter he early bid me give his father,

And threaten'd me with death, going in the vault,
If I departed not and left him there.

PRINCE

Give me the letter; I will look on it.
Where is the county's page, that raised the watch?
Sirrah, what made your master in this place?

PAGE

He came with flowers to strew his lady's grave;
And bid me stand aloof, and so I did:
Anon comes one with light to ope the tomb;
And by and by my master drew on him;
And then I ran away to call the watch.

PRINCE

This letter doth make good the friar's words,
Their course of love, the tidings of her death:
And here he writes that he did buy a poison
Of a poor 'pothecary, and therewithal
Came to this vault to die, and lie with Juliet.
Where be these enemies? Capulet! Montague!
See, what a scourge is laid upon your hate,
That heaven finds means to kill your joys with love.
And I for winking at your discords too
Have lost a brace of kinsmen: all are punish'd.

CAPULET

O brother Montague, give me thy hand:
This is my daughter's jointure, for no more
Can I demand.

MONTAGUE

But I can give thee more:
For I will raise her statue in pure gold;
That while Verona by that name is known,
There shall no figure at such rate be set
As that of true and faithful Juliet.

CAPULET

As rich shall Romeo's by his lady's lie;
Poor sacrifices of our enmity!

PRINCE

A glooming peace this morning with it brings;
The sun, for sorrow, will not show his head:
Go hence, to have more talk of these sad things;
Some shall be pardon'd, and some punished:
For never was a story of more woe
Than this of Juliet and her Romeo.

[*Exeunt.*

Notes

1. PROLOGUE, Omitted in Folios.
2. Cruel; – so Quartos 4, 5; Quartos 2, 3, Folios read *'ciuil,'* and *'civil.'*
3. Farther; – so Quartos 2, 4; Quarto 5, *'further'*; Quarto 3, Folios 1, 2, 3, *'Fathers'*; Folio 4, *'Father's.'*
4. Drave me to walk abroad; – Pope (from Quarto 1), *'drew me from company'*; Theobald, *'drew me to walk abroad.'*
5. Which then most sought where most might not be found; – Pope (from Quarto 1), *'That most are busied, when they're most alone'*; Keightley, *'Which there … ,'* &c. Herr conjectured *'Which then most sought where many …'*; Allen conjectured *'which then most sought where more …'*
6. Sun; – Theobald's emendation of Quartos and Folios, *'same.'*
7. See pathways to his will; – Staunton conjectured *'set pathways to our will'*; Hanmer, *'… ill.'*
8. Why such is; – Seymour conjectured *'Why such is, merely'*; Collier MS., *'Why such, Benvolio, is'*; Mommsen conjectured *'Why, such, Benvolio, such is'*; Keightley, *'Why, gentle cousin, such is'*; Orger conjectured *'Why, such a love is.'*
9. Raised; – Pope's correction (from Quarto 1); Quartos, Folios, *'made.'*
10. Bid a sick man in sadness make; – so (Quarto 1) Quartos 4, 5; Quartos 2, 3, Folio 1, read *'A sicke man in sadnesse makes'*; Folios 2, 3, 4, *'A sicke man in good sadnesse makes.'*
11. From love's weak childish bow she lives unharm'd; – Grant White conjectured *''Gainst … encharm'd'*; Quartos, Folios, *'uncharmd'*; Collier MS., *'encharm'd.'*
12. With beauty dies her store; – Theobald reads *'with her dies Beauty's Store'*; Keightley, *'with her dies beauty store.'*
13. She is the hopeful lady of my earth; – Johnson conjectured *'She is the hope and stay of my full years.'*
14. Made dark heaven light; – Theobald reads *'make dark heaven's light'*; Warburton, *'make dark even light'*; Jackson conjectured *'mask dark heaven's light'*; Daniel conjectured *'mock dark heaven's light.'*
15. Young men; – Johnson conjectured *'yeomen.'*
16. Which on more view, – &c.; so Quartos 4, 5; Quartos 2, 3, Folios, *'one'* for *'on'*; (Quarto 1), *'Such, amongst view of many myne being one'*; perhaps we should read with Mason, *'Whilst on more view of many, mine being one'*; many readings have been proposed.
17. Shake, quoth the dove-house, – referring to the effects of the earthquake; Daniel conjectured *'goeth'* for *'quoth.'*
18. Honour; – Pope's emendation (from Quarto 1); Quartos, Folios, *'houre'* and *'hour.'*
19. The game was ne'er so fair, and I am done; – "an allusion to an old proverbial saying which advises to give over when the game is at the fairest" (Ritson).
20. Cp. – Chaucer's *Manciple's Prologue:*—

    "Ther gan our hoste for to jape and pleye,
    And seyde, sirs, what!
    Dun is in the myre!"

    A proverbial expression originally used in an old rural sport, and meaning, "we are all at a standstill!" or, "let us make an effort to move on" *(vide* Prof. Skeat's *Notes to Canterbury Tales,* Vol. v. p. 435-6).
21. Of this sir-reverence love; – Singer's emendation from (Quarto 1); Quartos read *'Or saue you reuerence loue.'*; Folios 1, 2, 3, *'Or saue your reuerence loue.'*
22. Capell's emendation; (Quarto 1) reads *'We burne our lights by night, like Lampes by day'*; Quartos, *'We waste our*

lights in vaine, lights lights by day'; Folios, *'We wast our lights in vaine, lights, lights, by day.'*

23. Maid; – Pope's reading (from Quarto 1); Quartos, Folio 1, *'man'*; Folios 2, 3, 4, *'woman'*; Ulrici (from Collier MS.), *'milk-maid.'*
24. Courtier's; – Pope (from Quarto 1) reads *'lawyer's'*; Theobald conjectured *'taylor's.'*
25. Of healths; – Thrilby conjectured *'Of delves'*; Keightley conjectured *'Trenches'*; Clark MS., *'Of hilts.'*
26. Untangled; "which once u." – the untangling of which.
27. Face; – Pope's reading (from Quarto 1); Quartos, Folios, *'side'*; Collier MS., *'tide.'*
28. Will have a bout; – (Quarto 1); *'will haue about'*; Quartos, Folios, *'will walke about'*; Pope, *'we'll have a bout;* Daniel, *'will walke a bout.'*
29. It seems she; – so (Quarto 1); Quartos, Folio 1; Folios 2, 3, 4, read *'Her beauty'*; Bulloch conjectured *'In streams she'*; &c.
30. Pronounce; – Quartos 2, 3, *'prouaunt'*; Folio 1, *'Prouant'*; Folios 2, 3, 4, *'Couply'*; Rowe, *'couple.'*
31. Trim, – Steevens (from Quarto 1); Quartos, Folios, *'true.'*
32. Young Adam Cupid, he that shot so trim; – all the early editions read *'Abraham Cupid'*; Theobald conjectured *'auborn'*; Upton, *'Adam,'* referring to Adam Bell, the famous archer. It must be borne in mind, however, that *'Abram,' 'Abraham,'* was a regular corrupt form of *auburn,* formerly often written *abern, abron.*
33. Nor any other part Belonging to a man. O, be some other name! – Malone's emendation; Pope (from Quarto 1) reads *'nor any other part'*; Quartos, Folios, *'O be some other name Belonging to a man.'*
34. Name, – so Pope (from Quarto 1); Quartos, Folios, *'word.'*
35. Fair maid, if either thee dislike; – so Quartos, Folios; Pope (from Quarto 1) reads *'fair saint ... displease'*; Theobald, *'fair saint ... dislike'*; Grant White, *'fair maid ... displease'*; Anon. conjectured *'fair maid ... mislike.'*
36. Blessed moon I swear; – so (Quarto 1) Quartos; Folios read *'moon I vow.'*
37. Suit; – so Quarto 5; Quarto 4, *'sute'*; Quartos 2, 3, Folios, *'strife.'*
38. Father's cell; – Capell's reading (from Quarto 1); Quartos, Folios 3, 4, *'Friers close cell'*; Folios 1, 2, *'Fries close cell.'*
39. 1–4 Omitted in Folios 2, 3, 4.
40. Day's path and Titan's fiery wheels; – Malone's reading (from Quarto 1); Quartos, Folio 1, *'day's path, and Titans burning wheels'*; Pope, *'day's pathway, made by Titan's wheels.'*
41. Small, – so Pope from (Quarto 1); Quartos, Folios, *'weake.'*
42. I am none of his skains-mates'; skains-mates – occurs nowhere else, its origin is uncertain; it is perhaps connected with *skain, skein,* 'as if associated in winding yarns' (or *skain's = gen.* of *skain, skean* = dagger; 'as if a brother in arms').
43. Sum up sum of half my; – so Quartos 2, 3; Quartos 4, 5, *'summe up some of halfe my'*; Folios, *'sum up some of halfe my,'* &c.
44. Kinsman, – *Capell's reading from (Quarto 1); Quarto 5, other texts,* 'cousin.'
45. Agile; – (Quarto 1) Quartos 4, 5, *'agill'*; Quartos 2, 3, Folio 1, *'aged'*; Folios 2, 3, 4, *'able.'*
46. Hate's'; – Knight's emendation; Quartos, Folios, read *'hearts'*; Hanmer, *'heats"*; Johnson, *'hearts'.'*
47. That runaways' eyes may wink; – an epitome of the various interpretations of these words filling no less than twenty-eight pages of Furness' variorum edition; the Quartos and Folios do not mark the possessive, and scholars are divided on the subject of the singular or plural possessive. The Cambridge editors evidently make *'runaways'* = runagates, night-prowlers. The present editor cannot bring himself to believe that Shakespeare intended this reading, and would fain substitute *'Runaway's'* in the sense of 'Day's'; 'Runaway' may have belonged to the playful phraseology of Elizabethan girls, and savours of the expressive language of children's rhymes.
48. Dear-loved; – Pope's reading (from Quarto 1); Quartos, Folios, read *'dearest.'*
49. Dove-feather'd raven; – Theobald's emendation of Quartos 2, 3, Folio 1, *'Rauenous douefeathered Rauen'*; Quartos 4, 5, Folios 2, 3, 4, *'Rauenous doue, feathred Rauen.'*
50. Damned saint; – so Quartos 4, 5, Folios 2, 3, 4; Quartos 2, 3, *'dimme saint'*; Folio 1, *'dimne saint.'*
51. Thou fond mad man, hear me but speak a word; – Malone's emendation (from Quarto 1); Quartos 2, 3, *'Then fond mad man, heare me a little speake'*; Quartos 4, 5, *'Thou fond mad man, heare me a little speake'*; Folio 1, *'Then fond mad man, heare me speake'*; Folios 2, 3, 4, *'Fond mad man, heare me speake.'*
52. According to Warburton there is a popular saying to this effect, due to the fact that the toad has very fine eyes and the lark very ugly ones.
53. Below; – Pope's reading from (Quarto 1); Quartos, Folios, *'so lowe.'*
54. Omitted in Folios.
55. Lent; – Pope (from Quarto 1) reads *'sent'*; Cowden Clarke conjectured *'left.'*
56. So Quarto 2 and the other Quartos; Quarto 1 reads:—

    "Gods blessed mother wife it mads me,
    Day, night, early, late, at home, abroad,
    Alone, in company, waking or sleeping,
    Still my care hath been to see her matcht."

    Many attempts have been made to smooth the lines, but perhaps they express Capulet's excitement.
57. Train'd; – Capell's reading (from Quarto 1); Quartos 3, 4, 5, Folios *'allied'*; Quarto 2, *'liand'*; &c.
58. Nothing slow to slack his haste; – Collier conjectured *'something slow,'* &c.; Quarto 1, *'nothing slack to slow his haste'*; Johnson conjectured *'nothing slow to back his haste.'*
59. Omitted in Quartos, Folios.
60. Cure, – so (Quarto 1) Quarto 5; Quartos 2, 3, 4, Folios, *'care.'*
61. And he and I Will watch thy waking; – the reading of Quartos 3, 4, 5; omitted in Folios.

62. O play me some merry dump, to comfort me; – the reading of Quartos; omitted in Folios.
63. These lines are from Richard Edwards' *Paradise of Dainty Devises,* 1576.
64. Flattering truth; – so Quartos, Folios; Malone following (Quarto 1) reads *'flattering eye';* Collier MS., *'flattering death';* Grant White, *'flattering sooth';* &c.
65. I defy you; – Pope's reading; (Quarto 1), *'I defie my';* Quartos 2, 3, 4, Folio 1, *'I denie you';* Folios 2, 3, 4, Quarto 5, *'I deny you.'*
66. I do beseech you, sir, have patience; – Pope (from Quarto 1) reads *'Pardon me sir, I dare not leave you thus';* Steevens (1793) reads *'Pardon me, sir, I will not leave you thus.'*
67. Stumbled at graves, – &c:—

> *"For many men that stumble at the threshold*
> *Are well foretold that danger lurks within";*

3 *Henry VI.,* IV. vii. 11, 12.
68. Rust; – so Quartos, Folios; Hazlitt (from Quarto 1) reads *'rest.'*
69. It, i.e. – the dagger; so Quarto 2; the rest read *'is.'* —— *'mis-sheathed';* the reading of Folio 4; Folios 1, 2, 3, Quarto 5, *'misheathed';* Quarto 3, 4, *'missheath'd';* Jackson conjectured *'mi-sheath'd.'*
70. After this line (Quarto 1) reads *'and young Benvolio is deceased too.'*

TIMON OF ATHENS

TIMON OF ATHENS

DRAMATIS PERSONAE

TIMON, of Athens.
LUCIUS, flattering lord.
LUCULLUS, flattering lord.
SEMPRONIUS, flattering lord.
VENTIDIUS, one of Timon's false friends.
ALCIBIADES, an Athenian captain.
APEMANTUS, a churlish philosopher.
FLAVIUS, steward to Timon.
Poet, Painter, Jeweller, and Merchant.
An old Athenian.
FLAMINIUS, servant to Timon.
LUCILIUS, servant to Timon.
SERVILIUS, servant to Timon.
CAPHIS, servant to Timon's creditors.
PHILOTUS, servant to Timon's creditors.
TITUS, servant to Timon's creditors.
LUCIUS, servant to Timon's creditors.
HORTENSIUS, servant to Timon's creditors.
And others, servants to Timon's creditors.
A Page.
A Fool.
Three Strangers.
PHRYNIA, mistress to Alcibiades.
TIMANDRA, mistress to Alcibiades.
Cupid and Amazons in the mask.
Other Lords, Senators, Officers, Soldiers, Banditti, and Attendants.

SCENE : *Athens, and the neighbouring woods.*

ACT ONE SCENE ONE

Athens. A hall in Timon's house.

Enter Poet, Painter, Jeweller, Merchant, *and others, at several doors.*

POET
Good day, sir.
PAINTER
I am glad you're well.
POET
I have not seen you long: how goes the world?
PAINTER
It wears, sir, as it grows.
POET
Ay, that's well known:
But what particular rarity? what strange,
Which manifold record not matches? See,
Magic of bounty! all these spirits thy power
Hath conjured to attend. I know the merchant.
PAINTER
I know them both; th' other's a jeweller.
MERCHANT
O, 'tis a worthy lord.
JEWELLER
Nay, that's most fix'd.
MERCHANT
A most incomparable man, breathed, as it were, 13
To an untirable and continuate goodness:
He passes.
JEWELLER
I have a jewel here—

MERCHANT
O, pray, let's see't: for the Lord Timon, sir?
JEWELLER
If he will touch the estimate: but, for that—
POET
[*Reciting to himself*] 'When we for recompense have praised the vile,
It stains the glory in that happy verse
Which aptly sings the good.'
MERCHANT
'Tis a good form. [*Looking at the jewel.*
JEWELLER
And rich: here is a water, look ye.
PAINTER
You are rapt, sir, in some work, some dedication
To the great lord.
POET
A thing slipp'd idly from me. 27
Our poesy is as a gum, which oozes [1]
From whence 'tis nourish'd: the fire i' the flint
Shows not till it be struck; our gentle flame
Provokes itself and like the current flies [2]
Each bound it chafes. What have you there?
PAINTER
A picture, sir. When comes your book forth?
POET
Upon the heels of my presentment, sir.
Let's see your piece.
PAINTER
'Tis a good piece.
POET
So 'tis: this comes off well and excellent.
PAINTER
Indifferent.
POET
Admirable: how this grace [3]
Speaks his own standing! what a mental power 40
This eye shoots forth! how big imagination
Moves in this lip! to the dumbness of the gesture
One might interpret.
PAINTER
It is a pretty mocking of the life.
Here is a touch; is't good?
POET
I will say of it,
It tutors nature: artificial strife
Lives in these touches, livelier than life.

Enter certain Senators, *and pass over.*

PAINTER
How this lord is follow'd!
POET
The senators of Athens: happy man! [4]
PAINTER
Look, more! 52
POET
You see this confluence, this great flood of visitors.
I have, in this rough work, shaped out a man,
Whom this beneath world doth embrace and hug
With amplest entertainment: my free drift
Halts not particularly, but moves itself
In a wide sea of wax: no levell'd malice [5]
Infects one comma in the course I hold;
But flies an eagle flight, bold and forth on,
Leaving no tract behind. 61
PAINTER
How shall I understand you?
POET
I will unbolt to you.
You see how all conditions, how all minds,
As well of glib and slippery creatures as
Of grave and austere quality, tender down
Their services to Lord Timon: his large fortune
Upon his good and gracious nature hanging
Subdues and properties to his love and tendance
All sorts of hearts; yea, from the glass-faced flatterer
To Apemantus, that few things loves better
Than to abhor himself: even he drops down
The knee before him and returns in peace
Most rich in Timon's nod.
PAINTER
I saw them speak together.
POET
Sir, I have upon a high and pleasant hill
Feign'd Fortune to be throned: the base o' the mount
Is rank'd with all deserts, all kind of natures,
That labour on the bosom of this sphere
To propagate their states: amongst them all,
Whose eyes are on this sovereign lady fix'd,
One do I personate of Lord Timon's frame,
Whom fortune with her ivory hand wafts to her; 84
Whose present grace to present slaves and servants
Translates his rivals.
PAINTER
'Tis conceived to scope.
This throne, this Fortune, and this hill, methinks,
With one man beckon'd from the rest below,
Bowing his head against the sleepy mount
To climb his happiness, would be well express'd
In our condition.
POET
Nay, sir, but hear me on.
All those which were his fellows but of late,
Some better than his value, on the moment
Follow his strides, his lobbies fill with tendance, 97

Rain sacrificial whispering in his ear,
Make sacred even his stirrup, and through him
Drink the free air.

PAINTER
Ay, marry, what of these?

POET
When Fortune in her shift and change of mood
Spurns down her late beloved, all his dependants
Which labour'd after him to the mountain's top
Even on their knees and hands, let him slip down, [6]
Not one accompanying his declining foot.

PAINTER
'Tis common:
A thousand moral paintings I can show 108
That shall demonstrate these quick blows of Fortune's
More pregnantly than words. Yet you do well
To show Lord Timon that mean eyes have seen
The foot above the head.

Trumpets sound. Enter LORD TIMON, *addressing himself courteously to every suitor; a* Messenger *from* VENTIDIUS *talking with him*; LUCILIUS *and other servants following.*

TIMON
Imprison'd is he, say you?

MESSENGER
Ay, my good lord: five talents is his debt,
His means most short, his creditors most strait:
Your honourable letter he desires
To those have shut him up; which failing,
Periods his comfort.

TIMON
Noble Ventidius! Well;
I am not of that feather to shake off 121
My friend when he must need me. I do know him
A gentleman that well deserves a help:
Which he shall have: I'll pay the debt, and free him.

MESSENGER
Your lordship ever binds him.

TIMON
Commend me to him: I will send his ransom;
And being enfranchised, bid him come to me.
'Tis not enough to help the feeble up,
But to support him after. Fare you well.

MESSENGER
All happiness to your honour! [*Exit.*

Enter an old Athenian.

OLD ATHENIAN
Lord Timon, hear me speak.

TIMON
Freely, good father. 132

OLD ATHENIAN
Thou hast a servant named Lucilius.

TIMON
I have so: what of him?

OLD ATHENIAN
Most noble Timon, call the man before thee.

TIMON
Attends he here, or no? Lucilius!

LUCILIUS
Here, at your lordship's service.

OLD ATHENIAN
This fellow here, Lord Timon, this thy creature,
By night frequents my house. I am a man
That from my first have been inclined to thrift;
And my estate deserves an heir more raised
Than one which holds a trencher.

TIMON
Well; what further? 143

OLD ATHENIAN
One only daughter have I, no kin else,
On whom I may confer what I have got:
The maid is fair, o' the youngest for a bride,
And I have bred her at my dearest cost
In qualities of the best. This man of thine
Attempts her love: I prithee, noble lord,
Join with me to forbid him her resort;
Myself have spoke in vain.

TIMON
The man is honest. [7]

OLD ATHENIAN
Therefore he will be, Timon:
His honesty rewards him in itself; 154
It must not bear my daughter.

TIMON
Does she love him?

OLD ATHENIAN
She is young and apt:
Our own precedent passions do instruct us
What levity's in youth.

TIMON
[*To* Lucilius] Love you the maid?

LUCILIUS
Ay, my good lord, and she accepts of it.

OLD ATHENIAN
If in her marriage my consent be missing,
I call the gods to witness, I will choose
Mine heir from forth the beggars of the world,
And dispossess her all.

TIMON
How shall she be endow'd, if she be mated with an equal husband? 167

OLD ATHENIAN
Three talents on the present; in future, all.

TIMON
This gentleman of mine hath served me long:
To build his fortune I will strain a little,

For 'tis a bond in men. Give him thy daughter:
What you bestow, in him I'll counterpoise,
And make him weigh with her.

OLD ATHENIAN
Most noble lord,
Pawn me to this your honour, she is his.

TIMON
My hand to thee; mine honour on my promise.

LUCILIUS
Humbly I thank your lordship: never may
That state or fortune fall into my keeping, 178
Which is not owed to you!
[*Exeunt Lucilus and Old Athenian.*

POET
Vouchsafe my labour, and long live your lordship!

TIMON
I thank you; you shall hear from me anon:
Go not away. What have you there, my friend?

PAINTER
A piece of painting, which I do beseech
Your lordship to accept.

TIMON
Painting is welcome.
The painting is almost the natural man;
For since dishonour traffics with man's nature,
He is but outside: these pencill'd figures are
Even such as they give out. I like your work;
And you shall find I like it: wait attendance
Till you hear further from me.

PAINTER
The gods preserve ye!

TIMON
Well fare you, gentleman: give me your hand;
We must needs dine together. Sir, your jewel
Hath suffer'd under praise.

JEWELLER
What, my lord! dispraise?

TIMON
A mere satiety of commendations.
If I should pay you for't as 'tis extoll'd,
It would unclew me quite.

JEWELLER
My lord, 'tis rated
As those which sell would give: but you well know,
Things of like value differing in the owners
Are prized by their masters: believe't, dear lord,
You mend the jewel by the wearing it.

TIMON
Well mock'd.

MERCHANT
No, my good lord; he speaks the common tongue,
Which all men speak with him.

TIMON
Look, who comes here: will you be chid?

Enter APEMANTUS.

JEWELLER
We'll bear, with your lordship.

MERCHANT
He'll spare none.

TIMON
Good morrow to thee, gentle Apemantus!

APEMANTUS
Till I be gentle, stay thou for thy good morrow;
When thou art Timon's dog, and these knaves honest. 214

TIMON
Why dost thou call them knaves? thou know'st them not.

APEMANTUS
Are they not Athenians?

TIMON
Yes.

APEMANTUS
Then I repent not.

JEWELLER
You know me, Apementus?

APEMANTUS
Thou know'st I do: I call'd thee by thy name.

TIMON
Thou art proud, Apemantus.

APEMANTUS
Of nothing so much as that I am not like Timon. 224

TIMON
Whither art going?

APEMANTUS
To knock out an honest Athenian's brains.

TIMON
That's a deed thou'lt die for.

APEMANTUS
Right, if doing nothing be death by the law.

TIMON
How likest thou this picture, Apemantus?

APEMANTUS
The best, for the innocence. 230

TIMON
Wrought he not well that painted it?

APEMANTUS
He wrought better that made the painter; and yet he's but a filthy piece of work.

PAINTER
You're a dog.

APEMANTUS
Thy mother's of my generation: what's she, if I be a dog?

TIMON
Wilt dine with me, Apemantus?

APEMANTUS
No; I eat not lords.

TIMON
An thou shouldst, thou 'ldst anger ladies.
APEMANTUS
O, they eat lords; so they come by great bellies. 239
TIMON
That's a lascivious apprehension.
APEMANTUS
So thou apprehendest it: take it for thy labour.
TIMON
How dost thou like this jewel, Apemantus?
APEMANTUS
Not so well as plain-dealing, which will not cost a man a doit.
TIMON
What dost thou think 'tis worth?
APEMANTUS
Not worth my thinking. How now, poet! 246
POET
How now, philosopher!
APEMANTUS
Thou liest.
POET
Art not one?
APEMANTUS
Yes.
POET
Then I lie not.
APEMANTUS
Art not a poet?
POET
Yes.
APEMANTUS
Then thou liest: look in thy last work, where thou hast feigned him a worthy fellow.
POET
That's not feigned; he is so. 256
APEMANTUS
Yes, he is worthy of thee, and to pay thee for thy labour: he that loves to be flattered is worthy o' the flatterer. Heavens, that I were a lord!
TIMON
What wouldst do then, Apemantus?
APEMANTUS
E'en as Apemantus does now; hate a lord with my heart.
TIMON
What, thyself?
APEMANTUS
Ay.
TIMON
Wherefore? 265
APEMANTUS
That I had no angry wit to be a lord. [8]
Art not thou a merchant?
MERCHANT
Ay, Apemantus.
APEMANTUS
Traffic confound thee, if the gods will not!
MERCHANT
If traffic do it, the gods do it.
APEMANTUS
Traffic's thy god; and thy god confound thee!

Trumpet sounds. Enter a Messenger.

TIMON
What trumpet's that?
MESSENGER
'Tis Alcibiades, and some twenty horse,
All of companionship. 274
TIMON
Pray, entertain them; give them guide to us.
[*Exeunt some Attendants.*
You must needs dine with me: go not you hence
Till I have thank'd you: when dinner's done,
Show me this piece. I am joyful of your sights.

Enter ALCIBIADES, *with the rest.*

Most welcome, sir!
APEMANTUS
So, so, there!
Aches contract and starve your supple joints!
That there should be small love 'mongst these sweet knaves,
And all this courtesy! The strain of man's bred out
Into baboon and monkey. 285
ALCIBIADES
Sir, you have saved my longing, and I feed
Most hungerly on your sight.
TIMON
Right welcome, sir!
Ere we depart, we'll share a bounteous time
In different pleasures. Pray you, let us in.
[*Exeunt all except Apemantus.*

Enter two Lords.

FIRST LORD
What time o' day is't, Apemantus?
APEMANTUS
Time to be honest.
FIRST LORD
That time serves still.
APEMANTUS
The more accursed thou, that still omitt'st it.
SECOND LORD
Thou art going to Lord Timon's feast? 295
APEMANTUS
Ay, to see meat fill knaves and wine heat fools.
SECOND LORD
Fare thee well, fare thee well.

APEMANTUS
Thou art a fool to bid me farewell twice.
SECOND LORD
Why, Apemantus?
APEMANTUS
Shouldst have kept one to thyself, for I mean to give thee none.
FIRST LORD
Hang thyself!
APEMANTUS
No, I will do nothing at thy bidding: make thy requests to thy friend.
SECOND LORD
Away, unpeaceable dog, or I'll spurn thee hence!
APEMANTUS
I will fly, like a dog, the heels o' the ass. [*Exit.*
FIRST LORD
He's opposite to humanity. Come, shall we in,
And taste Lord Timon's bounty? he outgoes
The very heart of kindness.
SECOND LORD
He pours it out; Plutus, the god of gold,
Is but his steward: no meed, but he repays
Sevenfold above itself; no gift to him,
But breeds the giver a return exceeding
All use of quittance.
FIRST LORD
The noblest mind he carries
That ever govern'd man.
SECOND LORD
Long may he live in fortunes! Shall we in?
FIRST LORD
I'll keep you company. [*Exeunt.*

ACT ONE SCENE TWO

A banqueting-room in Timon's house.

Hautboys playing loud music. A great banquet served in; FLAVIUS *and others attending; then enter,* TIMON, ALCIBIADES, LORDS, SENATORS, *and* VENTIDIUS. *Then comes, dropping, after all,* APEMANTUS, *discontentedly, like himself.*

VENTIDIUS
Most honour'd Timon,
It hath pleased the gods to remember my father's age,
And call him to long peace.
He is gone happy, and has left me rich:
Then, as in grateful virtue I am bound
To your free heart, I do return those talents,
Doubled with thanks and service, from whose help
I derived liberty.
TIMON
O, by no means,
Honest Ventidius; you mistake my love:
I gave it freely ever; and there's none
Can truly say he gives, if he receives:
If our betters play at that game, we must not dare
To imitate them; faults that are rich are fair.
VENTIDIUS
A noble spirit!
TIMON
Nay, my lords,
[*They all stand ceremoniously looking on Timon.*
Ceremony was but devised at first
To set a gloss on faint deeds, hollow welcomes,
Recanting goodness, sorry ere 'tis shown;
But where there is true friendship, there needs none.
Pray, sit; more welcome are ye to my fortunes
Than my fortunes to me. [*They sit.*
FIRST LORD
My lord, we always have confess'd it.
APEMANTUS
Ho, ho, confess'd it! hang'd it, have you not?
TIMON
O, Apemantus, you are welcome.
APEMANTUS
No;
You shall not make me welcome:
I come to have thee thrust me out of doors.
TIMON
Fie, thou'rt a churl; ye've got a humour there
Does not become a man: 'tis much to blame.
They say, my lords, 'ira furor brevis est;' but yond man is ever angry. Go, let him have a table by himself, for he does neither affect company, nor is he fit for't, indeed.
APEMANTUS
Let me stay at thine apperil, Timon: I come to observe; I give thee warning on't.
TIMON
I take no heed of thee; thou'rt an Athenian, therefore welcome: I myself would have no power; prithee, let my meat make thee silent.
APEMANTUS
I scorn thy meat; 'twould choke me, for I should ne'er flatter thee. O you gods, what a number of men eat Timon, and he sees 'em not! It grieves me to see so many dip their meat in one man's blood; and all the madness is, he cheers them up too.
I wonder men dare trust themselves with men:
Methinks they should invite them without knives; [9]
Good for their meat, and safer for their lives.
There's much example for't; the fellow that sits next him now, parts bread with him, pledges the breath of

him in a divided draught, is the readiest man to kill him: 't has been proved. If I were a huge man, I should fear to drink at meals; 53

Lest they should spy my windpipe's dangerous notes:
Great men should drink with harness on their throats.

TIMON
My lord, in heart; and let the health go round.

SECOND LORD
Let it flow this way, my good lord.

APEMANTUS
Flow this way! A brave fellow! he keeps his tides well. Those healths will make thee and thy state look ill, Timon. Here's that which is too weak to be a sinner, honest water, which ne'er left man i' the mire: 62
This and my food are equals; there's no odds:
Feasts are too proud to give thanks to the gods.

[*Apemantus' grace.*]

Immortal gods, I crave no pelf;
I pray for no man but myself:
Grant I may never prove so fond,
To trust man on his oath or bond;
Or a harlot, for her weeping;
Or a dog, that seems a-sleeping:
Or a keeper with my freedom;
Or my friends, if I should need 'em. 72
Amen. So fall to't:
Rich men sin, and I eat root. [10]

[*Eats and drinks.*

Much good dich thy good heart, Apemantus!

TIMON
Captain Alcibiades, your heart's in the field now.

ALCIBIADES
My heart is ever at your service, my lord.

TIMON
You had rather be at a breakfast of enemies than a dinner of friends. 79

ALCIBIADES
So the were bleeding-new, my lord, there's no meat like 'em: I could wish my best friend at such a feast.

APEMANTUS
Would all those fatterers were thine enemies then, that then thou mightst kill 'em and bid me to 'em!

FIRST LORD
Might we but have that happiness, my lord, that you would once use our hearts, whereby we might express some part of our zeals, we should think ourselves for ever perfect. 87

TIMON
O, no doubt, my good friends, but the gods themselves have provided that I shall have much help from you: how had you been my friends else? why have you that charitable title from thousands, did not you chiefly belong to my heart? I have told more of you to myself than you can with modesty speak in your own behalf; and thus far I confirm you. O you gods, think I, what need we have any friends, if we should ne'er have need of 'em? they were the most needless creatures living, should we ne'er have use for 'em, and would most resemble sweet instruments hung up in cases that keep their sounds to themselves. Why, I have often wished myself poorer, that I might come nearer to you. We are born to do benefits: and what better or properer can we can our own than the riches of our friends? O, what a precious comfort 'tis, to have so many, like brothers, commanding one another's fortunes! O joy, e'en made away ere 't can be born! Mine eyes cannot hold out water, methinks: to forget their faults, I drink to you.

APEMANTUS
Thou weepest to make them drink, Timon.

SECOND LORD
Joy had the like conception in our eyes
And at that instant like a babe sprung up.

APEMANTUS
Ho, ho! I laugh to think that babe a bastard.

THIRD LORD
I promise you, my lord, you moved me much.

APEMANTUS
Much! [*Tucket, within.*

TIMON
What means that trump?

Enter a Servant.

How now?

SERVANT
Please you, my lord, there are certain ladies most desirous of admittance.

TIMON
Ladies! what are their wills?

SERVANT
There comes with them a forerunner, my lord, which bears that office, to signify their pleasures.

TIMON
I pray, let them be admitted.

Enter CUPID.

CUPID
Hail to thee, worthy Timon, and to all [11]
That of his bounties taste! The five best senses
Acknowledge thee their patron; and come freely 125
To gratulate thy plenteous bosom: th' ear,
Taste, touch and smell, pleased from thy tale rise;
They only now come but to feast thine eyes.

TIMON
They're welcome all; let 'em have kind admittance:
Music, make their welcome! [12] [*Exit Cupid.*

FIRST LORD
You see, my lord, how ample you're beloved.

Music. Re-enter CUPID, *with a mask of Ladies as Amazons, with lutes in their hands, dancing and playing.*

APEMANTUS
Hoy-day, what a sweep of vanity comes this way!
They dance! they are mad women.
Like madness is the glory of this life.
As this pomp shows to a little oil and root.
We make ourselves fools, to disport ourselves;
And spend our flatteries, to drink those men
Upon whose age we void it up again,
With poisonous spite and envy.
Who lives that's not depraved or depraves?
Who dies, that bears not one spurn to their graves
Of their friends' gift?
I should fear those that dance before me now
Would one day stamp upon me: 't has been done;
Men shut their doors against a setting sun.

The Lords rise from table, with much adoring of TIMON*; and to show their loves, each singles out an* Amazon, *and all dance, men with women, a lofty strain or two to the hautboys, and cease*

TIMON
You have done our pleasures much grace, fair ladies,
Set a fair fashion on our entertainment,
Which was not half so beautiful and kind;
You have added worth unto 't and lustre,
And entertain'd me with mine own device;
I am to thank you for 't.

FIRST LADY
My lord, you take us even at the best.

APEMANTUS
'Faith, for the worst is filthy; and would not hold taking, I doubt me.

TIMON
Ladies, there is an idle banquet attends you:
Please you to dispose yourselves.

ALL LADIES
Most thankfully, my lord.
[*Exeunt Cupid and Ladies.*

TIMON
Flavius.

FLAVIUS
My lord?

TIMON
The little casket bring me hither.

FLAVIUS
Yes, my lord. More jewels yet! [*Aside*] There is no crossing him in 's humour;
Else I should tell him,—well, i' faith I should,
When all's spent, he 'ld be cross'd then, an he could.
'Tis pity bounty had not eyes behind
That man might ne'er be wretched for his mind.
[*Exit.*

FIRST LORD
Where be our men?

SERVANT
Here, my lord, in readiness.

SECOND LORD
Our horses!

*Re-enter*FLAVIUS, *with the casket.*

TIMON
O my friends,
I have one word to say to you: look you, my good lord,
I must entreat you, honour me so much
As to advance this jewel; accept it and wear it,
Kind my lord.

FIRST LORD
I am so far already in your gifts,—

ALL
So are we all.

Enter a Servant.

SERVANT
My lord, there are certain nobles of the senate
Newly alighted, and come to visit you.

TIMON
They are fairly welcome.

FLAVIUS
I beseech your honour,
Vouchsafe me a word; it does concern you near.

TIMON
Near! why then, another time I'll hear thee:
I prithee, let's be provided to show them entertainment.

FLAVIUS
[*Aside*] I scarce know how.

Enter a Second Servant.

SECOND SERVANT
May it please your honour, Lord Lucius,
Out of his free love, hath presented to you
Four milk-white horses, trapp'd in silver.

TIMON
I shall accept them fairly; let the presents
Be worthily entertain'd.

Enter a third Servant.

How now! what news?

THIRD SERVANT
Please you, my lord, that honourable gentleman, Lord Lucullus, entreats your company to-morrow to hunt with him, and has sent your honour two brace of greyhounds.

TIMON
I'll hunt with him; and let them be received,
Not without fair reward.
FLAVIUS
[*Aside*] What will this come to?
He commands us to provide, and give great gifts,
And all out of an empty coffer:
Nor will he know his purse, or yield me this,
To show him what a beggar his heart is,
Being of no power to make his wishes good:
His promises fly so beyond his state
That what he speaks is all in debt; he owes
For every word: he is so kind that he now
Pays interest for 't; his land's put to their books.
Well, would I were gently put out of office
Before I were forced out!
Happier is he that has no friend to feed
Than such that do e'en enemies exceed.
I bleed inwardly for my lord. [*Exit.*
TIMON
You do yourselves
Much wrong, you bate too much of your own merits:
Here, my lord, a trifle of our love.
SECOND LORD
With more than common thanks I will receive it.
THIRD LORD
O, he's the very soul of bounty!
TIMON
And now I remember, my lord, you gave
Good words the other day of a bay courser
I rode on: it is yours, because you liked it.
SECOND LORD
O, I beseech you, pardon me, my lord, in that.
TIMON
You may take my word, my lord; I know, no man
Can justly praise but what he does affect:
I weigh my friend's affection with mine own;
I'll tell you true. I'll call to you.
ALL LORDS
O, none so welcome.
TIMON
I take all and your several visitations
So kind to heart, 'tis not enough to give;
Methinks, I could deal kingdoms to my friends,
And ne'er be weary. Alcibiades,
Thou art a soldier, therefore seldom rich;
It comes in charity to thee: for all thy living
Is 'mongst the dead, and all the lands thou hast
Lie in a pitch'd field.
ALCIBIADES
Ay, defiled land, my lord.
FIRST LORD
We are so virtuously bound—
TIMON
And so
Am I to you.
SECOND LORD
So infinitely endear'd—
TIMON
All to you. Lights, more lights!
FIRST LORD
The best of happiness,
Honour and fortunes, keep with you, Lord Timon!
TIMON
Ready for his friends.
[*Exeunt all but* APEMANTUS *and* TIMON.
APEMANTUS
What a coil's here!
Serving of becks and jutting-out of bums!
I doubt whether their legs be worth the sums
That are given for 'em. Friendship's full of dregs:
Methinks, false hearts should never have sound legs.
Thus honest fools lay out their wealth on court'sies.
TIMON
Now, Apemantus, if thou wert not sullen,
I would be good to thee.
APEMANTUS
No, I'll nothing: for if I should be bribed too, there would be none left to rail upon thee, and then thou wouldst sin the faster. Thou givest so long,
Timon, I fear me thou wilt give away thyself in paper shortly: what need these feasts, pomps and vain-glories?
TIMON
Nay, an you begin to rail on society once, I am sworn not to give regard to you. Farewell; and come with better music. [*Exit.*
APEMANTUS
So:
Thou wilt not hear me now; thou shalt not then:
I'll lock thy heaven from thee.
O, that men's ears should be
To counsel deaf, but not to flattery! [*Exit.*

ACT TWO SCENE ONE

A Senator's house.

Enter a Senator, *with papers in his hand.*

SENATOR
And late, five thousand: to Varro and to Isidore
He owes nine thousand; besides my former sum,
Which makes it five and twenty. Still in motion
Of raging waste? It cannot hold; it will not.
If I want gold, steal but a beggar's dog,

And give it Timon, why, the dog coins gold.
If I would sell my horse, and buy twenty more
Better than he, why, give my horse to Timon,
Ask nothing, give it him, it foals me, straight,
And able horses. No porter at his gate, [13]
But rather one that smiles and still invites
All that pass by. It cannot hold; no reason
Can found his state in safety. Caphis, ho! [14]
Caphis, I say!

Enter CAPHIS.

CAPHIS
Here, sir; what is your pleasure?
SENATOR
Get on your cloak, and haste you to Lord Timon;
Importune him for my moneys; be not ceased
With slight denial, nor then silenced when—
'Commend me to your master'—and the cap
Plays in the right hand, thus: but tell him,
My uses cry to me, I must serve my turn
Out of mine own; his days and times are past
And my reliances on his fracted dates
Have smit my credit: I love and honour him,
But must not break my back to heal his finger;
Immediate are my needs, and my relief
Must not be toss'd and turn'd to me in words,
But find supply immediate. Get you gone:
Put on a most importunate aspect,
A visage of demand; for, I do fear,
When every feather sticks in his own wing,
Lord Timon will be left a naked gull,
Which flashes now a phoenix. Get you gone.
CAPHIS
I go, sir.
SENATOR
'I go, sir!'—Take the bonds along with you,
And have the dates in conpt.
CAPHIS
I will, sir.
SENATOR
Go. [*Exeunt.*

ACT TWO SCENE TWO

The same. A hall in Timon's house.

Enter FLAVIUS, *with many bills in his hand.*

FLAVIUS
No care, no stop! so senseless of expense,
That he will neither know how to maintain it,

Nor cease his flow of riot: takes no account
How things go from him, nor resumes no care
Of what is to continue: never mind
Was to be so unwise, to be so kind.
What shall be done? he will not hear, till feel:
I must be round with him, now he comes from hunting.
Fie, fie, fie, fie!

Enter CAPHIS, *and the* Servants *of* ISIDORE *and* VARRO.

CAPHIS
Good even, Varro: what,
You come for money?
VARRO'S SERVANT
Is't not your business too?
CAPHIS
It is: and yours too, Isidore?
ISIDORE'S SERVANT
It is so.
CAPHIS
Would we were all discharged!
VARRO'S SERVANT
I fear it.
CAPHIS
Here comes the lord.

Enter TIMON, ALCIBIADES, *and* Lords, *&c.*

TIMON
So soon as dinner's done, we'll forth again,
My Alcibiades. With me? what is your will?
CAPHIS
My lord, here is a note of certain dues.
TIMON
Dues! Whence are you?
CAPHIS
Of Athens here, my lord.
TIMON
Go to my steward.
CAPHIS
Please it your lordship, he hath put me off
To the succession of new days this month:
My master is awaked by great occasion
To call upon his own, and humbly prays you
That with your other noble parts you'll suit
In giving him his right.
TIMON
Mine honest friend,
I prithee, but repair to me next morning.
CAPHIS
Nay, good my lord,—
TIMON
Contain thyself, good friend.
VARRO'S SERVANT
One Varro's servant, my good lord,—
ISIDORE'S SERVANT
From Isidore;
He humbly prays your speedy payment.
CAPHIS
If you did know, my lord, my master's wants—
VARRO'S SERVANT
'Twas due on forfeiture, my lord, six weeks
And past.
ISIDORE'S SERVANT
Your steward puts me off, my lord;
And I am sent expressly to your lordship.
TIMON
Give me breath.
I do beseech you, good my lords, keep on;
I'll wait upon you instantly.
[*Exeunt* ALCIBIADES *and Lords.*
[*To Flavius*]
Come hither: pray you,
How goes the world, that I am thus encounter'd
With clamorous demands of date-broke bonds,
And the detention of long-since-due debts,
Against my honour?
FLAVIUS
Please you, gentlemen,
The time is unagreeable to this business:
Your importunacy cease till after dinner,
That I may make his lordship understand
Wherefore you are not paid.
TIMON
Do so, my friends. See them well entertain'd. [*Exit.*
FLAVIUS
Pray, draw near. [*Exit.*

Enter APEMANTUS *and* Fool.

CAPHIS
Stay, stay, here comes the fool with Apemantus: let's ha' some sport with 'em.
VARRO'S SERVANT
Hang him, he'll abuse us.
ISIDORE'S SERVANT
A plague upon him, dog!
VARRO'S SERVANT
How dost, fool?
APEMANTUS
Dost dialogue with thy shadow?
VARRO'S SERVANT
I speak not to thee.
APEMANTUS
No, 'tis to thyself.
[*To the Fool*] Come away.
ISIDORE'S SERVANT
There's the fool hangs on your back already.
APEMANTUS
No, thou stand'st single, thou'rt not on him yet.

CAPHIS
Where's the fool now? 68

APEMANTUS
He last asked the question. Poor rogues, and usurers' men! bawds between gold and want!

ALL SERVANT
What are we, Apemantus?

APEMANTUS
Asses.

ALL SERVANT
Why?

APEMANTUS
That you ask me what you are, and do not know yourselves. Speak to 'em, fool.

FOOL
How do you, gentlemen?

ALL SERVANT
Gramercies, good fool: how does your mistress? [16]

FOOL
She's e'en setting on water to scald such chickens as you are. Would we could see you at Corinth!

APEMANTUS
Good! Gramercy.

Enter Page.

FOOL
Look you, here comes my mistress' page.

PAGE
[*To the Fool*] Why, how now, captain! what do you in this wise company? How dost thou, Apemantus?

APEMANTUS
Would I had a rod in my mouth, that I might answer thee profitably. 86

PAGE
Prithee, Apemantus, read me the superscription of these letters: I know not which is which.

APEMANTUS
Canst not read?

PAGE
No.

APEMANTUS
There will little learning die then, that day thou art hanged. This is to Lord Timon; this to Alcibiades. Go; thou wast born a bastard, and thou't die a bawd. 93

PAGE
Thou wast whelped a dog, and thou shalt famish a dog's death. Answer not; I am gone. [*Exit.*

APEMANTUS
E'en so thou outrunnest grace. Fool, I will go with you to Lord Timon's.

FOOL
Will you leave me there?

APEMANTUS
If Timon stay at home. You three serve three usurers?

ALL SERVANT
Ay; would they served us!

APEMANTUS
So would I,—as good a trick as ever hangman served thief. 103

FOOL
Are you three usurers' men?

ALL SERVANT
Ay, fool.

FOOL
I think no usurer but has a fool to his servant: my mistress is one, and I am her fool. When men come to borrow of your masters, they approach sadly, and go away merry; but they enter my mistress' house merrily, and go away sadly: the reason of this?

VARRO'S SERVANT
I could render one. 111

APEMANTUS
Do it then, that we may account thee a whoremaster and a knave; which not-withstanding, thou shalt be no less esteemed.

VARRO'S SERVANT
What is a whoremaster, fool?

FOOL
A fool in good clothes, and something like thee. 'Tis a spirit: sometime't appears like a lord; sometime like a lawyer; sometime like a philosopher, with two stones moe than's artificial one: he is very often like a knight; and, generally, in all shapes that man goes up and down in from fourscore to thirteen, this spirit walks in. 122

VARRO'S SERVANT
Thou art not altogether a fool.

FOOL
Nor thou altogether a wise man: as much foolery as I have, so much wit thou lackest.

APEMANTUS
That answer might have become Apemantus.

ALL SERVANT
Aside, aside; here comes Lord Timon.

Re-enter TIMON *and* FLAVIUS.

APEMANTUS
Come with me, fool, come.

FOOL
I do not always follow lover, elder brother and woman; sometime the philosopher.

[*Exeunt Apemantus and Fool.*

FLAVIUS
Pray you, walk near: I'll speak with you anon.

[*Exeunt Servants.*

TIMON
You make me marvel: wherefore ere this time
Had you not fully laid my state before me,
That I might so have rated my expense,
As I had leave of means?
FLAVIUS
You would not hear me,
At many leisures I proposed.
TIMON
Go to:
Perchance some single vantages you took.
When my indisposition put you back:
And that unaptness made your minister, 141
Thus to excuse yourself.
FLAVIUS
O my good lord,
At many times I brought in my accounts,
Laid them before you; you would throw them off,
And say, you found them in mine honesty.
When, for some trifling present, you have bid me
Return so much, I have shook my head and wept;
Yea, 'gainst the authority of manners, pray'd you
To hold your hand more close: I did endure
Not seldom, nor no slight cheques, when I have
Prompted you in the ebb of your estate 153
And your great flow of debts. My loved lord, [17]
Though you hear now, too late—yet now's a time— [18]
The greatest of your having lacks a half
To pay your present debts.
TIMON
Let all my land be sold.
FLAVIUS
'Tis all engaged, some forfeited and gone;
And what remains will hardly stop the mouth
Of present dues: the future comes apace:
What shall defend the interim? and at length
How goes our reckoning?
TIMON
To Lacedaemon did my land extend.
FLAVIUS
O my good lord, the world is but a word: 166
Were it all yours to give it in a breath,
How quickly were it gone!
TIMON
You tell me true.
FLAVIUS
If you suspect my husbandry or falsehood,
Call me before the exactest auditors
And set me on the proof. So the gods bless me,
When all our offices have been oppress'd
With riotous feeders, when our vaults have wept
With drunken spilth of wine, when every room
Hath blazed with lights and bray'd with minstrelsy, 177
I have retired me to a wasteful cock, [19]
And set mine eyes at flow.
TIMON
Prithee, no more.
FLAVIUS
Heavens, have I said, the bounty of this lord!
How many prodigal bits have slaves and peasants
This night englutted! Who is not Timon's?
What heart, head, sword, force, means, but is Lord Timon's?
Great Timon, noble, worthy, royal Timon!
Ah, when the means are gone that buy this praise,
The breath is gone whereof this praise is made:
Feast-won, fast-lost; one cloud of winter showers, 190
These flies are couch'd.
TIMON
Come, sermon me no further;
No villanous bounty yet hath pass'd my heart;
Unwisely, not ignobly, have I given.
Why dost thou weep? Canst thou the conscience lack,
To think I shall lack friends? Secure thy heart;
If I would broach the vessels of my love,
And try the argument of hearts by borrowing,
Men and men's fortunes could I frankly use
As I can bid thee speak.
FLAVIUS
Assurance bless your thoughts!
TIMON
And, in some sort, these wants of mine are crown'd, 204
That I account them blessings; for by these
Shall I try friends: you shall perceive how you
Mistake my fortunes; I am wealthy in my friends.
Within there! Flaminius! Servilius!

Enter FLAMINIUS, SERVILIUS, *and other* Servants.

SERVANTS
My lord? my lord?
TIMON
I will dispatch you severally; you to Lord Lucius; to Lord Lucullus you: I hunted with his honour to-day: you, to Sempronius: commend me to their loves, and, I am proud, say, that my occasions have found time to use 'em toward a supply of money: let the request be fifty talents.
FLAMINIUS
As you have said, my lord.
FLAVIUS
[*Aside*] Lord Lucius and Lucullus? hum!

TIMON

Go you, sir, to the senators—
Of whom, even to the state's best health, I have
Deserved this hearing—bid 'em send o' the instant
A thousand talents to me.

FLAVIUS

I have been bold—
For that I knew it the most general way—
To them to use your signet and your name;
But they do shake their heads, and I am here
No richer in return.

TIMON

Is't true? can't be?

FLAVIUS

They answer, in a joint and corporate voice,
That now they are at fall, want treasure, cannot
Do what they would; are sorry—you are honourable,—
But yet they could have wish'd—they know not—
Something hath been amiss—a noble nature
May catch a wrench—would all were well—'tis pity;—
And so, intending other serious matters,
After distasteful looks and these hard fractions,
With certain half-caps and cold-moving nods
They froze me into silence.

TIMON

You gods, reward them!
Prithee, man, look cheerly. These old fellows
Have their ingratitude in them hereditary:
Their blood is caked, 'tis cold, it seldom flows;
'Tis lack of kindly warmth they are not kind;
And nature, as it grows again toward earth,
Is fashion'd for the journey, dull and heavy.
[*To a Servant*] Go to Ventidius.
[*To Flavius*]
Prithee, be not sad,
Thou art true and honest; ingeniously I speak.
No blame belongs to thee. [*To Servant*] Ventidius lately
Buried his father; by whose death he's stepp'd
Into a great estate: when he was poor,
Imprison'd and in scarcity of friends,
I clear'd him with five talents: greet him from me;
Bid him suppose some good necessity
Touches his friend, which craves to be remember'd
With those five talents. [*Exit Servant.*
[*To Flavius*] That had, give't these fellows
To whom 'tis instant due. Ne'er speak, or think,
That Timon's fortunes 'mong his friends can sink.

FLAVIUS

I would I could not think it: that thought is bounty's foe;
Being free itself, it thinks all others so. [*Exeunt.*

ACT THREE SCENE ONE

A room in Lucullus' house.

FLAMINIUS *waiting. Enter a* Servant *to him.*

SERVANT

I have told my lord of you; he is coming down to you.

FLAMINIUS

I thank you, sir.

Enter LUCULLUS.

SERVANT

Here's my lord.

LUCULLUS

[*Aside*] One of Lord Timon's men? a gift, I warrant. Why, this hits right; I dreamt of a silver basin and ewer to-night. Flaminius, honest
Flaminius; you are very respectively welcome, sir.
Fill me some wine. [*Exit Servant.*
And how does that honourable, complete, free-hearted gentleman of Athens, thy very bountiful good lord and master?

FLAMINIUS

His health is well, sir.

LUCULLUS

I am right glad that his health is well, sir: and what hast thou there under thy cloak, pretty Flaminius?

FLAMINIUS

'Faith, nothing but an empty box, sir; which, in my lord's behalf, I come to entreat your honour to supply; who, having great and instant occasion to use fifty talents, hath sent to your lordship to furnish him, nothing doubting your present assistance therein.

LUCILIUS

La, la, la, la! 'nothing doubting,' says he? Alas, good lord! a noble gentleman 'tis, if he would not keep so good a house. Many a time and often I ha' dined with him, and told him on't, and come again to supper to him, of purpose to have him spend less, and yet he would embrace no counsel, take no warning by my coming. Every man has his fault, and honesty is his: I ha' told him on't, but I could ne'er get him from't.

Re-enter Servant, *with wine.*

SERVANT

Please your lordship, here is the wine.

LUCULLUS

Flaminius, I have noted thee always wise. Here's to thee.

FLAMINIUS

Your lordship speaks your pleasure.

LUCULLUS

I have observed thee always for a towardly prompt spirit—give thee thy due—and one that knows what belongs to reason; and canst use the time well, if the time use thee well: good parts in thee. [*To Servant*] Get you gone, sirrah. [*Exit Servant*] Draw nearer, honest Flaminius. Thy lord's a bountiful gentleman: but thou art wise; and thou knowest well enough, although thou comest to me, that this is no time to lend money, especially upon bare friendship, without security. Here's three solidares for thee: good boy, wink at me, and say thou sawest me not. Fare thee well.

FLAMINIUS

Is't possible the world should so much differ,
And we alive that lived? Fly, damned baseness, [20]
To him that worships thee! 47

[*Throwing the money back.*

LUCULLUS

Ha! now I see thou art a fool, and fit for thy master.

[*Exit.*

FLAMINIUS

May these add to the number that may scald thee!
Let moulten coin be thy damnation, [21]
Thou disease of a friend, and not himself!
Has friendship such a faint and milky heart,
It turns in less than two nights? O you gods,
I feel my master's passion! this slave, [22]
Unto his honour, has my lord's meat in him: 55
Why should it thrive and turn to nutriment,
When he is turn'd to poison?
O, may diseases only work upon't!
And, when he's sick to death, let not that part of nature
Which my lord paid for, be of any power
To expel sickness, but prolong his hour! [*Exit.*

ACT THREE SCENE TWO

A public place.

Enter LUCILIUS, with three *Strangers.*

LUCILIUS

Who, the Lord Timon? he is my very good friend, and an honourable gentleman.

FIRST STRANGER

We know him for no less, though we are but strangers to him. But I can tell you one thing, my lord, and which I hear from common rumours: now Lord Timon's happy hours are done and past, and his estate shrinks from him.

LUCILIUS

Fie, no, do not believe it; he cannot want for money. 10

SECOND STRANGER

But believe you this, my lord, that, not long ago, one of his men was with the Lord Lucullus to borrow so many talents, nay, urged extremely for't and showed what necessity belonged to't, and yet was denied. [23]

LUCILIUS

How!

SECOND STRANGER

I tell you, denied, my lord.

LUCILIUS

What a strange case was that! now, before the gods,

I am ashamed on't. Denied that honourable man! there was very little honour showed in't. For my own part, I must needs confess, I have received some small kindnesses from him, as money, plate, jewels and such-like trifles, nothing comparing to his; yet, had he mistook him and sent to me, I should ne'er have denied his occasion so many talents. [24]

Enter SERVILIUS.

SERVILIUS

See, by good hap, yonder's my lord;
I have sweat to see his honour. My honoured lord,—

[*To Lucius.*

LUCILIUS

Servilius! you are kindly met, sir. Fare thee well: commend me to thy honourable virtuous lord, my very exquisite friend.

SERVILIUS

May it please your honour, my lord hath sent—

LUCILIUS

Ha! what has he sent? I am so much endeared to that lord; he's ever sending: how shall I thank him, thinkest thou? And what has he sent now?

SERVILIUS

Has only sent his present occasion now, my lord; requesting your lordship to supply his instant use with so many talents. 37

LUCILIUS

I know his lordship is but merry with me;
He cannot want fifty five hundred talents.

SERVILIUS

But in the mean time he wants less, my lord.
If his occasion were not virtuous,
I should not urge it half so faithfully.

LUCILIUS

Dost thou speak seriously, Servillius?

SERVILIUS

Upon my soul, 'tis true, sir.

LUCILIUS

What a wicked beast was I to disfurnish myself against such a good time, when I might ha' shown myself honourable! how unluckily it happened, that I should purchase the day before for a little part, and undo a great deal of honour! Servillius, now, before the gods, I am not able to do,—the more beast, I say:—I was sending to use Lord Timon myself, these gentlemen can witness! but I would not, for the wealth of Athens, I had done't now. Commend me bountifully to his good lordship; and I hope his honour will conceive the fairest of me, because I have no power to be kind: and tell him this from me, I count it one of my greatest afflictions, say, that I cannot pleasure such an honourable gentleman. Good Servilius, will you befriend me so far, as to use mine own words to him? [25]

SERVILIUS
Yes, sir, I shall.

LUCILIUS
I'll look you out a good turn, Servilius.
[*Exit Servilius.*
True, as you said, Simon is shrunk indeed;
And he that's once denied will hardly speed.
[*Exit.*

FIRST STRANGER
Do you observe this, Hostilius?

SECOND STRANGER
Why, this is the world's soul; and just of the same piece
Is every flatterer's spirit. Who can call him [26]
His friend that dips in the same dish? for, in
My knowing, Timon has been this lord's father,
And kept his credit with his purse,
Supported his estate; nay, Timon's money
Has paid his men their wages: he ne'er drinks,
But Timon's silver treads upon his lip;
And yet—O, see the monstrousness of man
When he looks out in an ungrateful shape!—
He does deny him, in respect of his, [27]
What charitable men afford to beggars.

THIRD STRANGER
Religion groans at it.

FIRST STRANGER
For mine own part,
I never tasted Timon in my life,
Nor came any of his bounties over me,
To mark me for his friend; yet, I protest,
For his right noble mind, illustrious virtue
And honourable carriage,
Had his necessity made use of me,
I would have put my wealth into donation,
And the best half should have return'd to him,
So much I love his heart: but, I perceive,
Men must learn now with pity to dispense;
For policy sits above conscience. [*Exeunt.*

ACT THREE SCENE THREE

A room in Sempronius' house.

Enter SEMPRONIUS, *and a* Servant *of* TIMON'S.

SEMPRONIUS
Must he needs trouble me in't,—hum!—'bove all others?
He might have tried Lord Lucius or Lucullus;
And now Ventidius is wealthy too,
Whom he redeem'd from prison: all these
Owe their estates unto him.

SERVANT
My lord,
They have all been touch'd and found base metal, for
They have all denied him.

SEMPRONIUS
How! have they denied him?
Has Ventidius and Lucullus denied him?
And does he send to me? Three? hum!
It shows but little love or judgment in him:
Must I be his last refuge! His friends, like physicians,
Thrive, give him over: must I take the cure upon me? [28]
Has much disgraced me in't; I'm angry at him,
That might have known my place: I see no sense for't, [29]
But his occasions might have woo'd me first;
For, in my conscience, I was the first man
That e'er received gift from him:
And does he think so backwardly of me now,
That I'll requite its last? No:
So it may prove an argument of laughter
To the rest, and 'mongst lords I be thought a fool.
I'ld rather than the worth of thrice the sum,
Had sent to me first, but for my mind's sake;
I'd such a courage to do him good. But now return,
And with their faint reply this answer join;
Who bates mine honour shall not know my coin.
[*Exit.*

SERVANT
Excellent! Your lordship's a goodly villain. The devil knew not what he did when he made man politic; he crossed himself by 't: and I cannot think but, in the end, the villanies of man will set him clear. How fairly this lord strives to appear foul! takes virtuous copies to be wicked, like those that under hot ardent zeal would set whole realms on fire:
Of such nature is his politic love.
This was my lord's best hope; now all are fled,
Save only the gods: now his friends are dead,
Doors, that were ne'er acquainted with their wards
Many a bounteous year must be employ'd

Now to guard sure their master.
And this is all a liberal course allows;
Who cannot keep his wealth must keep his house.
[*Exit.*

ACT THREE SCENE FOUR

The same. A hall in Timon's house.

Enter two Servants *of* VARRO, *and the* Servant *of* LUCIUS, *meeting* TITUS, HORTENSIUS, *and other* Servants *of* TIMON'S *creditors, waiting his coming out.*

FIRST SERVANT
Well met; good morrow, Titus and Hortensius.
TITUS
The like to you kind Varro.
HORTENSIUS
Lucius!
What, do we meet together?
LUCILIUS'S SERVANT
Ay, and I think
One business does command us all; for mine Is money.
TITUS
So is theirs and ours.

Enter PHILOTUS.

LUCILIUS'S SERVANT
And Sir Philotus too!
PHILOTUS
Good day at once.
LUCILIUS'S SERVANT
Welcome, good brother.
What do you think the hour?
PHILOTUS
Labouring for nine.
LUCILIUS'S SERVANT
So much?
PHILOTUS
Is not my lord seen yet?
LUCILIUS'S SERVANT
Not yet.
PHILOTUS
I wonder on't; he was wont to shine at seven.
LUCILIUS'S SERVANT
Ay, but the days are wax'd shorter with him:
You must consider that a prodigal course
Is like the sun's; but not, like his, recoverable.
I fear 'tis deepest winter in Lord Timon's purse;
That is, one may reach deep enough, and yet
Find little.
PHILOTUS
I am of your fear for that.
TITUS
I'll show you how to observe a strange event.
Your lord sends now for money.
HORTENSIUS
Most true, he does.
TITUS
And he wears jewels now of Timon's gift,
For which I wait for money.
HORTENSIUS
It is against my heart.
LUCILIUS'S SERVANT
Mark, how strange it shows,
Timon in this should pay more than he owes:
And e'en as if your lord should wear rich jewels,
And send for money for 'em.
HORTENSIUS
I'm weary of this charge, the gods can witness:
I know my lord hath spent of Timon's wealth,
And now ingratitude makes it worse than stealth.
FIRST SERVANT
Yes, mine's three thousand crowns: what's yours?
LUCILIUS'S SERVANT
Five thousand mine.
FIRST SERVANT
'Tis much deep: and it should seem by the sum,
Your master's confidence was above mine;
Else, surely, his had equall'd.

Enter FLAMINIUS.

TITUS
One of Lord Timon's men.
LUCILIUS'S SERVANT
Flaminius! Sir, a word: pray, is my lord ready to come forth?
FLAMINIUS
No, indeed, he is not.
TITUS
We attend his lordship; pray, signify so much.
FLAMINIUS
I need not tell him that; he knows you are too diligent. [*Exit.*

Enter FLAVIUS *in a cloak, muffled.*

LUCILIUS'S SERVANT
Ha! is not that his steward muffled so?
He goes away in a cloud: call him, call him.
TITUS
Do you hear, sir?
SECOND SERVANT
By your leave, sir,—
FLAVIUS
What do ye ask of me, my friend?
TITUS
We wait for certain money here, sir.

FLAVIUS
Ay,
If money were as certain as your waiting,
'Twere sure enough.
Why then preferr'd you not your sums and bills, 60
When your false masters eat of my lord's meat?
Then they could smile and fawn upon his debts
And take down the interest into their gluttonous maws.
You do yourselves but wrong to stir me up;
Let me pass quietly:
Believe 't, my lord and I have made an end;
I have no more to reckon, he to spend.

LUCILIUS'S SERVANT
Ay, but this answer will not serve.

FLAVIUS
If 'twill not serve, 'tis not so base as you;
For you serve knaves. [*Exit.*

FIRST SERVANT
How! what does his cashiered worship mutter? 72

SECOND SERVANT
No matter what; he's poor, and that's revenge enough. Who can speak broader than he that has no house to put his head in? such may rail against great buildings.

Enter SERVILIUS.

TITUS
O, here's Servilius; now we shall know some answer.

SERVILIUS
If I might beseech you, gentlemen, to repair some other hour, I should derive much from't; for, take't of my soul, my lord leans wondrously to discontent: his comfortable temper has forsook him; he's much out of health, and keeps his chamber.

LUCILIUS'S SERVANT
Many do keep their chambers are not sick:
And, if it be so far beyond his health,
Methinks he should the sooner pay his debts,
And make a clear way to the gods.

SERVILIUS
Good gods!

TITUS
We cannot take this for answer, sir.

FLAMINIUS
[*Within.*] Servilius, help! My lord! my lord!

Enter TIMON, *in a rage*; FLAMINIUS *following*.

TIMON
What, are my doors opposed against my passage? 92
Have I been ever free, and must my house
Be my retentive enemy, my gaol?
The place which I have feasted, does it now,
Like all mankind, show me an iron heart?

LUCILIUS'S SERVANT
Put in now, Titus.

TITUS
My lord, here is my bill.

LUCILIUS'S SERVANT
Here's mine.

HORTENSIUS
And mine, my lord.

VARRO'S SERVANTS
And ours, my lord.

PHILOTUS
All our bills. 102

TIMON
Knock me down with 'em: cleave me to the girdle.

LUCILIUS'S SERVANT
Alas, my lord,—

TIMON
Cut my heart in sums.

TITUS
Mine, fifty talents.

TIMON
Tell out my blood.

LUCILIUS'S SERVANT
Five thousand crowns, my lord.

TIMON
Five thousand drops pays that.
What yours?—and yours?

FIRST SERVANT
My lord,—

SECOND SERVANT
My lord,—

TIMON
Tear me, take me, and the gods fall upon you!
[*Exit.* 114

HORTENSIUS
'Faith, I perceive our masters may throw their caps at their money: these debts may well be called desperate ones, for a madman owes 'em. [*Exeunt.*

Re-enter TIMON *and* FLAVIUS.

TIMON
They have e'en put my breath from me, the slaves.
Creditors? devils!

FLAVIUS
My dear lord,—

TIMON
What if it should be so?

FLAVIUS
My lord,—

TIMON
I'll have it so. My steward!

FLAVIUS
Here, my lord.
TIMON
So fitly? Go, bid all my friends again,
Lucius, Lucullus, and Sempronius: [30]
All, sirrah, all:
I'll once more feast the rascals.
FLAVIUS
O, my lord,
You only speak from your distracted soul;
There is not so much left, to furnish out
A moderate table.
TIMON
Be't not in thy care; go,
I charge thee, invite them all: let in the tide
Of knaves once more; my cook and I'll provide.
[*Exeunt.*

ACT THREE SCENE FIVE

The same. The senate-house.

The Senate sitting.

FIRST SENATOR
My lord, you have my voice to it; the fault's
Bloody; 'tis necessary he should die:
Nothing emboldens sin so much as mercy.
SECOND SENATOR
Most true; the law shall bruise him.

Enter ALCIBIADES, *with* Attendants.

ALCIBIADES
Honour, health, and compassion to the senate!
FIRST SENATOR
Now, captain?
ALCIBIADES
I am an humble suitor to your virtues;
For pity is the virtue of the law,
And none but tyrants use it cruelly.
It pleases time and fortune to lie heavy
Upon a friend of mine, who, in hot blood,
Hath stepp'd into the law, which is past depth
To those that, without heed, do plunge into 't.
He is a man, setting his fate aside,
Of comely virtues:
Nor did he soil the fact with cowardice—
An honour in him which buys out his fault—
But with a noble fury and fair spirit,
Seeing his reputation touch'd to death,
He did oppose his foe:
And with such sober and unnoted passion
He did behave his anger, ere 'twas spent, [31]
As if he had but proved an argument.
FIRST SENATOR
You undergo too strict a paradox,
Striving to make an ugly deed look fair:
Your words have took such pains as if they labour'd
To bring manslaughter into form and set quarrelling
Upon the head of valour; which indeed
Is valour misbegot and came into the world
When sects and factions were newly born:
He's truly valiant that can wisely suffer
The worst that man can breathe, and make his wrongs
His outsides, to wear them like his raiment, carelessly,
And ne'er prefer his injuries to his heart,
To bring it into danger.
If wrongs be evils and enforce us kill,
What folly 'tis to hazard life for ill!
ALCIBIADES
My lord,—
FIRST SENATOR
You cannot make gross sins look clear:
To revenge is no valour, but to bear.
ALCIBIADES
My lords, then, under favour, pardon me,
If I speak like a captain.
Why do fond men expose themselves to battle,
And not endure all threats? sleep upon't,
And let the foes quietly cut their throats,
Without repugnancy? If there be
Such valour in the bearing, what make we
Abroad? why then, women are more valiant
That stay at home, if bearing carry it,
And the ass more captain than the lion, the felon
Loaden with irons wiser than the judge,
If wisdom be in suffering. O my lords,
As you are great, be pitifully good:
Who cannot condemn rashness in cold blood?
To kill, I grant, is sin's extremest gust;
But, in defence, by mercy, 'tis most just.
To be in anger is impiety;
But who is man that is not angry?
Weigh but the crime with this.
SECOND SENATOR
You breathe in vain.
ALCIBIADES
In vain! his service done
At Lacedaemon and Byzantium
Were a sufficient briber for his life.
FIRST SENATOR
What's that?
ALCIBIADES
I say, my lords, he has done fair service, [32]
And slain in fight many of our enemies:
How full of valour did he bear himself
In the last conflict, and made plenteous wounds!

SECOND SENATOR

He has made too much plenty with 'em;
He's a sworn rioter: he has a sin that often
Drowns him, and takes his valour prisoner:
If there were no foes, that were enough
To overcome him: in that beastly fury
He has been known to commit outrages,
And cherish factions: 'tis inferr'd to us,
His days are foul and his drink dangerous.

FIRST SENATOR

He dies.

ALCIBIADES

Hard fate! he might have died in war.
My lords, if not for any parts in him—
Though his right arm might purchase his own time
And be in debt to none—yet, more to move you,
Take my deserts to his, and join 'em both:
And, for I know your reverend ages love
Security, I'll pawn my victories, all
My honours to you, upon his good returns.
If by this crime he owes the law his life,
Why, let the war receive't in valiant gore
For law is strict, and war is nothing more.

FIRST SENATOR

We are for law: he dies; urge it no more,
On height of our displeasure: friend or brother,
He forfeits his own blood that spills another.

ALCIBIADES

Must it be so? it must not be. My lords,
I do beseech you, know me.

SECOND SENATOR

How!

ALCIBIADES

Call me to your remembrances.

THIRD SENATOR

What!

ALCIBIADES

I cannot think but your age has forgot me;
It could not else be, I should prove so base,
To sue, and be denied such common grace:
My wounds ache at you.

FIRST SENATOR

Do you dare our anger?
'Tis in few words, but spacious in effect;
We banish thee for ever.

ALCIBIADES

Banish me!
Banish your dotage; banish usury,
That makes the senate ugly.

FIRST SENATOR

If, after two days' shine, Athens contain thee,
Attend our weighing judgment. And, not to swell our spirit, [33]
He shall be executed presently. [*Exeunt Senators.*

ALCIBIADES

Now the gods keep you old enough; that you may live
Only in bone, that none may look on you! [34]
I'm worse than mad: I have kept back their foes,
While they have told their money and let out
Their coin upon large interest, I myself
Rich only in large hurts. All those for this?
Is this the balsam that the usuring senate
Pours into captains' wounds? Banishment!
It comes not ill; I hate not to be banish'd;
It is a cause worthy my spleen and fury,
That I may strike at Athens. I'll cheer up
My discontented troops, and lay for hearts.
'Tis honour with most lands to be at odds; [35]
Soldiers should brook as little wrongs as gods.
[*Exit.*

ACT THREE SCENE SIX

The same. A banqueting-room in Timon's house.

Music. Tables set out: Servants *attending. Enter divers Lords, Senators and others, at several doors.*

FIRST LORD

The good time of day to you, sir.

SECOND LORD

I also wish it to you. I think this honourable lord did but try us this other day.

FIRST LORD

Upon that were my thoughts tiring, when we encountered: I hope it is not so low with him as he made it seem in the trial of his several friends.

SECOND LORD

It should not be, by the persuasion of his new feasting.

FIRST LORD

I should think so: he hath sent me an earnest inviting, which many my near occasions did urge me to put off; but he hath conjured me beyond them, and
I must needs appear.

SECOND LORD

In like manner was I in debt to my importunate business, but he would not hear my excuse. I am sorry, when he sent to borrow of me, that my provision was out.

FIRST LORD

I am sick of that grief, too, as I understand how all things go.

SECOND LORD

Every man here's so. What would he have borrowed of you?

FIRST LORD

A thousand pieces.

SECOND LORD
A thousand pieces!
FIRST LORD
What of you?
SECOND LORD
He sent to me, sir,—Here he comes.

Enter TIMON *and* Attendants.

TIMON
With all my heart, gentlemen both; and how fare you?
FIRST LORD
Ever at the best, hearing well of your lordship.
SECOND LORD
The swallow follows not summer more willing than we your lordship. 28
TIMON
[*Aside*] Nor more willingly leaves winter; such summer-birds are men. Gentlemen, our dinner will not recompense this long stay: feast your ears with the music awhile, if they will fare so harshly o' the trumpet's sound; we shall to't presently. [36]
FIRST LORD
I hope it remains not unkindly with your lordship that I returned you an empty messenger. 35
TIMON
O, sir, let it not trouble you.
SECOND LORD
My noble lord,—
TIMON
Ah, my good friend, what cheer?
SECOND LORD
My most honourable lord, I am e'en sick of shame, that, when your lordship this other day sent to me,
I was so unfortunate a beggar.
TIMON
Think not on't, sir.
SECOND LORD
If you had sent but two hours before,— 43
TIMON
Let it not cumber your better remembrance. [*The banquet brought in.*] Come, bring in all together.
SECOND LORD
All covered dishes!
FIRST LORD
Royal cheer, I warrant you.
THIRD LORD
Doubt not that, if money and the season can yield it.
FIRST LORD
How do you? What's the news?
THIRD LORD
Alcibiades is banished: hear you of it? 50
FIRST LORD, SECOND LORD
Alcibiades banished!
THIRD LORD
'Tis so, be sure of it.
FIRST LORD
How! how!
SECOND LORD
I pray you, upon what?
TIMON
My worthy friends, will you draw near?
THIRD LORD
I'll tell you more anon. Here's a noble feast toward.
SECOND LORD
This is the old man still.
THIRD LORD
Will 't hold? will 't hold? 58
SECOND LORD
It does: but time will—and so—
THIRD LORD
I do conceive.
TIMON
Each man to his stool, with that spur as he would to the lip of his mistress: your diet shall be in all places alike. Make not a city feast of it, to let the meat cool ere we can agree upon the first place: sit, sit. The gods require our thanks.

You great benefactors, sprinkle our society with thankfulness. For your own gifts, make yourselves praised: but reserve still to give, lest your deities be despised. Lend to each man enough, that one need not lend to another; for, were your godheads to borrow of men, men would forsake the gods. Make the meat be beloved more than the man that gives it. Let no assembly of twenty be without a score of villains: if there sit twelve women at the table, let a dozen of them be—as they are. The rest of your fees, O gods—the senators of Athens, together with the common lag of people—what is amiss in them, you gods, make suitable for destruction. For these my present friends, as they are to me nothing, so in nothing bless them, and to nothing are they welcome.

Uncover, dogs, and lap.

[*The dishes are uncovered and seen to be full of warm water.*

SOME SPEAK
What does his lordship mean?
SOME OTHER
I know not.
TIMON
May you a better feast never behold,
You knot of mouth-friends! smoke and lukewarm water
Is your perfection. This is Timon's last; 86
Who, stuck and spangled with your flatteries, [37]
Washes it off, and sprinkles in your faces
Your reeking villany.

[*Throwing the water in their faces.*

Live loathed and long,
Most smiling, smooth, detested parasites,
Courteous destroyers, affable wolves, meek bears,
You fools of fortune, trencher-friends, time's flies,
Cap and knee slaves, vapours, and minute-jacks!
Of man and beast the infinite malady
Crust you quite o'er! What, dost thou go?
Soft! take thy physic first—thou too—and thou;— 98
Stay, I will lend thee money, borrow none.
[*Throws the dishes at them, and drives them out*]
What, all in motion? Henceforth be no feast,
Whereat a villain's not a welcome guest.
Burn, house! sink, Athens! henceforth hated be
Of Timon man and all humanity! [*Exit.*

Re-enter the Lords, Senators, *&c.*

FIRST LORD
How now, my lords!
SECOND LORD
Know you the quality of Lord Timon's fury?
THIRD LORD
Push! did you see my cap?
FOURTH LORD
I have lost my gown. 107
FIRST LORD
He's but a mad lord, and nought but humour sways him.
He gave me a jewel th' other day, and now he has beat it out of my hat: did you see my jewel?
THIRD LORD
Did you see my cap?
SECOND LORD
Here 'tis.
FOURTH LORD
Here lies my gown.
FIRST LORD
Let's make no stay.
SECOND LORD
Lord Timon's mad.
THIRD LORD
I feel 't upon my bones.
FOURTH LORD
One day he gives us diamonds, next day stones.
[*Exeunt.*

ACT FOUR SCENE ONE

Without the walls of Athens.

Enter TIMON.

TIMON
Let me look back upon thee. O thou wall,
That girdlest in those wolves, dive in the earth,
And fence not Athens! Matrons, turn incontinent!
Obedience fail in children! slaves and fools,
Pluck the grave wrinkled senate from the bench,
And minister in their steads! to general filths
Convert o' the instant, green virginity,
Do 't in your parents' eyes! bankrupts, hold fast;
Rather than render back, out with your knives,
And cut your trusters' throats! bound servants, steal! 11
Large-handed robbers your grave masters are,
And pill by law. Maid, to thy master's bed;
Thy mistress is o' the brothel! Son of sixteen,
Pluck the lined crutch from thy old limping sire,
With it beat out his brains! Piety, and fear,
Religion to the gods, peace, justice, truth,
Domestic awe, night-rest, and neighbourhood,
Instruction, manners, mysteries, and trades,
Degrees, observances, customs, and laws,
Decline to your confounding contraries. 21
And let confusion live! Plagues, incident to men, [38]
Your potent and infectious fevers heap
On Athens, ripe for stroke! Thou cold sciatica,
Cripple our senators, that their limbs may halt
As lamely as their manners. Lust and liberty
Creep in the minds and marrows of our youth,
That 'gainst the stream of virtue they may strive,
And drown themselves in riot! Itches, blains,
Sow all the Athenian bosoms; and their crop
Be general leprosy! Breath infect breath, 33
That their society, as their friendship, may
Be merely poison! Nothing I'll bear from thee,
But nakedness, thou detestable town!
Take thou that too, with multiplying bans!
Timon will to the woods; where he shall find
The unkindest beast more kinder than mankind.
The gods confound—hear me, you good gods all—
The Athenians both within and out that wall!
And grant, as Timon grows, his hate may grow
To the whole race of mankind, high and low! Amen.
[*Exit.*

ACT FOUR SCENE TWO

Athens. A room in Timon's house.

Enter FLAVIUS, *with two or three* Servants.

FIRST SERVANT
Hear you, master steward, where's our master?
Are we undone? cast off? nothing remaining?

FLAVIUS
Alack, my fellows, what should I say to you?
Let me be recorded by the righteous gods,
I am as poor as you.
FIRST SERVANT
Such a house broke!
So noble a master fall'n! All gone! and not
One friend to take his fortune by the arm,
And go along with him!
SECOND SERVANT
As we do turn our backs
From our companion thrown into his grave,
So his familiars to his buried fortunes 12
Slink all away, leave their false vows with him,
Like empty purses pick'd; and his poor self,
A dedicated beggar to the air,
With his disease of all-shunn'd poverty,
Walks, like contempt, alone. More of our fellows.

Enter other Servants.

FLAVIUS
All broken implements of a ruin'd house.
THIRD SERVANT
Yet do our hearts wear Timon's livery;
That see I by our faces; we are fellows still,
Serving alike in sorrow: leak'd is our bark,
And we, poor mates, stand on the dying deck,
Hearing the surges threat: we must all part
Into this sea of air.
FLAVIUS
Good fellows all,
The latest of my wealth I'll share amongst you.
Wherever we shall meet, for Timon's sake,
Let's yet be fellows; let's shake our heads, and say,
As 'twere a knell unto our master's fortunes,
'We have seen better days.' Let each take some;
Nay, put out all your hands. Not one word more:
Thus we part rich in sorrow, parting poor. 32
[*Servants embrace, and part several ways.*
O, the fierce wretchedness that glory brings us!
Who would not wish to be from wealth exempt,
Since riches point to misery and contempt?
Who would be so mock'd with glory? or to live
But in a dream of friendship?
To have his pomp and all what state compounds [39]
But only painted, like his varnish'd friends?
Poor honest lord, brought low by his own heart,
Undone by goodness! Strange, unusual blood,
When man's worst sin is, he does too much good!
Who, then, dares to be half so kind again? 43
For bounty, that makes gods, does still mar men.
My dearest lord, bless'd, to be most accursed,
Rich, only to be wretched, thy great fortunes
Are made thy chief afflictions. Alas, kind lord!
He's flung in rage from this ingrateful seat
Of monstrous friends, nor has he with him to
Supply his life, or that which can command it.
I'll follow and inquire him out:
I'll ever serve his mind with my best will;
Whilst I have gold, I'll be his steward still. [*Exit.*

ACT FOUR SCENE THREE

Woods and cave, near the sea-shore.

Enter TIMON, *from the cave.*

TIMON
O blessed breeding sun, draw from the earth
Rotten humidity; below thy sister's orb
Infect the air! Twinn'd brothers of one womb,
Whose procreation, residence, and birth,
Scarce is dividant, touch them with several fortunes;
The greater scorns the lesser: not nature,
To whom all sores lay siege, can bear great fortunes,
But thy contempt of nature.
Raise me this beggar, and deny't that lord; [40]
The senator shall bear contempt hereditary, 10
The beggar native honour.
It is the pasture lards the rother's sides, [41]
The want that makes him lean. Who dares, who dares,
In purity of manhood stand upright,
And say 'This man's a flatterer?' if one be,
So are they all; for every grise of fortune
Is smooth'd by that below: the learned pate
Ducks to the golden fool: all is oblique; [42]
There's nothing level in our cursed natures,
But direct villany. Therefore, be abhorr'd 21
All feasts, societies, and throngs of men!
His semblable, yea, himself, Timon disdains:
Destruction fang mankind! Earth, yield me roots!
[*Digging.*
Who seeks for better of thee, sauce his palate
With thy most operant poison! What is here?
Gold? yellow, glittering, precious gold? No, gods,
I am no idle votarist: roots, you clear heavens!
Thus much of this will make black white, foul fair,
Wrong right, base noble, old young, coward valiant.
Ha, you gods! why this? what this, you gods? Why, this 32
Will lug your priests and servants from your sides,
Pluck stout men's pillows from below their heads:
This yellow slave
Will knit and break religions, bless the accursed,
Make the hoar leprosy adored, place thieves
And give them title, knee and approbation
With senators on the bench: this is it

That makes the wappen'd widow wed again;
She, whom the spital-house and ulcerous sores
Would cast the gorge at, this embalms and spices
To the April day again. Come, damned earth,
Thou common whore of mankind, that put'st odds
Among the rout of nations, I will make thee
Do thy right nature. [*March afar off.*] Ha! a drum? Thou'rt quick,
But yet I'll bury thee: thou'lt go, strong thief,
When gouty keepers of thee cannot stand.
Nay, stay thou out for earnest.
[*Keeping some gold.*

Enter ALCIBIADES, *with drum and fife, in warlike manner*; PHRYNIA *and* TIMANDRA.

ALCIBIADES
What art thou there? speak.

TIMON
A beast, as thou art. The canker gnaw thy heart,
For showing me again the eyes of man!

ALCIBIADES
What is thy name? Is man so hateful to thee,
That art thyself a man?

TIMON
I am Misanthropos, and hate mankind.
For thy part, I do wish thou wert a dog,
That I might love thee something.

ALCIBIADES
I know thee well;
But in thy fortunes am unlearn'd and strange.

TIMON
I know thee too; and more than that I know thee,
I desire not to know. Follow thy drum;
With man's blood paint the ground, gules, gules:
Religious canons, civil laws are cruel;
Then what should war be? This fell whore of thine
Hath in her more destruction than thy sword,
For all her cherubin look.

PHRYNIA
Thy lips rot off!

TIMON
I will not kiss thee; then the rot returns
To thine own lips again.

ALCIBIADES
How came the noble Timon to this change?

TIMON
As the moon does, by wanting light to give:
But then renew I could not, like the moon;
There were no suns to borrow of.

ALCIBIADES
Noble Timon,
What friendship may I do thee?

TIMON
None, but to
Maintain my opinion.

ALCIBIADES
What is it, Timon?

TIMON
Promise me friendship, but perform none: if thou wilt not promise, the gods plague thee, for thou art a man! if thou dost perform, confound thee, for thou art a man!

ALCIBIADES
I have heard in some sort of thy miseries.

TIMON
Thou saw'st them, when I had prosperity.

ALCIBIADES
I see them now; then was a blessed time.

TIMON
As thine is now, held with a brace of harlots.

TIMANDRA
Is this the Athenian minion, whom the world
Voiced so regardfully?

TIMON
Art thou Timandra?

TIMANDRA
Yes.

TIMON
Be a whore still: they love thee not that use thee;
Give them diseases, leaving with thee their lust.
Make use of thy salt hours: season the slaves
For tubs and baths; bring down rose-cheeked youth
To the tub-fast and the diet.

TIMANDRA
Hang thee, monster!

ALCIBIADES
Pardon him, sweet Timandra; for his wits
Are drown'd and lost in his calamities.
I have but little gold of late, brave Timon,
The want whereof doth daily make revolt
In my penurious band: I have heard, and grieved,
How cursed Athens, mindless of thy worth,
Forgetting thy great deeds, when neighbour states,
But for thy sword and fortune, trod upon them,—

TIMON
I prithee, beat thy drum, and get thee gone.

ALCIBIADES
I am thy friend, and pity thee, dear Timon.

TIMON
How dost thou pity him whom thou dost trouble?
I had rather be alone.

ALCIBIADES
Why, fare thee well:
Here is some gold for thee.

TIMON
Keep it, I cannot eat it.

ALCIBIADES
When I have laid proud Athens on a heap,—
TIMON
Warr'st thou 'gainst Athens?
ALCIBIADES
Ay, Timon, and have cause.
TIMON
The gods confound them all in thy conquest;
And thee after, when thou hast conquer'd! [44]
ALCIBIADES
Why me, Timon?
TIMON
That, by killing of villains,
Thou wast born to conquer my country.
Put up thy gold: go on,—here's gold,—go on;
Be as a planetary plague, when Jove
Will o'er some high-viced city hang his poison
In the sick air: let not thy sword skip one: 126
Pity not honour'd age for his white beard;
He is an usurer: strike me the counterfeit matron;
It is her habit only that is honest,
Herself's a bawd: let not the virgin's cheek
Make soft thy trenchant sword; for those milk-paps,
That through the window-bars bore at men's eyes, [45]
Are not within the leaf of pity writ,
But set them down horrible traitors: spare not the babe,
Whose dimpled smiles from fools exhaust their mercy;
Think it a bastard, whom the oracle 139
Hath doubtfully pronounced thy throat shall cut,
And mince it sans remorse: swear against objects;
Put armour on thine ears and on thine eyes;
Whose proof, nor yells of mothers, maids, nor babes,
Nor sight of priests in holy vestments bleeding,
Shall pierce a jot. There's gold to pay thy soldiers:
Make large confusion; and, thy fury spent,
Confounded be thyself! Speak not, be gone.
ALCIBIADES
Hast thou gold yet? I'll take the gold thou givest me,
Not all thy counsel. 150
TIMON
Dost thou, or dost thou not, heaven's curse upon thee!
PHRYNIA, TIMANDRA
Give us some gold, good Timon: hast thou more?
TIMON
Enough to make a whore forswear her trade,
And to make whores, a bawd. Hold up, you sluts,
Your aprons mountant: you are not oathable,—
Although, I know, you 'll swear, terribly swear
Into strong shudders and to heavenly agues
The immortal gods that hear you,—spare your oaths,
I'll trust to your conditions: be whores still;
And he whose pious breath seeks to convert you, 162
Be strong in whore, allure him, burn him up;
Let your close fire predominate his smoke,
And be no turncoats: yet may your pains, six months,
Be quite contrary: and thatch your poor thin roofs
With burthens of the dead;—some that were hang'd,
No matter:—wear them, betray with them: whore still;
Paint till a horse may mire upon your face:
A pox of wrinkles!
PHRYNIA, TIMANDRA
Well, more gold: what then?
Believe't, that we'll do any thing for gold.
TIMON
Consumptions sow
In hollow bones of man; strike their sharp shins,
And mar men's spurring. Crack the lawyer's voice, [46]
That he may never more false title plead,
Nor sound his quillets shrilly: hoar the flamen,
That scolds against the quality of flesh,
And not believes himself: down with the nose,
Down with it flat; take the bridge quite away
Of him that, his particular to foresee,
Smells from the general weal: make curl'd-pate ruffians bald; 187
And let the unscarr'd braggarts of the war
Derive some pain from you: plague all;
That your activity may defeat and quell
The source of all erection. There's more gold:
Do you damn others, and let this damn you,
And ditches grave you all!
PHRYNIA, TIMANDRA
More counsel with more money, bounteous Timon.
TIMON
More whore, more mischief first; I have given you earnest.
ALCIBIADES
Strike up the drum towards Athens! Farewell, Timon:
If I thrive well, I'll visit thee again. 199
TIMON
If I hope well, I'll never see thee more.
ALCIBIADES
I never did thee harm.
TIMON
Yes, thou spokest well of me.
ALCIBIADES
Call'st thou that harm?

TIMON
Men daily find it. Get thee away, and take
Thy beagles with thee.
ALCIBIADES
We but offend him. Strike!
[*Drum beats. Exeunt Alcibiades, Phrynia, and Timandra.*
TIMON
That nature, being sick of man's unkindness,
Should yet be hungry! Common mother, thou, [*Digging.*
Whose womb unmeasurable, and infinite breast,
Teems, and feeds all; whose self-same mettle,
Whereof thy proud child, arrogant man, is puff'd,
Engenders the black toad and adder blue,
The gilded newt and eyeless venom'd worm,
With all the abhorred births below crisp heaven
Whereon Hyperion's quickening fire doth shine;
Yield him, who all thy human sons doth hate,
From forth thy plenteous bosom, one poor root!
Ensear thy fertile and conceptious womb,
Let it no more bring out ingrateful man!
Go great with tigers, dragons, wolves, and bears;
Teem with new monsters, whom thy upward face
Hath to the marbled mansion all above
Never presented!—O, a root,—dear thanks!—
Dry up thy marrows, vines, and plough-torn leas;
Whereof ungrateful man, with liquorish draughts
And morsels unctuous, greases his pure mind,
That from it all consideration slips!

Enter APEMANTUS.

More man? plague, plague!
APEMANTUS
I was directed hither: men report
Thou dost affect my manners, and dost use them.
TIMON
'Tis, then, because thou dost not keep a dog,
Whom I would imitate: consumption catch thee!
APEMANTUS
This is in thee a nature but infected;
A poor unmanly melancholy sprung
From change of fortune. Why this spade? This place?
This slave-like habit? and these looks of care?
Thy flatterers yet wear silk, drink wine, lie soft;
Hug their diseased perfumes, and have forgot
That ever Timon was. Shame not these woods,
By putting on the cunning of a carper.
Be thou a flatterer now, and seek to thrive
By that which has undone thee: hinge thy knee,
And let his very breath, whom thou'lt observe,
Blow off thy cap; praise his most vicious strain,
And call it excellent: thou wast told thus;
Thou gavest thine ears like tapsters that bid welcome [47]
To knaves and all approachers: 'tis most just
That thou turn rascal; hadst thou wealth again,
Rascals should have 't. Do not assume my likeness.
TIMON
Were I like thee, I'ld throw away myself.
APEMANTUS
Thou hast cast away thyself, being like thyself;
A madman so long, now a fool. What, think'st
That the bleak air, thy boisterous chamberlain,
Will put thy shirt on warm? will these moss'd trees,
That have outlived the eagle, page thy heels,
And skip where thou point'st out? will the cold brook, [48]
Candied with ice, caudle thy morning taste,
To cure thy o'er-night's surfeit? Call the creatures
Whose naked natures live in an the spite
Of wreakful heaven, whose bare unhoused trunks,
To the conflicting elements exposed,
Answer mere nature; bid them flatter thee;
O, thou shalt find—
TIMON
A fool of thee: depart.
APEMANTUS
I love thee better now than e'er I did.
TIMON
I hate thee worse.
APEMANTUS
Why?
TIMON
Thou flatter'st misery.
APEMANTUS
I flatter not; but say thou art a caitiff.
TIMON
Why dost thou seek me out?
APEMANTUS
To vex thee.
TIMON
Always a villain's office or a fool's.
Dost please thyself in't?
APEMANTUS
Ay.
TIMON
What! a knave too?
APEMANTUS
If thou didst put this sour-cold habit on
To castigate thy pride, 'twere well: but thou
Dost it enforcedly; thou'ldst courtier be again,
Wert thou not beggar. Willing misery
Outlives incertain pomp, is crown'd before: [49]
The one is filling still, never complete;
The other, at high wish: best state, contentless,

Hath a distracted and most wretched being,
Worse than the worst, content.
Thou shouldst desire to die, being miserable.

TIMON

Not by his breath that is more miserable.
Thou art a slave, whom Fortune's tender arm
With favour never clasp'd; but bred a dog.
Hadst thou, like us from our first swath, proceeded
The sweet degrees that this brief world affords
To such as may the passive drugs of it [50]
Freely command, thou wouldst have plunged thyself
In general riot; melted down thy youth
In different beds of lust; and never learn'd
The icy precepts of respect, but follow'd
The sugar'd game before thee. But myself,
Who had the world as my confectionary, 302
The mouths, the tongues, the eyes and hearts of men
At duty, more than I could frame employment,
That numberless upon me stuck as leaves
Do on the oak, have with one winter's brush
Fell from their boughs and left me open, bare
For every storm that blows: I, to bear this,
That never knew but better, is some burden:
Thy nature did commence in sufferance, time
Hath made thee hard in't. Why shouldst thou hate men?
They never flatter'd thee: what hast thou given? 314
If thou wilt curse, thy father, that poor rag,
Must be thy subject, who in spite put stuff
To some she beggar and compounded thee
Poor rogue hereditary. Hence, be gone!
If thou hadst not been born the worst of men,
Thou hadst been a knave and flatterer.

APEMANTUS

Art thou proud yet?

TIMON

Ay, that I am not thee.

APEMANTUS

I, that I was
No prodigal.

TIMON

I, that I am one now:
Were all the wealth I have shut up in thee,
I'ld give thee leave to hang it. Get thee gone.
That the whole life of Athens were in this!
Thus would I eat it. [*Eating a root.*

APEMANTUS

Here; I will mend thy feast.
[*Offering him a root.*

TIMON

First mend my company, take away thyself. [51]

APEMANTUS

So I shall mend mine own, by the lack of thine.

TIMON

'Tis not well mended so, it is but botch'd; if not, I would it were.

APEMANTUS

What wouldst thou have to Athens?

TIMON

Thee thither in a whirlwind. If thou wilt,
Tell them there I have gold; look, so I have.

APEMANTUS

Here is no use for gold.

TIMON

The best and truest; 339
For here it sleeps, and does no hired harm.

APEMANTUS

Where liest o' nights, Timon?

TIMON

Under that's above me.
Where feed'st thou o' days, Apemantus?

APEMANTUS

Where my stomach finds meat; or, rather, where I eat it.

TIMON

Would poison were obedient and knew my mind!

APEMANTUS

Where wouldst thou send it?

TIMON

To sauce thy dishes. 348

APEMANTUS

The middle of humanity thou never knewest, but the extremity of both ends: when thou wast in thy gilt and thy perfume, they mocked thee for too much curiosity; in thy rags thou knowest none, but art despised for the contrary. There's a medlar for thee, eat it.

TIMON

On what I hate I feed not.

APEMANTUS

Dost hate a medlar?

TIMON

Ay, though it look like thee.

APEMANTUS

An thou hadst hated medlears sooner, thou shouldst have loved thyself better now. What man didst thou ever know unthrift that was beloved after his means? [52]

TIMON

Who, without those means thou talkest of, didst thou ever know beloved?

APEMANTUS

Myself.

TIMON

I understand thee; thou hadst some means to keep a dog.

APEMANTUS

What things in the world canst thou nearest compare to thy flatterers? 367

TIMON

Women nearest; but men, men are the things themselves. What wouldst thou do with the world, Apemantus, if it lay in thy power?

APEMANTUS

Give it the beasts, to be rid of the men.

TIMON

Wouldst thou have thyself fall in the confusion of men, and remain a beast with the beasts?

APEMANTUS

Ay, Timon.

TIMON

A beastly ambition, which the gods grant thee t' attain to! If thou wert the lion, the fox would beguile thee; if thou wert the lamb, the fox would eat thee: if thou wert the fox, the lion would suspect thee, when peradventure thou wert accused by the ass: if thou wert the ass, thy dulness would torment thee, and still thou livedst but as a breakfast to the wolf: if thou wert the wolf, thy greediness would afflict thee, and oft thou shouldst hazard thy life for thy dinner: wert thou the unicorn, pride and wrath would confound thee and make thine own self the conquest of thy fury: wert thou a bear, thou wouldst be killed by the horse: wert thou a horse, thou wouldst be seized by the leopard: wert thou a leopard, thou wert german to the lion and the spots of thy kindred were jurors on thy life: all thy safety were remotion and thy defence absence. What beast couldst thou be, that were not subject to a beast? and what a beast art thou already, that seest not thy loss in transformation! 393

APEMANTUS

If thou couldst please me with speaking to me, thou mightst have hit upon it here: the commonwealth of Athens is become a forest of beasts.

TIMON

How has the ass broke the wall, that thou art out of the city?

APEMANTUS

Yonder comes a poet and a painter: the plague of company light upon thee! I will fear to catch it and give way: when I know not what else to do, I'll see thee again. 402

TIMON

When there is nothing living but thee, thou shalt be welcome. I had rather be a beggar's dog than Apemantus.

APEMANTUS

Thou art the cap of all the fools alive.

TIMON

Would thou wert clean enough to spit upon!

APEMANTUS

A plague on thee! thou art too bad to curse.

TIMON

All villains that do stand by thee are pure.

APEMANTUS

There is no leprosy but what thou speak'st.

TIMON

If I name thee.
I'll beat thee, but I should infect my hands.

APEMANTUS

I would my tongue could rot them off! 413

TIMON

Away, thou issue of a mangy dog!
Choler does kill me that thou art alive;
I swound to see thee.

APEMANTUS

Would thou wouldst burst!

TIMON

Away,
Thou tedious rogue! I am sorry I shall lose
A stone by thee. [*Throws a stone at him.*

APEMANTUS

Beast!

TIMON

Slave!

APEMANTUS

Toad!

TIMON

Rogue, rogue, rogue!
I am sick of this false world, and will love nought
But even the mere necessities upon 't.
Then, Timon, presently prepare thy grave;
Lie where the light foam the sea may beat
Thy grave-stone daily: make thine epitaph,
That death in me at others' lives may laugh.
[*To the gold*] O thou sweet king-killer, and dear divorce
'Twixt natural son and sire! thou bright defiler
Of Hymen's purest bed! thou valiant Mars!
Thou ever young, fresh, loved and delicate wooer,
Whose blush doth thaw the consecrated snow
That lies on Dian's lap! thou visible god,
That solder'st close impossibilities,
And makest them kiss! that speak'st with every tongue, 439
To every purpose! O thou touch of hearts!
Think, thy slave man rebels, and by thy virtue
Set them into confounding odds, that beasts
May have the world in empire!

APEMANTUS

Would 'twere so!
But not till I am dead. I'll say thou'st gold:
Thou wilt be throng'd to shortly.

TIMON

Throng'd to!

TIMON I had rather be a beggar's dog, than Apemantus.

APEMANTUS
Ay.
TIMON
Thy back, I prithee.
APEMANTUS
Live, and love thy misery.
TIMON
Long live so, and so die. [*Exit Apemantus.*
I am quit.
Moe things like men! Eat, Timon, and abhor them.

Enter Banditti.

FIRST BANDIT
Where should he have this gold? It is some poor fragment, some slender ort of his remainder: the mere want of gold, and the falling-from of his friends, drove him into this melancholy.
SECOND BANDIT
It is noised he hath a mass of treasure.
THIRD BANDIT
Let us make the assay upon him: if he care not for't, he will supply us easily; if he covetously reserve it, how shall's get it?
SECOND BANDIT
True; for he bears it not about him, 'tis hid.
FIRST BANDIT
Is not this he? 463
BANDITTI
Where?
SECOND BANDIT
'Tis his description.
THIRD BANDIT
He; I know him.
BANDITTI
Save thee, Timon.
TIMON
Now, thieves?
BANDITTI
Soldiers, not thieves.
TIMON
Both too; and women's sons.
BANDITTI
We are not thieves, but men that much do want.
TIMON
Your greatest want is, you want much of
meat. [53]

Why should you want? Behold, the earth hath roots; [54]
Within this mile break forth a hundred springs;
The oaks bear mast, the briers scarlet hips;
The bounteous housewife, nature, on each bush
Lays her full mess before you. Want! why want?

FIRST BANDIT
We cannot live on grass, on berries, water,
As beasts and birds and fishes.

TIMON
Nor on the beasts themselves, the birds, and fishes;
You must eat men. Yet thanks I must you con
That you are thieves profess'd, that you work not
In holier shapes: for there is boundless theft
In limited professions. Rascal thieves,
Here's gold. Go, suck the subtle blood o' the grape,
Till the high fever seethe your blood to froth,
And so 'scape hanging: trust not the physician;
His antidotes are poison, and he slays
Moe than you rob: take wealth and lives together;
Do villany, do, since you protest to do't, [55]
Like workmen. I'll example you with thievery:
The sun's a thief, and with his great attraction
Robs the vast sea: the moon's an arrant thief,
And her pale fire she snatches from the sun:
The sea's a thief, whose liquid surge resolves
The moon into salt tears: the earth's a thief, [56]
That feeds and breeds by a composture stolen
From general excrement: each thing's a thief:
The laws, your curb and whip, in their rough power
Have uncheque'd theft. Love not yourselves: away,
Rob one another. There's more gold. Cut throats:
All that you meet are thieves: to Athens go,
Break open shops; nothing can you steal,
But thieves do lose it: steal no less for this
I give you; and gold confound you whosoe'er! Amen.

THIRD BANDIT
Has almost charmed me from my profession, by persuading me to it.

FIRST BANDIT
'Tis in the malice of mankind that he thus advises us; not to have us thrive in our mystery.

SECOND BANDIT
I'll believe him as an enemy, and give over my trade.

FIRST BANDIT
Let us first see peace in Athens: there is no time so miserable but a man may be true. [*Exeunt Banditti.*

Enter FLAVIUS.

FLAVIUS
O you gods!
Is yond despised and ruinous man my lord?
Full of decay and failing? O monument
And wonder of good deeds evilly bestow'd!
What an alteration of honour
Has desperate want made!
What viler thing upon the earth than friends
Who can bring noblest minds to basest ends!
How rarely does it meet with this time's guise,
When man was wish'd to love his enemies!
Grant I may ever love, and rather woo
Those that would mischief me than those that do!
Has caught me in his eye: I will present
My honest grief unto him; and, as my lord,
Still serve him with my life. My dearest master!

TIMON
Away! what art thou?

FLAVIUS
Have you forgot me, sir?

TIMON
Why dost ask that? I have forgot all men;
Then, if thou grant'st thou'rt a man, I have forgot all men;

FLAVIUS
An honest poor servant of yours.

TIMON
Then I know thee not:
I never had honest man about me, I; all
I kept were knaves, to serve in meat to villains.

FLAVIUS
The gods are witness,
Ne'er did poor steward wear a truer grief
For his undone lord than mine eyes for you.

TIMON
What, dost thou weep? Come nearer. Then I love thee,
Because thou art a woman, and disclaim'st
Flinty mankind; whose eyes do never give
But thorough lust and laughter. Pity's sleeping:
Strange times, that weep with laughing, not with weeping!

FLAVIUS
I beg of you to know me, good my lord,
To accept my grief and whilst this poor wealth lasts
To entertain me as your steward still.

TIMON
Had I a steward
So true, so just, and now so comfortable?
It almost turns my dangerous nature mild. [57]
Let me behold thy face. Surely, this man
Was born of woman.
Forgive my general and exceptless rashness,
You perpetual-sober gods! I do proclaim
One honest man—mistake me not—but one;
No more, I pray,—and he's a steward.
How fain would I have hated all mankind!
And thou redeem'st thyself: but all, save thee,
I fell with curses.

Methinks thou art more honest now than wise;
For, by oppressing and betraying me,
Thou mightst have sooner got another service:
For many so arrive at second masters,
Upon their first lord's neck. But tell me true—
For I must ever doubt, though ne'er so sure—
Is not thy kindness subtle, covetous,
If not a usuring kindness, and, as rich men deal gifts,
Expecting in return twenty for one?

FLAVIUS

No, my most worthy master; in whose breast
Doubt and suspect, alas, are placed too late:
You should have fear'd false times when you did feast:
Suspect still comes where an estate is least.
That which I show, heaven knows, is merely love,
Duty and zeal to your unmatched mind,
Care of your food and living; and, believe it,
My most honour'd lord,
For any benefit that points to me,
Either in hope or present, I'ld exchange
For this one wish, that you had power and wealth
To requite me, by making rich yourself.

TIMON

Look thee, 'tis so! Thou singly honest man,
Here, take: the gods out of my misery
Have sent thee treasure. Go, live rich and happy;
But thus condition'd: thou shalt build from men;
Hate all, curse all, show charity to none,
But let the famish'd flesh slide from the bone,
Ere thou relieve the beggar; give to dogs
What thou deny'st to men; let prisons swallow 'em,
Debts wither 'em to nothing; be men like blasted woods,
And may diseases lick up their false bloods!
And so farewell and thrive.

FLAVIUS

O, let me stay,
And comfort you, my master.

TIMON

If thou hatest curses,
Stay not; fly, whilst thou art blest and free:
Ne'er see thou man, and let me ne'er see thee.

[*Exit Flavius. Timon retires to his cave.*

ACT FIVE SCENE ONE

The woods. Before Timon's cave.

Enter Poet *and* Painter; TIMON *watching them from his cave.*

PAINTER

As I took note of the place, it cannot be far where he abides.

POET

What's to be thought of him? does the rumour hold for true, that he's so full of gold?

PAINTER

Certain: Alcibiades reports it; Phrynia and Timandra had gold of him: he likewise enriched poor straggling soldiers with great quantity: 'tis said he gave unto his steward a mighty sum.

POET

Then this breaking of his has been but a try for his friends.

PAINTER

Nothing else: you shall see him a palm in Athens again, and flourish with the highest. Therefore 'tis not amiss we tender our loves to him, in this supposed distress of his: it will show honestly in us; and is very likely to load our purposes with what they travail for, if it be a just and true report that goes of his having.

POET

What have you now to present unto him?

PAINTER

Nothing at this time but my visitation: only I will promise him an excellent piece.

POET

I must serve him so too, tell him of an intent that's coming toward him.

PAINTER

Good as the best. Promising is the very air o' the time: it opens the eyes of expectation: performance is ever the duller for his act; and, but in the plainer and simpler kind of people, the deed of saying is quite out of use. To promise is most courtly and fashionable: performance is a kind of will or testament which argues a great sickness in his judgment that makes it.

[*Timon comes from his cave, behind.*

TIMON

[*Aside*] Excellent workman! thou canst not paint a man so bad as is thyself.

POET

I am thinking what I shall say I have provided for him: it must be a personating of himself; a satire against the softness of prosperity, with a discovery of the infinite flatteries that follow youth and opulency.

TIMON

[*Aside*] Must thou needs stand for a villain in thine own work? wilt thou whip thine own faults in other men? Do so, I have gold for thee.

POET

Nay, let's seek him:
Then do we sin against our own estate,
When we may profit meet, and come too late.

PAINTER

True;
When the day serves, before black-corner'd night,

Find what thou want'st by free and offer'd light.
Come.

TIMON
[*Aside*] I'll meet you at the turn. What a god's gold, 46
That he is worshipp'd in a baser temple
Than where swine feed!
'Tis thou that rigg'st the bark and plough'st the foam,
Settlest admired reverence in a slave:
To thee be worship! and thy saints for aye
Be crown'd with plagues that thee alone obey!
Fit I meet them. [*Coming forward.*

POET
Hail, worthy Timon!

PAINTER
Our late noble master!

TIMON
Have I once lived to see two honest men?

POET
Sir, 58
Having often of your open bounty tasted,
Hearing you were retired, your friends fall'n off,
Whose thankless natures—O abhorred spirits!—
Not all the whips of heaven are large enough:
What! to you,
Whose star-like nobleness gave life and influence
To their whole being! I am rapt and cannot cover
The monstrous bulk of this ingratitude
With any size of words.

TIMON
Let it go naked, men may see't the better: 68
You that are honest, by being what you are,
Make them best seen and known.

PAINTER
He and myself
Have travail'd in the great shower of your gifts,
And sweetly felt it.

TIMON
Ay, you are honest men.

PAINTER
We are hither come to offer you our service.

TIMON
Most honest men! Why, how shall I requite you?
Can you eat roots, and drink cold water? no.

BOTH
What we can do, we'll do, to do you service.

TIMON
Ye're honest men: ye've heard that I have gold;
I am sure you have: speak truth; ye're honest men. 81

PAINTER
So it is said, my noble lord; but therefore
Came not my friend nor I.

TIMON
Good honest men! Thou draw'st a counterfeit
Best in all Athens: thou'rt, indeed, the best;
Thou counterfeit'st most lively.

PAINTER
So, so, my lord.

TIMON
E'en so, sir, as I say. And, for thy fiction,
Why, thy verse swells with stuff so fine and smooth
That thou art even natural in thine art.
But, for all this, my honest-natured friends,
I must needs say you have a little fault: 92
Marry, 'tis not monstrous in you, neither wish I
You take much pains to mend.

BOTH
Beseech your honour
To make it known to us.

TIMON
You'll take it ill.

BOTH
Most thankfully, my lord.

TIMON
Will you, indeed?

BOTH
Doubt it not, worthy lord.

TIMON
There's never a one of you but trusts a knave,
That mightily deceives you.

BOTH
Do we, my lord?

TIMON
Ay, and you hear him cog, see him dissemble,
Know his gross patchery, love him, feed him,
Keep in your bosom: yet remain assured 106
That he's a made-up villain.

PAINTER
I know none such, my lord.

POET
Nor I.

TIMON
Look you, I love you well; I'll give you gold,
Rid me these villains from your companies:
Hang them or stab them, drown them in a draught,
Confound them by some course, and come to me,
I'll give you gold enough.

BOTH
Name them, my lord, let's know them.

TIMON
You that way and you this, but two in company;
Each man apart, all single and alone, 117
Yet an arch-villain keeps him company.
If where thou art two villains shall not be,
Come not near him. If thou wouldst not reside
But where one villain is, then him abandon.

FLAVIUS Lord Timon! Timon! Look out, and speak to friends.

Hence, pack! there's gold; you came for gold, ye slaves:
[*To Painter*] You have work'd for me; there's payment for you: hence! [59]
[*To Poet*] You are an alchemist; make gold of that.
Out, rascal dogs!
[*Beats them out, and then retires to his cave.*

Enter FLAVIUS *and two* Senators.

FLAVIUS
It is in vain that you would speak with Timon;
For he is set so only to himself 129
That nothing but himself which looks like man
Is friendly with him.

FIRST SENATOR
Bring us to his cave:
It is our part and promise to the Athenians
To speak with Timon.

SECOND SENATOR
At all times alike
Men are not still the same: 'twas time and griefs
That framed him thus: time, with his fairer hand,
Offering the fortunes of his former days,
The former man may make him. Bring us to him,
And chance it as it may.

FLAVIUS
Here is his cave.
Peace and content be here! Lord Timon!
Timon! 143
Look out, and speak to friends: the Athenians,
By two of their most reverend senate, greet thee:
Speak to them, noble Timon.

TIMON *comes from his cave.*

TIMON
Thou sun, that comfort'st, burn! Speak, and be hang'd:
For each true word, a blister! and each false
Be as a cauterizing to the root o' the tongue, [60]
Consuming it with speaking!

FIRST SENATOR
Worthy Timon,—
TIMON
Of none but such as you, and you of Timon.
FIRST SENATOR
The senators of Athens greet thee, Timon.
TIMON
I thank them; and would send them back the plague,
Could I but catch it for them.
FIRST SENATOR
O, forget
What we are sorry for ourselves in thee.
The senators with one consent of love
Entreat thee back to Athens; who have thought
On special dignities, which vacant lie
For thy best use and wearing.
SECOND SENATOR
They confess
Toward thee forgetfulness too general, gross: [61]
Which now the public body, which doth seldom
Play the recanter, feeling in itself
A lack of Timon's aid, hath sense withal
Of its own fail, restraining aid to Timon;
And send forth us, to make their sorrow'd render,
Together with a recompense more fruitful
Than their offence can weigh down by the dram;
Ay, even such heaps and sums of love and wealth
As shall to thee blot out what wrongs were theirs
And write in thee the figures of their love,
Ever to read them thine.
TIMON
You witch me in it;
Surprise me to the very brink of tears:
Lend me a fool's heart and a woman's eyes,
And I'll beweep these comforts, worthy senators.
FIRST SENATOR
Therefore, so please thee to return with us
And of our Athens, thine and ours, to take
The captainship, thou shalt be met with thanks,
Allow'd with absolute power and thy good name
Live with authority: so soon we shall drive back
Of Alcibiades the approaches wild,
Who, like a boar too savage, doth root up
His country's peace.
SECOND SENATOR
And shakes his threatening sword
Against the walls of Athens.
FIRST SENATOR
Therefore, Timon,—
TIMON
Well, sir, I will; therefore, I will, sir; thus:
If Alcibiades kill my countrymen,
Let Alcibiades know this of Timon,
That Timon cares not. But if be sack fair Athens,
And take our goodly aged men by the beards,
Giving our holy virgins to the stain
Of contumelious, beastly, mad-brain'd war,
Then let him know, and tell him Timon speaks it,
In pity of our aged and our youth,
I cannot choose but tell him, that I care not,
And let him take't at worst; for their knives care not,
While you have throats to answer: for myself,
There's not a whittle in the unruly camp
But I do prize it at my love before
The reverend'st throat in Athens. So I leave you
To the protection of the prosperous gods,
As thieves to keepers.
FLAVIUS
Stay not, all's in vain.
TIMON
Why, I was writing of my epitaph; it will be seen to-morrow: my long sickness
Of health and living now begins to mend,
And nothing brings me all things. Go, live still;
Be Alcibiades your plague, you his,
And last so long enough!
FIRST SENATOR
We speak in vain.
TIMON
But yet I love my country, and am not
One that rejoices in the common wreck,
As common bruit doth put it.
FIRST SENATOR
That's well spoke.
TIMON
Commend me to my loving countrymen,—
FIRST SENATOR
These words become your lips as they pass thorough them.
SECOND SENATOR
And enter in our ears like great triumphers
In their applauding gates.
TIMON
Commend me to them,
And tell them that, to ease them of their griefs,
Their fears of hostile strokes, their aches, losses,
Their pangs of love, with other incident throes
That nature's fragile vessel doth sustain
In life's uncertain voyage, I will some kindness do them:
I'll teach them to prevent wild Alcibiades' wrath.
FIRST SENATOR
I like this well; he will return again.
TIMON
I have a tree, which grows here in my close,
That mine own use invites me to cut down,

And shortly must I fell it: tell my friends,
Tell Athens, in the sequence of degree
From high to low throughout, that whoso please
To stop affliction, let him take his haste, [62]
Come hither, ere my tree hath felt the axe,
And hang himself. I pray you, do my greeting.

FLAVIUS
Trouble him no further; thus you still shall find him.

TIMON
Come not to me again: but say to Athens,
Timon hath made his everlasting mansion
Upon the beached verge of the salt flood;
Who once a day with his embossed froth
The turbulent surge shall cover: thither come,
And let my grave-stone be your oracle.
Lips, let sour words go by and language end:
What is amiss plague and infection mend!
Graves only be men's works and death their gain!
Sun, hide thy beams! Timon hath done his reign.
[*Retires to his cave.*

FIRST SENATOR
His discontents are unremoveably
Coupled to nature.

SECOND SENATOR
Our hope in him is dead: let us return,
And strain what other means is left unto us
In our dear peril.

FIRST SENATOR
It requires swift foot. [*Exeunt.*

ACT FIVE SCENE TWO

Before the walls of Athens.

Enter two Senators *and a* Messenger.

FIRST SENATOR
Thou hast painfully discover'd: are his files
As full as thy report?

MESSENGER
I have spoke the least:
Besides, his expedition promises
Present approach.

SECOND SENATOR
We stand much hazard, if they bring not Timon.

MESSENGER
I met a courier, one mine ancient friend;
Whom, though in general part we were opposed, [63]
Yet our old love made a particular force, [64]
And made us speak like friends: this man was riding
From Alcibiades to Timon's cave,
With letters of entreaty, which imported
His fellowship i' the cause against your city,
In part for his sake moved.

FIRST SENATOR
Here come our brothers.

Enter the Senators *from* TIMON.

THIRD SENATOR
No talk of Timon, nothing of him expect.
The enemies' drum is heard, and fearful scouring
Doth choke the air with dust: in, and prepare:
Ours is the fall, I fear; our foes the snare. [*Exeunt.*

ACT FIVE SCENE THREE

The woods. Timon's cave, and a rude tomb seen.

Enter a Soldier, *seeking* TIMON.

SOLDIER
By all description this should be the place.
Who's here? speak, ho! No answer! What is this?
Timon is dead, who hath outstretch'd his span:
Some beast rear'd this; there does not live a man. [65]
Dead, sure; and this his grave. What's on this tomb
I cannot read; the character I'll take with wax:
Our captain hath in every figure skill,
An aged interpreter, though young in days:
Before proud Athens he's set down by this,
Whose fall the mark of his ambition is.
[*Exit.*

ACT FIVE SCENE FOUR

Before the walls of Athens.

Trumpets sound. Enter ALCIBIADES *with his powers.*

ALCIBIADES
Sound to this coward and lascivious town
Our terrible approach. [*A parley sounded.*

Enter Senators *on the walls.*

Till now you have gone on and fill'd the time
With all licentious measure, making your wills
The scope of justice; till now myself and such
As slept within the shadow of your power
Have wander'd with our traversed arms and breathed
Our sufferance vainly: now the time is flush,
When crouching marrow in the bearer strong
Cries of itself 'No more:' now breathless wrong
Shall sit and pant in your great chairs of ease,

And pursy insolence shall break his wind
With fear and horrid flight.

FIRST SENATOR
Noble and young,
When thy first griefs were but a mere conceit,
Ere thou hadst power or we had cause of fear,
We sent to thee, to give thy rages balm,
To wipe out our ingratitude with loves
Above their quantity.

SECOND SENATOR
So did we woo
Transformed Timon to our city's love
By humble message and by promised means:
We were not all unkind, nor all deserve
The common stroke of war.

FIRST SENATOR
These walls of ours
Were not erected by their hands from whom
You have received your griefs; nor are they such
That these great towers, trophies and schools should fall
For private faults in them.

SECOND SENATOR
Nor are they living
Who were the motives that you first went out;
Shame that they wanted cunning, in excess [66]
Hath broke their hearts. March, noble lord,
Into our city with thy banners spread:
By decimation, and a tithed death—
If thy revenges hunger for that food
Which nature loathes—take thou the destined tenth,
And by the hazard of the spotted die
Let die the spotted.

FIRST SENATOR
All have not offended;
For those that were, it is not square to take
On those that are, revenges: crimes, like lands,
Are not inherited. Then, dear countryman,
Bring in thy ranks, but leave without thy rage:
Spare thy Athenian cradle and those kin
Which in the bluster of thy wrath must fall
With those that have offended: like a shepherd,
Approach the fold and cull the infected forth,
But kill not all together.

SECOND SENATOR
What thou wilt,
Thou rather shalt enforce it with thy smile
Than hew to't with thy sword.

FIRST SENATOR
Set but thy foot
Against our rampired gates, and they shall ope;
So thou wilt send thy gentle heart before,
To say thou'lt enter friendly.

SECOND SENATOR
Throw thy glove,
Or any token of thine honour else,
That thou wilt use the wars as thy redress
And not as our confusion, all thy powers
Shall make their harbour in our town, till we
Have seal'd thy full desire.

ALCIBIADES
Then there's my glove;
Descend, and open your uncharged ports:
Those enemies of Timon's and mine own
Whom you yourselves shall set out for reproof
Fall and no more: and, to atone your fears
With my more noble meaning, not a man
Shall pass his quarter, or offend the stream
Of regular justice in your city's bounds,
But shall be render'd to your public laws [67]
At heaviest answer.

BOTH
'Tis most nobly spoken.

ALCIBIADES
Descend, and keep your words.
[*The Senators descend, and open the gates.*

Enter Soldier.

SOLDIER
My noble general, Timon is dead;
Entomb'd upon the very hem o' the sea;
And on his grave-stone this insculpture, which
With wax I brought away, whose soft impression
Interprets for my poor ignorance.

ALCIBIADES
[*Reads the epitaph*] 'Here lies a wretched corse, of wretched soul bereft:
Seek not my name: a plague consume you wicked caitiffs left!
Here lie I, Timon; who, alive, all living men did hate:
Pass by and curse thy fill, but pass and stay not here thy gait.'
These well express in thee thy latter spirits:
Though thou abhorr'dst in us our human griefs,
Scorn'dst our brain's flow and those our droplets which
From niggard nature fall, yet rich conceit
Taught thee to make vast Neptune weep for aye
On thy low grave, on faults forgiven. Dead [68]
Is noble Timon: of whose memory
Hereafter more. Bring me into your city,
And I will use the olive with my sword,
Make war breed peace, make peace stint war, make each
Prescribe to other as each other's leech.
Let our drums strike. [*Exeunt.*

Notes

1. Gum, which oozes; – Johnson's reading; Folios read *'grown, which uses'*; Pope, *'gum which issues.'*
2. Flies Each bound it chafes; – Folios, *'chases'*; Becket conjectured *'flies. Eche (bound) it chafes'*; Schmidt *'chafes with.'*
3. Grace Speaks his own standing; – Johnson conjectured *'standing ... graces'* or *'grace Speaks understanding'*; Mason conjectured *'Grace Speaks its own standing'*; Jackson conjectured *'grace Speaks! 'tis one standing'*; Orger conjectured *'grace ... seeming.'*
4. Happy man; – Theobald's emendation of Folios, *'happy men.'*
5. Sea of wax; – Bailey conjectured *'sweep of taxing'*; Collier MS., *'sea of verse'*; &c.; but there is evidently a reference to writing-tablets covered with wax.
6. Slip; – Folios, *'sit'*; Delius conjectured *'sink.'*
7. The line is supposed by some to be corrupt, and many emendations have been proposed, but Coleridge's interpretation commends itself:—"The meaning of the first line the poet himself explains, or rather unfolds, in the second. 'The man is honest!'—True; and for that very cause, and with no additional or extrinsic motive, he will be so. No man can be justly called honest, who is not so for honesty's sake, itself including its reward."
8. That I had no angry wit to be a lord; – Blackstone conjectured *'Angry that I had no wit,—to be a lord'*; Malone conjectured *'That I had no angry wit.—To be a lord!'*; Anon. conjectured *'That I had no ampler wit than be a lord'*; Warburton, *'That I had so hungry a wit to be a lord'*; Heath conjectured *'That ... so wrong'd my wit to be a lord'*; &c., &c.
9. Alluding to the then custom of each guest bringing his own knife to a feast.
10. Sin; – Farmer conjectured *'sing'*; Singer conjectured *'dine'*; Kinnear conjectured *'surfeit.'*
11. The arrangement of these lines was first suggested by Rann, and followed by Steevens in his edition of 1793.
12. Music, make their welcome; – Pope reads *'Let musick make their welcome'*; Capell, *'Musick, make known their welcome.'*
13. And able horses; – so Folios 1, 2; Folios 3, 4, *'An able horse'*; Theobald, *'ten able horse'*; Jackson conjectured *'Ay, able horses'*; Collier MS., *'a stable o' horses'*; Singer conjectured *'Two able horses.'*
14. Found his state in safety; – Hanmer's reading; Folios, *'sound ...'*; Capell, *'found ... on safety'*; Capell conjectured *'find ... in safety.'*
15. Was to be; – Heath conjectured *'Was made to be'*; Long MS., *'Was'*; Mason conjectured *'Was formed'*; Singer MS., *'Was truly'*; Collier MS., *'Was surely.'*
16. Mistress; – (so 1. 107).
17. Loved lord; – Folios 2, 3, 4, *'dear lov'd lord'*; S. Walker conjectured *'belov'd.'*
18. Folios read *'Though you heare now (too late) yet nowes a time, The'*; Hanmer, *'Though ... yet now's too late a time'*; Collier MS., *'Though ... yet now's a time too late.'*
19. Wasteful cock; – Pope reads *'lonely room'*; Collier MS., *'wasteful nook'*; Jackson conjectured *'wakeful cock'*; Jervis conjectured *'wakeful couch'*; Keightley, *'wasteful cock-loft'*; Daniel conjectured *'wakeful cot'*; Jackson's conjecture seems best, *'wakeful cock,' i.e.* 'cock-loft,' unless *'cock'* = wine-tap.
20. And we alive that lived; i.e. – in so short a time.
21. Let molten coin be thy damnation; cp. – the old ballad, *"The Dead Man's Song"*:

    "And ladies full of melted gold
    Were poured down their throats."

22. Slave, Unto his honour; – Steevens' reading; Folios, *'Slave unto his honour'*; Pope, *'slave Unto this hour'*; Collier MS., *'slave unto his humour'*; Staunton, *'slave Unto dishonour'*; but the words are probably spoken ironically.
23. So many; – changed by Theobald to *'fifty'*; so, too, in 1. 41; but the figures are very doubtful, and *'fifty-five hundred talents,'* in 1. 43, is obviously a mere exaggeration.
24. Mistook him, – &c., *i.e.* 'made the mistake and applied to me'; Hanmer, *'o'erlook'd'*; Warburton, *'mislook'd'*; Johnson conjectured *'not mistook.'*
25. For a little part; – Theobald, *'for a little dirt'*; Hanmer, *'a little dirt'*; Heath conjectured *'for a little profit'*; Johnson conjectured *'for a little park'*; Mason conjectured *'for a little port'*; Jackson conjectured *'for a little part'*; Bailey conjectured *'for a little sport'*; Kinnear conjectured *'for a little pomp.'* Steevens explains the passage thus:—"By purchasing what brought me little honour, I have lost the more honourable opportunity of supplying the wants of my friends."
26. Spirit, – Theobald's correction of Folios, *'sport'*; Collier MS., *'port.'*
27. In respect of his; – Staunton conjectured *'this.'*
28. Thrive, give him over; – so Folio 1; Folios 2, 3, 4, *'That thriv'd, give him over'*; Pope, *'Three give him over?'*; Hanmer, *'Tried give him over'*; Theobald, *'Thriv'd, give him over?'*; Tyrwhitt conjectured *'Shriv'd give him over:'*; Johnson conjectured *'Thrice give him over,'* &c.
29. Sense; – Collier conjectured *'scuse.'*
30. Sempronius: all:; – so Folios 3, 4; Folio 1, *'Sempronius Vllorxa: All'*; Folio 2, *'Semprovius: All'*; Malone, *'Sempronius: Ullorxa, all'*; Grant White suggested that *'Vllorxa'* was a misprint for *'Ventidius.'*
31. Behave his anger, ere 'twas spent; – Folios, *'behooue his ...'*; Johnson conjectured *'behold his adversary shent'*; Steevens conjectured *'behave, ere was his anger spent'*; Becket conjectured *'behave; his anger was, 'ere spent'*; Hanmer, *'behave in's ...'*; Malone conjectured *'behave his ...'*; Collier MS., *'reprove his ...'*, &c.
32. I say, my lords, has; – Pope reads *'I say my lords h'as'*; Folio 1. *'Why say my Lords ha's'*; Folios 2, 3, *'Why I say my Lords ha's'*; Folio 4, *'Why, I say my Lords h'as'*; Capell, *Why, I say, my lords, he has'*; Dyce, *'Why, I say, my lords, has'*; Globe edd., *'I say my lords, he has.'*
33. And, not to swell our spirit, i.e. – 'not to swell our spirit with anger, not to become exasperated'; Theobald, *'And note, to swell your spirit'*; Capell. *'And, not to swell your spirit'*; Singer. *'quell'*; Kinnear, *'quail.'*
34. Only in bone, i.e. – 'as a mere skeleton'; Staunton conjectured *'Only at home,'* or *'Only in doors'*; Ingleby conjectured *'only in bed'*; Hudson conjectured *'only alone.'*

35. Most lands; – Warburton, *'most hands'*; Malone conjectured *'most lords'*; Mason conjectured *'my stains'*; Becket conjectured *'most brands'*; Jackson conjectured, *'most bands.'*
36. Harshly o' the trumpet's; – Rowe, *'harshly as o' the Trumpets'*; Steevens (1793), *'harshly on the trumpet's'*; Grant White conjectured *'harshly. O, the trumpets,'* &c.
37. You with flatteries; – so Folios; Warburton, *'with your flatteries'*; Keightley, *'by you with flatteries'*; Folio 2 reads *'flatteries'*; S. Walker conjectured *'flattery.'*
38. Let; – Hanmer's emendations of Folios, *'yet.'*
39. What state compounds; – S. Walker conjectured *'state comprehends'*; Grant White conjectured *'that state compounds'*; Watkiss Lloyd conjectured *'whate'er state comprehends.'*
40. Deny't; – Warburton, *'denude'*; Hanmer, *'degrade'*; Heath conjectured *'deprive'*; Steevens conjectured *'devest'*; Collier MS., *'decline'*; &c.; the indefinite *'it'* refers to the implied noun in *'raise,' i.e.* 'give elevation to.'
41. Pasture lards the rother's sides; – *'rother,'* Singer's emendation for Folios *'brothers.'* Folio 1, *'Pastour'*; Folios 2, 3, 4, *'pastor'*; Farmer and Steevens conjectured *'pasterer'*: *'lards'*; Rowe's reading, Folio 1, *'Lards'*; Folios 2, 3, 4, *'Lords.'*
42. All is oblique; – Pope's emendation, Folio 1, *'All's obliquie'*; Folios 2, 3, *'Alls obliquy'*; Folio 4, *'All's obliquy'*; Rowe, *'all's obloquy'*; Lettsom conjectured *'all, all's oblique.'*
43. Wappen'd; – so Folios 1, 2; Folios 3, 4, *'wapen'd'*; Warburton, *'waped'*; Johnson conjectured *'wained'*; Malone conjectured *'wapper'd'*; Anon. conjectured, *'Wapping'*; Steevens conjectured *'weeping'*; Seymour conjectured *'vapid'*; Staunton conjectured *'woe-pin'd'*; Fleay, *'wop-eyed'*; *i.e.* having waterish eyes (*vide* Glossary).
44. Conquer my country; – Kinnear conjectured *'confound my countrymen'*; Hanmer, *'make conquest of my country;* Capell, *'conquer thy own country'*; S. Walker conjectured *'scourge thy country'*; Hudson, *'scourge my country.'*
45. Window-bars; – Johnson conjectured; Folios, *'window Barn'*; Pope, *'window-barn'*; Warburton, *'window-lawn'*; Tyrwhitt conjectured *'widow's barb.'*
46. Spurring; – Hanmer, *'sparring'*; Long MS., *'spurning'*; Seymour conjectured *'springing'*; there is no need to emend the text.
47. Bade; – Folio 1, *'bad'*; Folios 2, 3, 4, *'bid.'*
48. When; – S. Walker conjectured *'where.'*
49. Outlives incertain; – Rowe's emendation; Folio 1 reads *'Out-lives: incertaine'*; Folios 2, 3, 4, *'Out-lives: in certaine'*; Hanmer, *'Out-strips incertain'*; Capell, *'Outvies uncertain.'*
50. Drugs; – Folios 1, 2, *'drugges'*; Mason conjectured *'drudges'*; Collier MS., *'dugs'*; Capell conjectured MS. *'dregs'*; *'drugs'* = *'drudges.'*
51. My; – Rowe's correction of Folios, *'thy.'*
52. After his means, – i.e. *'after his means were gone.'*
53. Meat; – Theobald, *'meet' (i.e.* 'what you ought to be'); Hanmer, *'men'*; Steevens conjectured *'me'*; &c.
54. Behold, the earth hath roots, – &c.; *cp.* Hall's *Satires,* III. 1 (pub. 1598):—

   "Time was that, whiles the autumn full did last
   Our hungry sires gap'd for the falling mast," &c.

55. Villany; – Rowe's correction of Folios 1, 2, *'villaine.'*
56. Moon; – Theobald, *'mounds'*; Capell, *'earth'*; Tollet conjectured *'main.'*
57. Dangerous nature mild; – Thirlby conjectured; Folios, *'wild'*; Becket conjectured *'nature dangerous-wild'*; Jackson conjectured *'dolorous nature wild.'*
58. Black-corned'd, i.e. – 'hiding things in dark corners'; Hanmer, *'black-corneted'*; Warburton conjectured *'black-cornette'*; Farmer conjectured MS. *'black-coroned'*; Mason conjectured *'black-crowned'*; Jackson conjectured *'dark-horned'*; Singer conjectured, *'black-curtain'd,'* &c.
59. You have work; – so Folios; Hanmer, *'You have work'd'*; Malone, *'You have done work'*; Steevens conjectured *'You've work'd.'*
60. As a cauterizing; – Rowe's emendation; Folio 1, *'as a Cantherizing'*; Folios 2, 3, 4, *'as a Catherizing'*; Pope, *'cauterizing'*; Capell, *'cancerizing.'*
61. General, gross: – Pope's emendation of Folios, *'generall grosse:'* S. Walker's conjecture, adopted by Dyce, *'general-gross.'*
62. Haste; – Pope, *'taste'*; Warburtion conjectured MS., *'tatch'*; Collier MS., *'halter.'*
63. Whom, – instead of *'who,'* owing to confusion of construction; Pope, *'Who'*; Hanmer, *'And'*; Singer, *'When'*; &c.
64. Made a particular force; – Hanmer reads *'had ... force'*; Staunton conjectured *'took ... truce'*; Bailey conjectured *'had ... force with'*; &c.
65. These words are in all probability the reflection of the soldier; this view is certainly more acceptable than to believe them to be an inscription placed by Timon somewhere near the tomb. Nor is it necessary, with Warburton, to change *'read' into 'rear'd.'* The soldier, seeing the tomb, infers that Timon is dead, but he cannot read the inscription; 'some beast read this! there does not live a man able to do so' (*v.* Preface).
66. Shame, that they wanted cunning, in excess; – Theobald's emendation ('extreme shame for their folly in banishing you hath broken their hearts'); Folio 1 reads *'(Shame that they wanted, cunning in excesse)'*; Folios 2, 3, 4, *'Shame (that they wanted cunning in excesse)'*; Johnson conjectured *'Shame that they wanted, coming in excess.'*
67. Render'd to your; – the conjecture of *Chedworth,'* adopted by Dyce; Folio 1 reads *'remedied to your'*; Folios 2, 3, 4, *'remedied by your'*; Pope, *'remedied by'*; Johnson, *'remedied to'*; Malone, *'remedy'd, to your'*; Singer (ed. 2), *'remitted to your.'*
68. On thy low grave, on faults forgiven. Dead; – the reading of Folios; Theobald reads *'On thy low grave.—On: faults forgiven.—Dead'*; Hanmer, *'On thy low grave our faults—forgiv'n, since dead.'*

TITUS ANDRONICUS

TITUS ANDRONICUS

DRAMATIS PERSONAE

SATURNINUS, son to the late Emperor of Rome, and afterwards declared Emperor.
BASSIANUS, brother to Saturninus; in love with Lavinia.
TITUS ANDRONICUS, a noble Roman, general against the Goths.
MARCUS ANDRONICUS, tribune of the people, and brother to Titus.
LUCIUS, son to Titus Andronicus.
QUINTUS, son to Titus Andronicus.
MARTIUS, son to Titus Andronicus.
MUTIUS, son to Titus Andronicus.
Young LUCIUS, a boy, son to Lucius.
PUBLIUS, son to Marcus the Tribune.
SEMPRONIUS, kinsman to Titus.
CAIUS, kinsman to Titus.
VALENTINE, kinsman to Titus.
AEMILIUS, a noble Roman.
ALARBUS, son to Tamora.
DEMETRIUS, son to Tamora.
CHIRON, son to Tamora.
AARON, a Moor, beloved by Tamora.
A Captain, Tribune, Messenger, and Clown; Romans.
Goths and Romans.
TAMORA, Queen of the Goths.
LAVINIA, daughter of Titus Andronicus.
A Nurse.
Senators, Tribunes, Officers, Soldiers, and Attendants.

SCENE : *Rome, and the country near it.*

ACT ONE SCENE ONE

Rome. Before the Capitol.

The Tomb of ANDRONICI *appearing; the* Tribunes *and* Senators *aloft. Enter, below, from one side,* SATURNINUS *and his* Followers; *and, from the other side,* BASSIANUS *and his* Followers; *with drum and colours.*

SATURNINUS
Noble patricians, patrons of my right,
Defend the justice of my cause with arms,
And, countrymen, my loving followers,
Plead my successive title with your swords:
I am his first-born son, that was the last [1]
That ware the imperial diadem of Rome;
Then let my father's honours live in me,
Nor wrong mine age with this indignity.

BASSIANUS
Romans, friends, followers, favourers of my right,
If ever Bassianus, Caesar's son,
Were gracious in the eyes of royal Rome,
Keep then this passage to the Capitol
And suffer not dishonour to approach
The imperial seat, to virtue consecrate,
To justice, continence and nobility;
But let desert in pure election shine,
And, Romans, fight for freedom in your choice.

Enter MARCUS ANDRONICUS,
aloft, with the crown.

MARCUS ANDRONICUS
Princes, that strive by factions and by friends
Ambitiously for rule and empery,
Know that the people of Rome, for whom we stand
A special party, have, by common voice,
In election for the Roman empery,
Chosen Andronicus, surnamed Pius
For many good and great deserts to Rome:
A nobler man, a braver warrior,
Lives not this day within the city walls;
He by the senate is accited home
From weary wars against the barbarous Goths;
That, with his sons, a terror to our foes,
Hath yoked a nation strong, train'd up in arms.
Ten years are spent since first he undertook
This cause of Rome and chastised with arms
Our enemies' pride: five times he hath return'd
Bleeding to Rome, bearing his valiant sons
In coffins from the field;
And now at last, laden with honour's spoils,
Returns the good Andronicus to Rome,
Renowned Titus, flourishing in arms.
Let us entreat, by honour of his name,
Whom worthily you would have now succeed,
And in the Capitol and senate's right,
Whom you pretend to honour and adore,
That you withdraw you and abate your strength;
Dismiss your followers and, as suitors should,
Plead your deserts in peace and humbleness.

SATURNINUS
How fair the tribune speaks to calm my thoughts!

BASSIANUS
Marcus Andronicus, so I do affy
In thy uprightness and integrity,
And so I love and honour thee and thine,
Thy noble brother Titus and his sons,
And her to whom my thoughts are humbled all,
Gracious Lavinia, Rome's rich ornament,
That I will here dismiss thy loving friends,
And to my fortunes and the people's favour
Commit my cause in balance to be weigh'd.
[*Exeunt the Followers of Bassianus.*

SATURNINUS
Friends, that have been thus forward in my right,
I thank you all and here dismiss you all,
And to the love and favour of my country
Commit myself, my person and the cause.
[*Exeunt the Followers of Saturninus.*
Rome, be as just and gracious unto me
As I am confident and kind to thee.
Open the gates, and let me in. [2]

BASSIANUS
Tribunes, and me, a poor competitor.
[*Flourish. Saturninus and Bassianus go up into the Capitol.*

Enter a Captain.

CAPTAIN
Romans, make way: the good Andronicus,
Patron of virtue, Rome's best champion,
Successful in the battles that he fights,
With honour and with fortune is return'd
From where he circumscribed with his sword,
And brought to yoke, the enemies of Rome.

Drums and trumpets sounded. Enter MARTIUS *and* MUTIUS; *after them, two* Men *bearing a coffin covered with black; then* LUCIUS *and* QUINTUS. *After them,* TITUS ANDRONICUS; *and then* TAMORA, *with* ALARBUS, DEMETRIUS, CHIRON, AARON, *and other Goths, prisoners;* Soldiers *and* People *following. The* Bearers *set down the coffin, and* TITUS *speaks.*

TITUS ANDRONICUS
Hail, Rome, victorious in thy mourning weeds!
Lo, as the bark, that hath discharged her fraught,
Returns with precious lading to the bay
From whence at first she weigh'd her anchorage,
Cometh Andronicus, bound with laurel boughs,
To re-salute his country with his tears,
Tears of true joy for his return to Rome.
Thou great defender of this Capitol,
Stand gracious to the rites that we intend!
Romans, of five and twenty valiant sons,
Half of the number that King Priam had,
Behold the poor remains, alive and dead!
These that survive let Rome reward with love;
These that I bring unto their latest home,
With burial amongst their ancestors:
Here Goths have given me leave to sheathe my sword.
Titus, unkind and careless of thine own,
Why suffer'st thou thy sons, unburied yet,
To hover on the dreadful shore of Styx?
Make way to lay them by their brethren.
[*The tomb is opened.*
There greet in silence, as the dead are wont,
And sleep in peace, slain in your country's wars!
O sacred receptacle of my joys,
Sweet cell of virtue and nobility,
How many sons of mine hast thou in store,
That thou wilt never render to me more!

LUCIUS
Give us the proudest prisoner of the Goths,
That we may hew his limbs, and on a pile

Ad manes fratrum sacrifice his flesh,
Before this earthy prison of their bones;
That so the shadows be not unappeased.
Nor we disturb'd with prodigies on earth.

TITUS ANDRONICUS
I give him you, the noblest that survives,
The eldest son of this distressed queen.

TAMORA
Stay, Roman brethren! Gracious conqueror,
Victorious Titus, rue the tears I shed,
A mother's tears in passion for her son:
And if thy sons were ever dear to thee,
O, think my son to be as dear to me!
Sufficeth not that we are brought to Rome,
To beautify thy triumphs and return,
Captive to thee and to thy Roman yoke,
But must my sons be slaughter'd in the streets,
For valiant doings in their country's cause?
O, if to fight for king and commonweal
Were piety in thine, it is in these.
Andronicus, stain not thy tomb with blood:
Wilt thou draw near the nature of the gods?
Draw near them then in being merciful:
Sweet mercy is nobility's true badge:
Thrice noble Titus, spare my first-born son.

TITUS ANDRONICUS
Patient yourself, madam, and pardon me.
These are their brethren, whom you Goths beheld
Alive and dead, and for their brethren slain
Religiously they ask a sacrifice:
To this your son is mark'd, and die he must,
To appease their groaning shadows that are gone.

LUCIUS
Away with him! and make a fire straight;
And with our swords, upon a pile of wood,
Let's hew his limbs till they be clean consumed.
[Exeunt Lucius, Quintus, Martius, and Mutius, with Alarbus.

TAMORA
O cruel, irreligious piety!

CHIRON
Was ever Scythia half so barbarous?

DEMETRIUS
Oppose not Scythia to ambitious Rome.
Alarbus goes to rest; and we survive
To tremble under Titus' threatening looks.
Then, madam, stand resolved, but hope withal
The self-same gods that arm'd the Queen of Troy
With opportunity of sharp revenge
Upon the Thracian tyrant in his tent, [3]
May favour Tamora, the Queen of Goths—
When Goths were Goths and Tamora was queen—
To quit the bloody wrongs upon her foes.

Re-enter LUCIUS, QUINTUS, MARTIUS, *and* MUTIUS, *with their swords bloody.*

LUCIUS
See, lord and father, how we have perform'd
Our Roman rites: Alarbus' limbs are lopp'd,
And entrails feed the sacrificing fire,
Whose smoke, like incense, doth perfume the sky.
Remaineth nought, but to inter our brethren,
And with loud 'larums welcome them to Rome.

TITUS ANDRONICUS
Let it be so; and let Andronicus
Make this his latest farewell to their souls.
[Trumpets sounded, and the coffin laid in the tomb.
In peace and honour rest you here, my sons;
Rome's readiest champions, repose you here in rest,
Secure from worldly chances and mishaps!
Here lurks no treason, here no envy swells,
Here grow no damned grudges; here are no storms, [4]
No noise, but silence and eternal sleep:
In peace and honour, rest you here, my sons!

Enter LAVINIA.

LAVINIA
In peace and honour live Lord Titus long;
My noble lord and father, live in fame!
Lo, at this tomb my tributary tears
I render, for my brethren's obsequies;
And at thy feet I kneel, with tears of joy,
Shed on the earth, for thy return to Rome:
O, bless me here with thy victorious hand,
Whose fortunes Rome's best citizens applaud!

TITUS ANDRONICUS
Kind Rome, that hast thus lovingly reserved
The cordial of mine age to glad my heart!
Lavinia, live; outlive thy father's days,
And fame's eternal date, for virtue's praise!

Enter, below, MARCUS ANDRONICUS *and* Tribunes; *re-enter* SATURNINUS *and* BASSIANUS, *attended.*

MARCUS ANDRONICUS
Long live Lord Titus, my beloved brother,
Gracious triumpher in the eyes of Rome!

TITUS ANDRONICUS
Thanks, gentle tribune, noble brother Marcus.

MARCUS ANDRONICUS
And welcome, nephews, from successful wars,
You that survive, and you that sleep in fame!
Fair lords, your fortunes are alike in all,
That in your country's service drew your swords:
But safer triumph is this funeral pomp,

LAVINIA And at thy feet I kneel, with tears of joy.

That hath aspired to Solon's happiness
And triumphs over chance in honour's bed.
Titus Andronicus, the people of Rome, 184
Whose friend in justice thou hast ever been,
Send thee by me, their tribute and their trust,
This palliament of white and spotless hue;
And name thee in election for the empire,
With these our late-deceased emperor's sons:
Be candidatus then, and put it on,
And help to set a head on headless Rome.

TITUS ANDRONICUS
A better head her glorious body fits
Than this that shakes for age and feebleness:
What should I don this robe, and trouble you?
Be chosen with proclamations to-day, 195
To-morrow yield up rule, resign my life,
And set abroad new business for you all?
Rome, I have been thy soldier forty years,
And led my country's strength successfully,
And buried one and twenty valiant sons,
Knighted in field, slain manfully in arms,
In right and service of their noble country:
Give me a staff of honour for mine age,
But not a sceptre to control the world:
Upright he held it, lords, that held it last. 205

MARCUS ANDRONICUS
Titus, thou shalt obtain and ask the empery.

SATURNINUS
Proud and ambitious tribune, canst thou tell?

TITUS ANDRONICUS
Patience, Prince Saturninus.

SATURNINUS
Romans, do me right:
Patricians, draw your swords, and sheathe them not
Till Saturninus be Rome's emperor.
Andronicus, would thou wert shipp'd to hell,
Rather than rob me of the people's hearts!

LUCIUS
Proud Saturnine, interrupter of the good
That noble-minded Titus means to thee!

TITUS ANDRONICUS
Content thee, prince; I will restore to thee 216
The people's hearts, and wean them from themselves.

BASSIANUS
Andronicus, I do not flatter thee,

But honour thee, and will do till I die:
My faction if thou strengthen with thy friends,
I will most thankful be; and thanks to men
Of noble minds is honourable meed.

TITUS ANDRONICUS
People of Rome, and people's tribunes here,
I ask your voices and your suffrages:
Will you bestow them friendly on Andronicus?

TRIBUNES
To gratify the good Andronicus,
And gratulate his safe return to Rome,
The people will accept whom he admits.

TITUS ANDRONICUS
Tribunes, I thank you: and this suit I make,
That you create your emperor's eldest son,
Lord Saturnine; whose virtues will, I hope,
Reflect on Rome as Titan's rays on earth,
And ripen justice in this commonweal:
Then, if you will elect by my advice,
Crown him, and say 'Long live our emperor!'

MARCUS ANDRONICUS
With voices and applause of every sort,
Patricians and plebeians, we create
Lord Saturninus Rome's great emperor,
And say 'Long live our Emperor, Saturine!'
[A long flourish till they come down.

SATURNINUS
Titus Andronicus, for thy favours done
To us in our election this day,
I give thee thanks in part of thy deserts,
And will with deeds requite thy gentleness:
And, for an onset, Titus, to advance
Thy name and honourable family,
Lavinia will I make my empress,
Rome's royal mistress, mistress of my heart,
And in the sacred Pantheon her espouse:
Tell me, Andronicus, doth this motion please thee?

TITUS ANDRONICUS
It doth, my worthy lord; and in this match
I hold me highly honour'd of your grace:
And here in sight of Rome to Saturnine,
King and commander of our commonweal,
The wide world's emperor, do I consecrate
My sword, my chariot and my prisoners;
Presents well worthy Rome's imperial lord:
Receive them then, the tribute that I owe,
Mine honour's ensigns humbled at thy feet.

SATURNINUS
Thanks, noble Titus, father of my life!
How proud I am of thee and of thy gifts
Rome shall record, and when I do forget
The least of these unspeakable deserts,
Romans, forget your fealty to me.

TITUS ANDRONICUS
[*To Tamora*] Now, madam, are you prisoner to an emperor;
To him that, for your honour and your state,
Will use you nobly and your followers.

SATURNINUS
A goodly lady, trust me; of the hue
That I would choose, were I to choose anew.
Clear up, fair queen, that cloudy countenance:
Though chance of war hath wrought this change of cheer,
Thou comest not to be made a scorn in Rome:
Princely shall be thy usage every way.
Rest on my word, and let not discontent
Daunt all your hopes: madam, he comforts you
Can make you greater than the Queen of Goths.
Lavinia, you are not displeased with this?

LAVINIA
Not I, my lord; sith true nobility
Warrants these words in princely courtesy.

SATURNINUS
Thanks, sweet Lavinia. Romans, let us go:
Ransomless here we set our prisoners free:
Proclaim our honours, lords, with trump and drum.
[Flourish. Saturninus courts Tamora in dumb show.

BASSIANUS
Lord Titus, by your leave, this maid is mine.
[Seizing Lavinia.

TITUS ANDRONICUS
How, sir! are you in earnest then, my lord?

BASSIANUS
Ay, noble Titus; and resolved withal
To do myself this reason and this right.

MARCUS ANDRONICUS
'Suum cuique' is our Roman justice:
This prince in justice seizeth but his own.

LUCIUS
And that he will, and shall, if Lucius live.

TITUS ANDRONICUS
Traitors, avaunt! Where is the emperor's guard?
Treason, my lord! Lavinia is surprised!

SATURNINUS
Surprised! by whom?

BASSIANUS
By him that justly may
Bear his betroth'd from all the world away.
[Exeunt Bassianus and Marcus with Lavinia.

MUTIUS
Brothers, help to convey her hence away,
And with my sword I'll keep this door safe.
[Exeunt Lucius, Quintus, and Martius.

TITUS ANDRONICUS
Follow, my lord, and I'll soon bring her back.

MUTIUS
My lord, you pass not here.
TITUS ANDRONICUS
What, villain boy!
Barr'st me my way in Rome? [*Stabbing Mutius.*
MUTIUS
Help, Lucius, help! [*Dies.*
[*During the fray, Saturninus, Tamora, Demetrius, Chiron and Aaron go out and re-enter, above.*

Re-enter LUCIUS.

LUCIUS
My lord, you are unjust, and, more than so,
In wrongful quarrel you have slain your son.
TITUS ANDRONICUS
Nor thou, nor he, are any sons of mine;
My sons would never so dishonour me:
Traitor, restore Lavinia to the emperor.
LUCIUS
Dead, if you will; but not to be his wife,
That is another's lawful promised love. [*Exit.*
SATURNINUS
No, Titus, no; the emperor needs her not,
Nor her, nor thee, nor any of thy stock:
I'll trust, by leisure, him that mocks me once;
Thee never, nor thy traitorous haughty sons,
Confederates all thus to dishonour me.
Was there none else in Rome to make a stale,
But Saturnine? Full well, Andronicus.
Agree these deeds with that proud brag of thine,
That said'st I begg'd the empire at thy hands.
TITUS ANDRONICUS
O monstrous! what reproachful words are these?
SATURNINUS
But go thy ways; go, give that changing piece
To him that flourish'd for her with his sword:
A valiant son-in-law thou shalt enjoy;
One fit to bandy with thy lawless sons,
To ruffle in the commonwealth of Rome.
TITUS ANDRONICUS
These words are razors to my wounded heart.
SATURNINUS
And therefore, lovely Tamora, queen of Goths,
That like the stately Phoebe 'mongst her nymphs
Dost overshine the gallant'st dames of Rome,
If thou be pleased with this my sudden choice,
Behold, I choose thee, Tamora, for my bride,
And will create thee empress of Rome.
Speak, Queen of Goths, dost thou applaud my choice?
And here I swear by all the Roman gods,
Sith priest and holy water are so near
And tapers burn so bright and every thing
In readiness for Hymenaeus stand,
I will not re-salute the streets of Rome,
Or climb my palace, till from forth this place
I lead espoused my bride along with me.
TAMORA
And here, in sight of heaven, to Rome I swear,
If Saturnine advance the Queen of Goths,
She will a handmaid be to his desires,
A loving nurse, a mother to his youth.
SATURNINUS
Ascend, fair queen, Pantheon. Lords, accompany
Your noble emperor and his lovely bride,
Sent by the heavens for Prince Saturnine,
Whose wisdom hath her fortune conquered:
There shall we consummate our spousal rites.
[*Exeunt all but Titus.*
TITUS ANDRONICUS
I am not bid to wait upon this bride.
Titus, when wert thou wont to walk alone,
Dishonour'd thus, and challenged of wrongs?

Re-enter MARCUS, LUCIUS, QUINTUS, *and* MARTIUS.

MARCUS ANDRONICUS
O Titus, see, O, see what thou hast done!
In a bad quarrel slain a virtuous son.
TITUS ANDRONICUS
No, foolish tribune, no; no son of mine,
Nor thou, nor these, confederates in the deed
That hath dishonour'd all our family;
Unworthy brother, and unworthy sons!
LUCIUS
But let us give him burial, as becomes;
Give Mutius burial with our brethren.
TITUS ANDRONICUS
Traitors, away! he rests not in this tomb:
This monument five hundred years hath stood,
Which I have sumptuously re-edified:
Here none but soldiers and Rome's servitors
Repose in fame; none basely slain in brawls:
Bury him where you can; he comes not here.
MARCUS ANDRONICUS
My lord, this is impiety in you:
My nephew Mutius' deeds do plead for him;
He must be buried with his brethren.
QUINTUS, MARTIUS
And shall, or him we will accompany.
TITUS ANDRONICUS
'And shall!' what villain was it spake that word?
QUINTUS
He that would vouch it in any place but here.
TITUS ANDRONICUS
What, would you bury him in my despite?
MARCUS ANDRONICUS
No, noble Titus, but entreat of thee
To pardon Mutius and to bury him.

TITUS ANDRONICUS
Marcus, even thou hast struck upon my crest,
And, with these boys, mine honour thou hast wounded:
My foes I do repute you every one;
So, trouble me no more, but get you gone.
MARTIUS
He is not with himself; let us withdraw.
QUINTUS
Not I, till Mutius' bones be buried.
[*Marcus and the Sons of Titus kneel.*
MARCUS ANDRONICUS
Brother, for in that name doth nature plead,—
QUINTUS
Father, and in that name doth nature speak,—
TITUS ANDRONICUS
Speak thou no more, if all the rest will speed.
MARCUS ANDRONICUS
Renowned Titus, more than half my soul,—
LUCIUS
Dear father, soul and substance of us all,—
MARCUS ANDRONICUS
Suffer thy brother Marcus to inter
His noble nephew here in virtue's nest,
That died in honour and Lavinia's cause.
Thou art a Roman; be not barbarous:
The Greeks upon advice did bury Ajax
That slew himself; and wise Laertes' son
Did graciously plead for his funerals:
Let not young Mutius, then, that was thy joy,
Be barr'd his entrance here.
TITUS ANDRONICUS
Rise, Marcus, rise.
The dismall'st day is this that e'er I saw,
To be dishonour'd by my sons in Rome!
Well, bury him, and bury me the next.
[*Mutius is put into the tomb.*
LUCIUS
There lie thy bones, sweet Mutius, with thy friends,
Till we with trophies do adorn thy tomb.
ALL
[*Kneeling*] No man shed tears for noble Mutius;
He lives in fame that died in virtue's cause.
MARCUS ANDRONICUS
My lord, to step out of these dreary dumps,
How comes it that the subtle Queen of Goths
Is of a sudden thus advanced in Rome?
TITUS ANDRONICUS
I know not, Marcus; but I know it is:
Whether by device or no, the heavens can tell:
Is she not then beholding to the man
That brought her for this high good turn so far?
Yes, and will nobly him remunerate.

Flourish. Re-enter, from one side, SATURNINUS *attended,* TAMORA, DEMETRIUS, CHIRON *and* AARON; *from the other,* BASSIANUS, LAVINIA, *and others.*

SATURNINUS
So, Bassianus, you have play'd your prize:
God give you joy, sir, of your gallant bride!
BASSIANUS
And you of yours, my lord! I say no more,
Nor wish no less; and so, I take my leave.
SATURNINUS
Traitor, if Rome have law or we have power,
Thou and thy faction shall repent this rape.
BASSIANUS
Rape, call you it, my lord, to seize my own,
My truth-betrothed love and now my wife?
But let the laws of Rome determine all;
Meanwhile I am possess'd of that is mine.
SATURNINUS
'Tis good, sir: you are very short with us;
But, if we live we'll be as short with you.
BASSIANUS
My lord, what I have done, as best I may,
Answer I must and shall do with my life.
Only thus much I give your grace to know:
By all the duties that I owe to Rome,
This noble gentleman, Lord Titus here,
Is in opinion and in honour wrong'd;
That in the rescue of Lavinia
With his own hand did slay his youngest son,
In zeal to you and highly moved to wrath
To be controll'd in that he frankly gave:
Receive him, then, to favour, Saturnine,
That hath express'd himself in all his deeds
A father and a friend to thee and Rome.
TITUS ANDRONICUS
Prince Bassianus, leave to plead my deeds:
'Tis thou and those that have dishonour'd me.
Rome and the righteous heavens be my judge,
How I have loved and honour'd Saturnine!
TAMORA
My worthy lord, if ever Tamora
Were gracious in those princely eyes of thine,
Then hear me speak indifferently for all;
And at my suit, sweet, pardon what is past.
SATURNINUS
What, madam, be dishonour'd openly,
And basely put it up without revenge?
TAMORA
Not so, my lord; the gods of Rome forfend
I should be author to dishonour you!

But on mine honour dare I undertake
For good Lord Titus' innocence in all;
Whose fury not dissembled speaks his griefs:
Then, at my suit, look graciously on him;
Lose not so noble a friend on vain suppose,
Nor with sour looks afflict his gentle heart.
[*Aside to Saturninus.*] My lord, be ruled by me, be won at last;
Dissemble all your griefs and discontents:
You are but newly planted in your throne;
Lest, then, the people, and patricians too,
Upon a just survey, take Titus' part,
And so supplant you for ingratitude,
Which Rome reputes to be a heinous sin,
Yield at entreats; and then let me alone:
I'll find a day to massacre them all
And raze their faction and their family.
The cruel father and his traitorous sons,
To whom I sued for my dear son's life,
And make them know what 'tis to let a queen
Kneel in the streets and beg for grace in vain.
Come, come, sweet emperor; come, Andronicus;
Take up this good old man, and cheer the heart
That dies in tempest of thy angry frown.

SATURNINUS
Rise, Titus, rise; my empress hath prevail'd.

TITUS ANDRONICUS
I thank your majesty, and her, my lord:
These words, these looks, infuse new life in me.

TAMORA
Titus, I am incorporate in Rome,
A Roman now adopted happily,
And must advise the emperor for his good.
This day all quarrels die, Andronicus;
And let it be mine honour, good my lord,
That I have reconciled your friends and you.
For you, Prince Bassianus, I have pass'd
My word and promise to the emperor,
That you will be more mild and tractable.
And fear not, lords, and you, Lavinia;
By my advice, all humbled on your knees,
You shall ask pardon of his majesty.

LUCIUS
We do, and vow to heaven and to his highness,
That what we did was mildly as we might,
Tendering our sister's honour and our own.

MARCUS ANDRONICUS
That, on mine honour, here I do protest.

SATURNINUS
Away, and talk not; trouble us no more.

TAMORA
Nay, nay, sweet emperor, we must all be friends:
The tribune and his nephews kneel for grace;
I will not be denied: sweet heart, look back.

SATURNINUS
Marcus, for thy sake and thy brother's here,
And at my lovely Tamora's entreats,
I do remit these young men's heinous faults:
Stand up. [5]
Lavinia, though you left me like a churl,
I found a friend, and sure as death I swore
I would not part a bachelor from the priest.
Come, if the emperor's court can feast two brides,
You are my guest, Lavinia, and your friends.
This day shall be a love-day, Tamora.

TITUS ANDRONICUS
To-morrow, an it please your majesty
To hunt the panther and the hart with me,
With horn and hound we'll give your grace bonjour.

SATURNINUS
Be it so, Titus, and gramercy too. [*Flourish. Exeunt.*

ACT TWO SCENE ONE

Rome. Before the Palace.

Enter AARON.

AARON
Now climbeth Tamora Olympus' top,
Safe out of fortune's shot; and sits aloft,
Secure of thunder's crack or lightning flash;
Advanced above pale envy's threatening reach.
As when the golden sun salutes the morn,
And, having gilt the ocean with his beams,
Gallops the zodiac in his glistering coach,
And overlooks the highest-peering hills;
So Tamora:
Upon her wit doth earthly honour wait,
And virtue stoops and trembles at her frown.
Then, Aaron, arm thy heart, and fit thy thoughts,
To mount aloft with thy imperial mistress,
And mount her pitch, whom thou in triumph long
Hast prisoner held, fetter'd in amorous chains
And faster bound to Aaron's charming eyes
Than is Prometheus tied to Caucasus.
Away with slavish weeds and servile thoughts!
I will be bright, and shine in pearl and gold,
To wait upon this new-made empress.
To wait, said I? to wanton with this queen,
This goddess, this Semiramis, this nymph,
This siren, that will charm Rome's Saturnine,
And see his shipwreck and his commonweal's.
Holloa! what storm is this?

Enter DEMETRIUS *and* CHIRON, *braving.*

DEMETRIUS
Chiron, thy years want wit, thy wit wants edge,

And manners, to intrude where I am graced;
And may, for aught thou know'st, affected be.
CHIRON
Demetrius, thou dost over-ween in all;
And so in this, to bear me down with braves.
'Tis not the difference of a year or two
Makes me less gracious or thee more fortunate:
I am as able and as fit as thou
To serve, and to deserve my mistress' grace;
And that my sword upon thee shall approve,
And plead my passions for Lavinia's love.
AARON
[*Aside*] Clubs, clubs! These lovers will not keep the peace.
DEMETRIUS
Why, boy, although our mother, unadvised,
Gave you a dancing rapier by your side,
Are you so desperate grown, to threat your friends? 42
Go to; have your lath glued within your sheath
Till you know better how to handle it.
CHIRON
Meanwhile, sir, with the little skill I have,
Full well shalt thou perceive how much I dare.
DEMETRIUS
Ay, boy, grow ye so brave? [*They draw.*
AARON
[*Coming forward*] Why, how now, lords!
So near the emperor's palace dare you draw,
And maintain such a quarrel openly?
Full well I wot the ground of all this grudge:
I would not for a million of gold
The cause were known to them it most concerns; 54
Nor would your noble mother for much more
Be so dishonour'd in the court of Rome.
For shame, put up.
DEMETRIUS
Not I, till I have sheathed
My rapier in his bosom and withal
Thrust these reproachful speeches down his throat
That he hath breathed in my dishonour here.
CHIRON
For that I am prepared and full resolved.
Foul-spoken coward, that thunder'st with thy tongue,
And with thy weapon nothing darest perform!
AARON
Away, I say! 66
Now, by the gods that warlike Goths adore,
This petty brabble will undo us all.
Why, lords, and think you not how dangerous
It is to jet upon a prince's right?
What, is Lavinia then become so loose,
Or Bassianus so degenerate,
That for her love such quarrels may be broach'd
Without controlment, justice, or revenge?
Young lords, beware! and should the empress know
This discord's ground, the music would not please. 78
CHIRON
I care not, I, knew she and all the world:
I love Lavinia more than all the world.
DEMETRIUS
Youngling, learn thou to make some meaner choice:
Lavinia is thine elder brother's hope.
AARON
Why, are ye mad? or know ye not, in Rome
How furious and impatient they be,
And cannot brook competitors in love?
I tell you, lords, you do but plot your deaths
By this device.
CHIRON
Aaron, a thousand deaths
Would I propose to achieve her whom I love.
AARON
To achieve her! how?
DEMETRIUS
Why makest thou it so strange?
She is a woman, therefore may be woo'd; [6]
She is a woman, therefore may be won;
She is Lavinia, therefore must be loved.
What, man! more water glideth by the mill
Than wots the miller of; and easy it is
Of a cut loaf to steal a shive, we know:
Though Bassianus be the emperor's brother,
Better than he have worn Vulcan's badge.
AARON
[*Aside*] Ay, and as good as Saturninus may. 100
DEMETRIUS
Then why should he despair that knows to court it
With words, fair looks and liberality?
What, hast not thou full often struck a doe,
And borne her cleanly by the keeper's nose?
AARON
Why, then, it seems, some certain snatch or so
Would serve your turns.
CHIRON
Ay, so the turn were served.
DEMETRIUS
Aaron, thou hast hit it.
AARON
Would you had hit it too!
Then should not we be tired with this ado.
Why, hark ye, hark ye! and are you such fools
To square for this? would it offend you, then,
That both should speed? 113

CHIRON
Faith, not me.

DEMETRIUS
Nor me, so I were one.

AARON
For shame, be friends, and join for that you jar:
'Tis policy and stratagem must do
That you affect; and so must you resolve,
That what you cannot as you would achieve,
You must perforce accomplish as you may.
Take this of me: Lucrece was not more chaste
Than this Lavinia, Bassianus' love. 122
A speedier course than lingering languishment
Must we pursue, and I have found the path.
My lords, a solemn hunting is in hand;
There will the lovely Roman ladies troop:
The forest walks are wide and spacious;
And many unfrequented plots there are
Fitted by kind for rape and villany:
Single you thither then this dainty doe,
And strike her home by force, if not by words:
This way, or not at all, stand you in hope.
Come, come, our empress, with her sacred wit
To villany and vengeance consecrate, 134
Will we acquaint with all that we intend;
And he shall file our engines with advice,
That will not suffer you to square yourselves,
But to your wishes' height advance you both.
The emperor's court is like the house of Fame,
The palace full of tongues, of eyes, and ears:
The woods are ruthless, dreadful, deaf, and dull;
There speak, and strike, brave boys, and take your turns;
There serve your lusts, shadow'd from heaven's eye, 145
And revel in Lavinia's treasury.

CHIRON
Thy counsel, lad, smells of no cowardice,

DEMETRIUS
Sit fas aut nefas, till I find the stream
To cool this heat, a charm to calm these fits,
Per Styga, per manes vehor. [*Exeunt.*

ACT TWO SCENE TWO

A forest near Rome. Horns and cry of hounds heard.
Enter TITUS ANDRONICUS, *with* Hunters, *&c.*, MARCUS, LUCIUS, QUINTUS, *and* MARTIUS.

TITUS ANDRONICUS
The hunt is up, the morn is bright and grey,
The fields are fragrant and the woods are green:
Uncouple here and let us make a bay
And wake the emperor and his lovely bride
And rouse the prince and ring a hunter's peal,
That all the court may echo with the noise.
Sons, let it be your charge, as it is ours,
To attend the emperor's person carefully:
I have been troubled in my sleep this night,
But dawning day new comfort hath inspired.

A cry of hounds, and horns winded in a peal. Enter SATURNINUS, TAMORA, BASSIANUS, LAVINIA, DEMETRIUS, CHIRON, *and* Attendants.

Many good morrows to your majesty;
Madam, to you as many and as good:
I promised your grace a hunter's peal.

SATURNINUS
And you have rung it lustily, my lord;
Somewhat too early for new-married ladies.

BASSIANUS
Lavinia, how say you?

LAVINIA
I say, no;
I have been broad awake two hours and more.

SATURNINUS
Come on, then; horse and chariots let us have,
And to our sport. [*To Tamora*] Madam, now shall ye see
Our Roman hunting.

MARCUS ANDRONICUS
I have dogs, my lord, 24
Will rouse the proudest panther in the chase,
And climb the highest promontory top.

TITUS ANDRONICUS
And I have horse will follow where the game
Makes way, and run like swallows o'er the plain.

DEMETRIUS
Chiron, we hunt not, we, with horse nor hound,
But hope to pluck a dainty doe to ground.
[*Exeunt.*

ACT TWO SCENE THREE

A lonely part of the forest.
Enter AARON, *with a bag of gold.*

AARON
He that had wit would think that I had none,
To bury so much gold under a tree,
And never after to inherit it.
Let him that thinks of me so abjectly
Know that this gold must coin a stratagem,
Which, cunningly effected, will beget
A very excellent piece of villany:

And so repose, sweet gold, for their unrest
[*Hides the gold.*
That have their alms out of the empress' chest.

Enter TAMORA.

TAMORA
My lovely Aaron, wherefore look'st thou sad,
When every thing doth make a gleeful boast?
The birds chant melody on every bush,
The snake lies rolled in the cheerful sun,
The green leaves quiver with the cooling wind
And make a chequer'd shadow on the ground:
Under their sweet shade, Aaron, let us sit,
And, whilst the babbling echo mocks the hounds,
Replying shrilly to the well-tuned horns,
As if a double hunt were heard at once,
Let us sit down and mark their yelping noise; [7]
And, after conflict such as was supposed
The wandering prince and Dido once enjoy'd,
When with a happy storm they were surprised
And curtain'd with a counsel-keeping cave,
We may, each wreathed in the other's arms,
Our pastimes done, possess a golden slumber;
Whiles hounds and horns and sweet melodious birds
Be unto us as is a nurse's song
Of lullaby to bring her babe asleep.

AARON
Madam, though Venus govern your desires,
Saturn is dominator over mine:
What signifies my deadly-standing eye,
My silence and my cloudy melancholy,
My fleece of woolly hair that now uncurls
Even as an adder when she doth unroll
To do some fatal execution?
No, madam, these are no venereal signs:
Vengeance is in my heart, death in my hand,
Blood and revenge are hammering in my head.
Hark, Tamora, the empress of my soul,
Which never hopes more heaven than rests in thee,
This is the day of doom for Bassianus:
His Philomel must lose her tongue to-day,
Thy sons make pillage of her chastity
And wash their hands in Bassianus' blood.
Seest thou this letter? take it up, I pray thee,
And give the king this fatal-plotted scroll.
Now question me no more; we are espied;
Here comes a parcel of our hopful booty,
Which dreads not yet their lives' destruction.

TAMORA
Ah, my sweet Moor, sweeter to me than life!

AARON
No more, great empress; Bassianus comes:
Be cross with him: and I'll go fetch thy sons
To back thy quarrels, whatsoe'er they be. [*Exit.*

Enter BASSIANUS *and* LAVINIA.

BASSIANUS
Who have we here? Rome's royal empress,
Unfurnish'd of her well-beseeming troop?
Or is it Dian, habited like her,
Who hath abandoned her holy groves
To see the general hunting in this forest?

TAMORA
Saucy controller of our private steps!
Had I the power that some say Dian had,
Thy temples should be planted presently
With horns, as was Actaeon's; and the hounds
Should drive upon thy new-transformed limbs,
Unmannerly intruder as thou art!

LAVINIA
Under your patience, gentle empress,
'Tis thought you have a goodly gift in horning;
And to be doubted that your Moor and you
Are singled forth to try experiments:
Jove shield your husband from his hounds
to-day!
'Tis pity they should take him for a stag.

BASSIANUS
Believe me, queen, your swarth Cimmerian
Doth make your honour of his body's hue,
Spotted, detested, and abominable.
Why are you sequester'd from all your train,
Dismounted from your snow-white goodly steed,
And wander'd hither to an obscure plot,
Accompanied but with a barbarous Moor,
If foul desire had not conducted you?

LAVINIA
And, being intercepted in your sport,
Great reason that my noble lord be rated
For sauciness. I pray you, let us hence,
And let her joy her raven-colour'd love;
This valley fits the purpose passing well.

BASSIANUS
The king my brother shall have note of this.

LAVINIA
Ay, for these slips have made him noted long:
Good king, to be so mightily abused!

TAMORA
Why have I patience to endure all this?

Enter DEMETRIUS *and* CHIRON.

DEMETRIUS
How now, dear sovereign, and our gracious mother!
Why doth your highness look so pale and wan?

TAMORA
Have I not reason, think you, to look pale?
These two have 'ticed me hither to this place:
A barren detested vale, you see it is; [8]
The trees, though summer, yet forlorn and lean,

O'ercome with moss and baleful mistletoe:
Here never shines the sun; here nothing breeds,
Unless the nightly owl or fatal raven:
And when they show'd me this abhorred pit,
They told me, here, at dead time of the night,
A thousand fiends, a thousand hissing snakes,
Ten thousand swelling toads, as many urchins,
Would make such fearful and confused cries
As any mortal body hearing it
Should straight fall mad, or else die suddenly.
No sooner had they told this hellish tale,
But straight they told me they would bind me here
Unto the body of a dismal yew,
And leave me to this miserable death:
And then they call'd me foul adulteress,
Lascivious Goth, and all the bitterest terms
That ever ear did hear to such effect:
And, had you not by wondrous fortune come,
This vengeance on me had they executed.
Revenge it, as you love your mother's life,
Or be ye not henceforth call'd my children.

DEMETRIUS
This is a witness that I am thy son.
[*Stabs Bassianus.*

CHIRON
And this for me, struck home to show my strength.
[*Also stabs Bassianus, who dies.*

LAVINIA
Ay, come, Semiramis, nay, barbarous Tamora,
For no name fits thy nature but thy own!

TAMORA
Give me thy poniard; you shall know, my boys,
Your mother's hand shall right your mother's wrong.

DEMETRIUS
Stay, madam; here is more belongs to her;
First thrash the corn, then after burn the straw:
This minion stood upon her chastity,
Upon her nuptial vow, her loyalty,
And with that painted hope braves your mightiness: [9]
And shall she carry this unto her grave?

CHIRON
An if she do, I would I were an eunuch.
Drag hence her husband to some secret hole,
And make his dead trunk pillow to our lust.

TAMORA
But when ye have the honey ye desire,
Let not the wasp outlive, us both to sting. [10]

CHIRON
I warrant you, madam, we will make that sure.
Come, mistress, now perforce we will enjoy
That nice-preserved honesty of yours.

LAVINIA
O Tamora! thou bear'st a woman's face,—

TAMORA
I will not hear her speak; away with her!

LAVINIA
Sweet lords, entreat her hear me but a word.

DEMETRIUS
Listen, fair madam: let it be your glory
To see her tears; but be your heart to them
As unrelenting flint to drops of rain.

LAVINIA
When did the tiger's young ones teach the dam?
O, do not learn her wrath; she taught it thee;
The milk thou suck'dst from her did turn to marble;
Even at thy teat thou hadst thy tyranny.
Yet every mother breeds not sons alike:
[*To Chiron*] Do thou entreat her show a woman pity.

CHIRON
What, wouldst thou have me prove myself a bastard?

LAVINIA
'Tis true; the raven doth not hatch a lark:
Yet have I heard,—O, could I find it now!—
The lion moved with pity did endure
To have his princely paws pared all away: [11]
Some say that ravens foster forlorn children,
The whilst their own birds famish in their nests:
O, be to me, though thy hard heart say no,
Nothing so kind, but something pitiful!

TAMORA
I know not what it means; away with her!

LAVINIA
O, let me teach thee! for my father's sake,
That gave thee life, when well he might have slain thee,
Be not obdurate, open thy deaf ears.

TAMORA
Hadst thou in person ne'er offended me,
Even for his sake am I pitiless.
Remember, boys, I pour'd forth tears in vain,
To save your brother from the sacrifice;
But fierce Andronicus would not relent:
Therefore, away with her, and use her as you will,
The worse to her, the better loved of me.

LAVINIA
O Tamora, be call'd a gentle queen,
And with thine own hands kill me in this place!
For 'tis not life that I have begg'd so long;
Poor I was slain when Bassianus died.

TAMORA
What begg'st thou, then? fond woman, let me go.

LAVINIA
'Tis present death I beg; and one thing more
That womanhood denies my tongue to tell:
O, keep me from their worse than killing lust,
And tumble me into some loathsome pit,

Where never man's eye may behold my body:
Do this, and be a charitable murderer.

TAMORA
So should I rob my sweet sons of their fee:
No, let them satisfy their lust on thee.

DEMETRIUS
Away! for thou hast stay'd us here too long.

LAVINIA
No grace? no womanhood? Ah, beastly creature!
The blot and enemy to our general name!
Confusion fall—

CHIRON
Nay, then I'll stop your mouth. Bring thou her husband:
This is the hole where Aaron bid us hide him.
[*Demetrius throws the body of Bassianus into the pit; then exeunt Demetrius and Chiron, dragging off Lavinia.*

TAMORA
Farewell, my sons: see that you make her sure.
Ne'er let my heart know merry cheer indeed,
Till all the Andronici be made away.
Now will I hence to seek my lovely Moor,
And let my spleenful sons this trull deflour.
[*Exit.*

Re-enter AARON, *with* QUINTUS *and* MARTIUS.

AARON
Come on, my lords, the better foot before:
Straight will I bring you to the loathsome pit
Where I espied the panther fast asleep.

QUINTUS
My sight is very dull, whate'er it bodes.

MARTIUS
And mine, I promise you; were't not for shame,
Well could I leave our sport to sleep awhile.
[*Falls into the pit.*

QUINTUS
What, art thou fall'n? What subtle hole is this,
Whose mouth is cover'd with rude-growing briers,
Upon whose leaves are drops of new-shed blood
As fresh as morning dew distill'd on flowers?
A very fatal place it seems to me.
Speak, brother, hast thou hurt thee with the fall?

MARTIUS
O, brother, with the dismall'st object hurt
That ever eye with sight made heart lament!

AARON
[*Aside*] Now will I fetch the king to find them here,
That he thereby may give a likely guess
How these were they that made away his brother.
[*Exit.*

MARTIUS
Why dost not comfort me, and help me out
From this unhallowed and blood-stained hole?

QUINTUS
I am surprised with an uncouth fear:
A chilling sweat o'er-runs my trembling joints:
My heart suspects more than mine eye can see.

MARTIUS
To prove thou hast a true-divining heart,
Aaron and thou look down into this den,
And see a fearful sight of blood and death.

QUINTUS
Aaron is gone, and my compassionate heart
Will not permit mine eyes once to behold
The thing whereat it trembles by surmise:
O, tell me how it is; for ne'er till now
Was I a child to fear I know not what.

MARTIUS
Lord Bassianus lies embrewed here,
All on a heap, like to a slaughter'd lamb,
In this detested, dark, blood-drinking pit.

QUINTUS
If it be dark, how dost thou know 'tis he?

MARTIUS
Upon his bloody finger he doth wear
A precious ring, that lightens all the hole,
Which, like a taper in some monument,
Doth shine upon the dead man's earthy cheeks,
And shows the ragged entrails of the pit:
So pale did shine the moon on Pyramus
When he by night lay bathed in maiden blood.
O brother, help me with thy fainting hand—
If fear hath made thee faint, as me it hath—
Out of this fell devouring receptacle,
As hateful as Cocytus' misty mouth.

QUINTUS
Reach me thy hand, that I may help thee out;
Or, wanting strength to do thee so much good,
I may be pluck'd into the swallowing womb
Of this deep pit, poor Bassianus' grave.
I have no strength to pluck thee to the brink.

MARTIUS
Nor I no strength to climb without thy help.

QUINTUS
Thy hand once more; I will not loose again,
Till thou art here aloft, or I below:
Thou canst not come to me: I come to thee.
[*Falls in.*

Enter SATURNINUS *with* AARON.

SATURNINUS
Along with me: I'll see what hole is here,
And what he is that now is leap'd into it.

Say, who art thou that lately didst descend
Into this gaping hollow of the earth?

MARTIUS

The unhappy son of old Andronicus;
Brought hither in a most unlucky hour,
To find thy brother Bassianus dead.

SATURNINUS

My brother dead! I know thou dost but jest:
He and his lady both are at the lodge
Upon the north side of this pleasant chase;
'Tis not an hour since I left him there.

MARTIUS

We know not where you left him all alive;
But, out, alas! here have we found him dead.

Re-enter TAMORA, *with* Attendants; TITUS ANDRONICUS, *and* LUCIUS.

TAMORA

Where is my lord the king?

SATURNINUS

Here, Tamora, though grieved with killing grief.

TAMORA

Where is thy brother Bassianus?

SATURNINUS

Now to the bottom dost thou search my wound:
Poor Bassianus here lies murdered.

TAMORA

Then all too late I bring this fatal writ,
The complot of this timeless tragedy;
And wonder greatly that man's face can fold
In pleasing smiles such murderous tyranny.
[*She giveth Saturnine a letter.*

SATURNINUS

[*Reads*] 'An if we miss to meet him handsomely—
Sweet huntsman, Bassianus 'tis we mean—
Do thou so much as dig the grave for him:
Thou know'st our meaning. Look for thy reward
Among the nettles at the elder-tree
Which overshades the mouth of that same pit
Where we decreed to bury Bassianus.
Do this, and purchase us thy lasting friends.'
O Tamora! was ever heard the like?
This is the pit, and this the elder-tree.
Look, sirs, if you can find the huntsman out
That should have murder'd Bassianus here.

AARON

My gracious lord, here is the bag of gold.

SATURNINUS

[*To Titus*] Two of thy whelps, fell curs of bloody kind,
Have here bereft my brother of his life.
Sirs, drag them from the pit unto the prison:
There let them bide until we have devised
Some never-heard-of torturing pain for them.

TAMORA

What, are they in this pit? O wondrous thing!
How easily murder is discovered!

TITUS ANDRONICUS

High emperor, upon my feeble knee
I beg this boon, with tears not lightly shed,
That this fell fault of my accursed sons,
Accursed, if the fault be proved in them,—

SATURNINUS

If it be proved! you see it is apparent.
Who found this letter? Tamora, was it you?

TAMORA

Andronicus himself did take it up.

TITUS ANDRONICUS

I did, my lord: yet let me be their bail;
For, by my father's reverend tomb, I vow
They shall be ready at your highness' will
To answer their suspicion with their lives.

SATURNINUS

Thou shalt not bail them: see thou follow me.
Some bring the murder'd body, some the murderers:
Let them not speak a word; the guilt is plain;
For, by my soul, were there worse end than death,
That end upon them should be executed.

TAMORA

Andronicus, I will entreat the king:
Fear not, thy sons; they shall do well enough.

TITUS ANDRONICUS

Come, Lucius, come; stay not to talk with them.
[*Exeunt.*

ACT TWO SCENE FOUR

Another part of the forest.

Enter DEMETRIUS *and* CHIRON *with* LAVINIA, *ravished; her hands cut off, and her tongue cut out.*

DEMETRIUS

So, now go tell, an if thy tongue can speak,
Who 'twas that cut thy tongue and ravish'd thee.

CHIRON

Write down thy mind, bewray thy meaning so,
An if thy stumps will let thee play the scribe.

DEMETRIUS

See, how with signs and tokens she can scrowl. [12]

CHIRON

Go home, call for sweet water, wash thy hands.

DEMETRIUS

She hath no tongue to call, nor hands to wash;
And so let's leave her to her silent walks.

CHIRON
An 'twere my case, I should go hang myself. [13]
DEMETRIUS
If thou hadst hands to help thee knit the cord.
[Exeunt Demetrius and Chiron.

Enter MARCUS.

MARCUS
Who is this? my niece, that flies away so fast!
Cousin, a word; where is your husband?
If I do dream, would all my wealth would wake me!
If I do wake, some planet strike me down,
That I may slumber in eternal sleep!
Speak, gentle niece, what stern ungentle hands
Have lopp'd and hew'd and made thy body bare
Of her two branches, those sweet ornaments,
Whose circling shadows kings have sought to sleep in,
And might not gain so great a happiness
As have thy love? Why dost not speak to me?
Alas, a crimson river of warm blood,
Like to a bubbling fountain stirr'd with wind,
Doth rise and fall between thy rosed lips,
Coming and going with thy honey breath.
But, sure, some Tereus hath deflowered thee,
And, lest thou shouldst detect him, cut thy tongue.
Ah, now thou turn'st away thy face for shame!
And, notwithstanding all this loss of blood,
As from a conduit with three issuing spouts,
Yet do thy cheeks look red as Titan's face
Blushing to be encounter'd with a cloud.
Shall I speak for thee? shall I say 'tis so?
O, that I knew thy heart; and knew the beast,
That I might rail at him, to ease my mind!
Sorrow concealed, like an oven stopp'd,
Doth burn the heart to cinders where it is.
Fair Philomela, she but lost her tongue,
And in a tedious sampler sew'd her mind:
But, lovely niece, that mean is cut from thee;
A craftier Tereus, cousin, hast thou met,
And he hath cut those pretty fingers off,
That could have better sew'd than Philomel.
O, had the monster seen those lily hands
Tremble, like aspen-leaves, upon a lute,
And make the silken strings delight to kiss them,
He would not then have touch'd them for his life!
Or, had he heard the heavenly harmony
Which that sweet tongue hath made, [14]
He would have dropp'd his knife, and fell asleep
As Cerberus at the Thracian poet's feet.
Come, let us go, and make thy father blind;
For such a sight will blind a father's eye:
One hour's storm will drown the fragrant meads;
What will whole months of tears thy father's eyes?
Do not draw back, for we will mourn with thee:
O, could our mourning ease thy misery! *[Exeunt.*

ACT THREE SCENE ONE

Rome. A street.

Enter Judges, Senators *and* Tribunes, *with* MARTIUS *and* QUINTUS , *bound, passing on to the place of execution*; TITUS *going before, pleading.*

TITUS ANDRONICUS
Hear me, grave fathers! noble tribunes, stay!
For pity of mine age, whose youth was spent
In dangerous wars, whilst you securely slept;
For all my blood in Rome's great quarrel shed;
For all the frosty nights that I have watch'd;
And for these bitter tears, which now you see
Filling the aged wrinkles in my cheeks;
Be pitiful to my condemned sons,
Whose souls are not corrupted as 'tis thought.
For two and twenty sons I never wept,
Because they died in honour's lofty bed.
[Lieth down; the Judges, &c., pass by him, and Exeunt.
For these, these, tribunes, in the dust I write [15]
My heart's deep languor and my soul's sad tears:
Let my tears staunch the earth's dry appetite;
My sons' sweet blood will make it shame and blush.
O earth, I will befriend thee more with rain,
That shall distil from these two ancient urns, [16]
Than youthful April shall with all his showers:
In summer's drought I'll drop upon thee still;
In winter with warm tears I'll melt the snow,
And keep eternal spring-time on thy face,
So thou refuse to drink my dear sons' blood.

Enter LUCIUS, *with his sword drawn.*

O reverend tribunes! O gentle, aged men!
Unbind my sons, reverse the doom of death;
And let me say, that never wept before,
My tears are now prevailing orators.
LUCIUS
O noble father, you lament in vain:
The tribunes hear you not; no man is by;
And you recount your sorrows to a stone.
TITUS ANDRONICUS
Ah, Lucius, for thy brothers let me plead.
Grave tribunes, once more I entreat of you,—
LUCIUS
My gracious lord, no tribune hears you speak.
TITUS ANDRONICUS
Why, 'tis no matter, man; if they did hear,
They would not mark me, or if they did mark, [17]

They would not pity me, yet plead I must;
And bootless unto them.
Therefore I tell my sorrows to the stones;
Who, though they cannot answer my distress,
Yet in some sort they are better than the tribunes,
For that they will not intercept my tale: 40
When I do weep, they humbly at my feet
Receive my tears and seem to weep with me;
And, were they but attired in grave weeds,
Rome could afford no tribune like to these.
A stone is soft as wax,—tribunes more hard than stones;
A stone is silent, and offendeth not,
And tribunes with their tongues doom men to death. [*Rises.*
But wherefore stand'st thou with thy weapon drawn?

LUCIUS
To rescue my two brothers from their death:
For which attempt the judges have pronounced
My everlasting doom of banishment. 54

TITUS ANDRONICUS
O happy man! they have befriended thee.
Why, foolish Lucius, dost thou not perceive
That Rome is but a wilderness of tigers?
Tigers must prey, and Rome affords no prey
But me and mine: how happy art thou, then,
From these devourers to be banished!
But who comes with our brother Marcus here?

Enter MARCUS *and* LAVINIA.

MARCUS ANDRONICUS
Titus, prepare thy aged eyes to weep
Or, if not so, thy noble heart to break: 63
I bring consuming sorrow to thine age.

TITUS ANDRONICUS
Will it consume me? let me see it, then.

MARCUS ANDRONICUS
This was thy daughter.

TITUS ANDRONICUS
Why, Marcus, so she is.

LUCIUS
Ay me, this object kills me!

TITUS ANDRONICUS
Faint-hearted boy, arise, and look upon her.
Speak, Lavinia, what accursed hand
Hath made thee handless in thy father's sight? [18]
What fool hath added water to the sea,
Or brought a faggot to bright-burning Troy?
My grief was at the height before thou camest,
And now, like Nilus, it disdaineth bounds. 75
Give me a sword, I'll chop off my hands too;
For they have fought for Rome, and all in vain;
And they have nursed this woe, in feeding life;
In bootless prayer have they been held up,
And they have served me to effectless use:
Now all the service I require of them
Is that the one will help to cut the other.
'Tis well, Lavinia, that thou hast no hands;
For hands, to do Rome service, are but vain. 84

LUCIUS
Speak, gentle sister, who hath martyr'd thee?

MARCUS ANDRONICUS
O, that delightful engine of her thoughts,
That blabb'd them with such pleasing eloquence,
Is torn from forth that pretty hollow cage,
Where, like a sweet melodious bird, it sung
Sweet varied notes, enchanting every ear! [19]

LUCIUS
O, say thou for her, who hath done this deed?

MARCUS ANDRONICUS
O, thus I found her, straying in the park,
Seeking to hide herself, as doth the deer
That hath received some unrecuring wound. 94

TITUS ANDRONICUS
It was my deer; and he that wounded her
Hath hurt me more than had he kill'd me dead:
For now I stand as one upon a rock
Environ'd with a wilderness of sea,
Who marks the waxing tide grow wave by wave,
Expecting ever when some envious surge
Will in his brinish bowels swallow him.
This way to death my wretched sons are gone;
Here stands my other son, a banish'd man,
And here my brother, weeping at my woes: 104
But that which gives my soul the greatest spurn,
Is dear Lavinia, dearer than my soul.
Had I but seen thy picture in this plight,
It would have madded me: what shall I do
Now I behold thy lively body so?
Thou hast no hands, to wipe away thy tears,
Nor tongue, to tell me who hath martyr'd thee:
Thy husband he is dead; and for his death
Thy brothers are condemn'd, and dead by this.
Look, Marcus! ah, son Lucius, look on her! 114
When I did name her brothers, then fresh tears
Stood on her cheeks, as doth the honey-dew
Upon a gather'd lily almost wither'd.

MARCUS ANDRONICUS
Perchance she weeps because they kill'd her husband;
Perchance because she knows them innocent.

TITUS ANDRONICUS
If they did kill thy husband, then be joyful,
Because the law hath ta'en revenge on them.
No, no, they would not do so foul a deed;
Witness the sorrow that their sister makes.
Gentle Lavinia, let me kiss thy lips; 125

Or make some sign how I may do thee ease:
Shall thy good uncle, and thy brother Lucius,
And thou, and I, sit round about some fountain,
Looking all downwards, to behold our cheeks
How they are stain'd as meadows, yet not dry, [20]
With miry slime left on them by a flood?
And in the fountain shall we gaze so long
Till the fresh taste be taken from that clearness,
And made a brine-pit with our bitter tears?
Or shall we cut away our hands, like thine?
Or shall we bite our tongues, and in dumb shows
Pass the remainder of our hateful days?
What shall we do? let us, that have our tongues,
Plot some device of further misery,
To make us wonder'd at in time to come.

LUCIUS
Sweet father, cease your tears; for, at your grief,
See how my wretched sister sobs and weeps.

MARCUS ANDRONICUS
Patience, dear niece. Good Titus, dry thine eyes.

TITUS ANDRONICUS
Ah, Marcus, Marcus! brother, well I wot
Thy napkin cannot drink a tear of mine,
For thou, poor man, hast drown'd it with thine own.

LUCIUS
Ah, my Lavinia, I will wipe thy cheeks.

TITUS ANDRONICUS
Mark, Marcus, mark! I understand her signs:
Had she a tongue to speak, now would she say
That to her brother which I said to thee:
His napkin, with his true tears all bewet,
Can do no service on her sorrowful cheeks.
O, what a sympathy of woe is this,
As far from help as Limbo is from bliss!

Enter AARON.

AARON
Titus Andronicus, my lord the emperor
Sends thee this word,—that, if thou love thy sons,
Let Marcus, Lucius, or thyself, old Titus,
Or any one of you, chop off your hand,
And send it to the king: he for the same
Will send thee hither both thy sons alive;
And that shall be the ransom for their fault.

TITUS ANDRONICUS
O gracious emperor! O gentle Aaron!
Did ever raven sing so like a lark,
That gives sweet tidings of the sun's uprise?
With all my heart, I'll send the emperor
My hand:
Good Aaron, wilt thou help to chop it off?

LUCIUS
Stay, father! for that noble hand of thine,
That hath thrown down so many enemies,
Shall not be sent: my hand will serve the turn:
My youth can better spare my blood than you:
And therefore mine shall save my brothers' lives.

MARCUS ANDRONICUS
Which of your hands hath not defended Rome,
And rear'd aloft the bloody battle-axe,
Writing destruction on the enemy's castle?
O, none of both but are of high desert:
My hand hath been but idle; let it serve
To ransom my two nephews from their death;
Then have I kept it to a worthy end.

AARON
Nay, come, agree whose hand shall go along,
For fear they die before their pardon come.

MARCUS ANDRONICUS
My hand shall go.

LUCIUS
By heaven, it shall not go!

TITUS ANDRONICUS
Sirs, strive no more: such wither'd herbs as these
Are meet for plucking up, and therefore mine.

LUCIUS
Sweet father, if I shall be thought thy son,
Let me redeem my brothers both from death.

MARCUS ANDRONICUS
And, for our father's sake and mother's care,
Now let me show a brother's love to thee.

TITUS ANDRONICUS
Agree between you; I will spare my hand.

LUCIUS
Then I'll go fetch an axe.

MARCUS ANDRONICUS
But I will use the axe. [*Exeunt Lucius and Marcus.*

TITUS ANDRONICUS
Come hither, Aaron; I'll deceive them both:
Lend me thy hand, and I will give thee mine.

AARON
[*Aside*] If that be call'd deceit, I will be honest,
And never, whilst I live, deceive men so:
But I'll deceive you in another sort,
And that you'll say, ere half an hour pass.
[*Cuts off Titus' hand.*

Re-enter LUCIUS *and* MARCUS.

TITUS ANDRONICUS
Now stay your strife: what shall be is dispatch'd.
Good Aaron, give his majesty my hand:
Tell him it was a hand that warded him
From thousand dangers; bid him bury it
More hath it merited; that let it have.
As for my sons, say I account of them
As jewels purchased at an easy price;
And yet dear too, because I bought mine own.

AARON
I go, Andronicus: and for thy hand
Look by and by to have thy sons with thee.
[*Aside*] Their heads, I mean. O, how this villany
Doth fat me with the very thoughts of it!
Let fools do good, and fair men call for grace.
Aaron will have his soul black like his face. [*Exit.*

TITUS ANDRONICUS
O, here I lift this one hand up to heaven,
And bow this feeble ruin to the earth:
If any power pities wretched tears,
To that I call! [*To Lavinia*] What, wilt thou kneel with me? [21]
Do, then, dear heart; for heaven shall hear our prayers;
Or with our sighs we'll breathe the welkin dim,
And stain the sun with fog, as sometime clouds
When they do hug him in their melting bosoms.

MARCUS ANDRONICUS
O brother, speak with possibilities,
And do not break into these deep extremes.

TITUS ANDRONICUS
Is not my sorrow deep, having no bottom?
Then be my passions bottomless with them.

MARCUS ANDRONICUS
But yet let reason govern thy lament.

TITUS ANDRONICUS
If there were reason for these miseries,
Then into limits could I bind my woes:
When heaven doth weep, doth not the earth o'erflow?
If the winds rage, doth not the sea wax mad,
Threatening the welkin with his big-swoln face?
And wilt thou have a reason for this coil?
I am the sea; hark, how her sighs do blow! [22]
She is the weeping welkin, I the earth:
Then must my sea be moved with her sighs;
Then must my earth with her continual tears
Become a deluge, overflow'd and drown'd
For why my bowels cannot hide her woes,
But like a drunkard must I vomit them.
Then give me leave, for losers will have leave
To ease their stomachs with their bitter tongues.

Enter a Messenger, *with two heads and a hand.*

MESSENGER
Worthy Andronicus, ill art thou repaid
For that good hand thou sent'st the emperor.
Here are the heads of thy two noble sons;
And here's thy hand, in scorn to thee sent back;
Thy griefs their sports, thy resolution mock'd;
That woe is me to think upon thy woes
More than remembrance of my father's death.
[*Exit.*

MARCUS ANDRONICUS
Now let hot Aetna cool in Sicily,
And be my heart an ever-burning hell!
These miseries are more than may be borne.
To weep with them that weep doth ease some deal;
But sorrow flouted at is double death.

LUCIUS
Ah, that this sight should make so deep a wound,
And yet detested life not shrink thereat!
That ever death should let life bear his name,
Where life hath no more interest but to breathe!
[*Lavinia kisses Titus.*

MARCUS ANDRONICUS
Alas, poor heart, that kiss is comfortless
As frozen water to a starved snake.

TITUS ANDRONICUS
When will this fearful slumber have an end?

MARCUS ANDRONICUS
Now, farewell, flattery: die, Andronicus;
Thou dost not slumber: see, thy two sons' heads,
Thy warlike hand, thy mangled daughter here;
Thy other banish'd son, with this dear sight
Struck pale and bloodless; and thy brother, I,
Even like a stony image, cold and numb.
Ah, now no more will I control thy griefs:
Rend off thy silver hair, thy other hand
Gnawing with thy teeth; and be this dismal sight
The closing up of our most wretched eyes:
Now is a time to storm; why art thou still?

TITUS ANDRONICUS
Ha, ha, ha!

MARCUS ANDRONICUS
Why dost thou laugh? it fits not with this hour.

TITUS ANDRONICUS
Why, I have not another tear to shed:
Besides, this sorrow is an enemy,
And would usurp upon my watery eyes
And make them blind with tributary tears:
Then which way shall I find Revenge's cave?
For these two heads do seem to speak to me,
And threat me I shall never come to bliss
Till all these mischiefs be return'd again
Even in their throats that have committed them.
Come, let me see what task I have to do.
You heavy people, circle me about,
That I may turn me to each one of you,
And swear unto my soul to right your wrongs.
The vow is made. Come, brother, take a head;
And in this hand the other I will bear.
Lavinia, thou shalt be employ'd: these arms! [23]
Bear thou my hand, sweet wench, between thy teeth.

As for thee, boy, go get thee from my sight;
Thou art an exile, and thou must not stay:
Hie to the Goths, and raise an army there:
And, if you love me, as I think you do,
Let's kiss and part, for we have much to do.
[Exeunt Titus, Marcus, and Lavinia.

LUCIUS
Farewell, Andronicus, my noble father,
The wofull'st man that ever lived in Rome:
Farewell, proud Rome; till Lucius come again,
He leaves his pledges dearer than his life: [24]
Farewell, Lavinia, my noble sister;
O, would thou wert as thou tofore hast been!
But now nor Lucius nor Lavinia lives
But in oblivion and hateful griefs.
If Lucius live, he will requite your wrongs;
And make proud Saturnine and his empress
Beg at the gates, like Tarquin and his queen.
Now will I to the Goths, and raise a power,
To be revenged on Rome and Saturnine. *[Exit.*

ACT THREE SCENE TWO

A room in Titus' house. A banquet set out. [25]

Enter TITUS, MARCUS, LAVINIA *and young* LUCIUS, *a Boy.*

TITUS ANDRONICUS
So, so; now sit: and look you eat no more
Than will preserve just so much strength in us
As will revenge these bitter woes of ours.
Marcus, unknit that sorrow-wreathen knot:
Thy niece and I, poor creatures, want our hands,
And cannot passionate our tenfold grief
With folded arms. This poor right hand of mine
Is left to tyrannize upon my breast;
Who, when my heart, all mad with misery,
Beats in this hollow prison of my flesh,
Then thus I thump it down.
[*To Lavinia*] Thou map of woe, that thus dost talk in signs!
When thy poor heart heats with outrageous beating, [26]
Thou canst not strike it thus to make it still.
Wound it with sighing, girl, kill it with groans;
Or get some little knife between thy teeth,
And just against thy heart make thou a hole;
That all the tears that thy poor eyes let fall
May run into that sink, and soaking in
Drown the lamenting fool in sea-salt tears.

MARCUS ANDRONICUS
Fie, brother, fie! teach her not thus to lay
Such violent hands upon her tender life.

TITUS ANDRONICUS
How now! has sorrow made thee dote already?
Why, Marcus, no man should be mad but I.
What violent hands can she lay on her life?
Ah, wherefore dost thou urge the name of hands;
To bid Aeneas tell the tale twice o'er,
How Troy was burnt and he made miserable?
O, handle not the theme, to talk of hands,
Lest we remember still that we have none.
Fie, fie, how franticly I square my talk,
As if we should forget we had no hands,
If Marcus did not name the word of hands!
Come, let's fall to; and, gentle girl, eat this:
Here is no drink! Hark, Marcus, what she says;
I can interpret all her martyr'd signs;
She says she drinks no other drink but tears,
Brew'd with her sorrow, mesh'd upon her cheeks:
Speechless complainer, I will learn thy thought;
In thy dumb action will I be as perfect
As begging hermits in their holy prayers:
Thou shalt not sigh, nor hold thy stumps to heaven,
Nor wink, nor nod, nor kneel, nor make a sign,
But I of these will wrest an alphabet
And by still practice learn to know thy meaning.

BOY
Good grandsire, leave these bitter deep laments:
Make my aunt merry with some pleasing tale.

MARCUS ANDRONICUS
Alas, the tender boy, in passion moved,
Doth weep to see his grandsire's heaviness.

TITUS ANDRONICUS
Peace, tender sapling; thou art made of tears,
And tears will quickly melt thy life away.
[Marcus strikes the dish with a knife.
What dost thou strike at, Marcus, with thy knife?

MARCUS ANDRONICUS
At that that I have kill'd, my lord; a fly.

TITUS ANDRONICUS
Out on thee, murderer! thou kill'st my heart;
Mine eyes are cloy'd with view of tyranny:
A deed of death done on the innocent
Becomes not Titus' brother: get thee gone:
I see thou art not for my company.

MARCUS ANDRONICUS
Alas, my lord, I have but kill'd a fly.

TITUS ANDRONICUS
But how, if that fly had a father and mother?
How would he hang his slender gilded wings,
And buzz lamenting doings in the air!
Poor harmless fly,
That, with his pretty buzzing melody,
Came here to make us merry! and thou hast kill'd him.

MARCUS ANDRONICUS
Pardon me, sir; it was a black ill-favour'd fly,
Like to the empress' Moor; therefore I kill'd him.
TITUS ANDRONICUS
O, O, O,
Then pardon me for reprehending thee,
For thou hast done a charitable deed.
Give me thy knife, I will insult on him;
Flattering myself, as if it were the Moor
Come hither purposely to poison me.—
There's for thyself, and that's for Tamora.
Ah, sirrah!
Yet, I think, we are not brought so low,
But that between us we can kill a fly
That comes in likeness of a coal-black Moor.
MARCUS ANDRONICUS
Alas, poor man! grief has so wrought on him,
He takes false shadows for true substances.
TITUS ANDRONICUS
Come, take away. Lavinia, go with me:
I'll to thy closet; and go read with thee
Sad stories chanced in the times of old.
Come, boy, and go with me: thy sight is young,
And thou shalt read when mine begin to dazzle.
[*Exeunt.*

ACT FOUR SCENE ONE

Rome. Titus's garden.

Enter young LUCIUS , *and* LAVINIA *running after him, and the boy flies from her, with books under his arm. Then enter* TITUS *and* MARCUS.

YOUNG LUCIUS
Help, grandsire, help! my aunt Lavinia
Follows me every where, I know not why:
Good uncle Marcus, see how swift she comes.
Alas, sweet aunt, I know not what you mean.
MARCUS ANDRONICUS
Stand by me, Lucius; do not fear thine aunt.
TITUS ANDRONICUS
She loves thee, boy, too well to do thee harm.

YOUNG LUCIUS
Ay, when my father was in Rome she did.
MARCUS ANDRONICUS
What means my niece Lavinia by these signs?
TITUS ANDRONICUS
Fear her not, Lucius: somewhat doth she mean:
See, Lucius, see how much she makes of thee:
Somewhither would she have thee go with her.
Ah, boy, Cornelia never with more care
Read to her sons than she hath read to thee
Sweet poetry and Tully's Orator.
MARCUS ANDRONICUS
Canst thou not guess wherefore she plies thee thus?
YOUNG LUCIUS
My lord, I know not, I, nor can I guess,
Unless some fit or frenzy do possess her:
For I have heard my grandsire say full oft,
Extremity of griefs would make men mad;
And I have read that Hecuba of Troy
Ran mad sorrow: that made me to fear;
Although, my lord, I know my noble aunt
Loves me as dear as e'er my mother did,
And would not, but in fury, fright my youth:
Which made me down to throw my books, and fly—
Causeless, perhaps. But pardon me, sweet aunt:
And, madam, if my uncle Marcus go,
I will most willingly attend your ladyship.
MARCUS ANDRONICUS
Lucius, I will.
[Lavinia turns over with her stumps the books which Lucius has let fall.
TITUS ANDRONICUS
How now, Lavinia! Marcus, what means this?
Some book there is that she desires to see.
Which is it, girl, of these? Open them, boy.
But thou art deeper read, and better skill'd:
Come, and take choice of all my library,
And so beguile thy sorrow, till the heavens
Reveal the damn'd contriver of this deed.
Why lifts she up her arms in sequence thus?
MARCUS ANDRONICUS
I think she means that there was more than one
Confederate in the fact: ay, more there was;
Or else to heaven she heaves them for revenge.
TITUS ANDRONICUS
Lucius, what book is that she tosseth so?
YOUNG LUCIUS
Grandsire, 'tis Ovid's Metamorphoses;
My mother gave it me.
MARCUS ANDRONICUS
For love of her that's gone,
Perhaps she cull'd it from among the rest.
TITUS ANDRONICUS
Soft! see how busily she turns the leaves! [28]
[Helping her.
What would she find? Lavinia, shall I read?
This is the tragic tale of Philomel,
And treats of Tereus' treason and his rape;
And rape, I fear, was root of thine annoy.
MARCUS ANDRONICUS
See, brother, see; note how she quotes the leaves.
TITUS ANDRONICUS
Lavinia, wert thou thus surprised, sweet girl,
Ravish'd and wrong'd, as Philomela was,
Forced in the ruthless, vast, and gloomy woods?
See, see!
Ay, such a place there is, where we did hunt—
O, had we never hunted there!—
Pattern'd by that the poet here describes,
By nature made for murders and for rapes.
MARCUS ANDRONICUS
O, why should nature build so foul a den,
Unless the gods delight in tragedies?
TITUS ANDRONICUS
Give signs, sweet girl, for here are none but friends,
What Roman lord it was durst do the deed:
Or slunk not Saturnine, as Tarquin erst,
That left the camp to sin in Lucrece' bed?
MARCUS ANDRONICUS
Sit down, sweet niece: brother, sit down by me.
Apollo, Pallas, Jove, or Mercury,
Inspire me, that I may this treason find!
My lord, look here: look here, Lavinia:
This sandy plot is plain; guide, if thou canst,
This after me, when I have writ my name
Without the help of any hand at all.
[He writes his name with his staff, and guides it with feet and mouth.
Cursed be that heart that forced us to this shift!
Write thou, good niece; and here display, at last,
What God will have discover'd for revenge:
Heaven guide thy pen to print thy sorrows plain,
That we may know the traitors and the truth!
[She takes the staff in her mouth, and guides it with her stumps, and writes.
TITUS ANDRONICUS
O, do ye read, my lord, what she hath writ?
'Stuprum. Chiron. Demetrius.'
MARCUS ANDRONICUS
What, what! the lustful sons of Tamora
Performers of this heinous, bloody deed?
TITUS ANDRONICUS
Magni Dominator poli, [29]
Tam lentus audis scelera? tam lentus vides?

MARCUS ANDRONICUS
O, calm thee, gentle lord; although I know
There is enough written upon this earth
To stir a mutiny in the mildest thoughts
And arm the minds of infants to exclaims.
My lord, kneel down with me; Lavinia, kneel;
And kneel, sweet boy, the Roman Hector's hope;
And swear with me, as, with the woful fere
And father of that chaste dishonour'd dame,
Lord Junius Brutus sware for Lucrece' rape,
That we will prosecute by good advice
Mortal revenge upon these traitorous Goths,
And see their blood, or die with this reproach.

TITUS ANDRONICUS
'Tis sure enough, an you knew how.
But if you hunt these bear-whelps, then beware:
The dam will wake; and, if she wind you once,
She's with the lion deeply still in league,
And lulls him whilst she playeth on her back,
And when he sleeps will she do what she list.
You are a young huntsman, Marcus; let it alone;
And, come, I will go get a leaf of brass,
And with a gad of steel will write these words,
And lay it by: the angry northern wind
Will blow these sands, like Sibyl's leaves, abroad,
And where's your lesson, then? Boy, what say you?

YOUNG LUCIUS
I say, my lord, that if I were a man,
Their mother's bed-chamber should not be safe
For these bad bondmen to the yoke of Rome.

MARCUS ANDRONICUS
Ay, that's my boy! thy father hath full oft
For his ungrateful country done the like.

YOUNG LUCIUS
And, uncle, so will I, an if I live.

TITUS ANDRONICUS
Come, go with me into mine armoury;
Lucius, I'll fit thee; and withal, my boy,
Shalt carry from me to the empress' sons
Presents that I intend to send them both:
Come, come; thou'lt do thy message, wilt thou not?

YOUNG LUCIUS
Ay, with my dagger in their bosoms, grandsire.

TITUS ANDRONICUS
No, boy, not so; I'll teach thee another course.
Lavinia, come. Marcus, look to my house:
Lucius and I'll go brave it at the court;
Ay, marry, will we, sir; and we'll be waited on.
[*Exeunt Titus, Lavinia, and Young Lucius.*

MARCUS ANDRONICUS
O heavens, can you hear a good man groan,
And not relent, or not compassion him?
Marcus, attend him in his ecstasy,
That hath more scars of sorrow in his heart
Than foemen's marks upon his batter'd shield;
But yet so just that he will not revenge.
Revenge, ye heavens, for old Andronicus! [30]
[*Exit.*

ACT FOUR SCENE TWO

The same. A room in the palace.

Enter, from one side, AARON, DEMETRIUS, *and* CHIRON; *from the other side, young* LUCIUS, *and an* Attendant, *with a bundle of weapons, and verses writ upon them.*

CHIRON
Demetrius, here's the son of Lucius;
He hath some message to deliver us.

AARON
Ay, some mad message from his mad grandfather.

YOUNG LUCIUS
My lords, with all the humbleness I may,
I greet your honours from Andronicus.
[*Aside*] And pray the Roman gods confound you both!

DEMETRIUS
Gramercy, lovely Lucius: what's the news?

YOUNG LUCIUS
[*Aside*] That you are both decipher'd, that's the news,
For villains mark'd with rape.—May it please you,
My grandsire, well advised, hath sent by me
The goodliest weapons of his armoury
To gratify your honourable youth,
The hope of Rome; for so he bade me say;
And so I do, and with his gifts present
Your lordships, that, whenever you have need,
You may be armed and appointed well:
And so I leave you both: [*Aside*] like bloody villains.
[*Exeunt Young Lucius and Attendant.*

DEMETRIUS
What's here? A scroll; and written round about?
Let's see:
[Reads] 'Integer vitae, scelerisque purus, [31]
Non eget Mauri jaculis, nec arcu.'

CHIRON
O, 'tis a verse in Horace; I know it well:
I read it in the grammar long ago.

AARON
Ay, just; a verse in Horace; right, you have it.
[*Aside*] Now, what a thing it is to be an ass!
Here's no sound jest! the old man hath found their guilt; [32]
And sends them weapons wrapp'd about with lines,
That wound, beyond their feeling, to the quick.

But were our witty empress well afoot,
She would applaud Andronicus' conceit: 32
But let her rest in her unrest awhile.
And now, young lords, was't not a happy star
Led us to Rome, strangers, and more than so,
Captives, to be advanced to this height?
It did me good, before the palace gate
To brave the tribune in his brother's hearing.

DEMETRIUS
But me more good, to see so great a lord
Basely insinuate and send us gifts.

AARON
Had he not reason, Lord Demetrius?
Did you not use his daughter very friendly? 42

DEMETRIUS
I would we had a thousand Roman dames
At such a bay, by turn to serve our lust.

CHIRON
A charitable wish and full of love.

AARON
Here lacks but your mother for to say amen.

CHIRON
And that would she for twenty thousand more.

DEMETRIUS
Come, let us go; and pray to all the gods
For our beloved mother in her pains.

AARON
[*Aside*] Pray to the devils; the gods have given us over. [*Trumpets sound within.*

DEMETRIUS
Why do the emperor's trumpets flourish thus?

CHIRON
Belike, for joy the emperor hath a son.

DEMETRIUS
Soft! who comes here?

Enter a Nurse, *with a blackamoor* Child *in her arms.*

NURSE
Good morrow, lords:
O, tell me, did you see Aaron the Moor?

AARON
Well, more or less, or ne'er a whit at all,
Here Aaron is; and what with Aaron now?

NURSE
O gentle Aaron, we are all undone!
Now help, or woe betide thee evermore!

AARON
Why, what a caterwauling dost thou keep!
What dost thou wrap and fumble in thine arms?

NURSE
O, that which I would hide from heaven's eye,
Our empress' shame, and stately Rome's disgrace! 65
She is deliver'd, lords; she is deliver'd.

AARON
To whom?

NURSE
I mean, she is brought a-bed.

AARON
Well, God give her good rest! What hath he sent her?

NURSE
A devil.

AARON
Why, then she is the devil's dam; a joyful issue.

NURSE
A joyless, dismal, black, and sorrowful issue:
Here is the babe, as loathsome as a toad
Amongst the fairest breeders of our clime:
The empress sends it thee, thy stamp, thy seal,
And bids thee christen it with thy dagger's point. 78

AARON
'Zounds, ye whore! is black so base a hue?
Sweet blowse, you are a beauteous blossom, sure.

DEMETRIUS
Villain, what hast thou done?

AARON
That which thou canst not undo.

CHIRON
Thou hast undone our mother.

DEMETRIUS
And therein, hellish dog, thou hast undone. [33]
Woe to her chance, and damn'd her loathed choice!
Accursed the offspring of so foul a fiend!

CHIRON
It shall not live. 88

AARON
It shall not die.

NURSE
Aaron, it must; the mother wills it so.

AARON
What, must it, nurse? then let no man but I
Do execution on my flesh and blood.

DEMETRIUS
I'll broach the tadpole on my rapier's point:
Nurse, give it me; my sword shall soon dispatch it.

AARON
Sooner this sword shall plough thy bowels up.
[*Takes the child from the Nurse, and draws.*
Stay, murderous villains! will you kill your brother?
Now, by the burning tapers of the sky,
That shone so brightly when this boy was got,
He dies upon my scimitar's sharp point 99
That touches this my first-born son and heir!
I tell you, younglings, not Enceladus,
With all his threatening band of Typhon's brood,

Nor great Alcides, nor the god of war,
Shall seize this prey out of his father's hands.
What, what, ye sanguine, shallow-hearted boys!
Ye white-limed walls! ye alehouse painted signs!
Coal-black is better than another hue,
In that it scorns to bear another hue;
For all the water in the ocean
Can never turn the swan's black legs to white,
Although she lave them hourly in the flood.
Tell the empress from me, I am of age
To keep mine own, excuse it how she can.

DEMETRIUS
Wilt thou betray thy noble mistress thus?

AARON
My mistress is my mistress; this myself,
The vigour and the picture of my youth:
This before all the world do I prefer;
This maugre all the world will I keep safe,
Or some of you shall smoke for it in Rome.

DEMETRIUS
By this our mother is for ever shamed.

CHIRON
Rome will despise her for this foul escape.

NURSE
The emperor, in his rage, will doom her death.

CHIRON
I blush to think upon this ignomy.

AARON
Why, there's the privilege your beauty bears:
Fie, treacherous hue, that will betray with blushing
The close enacts and counsels of the heart!
Here's a young lad framed of another leer:
Look, how the black slave smiles upon the father,
As who should say 'Old lad, I am thine own.'
He is your brother, lords, sensibly fed
Of that self-blood that first gave life to you,
And from that womb where you imprison'd were
He is enfranchised and come to light:
Nay, he is your brother by the surer side,
Although my seal be stamped in his face.

NURSE
Aaron, what shall I say unto the empress?

DEMETRIUS
Advise thee, Aaron, what is to be done,
And we will all subscribe to thy advice:
Save thou the child, so we may all be safe.

AARON
Then sit we down, and let us all consult.
My son and I will have the wind of you:
Keep there: now talk at pleasure of your safety.
[They sit.

DEMETRIUS
How many women saw this child of his?

AARON
Why, so, brave lords! when we join in league,
I am a lamb: but if you brave the Moor,
The chafed boar, the mountain lioness,
The ocean swells not so as Aaron storms.
But say, again; how many saw the child?

NURSE
Cornelia the midwife and myself;
And no one else but the deliver'd empress.

AARON
The empress, the midwife, and yourself:
Two may keep counsel when the third's away:
Go to the empress, tell her this I said.
[He kills the nurse.
Weke, weke! so cries a pig prepared to the spit.

DEMETRIUS
What mean'st thou, Aaron? wherefore didst thou this?

AARON
O Lord, sir, 'tis a deed of policy:
Shall she live to betray this guilt of ours,
A long-tongued babbling gossip? no, lords, no:
And now be it known to you my full intent.
Not far, one Muli lives, my countryman;
His wife but yesternight was brought to bed;
His child is like to her, fair as you are:
Go pack with him, and give the mother gold,
And tell them both the circumstance of all;
And how by this their child shall be advanced,
And be received for the emperor's heir,
And substituted in the place of mine,
To calm this tempest whirling in the court;
And let the emperor dandle him for his own.
Hark ye, lords; ye see I have given her physic,
[Pointing to the nurse.
And you must needs bestow her funeral;
The fields are near, and you are gallant grooms:
This done, see that you take no longer days,[34]
But send the midwife presently to me.
The midwife and the nurse well made away,
Then let the ladies tattle what they please.

CHIRON
Aaron, I see thou wilt not trust the air
With secrets.

DEMETRIUS
For this care of Tamora,
Herself and hers are highly bound to thee.
[Exeunt Demetrius and Chiron bearing off the Nurse's body.

AARON
Now to the Goths, as swift as swallow flies;
There to dispose this treasure in mine arms,
And secretly to greet the empress' friends.
Come on, you thick-lipp'd slave, I'll bear you hence;

For it is you that puts us to our shifts:
I'll make you feed on berries and on roots,
And feed on curds and whey, and suck the goat,
And cabin in a cave, and bring you up
To be a warrior, and command a camp. *[Exit.*

ACT FOUR SCENE THREE

The same. A public place.

Enter TITUS, *bearing arrows with letters at the ends of them; with him,* MARCUS, *young* LUCIUS, PUBLIUS, SEMPRONIUS, CAIUS, *and other* Gentlemen, *with bows.*

TITUS ANDRONICUS
Come, Marcus; come, kinsman; this is the way.
Sir boy, now let me see your archery; [35]
Look ye draw home enough, and 'tis there straight.
Terras Astraea reliquit: [36]
Be you remember'd, Marcus, she's gone, she's fled.
Sirs, take you to your tools. You, cousins, shall
Go sound the ocean, and cast your nets;
Happily you may catch her in the sea;
Yet there's as little justice as at land:
No; Publius and Sempronius, you must do it;
'Tis you must dig with mattock and with spade,
And pierce the inmost centre of the earth:
Then, when you come to Pluto's region,
I pray you, deliver him this petition;
Tell him, it is for justice and for aid,
And that it comes from old Andronicus, [37]
Shaken with sorrows in ungrateful Rome.
Ah, Rome! Well, well; I made thee miserable
What time I threw the people's suffrages
On him that thus doth tyrannize o'er me.
Go, get you gone; and pray be careful all,
And leave you not a man-of-war unsearch'd:
This wicked emperor may have shipp'd her hence;
And, kinsmen, then may we go pipe for justice.
MARCUS ANDRONICUS
O Publius, is not this a heavy case,
To see thy noble uncle thus distract?
PUBLIUS
Therefore, my lord, it highly us concerns
By day and night to attend him carefully,
And feed his humour kindly as we may,
Till time beget some careful remedy.
MARCUS ANDRONICUS
Kinsmen, his sorrows are past remedy.
Join with the Goths; and with revengeful war
Take wreak on Rome for this ingratitude,
And vengeance on the traitor Saturnine.
TITUS ANDRONICUS
Publius, how now! how now, my masters!
What, have you met with her?
PUBLIUS
No, my good lord; but Pluto sends you word,
If you will have Revenge from hell, you shall:
Marry, for Justice, she is so employ'd,
He thinks, with Jove in heaven, or somewhere else,
So that perforce you must needs stay a time.
TITUS ANDRONICUS
He doth me wrong to feed me with delays.
I'll dive into the burning lake below,
And pull her out of Acheron by the heels.
Marcus, we are but shrubs, no cedars we
No big-boned men framed of the Cyclops' size;
But metal, Marcus, steel to the very back,
Yet wrung with wrongs more than our backs can bear:
And sith there's no justice in earth nor hell,
We will solicit heaven and move the gods
To send down Justice for to wreak our wrongs.
Come, to this gear. You are a good archer, Marcus;
[He gives them the arrows.
'Ad Jovem,' that's for you: here, 'Ad Apollinem:'
'Ad Martem,' that's for myself:
Here, boy, to Pallas: here, to Mercury:
To Saturn, Caius, not to Saturnine; [38]
You were as good to shoot against the wind.
To it, boy! Marcus, loose when I bid.
Of my word, I have written to effect;
There's not a god left unsolicited.
MARCUS ANDRONICUS
Kinsmen, shoot all your shafts into the court:
We will afflict the emperor in his pride.
TITUS ANDRONICUS
Now, masters, draw. [*They shoot.*] O, well said, Lucius!
Good boy, in Virgo's lap; give it Pallas.
MARCUS ANDRONICUS
My lord, I aim a mile beyond the moon;
Your letter is with Jupiter by this.
TITUS ANDRONICUS
Ha, ha!
Publius, Publius, what hast thou done?
See, see, thou hast shot off one of Taurus' horns.
MARCUS ANDRONICUS
This was the sport, my lord: when Publius shot,
The Bull, being gall'd, gave Aries such a knock
That down fell both the Ram's horns in the court;
And who should find them but the empress' villain?
She laugh'd, and told the Moor he should not choose
But give them to his master for a present.

TITUS ANDRONICUS Of my word, I have written to effect; there's not a god left unsolicited.

TITUS ANDRONICUS
Why, there it goes: God give his lordship joy!

Enter a Clown, *with a basket, and two pigeons in it.*

News, news from heaven! Marcus, the post is come.
Sirrah, what tidings? have you any letters?
Shall I have justice? what says Jupiter?

CLOWN
O, the gibbet-maker! he says that he hath taken them down again, for the man must not be hanged till the next week.

TITUS ANDRONICUS
But what says Jupiter, I ask her?

CLOWN
Alas, sir, I know not Jupiter; I never drank with him in all my life.

TITUS ANDRONICUS
Why, villain, art not thou the carrier?

CLOWN
Ay, of my pigeons, sir; nothing else.

TITUS ANDRONICUS
Why, didst thou not come from heaven?

CLOWN
From heaven! alas, sir, I never came there: God forbid I should be so bold to press to heaven in my young days. Why, I am going with my pigeons to the tribunal plebs, to take up a matter of brawl betwixt my uncle and one of the emperial's men.

MARCUS ANDRONICUS
Why, sir, that is as fit as can be to serve for your oration; and let him deliver the pigeons to the emperor from you.

TITUS ANDRONICUS
Tell me, can you deliver an oration to the emperor with a grace?

CLOWN
Nay, truly, sir, I could never say grace in all my life.

TITUS ANDRONICUS
Sirrah, come hither: make no more ado,
But give your pigeons to the emperor:
By me thou shalt have justice at his hands.
Hold, hold; meanwhile here's money for thy charges.

Give me pen and ink. Sirrah, can you with a grace deliver a supplication?

CLOWN

Ay, sir.

TITUS ANDRONICUS

Then here is a supplication for you. And when you come to him, at the first approach you must kneel, then kiss his foot, then deliver up your pigeons, and then look for your reward. I'll be at hand, sir; see you do it bravely.

CLOWN

I warrant you, sir, let me alone.

TITUS ANDRONICUS

Sirrah, hast thou a knife? come, let me see it.
Here, Marcus, fold it in the oration;
For thou hast made it like an humble suppliant.
And when thou hast given it the emperor,
Knock at my door, and tell me what he says.

CLOWN

God be with you, sir; I will. 125

TITUS ANDRONICUS

Come, Marcus, let us go. Publius, follow me.

[*Exeunt.*

ACT FOUR SCENE FOUR

The same. Before the palace.

Enter SATURNINUS, TAMORA, DEMETRIUS, CHIRON, Lords, *and others*; SATURNINUS *with the arrows in his hand that* TITUS *shot.*

SATURNINUS

Why, lords, what wrongs are these! was ever seen
An emperor in Rome thus overborne,
Troubled, confronted thus; and, for the extent
Of egal justice, used in such contempt?
My lords, you know, as know the mightful gods,
However these disturbers of our peace
Buz in the people's ears, there nought hath pass'd,
But even with law, against the wilful sons
Of old Andronicus. And what an if
His sorrows have so overwhelm'd his wits, 11
Shall we be thus afflicted in his wreaks,
His fits, his frenzy, and his bitterness?
And now he writes to heaven for his redress:
See, here's to Jove, and this to Mercury;
This to Apollo; this to the god of war;
Sweet scrolls to fly about the streets of Rome!
What's this but libelling against the senate,
And blazoning our injustice every where?
A goodly humour, is it not, my lords?
As who would say, in Rome no justice were.
But if I live, his feigned ecstasies
Shall be no shelter to these outrages:
But he and his shall know that justice lives
In Saturninus' health, whom, if she sleep,
He'll so awake as she in fury shall
Cut off the proud'st conspirator that lives.

TAMORA

My gracious lord, my lovely Saturnine,
Lord of my life, commander of my thoughts,
Calm thee, and bear the faults of Titus' age,
The effects of sorrow for his valiant sons, 31
Whose loss hath pierced him deep and scarr'd his heart;
And rather comfort his distressed plight
Than prosecute the meanest or the best
For these contempts. [*Aside*] Why, thus it shall become
High-witted Tamora to gloze with all:
But, Titus, I have touch'd thee to the quick,
Thy life-blood out: if Aaron now be wise, 39
Then is all safe, the anchor's in the port.

Enter Clown.

How now, good fellow! wouldst thou speak with us?

CLOWN

Yea, forsooth, an your mistership be emperial. 44

TAMORA

Empress I am, but yonder sits the emperor.

CLOWN

'Tis he. God and Saint Stephen give you good den: I have brought you a letter and a couple of pigeons here. [*Saturninus reads the letter.*

SATURNINUS

Go, take him away, and hang him presently.

CLOWN

How much money must I have?

TAMORA

Come, sirrah, you must be hanged.

CLOWN

Hanged! by'r lady, then I have brought up a neck to a fair end. [*Exit, guarded.*

SATURNINUS

Despiteful and intolerable wrongs! 54
Shall I endure this monstrous villany?
I know from whence this same device proceeds:
May this be borne?—as if his traitorous sons,
That died by law for murder of our brother,
Have by my means been butcher'd wrongfully!
Go, drag the villain hither by the hair;
Nor age nor honour shall shape privilege:
For this proud mock I'll be thy slaughterman;
Sly frantic wretch, that hop'st to make me great,
In hope thyself should govern Rome and me.

Enter AEMILIUS.

What news with thee, Aemilius?

AEMILIUS

Arm, arm, my lord;—Rome never had more cause.
The Goths have gather'd head; and with a power
Of high-resolved men, bent to the spoil,
They hither march amain, under conduct
Of Lucius, son to old Andronicus;
Who threats, in course of this revenge, to do
As much as ever Coriolanus did.

SATURNINUS

Is warlike Lucius general of the Goths?
These tidings nip me, and I hang the head 74
As flowers with frost or grass beat down with storms:
Ay, now begin our sorrows to approach:
'Tis he the common people love so much;
Myself hath often over-heard them say,
When I have walked like a private man,
That Lucius' banishment was wrongfully,
And they have wish'd that Lucius were their emperor

TAMORA

Why should you fear? is not your city strong?

SATURNINUS

Ay, but the citizens favour Lucius,
And will revolt from me to succour him. 86

TAMORA

King, be thy thoughts imperious, like thy name.
Is the sun dimm'd, that gnats do fly in it?
The eagle suffers little birds to sing,
And is not careful what they mean thereby,
Knowing that with the shadow of his wings
He can at pleasure stint their melody;
Even so mayst thou the giddy men of Rome.
Then cheer thy spirit : for know, thou emperor,
I will enchant the old Andronicus
With words more sweet, and yet more dangerous,
Than baits to fish, or honey-stalks to sheep, 97
When as the one is wounded with the bait,
The other rotted with delicious feed.

SATURNINUS

But he will not entreat his son for us.

TAMORA

If Tamora entreat him, then he will:
For I can smooth and fill his aged ear
With golden promises; that, were his heart
Almost impregnable, his old ears deaf,
Yet should both ear and heart obey my tongue.
[*To Aemilius*] Go thou before, be our ambassador: 107
Say that the emperor requests a parley
Of warlike Lucius, and appoint the meeting
Even at his father's house, the old Andronicus. [40]

SATURNINUS

Aemilius, do this message honourably:
And if he stand on hostage for his safety,
Bid him demand what pledge will please him best.

AEMILIUS

Your bidding shall I do effectually. [*Exit.*

TAMORA

Now will I to that old Andronicus,
And temper him with all the art I have,
To pluck proud Lucius from the warlike Goths.
And now, sweet emperor, be blithe again, 118
And bury all thy fear in my devices.

SATURNINUS

Then go successantly, and plead to him. [*Exeunt.*

ACT FIVE SCENE ONE

Plains near Rome.

Enter LUCIUS *with an army of* Goths, *with drum and colours.*

LUCIUS

Approved warriors, and my faithful friends,
I have received letters from great Rome,
Which signify what hate they bear their emperor
And how desirous of our sight they are.
Therefore, great lords, be, as your titles witness,
Imperious and impatient of your wrongs,
And wherein Rome hath done you any scath,
Let him make treble satisfaction.

FIRST GOTH

Brave slip, sprung from the great Andronicus,
Whose name was once our terror, now our comfort; 11
Whose high exploits and honourable deeds
Ingrateful Rome requites with foul contempt,
Be bold in us: we'll follow where thou lead'st,
Like stinging bees in hottest summer's day
Led by their master to the flowered fields,
And be avenged on cursed Tamora.

ALL THE GOTHS

And as he saith, so say we all with him. [41]

LUCIUS

I humbly thank him, and I thank you all.
But who comes here, led by a lusty Goth?

Enter a Goth, *leading* AARON *with his child in his arms.*

SECOND GOTH

Renowned Lucius, from our troops I stray'd 21
To gaze upon a ruinous monastery;
And, as I earnestly did fix mine eye
Upon the wasted building, suddenly

I heard a child cry underneath a wall.
I made unto the noise; when soon I heard
The crying babe controll'd with this discourse:
'Peace, tawny slave, half me and half thy dam!
Did not thy hue betray whose brat thou art,
Had nature lent thee but thy mother's look,
Villain, thou mightst have been an emperor:
But where the bull and cow are both milk-white,
They never do beget a coal-black calf.
Peace, villain, peace!'—even thus he rates the babe,—
'For I must bear thee to a trusty Goth;
Who, when he knows thou art the empress' babe,
Will hold thee dearly for thy mother's sake.'
With this, my weapon drawn, I rush'd upon him,
Surprised him suddenly, and brought him hither,
To use as you think needful of the man.

LUCIUS
O worthy Goth, this is the incarnate devil 41
That robb'd Andronicus of his good hand;
This is the pearl that pleased your empress' eye, [42]
And here's the base fruit of his burning lust.
Say, wall-eyed slave, whither wouldst thou convey
This growing image of thy fiend-like face?
Why dost not speak? what, deaf? not a word?
A halter, soldiers! hang him on this tree,
And by his side his fruit of bastardy.

AARON
Touch not the boy; he is of royal blood.

LUCIUS
Too like the sire for ever being good.
First hang the child, that he may see it sprawl;
A sight to vex the father's soul withal.
Get me a ladder.

[*A ladder is brought, which Aaron is made to ascend.*

AARON
Lucius, save the child,
And bear it from me to the empress.
If thou do this, I'll show thee wondrous things,
That highly may advantage thee to hear:
If thou wilt not, befall what may befall,
I'll speak no more but 'Vengeance rot you all!'

LUCIUS
Say on: an if it please me which thou speak'st
Thy child shall live, and I will see it nourish'd.

AARON
An if it please thee! why, assure thee, Lucius, 64
'Twill vex thy soul to hear what I shall speak;
For I must talk of murders, rapes and massacres,
Acts of black night, abominable deeds,
Complots of mischief, treason, villanies
Ruthful to hear, yet piteously perform'd:
And this shall all be buried by my death,
Unless thou swear to me my child shall live.

LUCIUS
Tell on thy mind; I say thy child shall live.

AARON
Swear that he shall, and then I will begin. 73

LUCIUS
Who should I swear by? thou believest no god:
That granted, how canst thou believe an oath?

AARON
What if I do not? as, indeed, I do not;
Yet, for I know thou art religious
And hast a thing within thee called conscience,
With twenty popish tricks and ceremonies,
Which I have seen thee careful to observe,
Therefore I urge thy oath; for that I know
An idiot holds his bauble for a god
And keeps the oath which by that god he swears, 83
To that I'll urge him: therefore thou shalt vow
By that same god, what god soe'er it be,
That thou adorest, and hast in reverence,
To save my boy, to nourish and bring him up;
Or else I will discover nought to thee.

LUCIUS
Even by my god, I swear to thee I will.

AARON
First know thou, I begot him on the empress.

LUCIUS
O most insatiate and luxurious woman!

AARON
Tut, Lucius, that was but a deed of charity
To that which thou shalt hear of me anon. 93
'Twas her two sons that murder'd Bassianus;
They cut thy sister's tongue and ravish'd her
And cut her hands and trimm'd her as thou saw'st. [43]

LUCIUS
O detestable villain! call'st thou that trimming?

AARON
Why, she was wash'd and cut and trimm'd, and 'twas
Trim sport for them that had the doing of it.

LUCIUS
O barbarous, beastly villains, like thyself!

AARON
Indeed, I was their tutor to instruct them:
That codding spirit had they from their mother,
As sure a card as ever won the set; 104
That bloody mind, I think, they learn'd of me,
As true a dog as ever fought at head.
Well, let my deeds be witness of my worth.
I train'd thy brethren to that guileful hole
Where the dead corpse of Bassianus lay:
I wrote the letter that thy father found
And hid the gold within the letter mention'd,
Confederate with the queen and her two sons:
And what not done, that thou hast cause to rue,

Wherein I had no stroke of mischief in it?
I play'd the cheater for thy father's hand,
And, when I had it, drew myself apart
And almost broke my heart with extreme laughter:
I pry'd me through the crevice of a wall
When, for his hand, he had his two sons' heads;
Beheld his tears, and laugh'd so heartily,
That both mine eyes were rainy like to his :
And when I told the empress of this sport,
She swooned almost at my pleasing tale,
And for my tidings gave me twenty kisses.

FIRST GOTH
What, canst thou say all this, and never blush?

AARON
Ay, like a black dog, as the saying is. [44]

LUCIUS
Art thou not sorry for these heinous deeds?

AARON
Ay, that I had not done a thousand more.
Even now I curse the day—and yet, I think,
Few come within the compass of my curse—
Wherein I did not some notorious ill,
As kill a man, or else devise his death,
Ravish a maid, or plot the way to do it,
Accuse some innocent and forswear myself,
Set deadly enmity between two friends,
Make poor men's cattle break their necks; [45]
Set fire on barns and hay-stacks in the night,
And bid the owners quench them with their tears.
Oft have I digg'd up dead men from their graves
And set them upright at their dear friends' doors,
Even when their sorrows almost were forgot;
And on their skins, as on the bark of trees,
Have with my knife carved in Roman letters,
'Let not your sorrow die, though I am dead.'
Tut, I have done a thousand dreadful things
As willingly as one would kill a fly,
And nothing grieves me heartily indeed
But that I cannot do ten thousand more.

LUCIUS
Bring down the devil, for he must not die
So sweet a death as hanging presently.

AARON
If there be devils, would I were a devil,
To live and burn in everlasting fire,
So I might have your company in hell,
But to torment you with my bitter tongue!

LUCIUS
Sirs, stop his mouth, and let him speak no more.

Enter a Goth.

THIRD GOTH
My lord, there is a messenger from Rome
Desires to be admitted to your presence.

LUCIUS
Let him come near.

Enter AEMILIUS.

Welcome, Aemilius: what's the news from Rome?

AEMILIUS
Lord Lucius, and you princes of the Goths,
The Roman emperor greets you all by me;
And, for he understands you are in arms,
He craves a parley at your father's house.
Willing you to demand your hostages,
And they shall be immediately deliver'd.

FIRST GOTH
What says our general?

LUCIUS
Aemilius, let the emperor give his pledges
Unto my father and my uncle Marcus,
And we will come. March away. [*Exeunt.*

ACT FIVE SCENE TWO

Rome. Before Titus's house.

Enter TAMORA, DEMETRIUS, *and* CHIRON, *disguised.*

TAMORA
Thus, in this strange and sad habiliment,
I will encounter with Andronicus,
And say I am Revenge, sent from below
To join with him and right his heinous wrongs.
Knock at his study, where, they say, he keeps,
To rummage strange plots of dire revenge;
Tell him Revenge is come to join with him,
And work confusion on his enemies. [*They knock.*

Enter TITUS, *above.*

TITUS ANDRONICUS
Who doth molest my contemplation?
Is it your trick to make me ope the door,
That so my sad decrees may fly away,
And all my study be to no effect?
You are deceived: for what I mean to do
See here in bloody lines I have set down;
And what is written shall be executed.

TAMORA
Titus, I am come to talk with thee.

TITUS ANDRONICUS
No, not a word; how can I grace my talk,
Wanting a hand to give it action?
Thou hast the odds of me; therefore no more.

TAMORA
If thou didst know me, thou wouldst talk with me.

TITUS ANDRONICUS
I am not mad; I know thee well enough:
Witness this wrecked stump, witness these crimson lines;
Witness these trenches made by grief and care;
Witness the tiring day and heavy night;
Witness all sorrow, that I know thee well
For our proud empress, mighty Tamora:
Is not thy coming for my other hand?
TAMORA
Know, thou sad man, I am not Tamora;
She is thy enemy, and I thy friend:
I am Revenge: sent from the infernal kingdom,
To ease the gnawing vulture of thy mind,
By working wreakful vengeance on thy foes.
Come down, and welcome me to this world's light;
Confer with me of murder and of death:
There's not a hollow cave or lurking-place,
No vast obscurity or misty vale,
Where bloody murder or detested rape
Can couch for fear, but I will find them out;
And in their ears tell them my dreadful name,
Revenge, which makes the foul offender quake.
TITUS ANDRONICUS
Art thou Revenge? and art thou sent to me,
To be a torment to mine enemies?
TAMORA
I am; therefore come down, and welcome me.
TITUS ANDRONICUS
Do me some service, ere I come to thee.
Lo, by thy side where Rape and Murder stands;
Now give me some surance that thou art Revenge,
Stab them, or tear them on thy chariot-wheels;
And then I'll come and be thy waggoner,
And whirl along with thee about the globe.
Provide thee two proper palfreys, black as jet,
To hale thy vengeful waggon swift away,
And find out murderers in their guilty caves:
And when thy car is loaden with their heads,
I will dismount and by the waggon-wheel
Trot, like a servile footman, all day long,
Even from Hyperion's rising in the east
Until his very downfall in the sea:
And day by day I'll do this heavy task,
So thou destroy Rapine and Murder there.
TAMORA
These are my ministers, and come with me.
TITUS ANDRONICUS
Are these thy ministers? what are they call'd?
TAMORA
Rapine and Murder; therefore called so,
Cause they take vengeance of such kind of men.
TITUS ANDRONICUS
Good Lord, how like the empress' sons they are!
And you, the empress! but we worldly men
Have miserable, mad, mistaking eyes.
O sweet Revenge, now do I come to thee;
And, if one arm's embracement will content thee,
I will embrace thee in it by and by. [*Exit above.*
TAMORA
This closing with him fits his lunacy:
Whate'er I forge to feed his brain-sick fits,
Do you uphold and maintain in your speeches,
For now he firmly takes me for Revenge;
And, being credulous in this mad thought,
I'll make him send for Lucius his son;
And, whilst I at a banquet hold him sure,
I'll find some cunning practice out of hand,
To scatter and disperse the giddy Goths,
Or, at least, make them his enemies.
See, here he comes, and I must ply my theme. [46]

Enter TITUS *below.*

TITUS ANDRONICUS
Long have I been forlorn, and all for thee:
Welcome, dread Fury, to my woful house:
Rapine and Murder, you are welcome too.
How like the empress and her sons you are!
Well are you fitted, had you but a Moor:
Could not all hell afford you such a devil?
For well I wot the empress never wags
But in her company there is a Moor;
And, would you represent our queen aright,
It were convenient you had such a devil:
But welcome, as you are. What shall we do?
TAMORA
What wouldst thou have us do, Andronicus?
DEMETRIUS
Show me a murderer, I'll deal with him.
CHIRON
Show me a villain that hath done a rape,
And I am sent to be revenged on him.
TAMORA
Show me a thousand that have done thee wrong,
And I will be revenged on them all.
TITUS ANDRONICUS
Look round about the wicked streets of Rome;
And when thou find'st a man that's like thyself.
Good Murder, stab him; he's a murderer.
Go thou with him; and when it is thy hap
To find another that is like to thee,
Good Rapine, stab him; he's a ravisher.
Go thou with them; and in the emperor's court
There is a queen, attended by a Moor;
Well may'st thou know her by thy own proportion,
For up and down she doth resemble thee:
I pray thee, do on them some violent death;
They have been violent to me and mine.

TAMORA
Well hast thou lesson'd us; this shall we do.
But would it please thee, good Andronicus,
To send for Lucius, thy thrice-valiant son,
Who leads towards Rome a band of warlike Goths,
And bid him come and banquet at thy house;
When he is here, even at thy solemn feast,
I will bring in the empress and her sons,
The emperor himself and all thy foes;
And at thy mercy shall they stoop and kneel,
And on them shalt thou ease thy angry heart.
What says Andronicus to this device?

TITUS ANDRONICUS
Marcus, my brother! 'tis sad Titus calls.

Enter MARCUS.

Go, gentle Marcus, to thy nephew Lucius;
Thou shalt inquire him out among the Goths:
Bid him repair to me, and bring with him
Some of the chiefest princes of the Goths;
Bid him encamp his soldiers where they are:
Tell him the emperor and the empress too
Feast at my house, and he shall feast with them.
This do thou for my love; and so let him,
As he regards his aged father's life.

MARCUS ANDRONICUS
This will I do, and soon return again. [*Exit.*

TAMORA
Now will I hence about thy business,
And take my ministers along with me.

TITUS ANDRONICUS
Nay, nay, let Rape and Murder stay with me;
Or else I'll call my brother back again,
And cleave to no revenge but Lucius.

TAMORA
[*Aside to her sons*] What say you, boys? will you bide with him,
Whiles I go tell my lord the emperor
How I have govern'd our determined jest?
Yield to his humour, smooth and speak him fair,
And tarry with him till I turn again.

TITUS ANDRONICUS
[*Aside*] I know them all, though they suppose me mad,
And will o'erreach them in their own devices:
A pair of cursed hell-hounds and their dam!

DEMETRIUS
Madam, depart at pleasure; leave us here.

TAMORA
Farewell, Andronicus: Revenge now goes
To lay a complot to betray thy foes.

TITUS ANDRONICUS
I know thou dost; and, sweet Revenge, farewell.
[*Exit Tamora.*

CHIRON
Tell us, old man, how shall we be employ'd?

TITUS ANDRONICUS
Tut, I have work enough for you to do.
Publius, come hither, Caius, and Valentine!

Enter PUBLIUS *and others.*

PUBLIUS
What is your will?

TITUS ANDRONICUS
Know you these two?

PUBLIUS
The empress' sons, I take them, Chiron and Demetrius.

TITUS ANDRONICUS
Fie, Publius, fie! thou art too much deceived;
The one is Murder, Rape is the other's name;
And therefore bind them, gentle Publius.
Caius and Valentine, lay hands on them.
Oft have you heard me wish for such an hour,
And now I find it; therefore bind them sure,[47]
And stop their mouths, if they begin to cry.
[*Exit.*
Publius, &c., lay hold on Chiron and Demetrius.

CHIRON
Villains, forbear! we are the empress' sons.

PUBLIUS
And therefore do we what we are commanded.
Stop close their mouths, let them not speak a word.
Is he sure bound? look that you bind them fast.

Re-enter TITUS, *with* LAVINIA; *he bearing a knife, and she a basin.*

TITUS ANDRONICUS
Come, come, Lavinia; look, thy foes are bound.
Sirs, stop their mouths, let them not speak to me;
But let them hear what fearful words I utter.
O villains, Chiron and Demetrius!
Here stands the spring whom you have stain'd with mud,
This goodly summer with your winter mix'd.
You kill'd her husband, and for that vile fault
Two of her brothers were condemn'd to death,
My hand cut off and made a merry jest;
Both her sweet hands, her tongue, and that more dear
Than hands or tongue, her spotless chastity,
Inhuman traitors, you constrain'd and forced.
What would you say, if I should let you speak?
Villains, for shame you could not beg for grace.
Hark, wretches! how I mean to martyr you.
This one hand yet is left to cut your throats,
Whilst that Lavinia 'tween her stumps doth hold
The basin that receives your guilty blood.

You know your mother means to feast with me,
And calls herself Revenge, and thinks me mad:
Hark, villains! I will grind your bones to dust
And with your blood and it I'll make a paste,
And of paste a coffin I will rear
And make two pasties of your shameful heads,
And bid that strumpet, your unhallow'd dam,
Like to the earth swallow her own increase.
This is the feast that I have bid her to,
And this the banquet she shall surfeit on;
For worse than Philomel you used my daughter,
And worse than Progne I will be revenged:
And now prepare your throats. Lavinia, come,
[He cuts their throats.
Receive the blood: and when that they are dead,
Let me go grind their bones to powder small
And with this hateful liquor temper it;
And in that paste let their vile heads be baked.
Come, come, be every one officious
To make this banquet; which I wish may prove
More stern and bloody than the Centaurs' feast.
So, now bring them in, for I'll play the cook,
And see them ready 'gainst their mother comes.
[Exeunt, bearing the dead bodies.

ACT FIVE SCENE THREE

Court of Titus' house. A banquet set out.

Enter LUCIUS, MARCUS, *and* Goths, *with* AARON *prisoner.*

LUCIUS
Uncle Marcus, since it is my father's mind
That I repair to Rome, I am content.
FIRST GOTH
And ours with thine, befall what fortune will.
LUCIUS
Good uncle, take you in this barbarous Moor,
This ravenous tiger, this accursed devil;
Let him receive no sustenance, fetter him,
Till he be brought unto the empress' face,
For testimony of her foul proceedings:
And see the ambush of our friends be strong;
I fear the emperor means no good to us.
AARON
Some devil whisper curses in mine ear,
And prompt me, that my tongue may utter forth
The venomous malice of my swelling heart!
LUCIUS
Away, inhuman dog! unhallow'd slave!
Sirs, help our uncle to convey him in.
[Exeunt Goths, with Aaron. Flourish within.
The trumpets show the emperor is at hand.

Enter SATURNINUS *and* TAMORA , *with* AEMILIUS, Tribunes, Senators, *and others.*

SATURNINUS
What, hath the firmament more suns than one?
LUCIUS
What boots it thee to call thyself a sun?
MARCUS ANDRONICUS
Rome's emperor, and nephew, break the parle;
These quarrels must be quietly debated.
The feast is ready, which the careful Titus
Hath ordain'd to an honourable end.
For peace, for love, for league, and good to Rome:
Please you, therefore, draw nigh, and take your places.
SATURNINUS
Marcus, we will.
[Hautboys sound. The Company sit down at table.

Enter TITUS *dressed like a Cook*, LAVINIA *veiled, young* LUCIUS, *and others.* TITUS *places the dishes on the table.*

TITUS ANDRONICUS
Welcome, my gracious lord; welcome, dread queen;
Welcome, ye warlike Goths; welcome Lucius;
And welcome, all: although the cheer be poor,
'Twill fill your stomachs; please you eat of it.
SATURNINUS
Why art thou thus attired, Andronicus?
TITUS ANDRONICUS
Because I would be sure to have all well,
To entertain your highness and your empress.
TAMORA
We are beholding to you, good Andronicus.
TITUS ANDRONICUS
An if your highness knew my heart, you were.
My lord the emperor, resolve me this:
Was it well done of rash Virginius
To slay his daughter with his own right hand,
Because she was enforced, stain'd, and deflower'd?
SATURNINUS
It was, Andronicus.
TITUS ANDRONICUS
Your reason, mighty lord?
SATURNINUS
Because the girl should not survive her shame,
And by her presence still renew his sorrows.
TITUS ANDRONICUS
A reason mighty, strong, and effectual;
A pattern, precedent, and lively warrant,
For me, most wretched, to perform the like.
Die, die, Lavinia, and thy shame with thee;
[Kills Lavinia.
And, with thy shame, thy father's sorrow die!
SATURNINUS
What hast thou done, unnatural and unkind?

TITUS ANDRONICUS
Kill'd her, for whom my tears have made me blind.
I am as woful as Virginius was,
And have a thousand times more cause than he
To do this outrage: and it now is done.
SATURNINUS
What, was she ravish'd? tell who did the deed.
TITUS ANDRONICUS
Will't please you eat? will't please your highness feed?
TAMORA
Why hast thou slain thine only daughter thus?
TITUS ANDRONICUS
Not I; 'twas Chiron and Demetrius:
They ravish'd her, and cut away her tongue;
And they, 'twas they, that did her all this wrong.
SATURNINUS
Go fetch them hither to us presently.
TITUS ANDRONICUS
Why, there they are both, baked in that pie;
Whereof their mother daintily hath fed,
Eating the flesh that she herself hath bred.
'Tis true, 'tis true; witness my knife's sharp point.
[Kills Tamora.
SATURNINUS
Die, frantic wretch, for this accursed deed!
[Kills Titus.
LUCIUS
Can the son's eye behold his father bleed?
There's meed for meed, death for a deadly deed!
[Kills Saturninus. A great tumult. Lucius, Marcus, and others go up into the balcony.
MARCUS ANDRONICUS
You sad-faced men, people and sons of Rome,
By uproar sever'd, like a flight of fowl
Scatter'd by winds and high tempestuous gusts,
O, let me teach you how to knit again
This scatter'd corn into one mutual sheaf,
These broken limbs again into one body;
Lest Rome herself be bane unto herself, [48]
And she whom mighty kingdoms court'sy to,
Like a forlorn and desperate castaway,
Do shameful execution on herself.
But if my frosty signs and chaps of age,
Grave witnesses of true experience,
Cannot induce you to attend my words,
[*To Lucius*] Speak, Rome's dear friend, as erst our ancestor,
When with his solemn tongue he did discourse
To love-sick Dido's sad attending ear
The story of that baleful burning night
When subtle Greeks surprised King Priam's Troy,
Tell us what Simon hath bewitch'd our ears,
Or who hath brought the fatal engine in
That gives our Troy, our Rome, the civil wound.
My heart is not compact of flint nor steel;
Nor can I utter all our bitter grief,
But floods of tears will drown my oratory,
And break my utterance, even in the time
When it should move you to attend me most,
Lending your kind commiseration.
Here is a captain, let him tell the tale;
Your hearts will throb and weep to hear him speak.
LUCIUS
Then, noble auditory, be it known to you,
That cursed Chiron and Demetrius
Were they that murdered our emperor's brother;
And they it were that ravished our sister:
For their fell faults our brothers were beheaded;
Our father's tears despised, and basely cozen'd
Of that true hand that fought Rome's quarrel out,
And sent her enemies unto the grave.
Lastly, myself unkindly banished,
The gates shut on me, and turn'd weeping out,
To beg relief among Rome's enemies:
Who drown'd their enmity in my true tears,
And oped their arms to embrace me as a friend.
I am the turned forth, be it known to you,
That have preserved her welfare in my blood;
And from her bosom took the enemy's point,
Sheathing the steel in my adventurous body.
Alas, you know I am no vaunter, I;
My scars can witness, dumb although they are,
That my report is just and full of truth.
But, soft! methinks I do digress too much,
Citing my worthless praise: O, pardon me;
For when no friends are by, men praise themselves.
MARCUS ANDRONICUS
Now is my turn to speak. Behold this child:
[Pointing to the child in the arms of an Attendant.
Of this was Tamora delivered;
The issue of an irreligious Moor,
Chief architect and plotter of these woes:
The villain is alive in Titus' house,
And as he is, to witness this is true. [49]
Now judge what cause had Titus to revenge
These wrongs, unspeakable, past patience,
Or more than any living man could bear.
Now you have heard the truth, what say you, Romans?
Have we done aught amiss,—show us wherein,
And, from the place where you behold us now,
The poor remainder of Andronici
Will, hand in hand, all headlong cast us down,
And on the ragged stones beat forth our brains,
And make a mutual closure of our house.
Speak, Romans, speak; and if you say we shall,
Lo, hand in hand, Lucius and I will fall.

AEMILIUS
Come, come, thou reverend man of Rome,
And bring our emperor gently in thy hand,
Lucius our emperor; for well I know
The common voice do cry it shall be so.
ALL
Lucius, all hail, Rome's royal emperor!
MARCUS ANDRONICUS
Go, go into old Titus' sorrowful house,
[*To Attendants.*
And hither hale that misbelieving Moor,
To be adjudged some direful slaughtering death,
As punishment for his most wicked life.
[*Exeunt Attendants.*
LUCIUS, MARCUS, *and the others descend.*
ALL
Lucius, all hail, Rome's gracious governor!
LUCIUS
Thanks, gentle Romans: may I govern so,
To heal Rome's harms, and wipe away her woe!
But, gentle people, give me aim awhile,
For nature puts me to a heavy task:
Stand all aloof: but, uncle, draw you near,
To shed obsequious tears upon this trunk.
O, take this warm kiss on thy pale cold lips,
[*Kissing Titus.*
These sorrowful drops upon thy blood-stained face,
The last true duties of thy noble son!
MARCUS ANDRONICUS
Tear for tear, and loving kiss for kiss,
Thy brother Marcus tenders on thy lips:
O were the sum of these that I should pay
Countless and infinite, yet would I pay them!
LUCIUS
Come hither, boy; come, come, and learn of us
To melt in showers: thy grandsire loved thee well:
Many a time he danced thee on his knee,
Sung thee asleep, his loving breast thy pillow:
Many a matter hath he told to thee,
Meet and agreeing with thine infancy;
In that respect, then, like a loving child,
Shed yet some small drops from thy tender spring,
Because kind nature doth require it so:
Friends should associate friends in grief and woe:
Bid him farewell; commit him to the grave;
Do him that kindness, and take leave of him.
YOUNG LUCIUS
O grandsire, grandsire! even with all my heart
Would I were dead, so you did live again!
O Lord, I cannot speak to him for weeping;
My tears will choke me, if I ope my mouth.

Re-enter Attendants *with* AARON.

AEMILIUS
You sad Andronici, have done with woes:
Give sentence on this execrable wretch,
That hath been breeder of these dire events.
LUCIUS
Set him breast-deep in earth, and famish him;
There let him stand, and rave, and cry for food:
If any one relieves or pities him,
For the offence he dies. This is our doom:
Some stay to see him fasten'd in the earth.
AARON
O, why should wrath be mute, and fury dumb?
I am no baby, I, that with base prayers
I should repent the evils I have done:
Ten thousand worse than ever yet I did
Would I perform, if I might have my will;
If one good deed in all my life I did,
I do repent it from my very soul.
LUCIUS
Some loving friends convey the emperor hence,
And give him burial in his father's grave:
My father and Lavinia shall forthwith
Be closed in our household's monument.
As for that heinous tiger, Tamora,
No funeral rite, nor man in mourning weeds,
No mournful bell shall ring her burial:
But throw her forth to beasts and birds of prey:
Her life was beast-like, and devoid of pity;
And, being so, shall have like want of pity.
See justice done on Aaron, that damn'd Moor,
By whom our heavy haps had their beginning:
Then, afterwards, to order well the state,
That like events may ne'er it ruinate. [*Exeunt.*

Notes

1. I am his first-born son, that was the last That ware; – so Quartos; Folios 1, 2, 3 read *'I was the first-born son, that was the last That wore'*; Folio 4, *'I was the first-born Son of him that last Wore'*; Pope, *'I am the firstborn son of him that last Wore'*; Collier, *'I am his son That wore'*; Collier MS., *'I am the first borne Sonne, of him the last That wore.'*
2. Gates; – Capell reads *'gates, tribunes'*; Collier MS., *'brazen gates.'*
3. His tent; – Theobald reads *'her tent'* (alluding to Hecuba beguiling Polymnestor into the tent where she and the other Trojan captives were).
4. Drugs; – Quarto 1, *'drugges'*; Quarto 2, *'grudgges'*; Folios, *'grudges.'*
5. Stand up; – perhaps these words were, as Pope suggested, merely a stage-direction.
6. Cf. – 1 *Henry VI.*, V. iii. 77, 78; *Richard III.*, I. ii. 228, 229.
7. Yellowing; – so Quartos; Folios read *'yelping'*; Pope, *'yelling.'*

8. Barren detested; – Rowe reads *'barren and detested'*; Capell, *'bare, detested.'*
9. Painted hope braves your mightiness; – so Quartos; Folio 1; Folios 2, 3, 4, *'painted hope, she …'*; Warburton, *'painted cope she …'*; Capell, *'paint now braves your mightiness'*; Steevens conjectured *'painted, braves your …'*; &c. &c.
10. Outlive us; – Theobald's pointing; Quartos, Folios. *'outliue us'*; Dyce (ed. 2). *'outlive ye.'*
11. Paws; – Collier MS., *'claws.'*
12. Scrowl; – Quartos, *'scrowle'*; Folios. 1, 2, *'scowle'*; Folios 3, 4, *'scowl'*; Delius, *'scrawl.'*
13. Case; – Pope's emendation of Quartos, Folios. *'cause.'*
14. Which that sweet tongue hath made; – so Quartos, Folios; Hanmer, *'Which that sweet tongue of thine hath often made'*; Collier MS., *'Which that sweet tongue hath made in minstrelsy'*; &c.
15. For these, tribunes; – so Quartos, Folio 1; Folio 4, *'For these, these Tribunes'*; Malone, *'For these, good tribunes'*; Jackson conjectured *'For these two tribunes'*; Collier conjectured *'For these, O tribunes.'*
16. Urns; – Hanmer's emendation of Quartos, Folios 1, 2, 3, *'ruines'*; Folio 4, *'ruins.'*
17. Quarto 2 reads *'or if they did marke, All bootlesse unto them'*; Folios, *'oh if they did heare They would not pity me'*; Capell, *'or, if they did mark, All bootless unto them, they would not pity me,'* &c.
18. Sight; – Theobald, *'spight.'*
19. Sweet varied notes, enchanting every ear; – Collier MS. reads *'Rich varied notes, enchanting old and young'*; Folio 4, *'Sweet various …'*; &c.
20. As; – the reading of Collier, from Collier MS. and Long MS.; Quartos, Folios, *'in'*; Rowe, *'like.'*
21. Would; – so Quartos; Folios *read 'wilt'*; Capell conjectured *'wou't.'*
22. Blow; – the reading of Folios 2, 3, 4; Folio 1, Quartos, *'flow.'*
23. Employ'd in these things, – &c.; so Folios; Quartos, *'imployds in these Armes'*; perhaps, as the Cambridge editors suggest, the original MS. had as follows:—

    "And thou, Lavinia, shalt be imployd,
    Bear thou my hand, sweet wench, between thy teeth,"

    the Quarto reading being due to a correction of *'teeth'* to *'armes'*; the latter being taken by the printer as belonging to the previous line.
24. Leaves; – Rowe's emendation of Quartos, Folios, *'loues.'*
25. The whole of this scene is omitted in Quartos.
26. With outrageous beating; – Folio 1 reads *'without ragious beating.'*
27. Fear her not; – so Quartos; Folios read *'Feare not'*; Rowe, *'Fear thou not.'*
28. Soft! so busily; – Quartos, Folios, reads *'Soft, so busily'*; Rowe, *'Soft! see how busily'*; Capell, *'Soft, soft; how busily'*; Knight, *'Soft! how busily'*; Keightley, *'Soft, soft! so busily'*; Collier MS., *'Soft! see how busily.'*
29. Magni Dominator poli, Tamlentus audis scelera? tam lentus vides?; i.e. – Great ruler of the skies, dost thou so tardily hear and see crimes committed? (Seneca's *Hippolytus*, ii. 671); Theobald, *'Magne Dominator'*; Hanmer, *'Magne Regnator.'*
30. Revenge, ye heavens, – Johnson conjectured; *'Reuenge the heauens,'* so Quarto, Folios.
31. "He who is pure in life, and free from sin, needs not the darts of the Moor, nor the bow" (Horace, *Odes* I. 22).
32. Sound; – Theobald conjectured *'Fond,' i.e.* foolish; but, *'sound'* is probably to be taken ironically.
33. Omitted in Folios.
34. Take no longer days; – Collier MS., *'make no longer delays.'*
35. Let; – so Quartos, Folio 1; Folios 2, 3, 4, *'now let.*
36. Terras Astroea reliquit; i.e. – Astraea (the goddess of Justice) left the earth (Ovid. *Metam.* i. 150.)
37. Then, – a misprint for *'that.'*
38. To Saturn, Caius; – Capell's emendation; Quartos, Folios read *'To Saturnine, to Caius'*; Rowe (ed. 1), *'To Coelus and to Saturn'*; (ed. 2), *'To Saturn and to Coelus.'*
39. Thy life-blood out; – Folio 2, *'ont'*; Folio 3, *'on't'*; Walker suggested that a previous line had been lost, but the text seems correct, = "and drawn thy life-blood out."
40. Omitted in Quarto 2 and Folios; the reading of Quarto 1.
41. All the Goths, – should be *'The other Goths,'* as 'the first Goth' is kept distinet.
42. An allusion to the old proverb, "A black man is a pearl in a fair woman's eye" (Malone).
43. And cut her hands; – so Quartos; Folios, *'And cut her hands off'*; Collier MS., *'Cut her hands off.'*
44. A proverb found in *Ray's* collection.
45. Break their necks; – Malone conjectured *'break their necks and die'*; Jackson conjectured *'stray and break their necks'*; Collier MS., *'ofttimes break their necks,'* &c.
46. Ply; – so Quartos; Folios, *'play,'*
47. Omitted in Folios.
48. Lest Rome; – Capell's reading; Quartos, Folios, *'Let Rome'*; Malone, *'Lest Rome.'*
49. And as he is; – so Quartos, Folios; Theobald reads *'Damn'd as he is.'*

ANTONY AND CLEOPATRA

ANTONY AND CLEOPATRA

DRAMATIS PERSONAE

MARK ANTONY, triumvir.
OCTAVIUS CAESAR, triumvir.
M. AEMILIUS LEPIDUS, triumvir.
SEXTUS POMPEIUS, friend to Antony.
DOMITIUS ENOBARBUS, friend to Antony.
VENTIDIUS, friend to Antony.
EROS, friend to Antony.
SCARUS, friend to Antony.
DERCETAS, friend to Antony.
DEMETRIUS, friend to Antony.
PHILO, friend to Antony.
MECAENAS, friend to Caesar.
AGRIPPA, friend to Caesar.
DOLABELLA, friend to Caesar.
PROCULEIUS, friend to Caesar.
THYREUS, friend to Caesar.
GALLUS, friend to Caesar.
MENAS, friend to Pompey.
MENECRATES, friend to Pompey.
VARRIUS, friend to Pompey.
TAURUS, lieutenant-general to Caesar.
CANIDIUS, lieutenant-general to Antony.
SILIUS, an officer in Ventidius's army.
EUPHRONIUS, an ambassador from Antony to Caesar.
ALEXAS, attendant on Cleopatra.
MARDIAN, a Eunuch, attendant on Cleopatra.
SELEUCUS, attendant on Cleopatra.
DIOMEDES, attendant on Cleopatra.
A Soothsayer.
A Clown.
CLEOPATRA, queen of Egypt.
OCTAVIA, sister to Caesar and wife to Antony.
CHARMIAN, attendant on Cleopatra.
IRAS, attendant on Cleopatra.
Officers, Soldiers, Messengers, and other Attendants.

SCENE: *In several parts of the Roman empire.*

ACT ONE SCENE ONE

Alexandria. A room in CLEOPATRA'S *palace.*
Enter DEMETRIUS *and* PHILO.

PHILO
Nay, but this dotage of our general's
O'erflows the measure: those his goodly eyes,
That o'er the files and musters of the war
Have glow'd like plated Mars, now bend, now turn,
The office and devotion of their view
Upon a tawny front: his captain's heart,
Which in the scuffles of great fights hath burst
The buckles on his breast, reneges all temper,
And is become the bellows and the fan
To cool a gipsy's lust.

Flourish. Enter ANTONY, CLEOPATRA, *her Ladies, the Train, with Eunuchs fannin her.*

Look, where they come: 11
Take but good note, and you shall see in him.
The triple pillar of the world transform'd
Into a strumpet's fool: behold and see.
CLEOPATRA
If it be love indeed, tell me how much.

MARK ANTONY
There's beggary in the love that can be reckon'd.
CLEOPATRA
I'll set a bourn how far to be beloved.
MARK ANTONY
Then must thou needs find out new heaven, new earth.

Enter an Attendant.

ATTENDANT
News, my good lord, from Rome.
MARK ANTONY
Grates me: the sum. [1]
CLEOPATRA
Nay, hear them, Antony:
Fulvia perchance is angry; or, who knows 23
If the scarce-bearded Caesar have not sent
His powerful mandate to you, 'Do this, or this;
Take in that kingdom, and enfranchise that;
Perform 't, or else we damn thee.'
MARK ANTONY
How, my love!
CLEOPATRA
Perchance! nay, and most like:
You must not stay here longer, your dismission
Is come from Caesar; therefore hear it, Antony.
Where's Fulvia's process? Caesar's I would say? both?
Call in the messengers. As I am Egypt's queen,
Thou blushest, Antony; and that blood of thine 36
Is Caesar's homager: else so thy cheek pays shame
When shrill-tongued Fulvia scolds. The messengers!
MARK ANTONY
Let Rome in Tiber melt, and the wide arch
Of the ranged empire fall! Here is my space.
Kingdoms are clay: our dungy earth alike
Feeds beast as man: the nobleness of life
Is to do thus; when such a mutual pair [*Embracing.*
And such a twain can do't, in which I bind,
On pain of punishment, the world to weet
We stand up peerless.
CLEOPATRA
Excellent falsehood! 47
Why did he marry Fulvia, and not love her?
I'll seem the fool I am not; Antony
Will be himself.
MARK ANTONY
But stirr'd by Cleopatra.
Now, for the love of Love and her soft hours,
Let's not confound the time with conference harsh:
There's not a minute of our lives should stretch
Without some pleasure now. What sport to-night?
CLEOPATRA
Hear the ambassadors.
MARK ANTONY
Fie, wrangling queen!
Whom every thing becomes, to chide, to laugh,
To weep; whose every passion fully strives 59
To make itself, in thee, fair and admired!
No messenger, but thine; and all alone
To-night we 'll wander through the streets and note
The qualities of people. Come, my queen;
Last night you did desire it: speak not to us. [*Exeunt Antony and Cleopatra with their train.*
DEMETRIUS
Is Caesar with Antonius prized so slight?
PHILO
Sir, sometimes, when he is not Antony,
He comes too short of that great property
Which still should go with Antony.
DEMETRIUS
I am full sorry
That he approves the common liar, who [2]
Thus speaks of him at Rome: but I will hope 72
Of better deeds to-morrow. Rest you happy! [*Exeunt.*

ACT ONE SCENE TWO

The same. Another room.

Enter CHARMIAN, IRAS, ALEXAS, *and a Soothsayer.*

CHARMIAN
Lord Alexas, sweet Alexas, most any thing Alexas, almost most absolute Alexas, where's the soothsayer that you praised so to the queen? O, that I knew this husband, which, you say, must charge his horns with garlands! [3]
ALEXAS
Soothsayer!
SOOTHSAYER
Your will?
CHARMIAN
Is this the man? Is't you, sir, that know things?
SOOTHSAYER
In nature's infinite book of secrecy
A little I can read.
ALEXAS
Show him your hand. 11

Enter ENOBARBUS.

DOMITIUS ENOBARBUS
Bring in the banquet quickly; wine enough
Cleopatra's health to drink.

CHARMIAN
Good sir, give me good fortune.
SOOTHSAYER
I make not, but foresee.
CHARMIAN
Pray, then, foresee me one.
SOOTHSAYER
You shall be yet far fairer than you are.
CHARMIAN
He means in flesh.
IRAS
No, you shall paint when you are old.
CHARMIAN
Wrinkles forbid!
ALEXAS
Vex not his prescience; be attentive.
CHARMIAN
Hush! 22
SOOTHSAYER
You shall be more beloving than beloved.
CHARMIAN
I had rather heat my liver with drinking.
ALEXAS
Nay, hear him.
CHARMIAN
Good now, some excellent fortune! Let me be married to three kings in a forenoon, and widow them all: let me have a child at fifty, to whom Herod of Jewry may do homage: find me to marry me with Octavius Caesar, and companion me with my mistress.
SOOTHSAYER
You shall outlive the lady whom you serve.
CHARMIAN
O excellent! I love long life better than figs.
SOOTHSAYER
You have seen and proved a fairer former fortune
Than that which is to approach.
CHARMIAN
Then belike my children shall have no
names: prithee, how many boys and wenches
must I have?
SOOTHSAYER
If every of your wishes had a womb,
And fertile every wish, a million. [4]
CHARMIAN
Out, fool! I forgive thee for a witch. 41
ALEXAS
You think none but your sheets are privy to your wishes.
CHARMIAN
Nay, come, tell Iras hers.
ALEXAS
We'll know all our fortunes.
DOMITIUS ENOBARBUS
Mine, and most of our fortunes, to-night, shall be—drunk to bed.
IRAS
There's a palm presages chastity, if nothing else.
CHARMIAN
E'en as the o'erflowing Nilus presageth famine. 49
IRAS
Go, you wild bedfellow, you cannot soothsay.
CHARMIAN
Nay, if an oily palm be not a fruitful prognostication, I cannot scratch mine ear. Prithee, tell her but a worky-day fortune.
SOOTHSAYER
Your fortunes are alike.
IRAS
But how, but how? give me particulars.
SOOTHSAYER
I have said.
IRAS
Am I not an inch of fortune better than she? 57
CHARMIAN
Well, if you were but an inch of fortune better than I, where would you choose it?
IRAS
Not in my husband's nose.
CHARMIAN
Our worser thoughts heavens mend! Alexas,—come, his fortune, his fortune! O, let him marry a woman that cannot go, sweet Isis, I beseech thee! and let her die too, and give him a worse! and let worse follow worse, till the worst of all follow him laughing to his grave, fifty-fold a cuckold! Good Isis, hear me this prayer, though thou deny me a matter of more weight; good Isis, I beseech thee! [5]
IRAS
Amen. Dear goddess, hear that prayer of the people! for, as it is a heartbreaking to see a handsome man loose-wived, so it is a deadly sorrow to behold a foul knave uncuckolded: therefore, dear Isis, keep decorum, and fortune him accordingly!
CHARMIAN
Amen. 74
ALEXAS
Lo, now, if it lay in their hands to make me a cuckold, they would make themselves whores, but they 'ld do 't!
DOMITIUS ENOBARBUS
Hush! here comes Antony.
CHARMIAN
Not he; the queen.

Enter CLEOPATRA.

CLEOPATRA
Saw you my lord? [6]

DOMITIUS ENOBARBUS
No, lady.
CLEOPATRA
Was he not here?
CHARMIAN
No, madam.
CLEOPATRA
He was disposed to mirth; but on the sudden
A Roman thought hath struck him. Enobarbus!
DOMITIUS ENOBARBUS
Madam?
CLEOPATRA
Seek him, and bring him hither.
Where's Alexas?
ALEXAS
Here, at your service. My lord approaches. 88
CLEOPATRA
We will not look upon him: go with us. [*Exeunt.*

Enter ANTONY *with a* Messenger *and* Attendants.

MESSENGER
Fulvia thy wife first came into the field.
MARK ANTONY
Against my brother Lucius?
MESSENGER
Ay:
But soon that war had end, and the time's state
Made friends of them, jointing their force 'gainst Caesar;
Whose better issue in the war, from Italy,
Upon the first encounter, drave them.
MARK ANTONY
Well, what worst?
MESSENGER
The nature of bad news infects the teller.
MARK ANTONY
When it concerns the fool or coward. On: 100
Things that are past are done with me. 'Tis thus;
Who tells me true, though in his tale lie death,
I hear him as he flatter'd. [7]
MESSENGER
Labienus—
This is stiff news—hath, with his Parthian force,
Extended Asia from Euphrates;
His conquering banner shook from Syria
To Lydia and to Ionia;
Whilst—
MARK ANTONY
Antony, thou wouldst say,—
MESSENGER
O, my lord!
MARK ANTONY
Speak to me home, mince not the general tongue:
Name Cleopatra as she is call'd in Rome; 113
Rail thou in Fulvia's phrase; and taunt my faults
With such full license as both truth and malice
Have power to utter. O, then we bring forth weeds,
When our quick minds lie still; and our ills told us [8]
Is as our earing. Fare thee well awhile.
MESSENGER
At your noble pleasure. [*Exit.*
MARK ANTONY
From Sicyon, ho, the news! Speak there!
FIRST ATTENDANT
The man from Sicyon,—is there such an one?
SECOND ATTENDANT
He stays upon your will.
MARK ANTONY
Let him appear.
These strong Egyptian fetters I must break,
Or lose myself in dotage.

Enter another Messenger.

What are you?
SECOND MESSENGER
Fulvia thy wife is dead.
MARK ANTONY
Where died she?
SECOND MESSENGER
In Sicyon:
Her length of sickness, with what else more serious
Importeth thee to know, this bears.
[*Gives a letter.*
MARK ANTONY
Forbear me. [*Exit Second Messenger.*
There's a great spirit gone! Thus did I desire it:
What our contempt doth often hurl from us,
We wish it ours again; the present pleasure,
By revolution lowering, does become
The opposite of itself: she's good, being gone;
The hand could pluck her back that shoved her on. 141
I must from this enchanting queen break off: [9]
Ten thousand harms, more than the ills I know,
My idleness doth hatch. How now! Enobarbus!

Re-enter DOMITIUS ENOBARBUS.

DOMITIUS ENOBARBUS
What's your pleasure, sir?
MARK ANTONY
I must with haste from hence.
DOMITIUS ENOBARBUS
Why, then, we kill all our women: we see how mortal an unkindness is to them; if they suffer our departure, death's the word.
MARK ANTONY
I must be gone. 151

DOMITIUS ENOBARBUS

Under a compelling occasion, let women die: it were pity to cast them away for nothing; though, between them and a great cause, they should be esteemed nothing. Cleopatra, catching but the least noise of this, dies instantly; I have seen her die twenty times upon far poorer moment: I do think there is mettle in death, which commits some loving act upon her, she hath such a celerity in dying. [10]

MARK ANTONY

She is cunning past man's thought.

DOMITIUS ENOBARBUS

Alack, sir, no; her passions are made of nothing but the finest part of pure love: we cannot call her winds and waters sighs and tears; they are greater storms and tempests than almanacs can report: this cannot be cunning in her; if it be, she makes a shower of rain as well as Jove.

MARK ANTONY

Would I had never seen her!

DOMITIUS ENOBARBUS

O, sir, you had then left unseen a wonderful piece of work; which not to have been blest withal would have discredited your travel.

MARK ANTONY

Fulvia is dead.

DOMITIUS ENOBARBUS

Sir?

MARK ANTONY

Fulvia is dead.

DOMITIUS ENOBARBUS

Fulvia!

MARK ANTONY

Dead.

DOMITIUS ENOBARBUS

Why, sir, give the gods a thankful sacrifice. When it pleaseth their deities to take the wife of a man from him, it shows to man the tailors of the earth; comforting therein, that when old robes are worn out, there are members to make new. If there were no more women but Fulvia, then had you indeed a cut, and the case to be lamented: this grief is crowned with consolation; your old smock brings forth a new petticoat: and indeed the tears live in an onion that should water this sorrow.

MARK ANTONY

The business she hath broached in the state
Cannot endure my absence. 187

DOMITIUS ENOBARBUS

And the business you have broached here cannot be without you; especially that of Cleopatra's, which wholly depends on your abode.

MARK ANTONY

No more light answers. Let our officers
Have notice what we purpose. I shall break
The cause of our expedience to the queen,
And get her leave to part. For not alone
The death of Fulvia, with more urgent touches,
Do strongly speak to us; but the letters too
Of many our contriving friends in Rome
Petition us at home: Sextus Pompeius 198
Hath given the dare to Caesar, and commands
The empire of the sea: our slippery people,
Whose love is never link'd to the deserver
Till his deserts are past, begin to throw
Pompey the Great and all his dignities
Upon his son; who, high in name and power,
Higher than both in blood and life, stands up
For the main soldier: whose quality, going on,
The sides o' the world may danger: much is
breeding, 208
Which, like the courser's hair, hath yet but life, [11]
And not a serpent's poison. Say, our pleasure,
To such whose place is under us, requires
Our quick remove from hence.

DOMITIUS ENOBARBUS

I shall do't. *[Exeunt.*

ACT ONE SCENE THREE

The same. Another room.

Enter CLEOPATRA, CHARMIAN, IRAS, *and* ALEXAS.

CLEOPATRA

Where is he?

CHARMIAN

I did not see him since.

CLEOPATRA

See where he is, who's with him, what he does:
I did not send you: if you find him sad,
Say I am dancing; if in mirth, report
That I am sudden sick: quick, and
return. *[Exit Alexas.*

CHARMIAN

Madam, methinks, if you did love him dearly,
You do not hold the method to enforce
The like from him.

CLEOPATRA

What should I do, I do not?

CHARMIAN

In each thing give him way, cross him in nothing.

CLEOPATRA

Thou teachest like a fool; the way to lose him. 13

CHARMIAN

Tempt him not so too far; I wish, forbear:
In time we hate that which we often fear.
But here comes Antony.

Enter ANTONY.

CLEOPATRA
I am sick and sullen.
MARK ANTONY
I am sorry to give breathing to my purpose,—
CLEOPATRA
Help me away, dear Charmian; I shall fall:
It cannot be thus long, the sides of nature
Will not sustain it.
MARK ANTONY
Now, my dearest queen,—
CLEOPATRA
Pray you, stand farther from me.
MARK ANTONY
What's the matter?
CLEOPATRA
I know, by that same eye, there's some good news. 26
What says the married woman? You may go:
Would she had never given you leave to come!
Let her not say 'tis I that keep you here:
I have no power upon you; hers you are.
MARK ANTONY
The gods best know,—
CLEOPATRA
O, never was there queen
So mightily betray'd! yet at the first
I saw the treasons planted.
MARK ANTONY
Cleopatra,—
CLEOPATRA
Why should I think you can be mine and true,
Though you in swearing shake the throned gods,
Who have been false to Fulvia? Riotous madness,
To be entangled with those mouth-made vows,
Which break themselves in swearing!
MARK ANTONY
Most sweet queen,— 41
CLEOPATRA
Nay, pray you, seek no colour for your going,
But bid farewell, and go: when you sued staying,
Then was the time for words: no going then;
Eternity was in our lips and eyes,
Bliss in our brows' bent; none our parts so poor,
But was a race of heaven: they are so still,
Or thou, the greatest soldier of the world,
Art turn'd the greatest liar.
MARK ANTONY
How now, lady!
CLEOPATRA
I would I had thy inches; thou shouldst know 51
There were a heart in Egypt.
MARK ANTONY
Hear me, queen:
The strong necessity of time commands
Our services awhile; but my full heart
Remains in use with you. Our Italy
Shines o'er with civil swords: Sextus Pompeius
Makes his approaches to the port of Rome:
Equality of two domestic powers
Breed scrupulous faction: the hated, grown to strength,
Are newly grown to love: the condemn'd Pompey,
Rich in his father's honour, creeps apace 63
Into the hearts of such as have not thrived
Upon the present state, whose numbers threaten;
And quietness, grown sick of rest, would purge
By any desperate change: my more particular,
And that which most with you should safe my going,
Is Fulvia's death.
CLEOPATRA
Though age from folly could not give me freedom,
It does from childishness: can Fulvia die?
MARK ANTONY
She's dead, my queen:
Look here, and at thy sovereign leisure read
The garboils she awaked; at the last, best:
See when and where she died.
CLEOPATRA
O most false love!
Where be the sacred vials thou shouldst fill
With sorrowful water? Now I see, I see,
In Fulvia's death, how mine received shall be.
MARK ANTONY
Quarrel no more, but be prepared to know
The purposes I bear; which are, or cease,
As you shall give the advice. By the fire
That quickens Nilus' slime, I go from hence
Thy soldier, servant; making peace or war 84
As thou affect'st.
CLEOPATRA
Cut my lace, Charmian, come;
But let it be: I am quickly ill, and well,
So Antony loves.
MARK ANTONY
My precious queen, forbear;
And give true evidence to his love, which stands
An honourable trial.
CLEOPATRA
So Fulvia told me.
I prithee, turn aside and weep for her;
Then bid adieu to me, and say the tears
Belong to Egypt: good now, play one scene
Of excellent dissembling; and let it look
Like perfect honour.

MARK ANTONY
You'll heat my blood: no more.
CLEOPATRA
You can do better yet; but this is meetly.
MARK ANTONY
Now, by my sword,—
CLEOPATRA
And target. Still he mends;
But this is not the best. Look, prithee, Charmian,
How this Herculean Roman does become
The carriage of his chafe.
MARK ANTONY
I'll leave you, lady.
CLEOPATRA
Courteous lord, one word.
Sir, you and I must part, but that's not it:
Sir, you and I have loved, but there's not it;
That you know well: something it is I would,—
O, my oblivion is a very Antony,
And I am all forgotten.
MARK ANTONY
But that your royalty
Holds idleness your subject, I should take you
For idleness itself.
CLEOPATRA
'Tis sweating labour
To bear such idleness so near the heart
As Cleopatra this. But, sir, forgive me;
Since my becomings kill me, when they do not
Eye well to you: your honour calls you hence;
Therefore be deaf to my unpitied folly.
And all the gods go with you! upon your sword
Sit laurel victory! and smooth success
Be strew'd before your feet!
MARK ANTONY
Let us go. Come;
Our separation so abides, and flies,
That thou, residing here, go'st yet with me,
And I, hence fleeting, here remain with thee. Away!
[*Exeunt.*

ACT ONE SCENE FOUR

Rome. CAESAR'S *house.*

Enter OCTAVIUS CAESAR, *reading a letter,* LEPIDUS, *and their Train.*

OCTAVIUS CAESAR
You may see, Lepidus, and henceforth know,
It is not Caesar's natural vice to hate.
Our great competitor: from Alexandria [12]
This is the news: he fishes, drinks, and wastes
The lamps of night in revel; is not more manlike
Than Cleopatra; nor the queen of Ptolemy
More womanly than he; hardly gave audience, or
Vouchsafed to think he had partners: you shall find there
A man who is the abstract of all faults
That all men follow.
LEPIDUS
I must not think there are
Evils enow to darken all his goodness:
His faults in him seem as the spots of heaven,
More fiery by night's blackness; hereditary,
Rather than purchased; what he cannot change,
Than what he chooses.
OCTAVIUS CAESAR
You are too indulgent. Let us grant, it is not
Amiss to tumble on the bed of Ptolemy;
To give a kingdom for a mirth; to sit
And keep the turn of tippling with a slave;
To reel the streets at noon, and stand the buffet
With knaves that smell of sweat: say this becomes him,—
As his composure must be rare indeed [13]
Whom these things cannot blemish,—yet must Antony
No way excuse his soils, when we do bear
So great weight in his lightness. If he fill'd
His vacancy with his voluptuousness,
Full surfeits, and the dryness of his bones,
Call on him for't: but to confound such time,
That drums him from his sport, and speaks as loud
As his own state and ours,—'tis to be chid
As we rate boys, who, being mature in knowledge,
Pawn their experience to their present pleasure,
And so rebel to judgment.

Enter a Messenger.

LEPIDUS
Here's more news.
MESSENGER
Thy biddings have been done; and every hour,
Most noble Caesar, shalt thou have report
How 'tis abroad. Pompey is strong at sea;
And it appears he is beloved of those
That only have fear'd Caesar: to the ports
The discontents repair, and men's reports
Give him much wrong'd.
OCTAVIUS CAESAR
I should have known no less.
It hath been taught us from the primal state,
That he which is was wish'd until he were;
And the ebb'd man, ne'er loved till ne'er worth love,

Comes dear'd by being lack'd. This common body,
Like to a vagabond flag upon the stream,
Goes to and back, lackeying the varying tide, *14*
To rot itself with motion.

MESSENGER
Caesar, I bring thee word,
Menecrates and Menas, famous pirates,
Make the sea serve them, which they ear and wound
With keels of every kind: many hot inroads
They make in Italy; the borders maritime
Lack blood to think on't, and flush youth revolt:
No vessel can peep forth, but 'tis as soon
Taken as seen; for Pompey's name strikes more
Than could his war resisted.

OCTAVIUS CAESAR
Antony,
Leave thy lascivious wassails. When thou once
Wast beaten from Modena, where thou slew'st
Hirtius and Pansa, consuls, at thy heel
Did famine follow; whom thou fought'st against,
Though daintily brought up, with patience more
Than savages could suffer: thou didst drink
The stale of horses, and the gilded puddle
Which beasts would cough at: thy palate then did deign
The roughest berry on the rudest hedge;
Yea, like the stag, when snow the pasture sheets,
The barks of trees thou browsed'st; on the Alps
It is reported thou didst eat strange flesh,
Which some did die to look on: and all this—
It wounds thine honour that I speak it now—
Was borne so like a soldier, that thy cheek 80
So much as lank'd not.

LEPIDUS
'Tis pity of him.

OCTAVIUS CAESAR
Let his shames quickly
Drive him to Rome: 'tis time we twain
Did show ourselves i' the field; and to that end
Assemble we immediate council: Pompey
Thrives in our idleness.

LEPIDUS
To-morrow, Caesar,
I shall be furnish'd to inform you rightly
Both what by sea and land I can be able
To front this present time.

OCTAVIUS CAESAR
Till which encounter,
It is my business too. Farewell. 93

LEPIDUS
Farewell, my lord: what you shall know meantime
Of stirs abroad, I shall beseech you, sir,
To let me be partaker.

OCTAVIUS CAESAR
Doubt not, sir;
I knew it for my bond. [*Exeunt.*

ACT ONE SCENE FIVE

Alexandria. CLEOPATRA'S *palace.*
Enter CLEOPATRA, CHARMIAN, IRAS, *and* MARDIAN.

CLEOPATRA
Charmian!

CHARMIAN
Madam?

CLEOPATRA
Ha, ha!
Give me to drink mandragora.

CHARMIAN
Why, madam?

CLEOPATRA
That I might sleep out this great gap of time
My Antony is away.

CHARMIAN
You think of him too much.

CLEOPATRA
O, 'tis treason!

CHARMIAN
Madam, I trust, not so.

CLEOPATRA
Thou, eunuch Mardian!

MARDIAN
What's your highness' pleasure?

CLEOPATRA
Not now to hear thee sing; I take no pleasure
In aught an eunuch has: 'tis well for thee, 14
That, being unseminar'd, thy freer thoughts
May not fly forth of Egypt. Hast thou affections?

MARDIAN
Yes, gracious madam.

CLEOPATRA
Indeed!

MARDIAN
Not in deed, madam; for I can do nothing
But what indeed is honest to be done:
Yet have I fierce affections, and think
What Venus did with Mars.

CLEOPATRA
O Charmian,
Where think'st thou he is now? Stands he, or sits he?
Or does he walk? or is he on his horse? 26
O happy horse, to bear the weight of Antony!
Do bravely, horse! for wot'st thou whom thou movest?

The demi-Atlas of this earth, the arm
And burgonet of men. He's speaking now,
Or murmuring 'Where's my serpent of old Nile?'
For so he calls me: now I feed myself
With most delicious poison. Think on me,
That am with Phoebus' amorous pinches black,
And wrinkled deep in time? Broad-fronted Caesar, 36
When thou wast here above the ground, I was
A morsel for a monarch: and great Pompey
Would stand and make his eyes grow in my brow;
There would he anchor his aspect and die
With looking on his life.

Enter ALEXAS.

ALEXAS
Sovereign of Egypt, hail!

CLEOPATRA
How much unlike art thou Mark Antony!
Yet, coming from him, that great medicine hath
With his tinct gilded thee.
How goes it with my brave Mark Antony?

ALEXAS
Last thing he did, dear queen,
He kiss'd,—the last of many doubled kisses,—
This orient pearl. His speech sticks in my heart. 51

CLEOPATRA
Mine ear must pluck it thence.

ALEXAS
'Good friend,' quoth he,
'Say, the firm Roman to great Egypt sends
This treasure of an oyster; at whose foot,
To mend the petty present, I will piece
Her opulent throne with kingdoms; all the east,
Say thou, shall call her mistress.' So he nodded,
And soberly did mount an arm-gaunt steed, [15]
Who neigh'd so high, that what I would have spoke
Was beastly dumb'd by him. [16]

CLEOPATRA
What, was he sad or merry? 62

ALEXAS
Like to the time o' the year between the extremes
Of hot and cold, he was nor sad nor merry.

CLEOPATRA
O well-divided disposition! Note him,
Note him, good Charmian, 'tis the man; but note him:
He was not sad, for he would shine on those
That make their looks by his; he was not merry,
Which seem'd to tell them his remembrance lay
In Egypt with his joy; but between both:
O heavenly mingle! Be'st thou sad or merry,
The violence of either thee becomes, 72
So does it no man else. Met'st thou my posts?

ALEXAS
Ay, madam, twenty several messengers:
Why do you send so thick?

CLEOPATRA
Who's born that day
When I forget to send to Antony,
Shall die a beggar. Ink and paper, Charmian.
Welcome, my good Alexas. Did I, Charmian,
Ever love Caesar so?

CHARMIAN
O that brave Caesar!

CLEOPATRA
Be choked with such another emphasis!
Say, the brave Antony.

CHARMIAN
The valiant Caesar!

CLEOPATRA
By Isis, I will give thee bloody teeth,
If thou with Caesar paragon again 86
My man of men.

CHARMIAN
By your most gracious pardon,
I sing but after you.

CLEOPATRA
My salad days,
When I was green in judgement: cold in blood,
To say as I said then! But, come, away;
Get me ink and paper:
He shall have every day a several greeting,
Or I'll unpeople Egypt. [*Exeunt.*

ACT TWO SCENE ONE

Messina. POMPEY'S *house.*

Enter POMPEY, MENECRATES, *and* MENAS, *in warlike manner.*

POMPEY
If the great gods be just, they shall assist
The deeds of justest men.

MENECRATES
Know, worthy Pompey,
That what they do delay, they not deny.

POMPEY
Whiles we are suitors to their throne, decays
The thing we sue for.

MENECRATES We, ignorant of ourselves,
Beg often our own harms, which the wise powers
Deny us for our good; so find we profit
By losing of our prayers.

POMPEY
I shall do well:

The people love me, and the sea is mine;
My powers are crescent, and my auguring hope 17
Says it will come to the full. Mark Antony
In Egypt sits at dinner, and will make
No wars without doors: Caesar gets money where
He loses hearts: Lepidus flatters both,
Of both is flatter'd; but he neither loves,
Nor either cares for him.

MENAS
Caesar and Lepidus
Are in the field: a mighty strength they carry.

POMPEY
Where have you this? 'tis false.

MENAS
From Silvius, sir.

POMPEY
He dreams: I know they are in Rome together,
Looking for Antony. But all the charms of love, 25
Salt Cleopatra, soften thy waned lip!
Let witchcraft join with beauty, lust with both!
Tie up the libertine in a field of feasts,
Keep his brain fuming; Epicurean cooks
Sharpen with cloyless sauce his appetite;
That sleep and feeding may prorogue his honour
Even till a Lethe'd dulness!

Enter VARRIUS.

How now, Varrius!

VARRIUS
This is most certain that I shall deliver:
Mark Antony is every hour in Rome
Expected: since he went from Egypt 'tis 36
A space for further travel.

POMPEY
I could have given less matter
A better ear. Menas, I did not think
This amorous surfeiter would have donn'd his helm
For such a petty war: his soldiership
Is twice the other twain: but let us rear
The higher our opinion, that our stirring
Can from the lap of Egypt's widow pluck
The ne'er-lust-wearied Antony.

MENAS
I cannot hope
Caesar and Antony shall well greet together:
His wife that's dead did trespasses to Caesar;
His brother warr'd upon him; although, I think,
Not moved by Antony.

POMPEY
I know not, Menas,
How lesser enmities may give way to greater.
Were't not that we stand up against them all,
'Twere pregnant they should square between themselves;
For they have entertained cause enough
To draw their swords: but how the fear of us
May cement their divisions and bind up
The petty difference, we yet not know.
Be't as our gods will have't! It only stands
Our lives upon to use our strongest hands.
Come, Menas. [*Exeunt.*

ACT TWO SCENE TWO

Rome. The house of LEPIDUS.

Enter ENOBARBUS *and* LEPIDUS.

LEPIDUS
Good Enobarbus, 'tis a worthy deed,
And shall become you well, to entreat your captain
To soft and gentle speech.

DOMITIUS ENOBARBUS
I shall entreat him
To answer like himself: if Caesar move him,
Let Antony look over Caesar's head
And speak as loud as Mars. By Jupiter,
Were I the wearer of Antonius' beard,
I would not shave't to-day.

LEPIDUS
'Tis not a time
For private stomaching.

DOMITIUS ENOBARBUS
Every time
Serves for the matter that is then born in't. 13

LEPIDUS
But small to greater matters must give way.

DOMITIUS ENOBARBUS
Not if the small come first.

LEPIDUS
Your speech is passion:
But, pray you, stir no embers up. Here comes
The noble Antony.

Enter ANTONY *and* VENTIDIUS.

DOMITIUS ENOBARBUS
And yonder, Caesar.

Enter OCTAVIUS CAESAR, MECAENAS, *and* AGRIPPA.

MARK ANTONY
If we compose well here, to Parthia
Hark, Ventidius.

OCTAVIUS CAESAR
I do not know,
Mecaenas; ask Agrippa.

LEPIDUS
Noble friends,
That which combined us was most great, and let not
A leaner action rend us. What's amiss,
May it be gently heard: when we debate 27
Our trivial difference loud, we do commit

Murder in healing wounds: then, noble partners,
The rather, for I earnestly beseech,
Touch you the sourest points with sweetest terms,
Nor curstness grow to the matter.

MARK ANTONY
'Tis spoken well.
Were we before our armies, and to fight.
I should do thus [*Flourish.*

OCTAVIUS CAESAR
Welcome to Rome.

MARK ANTONY
Thank you.

OCTAVIUS CAESAR
Sit.

MARK ANTONY
Sit, sir.

OCTAVIUS CAESAR
Nay, then.

MARK ANTONY
I learn, you take things ill which are not so,
Or being, concern you not.

OCTAVIUS CAESAR
I must be laugh'd at,
If, or for nothing or a little, I
Should say myself offended, and with you
Chiefly i' the world; more laugh'd at, that I should
Once name you derogately, when to sound your name
It not concern'd me.

MARK ANTONY
My being in Egypt, Caesar,
What was't to you?

OCTAVIUS CAESAR
No more than my residing here at Rome
Might be to you in Egypt: yet, if you there
Did practise on my state, your being in Egypt
Might be my question.

MARK ANTONY
How intend you, practised?

OCTAVIUS CAESAR
You may be pleased to catch at mine intent
By what did here befal me. Your wife and brother
Made wars upon me; and their contestation
Was theme for you, you were the word of war. [18]

MARK ANTONY
You do mistake your business; my brother never
Did urge me in his act: I did inquire it;
And have my learning from some true reports,
That drew their swords with you. Did he not rather
Discredit my authority with yours;
And make the wars alike against my stomach,
Having alike your cause? Of this my letters
Before did satisfy you. If you'll patch a quarrel,
As matter whole you have not to make it with,
It must not be with this.

OCTAVIUS CAESAR
You praise yourself
By laying defects of judgment to me; but
You patch'd up your excuses.

MARK ANTONY
Not so, not so;
I know you could not lack, I am certain on't,
Very necessity of this thought, that I,
Your partner in the cause 'gainst which he fought,
Could not with graceful eyes attend those wars
Which fronted mine own peace. As for my wife,
I would you had her spirit in such another:
The third o' the world is yours; which with a snaffle
You may pace easy, but not such a wife.

DOMITIUS ENOBARBUS
Would we had all such wives, that the men might go to wars with the women!

MARK ANTONY
So much uncurbable, her garboils, Caesar,
Made out of her impatience, which not wanted
Shrewdness of policy too, I grieving grant
Did you too much disquiet: for that you must
But say, I could not help it.

OCTAVIUS CAESAR
I wrote to you
When rioting in Alexandria; you
Did pocket up my letters, and with taunts
Did gibe my missive out of audience.

MARK ANTONY
Sir,
He fell upon me ere admitted: then
Three kings I had newly feasted, and did want
Of what I was i' the morning: but next day
I told him of myself; which was as much
As to have ask'd him pardon. Let this fellow
Be nothing of our strife; if we contend,
Out of our question wipe him.

OCTAVIUS CAESAR
You have broken
The article of your oath; which you shall never
Have tongue to charge me with.

LEPIDUS
Soft, Caesar!

MARK ANTONY
No,
Lepidus, let him speak:
The honour is sacred which he talks on now,
Supposing that I lack'd it. But, on, Caesar;
The article of my oath.

OCTAVIUS CAESAR
To lend me arms and aid when I required them;
The which you both denied.

MARK ANTONY
Neglected, rather;
And then when poison'd hours had bound me up

From mine own knowledge. As nearly as I may,
I'll play the penitent to you: but mine honesty
Shall not make poor my greatness, nor my power
Work without it. Truth is, that Fulvia,
To have me out of Egypt, made wars here;
For which myself, the ignorant motive, do
So far ask pardon as befits mine honour
To stoop in such a case.

LEPIDUS
'Tis noble spoken.

MECAENAS
If it might please you, to enforce no further
The griefs between ye: to forget them quite
Were to remember that the present need
Speaks to atone you.

LEPIDUS
Worthily spoken, Mecaenas.

DOMITIUS ENOBARBUS
Or, if you borrow one another's love for the instant, you may, when you hear no more words of Pompey, return it again: you shall have time to wrangle in when you have nothing else to do.

MARK ANTONY
Thou art a soldier only: speak no more.

DOMITIUS ENOBARBUS
That truth should be silent I had almost
forgot.

MARK ANTONY
You wrong this presence; therefore speak no more.

DOMITIUS ENOBARBUS
Go to, then; your considerate stone. [19]

OCTAVIUS CAESAR
I do not much dislike the matter, but
The manner of his speech; for't cannot be
We shall remain in friendship, our conditions
So differing in their acts. Yet if I knew
What hoop should hold us stanch, from edge to edge
O' the world I would pursue it.

AGRIPPA
Give me leave, Caesar,—

OCTAVIUS CAESAR
Speak, Agrippa.

AGRIPPA
Thou hast a sister by the mother's side,
Admired Octavia: great Mark Antony
Is now a widower.

OCTAVIUS CAESAR
Say not so, Agrippa:
If Cleopatra heard you, your reproof
Were well deserved of rashness.

MARK ANTONY
I am not married, Caesar: let me hear
Agrippa further speak.

AGRIPPA
To hold you in perpetual amity,
To make you brothers, and to knit your hearts
With an unslipping knot, take Antony
Octavia to his wife; whose beauty claims
No worse a husband than the best of men;
Whose virtue and whose general graces speak
That which none else can utter. By this marriage,
All little jealousies, which now seem great,
And all great fears, which now import their dangers,
Would then be nothing: truths would be tales,
Where now half tales be truths: her love to both
Would, each to other and all loves to both,
Draw after her. Pardon what I have spoke;
For 'tis a studied, not a present thought,
By duty ruminated.

MARK ANTONY
Will Caesar speak?

OCTAVIUS CAESAR
Not till he hears how Antony is touch'd
With what is spoke already.

MARK ANTONY
What power is in Agrippa,
If I would say, 'Agrippa, be it so,'
To make this good?

OCTAVIUS CAESAR
The power of Caesar, and
His power unto Octavia.

MARK ANTONY
May I never
To this good purpose, that so fairly shows,
Dream of impediment! Let me have thy hand:
Further this act of grace; and from this hour
The heart of brothers govern in our loves
And sway our great designs!

OCTAVIUS CAESAR
There is my hand.
A sister I bequeath you, whom no brother
Did ever love so dearly: let her live
To join our kingdoms and our hearts; and never
Fly off our loves again!

LEPIDUS
Happily, amen!

MARK ANTONY
I did not think to draw my sword 'gainst Pompey;
For he hath laid strange courtesies and great
Of late upon me: I must thank him only,
Lest my remembrance suffer ill report;
At heel of that, defy him.

LEPIDUS
Time calls upon's:
Of us must Pompey presently be sought,
Or else he seeks out us.

MARK ANTONY
Where lies he?

OCTAVIUS CAESAR
About the mount Misenum.

MARK ANTONY
What is his strength by land?
OCTAVIUS CAESAR
Great and increasing: but by sea
He is an absolute master.
MARK ANTONY
So is the fame.
Would we had spoke together! Haste we for it:
Yet, ere we put ourselves in arms, dispatch we
The business we have talk'd of.
OCTAVIUS CAESAR
With most gladness:
And do invite you to my sister's view, 207
Whither straight I'll lead you.
MARK ANTONY
Let us, Lepidus,
Not lack your company.
LEPIDUS
Noble Antony,
Not sickness should detain me. [*Flourish. Exeunt Octavius Caesar, Mark Antony, and Lepidus.*
MECAENAS
Welcome from Egypt, sir.
DOMITIUS ENOBARBUS
Half the heart of Caesar, worthy Mecaenas! My honourable friend, Agrippa!
AGRIPPA
Good Enobarbus!
MECAENAS
We have cause to be glad that matters are so well digested. You stayed well by 't in Egypt. 218
DOMITIUS ENOBARBUS
Ay, sir; we did sleep day out of countenance, and made the night light with drinking.
MECAENAS
Eight wild-boars roasted whole at a breakfast, and but twelve persons there; is this true?
DOMITIUS ENOBARBUS
This was but as a fly by an eagle: we had much more monstrous matter of feast, which worthily deserved noting.
MECAENAS
She's a most triumphant lady, if report be
square to her. 227
DOMITIUS ENOBARBUS
When she first met Mark Antony, she pursed up his heart, upon the river of Cydnus.
AGRIPPA
There she appeared indeed; or my reporter devised well for her.
DOMITIUS ENOBARBUS
I will tell you.
The barge she sat in, like a burnish'd throne,
Burn'd on the water: the poop was beaten gold;
Purple the sails, and so perfumed that
The winds were love-sick with them; the oars were silver,
Which to the tune of flutes kept stroke, and made 238
The water which they beat to follow faster,
As amorous of their strokes. For her own person,
It beggar'd all description: she did lie
In her pavilion— cloth-of-gold of tissue—
O'er-picturing that Venus where we see
The fancy outwork nature: on each side her
Stood pretty dimpled boys, like smiling Cupids,
With divers-colour'd fans, whose wind did seem
To glow the delicate cheeks which they did cool,
And what they undid did.
AGRIPPA
O, rare for Antony! 249
DOMITIUS ENOBARBUS
Her gentlewomen, like the Nereides,
So many mermaids, tended her i' the eyes,
And made their bends adornings: at the helm [20]
A seeming mermaid steers: the silken tackle
Swell with the touches of those flower-soft hands,
That yarely frame the office. From the barge
A strange invisible perfume hits the sense
Of the adjacent wharfs. The city cast
Her people out upon her; and Antony,
Enthroned i' the market-place, did sit alone,
Whistling to the air; which, but for vacancy,
Had gone to gaze on Cleopatra too,
And made a gap in nature.
AGRIPPA
Rare Egyptian!
DOMITIUS ENOBARBUS
Upon her landing, Antony sent to her,
Invited her to supper: she replied,
It should be better he became her guest;
Which she entreated: our courteous Antony,
Whom ne'er the word of 'No' woman heard speak,
Being barber'd ten times o'er, goes to the feast,
And for his ordinary pays his heart 270
For what his eyes eat only.
AGRIPPA
Royal wench!
She made great Caesar lay his sword to bed:
He plough'd her, and she cropp'd.
DOMITIUS ENOBARBUS
I saw her once
Hop forty paces through the public street;
And having lost her breath, she spoke, and panted,
That she did make defect perfection,
And, breathless, power breathe forth.
MECAENAS
Now Antony must leave her utterly.
DOMITIUS ENOBARBUS
Never; he will not:

Age cannot wither her, nor custom stale
Her infinite variety: other women cloy
The appetites they feed; but she makes hungry
Where most she satisfies: for vilest things
Become themselves in her; that the holy priests
Bless her when she is riggish.

MECAENAS
If beauty, wisdom, modesty, can settle
The heart of Antony, Octavia is
A blessed lottery to him.

AGRIPPA
Let us go.
Good Enobarbus, make yourself my guest
Whilst you abide here.

DOMITIUS ENOBARBUS
Humbly, sir, I thank you. [*Exeunt.*

ACT TWO SCENE THREE

The same. CAESAR'S *house.*

Enter ANTONY, CAESAR, OCTAVIA *between them, and* Attendants.

MARK ANTONY
The world and my great office will sometimes
Divide me from your bosom.

OCTAVIA
All which time
Before the gods my knee shall bow my prayers [21]
To them for you.

MARK ANTONY
Good night, sir. My Octavia,
Read not my blemishes in the world's report:
I have not kept my square; but that to come
Shall all be done by the rule. Good night, dear lady.
Good night, sir.

OCTAVIUS CAESAR
Good night. [*Exeunt Caesar and Octavia.*

Enter Soothsayer.

MARK ANTONY
Now, sirrah; you do wish yourself in Egypt?

SOOTHSAYER
Would I had never come from thence, nor you
Thither!

MARK ANTONY
If you can, your reason?

SOOTHSAYER
I see it in
My motion, have it not in my tongue: but yet
Hie you to Egypt again.

MARK ANTONY
Say to me,
Whose fortunes shall rise higher, Caesar's or mine?

SOOTHSAYER
Caesar's.
Therefore, O Antony, stay not by his side:
Thy demon, that's thy spirit which keeps thee, is
Noble, courageous, high, unmatchable,
Where Caesar's is not; but, near him, thy angel
Becomes a fear, as being o'erpower'd: therefore [22]
Make space enough between you.

MARK ANTONY
Speak this no more.

SOOTHSAYER
To none but thee; no more, but when to thee.
If thou dost play with him at any game,
Thou art sure to lose; and, of that natural luck,
He beats thee 'gainst the odds: thy lustre thickens,
When he shines by: I say again, thy spirit
Is all afraid to govern thee near him;
But, he away, 'tis noble. [23]

MARK ANTONY
Get thee gone:
Say to Ventidius I would speak with him: [*Exit Soothsayer.*
He shall to Parthia. Be it art or hap,
He hath spoken true: the very dice obey him;
And in our sports my better cunning faints
Under his chance: if we draw lots, he speeds;
His cocks do win the battle still of mine,
When it is all to nought; and his quails ever
Beat mine, inhoop'd, at odds. I will to Egypt: [24]
And though I make this marriage for my peace,
I' the east my pleasure lies.

Enter VENTIDIUS.

O, come, Ventidius,
You must to Parthia: your commission's ready;
Follow me, and receive't. [*Exeunt.*

ACT TWO SCENE FOUR

The same. A street.

Enter LEPIDUS, MECAENAS, *and* AGRIPPA.

LEPIDUS
Trouble yourselves no further: pray you, hasten
Your generals after.

AGRIPPA
Sir, Mark Antony
Will e'en but kiss Octavia, and we'll follow.

LEPIDUS
Till I shall see you in your soldier's dress,
Which will become you both, farewell.

MECAENAS
We shall,

As I conceive the journey, be at the Mount
Before you, Lepidus.
LEPIDUS
Your way is shorter;
My purposes do draw me much about:
You'll win two days upon me.
MECAENAS, AGRIPPA
Sir, good success!
LEPIDUS
Farewell. [*Exeunt.*
14

ACT TWO SCENE FIVE

Alexandria. CLEOPATRA'S *palace.*

Enter CLEOPATRA, CHARMIAN, IRAS, *and* ALEXAS.

CLEOPATRA
Give me some music; music, moody food
Of us that trade in love.
ATTENDANTS
The music, ho!

Enter MARDIAN *the Eunuch.*

CLEOPATRA
Let it alone; let's to billiards: come, Charmian.
CHARMIAN
My arm is sore; best play with Mardian.
CLEOPATRA
As well a woman with an eunuch play'd
As with a woman. Come, you'll play with me, sir?
MARDIAN
As well as I can, madam.
CLEOPATRA
And when good-will is show'd, though't come too short,
The actor may plead pardon. I'll none now:
Give me mine angle; we'll to the river: there,
My music playing far off, I will betray 13
Tawny-finn'd fishes; my bended hook shall pierce
Their slimy jaws; and, as I draw them up,
I'll think them every one an Antony,
And say 'Ah, ha! you're caught.'
CHARMIAN
'Twas merry when
You wager'd on your angling; when your diver
Did hang a salt-fish on his hook, which he
With fervency drew up.
CLEOPATRA
That time,—O times!—
I laugh'd him out of patience; and that night
I laugh'd him into patience; and next morn,
Ere the ninth hour, I drunk him to his bed;
Then put my tires and mantles on him, whilst
I wore his sword Philippan.

Enter a Messenger.

O, from Italy!
Ram thou thy fruitful tidings in mine ears,
That long time have been barren.
MESSENGER
Madam, madam,—
CLEOPATRA
Antonius dead!—If thou say so, villain,
Thou kill'st thy mistress: but well and free,
If thou so yield him, there is gold, and here
My bluest veins to kiss; a hand that kings
Have lipp'd, and trembled kissing. 37
MESSENGER
First, madam, he is well.
CLEOPATRA
Why, there's more gold.
But, sirrah, mark, we use
To say the dead are well: bring it to that,
The gold I give thee will I melt and pour
Down thy ill-uttering throat.
MESSENGER
Good madam, hear me.
CLEOPATRA
Well, go to, I will;
But there's no goodness in thy face: if Antony
Be free and healthful,—so tart a favour
To trumpet such good tidings! If not well,
Thou shouldst come like a Fury crown'd with snakes,
Not like a formal man.
MESSENGER
Will't please you hear me?
CLEOPATRA
I have a mind to strike thee ere thou speak'st:
Yet, if thou say Antony lives, is well,
Or friends with Caesar, or not captive to him,
I'll set thee in a shower of gold, and hail
Rich pearls upon thee.
MESSENGER
Madam, he's well.
CLEOPATRA
Well said.
MESSENGER
And friends with Caesar.
CLEOPATRA
Thou'rt an honest man.
MESSENGER
Caesar and he are greater friends than ever.
CLEOPATRA
Make thee a fortune from me.

MESSENGER
But yet, madam,—
CLEOPATRA
I do not like 'But yet,' it does allay
The good precedence; fie upon 'But yet'! 66
'But yet' is as a gaoler to bring forth
Some monstrous malefactor. Prithee, friend,
Pour out the pack of matter to mine ear,
The good and bad together: he's friends with Caesar:
In state of health thou say'st; and thou say'st free.
MESSENGER
Free, madam! no; I made no such report:
He's bound unto Octavia.
CLEOPATRA
For what good turn?
MESSENGER
For the best turn i' the bed.
CLEOPATRA
I am pale, Charmian.
MESSENGER
Madam, he's married to Octavia.
CLEOPATRA
The most infectious pestilence upon thee!
[*Strikes him down.*
MESSENGER
Good madam, patience.
CLEOPATRA
What say you? Hence,
[*Strikes him again.*
Horrible villain! or I'll spurn thine eyes
Like balls before me; I'll unhair thy head:
[*She hales him up and down.*
Thou shalt be whipp'd with wire, and stew'd in brine,
Smarting in lingering pickle.
MESSENGER
Gracious madam,
I that do bring the news made not the match.
CLEOPATRA
Say 'tis not so, a province I will give thee,
And make thy fortunes proud: the blow thou hadst
Shall make thy peace for moving me to rage;
And I will boot thee with what gift beside 92
Thy modesty can beg.
MESSENGER
He's married, madam.
CLEOPATRA
Rogue, thou hast lived too long.
[*Draws a knife.*

CLEOPATRA Rogue, thou hast lived too long.

MESSENGER
Nay, then I'll run.
What mean you, madam? I have made no fault. *[Exit.*

CHARMIAN
Good madam, keep yourself within yourself:
The man is innocent.

CLEOPATRA
Some innocents 'scape not the thunderbolt.
Melt Egypt into Nile! and kindly creatures
Turn all to serpents! Call the slave again:
Though I am mad, I will not bite him: call.

CHARMIAN
He is afeard to come.

CLEOPATRA
I will not hurt him. *[Exit Charmian.*
These hands do lack nobility, that they strike
A meaner than myself; since I myself
Have given myself the cause.

Re-enter CHARMIAN *and* a Messenger.

Come hither, sir.
Though it be honest, it is never good
To bring bad news: give to a gracious message.
An host of tongues; but let ill tidings tell
Themselves when they be felt.

MESSENGER
I have done my duty.

CLEOPATRA
Is he married?
I cannot hate thee worser than I do,
If thou again say 'Yes.'

MESSENGER
He's married, madam.

CLEOPATRA
The gods confound thee! dost thou hold there still?

MESSENGER
Should I lie, madam?

CLEOPATRA
O, I would thou didst,
So half my Egypt were submerged and made
A cistern for scaled snakes! Go, get thee hence:
Hadst thou Narcissus in thy face, to me
Thou wouldst appear most ugly. He is married?

MESSENGER
I crave your highness' pardon.

CLEOPATRA
He is married?

MESSENGER
Take no offence that I would not offend you:
To punish me for what you make me do.
Seems much unequal: he's married to Octavia.

CLEOPATRA
O, that his fault should make a knave of thee,
That art not what thou'rt sure of! Get thee hence: [26]
The merchandise which thou hast brought from Rome
Are all too dear for me: lie they upon thy hand,
And be undone by 'em! *[Exit Messenger.*

CHARMIAN
Good your highness, patience.

CLEOPATRA
In praising Antony, I have dispraised Caesar.

CHARMIAN
Many times, madam.

CLEOPATRA
I am paid for't now.
Lead me from hence;
I faint: O Iras, Charmian! 'tis no matter.
Go to the fellow, good Alexas; bid him
Report the feature of Octavia, her years,
Her inclination, let him not leave out
The colour of her hair: bring me word quickly. *[Exit Alexas.*
Let him for ever go:—let him not—Charmian,
Though he be painted one way like a Gorgon, [27]
The other way's a Mars. Bid you Alexas
[To Mardian.
Bring me word how tall she is. Pity me, Charmian,
But do not speak to me. Lead me to my chamber. *[Exeunt.*

ACT TWO SCENE SIX

Near Misenum.

Flourish. Enter POMPEY *and* MENAS *at one side, with drum and trumpet: at another,* CAESAR, ANTONY, LEPIDUS, ENOBARBUS, MECAENAS, *with Soldiers marching.*

POMPEY
Your hostages I have, so have you mine;
And we shall talk before we fight.

OCTAVIUS CAESAR
Most meet
That first we come to words; and therefore have we
Our written purposes before us sent;
Which, if thou hast consider'd, let us know
If 'twill tie up thy discontented sword,
And carry back to Sicily much tall youth
That else must perish here.

POMPEY
To you all three,
The senators alone of this great world,
Chief factors for the gods, I do not know
Wherefore my father should revengers want,
Having a son and friends; since Julius Caesar,

Who at Philippi the good Brutus ghosted,
There saw you labouring for him. What was't
That moved pale Cassius to conspire; and what
Made the all-honour'd, honest Roman, Brutus,
With the arm'd rest, courtiers of beauteous freedom,
To drench the Capitol; but that they would
Have one man but a man? And that is it
Hath made me rig my navy; at whose burthen
The anger'd ocean foams; with which I meant
To scourge the ingratitude that despiteful Rome
Cast on my noble father.

OCTAVIUS CAESAR
Take your time.

MARK ANTONY
Thou canst not fear us, Pompey, with thy sails;
We'll speak with thee at sea: at land, thou know'st
How much we do o'er-count thee.

POMPEY
At land, indeed,
Thou dost o'er-count me of my father's house:
But, since the cuckoo builds not for himself,
Remain in't as thou mayst.

LEPIDUS
Be pleased to tell us—
For this is from the present — how you take
The offers we have sent you.

OCTAVIUS CAESAR
There's the point.

MARK ANTONY
Which do not be entreated to, but weigh
What it is worth embraced.

OCTAVIUS CAESAR
And what may follow,
To try a larger fortune.

POMPEY
You have made me offer
Of Sicily, Sardinia; and I must
Rid all the sea of pirates; then, to send
Measures of wheat to Rome; this 'greed upon,
To part with unhack'd edges, and bear back
Our targes undinted.

OCTAVIUS CAESAR, MARK ANTONY,
LEPIDUS
That's our offer.

POMPEY
Know, then,
I came before you here a man prepared
To take this offer: but Mark Antony
Put me to some impatience: though I lose
The praise of it by telling, you must know,
When Caesar and your brother were at blows,
Your mother came to Sicily and did find
Her welcome friendly.

MARK ANTONY
I have heard it, Pompey;
And am well studied for a liberal thanks
Which I do owe you.

POMPEY
Let me have your hand:
I did not think, sir, to have met you here.

MARK ANTONY
The beds i' the east are soft; and thanks to you,
That call'd me timelier than my purpose hither;
For I have gain'd by 't.

OCTAVIUS CAESAR
Since I saw you last,
There is a change upon you.

POMPEY
Well, I know not
What counts harsh fortune casts upon my face;
But in my bosom shall she never come,
To make my heart her vassal.

LEPIDUS
Well met here.

POMPEY
I hope so, Lepidus. Thus we are agreed:
I crave our composition may be written,
And seal'd between us.

OCTAVIUS CAESAR
That's the next to do.

POMPEY
We'll feast each other ere we part; and let's
Draw lots who shall begin.

MARK ANTONY
That will I, Pompey.

POMPEY
No, Antony, take the lot: but, first
Or last, your fine Egyptian cookery
Shall have the fame. I have heard that Julius Caesar
Grew fat with feasting there.

MARK ANTONY
You have heard much.

POMPEY
I have fair meanings, sir.

MARK ANTONY
And fair words to them.

POMPEY
Then so much have I heard:
And I have heard, Apollodorus carried—

DOMITIUS ENOBARBUS
No more of that: he did so.

POMPEY
What, I pray you?

DOMITIUS ENOBARBUS
A certain queen to Caesar in a mattress.

POMPEY
I know thee now: how farest thou, soldier?
DOMITIUS ENOBARBUS
Well;
And well am like to do; for, I perceive,
Four feasts are toward.
POMPEY
Let me shake thy hand;
I never hated thee: I have seen thee fight,
When I have envied thy behavior.
DOMITIUS ENOBARBUS
Sir,
I never loved you much; but I ha' praised ye,
When you have well deserved ten times as much
As I have said you did.
POMPEY
Enjoy thy plainness, 103
It nothing ill becomes thee.
Aboard my galley I invite you all:
Will you lead, lords?
OCTAVIUS CAESAR, MARK ANTONY, LEPIDUS
Show us the way, sir.
POMPEY
Come. [*Exeunt all but Menas and Enobarbus.*
MENAS
[*Aside.* Thy father, Pompey, would ne'er have made this treaty. — You and I have known, sir.
DOMITIUS ENOBARBUS
At sea, I think.
MENAS
We have, sir.
DOMITIUS ENOBARBUS
You have done well by water.
MENAS
And you by land. 114
DOMITIUS ENOBARBUS
I will praise any man that will praise me; though it cannot be denied what I have done by land.
MENAS
Nor what I have done by water.
DOMITIUS ENOBARBUS
Yes, something you can deny for your own safety: you have been a great thief by sea.
MENAS
And you by land.
DOMITIUS ENOBARBUS
There I deny my land service. But give me your hand, Menas: if our eyes had authority, here they might take two thieves kissing. 123
MENAS
All men's faces are true, whatsome'er their hands are.
DOMITIUS ENOBARBUS
But there is never a fair woman has a true face.
MENAS
No slander; they steal hearts.
DOMITIUS ENOBARBUS
We came hither to fight with you.
MENAS
For my part, I am sorry it is turned to a drinking. Pompey doth this day laugh away his fortune. 129
DOMITIUS ENOBARBUS
If he do, sure, he cannot weep't back again.
MENAS
You've said, sir. We looked not for Mark Antony here: pray you, is he married to Cleopatra?
DOMITIUS ENOBARBUS
Caesar's sister is called Octavia.
MENAS
True, sir; she was the wife of Caius Marcellus.
DOMITIUS ENOBARBUS
But she is now the wife of Marcus Antonius.
MENAS
Pray ye, sir? 136
DOMITIUS ENOBARBUS
'Tis true.
MENAS
Then is Caesar and he for ever knit together.
DOMITIUS ENOBARBUS
If I were bound to divine of this unity, I would not prophesy so.
MENAS
I think the policy of that purpose made more in the marriage than the love of the parties.
DOMITIUS ENOBARBUS
I think so too. But you shall find the band that seems to tie their friendship together will be the very strangler of their amity: Octavia is of a holy, cold, and still conversation. 146
MENAS
Who would not have his wife so?
DOMITIUS ENOBARBUS
Not he that himself is not so; which is Mark Antony. He will to his Egyptian dish again: then shall the sighs of Octavia blow the fire up in Caesar; and, as I said before, that which is the strength of their amity shall prove the immediate author of their variance. Antony will use his affection where it is: he married but his occasion here. 154
MENAS
And thus it may be. Come, sir, will you aboard?
I have a health for you.
DOMITIUS ENOBARBUS
I shall take it, sir: we have used our throats in Egypt.
MENAS
Come, let's away. [*Exeunt.*

ACT TWO SCENE SEVEN

On board Pompey's galley, off Misenum.

Music plays. Enter two or three Servants with a banquet.

FIRST SERVANT
Here they'll be, man. Some o' their plants are ill-rooted already: the least wind i' the world will blow them down.

SECOND SERVANT
Lepidus is high-coloured.

FIRST SERVANT
They have made him drink alms-drink.

SECOND SERVANT
As they pinch one another by the disposition, he cries out 'No more;' reconciles them to his entreaty, and himself to the drink.

FIRST SERVANT
But it raises the greater war between him and his discretion.

SECOND SERVANT
Why, this is to have a name in great men's fellowship: I had as lief have a reed that will do me no service as a partisan I could not heave.

FIRST SERVANT
To be called into a huge sphere, and not to be seen to move in't, are the holes where eyes should be, which pitifully disaster the cheeks.

A sennet sounded. Enter CAESAR, ANTONY, LEPIDUS, POMPEY, AGRIPPA, MECAENAS, ENOBARBUS, MENAS, *with other captains.*

MARK ANTONY
[*To Caesar*] Thus do they, sir, they take the flow o' the Nile
By certain scales i' the pyramid; they know,
By the height, the lowness, or the mean, if dearth
Or foison follow: the higher Nilus swells,
The more it promises: as it ebbs, the seedsman
Upon the slime and ooze scatters his grain,
And shortly comes to harvest.

LEPIDUS
You've strange serpents there.

MARK ANTONY
Ay, Lepidus.

LEPIDUS
Your serpent of Egypt is bred now of your mud by the operation of your sun: so is your crocodile.

MARK ANTONY
They are so.

POMPEY
Sit,—and some wine! A health to Lepidus!

LEPIDUS
I am not so well as I should be, but I'll ne'er out.

DOMITIUS ENOBARBUS
Not till you have slept; I fear me you'll be in till then.

LEPIDUS
Nay, certainly, I have heard the Ptolemies' pyramises are very goodly things; without contradiction, I have heard that.

MENAS
[*Aside to Pompey*] Pompey, a word.

POMPEY
[*Aside to Menas*] Say in mine ear: what is't?

MENAS
[*Aside to Pompey*] Forsake thy seat, I do beseech thee, captain,
And hear me speak a word.

POMPEY
[*Aside to Menas*] Forbear me till anon.
This wine for Lepidus!

LEPIDUS
What manner o' thing is your crocodile?

MARK ANTONY
It is shaped, sir, like itself; and it is as broad as it hath breadth: it is just so high as it is, and moves with its own organs: it lives by that which nourisheth it; and the elements once out of it, it transmigrates.

LEPIDUS
What colour is it of?

MARK ANTONY
Of it own colour too.

LEPIDUS
'Tis a strange serpent.

MARK ANTONY
'Tis so. And the tears of it are wet.

OCTAVIUS CAESAR
Will this description satisfy him?

MARK ANTONY
With the health that Pompey gives him, else he is a very epicure.

POMPEY
[*Aside to Menas*] Go hang, sir, hang! Tell me of that? away!
Do as I bid you. Where's this cup I call'd for?

MENAS
[*Aside to Pompey*] If for the sake of merit thou wilt hear me,
Rise from thy stool.

POMPEY
[*Aside to Menas*] I think thou'rt mad.
The matter? [*Rises, and walks aside.*

MENAS
I have ever held my cap off to thy fortunes.

POMPEY
Thou hast served me with much faith. What's else to say?

Be jolly, lords.

MARK ANTONY
These quick-sands, Lepidus,
Keep off them, for you sink.

MENAS
Wilt thou be lord of all the world?

POMPEY
What say'st thou?

MENAS
Wilt thou be lord of the whole world? That's twice.

POMPEY
How should that be?

MENAS
But entertain it,
And, though thou think me poor, I am the man
Will give thee all the world.

POMPEY
Hast thou drunk well?

MENAS
Now, Pompey, I have kept me from the cup.
Thou art, if thou darest be, the earthly Jove:
Whate'er the ocean pales, or sky inclips,
Is thine, if thou wilt ha't.

POMPEY
Show me which way.

MENAS
These three world-sharers, these competitors,
Are in thy vessel: let me cut the cable;
And, when we are put off, fall to their throats:
All there is thine. [28]

POMPEY
Ah, this thou shouldst have done,
And not have spoke on't! In me 'tis villany;
In thee't had been good service. Thou must know,
'Tis not my profit that does lead mine honour;
Mine honour, it. Repent that e'er thy tongue
Hath so betray'd thine act: being done unknown,
I should have found it afterwards well done;
But must condemn it now. Desist, and drink.

MENAS
[*Aside*] For this,
I'll never follow thy pall'd fortunes more.
Who seeks, and will not take when once 'tis offer'd,
Shall never find it more.

POMPEY
This health to Lepidus!

MARK ANTONY
Bear him ashore. I'll pledge it for him, Pompey.

DOMITIUS ENOBARBUS
Here's to thee, Menas!

MENAS
Enobarbus, welcome!

POMPEY
Fill till the cup be hid.

DOMITIUS ENOBARBUS
There's a strong fellow, Menas.
[*Pointing to the Attendant, who carries off Lepidus.*

MENAS
Why?

DOMITIUS ENOBARBUS
A' bears the third part of the world, man; see'st not?

MENAS
The third part, then, is drunk: would it were all,
That it might go on wheels!

DOMITIUS ENOBARBUS
Drink thou; increase the reels. [29]

MENAS
Come.

POMPEY
This is not yet an Alexandrian feast.

MARK ANTONY
It ripens towards it. Strike the vessels, ho?
Here is to Caesar!

OCTAVIUS CAESAR
I could well forbear't.
It's monstrous labour, when I wash my brain,
And it grows fouler.

MARK ANTONY
Be a child o' the time.

OCTAVIUS CAESAR
Possess it, I'll make answer:
But I had rather fast from all four days
Than drink so much in one.

DOMITIUS ENOBARBUS
Ha, my brave emperor! [*To Antony.*
Shall we dance now the Egyptian Bacchanals,
And celebrate our drink?

POMPEY
Let's ha't, good soldier.

MARK ANTONY
Come, let's all take hands,
Till that the conquering wine hath steep'd our sense
In soft and delicate Lethe.

DOMITIUS ENOBARBUS
All take hands.
Make battery to our ears with the loud music:
The while I'll place you: then the boy shall sing;
The holding every man shall bear as loud [30]
As his strong sides can volley.
[*Music Plays. Enobarbus places them hand in hand.*

THE SONG.

Come, thou monarch of the vine,
Plumpy Bacchus with pink eyne!
In thy fats our cares be drown'd,
With thy grapes our hairs be crown'd:
Cup us, till the world go round,

Cup us, till the world go round!
OCTAVIUS CAESAR
What would you more? Pompey, good night. Good brother,
Let me request you off: our graver business
Frowns at this levity. Gentle lords, let's part;
You see we have burnt our cheeks: strong Enobarb
Is weaker than the wine; and mine own tongue
Splits what it speaks: the wild disguise hath almost 147
Antick'd us all. What needs more words? Good night.
Good Antony, your hand.
POMPEY
I'll try you on the shore.
MARK ANTONY
And shall, sir; give's your hand.
POMPEY
O Antony,
You have my father's house,—But, what? we are friends.
Come, down into the boat.
DOMITIUS ENOBARBUS
Take heed you fall not. [*Exeunt all but Enobarbus and Menas.*
Menas, I'll not on shore.
MENAS
No, to my cabin.
These drums! these trumpets, flutes! what!
Let Neptune hear we bid a loud farewell
To these great fellows: sound and be hang'd, sound out! [*Sound a flourish, with drums.*
DOMITIUS ENOBARBUS
Ho! says I. There's my cap. 163
MENAS
Ho! Noble captain, come. [*Exeunt.*

ACT THREE SCENE ONE

A plain in Syria.

Enter VENTIDIUS *as it were in triumph, with* SILIUS, *and other* Romans, Officers, *and* Soldiers; *the dead body of* PACORUS *borne before him.*

VENTIDIUS
Now, darting Parthia, art thou struck; and now
Pleased fortune does of Marcus Crassus' death
Make me revenger. Bear the king's son's body
Before our army. Thy Pacorus, Orodes,
Pays this for Marcus Crassus.
SILIUS
Noble Ventidius,
Whilst yet with Parthian blood thy sword is warm,
The fugitive Parthians follow; spur through Media,
Mesopotamia, and the shelters whither
The routed fly: so thy grand captain Antony
Shall set thee on triumphant chariots and 11
Put garlands on thy head.
VENTIDIUS
O Silius, Silius,
I have done enough; a lower place, note well,
May make too great an act: for learn this, Silius;
Better to leave undone, than by our deed
Acquire too high a fame when him we serve's away.
Caesar and Antony have ever won
More in their officer than person: Sossius,
One of my place in Syria, his lieutenant,
For quick accumulation of renown,
Which he achieved by the minute, lost his favour. 23
Who does i' the wars more than his captain can
Becomes his captain's captain: and ambition,
The soldier's virtue, rather makes choice of loss,
Than gain which darkens him.
I could do more to do Antonius good,
But 'twould offend him; and in his offence
Should my performance perish.
SILIUS
Thou hast, Ventidius, that
Without the which a soldier, and his sword,
Grants scarce distinction. Thou wilt write to Antony!
VENTIDIUS
I'll humbly signify what in his name,
That magical word of war, we have effected;
How, with his banners and his well-paid ranks,
The ne'er-yet-beaten horse of Parthia
We have jaded out o' the field.
SILIUS
Where is he now?
VENTIDIUS
He purposeth to Athens: whither, with what haste
The weight we must convey with's will permit,
We shall appear before him. On, there; pass along! [*Exeunt.*

ACT THREE SCENE TWO

Rome. An ante-chamber in CAESAR'S *house.*

Enter AGRIPPA *at one door*, ENOBARBUS *at another.*

AGRIPPA
What, are the brothers parted?
DOMITIUS ENOBARBUS
They have dispatch'd with Pompey, he is gone;
The other three are sealing. Octavia weeps
To part from Rome; Caesar is sad; and Lepidus,

Since Pompey's feast, as Menas says, is troubled
With the green sickness.

AGRIPPA
'Tis a noble Lepidus.

DOMITIUS ENOBARBUS
A very fine one: O, how he loves Caesar!

AGRIPPA
Nay, but how dearly he adores Mark Antony!

DOMITIUS ENOBARBUS
Caesar? Why, he's the Jupiter of men.

AGRIPPA
What's Antony? The god of Jupiter.

DOMITIUS ENOBARBUS
Spake you of Caesar? How! the nonpareil!

AGRIPPA
O Antony! O thou Arabian bird!

DOMITIUS ENOBARBUS
Would you praise Caesar, say 'Caesar:' go no further.

AGRIPPA
Indeed, he plied them both with excellent praises.

DOMITIUS ENOBARBUS
But he loves Caesar best; yet he loves Antony:
Ho! hearts, tongues, figures, scribes, bards, poets, cannot
Think, speak, cast, write, sing, number, ho!
His love for Antony. But as for Caesar,
Kneel down, kneel down, and wonder.

AGRIPPA
Both he loves.

DOMITIUS ENOBARBUS
They are his shards, and he their beetle.
[*Trumpets within*] So;
This is to horse. Adieu, noble Agrippa.

AGRIPPA
Good fortune, worthy soldier; and farewell.

Enter CAESAR, MARK ANTONY, LEPIDUS, *and* OCTAVIA.

MARK ANTONY
No further, sir.

OCTAVIUS CAESAR
You take from me a great part of myself;
Use me well in 't. Sister, prove such a wife
As my thoughts make thee, and as my farthest band
Shall pass on thy approof. Most noble Antony,
Let not the piece of virtue, which is set
Betwixt us as the cement of our love,
To keep it builded, be the ram to batter
The fortress of it; for better might we
Have loved without this mean, if on both parts
This be not cherish'd.

MARK ANTONY
Make me not offended
In your distrust.

OCTAVIUS CAESAR
I have said.

MARK ANTONY
You shall not find,
Though you be therein curious, the least cause
For what you seem to fear: so, the gods keep you,
And make the hearts of Romans serve your ends!
We will here part.

OCTAVIUS CAESAR
Farewell, my dearest sister, fare thee well:
The elements be kind to thee, and make
Thy spirits all of comfort! fare thee well.

OCTAVIA
My noble brother!

MARK ANTONY
The April's in her eyes: it is love's spring,
And these the showers to bring it on. Be cheerful.

OCTAVIA
Sir, look well to my husband's house; and—

OCTAVIUS CAESAR
What,
Octavia?

OCTAVIA
I'll tell you in your ear.

MARK ANTONY
Her tongue will not obey her heart, nor can
Her heart inform her tongue,—the swan's down-feather,
That stands upon the swell at full of tide,
And neither way inclines.

DOMITIUS ENOBARBUS
[*Aside to Agrippa*] Will Caesar weep?

AGRIPPA
[*Aside to Enobarbus*]
He has a cloud in's face.

DOMITIUS ENOBARBUS
[*Aside to Agrippa*] He were the worse for that, were he a horse;
So is he, being a man.

AGRIPPA
[*Aside to Enobarbus*] Why, Enobarbus,
When Antony found Julius Caesar dead,
He cried almost to roaring; and he wept
When at Philippi he found Brutus slain.

DOMITIUS ENOBARBUS
[*Aside to Agrippa*] That year, indeed, he was troubled with a rheum;
What willingly he did confound he wail'd,
Believe't, till I wept too.

OCTAVIUS CAESAR
No, sweet Octavia,
You shall hear from me still; the time shall not
Out-go my thinking on you.

MARK ANTONY
Come, sir, come;
I'll wrestle with you in my strength of love:
Look, here I have you; thus I let you go,
And give you to the gods.
OCTAVIUS CAESAR
Adieu; be happy!
LEPIDUS
Let all the number of the stars give light
To thy fair way!
OCTAVIUS CAESAR
Farewell, farewell! [*Kisses Octavia.*
MARK ANTONY
Farewell! [*Trumpets sound. Exeunt.*

ACT THREE SCENE THREE

Alexandria. Cleopatra's *palace.*

Enter CLEOPATRA, CHARMIAN, IRAS, *and* ALEXAS.

CLEOPATRA
Where is the fellow?
ALEXAS
Half afeard to come.
CLEOPATRA
Go to, go to.

Enter the Messenger *as before.*

Come hither, sir.
ALEXAS
Good majesty,
Herod of Jewry dare not look upon you
But when you are well pleased.
CLEOPATRA
That Herod's head
I'll have: but how, when Antony is gone
Through whom I might command it? Come thou near.
MESSENGER
Most gracious majesty,—
CLEOPATRA
Didst thou behold Octavia?
MESSENGER
Ay, dread queen.
CLEOPATRA
Where?
MESSENGER
Madam, in Rome;
I look'd her in the face, and saw her led
Between her brother and Mark Antony.
CLEOPATRA
Is she as tall as me?
MESSENGER
She is not, madam.
CLEOPATRA
Didst hear her speak? is she shrill-tongued or low?
MESSENGER
Madam, I heard her speak; she is low-voiced.
CLEOPATRA
That's not so good: he cannot like her long.
CHARMIAN
Like her! O Isis! 'tis impossible.
CLEOPATRA
I think so, Charmian: dull of tongue, and dwarfish!
What majesty is in her gait? Remember,
If e'er thou look'dst on majesty.
MESSENGER
She creeps:
Her motion and her station are as one;
She shows a body rather than a life,
A statue than a breather.
CLEOPATRA
Is this certain?
MESSENGER
Or I have no observance.
CHARMIAN
Three in Egypt
Cannot make better note.
CLEOPATRA
He's very knowing;
I do perceive't: there's nothing in her yet:
The fellow has good judgment.
CHARMIAN
Excellent.
CLEOPATRA
Guess at her years, I prithee.
MESSENGER
Madam,
She was a widow,—
CLEOPATRA
Widow! Charmian, hark.
MESSENGER
And I do think she's thirty.
CLEOPATRA
Bear'st thou her face in mind? is't long or round?
MESSENGER
Round even to faultiness.
CLEOPATRA
For the most part, too, they are foolish that are so.
Her hair, what colour?
MESSENGER
Brown, madam: and her forehead
As low as she would wish it.
CLEOPATRA
There's gold for thee.

Thou must not take my former sharpness ill:
I will employ thee back again; I find thee
Most fit for business: go make thee ready;
Our letters are prepared. [*Exit Messenger.*

CHARMIAN
A proper man.

CLEOPATRA
Indeed, he is so: I repent me much
That so I harried him. Why, methinks, by him,
This creature's no such thing.

CHARMIAN
Nothing, madam.

CLEOPATRA
The man hath seen some majesty, and should know.

CHARMIAN
Hath he seen majesty? Isis else defend,
And serving you so long!

CLEOPATRA
I have one thing more to ask him yet, good Charmian:
But 'tis no matter; thou shalt bring him to me
Where I will write. All may be well enough.

CHARMIAN
I warrant you, madam. [*Exeunt.*

ACT THREE SCENE FOUR

Athens. A room in Antony's *house.*

Enter ANTONY *and* OCTAVIA.

MARK ANTONY
Nay, nay, Octavia, not only that,—
That were excusable, that, and thousands more
Of semblable import,—but he hath waged
New wars 'gainst Pompey; made his will, and read it
To public ear:
Spoke scantly of me: when perforce he could not
But pay me terms of honour, cold and sickly
He vented them; most narrow measure lent me:
When the best hint was given him, he not took't,
Or did it from his teeth.

OCTAVIA
O my good lord,
Believe not all; or, if you must believe,
Stomach not all. A more unhappy lady,
If this division chance, ne'er stood between,
Praying for both parts:
The good gods mock me presently,
When I shall pray, 'O, bless my lord and husband!'
Undo that prayer, by crying out as loud,
'O, bless my brother!' Husband win, win brother,
Prays, and destroys the prayer; no midway
'Twixt these extremes at all.

MARK ANTONY
Gentle Octavia,
Let your best love draw to that point, which seeks
Best to preserve it: if I lose mine honour,
I lose myself: better I were not yours
Than yours so branchless. But, as you requested,
Yourself shall go between's: the mean time, lady,
I'll raise the preparation of a war
Shall stain your brother: make your soonest haste;
So your desires are yours.

OCTAVIA
Thanks to my lord.
The Jove of power make me most weak, most weak,
Your reconciler! Wars 'twixt you twain would be
As if the world should cleave, and that slain men
Should solder up the rift.

MARK ANTONY
When it appears to you where this begins,
Turn your displeasure that way: for our faults
Can never be so equal, that your love
Can equally move with them. Provide your going;
Choose your own company, and command what cost
Your heart has mind to. [*Exeunt.*

ACT THREE SCENE FIVE

The same. Another room.

Enter ENOBARBUS *and* EROS, *meeting.*

DOMITIUS ENOBARBUS
How now, friend Eros!

EROS
There's strange news come, sir.

DOMITIUS ENOBARBUS
What, man?

EROS
Caesar and Lepidus have made wars upon Pompey.

DOMITIUS ENOBARBUS
This is old: what is the success?

EROS
Caesar, having made use of him in the wars 'gainst Pompey, presently denied him rivality; would not let him partake in the glory of the action: and not resting here, accuses him of letters he had formerly wrote to Pompey; upon his own appeal, seizes him: so the poor third is up, till death enlarge his confine.

DOMITIUS ENOBARBUS
Then, world, thou hast a pair of chaps, no more; [31]
And throw between them all the food thou hast,
They'll grind the one the other. Where's Antony?

EROS
He's walking in the garden—thus; and spurns

The rush that lies before him; cries, 'Fool Lepidus!'
And threats the throat of that his officer
That murder'd Pompey.

DOMITIUS ENOBARBUS
Our great navy's rigg'd.

EROS
For Italy and Caesar. More, Domitius;
My lord desires you presently: my news
I might have told hereafter.

DOMITIUS ENOBARBUS
'Twill be naught:
But let it be. Bring me to Antony.

EROS
Come, sir. [*Exeunt.*

ACT THREE SCENE SIX

Rome. CAESAR'S *house.*

Enter CAESAR, AGRIPPA, *and* MECAENAS.

OCTAVIUS CAESAR
Contemning Rome, he has done all this, and more,
In Alexandria: here's the manner of 't:
I' the market-place, on a tribunal silver'd,
Cleopatra and himself in chairs of gold
Were publicly enthroned: at the feet sat
Caesarion, whom they call my father's son,
And all the unlawful issue that their lust
Since then hath made between them. Unto her
He gave the stablishment of Egypt; made her
Of lower Syria, Cyprus, Lydia,
Absolute queen.

MECAENAS
This in the public eye?

OCTAVIUS CAESAR
I' the common show-place, where they exercise.
His sons he there proclaim'd the kings of kings:
Great Media, Parthia, and Armenia,
He gave to Alexander; to Ptolemy he assign'd
Syria, Cilicia, and Phoenicia: she
In the habiliments of the goddess Isis
That day appear'd; and oft before gave audience,
As 'tis reported, so.

MECAENAS
Let Rome be thus Inform'd.

AGRIPPA
Who, queasy with his insolence
Already, will their good thoughts call from him.

OCTAVIUS CAESAR
The people know it; and have now received
His accusations.

AGRIPPA
Who does he accuse?

OCTAVIUS CAESAR
Caesar: and that, having in Sicily
Sextus Pompeius spoil'd, we had not rated him
His part o' the isle: then does he say, he lent me
Some shipping unrestored: lastly, he frets
That Lepidus of the triumvirate
Should be deposed; and, being, that we detain
All his revenue.

AGRIPPA
Sir, this should be answer'd.

OCTAVIUS CAESAR
'Tis done already, and the messenger gone.
I have told him, Lepidus was grown too cruel;
That he his high authority abused,
And did deserve his change: for what I have conquer'd,
I grant him part; but then, in his Armenia,
And other of his conquer'd kingdoms, I
Demand the like.

MECAENAS
He'll never yield to that.

OCTAVIUS CAESAR
Nor must not then be yielded to in this.

Enter OCTAVIA *with her train.*

OCTAVIA
Hail, Caesar, and my lord! hail, most dear Caesar!

OCTAVIUS CAESAR
That ever I should call thee castaway!

OCTAVIA
You have not call'd me so, nor have you cause.

OCTAVIUS CAESAR
Why have you stol'n upon us thus! You come not
Like Caesar's sister: the wife of Antony
Should have an army for an usher, and
The neighs of horse to tell of her approach
Long ere she did appear; the trees by the way
Should have borne men; and expectation fainted,
Longing for what it had not; nay, the dust
Should have ascended to the roof of heaven,
Raised by your populous troops: but you are come
A market-maid to Rome: and have prevented
The ostentation of our love, which, left unshown,
Is often left unloved: we should have met you [32]
By sea and land; supplying every stage
With an augmented greeting.

OCTAVIA
Good my lord,
To come thus was I not constrain'd, but did it
On my free will. My lord, Mark Antony,
Hearing that you prepared for war, acquainted
My grieved ear withal; whereon, I begg'd
His pardon for return.

OCTAVIUS CAESAR
Which soon he granted,
Being an obstruct 'tween his lust and him.
OCTAVIA
Do not say so, my lord.
OCTAVIUS CAESAR
I have eyes upon him,
And his affairs come to me on the wind.
Where is he now?
OCTAVIA
My lord, in Athens.
OCTAVIUS CAESAR
No, my most wronged sister; Cleopatra
Hath nodded him to her. He hath given his empire
Up to a whore; who now are levying
The kings o' the earth for war: he hath assembled
Bocchus, the king of Libya; Archelaus,
Of Cappadocia; Philadelphos, king 81
Of Paphlagonia; the Thracian king, Adallas;
King Malchus of Arabia; King of Pont;
Herod of Jewry; Mithridates, king
Of Comagene; Polemon and Amyntas,
The kings of Mede and Lycaonia,
With a more larger list of sceptres.
OCTAVIA
Ay me, most wretched,
That have my heart parted betwixt two friends
That do afflict each other!
OCTAVIUS CAESAR
Welcome hither:
Your letters did withhold our breaking forth;
Till we perceived, both how you were wrong led, 94
And we in negligent danger. Cheer your heart;
Be you not troubled with the time, which drives
O'er your content these strong necessities;
But let determined things to destiny
Hold unbewail'd their way. Welcome to Rome;
Nothing more dear to me. You are abused
Beyond the mark of thought: and the high gods,
To do you justice, make them ministers
Of us and those that love you. Best of comfort;
And ever welcome to us.
AGRIPPA
Welcome, lady. 105
MECAENAS
Welcome, dear madam.
Each heart in Rome does love and pity you:
Only the adulterous Antony, most large
In his abominations, turns you off;
And gives his potent regiment to a trull,
That noises it against us.
OCTAVIA
Is it so, sir?
OCTAVIUS CAESAR
Most certain. Sister, welcome: pray you,
Be ever known to patience: my dear'st sister! [*Exeunt.*

ACT THREE SCENE SEVEN

Near Actium. ANTONY'S *camp.*

Enter CLEOPATRA *and* ENOBARBUS.

CLEOPATRA
I will be even with thee, doubt it not.
DOMITIUS ENOBARBUS
But why, why, why?
CLEOPATRA
Thou hast forspoke my being in these wars,
And say'st it is not fit.
DOMITIUS ENOBARBUS
Well, is it, is it?
CLEOPATRA
If not denounced against us, why should not we [33]
Be there in person?
DOMITIUS ENOBARBUS
[*Aside*] Well, I could reply:
If we should serve with horse and mares together,
The horse were merely lost; the mares would bear
A soldier and his horse.
CLEOPATRA
What is't you say? 13
DOMITIUS ENOBARBUS
Your presence needs must puzzle Antony;
Take from his heart, take from his brain, from's time,
What should not then be spared. He is already
Traduced for levity; and 'tis said in Rome
That Photinus an eunuch and your maids
Manage this war.
CLEOPATRA
Sink Rome, and their tongues rot
That speak against us! A charge we bear i' the war,
And, as the president of my kingdom, will
Appear there for a man. Speak not against it;
I will not stay behind.
DOMITIUS ENOBARBUS
Nay, I have done. 25
Here comes the emperor.

Enter MARK ANTONY *and* CANIDIUS.

MARK ANTONY
Is it not strange, Canidius,
That from Tarentum and Brundusium
He could so quickly cut the Ionian sea,

And take in Toryne? You have heard on't, sweet?
CLEOPATRA
Celerity is never more admired
Than by the negligent.
MARK ANTONY
A good rebuke,
Which might have well becomed the best of men,
To taunt at slackness. Canidius, we
Will fight with him by sea.
CLEOPATRA
By sea! what else?
CANIDIUS
Why will my lord do so?
MARK ANTONY
For that he dares us to't.
DOMITIUS ENOBARBUS
So hath my lord dared him to single fight.
CANIDIUS
Ay, and to wage this battle at Pharsalia.
Where Caesar fought with Pompey: but these offers,
Which serve not for his vantage, be shakes off;
And so should you.
DOMITIUS ENOBARBUS
Your ships are not well mann'd;
Your mariners are muleters, reapers, people
Ingross'd by swift impress; in Caesar's fleet
Are those that often have 'gainst Pompey fought:
Their ships are yare; yours, heavy: no disgrace
Shall fall you for refusing him at sea,
Being prepared for land.
MARK ANTONY
By sea, by sea.
DOMITIUS ENOBARBUS
Most worthy sir, you therein throw away
The absolute soldiership you have by land;
Distract your army, which doth most consist
Of war-mark'd footmen; leave unexecuted
Your own renowned knowledge; quite forego
The way which promises assurance; and
Give up yourself merely to chance and hazard,
From firm security.
MARK ANTONY
I'll fight at sea.
CLEOPATRA
I have sixty sails, Caesar none better.
MARK ANTONY
Our overplus of shipping will we burn;
And, with the rest full-mann'd, from the head of Actium
Beat the approaching Caesar. But if we fail,
We then can do't at land.

Enter a Messenger.

Thy business?
MESSENGER
The news is true, my lord; he is descried;
Caesar has taken Toryne.
MARK ANTONY
Can he be there in person? 'tis impossible;
Strange that power should be. Canidius,
Our nineteen legions thou shalt hold by land,
And our twelve thousand horse. We'll to our ship:
Away, my Thetis!

Enter a Soldier.

How now, worthy soldier?
SOLDIER
O noble emperor, do not fight by sea;
Trust not to rotten planks: do you misdoubt
This sword and these my wounds? Let the Egyptians
And the Phoenicians go a-ducking: we
Have used to conquer, standing on the earth,
And fighting foot to foot.
MARK ANTONY
Well, well; away! [*Exeunt Antony, Cleopatra, and Enobarbus.*
SOLDIER
By Hercules, I think I am i' the right.
CANIDIUS
Soldier, thou art: but his whole action grows [34]
Not in the power on't: so our leader's led,
And we are women's men.
SOLDIER
You keep by land
The legions and the horse whole, do you not?
CANIDIUS
Marcus Octavius, Marcus Justeius,
Publicola, and Caelius, are for sea:
But we keep whole by land. This speed of Caesar's
Carries beyond belief.
SOLDIER
While he was yet in Rome,
His power went out in such distractions as
Beguiled all spies.
CANIDIUS
Who's his lieutenant, hear you?
SOLDIER
They say, one Taurus.
CANIDIUS
Well I know the man.

Enter a Messenger.

MESSENGER
The emperor calls Canidius.
CANIDIUS
With news the time's with labour, and throes forth,

Each minute, some. [*Exeunt.*

ACT THREE SCENE EIGHT

A plain near Actium.

Enter CAESAR, *and* TAURUS, *with his army, marching.*

OCTAVIUS CAESAR
Taurus!
TAURUS
My lord?
OCTAVIUS CAESAR
Strike not by land; keep whole: provoke not battle,
Till we have done at sea. Do not exceed
The prescript of this scroll: our fortune lies
Upon this jump. [*Exeunt.*

ACT THREE SCENE NINE

Another part of the plain.

Enter ANTONY *and* ENOBARBUS.

MARK ANTONY
Set we our squadrons on yon side o' the hill,
In eye of Caesar's battle; from which place
We may the number of the ships behold,
And so proceed accordingly. [*Exeunt.*

ACT THREE SCENE TEN

Another part of the plain.
[*CANIDIUS marcheth with his land army one way over the stage; and TAURUS, the lieutenant of CAESAR, the other way. After their going in, is heard the noise of a sea-fight.*

Alarum. Enter DOMITIUS ENOBARBUS.

DOMITIUS ENOBARBUS
Naught, naught, all naught! I can behold no longer:
The Antoniad, the Egyptian admiral,
With all their sixty, fly and turn the rudder:
To see't mine eyes are blasted.

Enter SCARUS.

SCARUS
Gods and goddesses,
All the whole synod of them!
DOMITIUS ENOBARBUS
What's thy passion?
SCARUS
The greater cantle of the world is lost
With very ignorance; we have kiss'd away
Kingdoms and provinces.
DOMITIUS ENOBARBUS
How appears the fight?
SCARUS
On our side like the token'd pestilence,
Where death is sure. Yon ribaudred nag of
Egypt,— 14
Whom leprosy o'ertake!—i' the midst o' the fight,
When vantage like a pair of twins appear'd,
Both as the same, or rather ours the elder,
The breese upon her, like a cow in June,
Hoists sails and flies.
DOMITIUS ENOBARBUS
That I beheld:
Mine eyes did sicken at the sight, and could not
Endure a further view.
SCARUS
She once being loof'd,
The noble ruin of her magic, Antony,
Claps on his sea-wing, and, like a doting
mallard, 26
Leaving the fight in height, flies after her:
I never saw an action of such shame;
Experience, manhood, honour, ne'er before
Did violate so itself.
DOMITIUS ENOBARBUS
Alack, alack!

Enter CANIDIUS.

CANIDIUS
Our fortune on the sea is out of breath,
And sinks most lamentably. Had our general
Been what he knew himself, it had gone well:
O, he has given example for our flight,
Most grossly, by his own!
DOMITIUS ENOBARBUS
Ay, are you thereabouts?
Why, then, good night indeed. 38
CANIDIUS
Toward Peloponnesus are they fled.
SCARUS
'Tis easy to't; and there I will attend
What further comes.
CANIDIUS
To Caesar will I render
My legions and my horse: six kings already
Show me the way of yielding.
DOMITIUS ENOBARBUS
I'll yet follow
The wounded chance of Antony, though my reason
Sits in the wind against me. [*Exeunt.*

ACT THREE SCENE ELEVEN

Alexandria. CLEOPATRA'S *palace.*

Enter MARK ANTONY *with* Attendants.

MARK ANTONY
Hark! the land bids me tread no more upon't;
It is ashamed to bear me! Friends, come hither:
I am so hated in the world, that I
Have lost my way for ever: I have a ship
Laden with gold; take that, divide it; fly,
And make your peace with Caesar.
ALL
Fly! not we.
MARK ANTONY
I have fled myself; and have instructed cowards
To run and show their shoulders. Friends, be gone; 9
I have myself resolved upon a course
Which has no need of you; be gone:
My treasure's in the harbour, take it. O,
I follow'd that I blush to look upon:
My very hairs do mutiny; for the white
Reprove the brown for rashness, and they them
For fear and doting. Friends, be gone: you shall
Have letters from me to some friends that will
Sweep your way for you. Pray you, look not sad,
Nor make replies of loathness: take the hint
Which my despair proclaims; let that be left
Which leaves itself: to the sea-side straightway:
I will possess you of that ship and treasure. 22
Leave me, I pray, a little: pray you now:
Nay, do so; for, indeed, I have lost command,
Therefore I pray you: I'll see you by and by.
[*Sits down.*

Enter CLEOPATRA *led by* CHARMIAN *and* IRAS; EROS *following.*

EROS
Nay, gentle madam, to him, comfort him.
IRAS
Do, most dear queen.
CHARMIAN
Do! why: what else?
CLEOPATRA
Let me sit down. O Juno!
MARK ANTONY
No, no, no, no, no.
EROS
See you here, sir? 31
MARK ANTONY
O fie, fie, fie!
CHARMIAN
Madam!
IRAS
Madam, O good empress!
EROS
Sir, sir,—
MARK ANTONY
Yes, my lord, yes; he at Philippi kept
His sword e'en like a dancer; while I struck
The lean and wrinkled Cassius; and 'twas I
That the mad Brutus ended: he alone
Dealt on lieutenantry, and no practise had
In the brave squares of war: yet now—No
matter. 42
CLEOPATRA
Ah, stand by.
EROS
The queen, my lord, the queen.
IRAS
Go to him, madam, speak to him:
He is unqualitied with very shame.
CLEOPATRA
Well then, sustain me: O!
EROS
Most noble sir, arise; the queen approaches:
Her head's declined, and death will seize her, but
Your comfort makes the rescue.
MARK ANTONY
I have offended reputation,—A most unnoble swerving.
EROS
Sir, the queen. 53
MARK ANTONY
O, whither hast thou led me, Egypt? See,
How I convey my shame out of thine eyes
By looking back what I have left behind
'Stroy'd in dishonour.
CLEOPATRA
O my lord, my lord,
Forgive my fearful sails! I little thought
You would have follow'd.
MARK ANTONY
Egypt, thou knew'st too well
My heart was to thy rudder tied by the strings,
And thou shouldst tow me after: o'er my spirit
Thy full supremacy thou knew'st, and that
Thy beck might from the bidding of the gods
Command me.
CLEOPATRA
O, my pardon!
MARK ANTONY
Now I must 68
To the young man send humble treaties, dodge
And palter in the shifts of lowness; who
With half the bulk o' the world play'd as I pleased,
Making and marring fortunes. You did know
How much you were my conqueror; and that
My sword, made weak by my affection, would
Obey it on all cause.

ANTONY I have offended reputation, — A most unnoble swerving.

CLEOPATRA
Pardon, pardon!
MARK ANTONY
Fall not a tear, I say; one of them rates
All that is won and lost: give me a kiss; 78
Even this repays me. We sent our schoolmaster;
Is he come back? Love, I am full of lead.
Some wine, within there, and our viands! Fortune knows
We scorn her most when most she offers blows. [*Exeunt*.

ACT THREE SCENE TWELVE

Egypt. CAESAR'S *camp*.
Enter CAESAR, DOLABELLA, THYREUS, *with others*.

OCTAVIUS CAESAR
Let him appear that's come from Antony.
Know you him?
DOLABELLA
Caesar, 'tis his schoolmaster:
An argument that he is pluck'd, when hither
He sends so poor a pinion of his wing,
Which had superfluous kings for messengers
Not many moons gone by.

Enter EUPHRONIUS, *ambassador from* ANTONY.

OCTAVIUS CAESAR
Approach, and speak.
EUPHRONIUS
Such as I am, I come from Antony:
I was of late as petty to his ends
As is the morn-dew on the myrtle-leaf
To his grand sea.
OCTAVIUS CAESAR
Be't so: declare thine office. 13
EUPHRONIUS
Lord of his fortunes he salutes thee, and
Requires to live in Egypt: which not granted,
He lessens his requests; and to thee sues
To let him breathe between the heavens and earth,
A private man in Athens: this for him.
Next, Cleopatra does confess thy greatness;
Submits her to thy might; and of thee craves
The circle of the Ptolemies for her heirs,
Now hazarded to thy grace.

OCTAVIUS CAESAR
For Antony,
I have no ears to his request. The queen 24
Of audience nor desire shall fail, so she
From Egypt drive her all-disgraced friend,
Or take his life there: this if she perform,
She shall not sue unheard. So to them both.

EUPHRONIUS
Fortune pursue thee!

OCTAVIUS CAESAR
Bring him through the bands. [*Exit Euphronius.*
[*To Thyreus.*] To try eloquence, now 'tis time: dispatch;
From Antony win Cleopatra: promise,
And in our name, what she requires; add more, *35*
From thine invention, offers: women are not
In their best fortunes strong; but want will perjure 37
The ne'er touch'd vestal: try thy cunning, Thyreus;
Make thine own edict for thy pains, which we
Will answer as a law.

THYREUS
Caesar, I go.

OCTAVIUS CAESAR
Observe how Antony becomes his flaw,
And what thou think'st his very action speaks
In every power that moves.

THYREUS
Caesar, I shall. [*Exeunt.*

ACT THREE SCENE THIRTEEN

Alexandria. Cleopatra's *palace.*

Enter CLEOPATRA, ENOBARBUS, CHARMIAN, *and* IRAS.

CLEOPATRA
What shall we do, Enobarbus?

DOMITIUS ENOBARBUS
Think, and die.

CLEOPATRA
Is Antony or we in fault for this?

DOMITIUS ENOBARBUS
Antony only, that would make his will
Lord of his reason. What though you fled
From that great face of war, whose several ranges
Frighted each other? why should he follow?
The itch of his affection should not then
Have nick'd his captainship; at such a point,
When half to half the world opposed, he being
The meered question: 'twas a shame no less
Than was his loss, to course your flying flags,
And leave his navy gazing.

CLEOPATRA
Prithee, peace.

Enter MARK ANTONY *and* EUPHRONIUS, *the Ambassador.*

MARK ANTONY
Is that his answer?

EUPHRONIUS
Ay, my lord.

MARK ANTONY
The queen shall then have courtesy, so she
Will yield us up.

EUPHRONIUS
He says so.

MARK ANTONY
Let her know't.
To the boy Caesar send this grizzled head,
And he will fill thy wishes to the brim
With principalities.

CLEOPATRA
That head, my lord?

MARK ANTONY
To him again: tell him he wears the rose 25
Of youth upon him; from which the world should note
Something particular: his coin, ships, legions,
May be a coward's; whose ministers would prevail
Under the service of a child as soon
As i' the command of Caesar: I dare him therefore
To lay his gay comparisons apart,
And answer me declined, sword against sword,
Ourselves alone. I'll write it: follow me. [*Exeunt Antony and Euphronius.*

DOMITIUS ENOBARBUS
[*Aside.*] Yes, like enough, high-battled Caesar will
Unstate his happiness, and be staged to the show, 38
Against a sworder! I see men's judgments are
A parcel of their fortunes; and things outward
Do draw the inward quality after them,
To suffer all alike. That he should dream,
Knowing all measures, the full Caesar will
Answer his emptiness! Caesar, thou hast subdued
His judgment too.

Enter an Attendant.

ATTENDANT
A messenger from Caesar.

CLEOPATRA
What, no more ceremony? See, my women!
Against the blown rose may they stop their nose
That kneel'd unto the buds. Admit him, sir. [*Exit Attendant.*

DOMITIUS ENOBARBUS
[*Aside.*] Mine honesty and I begin to square.
The loyalty well held to fools does make
Our faith mere folly: yet he that can endure
To follow with allegiance a fall'n lord
Does conquer him that did his master conquer,
And earns a place i' the story.

Enter THYREUS.

CLEOPATRA
Caesar's will?
THYREUS
Hear it apart.
CLEOPATRA
None but friends: say boldly.
THYREUS
So, haply, are they friends to Antony.
DOMITIUS ENOBARBUS
He needs as many, sir, as Caesar has;
Or needs not us. If Caesar please, our master
Will leap to be his friend: for us, you know
Whose he is we are, and that is, Caesar's.
THYREUS
So.
Thus then, thou most renown'd: Caesar entreats,
Not to consider in what case thou stand'st,
Further than he is Caesar.
CLEOPATRA
Go on: right royal.
THYREUS
He knows that you embrace not Antony
As you did love, but as you fear'd him.
CLEOPATRA
O!
THYREUS
The scars upon your honour, therefore, he
Does pity, as constrained blemishes,
Not as deserved.
CLEOPATRA
He is a god, and knows
What is most right: mine honour was not yielded,
But conquer'd merely.
DOMITIUS ENOBARBUS
[*Aside.*] To be sure of that,
I will ask Antony. Sir, sir, thou art so leaky,
That we must leave thee to thy sinking, for
Thy dearest quit thee. [*Exit.*
THYREUS
Shall I say to Caesar
What you require of him? for he partly begs
To be desired to give. It much would please him,
That of his fortunes you should make a staff
To lean upon: but it would warm his spirits,
To hear from me you had left Antony,
And put yourself under his shrowd,
The universal landlord.
CLEOPATRA
What's your name?
THYREUS
My name is Thyreus.
CLEOPATRA
Most kind messenger,
Say to great Caesar this: in deputation
I kiss his conquering hand: tell him, I am prompt
To lay my crown at's feet, and there to kneel:
Tell him from his all-obeying breath I hear
The doom of Egypt.
THYREUS
'Tis your noblest course.
Wisdom and fortune combating together,
If that the former dare but what it can,
No chance may shake it. Give me grace to lay
My duty on your hand.
CLEOPATRA
Your Caesar's father oft,
When he hath mused of taking kingdoms in,
Bestow'd his lips on that unworthy place,
As it rain'd kisses.

Re-enter ANTONY *and* ENOBARBUS.

MARK ANTONY
Favours, by Jove that thunders!
What art thou, fellow?
THYREUS
One that but performs
The bidding of the fullest man, and worthiest
To have command obey'd.
DOMITIUS ENOBARBUS
[*Aside.* You will be whipp'd.
MARK ANTONY
Approach, there! Ah, you kite! Now, gods
and devils!
Authority melts from me: of late, when
I cried 'Ho!'
Like boys unto a muss, kings would start forth,
And cry 'Your will?' Have you no ears? I am
Antony yet.

Enter Attendants.

Take hence this Jack, and whip him.
DOMITIUS ENOBARBUS
[*Aside.*] 'Tis better playing with a lion's whelp
Than with an old one dying.
MARK ANTONY
Moon and stars!
Whip him. Were't twenty of the greatest tributaries
That do acknowledge Caesar, should I find them
So saucy with the hand of she here,—what's her name,

Since she was Cleopatra? Whip him, fellows,
Till, like a boy, you see him cringe his face,
And whine aloud for mercy: take him hence.

THYREUS
Mark Antony!

MARK ANTONY
Tug him away: being whipp'd,
Bring him again: this Jack of Caesar's shall
Bear us an errand to him.
[*Exeunt Attendants with Thyreus.*
You were half blasted ere I knew you: ha!
Have I my pillow left unpress'd in Rome,
Forborne the getting of a lawful race,
And by a gem of women, to be abused
By one that looks on feeders?

CLEOPATRA
Good my lord,—

MARK ANTONY
You have been a boggler ever: 141
But when we in our viciousness grow hard—
O misery on't!—the wise gods seel our eyes;
In our own filth drop our clear judgments; make us
Adore our errors; laugh at's, while we strut
To our confusion.

CLEOPATRA
O, is't come to this?

MARK ANTONY
I found you as a morsel cold upon
Dead Caesar's trencher; nay, you were a fragment
Of Cneius Pompey's; besides what hotter hours,
Unregister'd in vulgar fame, you have
Luxuriously pick'd out: for, I am sure, 153
Though you can guess what temperance should be,
You know not what it is.

CLEOPATRA
Wherefore is this?

MARK ANTONY
To let a fellow that will take rewards
And say 'God quit you!' be familiar with
My playfellow, your hand, this kingly seal
And plighter of high hearts! O, that I were
Upon the hill of Basan, to outroar
The horned herd! for I have savage cause;
And to proclaim it civilly, were like
A halter'd neck which does the hangman thank
For being yare about him.

Re-enter Attendants *with* THYREUS.

Is he whipp'd? 166

FIRST ATTENDANT
Soundly, my lord.

MARK ANTONY
Cried he? and begg'd a' pardon?

FIRST ATTENDANT
He did ask favour.

MARK ANTONY
If that thy father live, let him repent
Thou wast not made his daughter; and be thou sorry
To follow Caesar in his triumph, since
Thou hast been whipp'd for following him: henceforth
The white hand of a lady fever thee,
Shake thou to look on 't. Get thee back to Caesar,
Tell him thy entertainment: look, thou say
He makes me angry with him; for he seems
Proud and disdainful, harping on what I am,
Not what he knew I was: he makes me angry;
And at this time most easy 'tis to do't,
When my good stars, that were my former guides,
Have empty left their orbs, and shot their fires
Into the abysm of hell. If he mislike
My speech and what is done, tell him he has
Hipparchus, my enfranched bondman, whom
He may at pleasure whip, or hang, or torture,
As he shall like, to quit me: urge it thou: 187
Hence with thy stripes, begone! [*Exit Thyreus.*

CLEOPATRA
Have you done yet?

MARK ANTONY
Alack, our terrene moon
Is now eclipsed; and it portends alone
The fall of Antony!

CLEOPATRA
I must stay his time.

MARK ANTONY
To flatter Caesar, would you mingle eyes
With one that ties his points?

CLEOPATRA
Not know me yet?

MARK ANTONY
Cold-hearted toward me?

CLEOPATRA
Ah, dear, if I be so,
From my cold heart let heaven engender hail,
And poison it in the source; and the first stone
Drop in my neck: as it determines, so 201
Dissolve my life! The next Caesarion smite! [36]
Till by degrees the memory of my womb,
Together with my brave Egyptians all,
By the discandying of this pelleted storm,
Lie graveless, till the flies and gnats of Nile
Have buried them for prey!

MARK ANTONY
I am satisfied.
Caesar sits down in Alexandria; where
I will oppose his fate. Our force by land
Hath nobly held; our sever'd navy too 211
Have knit again, and fleet, threatening most sea-like.

Where hast thou been, my heart? Dost thou hear, lady?
If from the field I shall return once more
To kiss these lips, I will appear in blood;
I and my sword will earn our chronicle:
There's hope in't yet.

CLEOPATRA
That's my brave lord!

MARK ANTONY
I will be treble-sinew'd, hearted, breathed,
And fight maliciously: for when mine hours
Were nice and lucky, men did ransom lives
Of me for jests; but now I'll set my teeth,
And send to darkness all that stop me. Come,
Let's have one other gaudy night: call to me
All my sad captains; fill our bowls once more;
Let's mock the midnight bell.

CLEOPATRA
It is my birth-day:
I had thought to have held it poor; but, since my lord
Is Antony again, I will be Cleopatra.

MARK ANTONY
We will yet do well.

CLEOPATRA
Call all his noble captains to my lord.

MARK ANTONY
Do so, we'll speak to them; and to-night I'll force 234
The wine peep through their scars. Come on, my queen;
There's sap in't yet. The next time I do fight,
I'll make death love me; for I will contend
Even with his pestilent scythe.
[*Exeunt all but Domitius Enobarbus.*

DOMITIUS ENOBARBUS
Now he'll outstare the lightning. To be furious,
Is to be frighted out of fear; and in that mood
The dove will peck the estridge; and I see still,
A diminution in our captain's brain
Restores his heart: when valour preys on reason,
It eats the sword it fights with. I will seek 245
Some way to leave him. [*Exit.*

ACT FOUR SCENE ONE

Before Alexandria. CAESAR'S *camp.*

Enter CAESAR, AGRIPPA, *and* MECAENAS, *with his army;* OCTAVIUS CAESAR *reading a letter.*

OCTAVIUS CAESAR
He calls me boy; and chides, as he had power
To beat me out of Egypt; my messenger
He hath whipp'd with rods; dares me to personal combat,
Caesar to Antony: let the old ruffian know
I have many other ways to die; meantime
Laugh at his challenge.

MECAENAS
Caesar must think,
When one so great begins to rage, he's hunted
Even to falling. Give him no breath, but now
Make boot of his distraction: never anger
Made good guard for itself.

OCTAVIUS CAESAR
Let our best heads 13
Know, that to-morrow the last of many battles
We mean to fight: within our files there are,
Of those that served Mark Antony but late,
Enough to fetch him in. See it done:
And feast the army; we have store to do't,
And they have earn'd the waste. Poor Antony! [*Exeunt.*

ACT FOUR SCENE TWO

Alexandria. CLEOPATRA'S *palace.*

Enter ANTONY, CLEOPATRA, ENOBARBUS, CHARMIAN, IRAS, ALEXAS, *with others.*

MARK ANTONY
He will not fight with me, Domitius.

DOMITIUS ENOBARBUS
No.

MARK ANTONY
Why should he not?

DOMITIUS ENOBARBUS
He thinks, being twenty times of better fortune,
He is twenty men to one.

MARK ANTONY
To-morrow, soldier,
By sea and land I'll fight: or I will live,
Or bathe my dying honour in the blood
Shall make it live again. Woo't thou fight well?

DOMITIUS ENOBARBUS
I'll strike, and cry 'Take all.'

MARK ANTONY
Well said; come on.
Call forth my household servants: let's to-night
Be bounteous at our meal.

Enter three or four Servitors.

Give me thy hand, 14
Thou hast been rightly honest;—so hast thou;—

Thou,—and thou,—and thou:—you have served me well,
And kings have been your fellows.
CLEOPATRA
[*Aside to Enobarbus*] What means this?
DOMITIUS ENOBARBUS
[*Aside to Cleopatra*]
'Tis one of those odd tricks which sorrow shoots
Out of the mind.
MARK ANTONY
And thou art honest too.
I wish I could be made so many men,
And all of you clapp'd up together in
An Antony, that I might do you service
So good as you have done.
ALL
The gods forbid!
MARK ANTONY
Well, my good fellows, wait on me to-night:
Scant not my cups; and make as much of me
As when mine empire was your fellow too,
And suffer'd my command.
CLEOPATRA
[*Aside to Enobarbus*] What does he mean?
DOMITIUS ENOBARBUS
[*Aside to Cleopatra*]
To make his followers weep.
MARK ANTONY
Tend me to-night:
May be it is the period of your duty:
Haply you shall not see me more; or if,
A mangled shadow: perchance to-morrow
You'll serve another master. I look on you
As one that takes his leave. Mine honest friends,
I turn you not away; but, like a master
Married to your good service, stay till death:
Tend me to-night two hours, I ask no more,
And the gods yield you for't!
DOMITIUS ENOBARBUS
What mean you, sir,
To give them this discomfort? Look, they weep;
And I, an ass, am onion-eyed: for shame,
Transform us not to women.
MARK ANTONY
Ho, ho, ho!
Now the witch take me, if I meant it thus!
Grace grow where those drops fall! My hearty friends,
You take me in too dolorous a sense;
For I spake to you for your comfort; did desire you
To burn this night with torches: know, my hearts,
I hope well of to-morrow; and will lead you
Where rather I'll expect victorious life
Than death and honour. Let's to supper, come,
And drown consideration. [*Exeunt.*

ACT FOUR SCENE THREE

The same. Before *the palace.*

Enter two Soldiers *to their guard.*

FIRST SOLDIER
Brother, good night: to-morrow is the day.
SECOND SOLDIER
It will determine one way: fare you well.
Heard you of nothing strange about the streets?
FIRST SOLDIER
Nothing. What news?
SECOND SOLDIER
Belike 'tis but a rumour. Good night to you.
FIRST SOLDIER
Well, sir, good night.

Enter two other Soldiers.

SECOND SOLDIER
Soldiers, have careful watch.
THIRD SOLDIER
And you. Good night, good night.
[*They place themselves in every corner of the stage.*
FOURTH SOLDIER
Here we: and if to-morrow
Our navy thrive, I have an absolute hope
Our landmen will stand up.
THIRD SOLDIER
'Tis a brave army,
And full of purpose.
[*Music of the hautboys as under the stage.*
FOURTH SOLDIER
Peace! what noise?
FIRST SOLDIER
List, list!
SECOND SOLDIER
Hark!
FIRST SOLDIER
Music i' the air.
THIRD SOLDIER
Under the earth.
FOURTH SOLDIER
It signs well, does it not?
THIRD SOLDIER
No.
FIRST SOLDIER
Peace, I say!
What should this mean?
SECOND SOLDIER
'Tis the god Hercules, whom Antony loved,
Now leaves him.

FIRST SOLDIER
Walk; let's see if other watchmen
Do hear what we do?
[*They advance to another post.*
SECOND SOLDIER
How now, masters!
ALL
[*Speaking together*] How now!
How now! do you hear this?
FIRST SOLDIER
Ay; is't not strange? 29
THIRD SOLDIER
Do you hear, masters? do you hear?
FIRST SOLDIER
Follow the noise so far as we have quarter;
Let's see how it will give off.
ALL
Content. 'Tis strange. [*Exeunt.*

ACT FOUR SCENE FOUR

The same. A room in the palace.

Enter ANTONY *and* CLEOPATRA, CHARMIAN, *and others attending.*

MARK ANTONY
Eros! mine armour, Eros!
CLEOPATRA
Sleep a little.
MARK ANTONY
No, my chuck. Eros, come; mine armour, Eros! [37]

Enter EROS *with armour.*

Come, good fellow, put mine iron on:
If fortune be not ours to-day, it is
Because we brave her: come.
CLEOPATRA
Nay, I'll help too.
What's this for?
MARK ANTONY
Ah, let be, let be! thou art
The armourer of my heart: false, false; this, this.
CLEOPATRA
Sooth, la, I'll help: thus it must be.
MARK ANTONY
Well, well;
We shall thrive now. Seest thou, my good fellow?
Go put on thy defences.
EROS
Briefly, sir. 15
CLEOPATRA
Is not this buckled well?
MARK ANTONY
Rarely, rarely:
He that unbuckles this, till we do please
To daff't for our repose, shall hear a storm.
Thou fumblest, Eros; and my queen's a squire
More tight at this than thou: dispatch. O love,
That thou couldst see my wars to-day, and knew'st
The royal occupation! thou shouldst see
A workman in't.

Enter an armed Soldier.

Good morrow to thee; welcome:
Thou look'st like him that knows a warlike charge:
To business that we love we rise betime, 27
And go to't with delight.
SOLDIER
A thousand, sir,
Early though't be, have on their riveted trim,
And at the port expect you.
[*Shout. Trumpets flourish.*

Enter Captains *and* Soldiers.

CAPTAIN
The morn is fair. Good morrow, general.
ALL
Good morrow, general.
MARK ANTONY
'Tis well blown, lads:
This morning, like the spirit of a youth
That means to be of note, begins betimes.
So, so; come, give me that: this way; well said.
Fare thee well, dame, whate'er becomes of me:
This is a soldier's kiss: rebukeable
[*Kisses her.*
And worthy shameful check it were, to stand
On more mechanic compliment; I'll leave thee
Now, like a man of steel. You that will fight,
Follow me close: I'll bring you to't. Adieu.
[*Exeunt Mark Antony, Eros, Captains, and Soldiers.*
CHARMIAN
Please you, retire to your chamber.
CLEOPATRA
Lead me.
He goes forth gallantly. That he and Caesar might
Determine this great war in single fight!
Then Antony,—but now— Well, on. [*Exeunt.*

ACT FOUR SCENE FIVE

Alexandria. ANTONY'S *camp.*

Trumpets sound. Enter ANTONY *and* EROS ; *a* Soldier *meeting them.*

SOLDIER
The gods make this a happy day to Antony!

MARK ANTONY
Would thou and those thy scars had once prevail'd
To make me fight at land!

SOLDIER
Hadst thou done so,
The kings that have revolted, and the soldier
That has this morning left thee, would have still
Follow'd thy heels.

MARK ANTONY
Who's gone this morning?

SOLDIER
Who!
One ever near thee: call for Enobarbus, [38]
He shall not hear thee; or from Caesar's camp
Say 'I am none of thine.'

MARK ANTONY
What say'st thou?

SOLDIER
Sir,
He is with Caesar.

EROS
Sir, his chests and treasure 17
He has not with him.

MARK ANTONY
Is he gone?

SOLDIER
Most certain.

MARK ANTONY
Go, Eros, send his treasure after; do it;
Detain no jot, I charge thee: write to him—
I will subscribe—gentle adieus and greetings;
Say that I wish he never find more cause
To change a master. O, my fortunes have
Corrupted honest men! Dispatch.—Enobarbus![39]
[*Exeunt.*

ACT FOUR SCENE SIX

Alexandria. CAESAR'S *camp.*

Flourish. Enter CAESAR, AGRIPPA, *with* ENOBARBUS, *and others.*

OCTAVIUS CAESAR
Go forth, Agrippa, and begin the fight:
Our will is Antony be took alive;
Make it so known.

AGRIPPA
Caesar, I shall. [*Exit.*

OCTAVIUS CAESAR
The time of universal peace is near:
Prove this a prosperous day, the three-nook'd world
Shall bear the olive freely.

Enter a Messenger.

MESSENGER
Antony
Is come into the field.

OCTAVIUS CAESAR
Go charge Agrippa
Plant those that have revolted in the van,
That Antony may seem to spend his fury 12
Upon himself. [*Exeunt all but Enobarbus.*

DOMITIUS ENOBARBUS
Alexas did revolt; and went to Jewry on
Affairs of Antony; there did persuade [40]
Great Herod to incline himself to Caesar,
And leave his master Antony: for this pains
Caesar hath hang'd him. Canidius and the rest
That fell away have entertainment, but
No honourable trust. I have done ill;
Of which I do accuse myself so sorely,
That I will joy no more.

Enter a Soldier *of* CAESAR'S.

SOLDIER
Enobarbus, Antony 23
Hath after thee sent all thy treasure, with
His bounty overplus: the messenger
Came on my guard; and at thy tent is now
Unloading of his mules.

DOMITIUS ENOBARBUS
I give it you.

SOLDIER
Mock not, Enobarbus.
I tell you true: best you safed the bringer
Out of the host; I must attend mine office,
Or would have done't myself. Your emperor
Continues still a Jove. [*Exit.*

DOMITIUS ENOBARBUS
I am alone the villain of the earth, 34
And feel I am so most. O Antony,
Thou mine of bounty, how wouldst thou have paid
My better service, when my turpitude
Thou dost so crown with gold! This blows my heart:
If swift thought break it not, a swifter mean
Shall outstrike thought: but thought will do't, I feel.
I fight against thee! No: I will go seek
Some ditch wherein to die; the foul'st best fits 43
My latter part of life. [*Exit.*

ACT FOUR SCENE SEVEN

Field of battle between the camps.

Alarum. Drums and trumpets. Enter AGRIPPA *and others.*

AGRIPPA
Retire, we have engaged ourselves too far:

Caesar himself has work, and our oppression
Exceeds what we expected. [*Exeunt.*

Alarums. Enter ANTONY *and* SCARUS *wounded.*

SCARUS
O my brave emperor, this is fought indeed!
Had we done so at first, we had droven them home
With clouts about their heads.

MARK ANTONY
Thou bleed'st apace.

SCARUS
I had a wound here that was like a T,
But now 'tis made an H.

MARK ANTONY
They do retire.

SCARUS
We'll beat 'em into bench-holes: I have yet
Room for six scotches more. 12

Enter EROS.

EROS
They are beaten, sir, and our advantage serves
For a fair victory.

SCARUS
Let us score their backs,
And snatch 'em up, as we take hares, behind:
'Tis sport to maul a runner.

MARK ANTONY
I will reward thee
Once for thy spritely comfort, and ten-fold
For thy good valour. Come thee on.

SCARUS
I'll halt after. [*Exeunt.*

ACT FOUR SCENE EIGHT

Under the walls of Alexandria.

Alarum. Enter ANTONY, *in a march*; SCARUS, *with others.*

MARK ANTONY
We have beat him to his camp: run one before,
And let the queen know of our gests. To-morrow,
Before the sun shall see's, we'll spill the blood
That has to-day escaped. I thank you all;
For doughty-handed are you, and have fought
Not as you served the cause, but as 't had been
Each man's like mine; you have shown all Hectors.
Enter the city, clip your wives, your friends,
Tell them your feats; whilst they with joyful tears
Wash the congealment from your wounds, and kiss 11
The honour'd gashes whole. [*To Scarus.*
Give me thy hand;

Enter CLEOPATRA, *attended.*

To this great fairy I'll commend thy acts,
Make her thanks bless thee. [*To Cleopatra*] O thou day o' the world,
Chain mine arm'd neck; leap thou, attire and all,
Through proof of harness to my heart, and there
Ride on the pants triumphing!

CLEOPATRA
Lord of lords!
O infinite virtue, comest thou smiling from
The world's great snare uncaught?

MARK ANTONY
My nightingale,
We have beat them to their beds. What, girl! though grey
Do something mingle with our younger brown, yet ha' we 27
A brain that nourishes our nerves, and can
Get goal for goal of youth. Behold this man;
Commend unto his lips thy favouring hand: [41]
Kiss it, my warrior: he hath fought to-day
As if a god, in hate of mankind, had
Destroy'd in such a shape.

CLEOPATRA
I'll give thee, friend,
An armour all of gold; it was a king's.

MARK ANTONY
He has deserved it, were it carbuncled
Like holy Phoebus' car. Give me thy hand:
Through Alexandria make a jolly march; 38
Bear our hack'd targets like the men that owe them:
Had our great palace the capacity
To camp this host, we all would sup together,
And drink carouses to the next day's fate,
Which promises royal peril. Trumpeters,
With brazen din blast you the city's ear;
Make mingle with our rattling tabourines;
That heaven and earth may strike their sounds together,
Applauding our approach. [*Exeunt.* 47

ACT FOUR SCENE NINE

Caesar's camp.

Sentinels at their post.

FIRST SOLDIER
If we be not relieved within this hour,
We must return to the court of guard: the night
Is shiny; and they say we shall embattle
By the second hour i' the morn.

SECOND SOLDIER
This last day was
A shrewd one to's.

Enter ENOBARBUS.

DOMITIUS ENOBARBUS
O, bear me witness, night,—
THIRD SOLDIER
What man is this?
SECOND SOLDIER
Stand close, and list him.
DOMITIUS ENOBARBUS
Be witness to me, O thou blessed moon,
When men revolted shall upon record
Bear hateful memory, poor Enobarbus did
Before thy face repent!
FIRST SOLDIER
Enobarbus!
THIRD SOLDIER
Peace!
Hark further.
DOMITIUS ENOBARBUS
O sovereign mistress of true melancholy,
The poisonous damp of night disponge upon me,
That life, a very rebel to my will,
May hang no longer on me: throw my heart
Against the flint and hardness of my fault;
Which, being dried with grief, will break to powder,
And finish all foul thoughts. O Antony,
Nobler than my revolt is infamous,
Forgive me in thine own particular;
But let the world rank me in register
A master-leaver and a fugitive:
O Antony! O Antony! [*Dies.*
SECOND SOLDIER
Let's speak
To him.
FIRST SOLDIER
Let's hear him, for the things he speaks
May concern Caesar.
THIRD SOLDIER
Let's do so. But he sleeps.
FIRST SOLDIER
Swoons rather; for so bad a prayer as his
Was never yet for sleep.
SECOND SOLDIER
Go we to him.
THIRD SOLDIER
Awake, sir, awake; speak to us.
SECOND SOLDIER
Hear you, sir?
FIRST SOLDIER
The hand of death hath raught him. [*Drums afar off.*] Hark! the drums
Demurely wake the sleepers. Let us bear him
To the court of guard; he is of note: our hour
Is fully out.
THIRD SOLDIER
Come on, then;
He may recover yet. [*Exeunt with the body.*

ACT FOUR SCENE TEN

Between the two camps.

Enter ANTONY *and* SCARUS, *with their Army.*

MARK ANTONY
Their preparation is to-day by sea;
We please them not by land.
SCARUS
For both, my lord.
MARK ANTONY
I would they'ld fight i' the fire or i' the air;
We'ld fight there too. But this it is; our foot
Upon the hills adjoining to the city
Shall stay with us: order for sea is given;
They have put forth the haven …
Where their appointment we may best discover,
And look on their endeavour. [*Exeunt.*

ACT FOUR SCENE ELEVEN

Another part of the same.

Enter CAESAR, *and his Army.*

OCTAVIUS CAESAR
But being charged, we will be still by land,
Which, as I take't, we shall; for his best force
Is forth to man his galleys. To the vales,
And hold our best advantage. [*Exeunt.*

ACT FOUR SCENE TWELVE

Another part of the same.

Enter ANTONY *and* SCARUS.

MARK ANTONY
Yet they are not join'd: where yond pine does stand,
I shall discover all: I'll bring thee word
Straight, how 'tis like to go. [*Exit.*
SCARUS
Swallows have built
In Cleopatra's sails their nests: the augurers
Say they know not, they cannot tell; look grimly,
And dare not speak their knowledge. Antony
Is valiant, and dejected; and, by starts,

His fretted fortunes give him hope, and fear,
Of what he has, and has not.
[*Alarum afar off, as at a sea-fight.*

Re-enter ANTONY.

MARK ANTONY
All is lost;
This foul Egyptian hath betrayed me: 12
My fleet hath yielded to the foe; and yonder
They cast their caps up and carouse together
Like friends long lost. Triple-turn'd whore! 'tis thou
Hast sold me to this novice; and my heart
Makes only wars on thee. Bid them all fly;
For when I am revenged upon my charm,
I have done all. Bid them all fly; begone.
[*Exit Scarus.*
O sun, thy uprise shall I see no more:
Fortune and Antony part here; even here
Do we shake hands. All come to this? The hearts 22
That spaniel'd me at heels, to whom I gave
Their wishes, do discandy, melt their sweets
On blossoming Caesar; and this pine is bark'd,
That overtopp'd them all. Betray'd I am:
O this false soul of Egypt! this grave
charm,— *42*
Whose eye beck'd forth my wars, and call'd them home;
Whose bosom was my crownet, my chief end,—
Like a right gipsy, hath, at fast and loose,
Beguiled me to the very heart of loss.
What, Eros, Eros!

Enter CLEOPATRA.

Ah, thou spell! Avaunt! 35

CLEOPATRA
Why is my lord enraged against his love?

MARK ANTONY
Vanish, or I shall give thee thy deserving,
And blemish Caesar's triumph. Let him take thee,
And hoist thee up to the shouting plebeians:
Follow his chariot, like the greatest spot
Of all thy sex; most monster-like, be shown
For poor'st diminutives, for doits; and let
Patient Octavia plough thy visage up
With her prepared nails. [*Exit Cleopatra.*
'Tis well thou'rt gone,
If it be well to live; but better 'twere 46
Thou fell'st into my fury, for one death
Might have prevented many. Eros, ho! 48
The shirt of Nessus is upon me: teach me,
Alcides, thou mine ancestor, thy rage:
Let me lodge Lichas on the horns o' the moon;
And with those hands, that grasp'd the heaviest club,
Subdue my worthiest self. The witch shall die:
To the young Roman boy she hath sold me,
and I fall
Under this plot; she dies for't. Eros, ho! [*Exit.*

ACT FOUR SCENE THIRTEEN

Alexandria. Cleopatra's palace.

Enter CLEOPATRA, CHARMIAN, IRAS, *and* MARDIAN.

CLEOPATRA
Help me, my women! O, he is more mad
Than Telamon for his shield; the boar of Thessaly
Was never so emboss'd.

CHARMIAN
To the monument!
There lock yourself, and send him word you are dead.
The soul and body rive not more in parting
Than greatness going off.

CLEOPATRA
To the monument!
Mardian, go tell him I have slain myself;
Say, that the last I spoke was 'Antony,'
And word it, prithee, piteously: hence, Mardian,
And bring me how he takes my death. To the
monument! [*Exeunt.* 13

ACT FOUR SCENE FOURTEEN

The same. Another room.

Enter ANTONY *and* EROS.

MARK ANTONY
Eros, thou yet behold'st me?

EROS
Ay, noble lord.

MARK ANTONY
Sometimes we see a cloud that's dragonish;
A vapour sometime like a bear or lion,
A tower'd citadel, a pendent rock,
A forked mountain, or blue promontory
With trees upon't, that nod unto the world,
And mock our eyes with air: thou hast seen these signs;
They are black vesper's pageants.

EROS
Ay, my lord,

MARK ANTONY
That which is now a horse, even with a thought
The rack dislimns, and makes it indistinct, 13
As water is in water.

EROS
It does, my lord.
MARK ANTONY
My good knave Eros, now thy captain is
Even such a body: here I am Antony:
Yet cannot hold this visible shape, my knave.
I made these wars for Egypt: and the queen,—
Whose heart I thought I had, for she had mine;
Which whilst it was mine had annex'd unto't
A million more, now lost,—she, Eros, has
Pack'd cards with Caesar, and false-play'd my glory
Unto an enemy's triumph. 25
Nay, weep not, gentle Eros; there is left us
Ourselves to end ourselves.

Enter MARDIAN.

O! thy vile lady!
She has robb'd me of my sword.
MARDIAN
No, Antony;
My mistress loved thee, and her fortunes mingled
With thine entirely.
MARK ANTONY
Hence, saucy eunuch; peace!
She hath betray'd me and shall die the death.
MARDIAN
Death of one person can be paid but once,
And that she has discharged: what thou wouldst do
Is done unto thy hand: the last she spake
Was 'Antony! most noble Antony!' 38
Then in the midst a tearing groan did break
The name of Antony; it was divided
Between her heart and lips: she render'd life,
Thy name so buried in her.
MARK ANTONY
Dead, then?
MARDIAN
Dead.
MARK ANTONY
Unarm, Eros; the long day's task is done,
And we must sleep. [*To Mardian*] That thou depart'st hence safe,
Does pay thy labour richly; go. [*Exit Mardian.*
Off, pluck off:
The seven-fold shield of Ajax cannot keep
The battery from my heart. O, cleave, my sides!
Heart, once be stronger than thy continent, 52
Crack thy frail case! Apace, Eros, apace.
No more a soldier: bruised pieces, go;
You have been nobly borne. From me awhile.
[*Exit Eros.*
I will o'ertake thee, Cleopatra, and
Weep for my pardon. So it must be, for now
All length is torture: since the torch is out,
Lie down, and stray no farther: now all labour
Mars what it does; yea, very force entangles
Itself with strength: seal them, and all is done.
Eros!—I come, my queen:—Eros!—Stay for me: 63
Where souls do couch on flowers, we'll hand in hand,
And with our sprightly port make the ghosts gaze:
Dido and her aeneas shall want troops,
And all the haunt be ours. Come, Eros, Eros!

Re-enter EROS.

EROS
What would my lord?
MARK ANTONY
Since Cleopatra died,
I have lived in such dishonour, that the gods
Detest my baseness. I, that with my sword
Quarter'd the world, and o'er green Neptune's back
With ships made cities, condemn myself to lack
The courage of a woman; less noble mind 74
Than she which by her death our Caesar tells
'I am conqueror of myself.' Thou art sworn, Eros,
That, when the exigent should come, which now
Is come indeed, when I should see behind me
The inevitable prosecution of
Disgrace and horror, that, on my command,
Thou then wouldst kill me: do't; the time is come:
Thou strikest not me, 'tis Caesar thou defeat'st.
Put colour in thy cheek.
EROS
The gods withhold me!
Shall I do that which all the Parthian darts,
Though enemy, lost aim, and could not?
MARK ANTONY
Eros, 87
Wouldst thou be window'd in great Rome and see
Thy master thus with pleach'd arms, bending down
His corrigible neck, his face subdued
To penetrative shame, whilst the wheel'd seat
Of fortunate Caesar, drawn before him, branded
His baseness that ensued?
EROS
I would not see't.
MARK ANTONY
Come, then; for with a wound I must be cured.
Draw that thy honest sword, which thou hast worn
Most useful for thy country.
EROS
O, sir, pardon me! 98
MARK ANTONY
When I did make thee free, sworest thou not then
To do this when I bade thee? Do it at once;
Or thy precedent services are all

But accidents unpurposed. Draw, and come.
EROS
Turn from me, then, that noble countenance,
Wherein the worship of the whole world lies.
MARK ANTONY
Lo thee![43] [*Turning from him.*
EROS
My sword is drawn.
MARK ANTONY
Then let it do at once
The thing why thou hast drawn it.
EROS
My dear master,
My captain, and my emperor, let me say,
Before I strike this bloody stroke, farewell.
MARK ANTONY
'Tis said, man; and farewell.
EROS
Farewell, great chief. Shall I strike now?
MARK ANTONY
Now, Eros.
EROS
Why, there then: thus I do escape the sorrow
Of Antony's death.
[*Kills himself.*
MARK ANTONY
Thrice-nobler than myself!
Thou teachest me, O valiant Eros, what
I should, and thou couldst not. My queen and Eros
Have by their brave instruction got upon me
A nobleness in record: but I will be
A bridegroom in my death, and run into't
As to a lover's bed. Come, then; and, Eros,
Thy master dies thy scholar: to do thus
[*Falling on his sword.*
I learn'd of thee. How! not dead? not dead?
The guard, ho! O, dispatch me!

Enter DERCETAS *and* Guard.

FIRST GUARD
What's the noise?
MARK ANTONY
I have done my work ill, friends: O, make an end
Of what I have begun.
SECOND GUARD
The star is fall'n.
FIRST GUARD
And time is at his period.
ALL
Alas, and woe!
MARK ANTONY
Let him that loves me strike me dead.
FIRST GUARD
Not I.
SECOND GUARD
Nor I.
THIRD GUARD
Nor any one.
[*Exeunt Guard.*
DERCETAS
Thy death and fortunes bid thy followers fly.
This sword but shown to Caesar, with this tidings,
Shall enter me with him.

Enter DIOMEDES.

DIOMEDES
Where's Antony?
DERCETAS
There, Diomed, there.
DIOMEDES
Lives he?
Wilt thou not answer, man? [*Exit Dercetas.*
MARK ANTONY
Art thou there, Diomed? Draw thy sword, and give me
Sufficing strokes for death.
DIOMEDES
Most absolute lord,
My mistress Cleopatra sent me to thee.
MARK ANTONY
When did she send thee?
DIOMEDES
Now, my lord.
MARK ANTONY
Where is she?
DIOMEDES
Lock'd in her monument. She had a prophesying fear
Of what hath come to pass: for when she saw—
Which never shall be found— you did suspect
She had disposed with Caesar, and that yourrage
Would not be purged, she sent you word she was dead;
But, fearing since how it might work, hath sent
Me to proclaim the truth; and I am come,
I dread, too late.
MARK ANTONY
Too late, good Diomed: call my guard, I prithee.
DIOMEDES
What, ho, the emperor's guard! The guard, what, ho!
Come, your lord calls!

Enter four or five of the Guard of ANTONY.

MARK ANTONY
Bear me, good friends, where Cleopatra bides;

'Tis the last service that I shall command you.
FIRST GUARD
Woe, woe are we, sir, you may not live to wear
All your true followers out.
ALL
Most heavy day!
MARK ANTONY
Nay, good my fellows, do not please sharp fate
To grace it with your sorrows: bid that welcome
Which comes to punish us, and we punish it
Seeming to bear it lightly. Take me up:
I have led you oft: carry me now, good friends,
And have my thanks for all. 177
[*Exeunt, bearing Mark Antony.*

ACT FOUR SCENE FIFTEEN

The same. A monument.

Enter CLEOPATRA *and her maids aloft, with* CHARMIAN *and* IRAS.

CLEOPATRA
O Charmian, I will never go from hence.
CHARMIAN
Be comforted, dear madam.
CLEOPATRA
No, I will not:
All strange and terrible events are welcome,
But comforts we despise; our size of sorrow,
Proportion'd to our cause, must be as great
As that which makes it.

Enter, below, DIOMEDES.

How now! is he dead?
DIOMEDES
His death's upon him, but not dead.
Look out o' the other side your monument;
His guard have brought him thither.

Enter, below, Antony, *borne by the Guard.*

CLEOPATRA
O sun,
Burn the great sphere thou movest in! darkling stand [44]
The varying shore o' the world. O Antony, [45]
Antony, Antony! Help, Charmian, help, Iras, help; 17
Help, friends below; let's draw him hither.
MARK ANTONY
Peace!
Not Caesar's valour hath o'erthrown Antony,
But Antony's hath triumph'd on itself.
CLEOPATRA
So it should be, that none but Antony
Should conquer Antony; but woe 'tis so!
MARK ANTONY
I am dying, Egypt, dying; only
I here importune death awhile, until
Of many thousand kisses the poor last 26
I lay up thy lips.
CLEOPATRA
I dare not, dear,— [46]
Dear my lord, pardon,—I dare not,
Lest I be taken: not the imperious show
Of the full-fortuned Caesar ever shall
Be brooch'd with me; if knife, drugs, serpents, have
Edge, sting, or operation, I am safe:
Your wife Octavia, with her modest eyes
And still conclusion, shall acquire no honour
Demuring upon me. But come, come, Antony,—
Help me, my women,—we must draw thee up:
Assist, good friends.
MARK ANTONY
O, quick, or I am gone. 39
CLEOPATRA
Here's sport indeed! How heavy weighs my lord!
Our strength is all gone into heaviness,
That makes the weight: had I great Juno's power,
The strong-wing'd Mercury should fetch thee up,
And set thee by Jove's side. Yet come a little,—
Wishes were ever fools,—O, come, come, come;
[*They heave Antony aloft to Cleopatra.*
And welcome, welcome! die where thou hast lived:
Quicken with kissing: had my lips that power,
Thus would I wear them out.
ALL
A heavy sight! 49
MARK ANTONY
I am dying, Egypt, dying:
Give me some wine, and let me speak a little.
CLEOPATRA
No, let me speak; and let me rail so high,
That the false housewife Fortune break her wheel,
Provoked by my offence.
MARK ANTONY
One word, sweet queen:
Of Caesar seek your honour, with your safety. O!
CLEOPATRA
They do not go together.
MARK ANTONY
Gentle, hear me:
None about Caesar trust but Proculeius.
CLEOPATRA
My resolution and my hands I'll trust;
None about Caesar. 61
MARK ANTONY
The miserable change now at my end
Lament nor sorrow at; but please your thoughts

In feeding them with those my former fortunes
Wherein I lived, the greatest prince o' the world,
The noblest; and do now not basely die,
Not cowardly put off my helmet to
My countryman,—a Roman by a Roman
Valiantly vanquish'd. Now my spirit is going;
I can no more.

CLEOPATRA
Noblest of men, woo't die?
Hast thou no care of me? shall I abide
In this dull world, which in thy absence is
No better than a sty? O, see, my women,
[*Antony dies.*
The crown o' the earth doth melt. My lord!
O, wither'd is the garland of the war,
The soldier's pole is fall'n: young boys and girls
Are level now with men; the odds is gone,
And there is nothing left remarkable
Beneath the visiting moon.
[*Faints.*

CHARMIAN
O, quietness, lady!

IRAS
She is dead too, our sovereign.

CHARMIAN
Lady!

IRAS
Madam!

CHARMIAN
O madam, madam, madam!

IRAS
Royal Egypt,
Empress!

CHARMIAN
Peace, peace, Iras!

CLEOPATRA
No more, but e'en a woman, and commanded [47]
By such poor passion as the maid that milks
And does the meanest chares. It were for me
To throw my sceptre at the injurious gods;
To tell them that this world did equal theirs
Till they had stol'n our jewel. All's but naught;
Patience is sottish, and impatience does
Become a dog that's mad: then is it sin
To rush into the secret house of death,
Ere death dare come to us? How do you, women?
What, what! good cheer! Why, how now,
Charmian!
My noble girls! Ah, women, women, look,
Our lamp is spent, it's out! Good sirs, take heart:
We'll bury him; and then, what's brave, what's noble,
Let's do it after the high Roman fashion,
And make death proud to take us. Come, away:
This case of that huge spirit now is cold:
Ah, women, women! come; we have no friend
But resolution, and the briefest end.
[*Exeunt; those above bearing off Antony's body.*

ACT FIVE SCENE ONE

Alexandria. Caesar's *camp.*

Enter CAESAR, AGRIPPA, DOLABELLA, MECAENAS, GALLUS, PROCULEIUS, *and others, his council of war.*

OCTAVIUS CAESAR
Go to him, Dolabella, bid him yield;
Being so frustrate, tell him he mocks
The pauses that he makes.

DOLABELLA
Caesar, I shall.
[*Exit.*

Enter DERCETAS, *with the sword of* ANTONY.

OCTAVIUS CAESAR
Wherefore is that? and what art thou that darest
Appear thus to us?

DERCETAS
I am call'd Dercetas;
Mark Antony I served, who best was worthy
Best to be served: whilst he stood up and spoke,
He was my master; and I wore my life
To spend upon his haters. If thou please
To take me to thee, as I was to him
I'll be to Caesar; if thou pleasest not,
I yield thee up my life.

OCTAVIUS CAESAR
What is't thou say'st?

DERCETAS
I say, O Caesar, Antony is dead.

OCTAVIUS CAESAR
The breaking of so great a thing should make
A greater crack: the round world [48]
Should have shook lions into civil streets,
And citizens to their dens: the death of Antony
Is not a single doom; in the name lay
A moiety of the world.

DERCETAS
He is dead, Caesar:
Not by a public minister of justice,
Nor by a hired knife; but that self hand,
Which writ his honour in the acts it did,
Hath, with the courage which the heart did lend it,
Splitted the heart. This is his sword; [49]
I robb'd his wound of it; behold it stain'd
With his most noble blood.

OCTAVIUS CAESAR
Look you sad, friends?

The gods rebuke me, but it is tidings
To wash the eyes of kings.
AGRIPPA
And strange it is,
That nature must compel us to lament
Our most persisted deeds.
MECAENAS
His taints and honours 37
Waged equal with him.
AGRIPPA
A rarer spirit never
Did steer humanity: but you, gods, will give us
Some faults to make us men. Caesar is touch'd.
MECAENAS
When such a spacious mirror's set before him,
He needs must see himself.
OCTAVIUS CAESAR
O Antony!
I have follow'd thee to this; but we do lance
Diseases in our bodies: I must perforce
Have shown to thee such a declining day,
Or look on thine; we could not stall together
In the whole world: but yet let me lament, 49
With tears as sovereign as the blood of hearts,
That thou, my brother, my competitor
In top of all design, my mate in empire,
Friend and companion in the front of war,
The arm of mine own body, and the heart
Where mine his thoughts did kindle,—that our stars,
Unreconciliable, should divide
Our equalness to this. Hear me, good friends—
But I will tell you at some meeter season:

Enter an Egyptian.

The business of this man looks out of him;
We'll hear him what he says. Whence are you?
EGYPTIAN
A poor Egyptian yet. The queen my mistress,
Confined in all she has, her monument,
Of thy intents desires instruction,
That she preparedly may frame herself
To the way she's forced to.
OCTAVIUS CAESAR
Bid her have good heart:
She soon shall know of us, by some of ours,
How honourable and how kindly we
Determine for her; for Caesar cannot live [50]
To be ungentle.
EGYPTIAN
So the gods preserve thee! [*Exit.* 72
OCTAVIUS CAESAR
Come hither, Proculeius. Go and say,
We purpose her no shame: give her what comforts
The quality of her passion shall require,
Lest, in her greatness, by some mortal stroke
She do defeat us; for her life in Rome
Would be eternal in our triumph: go,
And with your speediest bring us what she says,
And how you find of her.
PROCULEIUS
Caesar, I shall. [*Exit.*
OCTAVIUS CAESAR
Gallus, go you along. [*Exit Gallus.*
Where's Dolabella,
To second Proculeius?
ALL
Dolabella! 85
OCTAVIUS CAESAR
Let him alone, for I remember now
How he's employ'd: he shall in time be ready.
Go with me to my tent; where you shall see
How hardly I was drawn into this war;
How calm and gentle I proceeded still
In all my writings: go with me, and see
What I can show in this. [*Exeunt.*

ACT FIVE SCENE TWO

Alexandria. A room in the monument.

Enter CLEOPATRA, CHARMIAN, *and* IRAS.

CLEOPATRA
My desolation does begin to make
A better life. 'Tis paltry to be Caesar;
Not being Fortune, he's but Fortune's knave,
A minister of her will: and it is great
To do that thing that ends all other deeds;
Which shackles accidents and bolts up change;
Which sleeps, and never palates more the dug, [51]
The beggar's nurse and Caesar's.

Enter, to the gates of the monument,
PROCULEIUS, GALLUS *and Soldiers*

PROCULEIUS
Caesar sends greeting to the Queen of Egypt;
And bids thee study on what fair demands 10
Thou mean'st to have him grant thee.
CLEOPATRA
What's thy name?
PROCULEIUS
My name is Proculeius.
CLEOPATRA
Antony
Did tell me of you, bade me trust you; but,
I do not greatly care to be deceived,

That have no use for trusting. If your master
Would have a queen his beggar, you must tell him,
That majesty, to keep decorum, must
No less beg than a kingdom: if he please
To give me conquer'd Egypt for my son,
He gives me so much of mine own, as I 23
Will kneel to him with thanks.

PROCULEIUS
Be of good cheer;
You're fall'n into a princely hand, fear nothing:
Make your full reference freely to my lord,
Who is so full of grace, that it flows over
Of all that need: let me report to him
Your sweet dependency; and you shall find
A conqueror that will pray in aid for kindness,
Where he for grace is kneel'd to.

CLEOPATRA
Pray you, tell him
I am his fortune's vassal, and I send him
The greatness he has got. I hourly learn 35
A doctrine of obedience; and would gladly
Look him i' the face.

PROCULEIUS
This I'll report, dear lady.
Have comfort, for I know your plight is pitied
Of him that caused it.

GALLUS
You see how easily she may be surprised:
[Here Proculeius and two of the Guard ascend the monument by a ladder placed against a window, and, having descended, come behind Cleopatra. Some of the Guard unbar and open the gates.
[To Proculeius and the Guard] Guard her till Caesar come. *[Exit.*

IRAS
Royal queen!

CHARMIAN
O Cleopatra! thou art taken, queen:

CLEOPATRA
Quick, quick, good hands. *[Drawing a dagger.*

PROCULEIUS
Hold, worthy lady, hold: *[Seizes and disarms her.*
Do not yourself such wrong, who are in this
Relieved, but not betray'd.

CLEOPATRA
What, of death too,
That rids our dogs of languish?

PROCULEIUS
Cleopatra,
Do not abuse my master's bounty by
The undoing of yourself: let the world see
His nobleness well acted, which your death
Will never let come forth.

CLEOPATRA
Where art thou, death?
Come hither, come! come, come, and take a queen
Worth many babes and beggars!

PROCULEIUS
O, temperance, lady!

CLEOPATRA
Sir, I will eat no meat, I'll not drink, sir;
If idle talk will once be necessary, [52]
I'll not sleep neither: this mortal house I'll ruin, 67
Do Caesar what he can. Know, sir, that I
Will not wait pinion'd at your master's court;
Nor once be chastised with the sober eye
Of dull Octavia. Shall they hoist me up
And show me to the shouting varletry
Of censuring Rome? Rather a ditch in Egypt
Be gentle grave unto me! rather on Nilus' mud
Lay me stark naked, and let the water-flies
Blow me into abhorring! rather make 76
My country's high pyramides my gibbet,
And hang me up in chains!

PROCULEIUS
You do extend
These thoughts of horror further than you shall
Find cause in Caesar.

Enter DOLABELLA.

DOLABELLA
Proculeius,
What thou hast done thy master Caesar knows,
And he hath sent for thee: for the queen,
I'll take her to my guard.

PROCULEIUS
So, Dolabella,
It shall content me best: be gentle to her.
[To Cleopatra]
To Caesar I will speak what you shall please,
If you'll employ me to him.

CLEOPATRA
Say, I would die. 90
[Exeunt Proculeius and Soldiers.

DOLABELLA
Most noble empress, you have heard of me?

CLEOPATRA
I cannot tell.

DOLABELLA
Assuredly you know me.

CLEOPATRA
No matter, sir, what I have heard or known.
You laugh when boys or women tell their dreams;
Is't not your trick?

DOLABELLA
I understand not, madam.

CLEOPATRA
I dream'd there was an Emperor Antony:
O, such another sleep, that I might see
But such another man!
DOLABELLA
If it might please ye,—
CLEOPATRA
His face was as the heavens; and therein stuck
A sun and moon, which kept their course, and lighted
The little O, the earth.
DOLABELLA
Most sovereign creature,—
CLEOPATRA
His legs bestrid the ocean: his rear'd arm
Crested the world: his voice was propertied
As all the tuned spheres, and that to friends;
But when he meant to quail and shake the orb,
He was as rattling thunder. For his bounty,
There was no winter in't; an autumn 'twas [53]
That grew the more by reaping: his delights
Were dolphin-like; they show'd his back above
The element they lived in: in his livery
Walk'd crowns and crownets; realms and islands were
As plates dropp'd from his pocket.
DOLABELLA
Cleopatra!
CLEOPATRA
Think you there was, or might be, such a man
As this I dream'd of?
DOLABELLA
Gentle madam, no.
CLEOPATRA
You lie, up to the hearing of the gods.
But, if there be, or ever were, one such,
It's past the size of dreaming: nature wants stuff
To vie strange forms with fancy; yet, to imagine
An Antony, were nature's piece 'gainst fancy,
Condemning shadows quite.
DOLABELLA
Hear me, good madam.
Your loss is as yourself, great; and you bear it
As answering to the weight: would I might never
O'ertake pursued success, but I do feel,
By the rebound of yours, a grief that smites [54]
My very heart at root.
CLEOPATRA
I thank you, sir.
Know you what Caesar means to do with me?
DOLABELLA
I am loath to tell you what I would you knew.
CLEOPATRA
Nay, pray you, sir,—
DOLABELLA
Though he be honourable,—
CLEOPATRA
He'll lead me, then, in triumph?
DOLABELLA
Madam, he will; I know't.
[Flourish, and shout within, 'Make way there: Caesar!'

Enter CAESAR, GALLUS, PROCULEIUS, MECAENAS, SELEUCUS, *and others of his Train.*

OCTAVIUS CAESAR
Which is the Queen of Egypt?
DOLABELLA
It is the emperor, madam.
[CLEOPATRA kneels.
OCTAVIUS CAESAR
Arise, you shall not kneel:
I pray you, rise; rise, Egypt.
CLEOPATRA
Sir, the gods
Will have it thus; my master and my lord
I must obey.
OCTAVIUS CAESAR
Take to you no hard thoughts:
The record of what injuries you did us,
Though written in our flesh, we shall remember
As things but done by chance.
CLEOPATRA
Sole sir o' the world,
I cannot project mine own cause so well
To make it clear; but do confess I have
Been laden with like frailties which before
Have often shamed our sex.
OCTAVIUS CAESAR
Cleopatra, know,
We will extenuate rather than enforce:
If you apply yourself to our intents,
Which towards you are most gentle, you shall find
A benefit in this change; but if you seek
To lay on me a cruelty, by taking
Antony's course, you shall bereave yourself
Of my good purposes, and put your children
To that destruction which I'll guard them from,
If thereon you rely. I'll take my leave.
CLEOPATRA
And may, through all the world: 'tis yours; and we,
Your scutcheons and your signs of conquest, shall
Hang in what place you please. Here, my good lord.
OCTAVIUS CAESAR
You shall advise me in all for Cleopatra.
CLEOPATRA
This is the brief of money, plate, and jewels,
I am possess'd of: 'tis exactly valued;
Not petty things admitted. Where's Seleucus?
SELEUCUS
Here, madam.

CLEOPATRA
This is my treasurer: let him speak, my lord,
Upon his peril, that I have reserved
To myself nothing. Speak the truth, Seleucus.
SELEUCUS
Madam,
I had rather seal my lips, than, to my peril,
Speak that which is not.
CLEOPATRA
What have I kept back?
SELEUCUS
Enough to purchase what you have made known.
OCTAVIUS CAESAR
Nay, blush not, Cleopatra; I approve
Your wisdom in the deed.
CLEOPATRA
See, Caesar! O, behold,
How pomp is follow'd! mine will now be yours;
And, should we shift estates, yours would be mine.
The ingratitude of this Seleucus does
Even make me wild: O slave, of no more trust
Than love that's hired! What, goest thou back? thou shalt
Go back, I warrant thee; but I'll catch thine eyes,
Though they had wings: slave, soulless villain, dog!
O rarely base!
OCTAVIUS CAESAR
Good queen, let us entreat you.
CLEOPATRA
O Caesar, what a wounding shame is this,
That thou, vouchsafing here to visit me,
Doing the honour of thy lordliness
To one so meek, that mine own servant should
Parcel the sum of my disgraces by
Addition of his envy! Say, good Caesar,
That I some lady trifles have reserved,
Immoment toys, things of such dignity
As we greet modern friends withal; and say,
Some nobler token I have kept apart
For Livia and Octavia, to induce
Their mediation; must I be unfolded
With one that I have bred? The gods! it smites me
Beneath the fall I have. [*To Seleucus*] Prithee, go hence;
Or I shall show the cinders of my spirits
Through the ashes of my chance: wert thou a man, [55]
Thou wouldst have mercy on me.
OCTAVIUS CAESAR
Forbear, Seleucus. [*Exit Seleucus.*
CLEOPATRA
Be it known, that we, the greatest, are misthought
For things that others do; and, when we fall,
We answer others' merits in our name, [56]
Are therefore to be pitied.
OCTAVIUS CAESAR
Cleopatra,
Not what you have reserved, nor what acknowledged,
Put we i' the roll of conquest: still be't yours,
Bestow it at your pleasure; and believe,
Caesar's no merchant, to make prize with you
Of things that merchants sold. Therefore be cheer'd;
Make not your thoughts your prisons: no, dear queen;
For we intend so to dispose you as
Yourself shall give us counsel. Feed, and sleep:
Our care and pity is so much upon you,
That we remain your friend; and so, adieu.
CLEOPATRA
My master, and my lord!
OCTAVIUS CAESAR
Not so. Adieu.
[*Flourish. Exeunt Caesar and his train.*
CLEOPATRA
He words me, girls, he words me, that I should not
Be noble to myself: but, hark thee, Charmian.
[*Whispers Charmian.*
IRAS
Finish, good lady; the bright day is done,
And we are for the dark.
CLEOPATRA
Hie thee again:
I have spoke already, and it is provided;
Go put it to the haste.
CHARMIAN
Madam, I will.

Re-enter DOLABELLA.

DOLABELLA
Where is the queen?
CHARMIAN
Behold, sir. [*Exit.*
CLEOPATRA
Dolabella!
DOLABELLA
Madam, as thereto sworn by your command,
Which my love makes religion to obey,
I tell you this: Caesar through Syria
Intends his journey; and within three days
You with your children will he send before:
Make your best use of this: I have perform'd
Your pleasure and my promise.
CLEOPATRA
Dolabella,
I shall remain your debtor.
DOLABELLA
I your servant,
Adieu, good queen; I must attend on Caesar.

CLEOPATRA
Farewell, and thanks. [*Exit Dolabella.*
Now, Iras, what think'st thou?
Thou, an Egyptian puppet, shalt be shown
In Rome, as well as I: mechanic slaves
With greasy aprons, rules, and hammers, shall
Uplift us to the view; in their thick breaths,
Rank of gross diet, shall be enclouded,
And forced to drink their vapour.

IRAS
The gods forbid!

CLEOPATRA
Nay, 'tis most certain, Iras: saucy lictors
Will catch at us, like strumpets; and scald rhymers
Ballad us out o' tune: the quick comedians,
Extemporally will stage us, and present
Our Alexandrian revels; Antony
Shall be brought drunken forth, and I shall see
Some squeaking Cleopatra boy my greatness
I' the posture of a whore.

IRAS
O the good gods!

CLEOPATRA
Nay, that's certain.

IRAS
I'll never see 't; for, I am sure, my nails
Are stronger than mine eyes.

CLEOPATRA
Why, that's the way
To fool their preparation, and to conquer
Their most absurd intents.

Re-enter CHARMIAN.

Now, Charmian!
Show me, my women, like a queen: go fetch
My best attires: I am again for Cydnus,
To meet Mark Antony: sirrah Iras, go.
Now, noble Charmian, we'll dispatch indeed;
And, when thou hast done this chare, I'll give thee leave
To play till doomsday. Bring our crown and all.
Wherefore's this noise? [*Exit Iras. A noise within.*

Enter a Guardsman.

GUARD
Here is a rural fellow
That will not be denied your highness presence:
He brings you figs.

CLEOPATRA
Let him come in. [*Exit Guardsman.*
What poor an instrument
May do a noble deed! he brings me liberty.
My resolution's placed, and I have nothing
Of woman in me: now from head to foot
I am marble-constant; now the fleeting moon
No planet is of mine.

Re-enter Guardsman, *with* Clown *bringing in a basket.*

GUARD
This is the man.

CLEOPATRA
Avoid, and leave him. [*Exit Guardsman.*
Hast thou the pretty worm of Nilus there,
That kills and pains not?

CLOWN
Truly, I have him: but I would not be the party that should desire you to touch him, for his biting is immortal; those that do die of it do seldom or never recover.

CLEOPATRA
Rememberest thou any that have died on't?

CLOWN
Very many, men and women too. I heard of one of them no longer than yesterday: a very honest woman, but something given to lie; as a woman should not do, but in the way of honesty: how she died of the biting of it, what pain she felt: truly, she makes a very good report o' the worm; but he that will believe all that they say, shall never be saved by half that they do: but this is most fallible, the worm's an odd worm.

CLEOPATRA
Get thee hence; farewell.

CLOWN
I wish you all joy of the worm.
[*Setting down his basket.*

CLEOPATRA
Farewell.

CLOWN
You must think this, look you, that the worm will do his kind.

CLEOPATRA
Ay, ay; farewell.

CLOWN
Look you, the worm is not to be trusted but in the keeping of wise people; for, indeed, there is no goodness in the worm.

CLEOPATRA
Take thou no care; it shall be heeded.

CLOWN
Very good. Give it nothing, I pray you, for it is not worth the feeding.

CLEOPATRA
Will it eat me?

CLOWN
You must not think I am so simple but I know the devil himself will not eat a woman: I know that a woman is a dish for the gods, if the devil dress her not. But, truly, these same whoreson devils do the gods

great harm in their women; for in every ten that they make, the devils mar five.

CLEOPATRA
Well, get thee gone; farewell. 335

CLOWN
Yes, forsooth: I wish you joy o' the worm. [*Exit.*

Re-enter IRAS *with a robe, crown, &c..*

CLEOPATRA
Give me my robe, put on my crown; I have
Immortal longings in me: now no more
The juice of Egypt's grape shall moist this lip:
Yare, yare, good Iras; quick. Methinks I hear
Antony call; I see him rouse himself
To praise my noble act; I hear him mock
The luck of Caesar, which the gods give men
To excuse their after wrath: husband, I come:
Now to that name my courage prove my title!
I am fire and air; my other elements
I give to baser life. So; have you done?
Come then, and take the last warmth of my lips.
Farewell, kind Charmian; Iras, long farewell.
[*Kisses them. Iras falls and dies.*
Have I the aspic in my lips? Dost fall?
If thou and nature can so gently part,
The stroke of death is as a lover's pinch,
Which hurts, and is desired. Dost thou lie still?
If thus thou vanishest, thou tell'st the world
It is not worth leave-taking. 355

CHARMIAN
Dissolve, thick cloud, and rain; that I may say,
The gods themselves do weep!

CLEOPATRA
This proves me base:
If she first meet the curled Antony,
He'll make demand of her, and spend that kiss
Which is my heaven to have. Come, thou mortal wretch,
[*To an asp, which she applies to her breast.*
With thy sharp teeth this knot intrinsicate
Of life at once untie: poor venomous fool,
Be angry, and dispatch. O, couldst thou speak,
That I might hear thee call great Caesar ass
Unpolicied!

CHARMIAN
O eastern star!

CLEOPATRA
Peace, peace! 369
Dost thou not see my baby at my breast,
That sucks the nurse asleep?

CHARMIAN
O, break! O, break!

CLEOPATRA
As sweet as balm, as soft as air, as gentle,—
O Antony!—Nay, I will take thee too.
[*Applying another asp to her arm.*
What should I stay— [*Dies.*

CHARMIAN
In this vile world? So, fare thee well.
Now boast thee, death, in thy possession lies
A lass unparallel'd. Downy windows, close;
And golden Phoebus never be beheld 379
Of eyes again so royal! Your crown's awry;
I'll mend it, and then play.

Enter the Guard, rushing in.

FIRST GUARD
Where is the queen?

CHARMIAN
Speak softly, wake her not.

FIRST GUARD
Caesar hath sent—

CHARMIAN
Too slow a messenger.
[*Applies an asp.*
O, come apace, dispatch! I partly feel thee.

FIRST GUARD
Approach, ho! All's not well: Caesar's beguiled.

SECOND GUARD
There's Dolabella sent from Caesar; call him.

FIRST GUARD
What work is here! Charmian, is this well done?

CHARMIAN
It is well done, and fitting for a princess
Descended of so many royal kings. 401
Ah, soldier! [*Dies.*

Re-enter DOLABELLA.

DOLABELLA
How goes it here?

SECOND GUARD
All dead.

DOLABELLA
Caesar, thy thoughts
Touch their effects in this: thyself art coming
To see perform'd the dreaded act which thou
So sought'st to hinder.
[*Within* 'A way there, a way for Caesar!'.

Re-enter CAESAR *and all his train, marching.*

DOLABELLA
O sir, you are too sure an augurer;
That you did fear is done.

OCTAVIUS CAESAR
Bravest at the last,
She levell'd at our purposes, and, being royal,
Took her own way. The manner of their deaths? 413
I do not see them bleed.

DOLABELLA
Who was last with them?
FIRST GUARD
A simple countryman, that brought her figs:
This was his basket.
OCTAVIUS CAESAR
Poison'd, then.
FIRST GUARD
O Caesar,
This Charmian lived but now; she stood and spake:
I found her trimming up the diadem
On her dead mistress; tremblingly she stood
And on the sudden dropp'd.
OCTAVIUS CAESAR
O noble weakness!
If they had swallow'd poison, 'twould appear
By external swelling: but she looks like sleep,
As she would catch another Antonys
In her strong toil of grace.
DOLABELLA
Here, on her breast,
There is a vent of blood and something blown:
The like is on her arm.
FIRST GUARD
This is an aspic's trail: and these fig-leaves
Have slime upon them, such as the aspic leaves
Upon the caves of Nile. [57]
OCTAVIUS CAESAR
Most probable
That so she died; for her physician tells me
She hath pursued conclusions infinite
Of easy ways to die. Take up her bed;
And bear her women from the monument:
She shall be buried by her Antony:
No grave upon the earth shall clip in it
A pair so famous. High events as these
Strike those that make them; and their story is
No less in pity than his glory which
Brought them to be lamented. Our army shall
In solemn show attend this funeral;
And then to Rome. Come, Dolabella, see
High order in this great solemnity. [*Exeunt.*

Notes

1. Grates me: the sum; – Folio 1, *'Grates me, the summe'*; Folios 2, 3, *'Rate me, the summe'*; Rowe, *'Rate me the sum'*; Pope, *'It grates me. Tell the sum'*; Capell, *"T grates me:—The sum'*; Steevens (1793), *'Grates me:—The sum.'*
2. Liar, who Thus speaks of him; – Pope reads *'liar Fame, Who speaks him thus.'*
3. Charge; – Warburton and Southern MS. conjectures, adopted by Theobald; Folios, *'change'*; Jackson conjectured *'chain'*; Williams conjectured *'hang.'*
4. Fertile; – Warburton conjecture, adopted by Theobald; Folios *'foretell'* and *'foretel'*; Pope, *'foretold'*; Collier MS., *'fruitful.'*
5. Alexas,—come; – Theobald's reading of the Folio text, where *Alexas* is erroneously printed as though the name of the speaker.
6. Saw you my lord?; – so Folios 2, 3, 4; Folio 1 reads *'Saue you, my lord.'*
7. The arrangement of the text was first given by Steevens.
8. Minds; – Warburton conjecture, adopted by Hanmer; Folios 1, 2, *'windes'*; Collier conjectured *'wints.'*
9. Enchanting; – so Folio 1; omitted in Folios 2, 3, 4; Rowe reads *'Aegyptian.'*
10. A compelling occasion; – Rowe's emendation of Folios, *'a compelling an occasion'*; Nicholson conjectured *'so compelling as occasion.'* &c.
11. Like the courser's hair, – &c., alluding to the popular notion that horsehair put into water will turn into a snake or worm.
12. Our; – Heath and Johnson conjecture, adopted by Singer; Folios, *'One'*; Hanmer, *'A.'*
13. As; – Johnson conjectured *'and.'*
14. Lackeying; lacquying, – Theobald's correction, from Anon. MS.; Folios, *'lacking'*; Pope, *'lashing'*; Southern MS., *'backing.'*
15. An arm-gaunt; – Folios, *'an Armegaunt'*; Hanmer, *'an arm-girt'*; Mason conjecture, adopted by Steevens, 1793, *'a termagant'*; Jackson conjectured *'a war-gaunt'*; Boaden conjectured, adopted by Singer, *'an arrogant'*; Lettsom conjectured *'a rampaunt'*; the latter ingenious emendation certainly commends itself; unless *'arm-gaunt'* = 'having lean fore-limbs.'
16. Beastly; – Hanmer, *'beast-like'*; Collier MS., *'boastfully'*; Becket conjectured *'basely.'*
17. Powers are crescent; – Theobald reads *'pow'r's a crescent'*; Becket conjectured *'power is crescent'*; Anon. conjectured *'power's a-crescent.'*
18. Was theme for you, i.e. – 'had you for its theme'; Johnson conjectured *'Had theme from you'*; Collier (ed. 2), *'For theme was you'*; Staunton conjectured *'Had you for theme'*; Orson conjectured *'Was known for yours,'* &c.
19. Your considerate stone, i.e. – 'I am silent as a stone'; Heath conjectured *'your confederates love'*; Johnson, *'your considerate ones'*; Blackstone conjectured *'your consideratest one.'* &c. &c.
20. And made their bends adornings; i.e. – "and made their very act of obeisance an improvement on their beauty" (Steevens); the passage has been variously interpreted, but this seems the simplest solution.
21. My prayers; – Rowe reads *'in prayers'*; Collier MS., *'with prayers.'*
22. A fear; – Collier (ed. 2), Thirlby conjectured *'afeard'*; S. Walker conjectured *'afear.'*
23. He away, 'tis; – Pope's emendation of Folio 1, *'he always 'tis'*; Folios 2, 3, 4, *'he always is.'*
24. Inhoop'd, i.e. – enclosed in a hoop; Hanmer, *'in-coop'd'*; Seward conjecture, adopted by Capell, *'in whoop'd-at.'*
25. Tawny-finn'd; – Theobald's emendation of Folios, *'Tawny-fine'*; Rowe reads *'Tawny-fin.'*

26. That art not what thou'rt sure of!; – Hanmer, *'That say'st but what thou'rt sure of'*; Johnson conjectured *'That art—not what?—Thou'rt sure on't,'* &c.; perhaps the words of the text mean 'that art not the evil thing of which thou art so certain'; other interpretations have been advanced.
27. Though he be painted one way like a Gorgon, – alluding to the old 'perspective' pictures showing one picture from one point of view, another from another standpoint.
28. There; – Pope, *'then'*; Steevens conjectured *'theirs.'*
29. Increase the reels; – Steevens conjectured *'and grease the wheels'*; Douce conjectured *'increase the revels.'*
30. Bear; – Theobald's emendation; Folios, *'beat.'*
31. Then, world, thou hast; – Hanmer's emendation; Folios, *'Then would thou hadst'*; Warburton MS., *'Then would thou hast': 'chaps, no,'* Theobald's reading of Folios, *'chaps no.'*
32. Left unloved; – Collier MS., *'held unloved'*; Singer conjectured, adopted by Hudson, *'felt unloved'*; Seymour conjectured *'left unvalued'*; Staunton conjectured *'left unpriz'd.'*
33. If not denounced against us; – Hanmer reads, *'Is't not denounc'd 'gainst us?'*; Jackson conjectured *'Is't not? Denounce against us!'*; &c.
34. His whole action grows Not in the power on't, i.e. – "his whole conduct in the war is not founded upon that which is his greatest strength, namely, his land force, but on the caprice of a woman," &c. (Malone).
35. And in our name, what she requires; add more, From thine invention, offers; – Grant White conjectured *'What she requires; and in our name add more Offers from thine invention'*; Walker, *'and more ... From thine invention offer.'*
36. Caesarion smite; – Hanmer's emendation; Folios, *'Caesarian smile.'*
37. Mine; – Folios, *'thine.'*
38. The text follows Malone's arrangement and reading (*vide* Cambridge Edition, Note VI.).
39. Dispatch. Enobarbus!; – Steevens (1773) reading; Folio 1, *'Dispatch Enobarbus'*; Folio 2, *'Dispatch Eros'*; Folios 3, 4. *'Dispatch, Eros'*; Pope *'dispatch my Eros'*; Johnson conjectured *'Dispatch! To Enobarbus!'*; Capell, *'Dispatch.—O Enobarbus!'*; Rann, *'Eros! Dispatch'*; Ritson conjectured, adopted by Steevens 1793, *'Eros, despatch'*; Anon. conjecture, *'Domitius Enorbarbus!'*
40. Persuade; – Rowe's correction of Folios, *'disswade.'*
41. Favouring; – Theobald's emendation of Folios *'savouring.'*
42. Soul; – Capell, *'soil'*; Singer (ed. 2) from Collier MS., *'spell'*; S. Walker conjectured *'snake': grave'*; Pope reads *'gay'*; Collier (ed. 2) from Collier MS., *'great'*; Singer (ed. 2), *'grand.'*
43. Lo thee; – Grant White conjectured *'Lo there.'*
44. Burn the great sphere; – Hanmer, *'Turn from the sphere'*; Warburton, *'Turn from th' great sphere.'*
45. Shore; – Staunton conjecture, adopted by Hudson, *'star.'*
46. I dare not; – Malone conjectured *'I dare not descend'*; Ritson conjecture, adopted by Wordsworth, *'I dare not come down'*; Anon. conjecture, from Plutarch, *'I dare not ope the gates'*; &c.
47. No more, but e'en a woman; – Capell's version; Folios read *'No more but in a Woman'*; Rowe, *'No more but a meer woman'*; Johnson conjecture, adopted by Steevens, 1773, 1778, *'No more—but e'en a woman.'*
48. Crack: the round world; – Steevens conjectured *'crack than this: the ruin'd world'*; Singer conjectured *'crack: the round world convulsive'*; Nicholson conjectured *'crack: the round world in rending'*; Daniel conjectured *'crack in the round world'*; &c., &c.
49. Splitted the heart; – Collier MS., *'Split that self noble heart'*; Elze conjectured *'Splitted that very heart.'*
50. Live To be ungentle, – Rowe (ed. 2) and Southern MS.; Folios read *'leaue to be ungentle'*; Capell, *'Leave to be gentle'*; Tyrwhitt conjectured *'learn To be ungentle'*; Gould conjectured *'bear to be ungentle.'*
51. Dug; – Warburton conjecture, adopted by Theobald, *'dugg'*; Folios, *'dung'*; Nicholson conjectured *'tongue'*; Cartwright conjectured *'wrong'*; Bailey conjectured *'doom.'*
52. Necessary; – Hanmer, *'accessory'*; Malone conjectured *'necessary, I'll not so much as syllable a word'*; Ritson conjectured *'necessary, I will not speak; if sleep be necessary.'*
53. An autumn 'twas; – Theobald and Thirlby conjectured; Folios read *'an Anthony it was'*; &c.
54. Smites; – Capell's emendation; Folios 1, 2, *'suites'*; Folios 3, 4, *'suits'*; Pope, *'shoots.'*
55. My chance, i.e. – my changed fortune, lot; Hanmer reads *'mischance'*; S. Walker conjectured *'my change'*; Ingleby conjecture, adopted by Hudson, *'my glance.'*
56. We answer others merits in our name, Are'; – Malone's reading; Folios, *'We answer others merits, in our name Are'*; &c.
57. Caves; – so Folios 2, 3, 4; Folio 1, *'caues'*; Barry conjectured *'canes'*; Anon. conjecture *'caves'*; Perring conjectured *'course.'*

GLOSSARY

ABATE: to shorten, to cast down, to blunt
ABATEMENT: diminution
ABIDE: to sojourn, to expiate (a corruption of 'Aby')
ABLE: to uphold
ABRIDGEMENT: a short play
ABROOK: to brook, abide
ABSEY-BOOK: a primer
ABSOLUTE: positive, certain, complete
ABUSE: to deceive
ABUSE: deception
ABY: to expiate a fault
ABYSM: abyss
ACCITE: to cite, summon
ACCUSE: accusation
ACHIEVE: to obtain
ACKNOWN: 'to be acknown' is to acknowledge
ACQUITTANCE: a receipt or discharge
ACTION-TAKING: litigious
ACTURE: action
ADDITION: title, attribute
ADDRESS: to prepare oneself
ADDRESSED: prepared
ADVANCE: to prefer, promote to honor
ADVERTISEMENT: admonition
ADVERTISING: attentive
ADVICE: consideration, discretion
ADVISE: sometimes *neuter*, sometimes *reflective* to consider, reflect
ADVISED: considerate
ADVOCATION: pleading, advocacy
AFEARD: afraid
AFFECT: to love
AFFEERED: assessed, confirmed
AFRONT: in front
AFFY: to affiance, to trust
AGAZED: looking in amazement
AGLET-BABY: the small figure engraved on a jewel
AGNISE: to acknowledge, confess
A-GOOD: a good deal, plenteously
A-HOLD: a sea-term
AIERY: the nest of a bird of prey
AIM: a guess
ALDER-LIEFEST: most loved of all
ALE: alehouse
ALLOW: to approve
ALLOWANCE: approval
AMES-ACE: two aces, the lowest throw of the dice
AMORT: dead, dejected
AN: if
ANCHOR: an anchorite, hermit
ANCIENT: an ensign bearer
ANGEL: a coin, so called because it bore the image of an angel
ANIGHT: by night
ANSWER: retaliation
ANTHROPOPHAGINIAN: a cannibal
ANTICK: the fool in the old plays
ANTRE: a cave
APPARENT: heir-apparent
APPEAL: accusation, to accuse
APPEARED: made apparent
APPLE-JOHN: a kind of apple
APPOINTMENT: preparation
APPREHENSION: opinion
APPREHENSIVE: apt to apprehend or understand
APPROBATION: probation
APPROOF: approbation, proof
APPROVE: to prove, to justify, make good
APPROVER: one who proves or tries
ARCH: chief
ARGAL: a ridiculous word intended for the Latin ergo
ARGENTINE: silver
ARGIER: Algiers
ARGOSY: originally a vessel of Ragusa or Ragosa, a Ragosine; hence any ship of burden
ARGUMENT: subject
ARMIGERO: a mistake for Armiger, the Latin for Esquire
AROINT: found only in the imperat, mood, get thee gone
A-ROW: in a row
ARTICULATE: to enter into articles of agreement, to exhibit in articles
ASK: to require
ASPECT: regard, looks
ASPERSION: sprinkling; hence blessing because before the Reformation benediction was generally accompanied by sprinkling of holy water
ASSAY: to attempt, test, make proof of
ASSINEGO: an ass
ASSUBJUGATE: to subjugate

ASSURANCE: deed of assurance
ASSURED: betrothed
ATOMY: an atom, used in contempt of a small person
ATONE: to put people at one, to reconcile, to agree
ATTACH: to seize, lay hold on
ATTASKED: taken to task, reprehended
ATTEND: to listen to
ATTENT: attentive
ATTORNEY: an agent, to employ as an agent, to perform by an agent
AUDACIOUS: spirited, daring, but without any note of blame attached to it
AUGUR: augury
AUTHENTIC: clothed with authority
AVAUNT: be gone, a word of abhorrence
AVE: the Latin for hail; hence acclamation
AVE-MARY: the angelic salutation addressed to the B. Virgin Mary
AVERRING: confirming
AWFUL: worshipful
AWKWARD: contrary

BACCARE: keep back
BACKWARD: the hinder part; hence, when applied to time, the past
BALKED: heaped, as on a ridge
BALLOW: a cudgel
BALM: the oil of consecration
BAN: to curse
BANK: to sail by the banks
BARM: yeast
BARN: a child
BARNACLE: a shell-fish, supposed to produce the sea-bird of the same name
BASE: a game, sometimes called Prisoners' base
BASES: an embroidered mantle worn by knights on horseback, and reaching from the middle to below the knees
BASILISK: a kind of ordnance
BASTA: (Italian), enough
BASTARD: raisin wine
BAT-FOWLING: catching birds with a clapnet by night
BATE: to flutter as a hawk, to except, to abate
BATLET: a small bat, used for beating clothes
BATTLE: army
BAVIN: a piece of waste wood, applied contemptuously to anything worthless
BAWCOCK: a fine fellow
BAY: the space between the main timbers of the roof
BEADSMAN: one who bids bedes, that is, prays prayers for another
BEARING-CLOTH: a rich cloth in which children were wrapt at their christening
BEAT: to flutter as a falcon, to meditate, consider earnestly
BEAVER: the lower part of a helmet
BEETLE: a mallet
BEING: dwelling
BEING: since, inasmuch as
BE-METE: to measure
BE-MOILED: daubed with dirt
BENDING: stooping under a weight
BENVENUTO: (Italian), welcome
BERGOMASK: a rustic dance
BESHREW: evil befal
BESTRAUGHT: distraught, distracted
BETEEM: to pour out
BETID: happened
BEZONIAN: a beggarly fellow
BIDING: abiding-place
BIGGEN: a night-cap
BILBERRY: the whortleberry
BILBO: a sword, from Bilboa, a town in Spain where they were made
BILBOES: fetters or stocks
BILL: a bill-hook, a weapon
BIN: been, are
BALLOW: a cudgel
BIRD-BOLT: a bolt to be shot from a crossbow at birds
BIRDING: hawking at partridges
BISSON: blind
BLANK: the white mark in the middle of a target; hence, metaphorically, that which is aimed at
BLENCH: to start aside, flinch
BLENT: blended
BLOOD-BOLTERED: smeared with blood
BLOW: to inflate
BOARD: to accost
BOB: a blow, metaph, a sarcasm, to strike, metaph, to ridicule, or to obtain by raillery
BODGE: to botch, bungle
BODIKIN: a corrupt word used as an oath
BOITIER VERT (FRENCH): green box
BOLD: to embolden
BOLLEN: swollen
BOLTER: a sieve
BOLTED: sifted, refined
BOLTING-HUTCH: a hutch in which meal was sifted
BOMBARD: a barrel, a drunkard
BOMBAST: padding
BONA-ROBA: a harlot
BOND: that to which one is bound
BOOK: a paper of conditions
BOOT: help, use, to help, to avail
BOOTLESS: without boot or advantage, useless
BOOTS: bots, a kind of worm
BORE: caliber of a gun; hence, metaph, size, weight, importance
BOSKY: covered with underwood
BOSOM: wish, heart's desire
BOTS: worms which infest horses
BOURN: a boundary, a brook
BRACE: armor for the arm, state of defence
BRACH: a hound bitch
BRAID: deceitful
BRAVE: handsome, well-dressed, boast
BRAVERY: finery, boastfulness
BRAWL: a kind of dance
BREED-BATE: a breeder of debate, a fomenter of quarrels
BREAST: voice
BREATHE: to exercise
BREATHING: exercising
BREECHING: liable to be whipt
BREESE: the gadfly
BRIDE-BUCK: a buck given away in presents
BRING: to attend one on a journey
BROCK: a badger, a term of contempt
BROKE: to act as a procurer
BROKEN: having lost some teeth by age
BROKEN MUSIC: the music of stringed instruments
BROKER: an agent

BROTHERHOOD: trading company
BROWNIST: a sectary, a follower of Brown, the founder of the Independents
BRUIT: noise, report, rumor, to noise abroad
BRUSH: rude assault
BUCK: suds or lye for washing clothes in
BUCK-BASKET: the basket in which clothes are carried to be washed
BUCKING: washing
BUCK-WASHING: washing in lye
BUG: a bugbear, a sceptre
BULLY-ROOK: a bragging cheater
BURGONET: a kind of helmet
BURST: to break
BUSKY: bushy
BUTT-SHAFT: a light arrow for shooting at a butt
BUXOM: obedient
BY'RLAKIN: by our little Lady: an oath

CADDIS: worsted galloon, so called because it resembles the caddis-worm
CADE: a cask or barrel
CAGE: a prison
CAIN-COLORED: red (applied to hair)
CAITIFF: a captive, a slave; hence, a witch
CALCULATE: prophesy
CALIVER: a hand-gun
CALLET: a trull
CALLING: appellation
CALM: qualm
CAN: to know, be skillful in
CANARY: a wine brought from the Canary Islands
CANDLE-WASTERS: persons who sit up all night to drink
CANAKIN: a little can
CANKER: a caterpillar, the dog-rose
CANSTICK: a candlestick
CANTLE: a slice, corner
CANTON: a canto
CANVAS: to sift; hence, metaphorically, to prove
CAPABLE: intelligent, capable of inheriting, ample, capacious
CAPITULATE: make head
CAPOCCHIA: a simpleton
CAPRICIO: (Italian), caprice
CAPRICIOUS: lascivious
CAPTIOUS: capacious
CARACK: a large ship of burden
CARBONADO: meat scotched for broiling
CARBONADO: to scotch for broiling
CARD: the paper on which the points of the compass are marked under the mariner's needle
CAREIRE: the curvetting of a horse
CARKANET: a necklace
CARL: a churl
CARLOT: a churl
CASTILIAN: a native of Castile; used as a cant term
CASTILIANO VULGO: a cant term, meaning, apparently, to use discreet language
CATALAN: a native of Cathay, a cant word
CATLING: cat-gut
CAVALERO: a cavalier, gentleman
CAVIARE: the roe of sturgeon pickled, a delicacy not appreciated by the vulgar
CAUTEL: deceit
CAUTELOUS: insidious
CEASE: decease
CEASE: put off, made to cease
CENSURE: judgment
CENSURE: to judge, criticise
CENTURY: a hundred of anything, whether men, prayers, or anything else
CEREMONY: a ceremonial vestment, religious rite, or anything ceremonial
CERTES: certainly
CESS: rate, reckoning
CHACE: a term at tennis
CHAMBER: a species of great gun
CHAMBERER: an effeminate man
CHANSON: a song
CHARACT: affected quality
CHARACTER: a letter, handwriting
CHARACTER: to carve or engrave
CHARACTERY: handwriting, that which is written
CHARE: a turn of work
CHARGE-HOUSE: a free-school
CHARLES' WAIN: the constellation called also Ursa Major, or the Great Bear
CHARNECO: a species of sweet wine
CHAUDRON: entrails
CHEATER: for escheator, an officer who collected the fines to be paid into the Exchequer, a decoy
CHECK: a technical term in falconry; when a falcon flies at a bird which is not her proper game she is said to check at it
CHECKS: perhaps intended for ethics
CHEER: fortune, countenance
CHERRY-PIT: a game played with cherrystones
CHEVERIL: kid leather
CHEWIT: cough
CHILDING: pregnant
CH'ILL: vulgar for 'I will.'
CHIRURGEONLY: in a manner becoming a surgeon
CHOPIN: a high shoe or clog
CHRISTOM: clothed with a chrisom, the white garment which used to be put on newly-baptized children
CHRISTENDOM: the state of being a Christian, name
CHUCK: chicken, a term of endearment
CHUFF: a coarse blunt clown
CINQUE PACE: a kind of dance
CIPHER: to decipher
CIRCUMSTANCE: an argument
CITAL: recital
CITE: to incite
CITTERN: a guitar
CLACK-DISH: a beggar's dish
CLAP I' THE CLOUT: to shoot an arrow into the bull's eye of the target
CLAW: to flatter
CLEPE: to call
CLIFF: clef, the key in music
CLING: to starve
CLINQUANT: glittering
CLIP: to embrace, to enclose
CLOUT: the mark in the middle of a target
COAST: to advance
COBLOAF: a big loaf
COCK: a cock boat, a euphemism for God
COCK-AND-PIE: an oath
COCKLE: tares or darnel

COCKNEY: a cock
COCK-SHUT-TIME: the twilight when cocks and hens go to roost
COG: to cheat, dissemble
COGNIZANCE: badge, token
COIGN: projecting corner stone
COIL: tumult, turmoil
COLLECTION: drawing a conclusion
COLLIED: blackened
COLOR: pretence
COLORABLE: specious
COLT: to defraud, befool
CO-MART: a joint bargain
COMBINATE: betrothed
COMBINE: to bind
COMMODITY: interest, profit
COMMONTY: used ludicrously for comedy.
COMPACT: compacted, composed
COMPARATIVE: rival
COMPARE: comparison
COMPASSIONATE: moving comparison
COMPETITOR: one who seeks the same thing, an associate in any object
COMPLEMENT: accomplishment
COMPLEXION: passion
COMPOSE: to agree
COMPOSITION: composition
COMPTIBLE: tractable
CON: to learn by heart, to acknowledge
CONCEIT: conception, opinion, fancy
CONCUPY: concubine
CONDITION: temper, quality
CONDOLEMENT: grief
CONDUCT: escort
CONFECT: to make up into sweetmeats
CONFOUND: to consume, destroy
CONJECT: conjecture
CONSIGN: to sign a common bond, to confederate
CONSORT: company
CONSORT: to accompany
CONSTANCY: consistency
CONSTANT: settled, determined
CONSTANTLY: firmly
CONSTER: to construe
CONTEMPTIBLE: contemptuous
CONTINENT: that which contains anything, that which is contained
CONTINUATE: uninterrupted
CONTRACTION: the marriage contract
CONTRARY: to oppose
CONTRIVE: to conspire, to wear away
CONTROL: to confute
CONVENT: to convene, summon, to be convenient
CONVERT: to change
CONVERTITE: a convert
CONVEY: to manage, to filch
CONVEYANCE: theft, fraud
CONVICT: convicted
CONVICTED: overpowered, vanquished, a doubtful word
CONVINCE: to conquer, subdue
CONVIVE: to feast together
CONVOY: escort
CONY-CATCH: to cheat
CONY-CATCHING: poaching, pilfering
COOLING CARD: used metaphorically for an insurmountable obstacle
COPATAIN HAT: a high-crowned hat
COPE: to reward, to give in return
COPPED: rising to a cop or head
COPY: theme
CORAGIO (Italian): courage!
CORAM: an ignorant mistake for Quorum
CORANTO: a lively dance
CORINTH: a cant term for a brothel
CORINTHIAN: a wencher
CORKY: dry like cork
CORNUTO (ITALIAN): a cuckold
COROLLARY: a surplus
CORPORAL: corporeal, bodily
CORPORAL OF THE FIELD: an aide-de-camp
CORRIVAL: rival
COSTARD: the head
COSTER-MONGER: peddling, mercenary
COT-QUEAN: an effeminate man, molly-coddle
COTE: a cottage, to quote, instance
COTE: to come alongside, overtake
COUCHINGS: crouchings
COUNTERVAIL: to counterpoise, outweigh
COUNTRY: belonging to one's country
COUPLEMENT: union
COURT HOLY-WATER: flattery
COUNT CONFECT: a nobleman composed of affectation
COUNTENANCE: fair shew
COUNTERFEIT: portrait, a piece of base coin
COUNTERPOINT: a counterpane
COUNTY: count, earl
COVENT: a convent
COVER: to lay the table for dinner
COWISH: cowardly
COWL-STAFF: the staff on which a vessel is supported between two men
COX MY PASSION: an oath, a euphemism for 'God's Passion.'
COY: to stroke, fondle, to condescend with difficulty
COYSTRILL: a kestril, a cowardly kind of hawk
COZEN: to cheat
COZENAGE: cheating
COZENER: a cheater
COZIER: a tailor
CRACK: to boast, a loud noise, clap, a forward boy
CRACKER: boaster
CRACK-HEMP: a gallows-bird
CRANK: a winding passage
CRANKING: winding
CRANTS: garlands, a doubtful word
CRARE: a ship of burden
CRAVEN: a dunghill cock
CREATE: formed, compounded
CREDENT: creditable, credible, credulous
CREDIT: report
CRESCIVE: increasing
CRESTLESS: not entitled to bear arms, lowborn
CRISP: curled, winding
CROSS: a piece of money, so called because coin was formerly stamped with a cross
CROW-KEEPER: one who scares crows
CROWNER: a coroner
CROWNET: a coronet
CRY: the yelping of hounds, a pack of hounds, a company, used contemptuously
CRY AIM: to encourage
CUE: the last words of an actor's speech, which is the signal for the next actor to begin
CUISSES: pieces of armor to cover the thighs

CULLION: a base fellow
CUNNING: skill, skillful
CURB: to bend, truckle
CURRENTS: occurrences
CURST: petulant, shrewish
CURSTNESS: shrewishness
CURTAIL: a cur
CURTAL: a docked horse
CURTAL-AXE: a cutlass
CUSTALORUM: a ludicrous mistake for Custos Rotulorum
CUSTARD-COFFIN: the crust of a custard-pudding
CUSTOMER: a common woman
CUT: a cheat, 'to draw cuts' is to draw lots
CYPRESS: a kind of crape

DAFF: to befool, to put off; this seems to be a corruption of 'doff.'
DAMN: to condemn
DANGER: reach, control, power
DANSKER: a Dane
DARE: to challenge
DARKLING: in the dark
DARRAIGN: to set in array
DAUB: to disguise
DAUBERY: imposition
DAY-WOMAN: a dairy-maid
DEAR: dire, that which has to do with the affections, piteous, important
DEARN: lonely. (Gower)
DEBOSHED: debauched, drunken
DECK: to bedew, this is probably a form of the verb 'to drag,' now a provincial word
DECK: a pack of cards
DECLINE: to enumerate, as in going through the cases of a noun
DECLINED: fallen
DEEM: doom, judgment
DEFEAT: to undo, destroy, destruction
DEFEATURE: disfigurement
DEFENCE: art of fencing
DEFEND: to forbid
DEFENSIBLE: having the power to defend
DEFTLY: dexterously
DEFY: renounce
DEGREES: a step
DELAY: to let slip by delaying
DEMERIT: merit, desert
DEMURELY: solemnly
DENAY: denial
DENIER: the 12th part of a French sol
DENOTEMENT: marking, note or manifestation
DENY: to refuse
DEPART: departure, to part
DEPARTING: parting, separation
DEPEND: to be in service
DERIVED: born, descended
DEROGATE: degraded
DESCANT: a variation upon a melody, hence, metaphorically, a comment on a given theme
DESIGN: to draw up articles
DESPATCH: to deprive, bereave
DESPERATE: determined, bold
DETECT: to charge, blame
DETERMINE: to conclude
DICH: optative mood, perhaps contracted for 'do it.'
DIET: food regulated by the rules of medicine
DIET: to have one's food regulated by the rules of medicine
DIFFUSED: confused
DIGRESSING: transgressing, going out of the right way
DIGRESSION: transgression
DIG-YOU-GOOD-DEN: give you good evening
DILDO: the chorus or burden of a song
DINT: stroke
DIRECTION: judgment, skill
DISABLE: to disparage
DISAPPOINTED: unprepared
DISCASE: to undress
DISCONTENT: a malcontent
DISCOURSE: power of reasoning
DISDAINED: disdainful
DISLIMN: to disfigure, transform
DISME: a tenth or tithe
DISPARK: to destroy a park
DISPONGE: to squeeze out as from a sponge
DISPOSE: disposal
DISPOSE: to conspire
DISPOSITION: maintenance
DISPUTABLE: disputation
DISPUTE: to argue, examine
DISSEMBLY: used ridiculously for assembly
DISTASTE: to corrupt
DISTEMPERED: discontented
DISTRACTION: a detached troop or company of soldiers
DISTRAUGHT: distracted, mad
DIVERTED: turned from the natural course
DIVISION: a phrase or passage in a melody
DIVULGED: published, spoken of
DOFF: to do off, strip., to put off with an excuse
DOIT: a small Dutch coin
DOLE: portion dealt, grief, lamentation
DON: to do on, put on
DONE: 'done to death,' put to death
DOTANT: one who dotes, a dotard
DOUT: to do out, quench
DOWLAS: a kind of coarse sacking
DOWLE: the swirl of a feather
DOWN-GYVED: hanging down like gyves or fetters
DRAB: a harlot
DRABBING: whoring
DRAUGHT: a privy
DRAWN: having his sword drawn
DRAWN: drunk, having taken a good draught
DRIBBLING: weak
DRIVE: to rush impetuously
DROLLERY: a puppet-show
DRUMBLE: to dawdle
DRY: thirsty
DUC-DAME: perhaps the Latin duc-ad-me, bring him to me
DUDGEON: a dagger
DULL: soothing
DULLARD: a dull person
DUMP: complaint
DUP: to do up, lift up

EAGER: sour, harsh, biting
EANLING: a yeanling, a lamb
EAR: to plough
ECHE: to eke out. (Gower)
ECSTASY: madness
EFT: ready, convenient
EISEL: vinegar
ELD: old age
EMBOSSED: swollen into protuberances, covered with foam
EMBOWELLED: disembowelled, emptied
EMBRASURE: embrace
EMINENCE: exalted station
EMPERY: empire

EMULATION: jealousy, mutiny
EMULOUS: jealous
ENCAVE: to place oneself in a cave
END: 'Still an end,' continually for ever
ENFEOFF: to place in possession in fee simple
ENGINE: a machine of war
ENGLUT: to swallow speedily
ENGROSS: to make gross or fat
ENGROSSMENT: immoderate acquisition
ENKINDLE: to make keen
ENMEW: to shut up, as a hawk is shut up in a mew
ENSCONCE: to cover as with a fort
ENSEAMED: fat, rank
ENSHIELD: hidden
ENTERTAIN: encounter, experience
ENTERTAINMENT: treatment, a disposition to entertain a proposal, service
ENTREATMENTS: interviews
EPHESIAN: interviews
EPHESIAN: a toper, a cant term
EQUIPAGE: attendance
EREWHILE: a short time since
ESCOT: to pay a man's reckoning, to maintain
ESPERANCE: hope, used as a war-cry
ESPIAL: a scout or spy
ESTIMATION: conjecture
ESTRIDGE: ostridge
ETERNE: eternal
EVEN: coequal
EVEN: to equal
EXAMINE: to question
EXCREMENT: that which grows outwardly from the body and has no sensation like the hair or nails, any outward show
EXECUTOR: an executioner
EXEMPT: excluded
EXERCISE: a religious service
EXHALE: to hale or draw out, to draw the sword
EXHIBITION: allowance, tension
EXIGENT: death, ending
EXION: ridiculously used for 'action.'
EXPECT: expectation
EXPEDIENCE: expedition, undertaking, haste
EXPEDIENT: expeditious, swift
EXPIATE: completed
EXPOSTULATE: to expound, discuss
EXPOSTURE: exposure
EXPRESS: to reveal
EXPULSE: to expel
EXSUFFICATE: that which has been hissed off, contemptible
EXTEND: to seize
EXTENT: a seizure
EXTERN: outward
EXTIRP: to extirpate
EXTRACTING: distracting
EXTRAUGHT: extracted, descended
EXTRAVAGANT: foreign, wandering
EXTREMES: extravagance of conduct, extremities
EYAS: a nestling hawk
EYAS-MUSKET: a nestling of the musket or merlin, the smallest species of British hawk
EYE: a glance, œillad
EYE: a shade of color, as in shot silk
EYNE: eyes

FACINOROUS: wicked
FACT: guilt
FACTIOUS: instant, importunate
FACULTY: essential virtue or power
FADGE: to suit
FADING: a kind of ending to a song
FAIN: glad, gladly
FAIR: beauty
FAITOR: a traitor
FALL: to let fall
FALLOW: fawn-colored
FALSE: falsehood
FALSING: deceptive
FAMILIAR: a familiar spirit
FANCY-FREE: untouched by love
FANG: to seize in the teeth
FANTASTIC: a fantastical person
FAP: drunk
FAR: farther
FARCED: stuffed
FARDEL: a burden
FARTUOUS: used ridiculously for 'virtuous.'
FAST: assuredly, unalterably
FAT: dull
FAVOR: countenance, complexion, quality
FEAR: the object of fear, to affright
FEARFUL: subject to fear, timorous
FEAT: dexterous
FEAT: to make fine
FEATER: more neatly
FEATLY: nimbly, daintily
FEATURE: beauty
FEDERARY: confederate
FEE-GRIEF: a grief held, as it were, in fee-simple, or the peculiar property of him who possesses it
FEEDER: agent, servant
FEERE: a companion, husband
FEHEMENTLY: used ridiculously for 'vehemently.'
FELL: the hide
FENCE: art or skill in defence
FEODARY: one who holds an estate by suit or service to a superior lord; hence one who acts under the direction of another
FESTER: to rankle, grow virulent
FESTINATELY: quickly
FET: fetched
FICO: a fig
FIELDED: in the field of battle
FIG: to insult
FIGHTS: clothes hung round a ship to conceal the men from the enemy
FILE: a list or catalogue
FILE: to defile, to smooth or polish, to make even
FILL-HORSE: shaft-horse
FILLS: the shafts
FILTH: a whore
FINE: end, to make fine or specious
FINELESS: endless
FIRAGO: ridiculously used for 'Virago.'
FIRE-DRAKE: Will o' the Wisp
FIRE-NEW: with the glitter of novelty on, like newly-forged metal
FIRK: to chastise
FIT: canto or division of a song, a trick or habit
FITCHEW: a polecat
FIVES: a disease incident to horses
FLAP-DRAGON: raisins in burning brandy
FLAP-JACK: a pan-cake
FLAT: certain
FLATNESS: lowness, depth
FLAW: a gust of wind, sudden emotion or the cause of it
FLAW: to make a flaw in, to break
FLECKED: spotted, streaked

FLEET: to float, to pass away, to pass the time
FLEETING: inconstant
FLESHMENT: the act of fleshing the sword, hence the first feat of arms
FLEWED: furnished with hang lips, as hounds are
FLIGHT: a particular mode of practising archery
FLIRT-GILL: a light woman
FLOURISH: an ornament
FLOURISH: to ornament, disguise with ornament
FLOTE: wave, sea
FLUSH: fresh, full of vigor
FOIL: defeat, disadvantage
FOIN: to fence, fight
FOISON: plenty
FOND: foolish, foolishly affectionate
FOOT-CLOTH: a saddle-cloth hanging down to the ground
FOR: for that, because
FORBID: accursed, outlawed
FORBODE: forbidden
FORCE: to stuff, for 'farce.'
FORCED: falsely attributed
FORDO: to kill, destroy, to weary
FORFEND: forbid
FOREIGN: obliged to live abroad
FOREPAST: former
FORESLOW: to delay
FORGETIVE: inventive
FORKED: horned
FORMAL: regular, retaining its proper and essential characteristic
FORSPENT: exhausted, weary
FORSPEAK: to speak against
FORTHRIGHT: a straight path; forthrights and meanders, straight paths and crooked ones
FORWEARY: to weary, exhaust
FOSSET-SELLER: one who sells the pipes inserted into a vessel to give vent to the liquor, and stopped by a spigot
FOX: a sword; a cant word
FOX-SHIP: the cunning of the fox
FRAMPOLD: peevish, unquiet
FRANK: the feeding place of swine
FRANKED: confined
FRANKLIN: a freeholder, a small squire
FRAUGHT: freighted
FRAUGHTAGE: freight
FRAUGHTING: of to fraught; loading or constituting the cargo of a ship
FRESH: a spring of fresh water
FRET: the stop of a guitar
FRET: to wear away, to variegate
FRIEND: to befriend
FRIPPERY: an old-clothes shop
FROM: contrary to
FRONT: to affront, oppose
FRONTIER: opposition
FRONTLET: that which is worn on the forehead
FRUSH: to break or bruise
FRUSTRATE: frustrated
FUB OFF: to put off
FULFILL: to fill full
FULL: complete.
FULLAM: a loaded die
FULSOME: lustful
FURNITOR: furnitory, an herb
FURNISHED: equipped

GABERDINE: a loose outer coat, or smock frock
GAD: a pointed instrument, a goad, upon the gad, with impetuous haste, upon the spur of the moment
GAIN-GIVING: misgiving
GAIT: going, steps
GALLIARD: a kind of dance
GALLIASSE: a kind of ship
GALLIMAUFRY: a ridiculous medley
GALLOW: to scare
GALLOWGLASS: the irregular infantry of Ireland, and the Highlands of Scotland
GAMESTER: a frolicsome person, a loose woman
GARBOIL: disorder, uproar
GARISH: gaudy, staring
GARNER: to lay by, as corn in a barn
GAST: frightened
GAUDY: festive
GAZE: an object of wonder
GEAR: matter of business of any kind
GECK: a fool
GENERAL: the generality, common people
GENERATIONS: children
GENEROSITY: noble birth
GENEROUS: noble
GENTILITY: good manners
GENTLE: gentlefolk, noble, to ennoble
GENTRY: complaisance, conduct becoming gentlefolk
GERMAN: akin, appropriate
GERMEN: seed, embryo
GEST: period
GIB: a he-cat
GIFTS: talents, endowment
GIGLOT: a wanton girl
GILDER: a coin of the value of or
GILT: money, state of wealth
GIMMAL: double
GIMMOR: contrivance
GING: gang
GIRD: to gibe
GIRD: a sarcasm or gibe
GLEEK: to scoff, a scoff
GLOSE: to comment; hence, to be garrulous
GLUT: to swallow
GNARL: to snarl
GOOD-DEED: indeed
GOOD-DEN: good-evening, contracted from 'Good-even.'
GOOD-YEAR OR GOOD-JER: a corruption of the French goujere; the venereal disease
GORBELLIED: corpulent
GOVERNMENT: discretion
GOURD: a species of game of chance
GOUT: a drop
GRACIOUS: abounding in grace Divine
GRAINED: engrained
GRAMERCY: grand mercy, much thanks
GRANGE: the farmstead attached to a monastery, a solitary farm-house
GRATILLITY: used ridiculously for 'gratuity.'
GRATULATE: to congratulate
GRAVE: to bury
GREASILY: grossly
GREEK: a bawd
GREEN: immature, fresh, unused
GREENLY: foolishly
GREET: to weep
GRIZE: a step
GROSSLY: palpably
GROUNDLING: one who sits in the pit of a theatre
GROWING: accruing
GUARD: decoration, to decorate

GUARDAGE: guardianship
GUINEA-HEN: the pitando, a cant term
GULES: red, a term in heraldry
GULF: the throat
GUN-STONE: a cannon ball
GUST: taste, relish
GYVE: to fetter

HACK: to become common
HAGGARD: a wild or unreclaimed hawk
HAG-SEED: seed or offspring of a hag
HAIR: course, order, grain
HALIDOM: holiness, sanctification, Christian fellowship; used as an oath, and analogous to 'By my faith.'
HALL: an open space to dance in
HALLOWMAS: All Hallow's Day
HAP: chance, fortune
HAPPILY: accidentally
HANDSAW: perhaps a corruption of Heronshaw; a hern
HARDIMENT: defiance, brave deeds
HARLOCK: charlock, wild mustard
HARRY: to annoy, harass
HAVING: property, fortune
HAVIOUR: behavior
HAUGHT: haughty
HAUNT: company
HAY: a term in fencing
HEADY: violent, headlong
HEAT: 'to heat,' heated
HEBENON: hebane
HEFT: a heaving
HEFT: furnished with a handle: hence, metaphorically, finished off, delicately formed
HELM: to steer, manage
HENCE: henceforward
HENCHMAN: a page or attendant
HENT: to seize, take
HERMIT: a beadsman, one bound to pray for another
HEST: command
HIGH: used in composition with adjectives to heighten or emphasize their signification, as, high-fantastical
HIGHT: called
HILD: held
HILDING: a paltry fellow
HINT: suggestion
HIREN: a prostitute, with a pun on the word 'iron.'
HIT: to agree
HOISE: to hoist, heave up on high
HOIST: hoisted
HOLP: to help; helped
HOME: to the utmost
HONEST: chaste
HONESTY: chastity
HONEY-STALKS: the red clover
HOODMAN-BLIND: the game now called blind-man's-buff
HORN-MAD: probably, that is, brain-mad
HOROLOGE: a clock
HOT-HOUSE: a brothel
HOX: to hamstring
HUGGER-MUGGER: secresy
HULL: to drift on the sea like a wrecked ship
HUMOROUS: fitful, or, perhaps, hurried
HUNT-COUNTER: to follow the scent the wrong way
HUNTS-UP: a holla used in hunting when the game was on foot
HURLY: noise, confusion
HURTLE: to clash
HURTLING: noise, confusion
HUSBANDRY: frugality, management
HUSWIFE: a jilt

ICE-BROOK: an icy-cold brook
I'FECKS: in faith, a euphemism
IGNOMY: ignominy
IMAGE: representation
IMBARE: to bare, lay open
IMMEDIACY: close connexion
IMMOMENT: unimportant
IMP: to graft, to splice a falcon's broken feathers
IMP: a scion, a child
IMPAWN: to stake, compromise
IMPEACH: to bring into question, impeachment
IMPEACHMENT: cause of censure, hindrance
IMPERCEIVERANT: dull of perception
IMPETICOS: to pocket
IMPORTANCE: importunity
IMPORTANT: importunate
IMPORTING: significant
IMPOSE: imposition, meaning command or task imposed upon any one
IMPOSITION: command
IMPRESE: a device with a motto
IMPRESS: to compel to serve
INCAPABLE: unconscious
INCARNARDINE: to dye red
INCENSED: incited, egged on
INCH-MEAL: by inch-meal, by portions of inches
INCLINING: compliant, inclination
INCLIP: to embrace
INCLUDE: conclude
INCONY: fine, delicate
INCORRECT: ill-regulated
IND: India
INDENT: to compound or bargain
INDEX: a preface
INDIFFERENT: ordinary
INDIGEST: disordered
INDITE: to invite, to convict
INDUCTION: introduction, beginning
INDURANCE: delay
INFINITE: infinite power
INGRAFT: to engraff, engrafted
INHABITABLE: uninhabitable
INHERIT: to possess
INHOOPED: penned up in hoops
INKHORN-MATE: a contemptuous term for an ecclesiastic, or man of learning
INKLE: a kind of narrow fillet or tape
INLAND: civilized, well-educated
INLY: inwardly
INQUISITION: enquiry
INSANE: that which causes insanity
INSCONCE: to arm, fortify
INSTANCE: example, information, reason, proof
INTEND: to pretend
INTENDING: regarding
INTENDMENT: intention
INTENTIVELY: attentively
INTERESSED: allied
INTERMISSION: pause, delay
INTRENCHMENT: not capable of being cut
INTRINSE: intricate
INTRINSICATE: intricate
INVENTION: imagination
INWARD: an intimate friend, intimate
INWARDNESS: intimacy

IRREGULOUS: lawless, licentious
ITERATION: reiteration

JACK: a mean fellow
JACK-A-LENT: a puppet thrown at in Lent
JACK GUARDANT: a jack in office
JADE: to whip, to treat with contempt
JAR: the ticking of a clock
JAR: to tick as a clock
JAUNCE: to prance
JESS: a strap of leather attached to the talons of a hawk, by which it is held on the fist
JEST: to tilt in a tournament
JET: to strut
JOVIAL: appertaining to Jove
JOURNAL: daily
JUDICIOUS: critical
JUMP: to agree, to hazard, hazard, exactly, nicely
JUSTICER: a judge, magistrate
JUT: to encroach
JUTTY: a projection, to jut out beyond
JUVENAL: youth, young man

KAM: crooked
KECKSY: hemlock
KEECH: a lump of tallow
KEEL: to skim
KEEP: to restrain
KEISAR: Caesar, Emperor
KERN: the rude foot soldiers of the Irish
KIBE: a chillblain
KICKSHAW: a made dish
KICKSY WICKSY: a wife, used in disdain
KILN-HOLE: the ash-hole under a kiln
KIND: nature
KINDLE: to bring forth young; used only of beasts
KINDLESS: unnatural
KINDLY: natural
KIRTLE: a gown
KNAVE: a boy, a serving-man
KNAP: to snap, crack
KNOT: a figure in garden beds
KNOW: to acknowledge

LABRAS: lips
LACED-MUTTON: a courtezan
LAG: the lowest of the people
LAG: late, behindhand
LAKIN: ladykin, little lady, an endearing term applied to the Virgin Mary in the oath, 'By our lakin.'
LAND-DAMN: perhaps to extirpate; Hanmer thinks it means to kill by stopping the urine
LAPSED: taken, apprehended
LARGE: licentious, free
LARGESS: a present
LASS-LORN: deserted by a mistress
LATCH: to smear, to catch
LATED: belated
LATTEN: made of brass
LAUND: lawn
LAVOLTA: a dance
LAY: wager
LEAGUE: besieging army
LEASING: lying
LEATHER-COATS: a kind of apple
LEECH: a physician
LEER: countenance, complexion
LEET: a manor court
LEGERITY: lightness
LEGE: to allege
LEIGER: an ambassador resident abroad
LEMAN: a lover or mistress
LENTEN: meagre, that which may be eaten in Lent
L'ENVOY: the farewell or moral at the end of a tale or poem
LET: to hinder, to hinder
LET: hindrance
LETHE: death
LEVEL: to aim, that which is aimed at
LEWD: ignorant, foolish
LEWDLY: wickedly
LEWDSTER: a lewd person
LIBBARD: a leopard
LIBERAL: licentious
LIBERTY: libertinism
LICENSE: licentiousness
LIEF: dear
LIFTER: a thief
LIGHT O' LOVE: a tune so called
LIGHTLY: easily, generally
LIKE: to please, to liken, compare, likely
LIKELIHOOD: promise, appearance
LIKING: condition
LIMBECK: an alembick, a still
LIMBO: or Limbo patrum, the place where good men under the Old Test. were believed to be imprisoned till released by Christ after his crucifixion
LIME: bird-lime
LIMN: to draw
LINE: to entangle as with bird-lime, to smear with bird-lime, to mix lime with beer or other liquor
LINE: to cover on the inside, to strengthen by inner works
LINSTOCK: a staff with a match at the end of it, used by gunners in firing cannon
LIST: a margin, hence a bound or enclosure
LITHER: lazy
LITTLE: miniature
LIVELIHOOD: appearance of life
LIVERY: a law phrase, signifying the act of delivering a freehold into the possession of the heir or purchaser
LIVING: lively, convincing
LOACH: a fish so called
LOB: a looby
LOCKRAM: a sort of coarse linen
LODE-STAR: the leading-star, pole-star
LOFFE: to laugh
LOGGATS: the game called nine-pins
LONGLY: longingly
LOOF: to luff, bring a vessel up to the wind
LOON: a low contemptible fellow
LOT: a prize in a lottery
LOTTERY: that which falls to a man by lot
LOWT: a clown
LOWT: to treat one as a lowt, with contempt
LOZEL: a spendthrift
LUBBER: a leopard
LUCE: the pike or jack, a fresh-water fish
LUMPISH: dull, dejected
LUNES: fits of lunacy
LURCH: to defeat, to win
LURCH: to shift, to play tricks
LURE: a thing stuffed to resemble a bird with which the falconer allures a hawk
LUSH: juicy, luxuriant

LUSTIG: lusty, cheerful
LUXURIOUS: lascivious
LUXURY: lust
LYM: a limer or slow hound

MADE: having his fortune made
MAGNIFICO: the chief magistrate at Venice
MAGOT-PIE: a magpie, a pie which feeds on magots
MAILED: covered as with a coat of mail
MAIN-COURSE: a sea-term
MAKE: to do up, bar, to do
MALKIN: a familiar name for Mary; hence a servant wench
MALLECHO: mischief
MAMMERING: hesitating
MAMMETS: a woman's breasts, a doll
MAMMOCK: to break, tear
MAN: to tame a hawk
MANAGE: management
MANDRAGORA, MANDRAKE: a plant of soporiferous quality, supposed to resemble a man
MANKIND: having a masculine nature
MARCHES: frontiers, borders
MARCHPANE: a kind of sweet biscuit
MARGENT: margin
MARRY TRAP: an oath
MARTLEMAS: the Feast of St. Martin, which occurs on the 11th of Nov. when the fine weather generally ends; hence applied to an old man
MATCH: an appointment
MATE: to confound, dismay
MEACOCK: tame, cowardly
MEALED: mingled
MEAN: instrument used to promote an end
MEAN: the tenor part in a harmony
MEAN: opportunity, power
MEASURE: reach, a stately dance
MEAZEL: a leper, spoken in contempt of a mean person
MEDAL: a portrait in a locket
MEDICINE: a physician
MEED: reward, hire
MEHERCLE: by Hercules
MEINY: retinue
MELL: to mix, to meddle
MEMORIZE: to cause to be remembered
MEPHISTOPHILUS: the name of a familiar spirit
MERCATANTE: (Italian), a foreign trader
MERELY: simply, absolutely
MESS: a company of four
METAPHYSICAL: supernatural
METE-YARD: measuring-wand
MEW UP: to confine
MICHER: a truant
MICKLE: much
MILL-SIXPENCE: a milled sixpence
MINCE: to do any thing affectedly
MINCING: affected
MISCREATE: illegitimate
MISDOUBT: to suspect
MISERY: avarice
MISPRISE: to despise, to mistake
MISPRISION: mistake
MISSIVE: messenger
MISTEMPERED: angry
MISTHINK: to think ill of
MISTRESS: the jack in bowling
MOBLED: muffled
MODERN: commonplace
MODULE: a model, image
MOE: more, of frequent occurrence
MOIETY: a portion
MOME: a stupid person
MOMENTARY: momentary
MONTHS-MIND: a monthly commemoration of the dead, but used ludicrously to mean a great mind or strong desire
MOOD: anger
MOON-CALF: a nick-name applied to Caliban
MOONISH: inconstant
MOP: nod
MORISCO: a Moor
MORRIS-PIKE: Moorish-pike
MORT: death, applied to animals of the chase
MORT-DU-VINAIGRE: (French), a ridiculous oath
MORTAL: fatal, deadly, murderous
MORTIFIED: ascetic
MOSE: a doubtful word, applied to some disease in a horse
MOTION: solicitation, emotion, a puppet
MOTIVE: one who moves, that which moves
MOTLEY: used as the many-colored coat of a fool, a fool
MOTLEY-MINDED: foolish
MOUSE-HUNT: a weasel
MOW: to make grimaces
MOY: a coin, probably a moidore
MUCH: significant of contempt, used ironically
MURE: a wall
MUST: a scramble
MUTINE: to mutiny, a mutineer

NAPKIN: a handkerchief
NATURAL: an idiot
NAYWARD: towards denial, a catch-word, by-word
NEB: the beak
NEELD: a needle
NEIF: hand
NEPHEW: a grandson
NETHER-STOCKS: stockings
NEXT: nearest
NICE: foolish
NICK: score or reckoning
NICK: to brand with folly
NIGHTED: black as night
NIGHT-RULE: nightly solemnity
NINE MEN'S MORRIS: a place set apart for a Moorish dance by nine men
NINNY: a fool, jester
NOBILITY: nobleness
NOBLE: a coin, worth
NODDY: a dolt
NONCE: for the nonce, corrupted from 'for then once,' for the occasion
NOOK-SHOTTEN: indented with bays and creeks
NOURISH: a nurse
NOVUM: a game at dice
NOWL: head
NUTHOOK: a hook for pulling down nuts, hence a thief

O: a circle
OAR: to row as with oars
OBSEQUIOUS: behaving as becomes one who attends funeral obsequies
OBSEQUIOUSLY: funereally
OBSTACLE: ridiculously used for 'obstinate.'

OCCUPATION: persons occupied in business
OCCURRENT: an incident
OD'S BODY, OD'S HEARTLINGS, OD'S PITTIKINS, OD'S PLESSED WILL: 'Od's in these and all similar exclamations is a euphemism for 'God's.'
OEILLIAD: an amorous glance
O'ERPARTED: having too important a part to act
O'ER-RAUGHT: overreached, overtasked
OFFERING: challenging
OFFICE: benefit, kindness, use, function
OLD: a cant term for great, as we say fine, or pretty
ONCE: some time
ONEYER: a banker, a doubtful word
OPE: open
OPE: to open, to open
OPEN: plain, public, to give tongue as a hound
OPERANT: active
OPINIONED: used ridiculously for pinioned
OPPOSITE: adversary
OPPOSITION: combat
OR: before
ORDER: measures
ORDINANCE: rank, order
ORGULOUS: proud
ORT: leaving, refuse
OSTENT: show, appearance
OSTENTATION: show, appearance
OUNCE: a beast of prey of the tiger kind
OUPHE: a fairy
OUSEL-COCK: the blackbird
OUT: all out, fully
OUT-LOOK: to face down
OUTWARD: not in the secret of affairs, outside
OWE: to own

PACK: to practice unlawful confederacy
PACK: a number of people confederated
PADDOCK: a toad
PAID: punished
PALABRAS: words, a cant term, from the Spanish
PALE: to enclose
PALL: to wrap as with a pall
PALLED: impaired
PALMER: one who bears a palm-branch, in token of having made a pilgrimage to Palestine
PALMY: victorious
PARCELLED: belonging to individuals
PARD: the leopard
PARITOR: an apparitor
PARLE: talk
PARLOUS: perilous, keen, shrewd
PARTED: endowed, gifted
PARTIZAN: a pike
PASH: the face
PASH: to strike violently, to bruise, crush
PASS: to practice, to surpass expectation
PASSANT: a term of heraldry, applied to animals represented on the shield as passing by at a trot
PASSING: surpassingly, exceedingly
PASSION: to have feelings
PASSIONATE: to suffer
PASSY-MEASURE: a kind of dance
PASTRY: the room where pastry was made
PATCH: a mean fellow
PATCHED: dressed in motley
PATCHERY: trickery
PATH: to walk
PATHETICAL: affected, hypocritical
PATIENT: to make patient, to compose
PATINE: the metal disc on which the bread is placed in the administration of the Eucharist
PATTERN: to give an example of, afford a pattern for
PAUCA VERBA: few words
PAUCAS: few, a cant term
PAVIN: a dance
PAX: a small image of Christ
PAY: to despatch
PEAT: a term of endearment for a child
PEDASCULE: a pedant, schoolmaster
PEER: to peep out
PEIZE: to balance, weigh down
PELTING: paltry
PERDU: lost
PERDURABLE: durable
PERDY: a euphemism for Par Dieu
PERFECT: certain
PERFECT: to inform perfectly
PERIAPTS: charms worn round the neck
PERJURE: a perjured person
PERSEVER: to persevere
PERSPECTIVE: a telescope, or some sort of optical glass
PEW-FELLOW: a comrade
PHEEZE: to comb, fleece, curry
PIA-MATER: the membrane covering the brain, the brain itself
PICK: to pitch, throw.
PICKED: chosen, selected
PICKERS (*and* STEALERS): the fingers, used ridiculously
PICKING: insignificant
PICKT-HATCH: a place noted for brothels
PIED: motley-coated, wearing the motley coat of a jester
PIELED: shaven
PIGHT: pitched
PILCHER: a scabbard
PILL: to pillage
PIN: a malady of the eyes, the centre of a target
PINFOLD: a pound, a place to confine lost cattle
PIONED: digged
PLACKET: a petticoat-front
PLAIN SONG: a simple air
PLAITED: intricate
PLANCHED: made of boards
PLANTATION: colonizing, planting a colony
PLAUSIVE: plausible
PLEACHED: interwoven
POINT: a lace furnished with a tag by which the breeches were held up
POINT-DE-VICE: derived from the French, faultless
POISE: balance, doubt
POLLED: bare
POMANDER: a perfumed ball
POMEWATER: a kind of apple
POOR-JOHN: a herring
POPINJAY: a parrot
PORT: pomp, state
PORT: a gate
PORTABLE: bearable
PORTANCE: conduct, behavior
POSSESS: to inform

POTCH: to push violently
POTENT: a potentate
POUNCET-BOX: a box for holding perfumes
POWER: forces, army
PRACTICE: wicked stratagem
PRACTISANT: a confederate
PRANK: to dress up
PRECEPT: a justice's summons
PRECIOUSLY: in business of great importance
PREGNANT: fertile of invention, ready, obvious
PRENOMINATE: to name beforehand, to prophesy
PRE-ORDINANCE: old-established law
PRESENCE: the presence-chamber, high bearing
PREST: ready
PRETENCE: design
PRETEND: to portend, to intend
PREVENT: to anticipate
PRICK: the mark denoting the hour on a dial
PRICK: to incite, to choose by pricking a hole with a pin opposite the name
PRICK-SONG: music sung in parts by note
PRICKET: a stag of two years
PRIDE: heat
PRIG: to steal
PRIME: rank, lecherous
PRIMER: more-important
PRIMERO: a game at cards
PRINCIPALITY: that which holds the highest place
PRINCOX: a coxcomb
PRISER: a prize-fighter
PROCURE: to bring
PROFACE: much good may it do you
PROFANE: outspoken
PROGRESS: a royal ceremonial journey
PROJECT: to shape or contrive
PROMPTURE: suggestion
PRONE: ready, willing
PROOF: strength of manhood
PROPAGATE: to advance, to forward
PROPAGATION: obtaining
PROPER-FALSE: natural falsehood
PROPERTIED: endowed with the properties of
PROPERTIES: scenes, dresses, &c. used in a theatre
PROPERTY: to take possession of
PROPOSE: to suppose, for the sake of argument, to converse
PROPOSE: conversation
PROROGUE: to defer
PROVAND: provender
PROVISION: forecast
PUCELLE: a virgin, the name given to Joan of Arc
PUDENCY: modesty
PUGGING: thieving
PUN: to pound
PURCHASE: to acquire, win
PURCHASE: gain, winnings
PUT: to compel
PUTTER-ON: an instigator
PUTTER-OUT: one who lends money at interest
PUTTING-ON: instigation
PUTTOCK: a kite

QUAIL: to faint, be languid, be afraid, to cause to quail
QUAINT: curiously beautiful
QUAKE: to cause to quake or tremble
QUALIFY: to moderate
QUALITY: those of the same nature, rank or condition
QUARREL: a suit, cause
QUARRY: game, a heap of game
QUART D'ÉCU: a quarter crown
QUARTER: the post allotted to a soldier
QUAT: a pimple; used in contempt of a person
QUEASY: squeamish, unsettled
QUELL: murder
QUENCH: to grow cool
QUERN: a hand-mill
QUEST: enquiry, search, inquest, jury
QUESTRIST: one who goes in search of another
QUICK: so far gone in pregnancy that the child is alive
QUICKEN: to come to life
QUIDDITY: QUIDDIT.} a subtle question
QUILLET: quidlibet, a subtle case in law
QUINTAIN: a post for tilting at
QUIP: sharp jest, a taunt
QUIRE: to sing in concert
QUIT: to requite, respond
QUIT: past tense of the verb to quit, quitted
QUITANCE: requital
QUIVER: active
QUOTE: to note

RABATO: a ruff
RABBIT-SUCKER: a weasel
RACE: breed; inherited nature
RACK: wreck, to enhance the price of anything, to drive as clouds
RAG: a term of contempt applied to persons
RAKE: to cover
RAPT: transported with emotion
RAPTURE: a fit
RASCAL: a lean deer
RASH: quick, violent
RATE: opinion, judgment, to assign, to value, to scold
RATOLORUM: a ludicrous mistake for Rotulorum
RAVIN: ravenous
RAVIN: to devour
RAUGHT: past tense of to reach
RAWLY: inadequately
RAWNESS: unprovided state
RAYED: arrayed, served
RAZED: slashed
REAR-MOUSE: the bat
REBATE: to deprive of keenness
REBECK: a three stringed fiddle
RECEIPT: money received
RECEIVING: capacity
RECHEAT: a point of the chase to call back the hounds
RECORD: to sing
RECORDER: a flute
RECURE: to cure, recover
RED-LATTICE: suitable to an ale-house, because ale-houses had commonly red lattices
RED PLAGUE: erysipelas
REDUCE: to bring back
REECHY: smoky, dirty
REFELL: to refute
REFER: to reserve to
REGIMENT: government
REGREET: a salutation
REGREET: to salute
REGUERDON: requital
RELATIVE: applicable
REMEMBER: to remind
REMORSE: pity

REMORSEFUL: full of pity, compassionate
REMOTION: removal
REMOVED: sequestered, remote
RENDER: to describe you
RENDER: account
RENEGE: to renounce, to deny
REPAIR: to renovate, comfort
REPEAL: to reverse the sentence of exile
REPROOF: confutation
REPUGN: to resist
REQUIEM: mass for the dead, so called because it begins with the words, Requiem eternam dona eis, Domine
RESOLVE: to satisfy, to dissolve
RESPECT: consideration
RESPECTIVE: respectful, thoughtful
RESPECTIVE: corresponding
RESPECTIVELY: respectfully
RETAILED: handed down
RETIRE: retreat
RETIRE: to draw back
REVERB: to echo
REVOLT: a rebel
RIB: to enclose as within ribs
RID: to destroy
RIFT: to split, a split
RIGGISH: wanton
RIGOL: a circle
RIPE: drunk
RIVAGE: the shore
RIVAL: a partner
RIVALITY: equal rank
RIVE: to fire
ROAD: the high road, applied to a common woman (traviata)
ROISTING: roistering, violent
ROMAGE: unusual stir
RONYON: a term of contempt applied to a woman
ROOD: the crucifix
ROOK: a cheater
ROPERY: roguery
ROPE-TRICKS: tricks such as are played by a rope-dancer
ROUND: to whisper, to become great with child, to finish off
ROUND: a diadem
ROUND: unceremonious
ROUNDEL: a dance or song
ROUNDURE: an enclosure
ROUSE: carousal
ROYNISH: mangy
RUBIOUS: ruddy
RUDDOCK: the redbreast
RUSH: to push
RUSHLING: rustling

SACRIFICIAL: reverent, as words used in religious worship
SACRING-BELL: the little bell rung at mass to give notice that the elements are consecrated
SAD: serious
SADLY: seriously
SADNESS: seriousness
SAFE: to make safe
SAG: to hang down
SALT: lascivious
SALT: taste
SANDED: marked with yellow spots
SANS: without
SAUCY: lascivious
SAW: moral saying
SAY: silken
SAY: assay, taste, relish
SCAFFOLDAGE: the gallery of a theatre
SCALD: scurvy, scabby
SCALE: to weigh in scales
SCALL: a scab, a word of reproach
SCAMBLE: to scramble
SCAMEL: probably a misprint for sea-mel, sea-mew
SCAN: to examine subtly
SCANT: to cut short, to spare
SCANT: scanty, short, scarcely
SCANTLING: a small portion
SCAPE: to escape
SCAPE: a sally
SCATHE: injury
SCATHE: to injure
SCATHFUL: destructive
SCONCE: the head
SCOTCH: to bruise or cut slightly
SCRIMER: a fencer
SCROYLE: a scabby fellow
SCULL: a shoal of fish
SCURVY: scabby; metaph, mean
SEAL: to set one's seal to a deed; hence, to confirm
SEAM: fat
SEAMY: showing the seam or sewing
SEAR: scorched, withered, to stigmatise
SEARCH: to probe; hence, to apply a healing remedy
SEATED: fixed, confirmed
SECT: a slip or scion, a political party
SECURELY: inconsiderately
SEEL: to close
SEELING: closing, blinding
SEEMING: seemly, becomingly
SEEMING: outward manner and appearance
SEEN: versed, instructed
SELD: seldom
SELF-BOUNTY: native goodness
SEMBLABLY: alike
SENIORY: seniority
SENNET: a flourish of trumpets
SEPULCHRE: to bury
SEQUESTRATION: separation
SERE: dry
SERJEANT: a bailiff
SERPIGO: a cutaneous disease
SERVICEABLE: 'serviceable vows,' vows that you will do her service, or be her servant
SETEBOS: the name of a fiend
SETTER: one who watches travellers to give information to thieves
SEVERAL: land which is not common but appropriated
SHAME: to be ashamed
SHAME: modesty
SHARDS: shreds, broken fragments of pottery
SHARDS: the wing cases of beetles; hence 'sharded.' and 'shard-bone.'
SHARKED: snatched up, as a shark does his prey
SHEEN: brilliancy
SHEER: pure, unmixed
SHENT: rebuked, blamed, hurt
SHERIFF'S-POST: a post at the door of a sheriff, to which royal proclamations were fixed
SHIVE: slice
SHOT: the reckoning at an ale-house
SHOUGHS: shaggy dogs
SHOULDERED: A doubtful word
SHOVEL-BOARD: game played by sliding metal pieces along a board at a mark
SHREWD: mischievous
SHRIFT: confession, absolution
SHRIVE: to confess
SHRIVING-TIME: time for confession
SHROUD: to enshroud oneself, cover oneself up

SIDE-SLEEVES: loose hanging sleeves
SIEGE: seat, stool, rank
SIGHT: an aperture in a helmet
SIGHTLESS: invisible, unsightly
SIGN: to give an omen
SILLY: simple, rustic
SIMULAR: counterfeit, feigned
SINGLE: feeble
SIR: a title applied to a bachelor of arts at the Universities
SITH: since
SITHENCE: since
SIZES: allowances
SKAINS-MATES: scapegraces
SKILL: to be of importance
SKILLESS: ignorant
SKIMBLE-SKAMBLE: rambling, disjointed
SKINKER: a drawer of liquor
SKIRR: to scour
SLACK: slacken
SLAVE: to turn to slavish uses
SLEAVE: floss-silk
SLEDDED: sledged
SLEIDED: untwisted, raw, applied to silk. (Gower)
SLEIGHTS: artifices
SLICE:
SLIPPER: slippery
SLIPS: a kind of noose, or leash, a piece of base money
SLIVER: to slice
SLIVER: a slice
SLOPS: loose breeches
SLUBBER: to slur over.
SMIRCHED: smeared, soiled
SMOOTH: to flatter
SMOOTHED: flattered, fawned upon
SNEAP: taunt, sarcasm
SNEAPED: pinched
SNEAPING:
SNECK-UP: go hang!
SNUFF: anger, 'to take in snuff' is to take offence
SOFTLY: gently
SOIL: spot, taint
SOLICIT: solicitation
SOLIDARE: a small coin
SOLVE: solution
SOMETIMES: formerly
SOOTH: truth, conciliation
SOOTH: true
SOREL: a buck of the third year
SORRIEST: most sorrowful
SORRY: sorrowful, dismal
SORT: a company, rank, condition, lot, 'In a sort,' in a manner
SORT: to choose, to suit, to consort
SOT: fool
SOUL-FEARING: soul-terrifying
SOWL: to lug, drag
SOWTER: name of a dog
SPECIALTY: a special contract
SPED: settled, done for
SPEED: fortune
SPERR: to bolt, fasten
SPIAL: spy
SPILL: to destroy
SPILTH: spilling
SPLEEN: violent haste, used of the lightning flash
SPRAG: quick
SPRING: shoot, bud, beginning
SPRINGHALT: stringhalt, a disease of horses
SPRITED: haunted
SPURS: roots of trees
SQUANDERED: scattered
SQUARE: to quarrel, the front part of a woman's dress, stomacher, equitable
SQUARER: quarreller
SQUASH: an unripe peascod
SQUIER: a square or rule
SQUINY: to squint
STAGGERS: a disease in horses, attended with giddiness: hence any bewildering distress
STAIN: to disfigure
STALE: a decoy, a gull, a prostitute
STALE: to make stale, deprive anything of its freshness
STAND UPON: to be incumbent on
STANIEL: an inferior kind of hawk
STARK: stiff
STARKLY: stiffly
STATE: a canopied chair
STATION: attitude, act of standing
STATIST: a statesman
STATUA: a statue
STATUE: image, picture
STATUTE: security, obligation
STATUTE-CAPS: woollen caps worn by citizens
STAY: a check
STEAD: to profit
STELLED: (a doubtful word) set or fixed
STERNAGE: steerage, course
STICKLER: an arbitrator in combats
STIGMATIC: a deformed person
STIGMATICAL: deformed
STILL: constant, constantly
STILLY: softly
STINT: to stop, to stop
STITHY: a smith's forge, to forge
STOCCADO: a stoccata, or thrust in fencing
STOCK: a stocking
STOMACH: courage, stubbornness, appetite, inclination
STONE-BOW: a cross-bow for throwing stones
STOUP: a cup
STOUT: strong, healthy
STOVER: folder
STRACHY: A word of doubtful meaning
STRAIGHT: immediately
STRAIN: lineage, disposition
STRAITED: straitened
STRANGE: foreign, coy, reserved, marvellous
STRANGENESS: coyness, reserve
STRANGER: foreigner
STRAPPADO: a kind of punishment
STRICTURE: strictness
STROSSERS: trowsers
STUCK: a thrust of a sword.
STUCK IN: corruption of stoccata
STUFF: baggage, material, substance
STUFFED: filled, stored
STY: to lodge as in a sty
SUBSCRIBE: to yield, to succumb
SUCCESS: issue, consequence, succession
SUCCESSIVE: succeeding
SUCCESSIVELY: in succession
SUDDEN: hasty, rash
SUDDENLY: hastily
SUFFERANCE: suffering
SUGGEST: to tempt, entice
SUGGESTION: temptation, enticement
SUITED: dressed
SULLEN: doleful, melancholy.
SUMPTER: a horse that carries provisions on a journey
SUPPOSE: a trick, imposition
SUPPOSED: counterfeit
SURCEASE: to cease
SURCEASE: cessation, end
SURPRISE: to capture by surprise

SUR-REINED: over-worked
SUSPECT: suspicion
SUSPIRE: to breathe
SWABBER: a sweeper of the deck of a ship
SWARTH: black, black quantity of grass cut down by one sweep of the scythe
SWASHER: swaggerer
SWASHING: dashing, smashing
SWATH: The same as 'swarth.'
SWATHLING: swaddling
SWAY: to move on
SWEAR: to adjure
SWEAR OVER: to out-swear
SWIFT: ready, quick
SWINGE-BUCKLER: a bully

TABLE: a tablet, note-book
TABLE-BOOK: note-book
TABLES: the game of backgammon, a note book
TABOR: a small side-drum
TABORER: a player on the tabor
TABOURINE: tambourine, drum
TAG: the rabble
TAINT: tainted
TAINTURE: defilement
TAKE: to infect, blast, bewitch
TAKE IN: to conquer
TAKE OUT: to copy
TAKE UP: to borrow money, or buy on credit, to make up a quarrel
TAKING: infection, malignant influence
TAKING UP: buying on credit
TALL: strong, valiant
TALE: counting, reckoning
TALLOW-CATCH: a lump of tallow
TANG: twang, sound, to sound
TANLING: anything tanned by the sun
TARRE: to excite, urge on
TARRIANCE: delay
TARTAR: Tartarus
TASK: to tax, challenge
TASKING: challenging
TASTE: to try
TAWDRY-LACE: a rustic necklace
TAXATION: satire, sarcasm
TAXING: satire
TEEN: grief
TELL: to count
TEMPER: to mix
TEMPERANCE: temperature
TEMPERED: mixed
TEND: to attend to
TENDER: to hold, to esteem, to have consideration for
TENT: to probe as a wound, a probe for searching a wound
TERCEL: the male of the goshawk
TERMAGANT: a ranting character in old plays
TESTED: pure, assayed
TESTERN: to reward with a tester, or sixpence
THARBOROUGH: (corrupted from 'third-borough') a constable
THEORICK: theory
THEWES: sinews, muscles
THICK: rapidly.
THICK-PLEACHED: thickly inter-twined
THIRD-BOROUGH: a constable
THOUGHT: anxiety, grief, so 'to take thoughts' is to give way to grief
THARSONICAL: boastful
THREE-MAN BEETLE: a wooden mallet worked by three men
THREE-MAN-SONG-MEN: singers of glees in three parts
THREE-PILE: three-piled velvet
THRENE: lament
THRID: thread, fibre
THROE: to put in agonies
THRUM: the tufted end of a thread in weaving
THRUMMED: made of coarse ends or tufts
TICKLE: ticklish
TIGHT: nimble, active
TIGHTLY: briskly, promptly
TIKE: a cur
TILLY-VALLY: an exclamation of contempt
TILTH: tillage
TIMELESS: untimely
TINET: stain, dye
TIRE: attire, head-dress
TIRE: to tear as a bird of prey, hence, metaphorically, to feed
TIRE: to attire, dress
TOD: to yield a tod of wool
TOKENS: plague spots
TOKENED: marked with plague spots
TOLL: to exact toll, to pay toll
TOO TOO: excessively
TOPLESS: supreme, without superior
TOUCH: touchstone for testing gold, trait, an acute feeling
TOUCHED: pricked
TOUSE: to pull, drag
TOWARDS: nearly ready
TOYS: trifles, foolish tricks
TRADE: beaten path
TRANECT: a ferry
TRASH: to check, as a huntsman his hounds
TRANSLATED: transformed
TRAVAIL: labor, toil
TRAY-TRIP: an old game played with dice
TREACHERS: traitors
TREATIES: entreaties
TRENCHED: carved
TRICK: technically, a copy of a coat of arms; hence, any peculiarity which distinguishes voice or feature
TRICK: to dress up
TRICKED: blazoned
TRICKING: ornament
TRICKSY: elegantly quaint
TRIPLE: third
TROJAN: a cant word for a thief
TROL-MY-DAMES: the name of a game; also called pigeon-holes
TROTH-PLIGHT: betrothed
TROW: to trust, think
TRUE: honest
TRUNDLE-TAIL: a long-tailed dog
TUCKET-SONANCE: a flourish on the trumpet
TUNDISH: a funnel
TURLYGOOD: a name adopted by bedlam-beggars
TURN: to modulate
TWANGLING: twanging
TWIGGEN: made of twigs, wicker
TWILLED: A doubtful word
TWINK: a twinkling
TWIRE: to peep, twinkle

UMBERED: stained, dark, as with umber
UNANELED: without extreme unction
UNAVOIDED: unavoidable
UNBARBED: untrimmed
UNBATED: unblunted
UNBOLT: to disclose
UNBOLTED: unsifted, unrefined
UNBREATHED: unpractised

UNCAPE: to throw off the hounds
UNCHARGED: undefended, applied to the gates of a city
UNCLEW: to unravel, undo
UNCOINED: unalloyed, unfeigned
UNDERGO: to undertake
UNDERTAKER: one who takes up another's quarrel
UNDER-WROUGHT: undermined
UNEATH: hardly
UNEXPRESSIVE: inexpressible
UNFAIR: to deprive of beauty
UNHAPPILY: censoriously
UNHAPPY: mischievous
UNHATCHED: undisclosed
UNHOUSELED: without receiving the sacrament
UNIMPROVED: unreproved
UNION: a pearl
UNJUST: dishonest
UNKIND: unnatural
UNLIVED: bereft of life
UNMANNED: untamed, applied to a hawk
UNOWED: unowned
UNPREGNANT: stupid
UNPROPER: common to all
UNQUESTIONABLE: not inquisitive
UNREADY: undressed
UNRESPECTIVE: inconsiderate
UNSISTING: unresting
UNSTANCHED: incontinent
UNTEMPERING: unsoftening
UNTENTED: unsearchable
UNTRADED: unused, uncommon
UNTRIMMED: spoiled of grace or ornament
UNTRUE: untruth
UNVALUED: invaluable
UNSPRING REEL: a boisterous dance
URCHIN: the hedge-hog
USANCE: usury
USE: interest
UTIS: riotous merriment, which accompanied the eighth day of a festival
UTTER: to expel, put forth
UTTERANCE: extremity

VADE: to fade
VAIL: to lower
VAILING: lowering
VAINNESS: vanity
VALANCED: adorned with a valance or fringe; applied to the beard
VALIDITY: value
VANTAGE: advantage
VANTBRACE: armor for the front of the arm
VARLET: a servant, valet
VAST: properly a waste-place, metaphorically, the dead of night, a gulf
VASTIDITY: immensity
VASTLY: like a waste
VASTY: vast, waste
VAUNT: the van, that which precedes
VAUNT-COURIERS: forerunners
VAWARD: the van, vanguard, advanced guard of an army, hence, metaphorically, the first of anything
VEGETIVES: herbs
VELURE: velvet
VELVET-GUARDS: literally, velvet trimmings; applied metaphorically to the citizens who wore them
VENEW: a bout in fencing, metaphorically applied to repartee and sallies of wit
VENEY: a bout at fencing
VENGE: to avenge
VENTAGES: holes in a flute or flageolet
VERBAL: wordy
VERY: true, real
VIA: off with you!
VICE: to screw, the buffoon in the old morality plays
VIE: to challenge; a term at cards, to play as for a wager
VIEWLESS: invisible
VILLAIN: a lowborn man
VINEWED: mouldy
VIOL-DE-GAMBOYS: a bass viol
VIRGINALLING: playing as on the virginals, a kind of a spinet
VIRTUE: the essential excellence
VIRTUOUS: excellent, endowed with virtues
VIZAMENT: advisement
VOLUBLE: fickle
VOLUNTARY: volunteer
VOTARIST: votary, one who has taken a vow
VULGAR: the common people, common
VULGARLY: publicly

WAFT: to wave, beckon, to turn
WAFTAGE: passage
WAFTURE: waving, beckoning
WAGE: to reward as with wages
WAILFUL: lamentable
WAIST: the middle of a ship
WANNION: 'With a wannion' = 'with a vengeance.'
WAPPENED: withered, overworn
WARD: guard, prison
WARDEN: a large pear used for baking
WARDER: truncheon
WARN: to summon
WASSAIL: a drinking bout, festivity
WAT: a familiar word for a hare
WATCH: a watch light
WATCH: to tame by keeping constantly awake
WATER-GALL: a secondary rainbow
WATER-WORK: painting in distemper
WATER-RUG: a kind of dog
WAX: to grow
WAXEN: perhaps, to hiccough
WEALTH: weal, advantage
WEAR: fashion
WEATHER-FEND: to defend from the weather
WEB AND PIN: the cataract in the eye
WEE: small, tiny
WEED: garment
WEE: to think
WEET: to wit, know
WEIGH OUT: to outweigh
WELKIN: the sky
WELKIN: sky-blue
WELL-LIKING: in good condition
WELL SAID: well done!
WEND: to go
WESAND: the wind-pipe
WHELK: a weal
WHELKED: marked with whelks or protuberances
WHEN AS: when
WHEN: an exclamation of impatience
WHERE: whereas, a place
WHIFFLER: an officer who clears the way in processions
WHILE-ERE: a little while ago
WHILES: until

WHIP-STOCK: handle of a whip
WHIST: hushed, silent
WHITE: the centre of an archery butt
WHITING-TIME: bleaching time
WHITSTER: bleacher
WHITELEY: pale-faced, a doubtful word
WHITTLE: a clasp knife
WHOO-BUB: hubbub
WHOOP: to cry out with astonishment
WICKED: noisome, baneful
WIDOW: to give a jointure to
WIDOWHOOD: widow's jointure
WIGHT: person
WILD: weald
WILDERNESS: wildness
WIMPLED: veiled, hooded
WINDOW-BARS: lattice-work across a woman's stomacher
WINDRING: winding
WINTER-GROUND: to protect (a plant) from frost
WIS: in the compound 'I wis,' certainly
WISH: to commend
WISTLY: wistfully
WIT: knowledge, wisdom
WITHOUT: beyond
WITS: five, the five senses
WITTOL: a contented cuckold
WITTY: intelligent
WOMAN-TIRED: hen-pecked
WONDERED: marvellously gifted
WOOD: mad
WOODCOCK: a simpleton
WOODMAN: a forester, huntsman, a cant term for a wencher
WOOLWARD: shirtless
WORD: to flatter or put off with words, to repeat the words of a song
WORLD: 'To go to the *world* is to get married, so 'a woman of the *world* is a married woman
WORM: a serpent
WORSER: worse
WORSHIP: to honor
WORTH: wealth, fortune
WORTS: cabbages
WOT: to know
WOUND: twisted about
WREAK: vengeance, to avenge
WREAKFUL: revengeful, avenging
WREST: an instrument used for tuning a harp
WRIT: gospel, truth. (Gower)
WRITHLED: shrivelled
WROTH: calamity, misfortune
WRY: to swerve
WRUNG: twisted, strained

YARE: ready, used as an int., 'be' being understood
YARELY: readily
Y-CLAD: clad
Y-CLEPED: called, named
YEARN: to grieve, vex
YELLOWNESS: jealousy
YELLOWS: a disease of horses
YEOMAN: a sheriff's officer
YIELD: to reward, to report
YOND: and yonder

ZANY: a clown, gull

INDEX OF CHARACTERS